Company Formation

A Practical Global Guide, Second Edition

General Editor **Agustí Jausàs**

General Editor
Agustí Jausàs

Publisher
Sian O'Neill

Marketing manager
Alan Mowat

Production
John Meikle, Russell Anderson

Publishing directors
Guy Davis, Tony Harriss, Mark Lamb

Company Formation: A Practical Global Guide, Second Edition
is published by
Globe Law and Business
Globe Business Publishing Ltd
New Hibernia House
Winchester Walk
London Bridge
London SE1 9AG
United Kingdom
Tel +44 20 7234 0606
Fax +44 20 7234 0808
Web www.gbplawbooks.com

Printed by CPI Antony Rowe

ISBN 978-1-905783-27-4

Company Formation: A Practical Global Guide, Second Edition
© 2009 Globe Business Publishing Ltd

DISCLAIMER
This publication is intended as a general guide only. The information and opinions which it contains are not intended to be a comprehensive study, nor to provide legal advice, and should not be treated as a substitute for legal advice concerning particular situations. Legal advice should always be sought before taking any action based on the information provided. The publishers bear no responsibility for any errors or omissions contained herein.

Table of contents

Preface

Agustí Jausàs
JAUSAS

As I explained in the preface to the first edition of this work, even with many years of professional experience as a company lawyer, I have never quite been able to overcome a feeling of unease when I have to participate in professional matters involving jurisdictions with whose laws I am unfamiliar. In these situations, needless to say, I always seek the advice of local professionals. However, being unfamiliar with basic principles can make conversations with local lawyers very uncomfortable. No matter how proficient you are in the law of your own country, you cannot help feeling at a disadvantage when you realise that you have less knowledge of the subject than some non-professional clients.

Every time I have had to deal with such a situation, I have tried to learn the basics of the legal framework of the new jurisdiction. This is never an easy task: it is extremely time consuming to review bulky legal texts in an attempt to extract useful information. I could never obtain all the necessary knowledge without constantly asking the local professionals for advice.

This type of problem arises most frequently in relation to the creation of companies with limited liability. You simply cannot have productive discussions with local counsel on this matter without a basic understanding of the available options; this allows you to evaluate the advantages and disadvantages of each and decide which option is best suited to your client's needs. A constructive dialogue in these cases assumes some familiarity with the alternatives on offer.

This book aims to give readers this understanding. To this end, we have collaborated with experts to explain the crucial issues involved in all the jurisdictions covered. Some of the authors have faithfully followed the standard template proposed, while others, due to the peculiarities of the regimes in their respective jurisdictions, have chosen to deal with these issues in a more flexible manner; in all cases, however, the key stages in the life cycle of these types of company – from incorporation to dissolution – are outlined.

In this way, the book paves the way for a critical evaluation of which options are best tailored to a client's needs, and should allow for constructive discussions with local professionals in the country where a new company is to be established.

The approach to this second edition has been based on two principles: to update the existing jurisdictions with any changes that have taken place and to extend the contents by including some new countries.

Again, I have to say that I owe an enormous debt of gratitude to each of the contributing authors for their generosity and efficiency in preparing their chapters, their efforts to focus exclusively on the proposed issues, and their benevolence in accepting suggested abridgements or amendments. I also want to thank Sian O'Neill of Globe Law and Business who, with her efforts and dedication, has once again been the elemental force behind this project.

Agustí Jausàs
5 May 2009

Agustí Jausàs is the founder of the law firm JAUSAS, with offices in Barcelona and Madrid. He has authored several books on company law and is the editor of two international publications on agency and distribution agreements; he is also a regular contributor to specialist journals.

Mr Jausàs served for eight years as chairman of the International Bar Association's Sub-committee on Agency and Distribution, Section of Business Law, and for four years as co-chairman of the Committee on International Sales and Related Commercial Transactions. He has participated in many national and international conferences and seminars on international commercial law and on the regulation of agency and distribution agreements. He has also been very active in advising on the formation of subsidiaries in different jurisdictions.

Argentina

Marcelo Gustavo Pozzetti
M & M Bomchil

1. Types of company with limited liability and applicable legislation

The most commonly used limited liability companies in Argentina are:

- the corporation (*sociedad anónima*); and
- the limited liability company (*sociedad de responsabilidad limitada*).

Both are regulated by the Commercial Companies Law of Argentina and resolutions issued by the local public commercial registries of each province. The Buenos Aires Public Commercial Registry is the *Inspección General de Justicia* (IGJ). Public corporations are also subject to the regulations of the National Securities Commission (*Comisión Nacional de Valores* (CNV)).

2. Incorporation procedure

2.1 Proceedings prior to incorporation

(a) Corporate name

IGJ regulations prohibit the use of the following terms as corporate names:

- terms that are contrary to the common good and public interest;
- terms that are identical to the corporate names of existing companies, or that are sufficiently similar as to cause confusion with other companies;
- terms such as '*Nacional*' and '*Oficial*', which may be used only in case of governmental or specially authorised activity;
- term such as 'Argentina' or other words that might suggest the existence of a foreign related company, which may be used only if the existence of such other company is proved at the time of incorporation;
- references to professional qualifications, which may be used only by companies incorporated as an instrument for the performance of such professional activities; and
- references to a group of companies, which may be used only if the existence of such a group is proved at the time of incorporation and the company undertakes to change its name should it leave the group.

(b) Capital contributions

Capital contributions may be made in cash or in kind (including ancillary contributions such as personal services or technical assistance). No other kind of contribution is accepted.

Cash contributions must be deposited with Banco de la Nación Argentina, which will issue a receipt that must be filed with the IGJ in order to complete the incorporation process. Alternatively, a public deed may be submitted in which a notary public confirms that the capital has been duly paid in. In the former case, once the IGJ has approved the incorporation and the company is duly registered, the shareholders can seek reimbursement of the bank deposit.

In-kind contributions must first be valued; for corporations, this valuation must be approved by the IGJ. The Commercial Companies Law provides that where goods are contributed, their value must be proved by:

- the market price, if any; or
- an expert report.

If the contributions are overvalued:

- the difference must be paid in by the shareholder that made the contribution; or
- the capital must be reduced accordingly.

Shareholders of limited liability companies are jointly and severally liable in a case of over-valuation of their in-kind contributions at the time of incorporation or a subsequent increase in capital stock. A creditor can challenge the valuation, in a case of bankruptcy or default of the company, within five years of the contribution; however, this remedy is unavailable in cases of judicial valuation.

(c)   ***Declaration of foreign investment***

Foreign investment is regulated by the Foreign Investment Financial Law and its amendments. The law enshrines three basic principles, which are further elaborated by Decree 1853/93:

- Foreign investors may invest in any economic activity in Argentina without any need for prior approval and under conditions equal to those applicable to domestic investors. No activities are excluded from this principle, save for certain specific exceptions (eg, broadcasting and the acquisition of real estate in border areas); nor are there any obligations to associate with domestic investors, or other restrictions or conditions.
- Foreign investors have the right to repatriate their investments and to remit profits abroad at any time. This notwithstanding, capital repatriation is currently (2009) limited due to Central Bank foreign exchange regulations.
- The principle of equal treatment between domestic and foreign investors is reaffirmed.

Foreign investors that make capital investments in Argentina for the promotion of economic activities, or for the extension or improvement of existing activities, have the same rights and obligations under the Constitution and local legislation as domestic investors.

Where a foreign company invests in Argentina by incorporating or participating in a local company, the foreign company must be registered with the IGJ, as explained in section 2.2(e).

(d) Tax identification number for foreign shareholders

Foreign shareholders should be registered with the tax authorities through a tax identification number (known as a 'CDI').

2.2 Incorporation

(a) Bylaws

(i) Essential clauses

The essential provisions that must be included in the bylaws are as follows:
- the name, age, marital status, nationality, profession, domicile and identification number of the shareholders;
- the corporate name and corporate domicile;
- the corporate purpose;
- the capital stock, expressed in Argentine currency, and a description of each shareholder's contribution;
- the duration of the company, which must be specific;
- details of the organisation of the corporate administration, internal controls, if any, and shareholders' meetings;
- rules on the distribution of profits and losses (and, where these are not included, profits and losses will be distributed in proportion to each shareholder's contribution);
- the shareholders' rights and obligations; and
- the procedure for dissolution and winding-up.

(ii) Clauses not foreseen by law

The Commercial Companies Law allows for the inclusion of optional clauses in the bylaws. However, such clauses cannot modify the main characteristics of each kind of company or mandatory rules established under the Commercial Companies Law. The clauses of the bylaws are enforceable as against the shareholders as from the date of incorporation, and as against third parties after registration with the IGJ.

(iii) Optional clauses governed by law

As long as clauses established within the bylaws do not affect legally protected public interests, there are no restrictions on the expansion of such clauses. Some corporate law principles apply in such cases, such as the protection of minority shareholders' rights, which cannot be altered by the partners.

(b) Execution of public deed

Corporations must be incorporated by way of public deed executed before a public notary; this is not mandatory for limited liability companies. There is no timeframe for registration of a company with the IGJ. Until registration, however, the benefits of limited liability have no effect.

Corporations and limited liability companies are incorporated as of the date of execution of the articles of incorporation or the social contract, but they do not acquire legal personality until registration with the IGJ.

(c)   Tax identification number

Corporations and limited liability companies must be registered with the tax authorities (obtaining a tax identification code number known as a 'CUIT') in order to fulfil their tax obligations.

(d)   Indirect taxes, incorporation fees and other levies

A company need not be registered with the tax authorities in order to register the incorporation with the IGJ.

Corporations and limited liability companies are not obliged to make any tax payments for incorporation. Tax obligations derive from the economic activities pursued by the company; consequently, if the company performs no economic activities then it will not be obliged to make tax payments.

This notwithstanding, a company must still comply with formal obligations (eg, provision of tax returns) and, if it does not perform economic activities, it must pay 1% of its total assets as the minimum deemed income tax at the end of the fiscal year.

The incorporation costs for corporations are approximately as follows for 2009:

- notarial expenses – approximately Ps2,900 (deed of incorporation and bylaws, notary report and notary fees);
- IGJ registration form – Ps94;
- *Official Gazette* publication – approximately Ps600;
- incorporation fee – Ps100;
- IGJ form to reserve the corporate name – Ps18 (reservation of the corporate name prior to incorporation is optional);
- deposit of at least 25% of the capital stock with Banco de la Nación Argentina – at least Ps3,000, depending on the corporate capital;
- commission to be paid to Banco de la Nación Argentina – Ps60;
- fee for registration of corporate books following incorporation – Ps900; and
- accounting books – Ps 200.

The incorporation costs for limited liability companies are approximately as follows for 2009:

- where the company is incorporated through a private document:
  - certification of signatures – approximately Ps56 per signature; and
  - certification of the signature of the lawyer who prepares the legal report for registration, which is effected by the bar association – Ps40;
- where the articles of incorporation and bylaws are filed by way of public deed – the fees and expenses are as detailed for corporations above;
- IGJ registration form – Ps94;
- *Official Gazette* publication – approximately Ps600;
- incorporation fee – Ps100;

- IGJ form to reserve the corporate name – Ps18 (reservation of the corporate name prior to incorporation is optional);
- deposit of at least 25% of the capital stock with Banco de la Nación Argentina (no minimum amount is required, but the stock capital must accord with the corporate purpose);
- commission to be paid to Banco de la Nación Argentina – Ps60;
- fee for registration of corporate books following incorporation – approximately Ps500; and
- accounting books – Ps 100.

(e) *Registration with Commercial Registry*

Along with the incorporation documents, the IGJ requires submission of, among other things:

- proof of payment of the corporate capital;
- public translations, where documents are filed in another language;
- the IGJ registration fee;
- the *Official Gazette* publication; and
- certification of the signature of the lawyer or notary public who files the presentation.

These requirements may vary depending on the kind of company.

Foreign companies that are interested in incorporating or participating in local companies must be registered with the IGJ. In order to comply with this obligation, the IGJ requires the submission of:

- a copy of the bylaws and any amendments thereto;
- the certificate of incorporation in the foreign company's country of origin;
- the corporate resolution appointing a legal representative;
- confirmation of whether the company is subject to prohibitions on the pursuit of activities relating to its corporate purpose in its country of origin; and
- confirmation of whether the company has agencies, branches or permanent representations outside Argentina, owns participations in companies as non-current assets outside Argentina, or owns fixed assets in its country of origin.

Documents establishing the ownership of assets outside Argentina must be filed annually.

Where a foreign company is incorporated for the sole purpose of acting as a vehicle for investment in other companies, and consequently cannot fulfil the above requirements, compliance can be achieved if the controlling company meets the above requirements – including submission of the proper documentation – and also files the following documents:

- a declaration of the board of directors or shareholders' meeting of the controlling company confirming the corporate purpose of the company; and
- a statement of the controlling company's legal representative in Argentina confirming the structure of the group of companies and personal

information on the partners of both the investing and the controlling companies.

(f) **Corporate books**

The Commercial Companies Law establishes that companies must keep the following books:

- board of directors' meeting book;
- shareholders' meeting book;
- shareholder register (corporations only);
- shareholders' meeting attendance book (corporations only);
- diary;
- inventory and balance sheet book;
- value added tax (VAT) sales (optional); and
- VAT purchases (optional).

The books must be registered with the IGJ following registration of incorporation.

(g) **Declaration of start date and other tax declarations**

According to Argentine tax law, a company must declare the start-up date of its activities using a registration procedure with the tax authorities. Additionally, a company should be registered for other applicable taxes, such as income tax, value added tax, minimum deemed income tax, and other federal taxes within local jurisdictions (eg turnover tax, if applicable).

The formal requirements, such as tax returns, may vary depending on the kind of tax and the system chosen by the taxpayer.

3. Number of shareholders

According to the Commercial Companies Law, a minimum of two shareholders is required. The law does not establish minimum or maximum amounts of capital or percentages that a person should own in a company or corporation in order to be considered a shareholder. However, current IGJ requirements state that the maximum participation a sole shareholder can hold is 98% of the capital stock; the other 2% of the capital stock should be owned by at least one other shareholder, based on the 'plurality of partners' requirement. Therefore, in principle, the IGJ will not register companies controlled by a shareholder holding more than 98% of the voting shares.

Limited liability companies must have between two and 50 partners. (The same criteria regarding maximum and minimum percentages of capital held by each partner apply to limited liability companies as to corporations.) Partners can also be domestic or foreign companies or individuals, and no nationality or residency requirements apply. However, corporations can be shareholders of other corporations only.

In corporations, shareholder liability is limited to full payment of the equity participation subscribed by each shareholder. In limited liability companies, all partners are jointly and severally liable for payment of the total amount of the capital.

4. Corporate name – limitations

Argentine law establishes that the corporate name of a limited liability company may include the personal names of one or more partners or a fanciful term, and must include the words *'sociedad de responsabilidad limitada'* or its abbreviation 'SRL'.

The corporate name of a corporation may include the names of real persons or a fanciful term, and must include the words *'sociedad anónima'* or its abbreviation 'SA'.

In both cases, if the appropriate corporate form or its abbreviation is not indicated, the partners or shareholders will not have the benefits of limited liability.

5. Corporate domicile

The corporate domicile must be located in the jurisdiction where the main administration of the business is located. The bylaws need only indicate the relevant jurisdiction; the actual address can be established separately, in order to allow for a change in address without any need to amend the bylaws.

6. Corporate purpose

The corporate purpose must be specific, determined, lawful and possible to achieve. It determines the activities on which the capital is to be invested. In this sense, the corporate purpose works as a guarantee to the shareholders, as the managers cannot undertake activities that diverge significantly from the corporate purpose.

Certain corporations are controlled by different public entities in addition to the IGJ, depending on their corporate purpose. For instance, banks are controlled by the Central Bank, insurance companies are controlled by the Insurance Superintendence and companies that manage retirement and pension funds are controlled by the Superintendence of Managers of Retirement and Pension Funds. These are usually sole-purpose corporations, forbidden to undertake secondary business that is unrelated to the main corporate purpose.

In specific cases, the corporate purpose also determines what kind of company can undertake such activities. For example, the public offer of titles and bourse activity may be performed by corporations only.

7. Capital stock

7.1 Minimum capital requirement

Corporations must have a minimum capital stock of Ps12,000. There is no minimum capital requirement for limited liability companies. While the capital stock of corporations is represented by shares, in limited liability companies it is represented by quotas.

IGJ regulations establish that the capital stock must be appropriate for the pursuit of the corporate purpose. Therefore, the IGJ may require that certain companies have a higher capital amount than the statutory minimum.

7.2 Nature of contributions

Please see section 2.1(b).

7.3   Partial payments

All shares or quotas must be subscribed at the time of incorporation.

Where the capital is paid in cash, at least 25% of the capital must be paid in at the time of incorporation and the remainder within the next two years. Where consideration for the stock is other than cash, subscriptions must be fully paid up upon incorporation.

7.4   Representation of shares

The capital stock of corporations is represented by shares. Shares must be nominative and non-endorsable, and may be represented by certificates. The issuance and ownership of registrable shares that are not represented by certificates are recorded in the company's share register, which may be kept by the company or by other entities (eg, banks, Caja de Valores SA).

The shares must all have equal value and may be divided into different classes according to the rights attached to each class. It is forbidden to establish different voting rights within the same class.

Each share certificate can represent one or more shares. Listed corporations are allowed to issue global bonds.

Provisional share certificates may be issued until all shares subscribed are fully paid up.

7.5   Transfer of shares

(a)   Restrictions

The shares of corporations are freely transferable. This notwithstanding, the shareholders may limit the transfer of shares by including relevant provisions in the bylaws, although the transfer of shares may not be excluded altogether.

(b)   Formalities

The transfer of shares must be notified in writing to the company or to the entity that keeps the share register, where applicable, and must be recorded in the share register. The signature of the transferor should be certified by a notary public. No other formalities are required.

7.6   Increase in capital stock

Increases and reductions in the capital stock must follow the procedures established by the Commercial Companies Law, and they are effective as against third parties only upon registration with the public Commercial Registry. This restriction is established in order to protect the rights of shareholders and creditors.

Where the bylaws so provide, corporations can increase the capital stock to more than five times the original capital stock without any need to amend the bylaws.

8. Equity

8.1 Equity–capital ratio

Under the Commercial Companies Law, loss of the capital stock – that is, where losses absorb 100% of the reserves and the capital stock – constitutes grounds for dissolution.

The Commercial Companies Law provides for two alternative methods to avoid dissolution and restore the balance between the company's assets and liabilities:

- increase of capital stock; or
- reimbursement of capital stock.

In both cases the shareholders must make cash or in-kind capital contributions or convert debt into capital contributions to pay in the capital increase.

The Commercial Companies Law also establishes that when losses absorb 100% of the reserves and 50% of the corporate capital, a capital reduction is mandatory. In such a case, the shareholders can decide to reduce the corporate capital or make capital contributions in order to cover the losses or increase the capital.

8.2 Convertible bonds

Corporations and branches of foreign companies registered according to the law can obtain financing or indirectly increase their capital stock by issuing convertible bonds. The bondholders are creditors of the company and, depending on the bond provisions, may convert their credit into shares.

Convertible bonds may be issued in classes and series. The issuance of a new series is forbidden until the previous series is fully subscribed.

Convertible bonds may be issued in foreign currency and are freely transferable to other countries. The Commercial Companies Law grants the shareholders a right of first refusal regarding the bonds at the time of their conversion into shares.

Simple bonds may also be issued; these have financial purposes only and do not grant the right to acquire shares in the company.

The terms of convertible bonds are determined not by law but by the issuer. In order to promote the issuance of long-term convertible bonds, local regulations provide for certain income-tax exemptions.

Corporations can issue convertible bonds even if this is not expressly contemplated in the bylaws; a bond issue may be decided by an extraordinary shareholders' meeting and, in the case of listed companies, by an ordinary shareholders' meeting. The company must publish the bond offer for one day in the *Official Gazette*, together with a detailed description of the terms of the offer.

9. Administration

9.1 General shareholders' meeting

Corporations: The shareholders' meeting is the governing body of a corporation. Except where shareholders' meetings must be unanimously convened (ie, 100% of the capital stock must be present at the meeting and all resolutions must be adopted unanimously), meetings should be called by means of publication for a five-day period in the *Official Gazette* and, in specific cases, in a national newspaper, between 10 and 30 days before the date of the meeting (or between 20 and 45 days before the meeting for public companies). These terms are calculated as of the last date of publication.

Fifteen days prior to the date of the meeting, the board must submit to the shareholders – either at the corporate domicile or by electronic means – all relevant information regarding the meeting, the documents to be considered at the meeting and the board's proposals.

Shareholders' meetings may be ordinary or extraordinary, depending on the issues to be decided. Ordinary shareholders' meetings must be held for:

- approval of the financial statements;
- appointment of directors; and
- payment of dividends.

All other business (eg, amendment of the bylaws, merger or spin-off) must be transacted at extraordinary shareholders' meetings.

In public companies, the shareholders' meeting decides on the following matters, in addition to those indicated in the Commercial Companies Law:

- sale of, or granting of liens over, all or a substantial part of the assets of the company, where such transactions take place outside the ordinary course of business; and
- entry into administration or management agreements.

Shareholders may authorise another person who is not a director, employee or syndic of the company to act on their behalf by proxy at shareholders' meetings.

According to recent IGJ regulations, only the registered legal representative of a foreign company, or a special agent appointed by the registered representative, can represent the foreign company at a shareholders' meeting. Consequently, a foreign company cannot appoint any other person to represent it.

Limited liability companies: Limited liability companies are governed by the partners' meeting or by corporate resolutions adopted in accordance with the provisions of the act of incorporation. The above provisions on notification of shareholders' meetings also apply to partners' meetings.

(a)   *Quorum requirements*

The quorum requirements for ordinary and extraordinary shareholders' and partners' meetings are set out in the table on the next page.

Type of meeting	Call	Quorum	Majorities
Ordinary	First	Majority of voting shares	Absolute majority of votes present, or qualified majorities as set out in the bylaws
	Second	Any number of shares present at the meeting	
Extraordinary	First	60% of the voting shares or higher, as set forth in the bylaws	Absolute majority of votes present, or qualified majorities as set out in the bylaws
	Second	60% of the voting shares, or higher or lower as set out in the bylaws	
Special matters (eg, transfer of domicile to another jurisdiction, change of corporate purpose, merger, dissolution)	–	Unanimous attendance required	Majority of all voting shares, without applying plurality of votes

9.2 Administrative body

Corporations: Corporations are administrated by the board of directors, which is in charge of managing the business of the corporation. As there is no required minimum number of members, the board may generally be composed of a sole director. The exceptions are corporations whose capital exceeds Ps2.1 million, publicly held corporations and public utilities, which must appoint at least three board members.

There are no nationality requirements, but a majority of the directors must reside in Argentina. The directors need not be shareholders. The board must appoint a president, who is the corporation's legal representative. One or more vice presidents may optionally be appointed. An absolute majority of the board constitutes a quorum and actions are taken as provided for in the bylaws.

Limited liability companies: Limited liability companies are managed by one or more managers, acting individually or jointly as set forth in the bylaws. Like the directors of a corporation, managers are subject to no nationality requirements but the majority must reside in Argentina. A manager need not be a partner in order to remain in office.

(a)   ***Term of office, resignation and removal of directors***

For corporations, the term of office of directors is specified in the bylaws and cannot exceed three fiscal years; as an exception, directors appointed by the surveillance committee can remain in office for five years. There is no term established by law for the directors of limited liability companies.

The resignation of a director should be accepted by the board whenever this does not affect the regular operations of the company and is not malicious or without due warning. The shareholders can remove a director from office at any time.

(b)   ***Directors' liability to third parties***

All board members are jointly and severally liable for acts performed pursuant to board resolutions. Each director is individually liable for such acts.

In addition, directors are jointly and severally liable to the corporation, shareholders and third parties for:
- improper exercise of their duties, according to the standards set forth in the Commercial Companies Law (see section 9.2(c));
- violation of the law, articles of incorporation or bylaws; and
- any other damage caused maliciously, abuse of power or gross negligence.

Section 274 of the Commercial Companies Law establishes an exception to the joint liability of all directors. A director who participated in, or was aware of, the offending resolution will be exempt from liability if his dissent is recorded in the minutes, or if he gives notice of his dissent to the syndic (where one has been appointed), the board of directors, the members of the surveillance committee, the shareholders meeting or any competent authority before any judicial action is filed.

Section 275 of the same law provides that the directors' liability is extinguished in the following circumstances:
- where performance of their duties is approved by the shareholders' meeting; or
- by express waiver of the right to start a claim, resolved by the shareholders' meeting.

However, liability will not be extinguished:
- where it arises from a violation of the law, the articles of incorporation or the bylaws;
- where at least 5% of the corporate capital opposes the extinguishment of liability at the shareholders' meeting; or
- in a case of bankruptcy.

(c)   ***Directors' duties***

Directors' duties are personal and cannot be transferred. The directors cannot participate, directly or indirectly, in activities that compete with the company, unless the shareholders' meeting gives its express authorisation. On the contrary, they will be held responsible for all damages that may result from their acts or omissions.

All directors must establish a domicile in Argentina and provide a guarantee, the amount of which is specified in the bylaws, for the fulfilment of their duties. According to IGJ regulations, this guarantee cannot be less than Ps10,000. For limited liability companies whose corporate capital is less than Ps12,000, the guarantee can be reduced to Ps2,000.

According to the Commercial Companies Law, the president is the company's legal representative and has the power to bind it against third parties for all acts that do not diverge significantly from its corporate purpose.

(d)   Special duties

The directors of public companies have additional duties, as outlined below.

(i)   Public offering duties

Directors and members of the surveillance committee must inform the CNV and self-regulating entities of:

- any fact or situation that, because of its importance, could substantially affect the underwriting of convertible bonds or the course of their negotiation; and
- holdings of shares, debt securities and debt certificates.

(ii)   Duty of secrecy

Certain persons identified under CNV resolutions – including directors and syndics of corporations – who have access to information that has not been publicly disclosed and that, because of its importance, might affect the price of a company's securities are subject to a strict duty of secrecy and must refrain from acting on this information until it becomes public.

(iii)   Duties of loyalty and diligence

Directors, administrators and syndics of public companies must:

- put the corporate interests of the company and the common interests of all partners ahead of any other interests, including those of the person or persons controlling the company;
- refrain from procuring any personal benefit on behalf of the company, other than the normal compensation for their office; and
- organise and implement preventive systems for the protection of corporate interests, so as to reduce the risk of permanent or occasional conflicts of interest in the course of their personal relationship with the company.

These duties refer, in particular, to:

- activities that compete with those of the company;
- the use or disposal of corporate assets;
- the determination of compensation or proposals related to compensation;
- the use of non-public information;
- the exploitation of business opportunities for their own benefit or that of third parties; and
- in general, any situation that causes or may cause a conflict of interest affecting the company.

Directors, administrators and syndics of public companies must also:

- ensure adequate means to carry out the company's activities and exercise such internal control as may be necessary to guarantee prudent management and prevent breach of duties imposed by the CNV and self-regulated entities; and

- act with the diligence of a 'good businessman' in the preparation and disclosure of information obtained on the market, and oversee the independence of external auditors.

(e)   Criminal liability

The Criminal Code includes no express provisions on the criminal liability of directors. A director may be held criminally liable for the commission of fraud, a crime that is not specifically related to company directors.

9.3   Others

(a)   Internal controllers and auditors

Internal control of corporations and limited liability companies is performed by the syndic or the surveillance committee. The syndic is a company officer entrusted with supervising compliance with the law and the bylaws. He must be an attorney or accountant. Appointment of the syndic is not mandatory, except for corporations whose capital exceeds Ps2.1 million, publicly held corporations and public utilities. Note that the bylaws of corporation may in any case establish the appointment of an alternate in order to cover a director's vacancy from time to time. This measure is mandatory in companies that do not have a syndic or a statutory auditing committee (eg in the case mentioned previously in this paragraph).

A syndic may also be appointed in limited liability companies, although this is rare. Limited liability companies with a capital stock of at least Ps2.1 million are obliged to appoint a syndic.

The following companies are obliged to appoint a surveillance committee:

- listed corporations;
- companies with a capital stock of at least Ps2.1 million;
- companies with government participation;
- companies which undertake financial activities or perform public services; and
- companies that control or are controlled by another company that is subject to government control.

The committee must have at least three members, and must have an odd number of members.

10.   Fiscal year

The fiscal year cannot exceed one calendar year in duration, and it ends on the date established in the bylaws.

11. Financial statements

11.1 Company tax

Companies in Argentina are, in principle, subject to income tax, VAT, minimum deemed income tax and, within local jurisdictions, turnover tax and municipal taxes. The main characteristics of each are outlined in the table below.

National taxes	Rate	Tax period
Income tax	35% of the profit.	Annually
VAT	21% (there are some special regimes for certain activities).	Monthly
Minimum deemed income tax	1% of the total assets.	Annually
Local taxes	Rate	Tax period
Turnover tax	Varies from 0.5% to 6%, according to jurisdiction and activity.	Monthly
Municipal taxes	Varies according to jurisdiction and activity.	Monthly or annually

11.2 Annual accounts

(a) Documents

The financial statements are composed of:
- the annual report to stockholders;
- the consolidated profit and loss statement;
- a statement on the net worth;
- complementary notes;
- the audit report; and
- where appropriate, the report of the syndic or surveillance committee.

(b) Audit report

According to accounting regulations, the audit report must comply with several rules in order to guarantee independence and objectivity. All annual financial statements must be audited by an independent auditor.

While all corporations must file their financial statements with the IGJ, only limited liability companies with a capital stock of more than Ps2.1 million are obliged to do so.

(c)   ***Approval and distribution of profits***

The governing body of the company approves and distributes the profits. The conditions under which they will be distributed are set out in the annual report to stockholders.

Dividends are not included in the tax base for income tax purposes (equalisation tax could be applicable, too). Dividends are not subject to VAT.

(d)   ***Deposit and publication***

The financial statements must be deposited at the corporate domicile at least 15 days prior to the date of the meeting at which they are to be approved. In case of breach of this regulation, the shareholders or partners can request the court to declare the meeting null and void.

Once the financial statements have been approved, corporations must submit them to the IGJ for publicity purposes. Limited liability companies are not required to do so unless they are subject to government control (eg, where the capital stock exceeds Ps2.1 million). Listed corporations must also file their financial statements with the CNV and the Buenos Aires Stock Exchange. The CNV publishes the financial statements online, while the stock exchange publishes them in its *Daily Gazette*.

12.   Company reorganisation

12.1   Merger

The Commercial Companies Law foresees two different types of merger (both of which must be registered with the IGJ):

- where a company absorbs one or more companies that are dissolved without liquidation; and
- when two or more companies are dissolved without liquidation in order to incorporate a new company.

Merger involves the full transfer of all assets and liabilities (considered as universal succession) of the absorbed companies to the absorbing company or new company, as appropriate.

The absorbed companies are dissolved without liquidation by right due to the sole fact of the merger, as of the effective date of the merger.

In order to effect a merger, a specific procedure must be followed that involves the following steps, among others:

- preparation of special merger financial statements;
- execution of a merger agreement between the participants, which must be approved by the boards of directors and shareholders' meetings of all participants; and
- publication of notice of the merger for three days in the *Official Gazette* and in an Argentine newspaper. Creditors may oppose the merger within 15 days of the final publication.

As a rule, the transfer of assets gives rise to liability for income tax, VAT and some local taxes (eg turnover tax or stamp tax). If certain requirements are met, the merger may qualify as a tax-free reorganisation under Article 77 of the Income Tax Law and also enjoy exemptions from VAT and local taxes, depending on the regulations of the local jurisdictions involved.

In the case of a merger of two companies, the requirements are as follows:

- Both companies must have been active within the last 18 months and have carried out the same or related activities for the last year preceding the merger;
- For the two years following the merger date, the surviving company must carry on the same activities as the predecessor company or companies;
- The shareholders of each predecessor company must receive a participation in the surviving company, the value of which may not be less than 80% of the capital of the predecessor company; the amount of this participation must further be maintained for two years following the merger;
- The Commercial Companies Law Provisions on publication and registration must be observed; and
- The reorganisation must be notified to the tax authorities according to certain proceedings.

12.2 Spin-off

A spin-off is defined in the Commercial Companies Law as a transaction through which a company:

- separates part of its assets and creates a new company along with the assets of another company;
- divests certain of its assets to one or more existing companies;
- creates a new company with certain of its relevant assets; or
- creates two or more new companies using all of its assets.

The extraordinary shareholders' meeting or partners' meeting must approve:

- the spin-off;
- the spin-off balance sheet;
- the amendment of the bylaws, or the bylaws of the new company or companies, as the case may be; and
- the distribution of shares.

The spin-off must be published in the *Official Gazette* and in a national newspaper for three days.

Once the 15-day period established by law to claim rights of withdrawal (shareholders) and creditors' rights has expired, the amendment of the company's bylaws or the incorporation of the new company or companies must be registered with the IGJ.

12.3 Transformation

The transformation of a company involves a change in corporate form (eg from a corporation to a limited liability company) without any modification of its assets and liabilities.

A transformation is effected through the following procedure:

- The extraordinary shareholders' meeting or partners' meeting approves the transformation, the transformation agreement and the transformation balance sheet.
- The details of the transformation are published for three days in the *Official Gazette* and in a national newspaper.
- Once the 15-day opposition period has expired, the documents are registered with the IGJ.

13. Eventual partner separation

According to the Commercial Companies Law, the shareholders can exercise their right of withdrawal in the case of certain changes to the bylaws, such as those involving transformation or spin-off, that are not approved unanimously. The law establishes a five-day term to exercise the right of withdrawal for shareholders who voted against the corresponding resolution and a 15-day term for shareholders who were absent from the meeting.

The withdrawal right is not effective if the shareholders' meeting revokes the resolution within 60 days of the last day on which absent shareholders could exercise the right of withdrawal.

The quotas or shares of withdrawing partners or shareholders will be evaluated based on the last financial statement approved or that should have been approved according to the law or, where appropriate, on the transformation or spin-off balance sheet.

14. Dissolution and liquidation

14.1 Dissolution

The partners or shareholders are free to set forth in the bylaws additional grounds for dissolution to those established by the Commercial Companies Law, which include:

- the will of the partners or shareholders;
- expiry of the specified duration;
- achievement of the corporate purpose or impossibility of achieving the corporate purpose;
- capital loss;
- bankruptcy;
- merger; and
- for corporations, cancellation of the authorisation to make public offers or cancellation of listing.

14.2 Liquidation

The company retains its legal personality during the liquidation, which is carried out by a liquidator appointed for such purpose (the administrative body may act as liquidator).

The company must register the appointment of a liquidator with the IGJ. The liquidator has 30 days from the date of appointment to prepare an inventory and balance sheet for consideration by the shareholders or partners, who may extend this term to a maximum of 120 days. Where appropriate, the annual balance sheet must still be filed during this time.

During the liquidation, the liquidator must sell the corporate assets, cancel debts and distribute any balance remaining. At the end of the liquidation procedure, the liquidator must prepare a final balance sheet and a distribution programme.

Once the liquidation has ended and any remaining assets have been distributed, de-registration of the company must be requested from the IGJ.

15. Branches

Foreign companies may perform business or activities in Argentina through a branch. A legal representative duly authorised to operate the branch must be appointed.

There is no minimum capital requirement for branches, with the exception of those acting in certain industries such as banking or insurance.

The branch must maintain separate accounts from its head office and file annual financial statements with the corresponding public registry of commerce. This notwithstanding, there is no limitation of liability of the branch with respect to its head office.

Branches must also comply with the requirements for foreign companies (see section 2.2(e)). Consequently, the same documentation must be filed with the IGJ at the time of registration and on an annual basis.

Australia

Louise M Chau
Frederick John Chilton
Allens Arthur Robinson

---

1.   Types of company with limited liability and applicable legislation

Companies in Australia are governed by the Corporations Act 2001 (Cth), which is a federal act. The following types of limited liability company may be registered under the act:

- proprietary company limited by shares;
- public company limited by shares;
- public company limited by guarantee; and
- public company with no liability.

Trading companies, whether proprietary or public, are generally limited by shares. In such companies, the liability of the members is limited to the amount, if any, unpaid on their respective shareholdings. Proprietary companies are the most common type of company, as they are not subject to some of the more onerous financial reporting requirements applicable to public companies (see section 11).

A proprietary company is a company that has no more than 50 non-employee shareholders and cannot engage in any activity involving public offers of its securities. If a proprietary company attempts to lodge a prospectus or exceeds 50 members, the Australian Securities and Investments Commission (ASIC) has the power to convert it to a public company. Only public companies can raise capital from the public or operate a registered managed investment scheme.

A company limited by guarantee is a company in which the members do not hold shares, but each member agrees to contribute an amount specified in the company's constitution in the event that the company is unable to meet its liabilities. This amount can be nominal. The amount guaranteed cannot be changed, nor can it be regarded as an asset of the company to be borrowed against. Non-profit and charitable organisations are generally registered as companies limited by guarantee. The advantage of incorporating as a company limited by guarantee over any other form of company is that members are not required to make capital contributions when the company is established. Companies limited by guarantee are unable to issue shares and instead can raise funds by way of grants, annual membership fees, donations and borrowing.

A company with no liability is a company that has a share capital and is unable to recover any amount unpaid on shares held by its members, and whose constitution states that its sole objects are mining purposes. This type of company is relatively uncommon.

2. Incorporation procedure

2.1 Proceedings prior to incorporation

(a)   *Name registration*
Unless the name of the proposed company will simply be its Australian company number, the proposed name of the company must be provided in the application for registration. A company may reserve a proposed name prior to incorporation, with such reservation lasting for two months from the lodgement date.

(b)   *Capital contributions*
Australia no longer has a system of par value for shares. The value of equity contributed in cash or in kind can now be reflected in any number of shares. However, it is normal to provide equity in cash.

(c)   *Declaration of foreign investment*
Generally, there is no requirement for a declaration of foreign investment other than the need to specify the name and address of each shareholder in the application for registration submitted to ASIC.

However, the Corporations Act does require disclosure of information about the ownership of shares held in listed public companies if a foreign company has a substantial holding in the listed company. The term 'substantial holding' is defined to mean 5% of the total votes attached to the voting shares in a company. This is measured by both the foreign company's direct interest as well as the interests held by its associates.

Further, under the Foreign Acquisition and Takeovers Act 1975 (Cth), new investments over a specific size, by foreign governments or in certain industries such as banking, civil aviation, shipping, airports, media and telecommunications, must be approved by the Australian treasurer, as advised by the Foreign Investment Review Board.

(d)   *Tax identification number for shareholders/directors*
Shareholders are required to provide the company with their Australian business number or tax file number if they wish to take advantage of the dividend imputation provisions. These allow the company to avoid withholding tax on dividends.

2.2 Incorporation

(a)   *Constitution*
The internal workings of companies are governed by a constitution. If a company does not adopt a constitution, then various replaceable rules set out in the Corporations Act will apply. However, the replaceable rules do not apply to proprietary companies where the same person is both the sole director and sole shareholder of the company.

A constitution is mandatory only for a company with no liability, a company limited by guarantee that wishes to be exempt from the requirement to include the word 'Limited' in its name, or a 'special purpose company' that wishes to obtain the reduced annual review fee under the Corporations (Review Fees) Regulations 2003.

(b)   *Documents to be lodged*

A public company must lodge a copy of its constitution. A proprietary company that adopts a constitution does not need to lodge a copy of the constitution with its application for registration, but the Constitution must be kept with the Company's records and made available if required. Each named member in the application must agree in writing to the terms of the constitution.

(c)   *Tax identification number*

Once a company is incorporated it can apply to the commissioner of taxation for an Australian business number, which also enables registration for goods and services tax (GST). The Australian business number also functions as a tax file number.

(d)   *Indirect taxes, incorporation fees*

Companies must file a monthly or quarterly business activity statement detailing GST received and GST paid, which may be claimed as an input tax. Any excess of receipts over deductions is payable to the Australian Taxation Office with the company's submission of its business activity statement.

Simple wholly owned subsidiaries can be established for less than A$2,000, including legal professional fees and ASIC filing fees. No government taxes are levied on incorporation.

(e)   *Registration*

Any person, whether natural or legal, may apply for the registration of a company. The applicant need not be a person who is to be a member or officer of the company. If the applicant is a corporation, at least one director or secretary of that corporation must sign the application.

The application for registration must be in the prescribed form (ie ASIC Form 201). The form requires the following statement of matters:

- The type of company that is proposed to be registered must be identified.
- The proposed company name must be provided, unless its name will simply be its Australian company number.
- The state or territory in which the company is to be registered must be nominated.
- The address of the proposed registered office must be provided. If the company does not occupy the premises at this address, an occupier's consent letter must be obtained from the occupier. For public companies, the proposed opening hours of the registered office must be provided. The address of the proposed principal place of business must also be supplied if it is different from the address of the proposed registered office.
- The application must set out the full present and former names, dates and places of birth and addresses of each director and secretary. A proprietary

company must have at least one director, and at least one director must ordinarily reside in Australia. A proprietary company need not have a secretary, but if it does then at least one secretary must ordinarily reside in Australia. A public company must have at least three directors and at least two directors must ordinarily reside in Australia. A public company must also have at least one secretary and at least one secretary must ordinarily reside in Australia.

- The full name and address of each proposed member must be provided.
- The application must provide details of the share structure of the proposed company. If the proposed company is to be a company limited by guarantee, the amount of each member's guarantee must be provided.
- If the proposed company will have an ultimate holding company, the application must state the name, Australian company number and country of incorporation of the ultimate holding company.

Once an application has been lodged, ASIC may register the company. Once the company is registered, it comes into existence as a body corporate.

(f) Official books

A company must keep minute books, a register of members, a register of option holders (if any) and a register of charges.

A company is required to record in its minute books, within one month, minutes of all general meetings and of directors' meetings, as well as resolutions passed by members and directors.

The register of members must contain:

- the name and address of each member, and the date on which the member's name was entered on the register;
- where the company has more than 50 members, an up-to-date index, unless the register is kept in a form that operates effectively as an index;
- where the company has a share capital, the date on which every allotment of shares takes place, the number of shares in each allotment, the shares held by each member, the class of shares, share numbers or share certificate numbers, the amount paid on the shares, whether the shares are fully paid and any amount unpaid on the shares; and
- the date on which any person ceased to be a member during the previous seven years and the name and details of that person.

Where a charge is created on property of the company, or the company acquires property subject to a charge, the following particulars must be entered in the register of charges:

- the date of creation of the charge, or the date on which the company acquired the property subject to a charge;
- a description of the liability (whether present or prospective) secured by the charge;
- a description of the property charged;

- the name of the trustee or chargee for debenture holders; and
- the name of the person whom the company believes to be the holder of the charge.

Each register should be kept at the company's registered office, an office at the principal place of business in Australia or another office in Australia approved by ASIC.

3. Number of shareholders

There must be at least one shareholder for a company limited by shares, and a proprietary company cannot have more than 50 shareholders.

4. Corporate name – limitations

A name is generally available for registration unless it is identical to a name that has already been reserved or registered under the Corporations Act, or is identical to a name that has been listed on the national Business Names Register.

A name is also unavailable for registration if it is of a kind declared to be unacceptable under Section 147 of the act. These include:

- names that are undesirable or likely to be offensive;
- names containing restricted words, as specified in the regulations (eg 'Made in Australia', 'Stock Exchange', 'Trust', 'GST' and 'RSL'); and
- names that are capable of suggesting a connection with the Crown, a government or the British royal family.

A further requirement is that:

- the name of every company with no liability must include the words 'No liability' or 'NL';
- the name of every proprietary company must include the word 'Proprietary' or 'Pty'; and
- the name of every company with limited liability must include the word 'Limited' or 'Ltd'.

However, ASIC may register a company limited by guarantee without including the word 'Limited' in its name if its constitution requires the company to pursue charitable purposes only and to apply its income in promoting those purposes. Such companies cannot make distributions to their members or pay fees to their directors.

If a company name is registered when it should not in fact have been, ASIC has the power to direct the company to change its name within two months.

5. Corporate domicile

The name of the state or territory in which the company is to be registered must be nominated upon registration. State and territory stamp duty legislation is currently (2009) undergoing significant reform. At the date of publication, no stamp duty is payable on the transfer of shares if a company is registered in Victoria, Western Australia, Queensland, Tasmania or the Northern Territory (although a general exemption is available for shares quoted on a relevant exchange). This often leads to a company declaring one of those states to be its domicile.

6. Corporate purpose

The doctrine of *ultra vires* (ie, acting beyond the scope of one's powers) has been overruled by statute. It is normal to provide in the constitution that the company will have the powers of a natural person. However, there are some unusual circumstances in which companies have limited powers. Examples of these include cooperatives and government-owned corporations.

7. Capital stock

7.1 Minimum capital requirement

No minimum amount is required to be subscribed, although it is usual to subscribe at least A$1.

7.2 Nature of contributions

With the abolition of par value, it has now become easier to make in-kind contributions.

7.3 Partial payments

It is possible to issue partly paid shares in respect of which directors can then make calls for unpaid amounts. Shareholders will be liable for these amounts. The unpaid capital is an asset of the company and thus, in an insolvency administration, it is possible for a receiver or liquidator to recover the unpaid amounts. The exception is a company with no liability, which can be used only in the mining industry, where shareholders are not liable for the unpaid amounts. However, these shares are forfeited if shareholders do not meet a call.

Partly paid shares usually carry diminished rights. For example, the voting rights and dividend rights that would otherwise apply are usually reduced in proportion to the amount that has been paid on the shares.

7.4 Representation of shares

A company must generally issue share certificates stating the name of the company, the class of shares and the amount unpaid on the shares (if any). Such a share certificate is prima facie evidence that the person named on the certificate is entitled to the shares and has paid the amount certified to have been paid. However, shares in listed companies are generally held without share certificates due to the listing rules of the Australian Stock Exchange (ASX). Instead, holding statements are issued to keep shareholders informed of the balance of their respective holdings.

7.5 Transfer of shares

(a) Restrictions

The company's constitution may impose restrictions on the transfer of shares. In fact, it is normal for proprietary companies to provide their directors with absolute discretion to refuse to register a transfer of shares. However, if a company is listed on the ASX, it is prevented from imposing any restrictions on the transfer of fully paid shares.

The Corporations Act and the ASX Listing Rules provide for restrictions in certain circumstances. The act provides that a transfer of shares while a company is under administration or after it commences winding-up is void. For listed companies or unlisted companies with more than 50 shareholders, a person must not acquire a relevant interest in issued voting shares if that person's or another person's voting power would increase to more than 20%, unless the person proceeds with a takeover offer for all shares of that class. Further, under the ASX Listing Rules, the prior approval of the shareholders in general meeting is required if a listed company transfers assets or securities in excess of 5% to a related party or subsidiary, a substantial holder in the listed company or a person whose relationship to the listed company is such that the transfer should be approved by the shareholders in general meeting.

The application of the Trade Practices Act 1974 (Cth) and the Foreign Acquisition and Takeovers Act 1975 (Cth) (see section 2.1(c)) should also be considered.

(b) *Formalities*

A transfer of shares is effective at law when a duly executed share transfer in proper form is registered and the old share certificates are handed over and new share certificates are issued. However, shares in listed companies can be transferred without delivery of share certificates, in accordance with the ASX Listing Rules.

8. Equity

8.1 Types of equity

It is possible to divide shares into different classes. Ordinary shares are the ordinary, default class of shares, and they carry rights and obligations that are usual for such shares, such as the right to vote at general meetings, to receive dividends that are declared by the directors and to participate in any distributions upon the winding-up of the company. Ordinary shares may be divided into different classes (eg, A class and B class) where there are different groups of shareholders. In those circumstances, the rights attaching to the different classes of shares must be set out in the company's constitution.

It is not uncommon, particularly with investors in start-up companies, to issue preference shares that give special rights to holders and usually entitle holders to rank ahead of ordinary holders upon winding-up. Depending on the circumstances, preference shares may also confer the right to receive dividends in preference to any dividends that may be declared by the company in respect of its ordinary shares. Preference shares may be cumulative or non-cumulative.

8.2 Convertible notes

Convertible notes are notes that are convertible into a security (usually ordinary shares) upon specified conversion events.

Convertible notes usually have a face value and accrue interest at a specified interest rate. The notes may be issued at their face value, or at a discount or premium to their face value.

There is usually a formula for determining how many shares are to be issued upon conversion of the note. Different conversion ratios will arise under the formula as the company's capital structure and share price change over time. Changes in capital that can impact on the conversion ratio may include the issue of additional shares by the company or the company undertaking a share buyback.

9. Administration

9.1 General shareholders' meeting

(a) *Calling a meeting*
The directors of a company must call a general meeting at the request of members with at least 5% of the votes that may be cast at the general meeting, or at the request of at least 100 members who are entitled to vote at the general meeting, unless a different number is prescribed by the regulations.

(b) *Notice*
Written notice of the meeting must be provided, containing all the information that shareholders would reasonably require in order to make an informed decision. A listed company must give at least 28 days' notice and other companies must give at least 21 days' notice. Shorter notice can be given where members with at least 95% of the votes that may be cast at the meeting agree beforehand. However, the provision for shorter notice does not apply to a resolution to remove or appoint a director or to remove an auditor.

(c) *Quorum requirements*

(i) *Attendance*
A company's constitution may state the quorum requirements. To the extent that the constitution does not do so, the replaceable rule contained within the Corporations Act states that a quorum for a meeting of a company's members is two members, and the quorum must be present at all times during the meeting. Proxies and body corporate representatives are counted once only for these purposes.

(ii) *Voting*
Ordinary resolutions must be passed by more than 50% of the votes cast by members entitled to vote on the resolution. Special resolutions must be passed by at least 75% of the votes cast by members entitled to vote on the resolution and shareholders must be given notice of the special resolution before the meeting.

(d) *Challenging resolutions*
In general terms, a resolution that has been certified by a chairman of the meeting to have been passed by the requisite majority is not subject to challenge.

The so-called 'indoor management' rule allows an outside party to assume that internal requirements that are not public have been complied with (eg, that the directors have been properly appointed, that board meetings are properly convened, that board members are properly informed and that the required quorum is present).

9.2 Administrative body

(a) Different systems of administration

All Australian companies are similar in that their management is vested in a board of directors, which can delegate some of its powers to a managing director. Some decisions may be required (by a company's constitution, a shareholder agreement, the ASX Listing Rules or the Corporations Act) to be made by the shareholders in general meeting.

(b) Term of office, resignation and removal of directors

A proprietary company may specify in its constitution how a director is to be removed. Where the replaceable rules apply, a proprietary company may by resolution remove a director from office and appoint another director to that office.

A public company may by resolution remove a director from office despite anything in the company's constitution, an agreement between the company and the director, or an agreement between any or all members of the company and the director. A company must notify ASIC within 14 days of a director's removal. The removal of a director of a public company is generally done at a shareholders' meeting by ordinary resolution.

(c) Directors' duties

(i) Duty to avoid conflicts

Under common law, directors must not allow their own interests to conflict with their duties to the company; nor are they entitled to make a profit without the knowledge and assent of the company.

The Corporations Act further requires a director with a material personal interest in a matter relating to the company's affairs to give the other directors notice of the interest, unless the act exempts the interest from having to be disclosed.

Such notice must be given as soon as practicable after the director becomes aware of the interest in the matter, and details of the notice must be recorded in the minutes of the meeting. Disclosure can be a standing disclosure; however, it must be updated as soon as the director becomes aware of a changed interest.

Directors of a listed public company must notify the stock exchange on which the company is listed of certain relevant interests the directors have in securities of the company and contracts to which the directors are party or under which they are entitled to a benefit or right.

A director of a proprietary company can be present and vote at a directors' meeting about a matter in which the director is materially interested as long as the director has disclosed that interest or the interest is one that need not be disclosed under the act.

In contrast, a director of a public company who has a material personal interest in a matter that is being considered at a directors' meeting must not be present while the matter is being considered at the meeting; nor can the director vote on the matter. There are some exceptions to this general prohibition.

Where it is not possible to constitute a quorum for a directors' meeting due to the prohibition, one or more of the directors (including those who have a material personal interest in that matter) may call a general meeting to consider a resolution to deal with the matter.

(ii)   *Duty to act in good faith*

Under common law, directors are required to act in good faith in the interests of the company, and to act honestly in what they consider to be the interests of the company.

Ignorance of the facts (as opposed to the law) will not ordinarily result in a breach of duty. It has been found that a director who makes a good-faith decision in ignorance of relevant facts will have discharged his or her duty to act in good faith.

However, directors must exercise independent judgement in order to avoid a breach of the duty of care. To the extent that a director relies upon the knowledge and experience of others in the corporate group, the exercise of independent judgement requires directors to listen to and assess what their colleagues have to say and bring their own mind to bear on the issue using such skill and judgement as they possess.

The Corporations Act further provides that directors must exercise their powers and discharge their duties in good faith and in the best interests of the corporation, and for a proper purpose.

Where a director of a wholly owned subsidiary has acted in good faith in the best interests of the holding company, this constitutes an act in good faith in the interests of the subsidiary if the constitution of the subsidiary expressly authorises the director to act in the best interests of the holding company.

(iii)   *Duty to act for a proper purpose*

Under common law, directors must exercise the powers conferred on them by the constitution for the purpose for which they were conferred. This involves an examination of the relevant director's motives, as well as an examination of the nature of the power in question and the limits for which it may be exercised.

Directors cannot bind themselves to act in accordance with the instructions of another person.

Under the Corporations Act, directors must not improperly use their positions to gain an advantage for themselves or someone else, or to cause detriment to the corporation.

Anyone who obtains information because he is, or has been, a director must not improperly use the information to gain an advantage for himself or someone else, or to cause detriment to the corporation.

(iv) *Duty of care and diligence*

Directors are subject to a common-law duty to take reasonable care in the performance of their office. The duty involves becoming familiar with the business of the company and how it is run, and ensuring that the board has available means to have effective oversight of the management so that it can satisfy itself that the company is being properly run. Directors cannot avoid their responsibilities simply by being insufficiently informed.

The Corporations Act provides that directors must exercise their powers and discharge their duties with the degree of care and diligence that a reasonable person would exercise if they:

- were a director or officer of a corporation in the corporation's circumstances; and
- occupied the office held by, and had the same responsibilities within the corporation as, the director or officer.

The business judgement rule provides that directors who make a business judgement are deemed to have satisfied the statutory and common-law duties of care and diligence if they:

- make the judgement in good faith for a proper purpose;
- do not have a material personal interest in the subject matter of the judgement;
- inform themselves about the subject matter of the judgement; and
- rationally believe that the judgement is in the best interests of the company.

(v) *Other statutory duties*

Directors have a number of other statutory duties, including a duty:

- to ensure that dividends are paid out of profits, not out of capital;
- to take all reasonable steps to ensure that the company's financial records are maintained;
- to prevent the company from incurring a debt where there are reasonable grounds to suspect that the company is insolvent or will become insolvent by incurring the debt;
- not to enter into an agreement or transaction with the intention of preventing the recovery of employee entitlements or significantly reducing the amount of employee entitlements that can be recovered; and
- to give the company any information affecting or relating to the director that the company needs or will need to comply with Chapter 6 of the Corporations Act dealing with takeovers.

(d) **Civil and criminal liability**

A breach of general law fiduciary duties entitles the company to avoid any associated transaction – that is, the actions of the director are voidable. A breach of the general law duty of care occasioned by some negligence on the part of the director gives rise only to an action in damages.

The statutory duties under the Corporations Act relating to care and diligence, good faith, use of position, use of information, maintenance of financial records and prevention of insolvent trading carry civil penalty provisions. Contravention of these provisions allows a court to award pecuniary penalties of up to A$200,000 and compensation orders where the contravention results in a loss to the company.

A breach of a duty under the act that constitutes a criminal offence will attract a fine and/or imprisonment. The following are criminal offences:

- reckless or dishonest breach of the statutory duty of good faith;
- breach of the statutory duties relating to use of information and position, if the contravener intentionally or recklessly sought to gain an advantage for himself or someone else, or to cause detriment to the company;
- breach of the statutory duty regarding prevention of insolvent trading, if it involves actual knowledge of the company's insolvency and dishonesty;
- breach of the statutory duty regarding the provision of information necessary for compliance with takeover provisions; and
- breach of the duty of directors of public companies regarding voting on matters in which they have a material personal interest.

9.3   Others

(a)   *Attorneys*

It is possible to grant a power of attorney to exercise powers on behalf of a company. This is normally used in relation to a specific transaction, rather than in a general sense.

(b)   *Internal controllers and auditors*

Auditors who conduct an audit of a financial report must report to the members of the company on whether they are of the opinion that the financial report accords with applicable accounting standards and provides a true and fair view of the company's financial position and performance.

Auditors must give the directors a written declaration that, to the best of their knowledge, there has been no contravention of:

- the auditor independence requirements of the Corporations Act in relation to the audit or review; and
- any applicable code of professional conduct in relation to the audit or review.

There is a general requirement of independence to avoid conflict-of-interest situations. In addition, there are prescribed independence requirements, which include restrictions on a range of employment, investment and commercial transactions and relationships between the auditors and the audited company.

Former auditors are also restricted from taking up positions with clients within two years of auditing them. Auditors of listed companies are required to rotate their team members to ensure that an individual who has played a significant role in an audit for a period of five years does not play a significant role for at least the next two years.

10. Fiscal year

The fiscal year in Australia ordinarily runs from July 1 to June 30. However, it is possible to apply for a variation if a company can show good cause – for example, the need to conform to an overseas parent company.

11. Financial statements

11.1 Reporting obligations

The financial reporting and disclosure obligations imposed on companies vary greatly, depending on the type and size of the company in question. As a general rule:

- large proprietary companies are subject to more onerous reporting and disclosure obligations than small proprietary companies; and
- public companies are subject to more extensive obligations than proprietary companies.

11.2 Company tax

Companies are liable to pay tax on their assessable income at the rate of 30%. Capital gains are taxed at the same rate. There are provisions that, in certain circumstances, allow past losses to be utilised to offset income or capital gains. Fringe benefits tax may be payable in certain circumstances on some benefits provided to employees. Payroll tax, based on wages paid or payable, may also apply. If a company has not contributed the mandatory 9% of an employee's salary to the employee's superannuation fund, the company may be subject to the Super Guarantee Charge.

11.3 Annual accounts

(a) Documents and reports

Proprietary companies: A large proprietary company must prepare and lodge a financial report and a directors' report with ASIC within four months of the end of its financial year. A small proprietary company only needs to lodge these reports if it is directed to do so by shareholders with at least 5% of the votes or by ASIC, or if it is controlled by a foreign company and class order relief is not available. Relief will depend on the size of the overseas group to which the Australian company belongs.

A proprietary company is a 'large' proprietary company for a financial year if it satisfies at least two of the following criteria:

- the consolidated revenue for the financial year of the company and the entities it controls (if any) is A$25 million or more;
- the value of the consolidated gross assets at the end of the financial year of the company and the entities it controls (if any) is A$12.5 million or more; and
- the company and the entities it controls (if any) have at least 50 employees at the end of the financial year.

A proprietary company is a 'small' proprietary company for a financial year if it satisfies at least two of the following criteria:

- the consolidated revenue for the financial year of the company and the entities it controls (if any) is less than A$25 million;
- the value of the consolidated gross assets at the end of the financial year of the company and the entities it controls (if any) is less than A$12.5 million; and
- the company and the entities it controls (if any) have fewer than 50 employees at the end of the financial year.

All companies must keep sufficient accounting records to allow true and fair financial statements to be prepared and audited. These records must be retained for a period of seven years after completion of the transactions to which they relate.

The financial report must contain specified financial statements, notes and a directors' declaration, and comply with applicable accounting standards. A company must also ensure that its financial report for a financial year is audited in accordance with the Corporations Act and that an auditors' report is obtained.

Public companies: All companies must keep sufficient accounting records to allow true and fair financial statements to be prepared and audited. These records must be retained for a period of seven years after the completion of the transactions to which they relate.

A public company must prepare and lodge a financial report and directors' report. The financial report must contain the specified financial statements, notes and a directors' declaration, and comply with applicable accounting standards. A company must also ensure that its financial report for a financial year is audited in accordance with the Corporations Act and that an auditors' report is obtained. A public company that is not a wholly owned subsidiary is also required to include in its directors' report details of:

- each director's and secretary's qualifications, experience and special responsibilities; and
- the number of directors' meetings and board committee meetings held during the year, and each director's attendance at those meetings.

(b)   *Approval and distribution of profits*

Dividends are usually recommended by the board of directors, subject to approval by the shareholders. In some circumstances, a company has the power both to approve and to decline dividends without shareholder approval. Dividends must be paid out of the profits of the company. Dividends remitted to an overseas shareholder will be subject to a dividend withholding tax of 30%. If a company has paid corporate income tax and thus has imputation credits available, these will be offset against the withholding tax. This is usually substantially reduced through double taxation agreements between Australia and other countries.

(c)   *Deposit and publication*

Each year, proprietary companies and public companies must give their members either the full reports or a concise financial report for the financial year.

If shareholders with 5% of the votes direct a small proprietary company to prepare a report, the company must report to members by the later of:

- two months after the date on which the direction is given; and
- four months after the end of the financial year.

Other proprietary companies must report to members within four months after the end of the financial year.

A public company must report to members by the earlier of:

- 21 days before the next annual general meeting after the end of the financial year; or
- four months after the end of the financial year.

A company that must prepare or obtain a report (including a concise report) for a full financial year must lodge the report with ASIC within four months of the end of the financial year. A small proprietary company that prepares a financial report in response to a shareholder direction is exempt from this requirement.

12. Company reorganisation

12.1 Transformation

(a) Converting a public company to a proprietary company

Generally, to convert a public company limited by shares to a proprietary company limited by shares, the company must:

- ensure that it has no more than 50 non-employee shareholders;
- pass a special resolution resolving to change its type;
- lodge a copy of the special resolution with ASIC within 14 days of its adoption; and
- lodge an application complying with Section 163 of the Corporations Act with ASIC, together with a copy of the special resolution.

(b) Converting a proprietary company to a public company

Generally, to convert a proprietary company limited by shares to a public company limited by shares, the company must:

- pass a special resolution resolving to change its type;
- lodge a copy of the special resolution with ASIC within 14 days of its adoption; and
- lodge an application complying with Section 163 of the Corporations Act with ASIC, together with a copy of the special resolution, a consolidated copy of the company's constitution and a copy of each document or resolution that is necessary to ascertain the rights attached to the company's issued and unissued shares.

A conversion does not:

- create a new legal entity;
- affect the company's existing property, rights or obligations; or

- render defective any legal proceedings by or against the company or its members.

12.2 Alteration of capital

A company may reduce its share capital if the reduction:
- is fair and reasonable to the shareholders as a whole;
- does not materially prejudice the company's ability to pay its creditors; and
- is approved by the shareholders.

No court approval is required, but the court will become involved if there is a legal challenge to the reduction.

There are two types of reduction: equal (ie, *pro rata*) or selective (eg, to buy back the shares of a particular shareholder). An equal reduction requires approval by resolution of the shareholders in general meeting. A selective reduction requires approval by special resolution. If there is also a cancellation of shares, the reduction must also be approved by a separate special resolution passed at a meeting of the shareholders whose shares are to be cancelled.

Information requirements: The notice of the meeting must include all information known to the company that is material, but not information that it would be unreasonable to require the company to disclose because it has previously disclosed the information. Before shareholders vote on a resolution to approve a share capital reduction, the company must properly inform the shareholders of:
- the effect of the reduction on them and other shareholders; and
- the scheme of which the reduction forms part.

Voting: For a selective reduction, no votes may be cast in favour of the resolution by anyone who is to receive consideration as part of the reduction.

Lodgement of documents with ASIC: Before the notice of meeting is sent to the shareholders, the company must lodge with ASIC a copy of:
- the notice of meeting; and
- any document relating to the reduction that will accompany the notice of meeting sent to shareholders.

In the case of a selective reduction requiring special shareholder approval, the company must lodge with ASIC a copy of any resolution within 14 days of its adoption. The company must not make the reduction until 14 days after the lodgement.

If the shares are cancelled, the company must lodge with ASIC a notice in the prescribed form within one month.

12.3 Merger

The common form of an M&A transaction in Australia is for the target company to become a subsidiary. It is possible to have a scheme of arrangement, including where the assets of the acquirer and target are merged (or for other purposes such as alteration of rights attaching to shares), but court approval is required for this to take place.

12.4   **Split-off**

It is possible to split off a subsidiary or transfer assets to a new entity. This requires shareholder approval.

13.   **Eventual shareholder separation**

Shareholders can dispose of their shares by selling them to one or more other shareholders (see section 7.5 above). In a closely held company, it is common to include in the constitution a system of pre-emptive rights. A company may only buy back its own shares if:

- the buy-back does not materially prejudice the company's ability to pay its creditors; and
- the company follows the procedures laid down in the Corporations Act.

14.   **Dissolution and liquidation**

Dissolution of a company can come about by way of receivership, administration or liquidation. A receiver is a person appointed by a court to take possession of property in order to enforce a creditor's security or to prevent improper disposal of the company's property. It is also common in Australia for a secured creditor to appoint a receiver and manager who takes control of the company and can manage it and realise assets for the benefit of the secured creditor. An administrator is a person appointed by the company itself to investigate the company and, for a limited period of its administration, the company is protected from creditors. A liquidator is a person who assumes control of a company's affairs to discharge its liabilities, and may be appointed by the court or members of the company.

15.   **Branches**

Instead of incorporating a company in Australia, it is possible to register a foreign company in Australia and operate through a branch. A number of tax and liability considerations should be thought through. As far as Australia is concerned, the branch is the entity that is registered. Thus, the branch has no separate limitation of liability from the main company.

A branch is required to file with ASIC certain information and copies of all filings made with governing authorities in its jurisdiction of incorporation.

Austria

Alexander Krilyszyn
Pistotnik Rechtsanwaltsgesellschaft mbH

---

1. Types of company with limited liability and applicable legislation

Austrian commercial law distinguishes between:

- companies with limited liability of shareholders; and
- partnerships with either limited or unlimited liability of partners.

The most common form of incorporation is the limited liability company (*Gesellschaft mit beschränkter Haftung*), which is governed by the Law on Limited Liability Companies. This chapter thus deals in detail with the establishment of limited liability companies.

Over the years, the distinction between stock corporations and limited liability companies of a certain size has almost disappeared. Accounting and bookkeeping provisions, and the rules on the establishment of a supervisory board, are now more or less identical. One of the main differences still remaining is that while shareholders of a stock corporation can be anonymous, shareholders of a limited liability company must always be registered with the Commercial Registry. Another difference is the minimum capital requirement, which stands at €70,000 for stock corporations but just €35,000 for limited liability companies.

Limited liability companies are the bread and butter of Austria's commerce and industry, and they are thus the most important form of legal entity established in the jurisdiction. A limited liability company may become a limited or unlimited partner in a partnership, an option that is mainly utilised in certain tax schemes within larger groups of companies.

2. Incorporation procedure

2.1 Proceedings prior to incorporation

(a) Name registration

The name of a limited liability company can:

- be derived from the business that the company plans to carry out;
- include the name of one or more shareholders;
- be an inverted name as long as it is specifiable; or
- be a mix of the business that the company plans to carry out and a shareholder's name.

The company name must be distinguishable from other names registered at the same commercial court and include the term *'Gesellschaft mit beschränkter Haftung'* or an abbreviation such as 'GmbH'. Pre-registration is not required, but it is advisable to contact the commercial registry in advance if some exceptional fanciful addition is desired, such as *'Smiling Holding Company GmbH'*. Here, 'Smiling' would be regarded as a fanciful addition, while 'holding company' is derived from the purpose of the business. In some cases the local chamber of commerce may be requested to issue an opinion.

Where the word 'Austria' or another regional reference is to be included in the company name, it will prove very helpful if the commercial registry can be furnished with evidence that the company is part of an international group of companies which distinguishes between its subsidiaries by adding the name of the respective country to the name of each local company. Otherwise, a complicated procedure must be undertaken that can easily take a few months and involves various opinions of the nine local Austrian chambers of commerce.

(b) Capital contributions

The minimum share capital is €35,000. The contributions can be made in cash or in kind. As a rule, 50% of any stated amount must be paid in prior to incorporation; proof of payment must be provided in the form of a bank declaration. The minimum amount to be contributed by an individual shareholder is €70.

(c) Declaration of foreign investment

No such declaration is required in Austria.

(d) Tax number for foreign partners/directors

No tax number is required, unless the foreign partner/director is granted payments by the Austrian company and does not reside in Austria.

2.2 Incorporation

(a) Bylaws

(i) Essential clauses

The articles of association must specify:
- the name and registered domicile of the company;
- the purpose of the business;
- the amount of the stated capital; and
- the amount to be contributed to the stated capital by each shareholder.

(ii) Clauses not foreseen by law

Clauses that are inconsistent with the provisions of the Law on Limited Liability Companies may not be included in the articles of association and shall have no legal effect (Section 4(2) of the Law on Limited Liability Companies).

(b) **Execution of public deed**

The articles of association must take the form of a notarial deed. If they are to be signed by a proxy, a special authorisation pertaining to this single business matter of establishing a company is required and the respective document must be notarised and affixed to the articles (Section 4(3) of the Law on Limited Liability Companies).

Any power of attorney signed outside Austria generally requires notarial legalisation and an apostille under the Hague Convention.

(c) **Tax identification number**

Like other legal entities, a limited liability company is subject to corporate income tax and value added tax. It must therefore register with the local tax office upon establishment.

(d) **Registration with the commercial registry**

The commercial register is established at the respective commercial court, which is the local district court. As registration is now administered electronically, solicitors, notaries and other authorised persons may request electronic excerpts from the commercial register regarding a specific company. A company will be registered in the commercial register only pursuant to an application signed by all managing directors.

The following information must be filed together with this application:

- the articles of association in the form of a notarial deed;
- a list signed by the managing directors setting out the name, occupation, domicile and usual place of residence of each shareholder, as well as the amount of the original contribution subscribed for and the payment made on it;
- a list of the managing directors, including the name, occupation, domicile and usual place of residence of each and a certificate of appointment/election in notarised form; and
- a bank declaration, as proof of payment of the contributed share capital. This declaration should not be older than 14 days.

Additionally, the managing directors must provide specimen signatures in notarised form.

The application must further include a statement that the amount of the original cash contributions as shown in the list has been paid in cash, and that the amount paid in is at the free disposal of the managing directors.

The articles of association do not usually limit the duration of the company. It is therefore usual to incorporate companies with unlimited duration, although the articles of association may provide otherwise.

(e) **Legalisation of official books**

Shareholder resolutions may be recorded in a book of minutes.

(f) **Declaration of start date and other tax declarations**

Costs incurred in relation to the founding and establishment of the company are deductible for corporate income tax purposes.

(g) *Costs of establishment and registration*

The costs relating to the establishment and registration of a company are as follows:

- companies tax at a rate of 1% of the paid-up capital; and
- a fee of 0.55% of the nominal capital payable to the commercial registry.

If the shareholder of the company to be formed or taken over has not been self–employed within the last 15 years, if he has not been a shareholder of another company and if he will control the company, he can ask for government aid and avoid the above-mentioned as well as other fees (*'Neugründungsförderungsgesetz'*).

The fees of the solicitor and the notary public must also be taken into account.

3. Number of shareholders

Austria has enacted the respective EU regulations and a limited liability company may therefore be established by one or more shareholders. In a case of sole ownership, the articles of association are known as a 'declaration of establishment' but their content remains unchanged. Shareholders may be natural or legal persons.

4. Corporate name – limitations

With the exception of those outlined in section 2.1(a) above, there are few surprising limitations with regard to company names. These limitations are laid down in various laws such as the Austrian Banking Act, which reserves use of the term 'bank' to financial institutions.

5. Corporate domicile

An Austrian limited liability company must choose a domicile in Austria. The address of the local solicitor or tax adviser is sufficient.

6. Object

A limited liability company may carry on any lawful type of business. Very few exceptions exist (eg insurance business must be conducted by a stock corporation).

7. Capital stock

7.1 Minimum capital requirement

The minimum capital requirement for limited liability companies is €35,000. Fifty per cent of the stated amount must be paid up in cash prior to registration of the company.

7.2 Nature of contributions

Limited liability companies may be established with contributions either in cash or in kind, whether fully or partially. Where in-kind contributions are made, a certified accountant/auditor must carry out a formation audit and prepare a written report stating in detail the actual value of the contributed assets. The assets must be described and determined in the articles of association. Such assets may be almost anything of value, such as:

- receivables;
- property, including machinery;
- company shares;
- patents, know-how, trademarks and similar intellectual property rights; and
- real estate.

Contributions in cash and in kind may be mixed. As a rule, at least 50% of the stated share capital must be paid in cash; but where a certified auditor's report on in-kind contributions is produced, these may amount to up to 100% of the share capital.

7.3   Partial payments
See section 7.1.

7.4   Shares
The shareholders of a limited liability company do not hold individual share certificates; the legal fiction is that a certain amount of the share capital is allotted to each shareholder in accordance with the articles of association. Such shareholding (as opposed to the individual shares of a stock corporation) may be transferred only by way of notarial deed. Any agreement regarding such shareholding (eg options, encumbrance) is legally binding only if concluded by way of notarial deed. The individual shareholding is registered in the commercial register, showing the name and domicile of the shareholder. The person named in the commercial register is therefore to be regarded as the existing shareholder. It is the responsibility of the managing directors to notify the commercial registry accordingly and keep the information up to date.

7.5   Transfer of shares

(a)   Restrictions
The articles of association may impose various restrictions on the transfer of shares; these are limited only by the imagination of the drafter. The usual forms are:
- rights of first refusal; and
- option rights, whereby the price is to be established on the basis of a price formula as at the date of exercise of the option.

These provisions may be mixed in any way that the shareholders deem proper.

(b)   Formalities
A shareholding in an Austrian limited liability company may be transferred only through a share purchase agreement in the form of a notarial deed. The same provisions apply with regard to the formalities of a power of attorney as described in connection with the establishment of the company (see section 2.2(b)).

8. Equity

8.1 Equity/capital ratio

The Corporate Income Tax Act of Austria contains no specific provisions in this respect. As a rule, an equity/capital ratio of between 4:1 and 6:1 is permissible. Any known agreements between the company and shareholders providing equity must be at arm's length; otherwise, the additional equity may be regarded as hidden capital and interest paid may not be deemed tax deductible at company level.

8.2 Convertible bonds

Convertible bonds are not permissible at the level of a limited liability company. They may be created for a stock corporation, entitling the holder to exchange the bond for share certificates.

However, other types of bonds based on the company's profits may be issued (eg *Genussrechte, Gewinnschuldverschreibung*).

9. Administration

9.1 General shareholders' meeting

Shareholder decisions may be taken at a shareholders' meeting or through resolution by written vote. In the event of a written vote, the majority required to pass a resolution of the shareholders' meeting according to the law or the articles of association shall be calculated on the basis of the aggregate number of votes to which the shareholders in total are entitled.

(a) Quorum requirements

(i) Attendance

Generally, 10% of the share capital must be represented at a shareholders' meeting, although the articles of association may provide otherwise and certain provisions may similarly require otherwise.

(ii) Voting

Unless the law or the articles of association provide otherwise, a resolution is deemed to be passed by simple majority. In the articles of association a certain shareholder can be granted more votes independent from the amount of shares he got or he can get the power of veto for certain topics.

A unanimous decision is required to change the corporate purpose of the company, although the articles of association may provide otherwise.

A 75% majority is required for resolutions concerning:

- important investments in excess of 20% of the stated capital of the company;
- changes to the articles of association, including changes in the size of the share capital;
- liquidation;
- merger;

- transformation; and
- demerger.

(b) **Challenging resolutions**

Resolutions adopted by the shareholders' meeting and those adopted by written vote will be entered in a separate minute book. A court action may be instituted to have a shareholder resolution declared void if:

- under the law or the articles of association, the resolution must be considered as not having been adopted; or
- the resolution violates mandatory provisions of the law, or is inconsistent with the articles of association and the rules on changes to the articles of association have not been complied with.

An action may be initiated by:

- any shareholder present at the meeting whose objection to the resolution was entered in the minutes; or
- any shareholder who was not present because he was unjustly not admitted, or whose participation was impeded because the meeting was called improperly.

If the resolution was adopted by written vote, any shareholder who voted against the resolution or who was passed over in the voting process may institute an action.

The managing directors and the supervisory board, where one exists, may also institute an action if implementation of the resolution would result in their personal liability. An action seeking invalidation of a shareholder resolution must be directed against the company and must be brought within one month of the entry of the resolution in the minute book – for practical purposes, one month after the shareholders' meeting or written vote took place.

(c) **Minority rights**

Shareholders representing 10% of the stated capital are entitled to:

- request the convening of a shareholders' meeting, or convene the meeting themselves if the managing directors do not act on their request;
- request that certain matters be included on the agenda for the shareholders' meeting;
- request the appointment of auditors for a special audit; and
- enforce compensation claims against the executive management and the supervisory board members.

They also have some other rights of no practical use. From the above list, resolutions needing a 75% majority under section 9.1(a) above means that 25% plus one vote will have a blocking minority.

9.2 Administrative body

(a) System of administration

The executive management (also called the 'managing board') may consist of one or more managing directors. They may represent the limited liability company jointly or severally. The managing directors must be natural persons and may be appointed regardless of their citizenship and place of residence. The appointment may be made by separate resolution of the shareholders or in the articles of association. In the latter case, a managing director may be dismissed only by amendment of the articles of association, which makes the removal of the managing director more complicated. On the application of any interested third party, the court may appoint a provisional Austrian resident as managing director either if no managing director remains or if none of the managing directors maintains his permanent residence in Austria.

The managing directors carry on the day-to-day business of the company; they represent the company in all matters and may therefore obligate the company in binding form. The articles of association may specify whether one or more managing directors are to be appointed and their rights of representation. They may also grant rights of representation through what is usually known as *'Prokurist'*. The managing directors have sole responsibility for keeping all necessary company books and for drafting the annual financial statements and report. The managing board has also got to summon the general meeting once a year or anytime necessary for the welfare of the company.

(b) Term of office, resignation and removal of directors

The term of office may be for a limited or unlimited period. Managing directors are usually also employees of the company and therefore the provisions of their employment contracts prevail. These contracts are customarily of indefinite duration. Managing directors may be removed from office by simple majority decision of the shareholders. Such removal does not preclude a managing director who is employed with the company from protecting his rights under the employment agreement. The employment agreement must then be terminated in accordance with the applicable legal provisions.

A managing director may resign from office at any time; however; he must ensure that the company will not suffer any damage where he does so without cause.

Any change in the managing directors must be reported to the commercial registry.

(c) Directors' liability to third parties

The managing directors have an obligation to the company to act with the care of an orderly businessperson in the management of the business (Section 25 of the Law on Limited Liability Companies). Managing directors who breach their duties will be jointly and severally liable to the company for resulting damages. In particular, they will be liable for damages if payments are made after the obligation to file a bankruptcy petition is triggered. In such cases each managing director will be personally liable to the company in an amount of up to €100,000 if he fails to take the necessary measures to restructure the company as provided for by law or does not file for bankruptcy within 60 days after the company has become insolvent.

A managing director will also be liable to the company for damages resulting from transactions with the company which he concludes for his own account or for the account of another party without first obtaining the consent of all other managing directors or, if one exists, of the supervisory board.

The managing directors are jointly and severally liable for their actions. They cannot invoke the privilege of limitation of liability as an ordinary employee could.

Under certain circumstances, managing directors may be held liable if they misrepresent the status of the company to its financial institutions.

(d) *Non-competition*

The managing directors may not transact business within the company's scope of business for their own account or the account of others; nor may they serve as general partner of a partnership or as a member of the managing or supervisory board of another company in the same line of business, unless the company has consented. Managing directors who violate this prohibition may be removed without indemnification payments. The company may also claim damages, which are time-barred for three months after the date on which the company learns of the violation.

(e) *Special duties of secrecy and loyalty*

See sections 9.2(c) and 9.2(d).

(f) *Civil and criminal liability*

A direct liability may be derived from the Law on Unfair Trade Practices. Managing directors may also be held personally liable under certain administrative law provisions.

(g) *Supervisory board*

Under certain circumstances, the Law on Limited Liability Companies requires the appointment or election of a supervisory board by the shareholders. The supervisory board may be compared to the non-executive board of UK, US or Swiss companies. The supervisory board oversees the performance of the managing directors, although it does not appoint or dismiss managing directors – this task falls to the shareholders.

A supervisory board must be appointed if:

- the stated capital exceeds €70,000 and the company has more than 50 shareholders;
- the average number of employees in the preceding year exceeded 300;
- the company centrally manages stock corporations, companies with limited liability with a mandatory supervisory board or companies with limited liability within the meaning of Section 2.1 (Section 15(1) of the Stock Corporation Law, going concern), or controls them by means of a direct interest exceeding 50%, and the total number of employees in the controlling and controlled companies together amounts to more than 300 on average; within a corporate group it is sufficient if the controlling company has a supervisory board;

- the company is a general partner of a limited partnership and the total number of employees in the company and the partnership's business together amounts to more than 300 on average; or
- the company is an investment company.

The supervisory board consists of at least three members appointed by the shareholders. In addition, at least two supervisory board members must be appointed by the works council; as a rule, for every two members appointed by the shareholders and if an uneven number is appointed, an additional member must be appointed by the works council. Because of this it is usual that the shareholders appoint four members to guarantee the majority of the members appointed by the shareholders. A managing director or employee of the company cannot be appointed as a member of the supervisory board; neither can a legal entity. There are certain other restrictions on the number of supervisory board seats that one person may hold.

The supervisory board must appoint one chairman and one deputy chairman. Several subcommittees may be established. The supervisory board must convene at least four times each fiscal year, preferably every three months. Minutes must be taken, and these must be signed by the chairman or his deputy.

The supervisory board must also approve the following matters before they are carried out by the executive management:

- the acquisition and sale of interests, as well as the acquisition, sale and closure of enterprises and plants;
- the acquisition, sale and encumbrance of real estate;
- the establishment and closure of branches;
- investments that exceed certain acquisition costs, in each particular case with respect to the total in the fiscal year;
- the issue of securities, and the taking of loans and credits that exceed a certain sum in each particular case and with respect to the total in the fiscal year;
- the granting of loans and credits outside the ordinary course of business;
- the establishment and abandonment of lines of business and types of production;
- the determination of general business policy principles; and
- the determination of principles on the distribution of profits or turnover sharing, and the granting of pensions to managing directors and senior employees.

Where the supervisory board fails to approve such matters, this does not *per se* render the relevant transaction void. If the managing directors do not request such prior approval, they may be held personally liable for any damages resulting from the transactions.

The supervisory board must also review and inspect the company's financial statements to approve the proposed profit distribution and the annual report. It must report to the shareholders' meeting on an annual basis.

9.3 Others

(a) Attorneys

There are two types of employee with special power of attorney, both of whom are appointed by the managing directors.

Prokura: The *Prokurist* must be registered in the commercial register and a specimen signature must be filed. No particular written power of attorney is required for the *Prokurist* to represent the company. The *Prokurist* must be appointed by all members of the managing board.

The *Prokurist* may undertake most kinds of commercial transaction and may represent the company in any matters required to carry on business. However, the *Prokurist* may not:

- sell or encumber real estate;
- appoint another *Prokurist*;
- liquidate the business; or
- sign the financial statements and annual report.

It is possible to appoint one or more *Prokuristen* with joint or single signatory power. Their signatory power may be limited to signing together with a member of the managing board.

The *Prokura* is a function granted to the individual and may be revoked at any time by a member of the managing board.

Handlungsvollmacht: This is often translated as 'commercial power of attorney' and is narrower in scope than the power granted to *Prokuristen*. The *Handlungsbevollmächtigter* (ie the holder of such commercial power of attorney) is limited to the conclusion of specific business and any transactions in its ordinary course. The *Handlungsvollmacht* is not registered in the commercial register.

(b) Internal controllers and auditors

No specific rules exist with regard to internal controllers and auditors. They are regarded as employees who have been given a specific task.

10. Shareholders' duties and partners' liability

The main duties of a shareholder are that he has to pay or contribute in kind his part of the registered capital and give additional contributions if this is stated in the articles of association. If the shareholder does not fulfil these duties, he will lose his shareholder rights and will still be liable to pay the difference between contributed and stated capital.

The shareholders can also be liable if:

- there is a qualified undercapitalisation;
- there is a mixture of company and shareholder assets;
- misuse of the company has occurred (eg to bypass a certain law); and
- the shareholder directs the managing directors not to take the necessary measures to restructure the company as provided for by law.

11. Fiscal year

The fiscal year may be determined in the articles of association. The first fiscal year cannot be longer than one year, but it can be shorter. Any change in the fiscal year must be approved by the local tax authority and be registered in the commercial register.

The company may commence activities even before it has been established. If it is properly established, then any business activities entered into before its establishment are regarded as being carried out on its behalf.

12. Financial statements

12.1 Company tax

The corporate income tax rate is currently (2009) 25%. Dividends distributed are subject to income tax at the shareholder's personal level at a rate of 25%.

12.2 Annual accounts

(a) Documents

The managing directors have the duty to ensure that proper accounts are drawn up. The directors must prepare the annual report, which must be audited by a firm of auditors appointed by the shareholders. The auditors should confirm that the accounts are correct. They can withhold this confirmation if they feel that it is appropriate.

Depending on the actual size of the company, different accounting provisions apply. The different categories are outlined in the following table.

Small company	<ul><li>Balance sheet total of €3,650,000 or less</li><li>Turnover of €7.3 million or under in the preceding business year</li><li>Annual average of fewer than 50 employees</li></ul>
Medium-sized company	Must exceed two of the above prerequisites for small companies and stay below two of the following prerequisites over two consecutive fiscal years:<ul><li>Balance sheet total of €14.6 million</li><li>turnover of €29 million in the preceding business year</li><li>annual average of 250 employees</li></ul>
Large company	By definition, exceeds two of the above prerequisites for mid-sized companies over two consecutive fiscal years

Regardless of the company's size, the annual report must contain the following:
- the management report;

- the balance sheet;
- the profit and loss statement; and
- an annex explaining and disclosing certain details and accounting policies.

There are strict rules on the format of the balance sheet.

(b)   *Approval and distribution of profits*

The financial statements must be approved by the shareholders. The managing director(s) must propose how to utilise the profits to the shareholders' meeting.

(c)   *Deposit and publication*

The managing directors must file the annual financial statements as soon as possible with the Commercial Registry. Large companies must also publish the balance sheet and the auditors' certificate in the *Official Gazette*.

13.   Company reorganisation

There are various methods of effecting mergers and acquisitions in Austria. The main governing laws are:

- the Split-off or Demerger Act;
- the Takeover Act;
- the Transformation Act; and
- specific tax regulations.

Although a generalisation, it is true to say that most company reorganisations are tax driven. The purpose of these laws is to avoid any detrimental tax consequences when using one of the restructuring vehicles. Aside from the tax consequences, it is important to ensure that universal succession from the original company to the restructured entity is assured. The respective legislative provisions address these concerns.

Needless to say, shareholder resolutions and various formalities and applications are required in order to carry out the restructuring steps.

14.   Eventual partner separation

The articles of association may contain provisions for the eventual separation of partners. These may take the form of option clauses or the right to buy out the other partners in accordance with a price formula; in the absence of such provisions, separation may be effected through litigation. When litigating, the removal for cause of another shareholder or the termination for cause of the company may be requested.

By law the main shareholder, holding at least 90% of the registered capital, can ask the other shareholders to transfer their shares to him for adequate cash compensation. In the articles of association such an action by the main shareholder can be prohibited or it may be constituted that the main shareholder needs a higher percentage of share.

15.   Dissolution and liquidation

The shareholders may decide to liquidate the company by a 75% majority. They must then appoint the liquidator, who is usually a former managing director. A balance sheet must be drawn up at the beginning of the liquidation and another at the end of the liquidation.

The managing directors must notify the Commercial Registry of the liquidation. The liquidators must inform creditors of the dissolution of the company and invite them to file their claims. This notice must be published in the *Official Gazette* and give creditors a period of at least three months in which to file their claims.

During the liquidation period, the company is represented by the liquidators, who are bound by the same principles as the managing directors.

Once the debts have been paid, any surplus may be distributed to the shareholders. After liquidation, the company is deleted from the commercial register. The books and documents of such company must be kept at a place designated by the court for seven years and must remain open for inspection by shareholders or creditors of the company.

16. Branches

A company may conduct business in Austria in the form of a branch, which must be registered in the commercial register where both the branch and the main company are located. Foreign companies that have their corporate seat inside the European Union may also carry out business via an Austrian registered branch.

The branch must use the name of the main company, together with an indication that it is doing business as a branch. Any changes in the parent company must also be registered in the commercial register where the branch is located. The branch office must maintain all records with regard to its own business and meet the same auditing and filing requirements as the parent company.

The branch of a non-Austrian parent company is taxed only on the income and profits that are generated by the branch. Generally speaking, there is little difference between the tax rules applicable to a branch and to a subsidiary of a foreign legal entity.

17. Business licence

In order to do business in Austria, a company must acquire a business or trade licence. With the exception of a few businesses/trades, notification to the local trade authority is sufficient. Only very specific businesses need a licence (eg production of ammunition).

Increasingly, the local trade authority can be notified online. Upon receiving notification, the trade authority will usually issue the business licence. Doing business without the necessary notification or licence may be subject to administrative penalties and give competitors the option to seek redress.

Any legal entity carrying on a business must nominate a representative to the trade authority. This representative may be a member of the managing board or a *Prokurist*, or even an ordinary employee. As a general rule, the representative must work at the company's premises. The representative is liable to the trade authority with regard to compliance with trade law obligations and provisions. If the representative is employed by the company, he must be registered with the Social

Insurance Carrier. The respective EU provisions have mitigated some of the rules pertaining to trade representatives who are citizens of another EU member state.

By registering for a trade licence, the company automatically becomes a member of the local chamber of commerce and the special department applicable to its business.

The author would like to acknowledge Dr Rudolf Krilyszyn, of Rechtsanwälte Dr Krilyszyn, as author of the chapter on Austria for the first edition of this book.

Belgium

Patrick Geeraert
NautaDutilh

1. Types of company with limited liability and applicable legislation

1.1 Overview

Under Belgian law, foreign companies or investors wishing to set up a public limited liability company for commercial or trading purposes can use any of the following types of company (no reference is made to European companies (ie the European Company (SE) and the European Cooperative Society (SCE)).

English	Dutch/French	Company Code provisions
Limited partnership	*gewone commanditaire vennootschap/société en commandite simple*	Articles 201 to 209
Private limited liability company	*besloten vennootschap met beperkte aansprakelijkheid/société privée à responsabilité limitée*	Articles 210 to 349
Cooperative company with limited liability	*coöperatieve vennootschap met beperkte aansprakelijkheid/société cooperative à responsabilité limitée*	Articles 350 to 436
Public limited liability company	*naamloze vennootschap/société anonyme*	Articles 437 to 653
Limited partnership with shares	*commanditaire vennootschap op aandelen/société en commandite par actions*	Articles 654 to 660
Agricultural company	*landbouwvennootschap/société agricole*	Articles 789 to 838

Statistics show that in more than 90% of the cases in which a company with limited liability is formed for commercial or trade purposes, only two of the above forms are used: the public limited liability company and the private limited liability company. These corporate forms generally offer the best mix of flexibility in terms of corporate structure, legal certainty (ie both are well developed in the Company Code – see section 1.2(a) above) and limited liability. Given their importance, this chapter is devoted exclusively to these two corporate forms; however, the other types of public limited liability company may be better suited for certain purposes.

Over the past few decades, the differences between the public limited liability company and the private limited liability company have gradually become less distinct, though both types have their own particularities. Thus, in certain respects the principles and rules governing the public limited liability company and the private limited liability company are identical or very similar.

Reference is not made to public or listed companies – only a public limited liability company can go public – as these are subject to quite stringent rules that fall outside the scope of this chapter.

1.2   Applicable legislation

(a)   Company Code

The Company Code, which was consolidated in 1999 by the Belgian legislature, is split into two parts (Article 55*bis* of the Company Code). The first deals with the principles applicable to all types of company, including companies with limited liability such as the public limited liability company and the private limited liability company. This part sets out general rules and principles relating to incorporation, accounting and bookkeeping, partnership agreements, annulment of decisions of the general meeting, winding-up and liquidation, and statutes of limitations. The second part contains specific rules applicable to each type of company, including public limited liability companies.

Some general rules and principles set out in the Company Code are further clarified and/or implemented by royal or ministerial decrees (as amended from time to time), the most important being the Royal Decree of January 30 2001 (published in the *Belgian State Gazette* on February 6 2001) relating to the implementation of the Company Code. This decree is especially important with respect to bookkeeping and accounting.

(b)   Civil and Commercial Codes

The provisions of the Civil Code and the Commercial Code apply to public limited liability companies and private liability companies except where the Company Code provides otherwise (Article 3 of the Company Code). The Civil Code is especially important for companies that do not exercise commercial or trading activities or that perform activities deemed non-commercial in nature (ie certain liberal professions such as doctors and lawyers) (Article 2*bis* of the Commercial Code). The Civil Code is important as it includes the basic rules on the law of contract and on liability in contract or in tort.

(c) **Crossroads Enterprise Bank**
By the Act of January 16 2003 (published in the *Belgian State Gazette* on February 5 2003), the legislature created the Crossroads Enterprise Bank (CEB), which incorporates and modernises the former registry of commerce. In effect, the CEB is a central database on which all companies, individuals exercising commercial activities and foreign companies conducting commercial activities in Belgium must be registered. In principle, only authorised organisations and governmental agencies can access the data in the CEB, although certain information is available online (http://mineco.fgov.be/kbo.htm) and certificates can be issued to the general public. Pursuant to the provisions of the act, companies incorporated in Belgium must file certain data with the CEB (see section 2.2(f)).

(d) **Private international law**
As a general rule, Belgian law applies to any company with its effective domicile or registered office in Belgium, irrespective of where its instrument of incorporation was executed (Article 110 of the Belgian Code on Private International Law of July 16 2004).

2. Incorporation procedure

2.1 Proceedings prior to incorporation

(a) **Registration**

(i) *Obligation to select a corporate name*
Under Belgian law, every company must have a name, which must not be the same as, or misleadingly similar to, that of another company. In the latter case, any interested party can request that the company's name be changed and/or claim damages from the company's founders or management organs (Article 65 of the Company Code).

(ii) *Formalities*
The company's name must appear on its instrument of incorporation (Article 69 of the Company Code) and must be registered with the CEB.

(b) **Capital contributions**

(i) *Public limited liability company*
General rules: The minimum share capital is €61,500 and must be fully paid in at the time of incorporation (Articles 439 and 448 of the Company Code).
In addition:
- at the time of incorporation, at least 25% of each share must be paid in; and
- within five years of the date of incorporation, any shares representing an in-kind contribution, in whole or in part, must be fully paid in (Articles 439 and 448 of the Company Code).

Cash contributions: Any cash contributed to the capital of a public limited liability company upon incorporation must be deposited in an escrow account in the name of the company with a financial institution located in Belgium. (The opening of a bank account can take from one day to two weeks or more, due to strict money-laundering policies and regulations.) The funds will be released when the institution receives instructions to this effect from the notary who executed the instrument of incorporation. A certificate of funds held in escrow must be appended to the instrument. The funds will be released automatically if incorporation does not occur within three months of deposit with the financial institution (Article 449 of the Company Code).

In-kind contributions: In principle, any tangible or intangible assets can be contributed to the capital of a public limited liability company, provided they can be valued in accordance with economic standards (Article 443 of the Company Code). If an in-kind contribution is made, the founders must appoint a certified auditor prior to incorporation to draft a valuation report on the assets and the valuation methods used. The report must indicate whether the values resulting from these methods correspond to the number and value of shares issued in return for the contribution and the actual value of the consideration. In a special report, the founders must explain why the in-kind contribution is in the interests of the company and whether they have followed the auditor's conclusions. Both reports must be filed with the clerk of the commercial court of the judicial district where the company will have its registered office (Article 444 of the Company Code). Since January 1 2009, special rules apply if the in-kind contribution is composed of certain financial instruments or assets that have previously been audited by a certified auditor.

(ii)   Private limited liability company

The minimum issued capital required by law amounts to €18,550, of which €6,200 must be paid in at the time of incorporation. However, if the private limited liability company has only one founder, €12,400 must be paid in (Articles 214 and 223 Company Code).

In addition:

- at the time of incorporation, at least 25% of each share representing a cash contribution must be paid in; and
- each share representing an in-kind contribution, in whole or in part, must be fully paid in upon incorporation (Articles 214 and 223 Company Code).

Cash contributions: The same rules as those applicable to the public limited liability company will apply *mutatis mutandis* (Article 224 of the Company Code).

In-kind contributions: The same rules as those applicable to the public limited liability company will apply *mutatis mutandis* (including the special rules on financial instruments or assets that have previously been audited by a certified auditor) (Articles 218 and 219 of the Company Code).

(c) **Declaration of foreign investment**

There is no general duty to file or register a declaration of foreign investment. However, special procedures may apply to specific sectors.

(d) **Tax number of foreign investors/administrators**

In general, foreign investors or administrators are not required to register with the value added tax (VAT) authorities, except if they intend to conduct commercial or trading activities (see section 2.2(h)(i)).

2.2 Incorporation

(a) **Articles of association**

(i) *Use of languages*

Dutch, French and German are the three official languages of Belgium.

For the purposes of this chapter and as a general rule, with the exception of employment matters (ie issues falling within the scope of the employer–employee relationship) and certain documents whose use is determined by law, there are no statutory requirements to use a specific language, although Dutch and French are most common.

For employment matters, the language depends on the company's place of business.

Place of business	Language
Flemish region	Dutch
Walloon region	French
German-speaking region	German
Brussels–Capital region	Either French or Dutch, depending on the language of the employee

The company's place of business is also the relevant criterion with respect to documents required by law (eg the instrument of incorporation and other corporate documents, such as minutes of general meetings and invoices). For the purposes of this chapter, a company's place of business shall be deemed the same as its registered office.

Registered office	Language
Flemish region	Dutch
Walloon region	French
German-speaking region	German
Brussels–Capital region	French or Dutch or both

(ii)   *Instrument of incorporation*

The incorporation of a public limited liability company or a private limited liability company requires the assistance of a notary to execute the instrument of incorporation in the presence of the founders or their proxies, each of whom must be in possession of a valid power of attorney (Article 66 of the Company Code). Within 15 days of execution, an extract from the instrument must be filed with the clerk of the commercial court of the judicial district where the company has its registered office (Articles 67, 68 and 69 of the Company Code). This formality is usually accomplished by the notary. Incorporation is complete only when this extract has been recorded (Article 2 of the Company Code).

In order to render an instrument of incorporation enforceable against third parties, an extract thereof must be published in the *Belgian State Gazette* within 15 days of recordation with the commercial court clerk (Articles 73 and 76 of the Company Code).

The extract from the instrument of incorporation of a public limited liability company or a private limited liability company must include at least the following information (Article 69 of the Company Code):

- the company's corporate form;
- the address of its registered office;
- a precise indication of the life of the company (unless it has been incorporated for an indefinite duration);
- a precise indication of the identity of the founders and any shareholders whose contributions have not been fully paid in;
- the company's capital and the amount paid in and authorised, if any;
- the make-up of the company's capital and the auditor's conclusions if an in-kind contribution has been made;
- the commencement and close of the fiscal year;
- provisions dealing with the formation of reserves, the distribution of profits and any liquidation proceeds;
- the appointment of persons authorised to represent and manage the company, the scope of their authority and the manner in which such authority can be exercised (ie jointly, severally or as a board);
- the name of the certified auditor, if any;
- a precise description of the company's corporate purpose; and
- the date, place and time of the annual general meeting of shareholders and the conditions for admission to the meeting and the exercise of voting rights.

(iii)   *Articles of association*

The articles of association regulate the operation of a company. The articles are sometimes very detailed but they may also be quite concise. However, the Company Code requires that they deal with at least the issues described below.

Public limited liability company: The articles of association of a public limited liability company must cover the following issues (Article 453 of the Company Code):

- compliance with the statutory requirements regarding issued and paid-in share capital;
- provisions on the number of and method for appointing directors, managing

director(s), authorised representatives and the certified auditor, as well as the division of powers among these individuals;

- the number and par or fractional value, if any, of the company's shares and any restrictions on the transfer of shares, as well as specifications for the different classes of shares, if any, and the rights vested in each class;
- the number of profit-sharing certificates, if any, and any restrictions on the transfer of such certificates, as well as specifications for the different classes of certificates, if any, and the rights vested in each class;
- the nature of the shares (ie registered or dematerialised);
- a description and details of any in-kind contributions and the shares issued to the contributor(s) in return;
- a description and details of any special benefits granted to any founder(s) of the company;
- the total cost of incorporation or an estimate thereof;
- details of the financial institution referred to under Section 2.1(b)(i);
- details of any transactions involving real property contributed to the company in the preceding five years;
- any mortgages, charges or pledges on property contributed to the company's capital; and
- the conditions under which any contributed option rights can be exercised.

Private limited liability company: The articles of association of a private limited liability company must deal with at least the following issues (Article 226 of the Company Code):

- compliance with the statutory requirements regarding issued and paid-in share capital;
- the number and par or fractional value of the shares and any transfer restrictions;
- a description and details of any in-kind contribution and the shares issued to the contributor(s) in return;
- a description and details of any special benefits granted to any founder(s);
- the total cost of incorporation or an estimate thereof;
- details of the financial institution referred to in section 2.1(b)(ii);
- details of any transactions involving real property contributed to the company in the preceding five years;
- any mortgages, charges or pledges on property contributed to the company's capital; and
- the conditions under which any of contributed option rights can be exercised.

(b) *Execution of public instruments*

(i) *Notary*
The assistance of a notary is required to incorporate a public limited liability company or a private limited liability company. The parties are free to select a notary of their choice.

The notary charges a fee for services rendered based on a percentage of the issued capital and ranging from 0.855% down to 0.0114%, with lower percentages applying to greater amounts of capital. In addition, stamp duties are charged for each page the notary must execute.

(ii) Belgian State Gazette

An extract from the instrument of incorporation must be published in the *Belgian State Gazette*, following which the information contained therein shall be deemed public and enforceable against third parties. As of January 2009, the publication fee stood at €185.70 (excluding VAT).

(c) **Business plan**

At the time of incorporating either a private limited liability company or a public limited liability company, the founders must provide the notary with a business plan (Articles 215 and 440 of the Company Code). The notary will keep the plan on file for three years. The plan should contain a forecast clearly showing that the company's capital is sufficient to cover its intended business activities for two years. Should the company go bankrupt within three years of incorporation, the courts can request the notary to produce the plan. If the plan clearly indicates that the company's capital was manifestly insufficient to cover its business activities for two years, the founders can be held liable for any liabilities incurred by the company.

(d) **VAT number**

See Section 2.2(h)(i).

(e) **Payment of indirect taxes**

No indirect taxes are due on the share capital at the time of incorporation.

If the company's activities are subject to VAT, it will need a VAT registration (see section 2.2(h)(i)), which will usually come together with registration with the CEB (see section 2.2(f)).

(f) **Registration with the CEB**

(i) *Formalities*

Every company incorporated in Belgium must register with the CEB prior to commencing activities (Article 33 of the Act of January 16 2003). Upon registration, the company receives a unique 10-digit number which it must use on all corporate documents (eg invoices) (Articles 5, 11 and 13 of the Act of January 16 2003).

Upon incorporation, the following information must be filed with the CEB (Article 6 of the Act of January 16 2003):

- the company's corporate name and form;
- the address(es) of the company's registered office and various places of business;
- the date of incorporation;
- the identity of the company's founders and members of its management organs;

- a description of the company's activities; and
- details of any permits granted by public authorities.

The company must update the information on file with the CEB should any changes occur or if the information is no longer valid (Article 6 of the Act of January 16 2003). Commercial activities that have not yet been recorded with the CEB may be commenced only once the CEB has been informed of the changes (Article 35 of the Act of January 16 2003).

(ii)   *Permits and governmental approvals*

For certain activities, the company must obtain a specific permit or governmental approval (eg for the production and trade of foodstuffs, real-estate brokerage, transport activities on behalf of third parties and leasing activities). Without a permit or approval, the company either:

- will not be able to register with the CEB, as the latter must verify whether it has obtained the requisite permits and approvals; or
- will be able to register but will not be authorised to exercise any of the activities for which a permit or governmental approval is required (Article 39 of the Act of January 16 2003).

(iii)   *Proof of professional expertise for SMEs*

Small and medium-sized enterprises (SMEs) must provide the CEB with proof of sufficient professional expertise to exercise their intended activities. In essence, the company must prove that its management has:

- the requisite administration skills to manage the business; and
- professional expertise to exercise its intended activities.

The Act of February 10 1998 on the promotion of entrepreneurship contains a set of rules that companies can use to prove that they have sufficient professional expertise. If a company cannot do so, it cannot register with the CEB (Article 1 of the Royal Decree of June 22 2003).

An SME is a company that meets all of the following criteria (Article 2 of the Act of February 10 1998):

- it employs fewer than 50 persons on average annually;
- less than 25% of its shares are held by companies that are not SMEs; and
- its annual turnover does not exceed €7 million or its balance sheet total is less than €5 million.

If the company does not meet any of the above criteria, it will not be regarded as an SME and the above restrictive rules regarding professional expertise will not apply.

Although the above procedure may appear to be burdensome, SMEs can, subject to certain conditions, benefit from preferential company tax rates (see section 11.1 below) and other tax benefits. As SMEs often also comply with the criteria of small companies (see section 11.2(a)) – and vice versa – SMEs can also benefit from the advantages of small companies (eg see sections 11.2(a) and (b)).

(iv) *Fees*

A fee is charged by the Business Gateway Office, the amount of which is set by royal decree. The fee for registration with the CEB is currently €73.

(g) **Recording of minutes**

A company must keep a record of the minutes of all meetings of its corporate bodies.

(h) **Declaration of start date and other tax filings**

(i) *Registration with the VAT authorities*

Prior to the start of its activities, a company must register with the VAT authorities of the district where its registered office will be located if it intends to conduct commercial or trading activities (Article 4 of the VAT Code). Upon registration, the company will receive a VAT number, composed of the same 10 digits as its company number preceded by the prefix 'BE'. This number must be used on all invoices and the like (Article 50 of the VAT Code). Registration with the local VAT authorities is usually handled by the Business Gateway Office. Special tax filings may apply if the company intends to trade in excise goods (eg tobacco or alcoholic beverages).

(ii) *Registration with the Social Security Administration*

If the company intends to employ or hire personnel, it must register with the Social Security Administration and the tax authorities for the payment of social security contributions and salary withholding tax, respectively (Article 21 of the Act of June 27 1969).

In addition, the following steps must be taken:
- registration with a family allowances fund;
- registration with an external service for prevention and protection at work;
- establishment of work rules;
- establishment and maintenance of payroll documents;
- application for work permits (non-EU citizens may not work in Belgium on the basis of an employment contract without a work permit); and
- taking out of occupational accident insurance.

Administrators of a company must register with the social security authorities for self-employed workers within 90 days of their appointment and may be required to pay social security contributions.

3. Number of shareholders

3.1 Private limited liability company

To incorporate a private limited liability company, there must be at least two shareholders, who can be either natural or legal persons; a private limited liability company may also be incorporated by a sole shareholder (Articles 211 and 212 of the Company Code). However, if the sole shareholder is not an individual, or if the individual has previously incorporated a private limited liability company of which he is the sole shareholder, that shareholder shall be jointly and severally liable with the private limited liability company for any obligations of the latter until another shareholder joins the company (Articles 212 and 213 of the Company Code).

3.2 Public limited liability company

To incorporate a public limited liability company, there must be at least two shareholders, who can be either natural or legal persons (Articles 437 and 454 of the Company Code). Should the number of shareholders be reduced to one, the company will not automatically be liquidated. However, the sole shareholder will be held jointly and severally liable for all obligations of the public limited liability company from the date on which the number of shareholders dropped to one if within 12 months: (i) no additional shareholder is brought in; (ii) the company has not been converted into a private limited liability company; and (iii) the company has not been dissolved (Article 646 of the Company Code).

4. Corporate name – restrictions

4.1 Corporate name

See section 2.1(a) above.

A company's corporate name and form must be mentioned on all documents for external use (eg invoices, letters and announcements) issued by the company (Article 78 of the Company Code).

4.2 Trade name

A distinction should be made between a corporate name and a trade name. A company's corporate name is the name under which it is registered with the CEB, while a trade name is the name under which a company usually does business. These two names can – but need not – be the same. Unlike corporate names, there are no specific registration requirements with respect to trade names. However, specific protection of a trade name can be obtained through registration of the name as a trademark. In addition, even if a trade name has not been registered as a trademark and no other specific IP protection applies, a trade name is automatically protected under Article 8 of the Paris Convention for the Protection of Industrial Property of March 20 1883. In order for this provision to apply, the company need only prove that it was the first to use the name visibly and consistently in trade.

5. Corporate domicile

5.1 Choice of registered office

Every company must have a registered office, the address of which must be mentioned in its instrument of incorporation, published in the *Belgian State Gazette* and recorded with the CEB (see Sections 2.2(a)(ii) and 2.2(f)(ii)). A company's registered office must, in principle, coincide with its place of effective management but need not be the same as its place of business.

The company's registered office should be located in Belgium. If this not the case but management decisions are consistently taken in Belgium, the company will nevertheless be subject to Belgian law (see also section 1.2(d)).

Depending on the exact location of the company's registered office, different language requirements will apply to corporate documents (see section 2.2(a)(i)).

The address of the company's registered office must appear on all of the company's outgoing documents (eg invoices, letters and announcements) (Article 78 of the Company Code).

5.2 Change of registered office

A company's management organ is usually empowered by the articles of association to change the location of its registered office without the prior approval of the general meeting.

If the registered office is moved from one linguistic region to another (see section 2.2(a)(i)), the articles of association must be translated.

6. Corporate purpose

6.1 Duty to describe

A company's corporate purpose must be detailed in its articles of association. The corporate purpose may not be illegal or contrary to public policy (Article 227 (private limited liability company) and Article 454 (public limited liability company) of the Company Code). To verify whether a particular activity is illegal, an extensive (but non-exhaustive) list can be consulted at the Business Gateway Office.

The corporate purpose should be described extensively, but not in terms that are too general. A company's corporate purpose should define the various areas of activity in which it is active.

6.2 Registration

A company's corporate purpose determines the scope of activities for which it must register with the CEB (see section 2.2(f)).

6.3 Change to corporate purpose

If the company wishes to change its corporate purpose, the Company Code provides a specific procedure, following which the general shareholders' meeting must approve the change by a special majority (Article 287 (private limited liability company) and Article 559 (public limited liability company) of the Company Code).

7. Capital stock

7.1 Minimum capital requirement

Public limited liability company: The minimum share capital required by law is €61,500 and this must be fully paid in at the time of incorporation (see Section 2.1(b)(i); Articles 439 and 448 of the Company Code).

Private limited liability company: The minimum share capital required by law amounts to €18,550, of which €6,200 (or €12,400 if there is only one shareholder) must be paid in upon incorporation (Articles 214 and 223 of the Company Code).

7.2 Nature of contributions

Contributions to capital can be made in cash or in kind (see section 2.1(b)(i) with respect to the public limited liability company and section 2.1(b)(ii) with respect to the private limited liability company).

7.3 Partial payments

See section 2.1(b)(i) with respect to the public limited liability company and section 2.1(b)(ii) with respect to the private limited liability company.

7.4 Representation of shares

Public limited liability company: A public limited liability company can issue two types of shares (Article 460 of the Company Code): registered and dematerialised.

Since January 1 2008 a public limited liability company can no longer issue bearer shares. Gradually all existing bearer shares (issued prior to January 1 2008) will have to be converted into registered or dematerialised shares (and this must be done in any event prior to January 1 2014). In either case, a shareholder still holding bearer shares can request that they be converted into registered shares at any time (Article 462 of the Company Code).

If a company issues registered shares, it must keep a shareholder register including the details of the shareholders, the numbers of shares held and all transactions relating to the shares (Article 463 of the Company Code). The shares must remain registered until they have been fully paid in (Article 477 of the Company Code). When they have been recorded in the shareholder register, the company will issue certificates to the shareholders (Article 465 of the Company Code).

If a company issues dematerialised shares, these will be recorded in an account in the name of the respective shareholder. To issue dematerialised shares, the company will first have to register with a clearing institution, which will manage the accounts (Article 468 of the Company Code).

Private limited liability company: A private limited liability company can issue registered shares only (Article 232 of the Company Code). The company must record the details of its shareholders, the number of shares held by each and all transactions related to its shares in a register (Article 234 of the Company Code). Shareholders are issued certificates representing their shares once these have been recorded in the register (Article 235 of the Company Code).

7.5 Transfer of shares

(a) Restrictions

Public limited liability company: Shares in a public limited liability company can in principle be transferred freely and without restriction to any third party, subject only to the requirements set out in section 7.5(b) below (Articles 504 and 506 of the Company Code) and provided the shares are fully paid in.

Transfer restrictions can be included in the articles of association or in any shareholder agreement (Article 510 of the Company Code). Special requirements apply in the event of a non-transferability clause, an approval clause or a clause granting a pre-emptive right (Article 510 of the Company Code).

Private limited liability company: Due to the very nature of the private limited liability company, the transfer of its shares is more restricted (Article 249 of the Company Code).

Unless there are more stringent transfer restrictions in the articles of association (see Section 2.2(a)(iii)), shares in a private limited liability company can be transferred only if at least half the shareholders representing 75% of the shares (not taking into account the shares to be transferred) agree to the transfer. Unless the articles of association provide otherwise, this approval is not required if the shares are transferred to:

- a shareholder;
- the spouse of the transferor or the testator;
- direct linear ascendants or descendants of the transferor; and
- other persons permitted by the articles of association.

Apart from special provisions in the articles of associations, any interested third party can bring summary proceedings for refusal to consent to an intended transfer (Article 251 of the Company Code).

(b) Formalities

A transfer of ownership occurs *solo consensu* and, in principle, no additional formalities are needed to transfer ownership. However, to make the transfer enforceable against the company and third parties, additional formalities are in place as set out next.

Public limited liability company: Registered shares can be transferred by making the appropriate entries in the shareholder register. Dematerialised shares can be transferred by recording the transfer in the acquirer's account (Article 504 of the Company Code). The transfer will be carried out by the clearing institution.

Private limited liability company: Registered shares can be transferred by making the appropriate entries in the shareholder register (Article 250 of the Company Code).

8. Equity

8.1 Debt–equity ratio

The Company Code does not impose a specific obligation with respect to the ratio between borrowed funds (debt) and shareholders' equity (see also section 2.2(c)).

8.2 Net assets – share capital ratio

If the value of the company's net assets falls below half its issued share capital, a general meeting must be convened by the board of directors within two months of the time the losses were or should have been reported. This is to determine whether the company should continue in existence or be liquidated (special majority rules apply) and the restructuring measures that need to be taken. To this effect, the board must draft a special report. In the absence of such a report, any decisions taken by the general meeting shall be deemed null and void (Article 332 (private limited liability company) and Article 633 (public limited liability company) of the Company Code).

If the value of the company's net assets falls below one-quarter of its issued share capital, the same also holds true, but the company can be liquidated with the approval of only 25% of the votes cast (Article 332 (private limited liability company) and Article 633 (public limited liability company) of the Company Code).

If a general meeting is not convened, the company shall be liable for any damage sustained by third parties as a result.

If the value of the company's net assets drops below €61,500 (public limited liability company) or €6,200 (private limited liability company), any interested party can petition the court to order that the company be involuntarily liquidated (Article 333 (private limited liability company) and Article 634 (public limited liability company) of the Company Code).

8.3   Convertible bonds

Public limited liability company: A public limited liability company can issue convertible bonds (Article 485 of the Company Code). Convertible bonds must be fully paid in at the time of issuance (Article 489 of the Company Code). The bonds must provide for a right of conversion within 10 years of the date of issuance. In no case may the company limit or restrict the rights of convertible bondholders (Article 490 of the Company Code).

Should the company decide to repay the bond prematurely, bondholders are entitled to exercise their right to conversion (Article 492 of the Company Code).

Private limited liability company: A private limited liability company may not issue convertible bonds (Article 232 of the Company Code).

9.   Administration

9.1   General shareholders' meeting

(a)   *Powers of the general meeting*

The general meeting has a number of powers reserved to it by law (Article 257 (private limited liability company) and Article 522 (public limited liability company) of the Company Code; (see also Section 9.2(a))). The general meeting has the power, among other things, to:

- appoint and remove directors (Article 256 (private limited liability company) and Article 518 (public limited liability company) of the Company Code);
- approve the company's annual accounts and discharge directors and the certified auditor, if any (Article 284 (private limited liability company) and Article 554 (public limited liability company) of the Company Code);
- amend the corporate purpose (Article 287 (private limited liability company)

and Article 559 (public limited liability company) of the Company Code);

- amend the articles of association (Article 286 (private limited liability company) and Article 558 (public limited liability company) of the Company Code); and
- modify the rights attached to the company's shares (Article 288 (private limited liability company) and Article 560 (public limited liability company) of the Company Code).

(b) Convening the general meeting

A general meeting of a private limited liability company or a public limited liability company must be held at least once per year at the date, time and place mentioned in the articles of association (Article 282 (private limited liability company) and Article 552 (public limited liability company) of the Company Code; see also section 2.2(a)(ii)).

In addition, the board of directors and the company's auditor, if any, each has the power to convene a general meeting (Article 268 (private limited liability company) and Article 532 (public limited liability company) of the Company Code). The board or the auditor must call a general meeting if shareholder(s) holding at least 20% of the company's shares request this.

Public limited liability company: To convene a general meeting of a public limited liability company, a notice including the agenda of the meeting must be published in the *Belgian State Gazette* at least 15 days in advance. The same notice must be published 15 days prior to the meeting in a national newspaper if the general meeting:

- will be held at a different place or on a different date or time than that specified in the articles of association; or
- will deliberate on issues other than approval of the annual accounts, the annual report and the auditor's report, if any, and the release from liability of the directors and the auditor, if any (Article 533 of the Company Code).

If all shares of the public limited liability company are registered, the notice of the meeting, including the agenda, can be sent by registered mail, thereby replacing publication, or communication by any other means (eg email), if each shareholder expressly consents (Article 533 of the Company Code).

Private limited liability company: To convene the general meeting of a private limited liability company, a notice must be sent by registered mail, as all shares of a private limited liability company are registered (Article 268 of the Company Code; see also Section 7.4(b)). However, the notice can be sent by other means if each shareholder expressly consents (Article 268 of the Company Code).

(c) Quorum requirements

(i) Attendance

No quorum is required for the annual general meeting.

The Company Code imposes a number of special quorum requirements (which can be made more stringent by the articles of association) if the general meeting is scheduled to vote on:

- an amendment to the articles of association, in which case half the share capital should be present or represented (Article 286 (private limited liability company) and Article 558 (public limited liability company) of the Company Code); or
- a change to the corporate purpose, in which case half the share capital should be present or represented (Article 287 (private limited liability company) and Article 559 (public limited liability company) of the Company Code).

A shareholder need not appear in person and may be represented by a proxy at the general meeting (Article 280 (private limited liability company) and Article 547 (public limited liability company) of the Company Code). However, the articles of association of a private limited liability company can exclude such a right (Article 280 of the Company Code).

(ii)   Voting

In a private limited liability company, each share carries one vote (Article 275 of the Company Code). The same holds true for a public limited liability company, provided that the shares are of the same value (Article 541 of the Company Code). Should their value differ, however, the votes shall be distributed among the shares in proportion to the capital each represents. The shares issued at the lowest par value have one vote while those representing a multiple of that same par value have multiple votes.

As a general rule, decisions in a public limited liability company or private limited liability company are taken by simple majority of votes cast, unless the articles of association provide otherwise.

Special majority rules apply (unless the articles contain more rigorous provisions) with respect to certain issues, such as:

- amendment of the articles of association, in which case the approval of 75% of the votes cast is required (Article 286 (private limited liability company) and Article 558 (public limited liability company) of the Company Code); and
- a change to the corporate purpose, in which case the approval of 80% of the votes cast is required (Article 287 (private limited liability company) and Article 559 (public limited liability company) of the Company Code).

(d)   Challenging resolutions

Any interested third party – with the exception of those who have agreed to a particular resolution – can file proceedings before the competent commercial court to set aside resolutions of a general meeting (Articles 64 and 178 of the Company Code). A decision to overturn a particular resolution must be recorded with the clerk of the commercial court and an extract published in the *Belgian State Gazette* (Article 179 of the Company Code).

9.2 Administrative body

(a) Different systems of administration

Public limited liability company: A public limited liability company is managed by a board of directors, which must be composed of at least three directors, or two if there are only two shareholders (Article 518 of the Company Code).

The directors must act jointly and are empowered to take any acts and decisions to further the corporate purpose, except for those reserved to the general meeting (Articles 521 and 522 of the Company Code). In principle, a company can be represented only by its board of directors. However, the articles can provide that one or more directors acting jointly can represent the company.

The articles of association can also provide that the board of directors can transfer certain powers to a management committee (Article 524*bis* of the Company Code). Members of the management committee need not be directors.

In addition, daily management can be entrusted to one or more managing directors, who need not be shareholders (Article 525 of the Company Code).

Private limited liability company: A private limited liability company is managed by one or more directors acting as a board (by majority), jointly two or more directors or each individually) as determined by the articles of association (Articles 255 and 256 of the Company Code). The directors need not be shareholders (Article 255 of the Company Code).

The directors may take all decisions to further the company's corporate purpose, except those reserved exclusively to the general shareholders' meeting (Article 257 of the Company Code).

(b) Term of office, resignation and removal of directors

Public limited liability company: The directors of a public limited liability company and a private limited liability company are appointed by the general meeting (see Section 9.1(a)).

Directors of a public limited liability company are appointed for a maximum term of six years, which shall automatically expire if not renewed (Article 518 of the Company Code). The general shareholders' meeting is empowered to remove a director from office at any time (Article 518 of the Company Code). In the event of a vacancy, the remaining directors can appoint a temporary replacement, who shall serve until the next general shareholders' meeting.

Private limited liability company: Directors in a private limited liability company can be appointed in the articles of association or, more often, by the general shareholders' meeting, either for a definite or indefinite duration (Article 256 of the Company Code). As a general rule, directors can be removed by the general meeting at any time, except if they have been appointed in the articles for an indefinite term (ie the life of the company), in which case they can be removed only for serious cause, unless all the shareholders unanimously agree to do so or the articles of association provide otherwise (Article 256 of the Company Code).

The appointment or resignation of a director must be recorded with the CEB and published in the *Belgian State Gazette*, following which time it shall be enforceable against third parties (Articles 74 and 76 of the Company Code; see also Section 2.2(f)(ii)).

(c) Civil and criminal liability

The Civil Code sets out the general rules on contractual (Article 1134 of the Civil Code) and tort (Article 1382 of the Civil Code) liability.

In addition, the Company Code contains four specific rules on directors' liability:

- Directors can be held liable for all damage incurred by the company resulting from their mismanagement (Article 262 (private limited liability company) and Article 527 (public limited liability company) of the Company Code).
- Directors can be held liable for all damage incurred by the company and/or third parties resulting from any acts or decisions taken by the company in breach of its articles of association or the Company Code (Article 263 (private limited liability company) and Article 528 (public limited liability company) of the Company Code). A director can avoid this liability only if he did not actively participate in/agree to the decision and voiced his disapproval or objection at the first general shareholders' meeting following the decision.
- Directors can be held liable for all damage incurred by the company and/or third parties resulting from any act or decision taken by the company in violation of the conflict-of-interest rules, if such act or decision resulted in a financial benefit to any director to the company's detriment (Article 264 (private limited liability company) and Article 529 (public limited liability company) of the Company Code).
- Directors can be held liable for all damage (ie some or all of the company's liabilities in excess of its assets) incurred by the company and/or third parties (ie creditors) if the company goes bankrupt as a result of a manifest gross breach by such directors (Article 265 (private limited liability company) and Article 530 (public limited liability company) of the Company Code). In addition, the Belgian Social Security Administration and the trustee in bankruptcy may bring a claim before the Commercial Court to have all persons entrusted with the management of a company's assets declared personally and jointly liable for the payment of social security contributions, penalties and late-payment interest. This will be triggered if one of the following conditions is met:
  - the director acted in a clearly and grossly negligent manner leading to the bankruptcy of the company; or
  - over the five-year period immediately preceding the bankruptcy, the director was involved in two or more other bankruptcies, liquidations or similar situations in which social security contributions remained unpaid. In the latter case, negligence shall be presumed.

As to criminal liability, the Criminal Code has one specific article on directors' liability with respect to the abuse of company property (Article 492*bis* of the Criminal Code). However, a wide variety of corporate law provisions are subject to criminal sanctions.

(d) ***Non-compete obligation***

Aside from the general rules on directors' liability, the Company Code does not contain a specific non-compete obligation.

If a director has a conflict of interest (ie a direct or indirect financial interest that conflicts with a decision or act falling within the authority of the board of directors), he should notify the board prior to taking the decision in question as well as the auditor, if any, who must mention the conflict in his report (Article 259 (private limited liability company) and Article 523 (public limited liability company) of the Company Code; see also Section 11.2(b)). The director's notification and justification should be recorded in the minutes of the appropriate board meeting. The company can ask that any decisions taken in violation of this rule be declared null and void. Different rules apply in a private limited liability company where each director can act singly (Article 260 of the Company Code) or where the sole director is also the shareholder (Article 261 of the Company Code).

(e) ***Special duties of secrecy and loyalty***

The Company Code does not include specific provisions on special duties of secrecy and loyalty.

9.3 Others

(a) ***Attorneys***

The Company Code does not contain special provisions on attorneys.

(b) ***Internal controllers and auditors***

The Company Code does not contain special provisions on internal controllers and auditors.

However, it does include special provisions on the appointment of certified auditors (Articles 130 and following of the Company Code).

10. Fiscal year

The articles of association determine the start and close of the fiscal year (see Section 2.2(a)(ii)).

In principle, a company's fiscal year is equal to a 365-day period, although it can be as long as up to two years less one day or as little as one day at the beginning or end of the life of a company, or at the time of amending the dates of the commencement or close of its fiscal year. In certain other instances a fiscal year may be shorter than one year. The annual accounts must specify which period they cover.

11. Financial statements

11.1 Company tax

Belgian companies are taxed on their worldwide income. However, income generated abroad is usually exempt pursuant to applicable tax treaties. The corporate tax rate is in principle 33.99% – that is, 33% to which a 3% crisis surcharge is added

(Articles 215 and 463bis of the Income Tax Code).

Different tax rates apply if the company's net income is less than €322,500 (Article 215 of the Income Tax Code), as shown in the table below. However, there are certain exceptions even to these rules (eg if 50% of the shares are held by another company).

Net income (bracket system)	Tax rate (to which a 3% crisis surcharge is added)
€0 to €25,000	24.25% (24.98% with the crisis surcharge)
€5,000 to €90,000	31% (31.93% with the crisis surcharge)
€90,000 to €322,500	34.5% (35.54% with the crisis surcharge)

All companies must submit an annual tax return no later than six months after the close of the previous fiscal year (Article 10 of the Income Tax Code).

11.2   Annual accounts

(a)   Documents

Annually, the directors must draft the annual accounts, which consist of:

- a balance sheet;
- an income statement; and
- explanatory notes (Article 92 of the Company Code).

In addition, the directors are obliged to draft an annual report, discussing the company's policy and the most important events of the previous fiscal year, among other issues (Article 96 of the Company Code). This obligation does not apply to small companies. A small company is one that does not employ more than 100 people or does not exceed more than one of the following criteria (to be calculated on a consolidated basis):

- an average of 50 employees on an annual basis;
- a turnover of €7.3 million; and
- a balance sheet total of €3.65 million.

(b)   Audit report

All companies, with the exception of small companies, must appoint a certified auditor to draft an audit report (Article 141 of the Company Code).

The audit report must specifically address certain issues, including the following (Article 144 of the Company Code):

- the auditor's activities;
- compliance of the annual accounts with statutory requirements; and
- whether the annual accounts provide a true and fair view of the company's financial position.

(c)   Approval of annual accounts and distribution of profits

The annual accounts must be submitted for approval to the general shareholders' meeting within six months of the close of the fiscal year (Article 92 of the Company Code).

The company can distribute profits only if, at the close of the previous fiscal year, the value of its net assets (ie assets minus reserves and liabilities), as they appear from the annual accounts, is not less than, or will not be less than following the distribution, the total of:

- the effectively contributed or called share capital, whichever is higher; and
- those reserves that cannot be distributed pursuant to the articles of association or the Company Code (Article 320 (private limited liability company) and Article 617 (public limited liability company) of the Company Code).

If the company makes a dividend distribution, 20% of this amount must be transferred to its statutory reserves until they equal at least 10% of the share capital (Article 319 (private limited liability company) and Article 616 (public limited liability company) of the Company Code).

(d)   Filing and publication requirements

The annual accounts must be filed with the National Bank of Belgium by the directors in the form required by the Company Code, either on paper or using an electronic version, within 30 days of approval, and in any event no later than seven months following the close of its fiscal year (Article 98 of the Company Code). Small companies (see section 11.2(a) above) can file their annual accounts in abridged form (Article 99 of the Company Code).

Within 15 days of filing, a notice to this effect is published in the *Belgian State Gazette* (Article 102 of the Company Code).

A filing fee is due for recording annual accounts with the National Bank of Belgium, ranging from €140.79 to €435.91, depending on whether the annual accounts are in abridged form and/or filed in electronic or paper version.

The annual accounts can be consulted by any third party at any National Bank of Belgium office or at the commercial courts.

12.   Company reorganisation

12.1   Conversion

The Company Code contains rules regarding the conversion of companies.

A public limited liability company can be converted into a private limited liability company and vice versa.

In the three months prior to taking a decision on the matter, the certified auditor, if any, or an external accountant must prepare a balance sheet of the company's assets and liabilities (Articles 776 and 777 of the Company Code). The draft balance sheet, the board's report clarifying the decision and the amended articles of association must be appended to the notice to shareholders, who are exclusively empowered to vote on the conversion (Articles 778 and 779 of the Company Code).

Unless the articles of association provide otherwise, half the share capital must be present or represented – including half the profit-sharing certificates, if any – at the general meeting, and 80% must approve the conversion (Article 781 of the Company Code).

The decision to convert the company must be enacted in a notarised document (Article 783 of the Company Code).

12.2 Merger

The Company Code contains rules on mergers that are applicable to all companies with legal personality, including the public limited liability company and the private limited liability company (Articles 670 and following of the Company Code).

The Company Code distinguishes between two types of merger:

- a merger by absorption, whereby all assets and liabilities of the company are transferred to one or more receiving companies, and the shareholders of the transferor company receive shares in the latter companies (Article 671 of the Company Code); and
- a merger by the creation of a new company, whereby all assets and liabilities of the company are transferred to a new company, and shareholders in the transferor company receive shares in the new company (Article 672 of the Company Code).

Specific procedures and special majority rules apply.

12.3 Split-off

The Company Code contains rules on split-offs which are applicable to all companies with legal personality, including the public limited liability company and the private limited liability company (Articles 670 and following of the Company Code).

The Company Code distinguishes between three types of split-off:

- a split-off by absorption, whereby all assets and liabilities of a company are transferred to two or more receiving companies and the shareholders of the first company receive shares in the absorbing companies (Article 673 of the Company Code);
- a split-off by the creation of a new company, whereby all assets and liabilities of a company are transferred to two or more newly created companies, and the shareholders of the first company receive shares in the new companies (Article 674 of the Company Code); and
- a mixed split-off, whereby all assets and liabilities of a company are transferred to one or more receiving companies and to one or more new companies, and the shareholders of the transferor company receive shares in the receiving companies and the new companies (Article 675 of the Company Code).

Specific procedures and special majority rules apply.

13. Forced partner or shareholder buy-out

As a general rule, shareholders representing at least 30% of the share capital and/or 30% of the par or fractional value of the shares can petition the competent court to order that a shareholder transfer its shares to them (Article 334 (private limited liability company) and Article 636 (public limited liability company) of the Company Code).

In addition, any shareholder with just cause for doing so can petition the commercial court of the place where the company has its registered office to order that its shares be acquired by the other shareholders (Article 340 (private limited liability company) and Article 642 (public limited liability company) of the Company Code).

14.   Dissolution and liquidation

A public limited liability company or a private limited liability company can be incorporated for a definite or indefinite duration. If the company is incorporated for a definite period of time, it will automatically dissolve and liquidate when this period comes to an end. However, the general meeting, subject to special majority rules, can decide to dissolve and liquidate the company at any time, as is the case with a company incorporated for an indefinite duration (Article 343 (private limited liability company) and Article 645 (public limited liability company) of the Company Code). Shareholders can also petition the court to order that the company be dissolved and liquidated for just cause.

After dissolution, the company is deemed to remain in existence for the purposes of liquidation (Article 183 of the Company Code). To this effect, one or more liquidators will be appointed by the general meeting whose appointment must be approved by the competent commercial court (Article 184 of the Company Code). The liquidation can be a lengthy process (three to six months on average) and can only be completed upon the approval by the competent commercial court of a liquidation and distribution plan (Article 190 of the Company Code).

15.   Branches

Foreign companies can set up branches in Belgium, but they must follow a special procedure (Articles 58, 81 and 82 of the Company Code). A branch must be registered with the CEB.

Branches do not have limited liability under Belgian law.

Brazil

Evy Cynthia Marques
Neil Montgomery
Felsberg, Pedretti, Mannrich e Aidar Advogados e Consultores Legais

1. Types of company with limited liability and applicable legislation

In accordance with the Brazilian Civil Code (Law 10,406/02), effective as from January 2003, companies incorporated in Brazil are classified either as business companies (*sociedades empresárias*) or as non-business companies (*sociedades simples*).

A business company conducts organised economic activities aimed at the production and circulation of goods or services. All corporate documents, including those establishing the company, must be filed with the Commercial Registry. An entity conducting any other activity (including intellectual, scientific, literary or artistic activities) is considered a non-business company. All corporate documents of a non-business company, including those establishing the same, must be filed with the Civil Registry for Corporate Entities.

Business companies and non-business companies are most commonly incorporated as limited liability companies (*sociedades limitadas*). Further, corporations (*sociedades por ações*) are always considered to be business companies, regardless of their corporate purpose.

In limited liability companies, quotaholders (a shareholder of a limited liability company is called a quotaholder, since the capital of the company is divided into quotas) are, in principle, not liable for the debts and other obligations of the company; however, they are jointly and severally liable for full payment of the subscribed capital. Further, limited liability companies cannot issue securities, such as debentures and commercial papers, and do not have access to capital markets.

Most Brazilian companies are incorporated as limited liability companies, since this corporate form has the simplest structure of all companies with limited liability. Limited liability companies are now regulated by the Brazilian Civil Code, which made the structure of limited liability companies more complex (similar to that of a closed corporation). Previously, this type of company was regulated by Decree 3,708/19. Nowadays, the company's articles of association may contemplate the subsidiary application of either the Civil Code provisions on non-business companies or the Corporations Law (6,404/76, as subsequently amended).

In corporations, shareholders are not liable for any debts or other obligations of the corporation. They are liable only for paying in the shares they have subscribed for. Further, Brazilian corporations may privately issue securities as provided for under Brazilian law, including debentures and warrants. Publicly held corporations may effect public and private offerings of any security negotiated on the capital markets, provided all applicable legal requirements are satisfied – for example, registration with the Brazilian Securities Commission (*Comissão de Valores Mobiliários* (CVM)).

Brazilian corporations are governed by the Corporations Law, which has been amended several times over the last few decades. The latest amendment was enacted in 2007 by Law 11,638. The enactment of the Civil Code has not affected the rules governing this type of company.

Brazilian corporations may be publicly held (listed) or closed (non-listed), depending on whether they are registered with the CVM, and their shares may be traded on stock exchanges or, as the case may be, on the over-the-counter market. The CVM was established by Law 6,385/76, most recently amended by Law 11,638/2007.

Publicly held corporations are subject to stricter rules than closed corporations, not only because of the provisions of the Corporations Law, but also because of the audit requirements and a number of rules issued by the CVM, usually referred to as directives and regulations.

The differences between limited liability companies and corporations (whether closed or publicly held) are indicated throughout this chapter. The principal differences are outlined in the table below.

	Limited liability companies	Corporations
Access to capital markets	Limited liability companies cannot issue securities and do not have access to capital markets	Publicly held corporations are permitted to trade their securities on stock exchanges or, as the case may be, on the over-the-counter market
Deliberations	Strict quota-holders' meeting call and instalment rules apply only for limited liability companies with more than 10 quota holders	Strict call and instalment rules apply for all general shareholders' meetings
Call notices	Must be published in the *Official Gazette* and a widely circulated newspaper three times if the limited liability company has more than 10 quota holders	Must be published in the *Official Gazette* and a widely circulated newspaper three times
Quorum	Depends on the type of deliberation; most require quota holders representing 75% of the company's capital	Majority of votes, except as otherwise established by law or the bylaws *continued*

Inspection committee	Facultative	Mandatory
Management	One or more Brazilian-resident individuals, whether quota holders or not	Board of directors (composed of shareholders) and executive board (composed of two or more Brazilian-resident individuals)
Financial statements	Financial statements need not be published and registered with the Commercial Registry	Financial statements must be published and registered with the Commercial Registry

2. Incorporation procedure

2.1 Proceedings prior to incorporation

(a) *Name search*

A search of the Commercial Registry database in the state where the company is to be incorporated and in other states where the company is considering opening any branches or offices should be conducted to reveal whether other companies already use the name (or a similar name) proposed to be used by the limited liability company or corporation to be incorporated. Further, a search on the Brazilian Trademark and Patent Office should also be conducted to check whether trademarks identical or similar to the proposed company name have already been registered in classes corresponding to the activities to be carried on by the company to be incorporated. This is because such trademark registration could ultimately prevent the use of the intended company name.

(b) *Foreign investment*

Brazilian law limits foreign investment in certain sectors, such as in connection with the acquisition of real estate in rural areas or at international borders, and investment in Brazilian airline companies and in cable television and media companies. As from 2002, foreign investors can indirectly (through a Brazilian subsidiary) hold up to 30% of the voting capital of Brazilian press and broadcasting companies.

2.2 Incorporation

Limited liability companies: Limited liability companies must be incorporated by at least two quotaholders. In order to incorporate the company, the quotaholders must execute the articles of association – a private document governing the rules between the quotaholders – and file them with the Commercial Registry (for business companies) or the Civil Registry for Corporate Entities (for non-business companies) in the state where the registered office is located.

Corporations: Corporations must also be incorporated by at least two shareholders, except where:

- the corporation is a wholly owned subsidiary (see section 3 below); or
- the corporation has a board of directors, in which case a minimum of three shareholders is required (since this is the minimum number of members required to form the board of directors, who must all be shareholders).

Corporations are generally established by a general meeting of incorporation, at which all shares that make up the company's capital are subscribed, the bylaws are approved and the members of the board of directors, if any, or the members of the executive board are appointed. The minutes of the general meeting of incorporation, which may be a private or public document (the latter being certified by a notary public), must be filed with the Commercial Registry in the state where the registered office of the corporation is located (and with the CVM, if necessary).

(a)   *Articles of association*

(i)   *Essential clauses*

Limited liability companies: The articles of association of a limited liability company must contain the following mandatory provisions:

- details of all quotaholders (and of the person(s) resident in Brazil who will act as attorneys in fact in Brazil for such quotaholders);
- the company name (see section 4 below);
- the corporate capital, in Brazilian currency, describing each quota holder's equity interest, as well as the means and deadline for paying in such corporate capital (see section 6);
- the full address of the company's registered office;
- a clear and precise description of the corporate purpose;
- the date on which the company will be dissolved or a statement confirming that the duration of the company is to be indefinite;
- the financial year, if this does not coincide with the calendar year (see section 9);
- the appointment of the director/manager, who must be an individual resident in Brazil (see section 8.2);
- the procedure for distribution of profits to quotaholders; and
- dispute resolution procedures (ie a jurisdiction or arbitration clause to resolve any controversies arising between the quotaholders in respect of the articles of association).

Closed corporations: The bylaws of a corporation must contain the following mandatory provisions:

- the company name (see section 4 below);
- the corporate capital, in Brazilian currency, divided into shares with or without par value, as well as the means and deadline for paying in such corporate capital (see section 6);

- the full address of the company's registered office;
- a clear and precise description of the corporate purpose;
- the date on which the company will be dissolved or a statement confirming that the duration of the company is to be indefinite;
- the financial year, if this does not coincide with the calendar year (see section 9);
- the appointment of at least two executive board officers, who must be individuals resident in Brazil but need not be shareholders (see section 8.2);
- whether the inspection committee is to operate on a permanent or non-permanent basis;
- rules on the procedures for calling the general meeting and approving resolutions;
- the procedure for distribution of profits to shareholders; and
- dispute resolution procedures (ie, a jurisdiction or arbitration clause to resolve any controversies arising between the shareholders in respect of the bylaws).

The inspection committee must be composed of between three and five members, who need not be shareholders. Shareholders representing 10% of the voting capital or 5% of the non-voting capital may request that the inspection committee be convened. As is the case with the board of directors, Brazilian law provides mechanisms to ensure that minority shareholders and holders of preferred shares may appoint some of the members of the inspection committee.

The inspection committee is established under the Corporations Law and its principal function is to audit the corporation's financial statements and management's accounts. Depending on the provisions in the bylaws, the inspection committee may fulfil the functions of the audit committee as contemplated by the US Sarbanes-Oxley Act of 2002.

Publicly held corporations: The rules applicable to closed corporations also apply to publicly held corporations. Where a publicly held corporation is to be incorporated by means of an initial public offering, it must first obtain a publicly held corporation registration statement and a share issuance registration statement from the CVM. Closed corporations may become publicly held corporations by obtaining the first above-mentioned registration statement. In order for a corporation to cancel its publicly held corporation registration statement with the CVM, it must effect a public offering to buy all outstanding shares on the market, except for those held by the controlling shareholder.

(ii)   *Clauses not contemplated by law*
Limited liability companies: The quotaholders of limited liability companies may agree on whether the articles of association will provide for the subsidiary application of either the Civil Code provisions on non-business entities or the Corporations Law.

They may also agree to include provisions on the extra-judicial exclusion of quotaholders from the company by decision of the majority of quotaholders holding at least a majority of the corporate capital, in the event of breach of a quotaholder's duties as provided for in the articles of association and by law.

The quotaholders may stipulate in the articles of association whether the company is to have an inspection committee. This must be composed of at least three members, who need not be quotaholders.

Further, limited liability companies with more than 10 quotaholders must approve matters under their responsibility at a quotaholders' meeting, which must observe specific Civil Code requirements regarding call notices, convening and adoption of resolutions. Companies with fewer than 10 quotaholders may hold quotaholders' meetings, subject to less stringent procedures, in accordance with the articles of association.

This notwithstanding, any resolution requiring the quotaholders' approval will be deemed valid without any need to hold a quotaholders' meeting if all quotaholders give their approval in writing.

Closed corporations: The capital of closed and publicly held corporations is divided into shares, which may be common or preferred. In addition, the shares of closed corporations may be divided into different classes, depending on the rights attached.

Preferred shares may not exceed more than half of the corporation's capital. For companies incorporated prior to the enactment of Law 10,303/2001, this ratio stands at two-thirds. Generally, each share entitles the shareholder to one vote. However, the bylaws may specify that preferred shares have no voting rights or may restrict this right to certain matters.

In closed corporations, preferred shares confer a pre-emptive right to receive dividends and/or reimbursement of capital if the corporation is dissolved, and may, in accordance with the bylaws, confer final or minimum dividends and/or a dividend of 10% above that paid to holders of common shares.

Corporations are required to hold an annual shareholders' meeting within four months of the end of the financial year, at which resolutions will be adopted on:

- the corporation's financial statements and management's accounts;
- the utilisation of net profits and distribution of dividends; and
- the election of directors and the inspection committee, where applicable.

Any other matters requiring shareholder approval must be resolved at an extraordinary shareholders' meeting.

The Corporations Law establishes the terms and procedures for the calling and installation of a general meeting and the adoption of resolutions. The bylaws must comply with these rules. Shareholders may be represented at meetings by duly appointed proxies, who must be shareholders, attorneys or directors of the corporation. In such cases the power of attorney must have a limited term of one year.

Shareholders who dissent in respect of certain matters provided by law may withdraw from the corporation upon reimbursement of the value of their shares, to be determined based on the attributable net worth or economic value, depending on the provisions contained in the bylaws.

Publicly held corporations: Common shares issued by publicly held corporations cannot be divided into classes. Preferred shares or shares with limited voting rights may be traded on the capital markets only if they confer at least one of the following rights:

- a dividend of at least 25% of the net income of the period, with shareholders having preference to receive such dividends in a total amount equal to at least 3% of the attributable value of the share;
- a dividend of at least 10% more than the dividends attributed to common shares; or
- so-called 'tag along', as guaranteed to common shares.

The sale of a majority interest in a publicly held corporation may be effected only if a public offering is implemented to acquire all of the outstanding voting shares. The price per share must be at least 80% of the price of the shares comprising the controlling block.

The disclosure information and trading shares of publicly held corporations are subject to CVM regulation, which requires the prior approval by the CVM of their information disclosure policies.

The Corporations Law establishes certain different terms and procedures for the calling and installation of a shareholders' general meeting and the approval of resolutions of publicly held corporations. For example, the CVM may postpone the opening of any shareholders' meeting whenever it verifies that the shareholders were not duly informed of the agenda to be discussed at such meeting.

(b) **Indirect taxes, incorporation fees and other levies**
The filing fees for registration of the articles of association of limited liability business companies with the Commercial Registry vary from state to state, but are normally in the region of R$60 (approximately £15), while the fees for registration of bylaws of a corporation are around R$130 (approximately £30). Publicly held corporations must pay other fees in order to obtain a publicly held corporation registration statement and a share issuance registration statement from the CVM. Such companies must also pay an annual inspection fee to the CVM.

(c) **Registration with the Commercial Registry**
A business company must file its articles of association or bylaws with the Commercial Registry in the state where its registered office is located (non-business companies must file their constitutive documents with the Civil Registry for Corporate Entities). The articles of association of a limited liability company must be submitted together with the powers of attorney granted by foreign quotaholders to their local attorneys in fact (accompanied by certified Portuguese translations). The company will be considered to have been formally incorporated under Brazilian law on the date of registration of the articles of association or bylaws with the Commercial Registry, which will issue the company with a company identification number.

(d) **Registration with Federal Corporate Taxpayers Registry**
Once the company has been formally incorporated, it must apply for all other

required registrations, authorisations and permits. The principal registration required is enrolment with the Federal Corporate Taxpayers Registry, which is done by filing the relevant documentation with the Federal Inland Revenue.

(e)   *Registration of foreign investment with the Brazilian Central Bank*

In accordance with Brazilian law, all capital contributions to Brazilian companies made by non-resident individuals and foreign corporate entities must be registered by the company or its foreign investors with SISBACEN (the online registration system of the Brazilian Central Bank) within 30 days of execution of the respective:

- foreign exchange agreement (converting into Brazilian currency the foreign currency received by the company from its foreign members);
- quota/share sale-and-purchase agreement; or
- corporate documentation (eg amendments to the articles of association, minutes of the quotaholders'/shareholders' meetings).

Equity interests acquired by non-resident individuals and foreign corporate entities through the financial and capital markets are also subject to registration with the Brazilian Central Bank. However, the procedure is different from that outlined below.

Once a Federal Corporate Taxpayers Registry number has been obtained for the company, it must open a bank account and obtain a SISBACEN access code. This code allows the company to access SISBACEN and register foreign investors with the Brazilian Central Bank Companies Registry. Such registration in turn allows each foreign investor to obtain an RDE-IED code – identifying both the respective Brazilian company and the foreign investor – on SISBACEN.

An RDE-IED code is required not only for the company to execute foreign exchange contracts to convert funds received from foreign investors into Brazilian currency, but also to register each investment on SISBACEN.

On March 5 2007, the Brazilian National Monetary Council (CMN) issued Resolution No 3,447 establishing the rules for registration of tainted capital with the Brazilian Central Bank – BACEN (such tainted capital corresponding to all unregistered foreign capital invested by non-residents in Brazilian corporate entities with BACEN, which is not subject to any other form of registration), in addition to providing applicable penalties in connection thereto. BACEN issued regulations for Resolution 3,447 through BACEN Circular No 3,344 of March 7 2007.

(f)   *Tax registration of foreign investors*

Non-resident individuals holding assets and/or rights located in Brazil (eg real estate, vehicles, vessels, aircraft, equity interests, current accounts and investments in the financial and capital markets) must register with the Federal Individual Taxpayers Registry, either through a branch of the Federal Inland Revenue, if the non-resident individual is in Brazil, or through the Brazilian diplomatic representation in his country of residence.

Likewise, the following foreign corporate entities must register with the Federal Corporate Taxpayers Registry:

- foreign companies with assets and/or rights located in Brazil (eg real estate, vehicles, vessels, aircraft, equity interests, current accounts, investments in the financial and capital markets, intangible assets payable within more than 360 days and financing); and
- foreign companies that perform financed imports, leasing transactions, equipment lease, chartering or the importation of assets that have not yet been paid in as capital contributions to Brazilian companies, or that grant loans to Brazilian residents or make foreign investments in Brazil.

In certain transactions (eg involving the acquisition of equity interests, intangible assets payable within more than 360 days, financing, financed imports and leasing transactions, equipment lease, chartering, importation of assets that have not yet been paid in as capital contributions to Brazilian companies and the granting of loans to Brazilian residents), the foreign corporate entity will be registered with the Federal Corporate Taxpayers Registry upon registration with the Brazilian Central Bank Companies Registry.

(g) *Legalisation of official books*
Limited liability companies and corporations must retain the following corporate books and register them before use with the Commercial Registry in the state where their registered office is located:
- minute book for general quotaholders'/shareholders' meetings;
- minute book of management meetings/resolutions;
- minute book of board of directors' meetings/resolutions (mandatory only for listed corporations and/or with the authorised capital);
- minute book of inspection committee meetings and opinions (mandatory only for corporations);
- attendance book for quotaholders'/shareholders' meetings;
- share register (mandatory only for corporations); and
- share transfer register (mandatory only for corporations).

Limited liability companies and corporations must also register their accounting books (eg the ledger) before use with the Commercial Registry in the state where their registered office is located.

(h) *Declaration of start date and other tax declarations*
Once a company has been incorporated, many other licences, registrations, permits and authorisations must be obtained for the performance of its purpose, as outlined in the table overleaf.

Fiscal licences, registrations, permits and authorisations	• State taxpayer registration • Municipal taxpayer registration • Invoice registration
Labour and social security licences, registrations, permits and authorisations	• Registration with relevant employers' union • Registration with Accrued Severance Pay Fund • Registration with Social Security Institute • Registration with Labour Inspection Register • Maintenance of employee register • Maintenance of each employee's individual registration file
Operational licences, registrations, permits and authorisations	• Sanitary operational registration with state health department • Municipality licence for localisation and operation • Building occupancy permit • Building permit • Inspection certificate issued by the fire department • Permit to operate the plant • Registration of trademarks with the National Industrial Property Institute • Registration of domain names with the São Paulo State Foundation for Research Assistance Registration with SISCOMEX (the Integrated Foreign Trade System) • Registration with RADAR (which tracks the activities of foreign trade players)
Environmental licences, registrations, permits and authorisations	• Preliminary environmental licence • Installation licence • Operational licence

3. Number of shareholders

Limited liability companies: Limited liability companies must have at least two quotaholders. If a company has only two quotaholders then, in the event of withdrawal of one quota holder, the company must ensure that at least one more quota holder is recruited within 180 days, under penalty of dissolution of the company.

Corporations: Corporations must also have at least two shareholders, except where the corporation is a wholly owned subsidiary. A wholly owned subsidiary must be incorporated by means of public deed. The sole shareholder of the wholly owned subsidiary must be a Brazilian company (either a limited liability company or a corporation).

4. Corporate name – limitations

The Civil Code requires that the main corporate purpose be included in the company's name. Further, the company name must be completely different from other names that have already been registered with the Commercial Registry, to prevent any disputes.

5. Corporate domicile

The articles of association (limited liability companies) or the bylaws (corporations) specify the location of the company's registered office. This registered office may be changed by amendment of the articles of association or the bylaws, as approved at the extraordinary shareholders' meeting (for corporations). Branches may also be opened in Brazil by amendment of the articles of association or by resolution of the extraordinary shareholders' meeting or quotaholders' meeting.

6. Capital stock

6.1 Minimum capital requirement

Limited liability companies: The articles of association must specify the corporate capital, but no minimum amount is required. As far as thin capitalisation restrictions are concerned, there are currently no rules in Brazil limiting the level of debt owed by a company to its quotaholders/shareholders or in respect of the reclassification of such debts as equity.

Corporations: The bylaws must likewise establish the corporate capital, but again no minimum amount is required (except for corporations operating in certain sectors, such as banks and insurance companies). This notwithstanding, if the corporation has a board of directors, it can increase the corporate capital up to a pre-determined authorised capital limit specified in the bylaws.

6.2 Nature of contributions

Limited liability companies: The corporate capital of a limited liability company is divided into quotas. Each quota usually grants the holder the right to one vote at the quotaholders' meeting. The Civil Code does not address the possibility of having non-voting quotas (preferred quotas).

Quotaholders may pay in their respective equity interests either in cash or in kind (rights and assets, but not services); in the latter instance, the in-kind contribution is subject to appraisal, which must be approved by the quotaholders.

Closed corporations: The corporate capital of corporations is divided into shares. Shareholders may pay in their respective equity interests either in cash or in kind (rights and assets, but not services); in the latter instance, the in-kind contribution is subject to appraisal, which must be approved by the shareholders' meeting.

Publicly held corporations: An increase in the corporate capital of a publicly held corporation and the public offering of shares, as well as any distribution of securities in the primary and secondary markets, are subject to CVM regulations, which stipulate a number of requirements that must be observed when carrying out these types of transaction.

6.3 Partial payments

Limited liability companies: Subscribed quotas must be paid in, whether in a lump sum or in instalments, within the timeframe envisaged in the articles of association. This timeframe may be modified by amendment of the articles of association.

Corporations: In accordance with the Corporations Law, at least 10% of the price of the issued shares subscribed in cash must be paid in before incorporation. Certain sectors (eg the banking and insurance sectors) require higher thresholds (eg 50%). The remaining shares must be paid in within the timeframe envisaged in the bylaws.

6.4 Transfer of shares

(a) Restrictions

Limited liability companies: Quotas may be assigned to third parties, depending on the provisions of the articles of association. Likewise, heirs and successors may be barred from becoming quotaholders, depending on the provisions of the articles of association.

Article 1,057 of the Civil Code establishes that in the absence of express provisions in the articles of association, any quotaholder may transfer his equity interest, whether totally or partially, to:

- another quotaholder, without any need to obtain the approval of the remaining quotaholders; or
- a third party, if quotaholders representing more than one-quarter of the capital do not object.

Corporations: Shares may be assigned to third parties, depending on the provisions of the bylaws. The corporation may acquire its own shares to hold them in treasury, or cancel or resell them, in special circumstances provided by law (eg redemption). Article 254–A of the Corporations Law contemplates tag-along rights for publicly held corporations only. This provision does not have direct application to limited liability companies unless expressly provided for in the articles of association or in a quotaholders' agreement.

(b) Formalities

Limited liability companies: In limited liability companies, the transfer of quotas is effected by amendment of the articles of association, which must be executed and filed with the Commercial Registry (or Civil Registry for Corporate Entities, as the case may be) in the state where the company's registered office is located within 30 days of its execution. The Federal Corporate Taxpayers Registry – and, depending on the circumstances, other public registries – must be informed of the transfer.

Corporations: The transfer of a corporation's shares is generally effected through the annotation of the shareholder register and share transfer register.

7. Equity

7.1 Equity–capital ratio

There is no regulation in Brazil governing the ratio between capital stock and equity. However, the Civil Code and the Corporations Law provide that a company may reduce its capital if it has suffered irreparable losses (in the case of limited liability companies, this remedy is available only if the capital is fully paid up), by way of amendment to the articles of association (limited liability company) or by shareholder resolution (corporation).

7.2 Convertible debentures

Only corporations may issue debentures, which grant the holder a credit against the company under the terms and conditions specified in the deed of issue. The debenture may be converted into shares under terms and conditions specified in the indenture. Except as otherwise contemplated in specific laws, the total amount of debentures issued cannot exceed the company's capital.

8. Administration

8.1 quotaholders'/shareholders' meetings

(a) *Quorum requirements*

(i) *Attendance*

Limited liability companies: At first call, in accordance with the Civil Code, there is a quorum where quotaholders representing three-quarters of the capital are present. At second call, there is a quorum regardless of the number of quotaholders present. The articles of association of limited liability companies with up to 10 quotaholders may specify alternative quorum requirements for this purpose.

Corporations: In accordance with the Corporations Law, there is a quorum at first call where shareholders representing at least one-quarter of the voting rights are present. At second call, there is a quorum regardless of the number of shareholders present.

(ii) *Voting*

Limited liability companies: Each quota usually entitles the holder to one vote at the quotaholders' meeting. Specific quorums required for the approval of certain matters are outlined in the table overleaf; these may be increased, but never reduced, by the articles of association.

Quorum	Resolution
Unanimous decision	• Appointment of non-quotaholder directors/ managers, where the capital is not fully paid up
Three-quarters of the capital	• Merger, winding-up, or cessation or desistance of liquidation • Amendment of the articles of association, including the appointment of directors/managers
Two-thirds of the capital	• Appointment of non-quotaholder directors/managers, where the capital is fully paid up • Dismissal of quotaholders appointed as directors/ managers in the articles of association, except where otherwise established by the articles of association
More than half of the capital	• Dismissal of non-quotaholder directors/managers • Request for extrajudicial or judicial restructuring by a director or quotaholder • Appointment of quotaholder directors/managers through the quotaholders' meeting • Remuneration of directors/managers, where this is not contemplated in the articles of association • Liquidation of the company for an indefinite term
Majority of the capital in attendance	• Appointment and dismissal of liquidators, and approval of their accounts • Approval of management's accounts • Other cases not contemplated by law or the articles of association (if these do not require a higher quorum)
Majority of the remaining quota holders	• Exclusion of quotaholders in default • Judicial exclusion by gross negligence or supervening default • No opposition by more than one-quarter of the capital assignment of quotas to third parties

Corporations: In general, matters submitted for resolution at a duly convened general shareholders' meeting may be approved by shareholders representing 50% of the voting capital plus one voting share. Applicable legislation establishes a higher quorum for certain matters. Further, the bylaws may specify a higher quorum than that established by law.

8.2 Management

Limited liability companies: Only individuals who reside in Brazil, whether quotaholders or not, may be appointed as directors/managers of limited liability companies. Foreigners wishing to occupy management positions must first obtain a permanent visa, in accordance with minimum legal requirements. The company may have one or more directors/managers, whose remuneration is determined by the quotaholders.

Where directors/managers are company employees, they are entitled to all rights and benefits afforded to them under Brazilian labour law. If they are not employees, they are entitled only to such amounts as are agreed with the company.

However, an employment relationship may be characterised as such, regardless of anything agreed to the contrary in a written service agreement (eg that entered into between a company and non-employee directors/managers) if the person providing his services to the company does so on a permanent basis, under the direction of the company and in exchange for a salary; subordination is also an essential factor in the characterisation of an employment relationship. Accordingly, in the event that a de facto relationship established between a company and a supposedly non-employee director/manager satisfies such requirements, it may be regarded as an employment relationship and may thus entitle the director/manager to all rights and benefits afforded under Brazilian labour law.

Corporations: The management of corporations may be undertaken by the board of directors (mandatory for publicly held corporations) and the executive board. The board of directors must be composed solely of shareholders, although they need not be resident in Brazil. Where an appointed member does not reside in Brazil, he must grant a power of attorney to a Brazilian resident who may receive service of process and represent the member in Brazil. Brazilian law contemplates mechanisms to ensure that minority shareholders and holders of preferred shares may appoint some members of the board of directors.

The executive board is composed of at least two officers, who must reside in Brazil. Foreigners who wish to occupy this position must obtain a permanent visa, in accordance with minimum legal requirements. If the corporation has a board of directors, only one-third of its members can be appointed as executive board officers.

8.3 Civil liability of directors and managers

Limited liability companies: The civil liability of directors and managers may be governed by the Civil Code (for non-business entities, as the specific chapter on limited liability companies does not contemplate rules in this regard) or the Corporations Law, depending on which of these laws the quotaholders have elected will have subsidiary application to the articles of association.

While in office, directors and managers must exercise the same caution and diligence as though they were running their own business.

Therefore, directors and managers may be held liable for all acts and omissions performed out of the ordinary course of the company's business, except for those previously approved by the quotaholders.

For example, in accordance with the Civil Code, a director or manager who, without the prior written approval of the quotaholders, invests corporate credits or assets for his own benefit or that of a third party must reimburse the company (ie pay the equivalent sum), together with all accrued profit. If any damage was caused to the company, the director or manager will be held liable.

Corporations: The Corporations Law further provides that directors and officers owe duties of secrecy and loyalty to the company. For instance, directors and officers must serve the company with loyalty and maintain discretion in respect of the company's business. They are prohibited from:

- using any business opportunities for their own benefit or that of a third party, whether this causes damage to the company or not;
- rejecting business opportunities that are in the company's interests; and
- acquiring, in order to resell at a profit, assets or rights that are essential to the company or that the company intends to acquire.

Directors and officers are also prohibited from:

- practising acts of concession at the company's expense;
- borrowing funds or assets from the company, or using company assets, services or credit for their own benefit or that of a third party, without the prior approval of the general shareholders' meeting or the board of directors; and
- obtaining, whether directly or indirectly, any personal advantages from third parties as a result of their position, without prior shareholder approval or authorisation in the bylaws.

In general, directors and officers are not liable for illicit acts performed by other directors or officers, except where, for instance, they:

- connive with the offending directors or officers;
- neglect to investigate such acts; or
- are aware of such acts.

A director or officer will escape liability for an illicit act performed by another director or officer if his dissent to the illicit action is recorded in the minutes of the meeting or if he gives written notice of such dissent to the inspection committee, where one has been established, or to the general shareholders' meeting.

8.4 Criminal liability of directors and managers

Law 8,137/90 contemplates crimes against the Brazilian fiscal regime, including those which may be committed by directors and managers of companies.

8.5 Liability to third parties

In accordance with the Civil Code, acts performed by a director or manager outside the ordinary course of business may be opposed with respect to third parties where the following conditions are satisfied:

- the limits to the director's or manager's powers were duly registered with the Commercial Registry;

- the third parties were aware of such limits; and
- the transaction was obviously outside the normal course of business.

8.6 Non-competition

Neither the Civil Code nor the Corporations Law expressly includes non-competition provisions applicable to directors and managers. These may be included in the employment agreement or service agreement entered into between the director or manager and the company.

9. Fiscal year

Usually, the fiscal year coincides with the calendar year. However, an alternative fiscal year may be followed where express provision is made in the articles of association/bylaws.

10. Financial statements

10.1 Company tax

Many taxes affect companies operating in Brazil, including income taxes, operations taxes (eg federal excise tax, sales and services tax) and withholding taxes (eg tax on financial transactions, provisional tax on banking transactions). These taxes may vary depending on the type of activity performed by the company and the state in which it is located.

Corporate income tax is a federal tax charged on the company's accounting profit, as adjusted by the additions (non-deductible expenses) and exclusions (non-taxable revenues) specified by tax law in order to determine the taxable income. The tax rate is 15%, plus a 10% surtax on annual taxable income in excess of R$240,000.

Social contribution tax is a federal tax on taxable income currently levied at a rate of 9%. The tax base is similar to that for corporate income tax, although some specific adjustments may be required for one tax and not for the other, pursuant to the legal provisions. Where the taxpayer fulfils certain legal requirements, a social contribution tax credit may be available, reducing the applicable rate to 8%.

In order to determine their taxable income, Brazilian companies that meet certain legal requirements can choose between:

- an actual profits system; or
- a presumed profits system, whereby the company's pre-tax profit is deemed to be equal to a fixed profit margin applied on its gross sales revenues.

Tax losses may be carried forward indefinitely against future profits. However, set-off is limited to 30% of the current year's taxable income. No carry-back of losses is permitted

10.2 Annual accounts

(a) Documents

Limited liability companies: At the end of each financial year, limited liability companies must draw up their balance sheet and profit and loss statement, as required under the Civil Code.

Corporations: At the end of each financial year, corporations must draw up the following, pursuant to the Corporations Law:

- the balance sheet;
- the accrued profit and loss statement;
- the income statement; and
- the statement of origin and appropriation of funds.

(b)   Auditors' report

Limited liability companies: Limited liability companies are not obliged to have their books and financial statements examined annually by an auditing firm.

However, in accordance with Law No 11,638/2007, large companies, whether incorporated as corporations or not, should comply with the provisions of such Law for keeping accounting records and drawing up financial statements, as well as in relation to the obligation to have their books and financial statements examined annually by an independent auditing firm. Under Law No 11,638/2007, large companies are defined as a legal entity (or a number of legal entities under the same control) with total assets in excess of R$240 million (approximately £60 million) or annual gross turnover above R$300 million (approximately £75 million).

Corporations: Closed corporation may also opt to have the books and financial statements audited by an auditing firm; where the corporation does not do so, the inspection committee may choose to engage the services of an auditing firm.

Publicly held corporations are required to engage an independent auditor, which is duly registered with the CVM.

(c)   Approval and distribution of profits

Limited liability companies: At least once a year, within four months of the end of the fiscal year, the quotaholders must approve the financial statements and management accounts, as well as the proposed distribution of profits. Limited liability companies are not required to publish their financial statements. The company may prepare interim balance sheets and financial statements on a semi-annual basis or over shorter periods of time to determine the net result of the relevant period and decide on the distribution of profits. Since 1996, the distribution of profits in Brazil has been tax free.

Corporations: Corporations are required to hold the annual shareholders' meeting within four months of the end of the financial year, for the adoption of resolutions on the financial statements and officers' accounts, as well as on the utilisation of profits and distribution of dividends. Again, the distribution of profits is tax free.

(d)   Deposit and publication

Limited liability companies: The financial statements of limited liability companies need not be filed with the Commercial Registry or published in the *Official Gazette*.

Corporations: The financial statements of corporations must be filed with the

Commercial Registry and published in the *Official Gazette*; although closed corporations with fewer than 20 shareholders and a net worth of under R1 million are not subject to the publication requirement.

Further, the financial statements of publicly held corporations and all related accounting issues are subject to CVM control, pursuant to several directives and regulations. Therefore, the CVM is authorised to order the correction of financial statements where applicable, and may further require republication of the amended financial statement. Publicly held corporations must send their financial information to the CVM on a quarterly basis, using the Quarterly Information Form, which is made available to all company shareholders and to the market. Publicly held corporations must also send an updated annual information report to the CVM each year. Both of these documents must be prepared in accordance with CVM rules.

11. Company reorganisation

The Civil Code and the Corporations Law include specific rules on the transformation, amalgamation, spin-off and merger of companies. The Civil Code rules apply to limited liability companies, while the Corporations Law provisions apply to corporations.

The amalgamation, merger or spin-off of publicly held corporations must further comply with CVM regulations on issues such as:
- the minimum information that must be disclosed to shareholders in regards to the transaction;
- disclosure deadlines;
- appraisals; and
- the pricing of shares in order to calculate the share swap value.

12. Eventual partner separation

Limited liability companies: The articles of association may allow for quotaholders to withdraw from the company upon notification of the other quotaholders.

Where no express provision to this effect is made and the articles of association establish that the Civil Code will have subsidiary application, quotaholders may withdraw from the company upon notification of the other quotaholders at least 60 days in advance.

On the other hand, where the articles of association establish that the Corporations Law will have subsidiary application, quotaholders may withdraw from the company only where they dissent from the amendment of the articles of association, amalgamation or merger.

The articles of association may further provide for the extrajudicial exclusion of quotaholders in the event of breach of their duties under the articles of association and under law.

Corporations: Shareholders may withdraw from a corporation where they dissent from resolutions on issues such as a reduction in the obligatory dividend, spin-off and merger.

13. Dissolution and liquidation

The rules on the voluntary dissolution and liquidation of limited liability companies are set out in the Civil Code and are similar to those included in the Corporations Law.

The members may decide at any time to dissolve the company. The decision must be taken at a quotaholders' meeting and must be approved by quotaholders representing at least 75% of the corporate capital. For corporations, the decision must be approved by shareholders representing a majority of the corporate capital.

Once the resolution to dissolve the company has been adopted, the company will enter into voluntary liquidation under the guidance of a liquidator. Liquidation may be carried out either before a court or extrajudicially. In the former case, the liquidator is appointed by the judge with jurisdiction over the company, while in the latter case he is appointed by the quotaholders/shareholders. As a general practice in Brazil, voluntary dissolutions are undertaken extrajudicially.

In extrajudicial liquidation, the liquidator is also appointed at the quotaholders'/shareholders' meeting which decides on the company's dissolution.

Article 1,104 of the Civil Code expressly provides that the liquidator's liabilities and obligations are identical to those of the company's administrators. Therefore, pursuant to the requirements established for the management of limited liability companies, the liquidator must be an individual resident in Brazil.

The liquidator's numerous duties include:

- filing with the Commercial Registry the minutes of the quotaholders'/ shareholders' meeting at which the decision to dissolve was taken, or the judicial award ordering such dissolution;
- collecting assets, accounting books and corporate documents;
- drawing up, within 15 days of his appointment and with the assistance of the administrators, the company inventory and balance sheet; and
- filing with the Commercial Registry the minutes of the quotaholders'/ shareholders' meeting at which the liquidation process is deemed to have ended, or the corresponding quotaholder/shareholder agreement.

The liquidator further has the power to represent the company and execute all acts necessary to achieve the liquidation. He is entitled to sell personal property and real estate, enter into compromises and grant and accept debt releases on behalf of the dissolving company. In all acts, documents and publications, the liquidator must use the company name followed by the words 'in liquidation' and identify himself as the liquidator.

The liquidator may be removed during the course of liquidation by decision of the quotaholders/shareholders.

In a Brazilian dissolution and liquidation process, the liquidator will pay off all debts *pro rata*, respecting the rights of preferred creditors. The order of preference in which creditors must be paid is set out in Article 961 of the Civil Code. Secured creditors (ie those whose claims are secured by mortgage or hypothec) have priority over unsecured creditors. Debts that are not yet due as at the date of liquidation are to be paid at normal bank discount rates. Once all debts have been paid, the remaining amounts, if any, are distributed to the quotaholders/shareholders.

Once the dissolution and liquidation procedure has ended, another quotaholders'/shareholders' meeting will be called to approve the accounts and close the company by filing with the Commercial Registry the appropriate documents (eg the minutes of the general meeting, debt clearance certificates and certificates attesting the cancellation of registration with the social security, labour and tax authorities). The accounts presented by the liquidator must be approved by the quotaholders/shareholders.

Where the full dissolution and liquidation process is unnecessary (ie where the company is not operative, has no liabilities to pay and no assets that need to be sold), the quotaholders/shareholders may choose to close the company in the same meeting at which the decision to dissolve is approved. In such case the capital will be distributed among the quotaholders/shareholders in proportion to their respective equity interests in the company. The company will be closed once the minutes of the quotaholders'/shareholders' meeting and other required documents are filed with the Commercial Registry.

14. Branches

A Brazilian company's head office and branches are different establishments of the same company. They are, therefore, jointly and severally liable for all of the company's obligations.

Furthermore, a foreign company may establish itself in Brazil either through a branch or a subsidiary. Branches are subject to prior approval being obtained from the Brazilian Federal Executive Branch and are most commonly used by foreign banks and airline companies (in the latter case, the approval is granted by the Brazilian Civil Aviation Authority – ANAC). Due to the extremely complex procedure involved, the opening of a branch in Brazil is not generally recommended.

British Virgin Islands

James McConvill
Appleby

1. Introduction

The BVI Business Companies Act (the act) came into effect on January 1 2005 and introduced a comprehensive regime that affected all incorporated companies or those to be incorporated in the British Virgin Islands (BVI), replacing both the International Business Companies Ordinance and the Companies Act (Cap 285) (together, the 'old legislation'). It was drafted to ensure the territory was fully compliant with the European Union (EU) Savings Tax Directive and the EU Code of Conduct on Business Taxation, as required by the United Kingdom of all its Overseas Territories.

In October 2004, however, the Chief Minister, Dr D Orlando Smith, informed the country's Legislative Council that a two-year transitional period would be put in place to smooth the changeover to the act from the old legislation, which lowered the income tax rate to 0% for both local and international companies, thereby effectively removing the distinction between 'offshore' and 'onshore' entities.

On January 1 2007 the transitional period ended and the act became the sole act under which companies could be incorporated in the BVI.

2. Classification

In response to the increasing concern that the range of corporate structures available in the BVI was limited in comparison to other jurisdictions, Section 5 of the act made it possible to incorporate five different types of companies, namely:

- a company limited by shares;
- a company limited by guarantee that is not authorised to issue shares;
- a company limited by guarantee that is authorised to issue shares;
- an unlimited company that is not authorised to issue shares; and
- an unlimited company that is authorised to issue shares.

For companies that are limited by shares or otherwise authorised to issue shares, the memorandum of the company must indicate whether or not the company is authorised to issue bearer shares.

If a company limited by shares has restricted purposes, capacity, rights or powers, it may be registered, on incorporation, as a restricted purpose company. The restricted purposes of the company need to be specified in its memorandum. Restricted purpose companies are intended to be especially useful as special purpose vehicles in structured finance and securitisation transactions.

Further, a company limited by shares may, with written approval of the BVI Financial Services Commission, be incorporated as a 'Segregated Portfolio Company', with or without restricted purposes. The option to register as a segregated portfolio company is currently limited to licensed insurers and mutual funds.

3.   Incorporation

Registration of a company in the BVI is straightforward when compared with other jurisdictions. However, prior to registration, the company proposing to be registered must appoint a 'registered agent' – as only a registered agent may make an application for the incorporation of a BVI company (Section 6(2) of the act).

The registered agent will apply to the registrar of corporate affairs (the registrar) for the incorporation of the company by filing the following documents, which must both be signed by the registered agent and tendered with a document signifying that they have consented to act as registered agent of the company (Section 6(1)):

- the company's memorandum of association (memorandum), which must contain such particulars as set out in the act; and
- the articles of association (articles), unless the company is an unlimited company that is not authorised to issue shares.

A company limited by shares may state in its memorandum that the company is a restricted purposes company (Section 10(1)), in which case the memorandum must state those purposes (Section 10(2)). A company proposing to have restricted purposes must be registered on incorporation as having restricted purposes, as a company that is not registered as a restricted purposes company on its incorporation will not subsequently be registered as a restricted purposes company (Section 8(2). Accordingly, the certificate of incorporation of a restricted purposes company will state that the company is a restricted purposes company (Section 8). Note, however, that a company that is not registered as a restricted purposes company is not restricted from limiting the purposes, capacity, rights, powers or privileges of the company (Section 10(3)).

If the company is to be incorporated as a segregated portfolio company (SPC), then the written approval of the BVI Financial Services Commission (the Commission) is required.

When satisfied that the company has fulfilled the requirements of the act in respect of incorporation, the registrar will register the aforementioned documents, allot the company with a unique number and issue a certificate of incorporation (Section 7(1)). The company will be officially incorporated on the date specified in the certificate of incorporation (Section 7(2)).

Incorporation can take as little as a day to complete.

4.   Constitution

Upon the issue by the registrar of a certificate of incorporation, the company is, from the date shown on the certificate, a legal entity in its own right separate from its members and continues in existence until it is dissolved (Section 27). When registered, the memorandum and articles are binding between the company and its members and between each member of the company (Section 11(1)). The company, the board, each director and each member of the company has the rights, powers, duties and obligations set out in the act, except to the extent that they are modified or negated, as permitted by the act, the memorandum or articles (Section 11(2)). The memorandum and articles will have no effect to the extent that they contravene or are inconsistent with the act (Section 11(3)).

4.1 Memorandum of association (the memorandum)

The memorandum of a company must state (Section 9(1)):

- the name of the company;
- whether the company is limited by shares, limited by guarantee (and whether it is or is not authorised to issue shares) or unlimited (and whether it is or is not authorised to issue shares);
- the address of the first registered office of the company, which must be in the BVI; and
- the name of the first registered agent of the company.

In addition, where a company is limited by shares or is otherwise authorised to issue shares, the memorandum must state:

- the maximum number of shares that the company is authorised to issue or that the company is authorised to issue an unlimited number of shares;
- the classes of shares that the company is authorised to issue and, if the company is authorised to issue two or more classes of shares, the rights, privileges, restrictions and conditions attaching to each class of shares; and
- if the company is prohibited from issuing bearer shares (by any legislation), that the company is not authorised to issue bearer shares, convert registered shares to bearer shares or exchange registered shares for bearer shares; or
- if the company is not prohibited from issuing bearer shares, either that the company is, or is not, authorised to issues bearer shares, convert registered shares to bearer shares or exchange registered shares for bearer shares.

Furthermore, in the case of a company limited by guarantee, whether or not it is authorised to issue shares, the memorandum must state:

- whether or not it is authorised to issue shares; and
- the amount that each member of the company is liable to contribute to the company's assets in the event that a voluntary liquidator or a liquidator appointed under the Insolvency Act (No 5 of 2003) is appointed while they are a member.

As stated above, the memorandum of a restricted purposes company must also state those purposes (Section 10(2)), though a company that does not have restricted purposes is not prevented from limiting the purposes, capacity, rights, powers or privileges of the company (Section 10(3)).

The act provides some clarification of the rights attaching to shares in a BVI company when the memorandum (or articles) is silent. These rights are (Section 34(1)):

- the right to one vote at a meeting of the company or on any resolution of the members of the company;
- the right to an equal share of any dividend paid pursuant to the Act; and
- the right to an equal share in the distribution of any surplus assets in the company.

Accordingly, it is important to ensure that the memorandum expressly deals with the above matters if the company does not want these default rights to apply.

(a)   *Amendment of memorandum or articles of association*

An amendment to the memorandum (or articles) of a company may only be effected by the members of a company, by resolution, in general meeting (Section 12(1)). The memorandum may provide, however, that (Section 12(2)):

- specific provisions of the memorandum or articles may not be amended;
- a resolution passed by a specified majority of members greater than 50% is required; and
- the memorandum or articles (or specified provisions thereof) may only be amended if certain specified conditions are met.

These provisions do not apply, however, to a company that is not a restricted purposes company where it aims to restrict its purposes (Section 12(3)).

The memorandum itself may also permit its amendment by the directors of a company (Section 12(4)) but in this case the directors will not have the power to amend the memorandum or articles if to do so would (Section 12(5)):

- restrict the rights or powers of the members to amend the memorandum or articles;
- change the percentage of members required to pass a resolution to amend the memorandum or articles; or
- result in the memorandum or articles not being able to be amended by the members.

A restricted purposes company is not allowed to amend its memorandum so that it is not a restricted purposes company (Section 14(1)), though a restricted purposes company may amend its memorandum to modify its purposes (Section 14(2)). Conversely, a company that is not a restricted purposes company is not allowed to amend its memorandum to state that it is a restricted purposes company (Section 14(3)).

(b)   *Filing of notice of amendment of memorandum and restated memorandum*

Where a resolution is passed to amend the memorandum or articles, the company must file for registration a notice of the amendment, or a restated memorandum or articles incorporating the amendment (Section 13(1)). A company may file a restated memorandum or articles at any time (Section 15(1)). The amendment will have effect from the date that the notice of amendment, or restated memorandum or articles incorporating the amendment, is registered by the registrar; however, a company, a member or director of a company, or any interested person may apply to the court for an order that an amendment should have effect from a date no earlier than the resolution to amend the memorandum or articles (Section 13(2) and (3)). The court may make such an order where it is satisfied that it would be just to do so (Section 13(5)).

The company's memorandum and articles are available for inspection at the registrar's office, as is the company's certificate of incorporation.

4.2   Objects

Subject to its memorandum and articles, a company has the full capacity of a natural person who is *sui juris*. Pursuant to the act, a company has, irrespective of corporate benefit, the full capacity to carry on or undertake any business or activity, do any act or enter into any transaction and the full rights, powers and privileges related thereto (Section 28(1)). This includes the power to:

- issue and cancel shares and hold treasury shares;
- grant options over unissued shares in the company and treasury shares;
- issue securities that are convertible into shares; and
- give financial assistance to any person in connection with the acquisition of its own shares (unless in each instance the company is not authorised to issue shares).

Subject to the rights or interests of any existing or subsequent creditor of the company in any assets of the company, which will not be affected by the following (Section 28(4)), a company will also have the power to (Section 28(2)):

- issue debt obligations of every kind and grant options, warrants and rights to acquire debt obligations;
- guarantee a liability or obligation of any person, and secure any of its obligations by mortgage, pledge or other charge on any of its assets for that purpose; and
- protect the assets of the company for the benefit of the company, its creditors and its members and, at the discretion of the directors, for any person having a direct or indirect interest in the company. To protect the assets of the company, the directors may transfer any of its assets in trust to one or more trustees, to be held for the benefit of the company, its creditors, its members, or any person having a direct or indirect interest in the company (Section 28(3)).

Provided that the company is not a restricted purposes company, no act of a company or transfer of real or personal property to or by a company will be invalid by reason only of the fact that the company was without capacity or power to perform the act, or to transfer or receive the property (Section 29), save that the lack of capacity may be pleaded in proceedings:

- by a member to prohibit the transfer of real or personal property to or by a company; or
- by the company against the incumbent or former directors of the company for loss due to their unauthorised act. The court has the power to set aside

and prohibit the performance of a contract in certain circumstances specified under the act.

4.3 Names and change of name

The registrar may, at the request of any person, reserve a name for a period of 90 days for future adoption by a company (Section 25(1)). 'Limited' 'Corporation', 'Incorporated', 'Société Anonyme' or 'Sociedad Anonima' or the abbreviation 'Ltd', 'Corp', 'Inc' or 'SA' must be a part of the name of every company (Section 17(1)), and an unlimited company's name must end with 'Unlimited' or 'Unltd' (Section 17(2)).

If the company is a restricted purpose company, the name of the company must end with the words '(SPV) Limited' or '(SPV) Ltd' (Section 17(3)). If the company is a segregated portfolio company, the name of the company must include the designation 'Segregated Portfolio Company' or 'SPC' (Section 17(4)).

The name of a BVI company can merely comprise the expression 'BVI Company Number' followed by the company's number in figures and one of the above endings (Section 19). A BVI company may also have an additional name in foreign characters, but the Registrar must also give his approval to this name (Section 20).

A company may not be incorporated with a name that is identical to the name of a company already in existence under the act nor be so similar to a name as to be calculated to confuse or mislead (Section 18(1)(b)), or with a name that is indecent, offensive or, in the opinion of the registrar, objectionable (Section 18(1)(e)). The use of certain words is also restricted, and the written consent of the registrar is required for their use. Restricted words include the words 'Assurance', 'Bank', 'Building Society', 'Chamber of Commerce', 'Chartered', 'Cooperative', 'Imperial', 'Insurance', 'Municipal', 'Royal', 'Trust Company', 'Trustee Company' and words conveying a similar meaning, or any other word that, in the opinion of the registrar, suggests or is calculated to suggest (Section 18(2)):

- the patronage of the sovereign of the United Kingdom or that of a member of the royal family;
- a connection with the UK Government or a department thereof; or
- a connection with a municipality or other local authority or with a society or body incorporated by UK royal charter.

Subject to its memorandum and articles, a company may apply to the registrar to change its name (Section 21(1)). The registrar will register the company's change of name and issue a certificate of change of name if satisfied that the above requirements are still complied with (Section 21(2)).

The registrar has the power to compulsorily change the name of a company that fails to comply with a notice from the registrar requiring it to change its name (Section 22).

Every BVI company must ensure that its full name and, if it has one, its foreign-character name, is clearly stated in every written communication sent by or on behalf of the company, and on every document issued or signed by or on behalf of the company that evidences or creates a legal obligation of the company (Section 26(1)).

4.4   Continuance and discontinuance

(a)   Continuance

A company incorporated outside the BVI (ie a foreign company) may apply to the registrar to be continued in the BVI as if it were incorporated under the Companies Act, provided the laws of the foreign jurisdiction in which it is registered permit this (Section 180(1)). A foreign company may not continue in the BVI if (Section 180(2)):

- the company is subject to insolvency proceedings;
- a receiver or manager has been appointed in relation to any of its assets;
- it has entered into an arrangement with creditors that has not been concluded, or
- an application has been made to the relevant jurisdiction's court to liquidate the company.

An application for a foreign company to continue into the BVI is made by filing the following documents with the registrar (Section 181):

- a certified copy of its certificate of incorporation;
- the memorandum and articles that, in addition to complying with the provisions of the act, also indicate the name of the company at the date of the application and the name under which it proposes to be continued; the jurisdiction under which it is incorporated, registered or formed; and the date on which it was incorporated, registered or formed;
- satisfactory evidence that the application to continue and the proposed memorandum and articles have been approved by the requisite majority of directors (or other persons) who are in charge with exercising the powers of the company or in such manner as may be established by the company for exercising its powers; and
- satisfactory evidence that the company is not disqualified from continuing in the BVI (ie evidence to show that the company is not subject to insolvency proceedings or has not entered into an arrangement with creditors – this evidence may include the company's financial statements and register of charges).

The memorandum and articles must also be signed by, or on behalf of, the persons who approved the application to continue (Section 181(4)).

Once satisfied that the requirements of the act have been complied with, the registrar will register the above documents, allot a unique number to the company, and issue a certificate of continuation, which is conclusive evidence that all the requirements of the act have been complied with and that the company is continued as a company incorporated under the act under the name designated in its memorandum on the date specified in the certificate of continuation (Section 182(1) and (2)). The registrar still has the prerogative, however, to refuse to continue a foreign company if he is of the opinion that it would be contrary to the public interest to do so (Section 182(3)).

Where a foreign company is continued under the act, the company continues as a body corporate under the name designated in its memorandum, capable of exercising all of the powers of a company under the act (Section 183(1)). The memorandum and articles filed pursuant to the act become the memorandum and articles of the company (Section 183(1)(d)). All property of the company continues to vest in the company and the continuation of a foreign company to the BVI does not affect the continuity of the company as a legal entity; nor does it affect the assets, rights, obligations or liabilities of the company (Section 183(2)), which includes any existing cause of action, claim or liability to prosecution in respect of the foreign company (Section 183(3)). All shares in the company that were outstanding prior to the issue by the registrar of a certificate of continuation are deemed to have been issued in conformity with the act (Section 183(4)).

(b) *Discontinuance*

Subject to its memorandum and articles, any BVI company to which the registrar would issue a Certificate of Good Standing may, by a resolution of the directors or a resolution of members, continue out of the BVI as a company incorporated under the laws of a foreign jurisdiction, provided that the laws of the foreign jurisdiction permit and the company has complied with those laws (Section 184). The registrar will issue a Certificate of Good Standing, on request, if he is satisfied that the company is on the register of companies and has paid all fees, annual fees and penalties due and payable (Section 235(1)).

In order to be discontinued in the BVI, the registered agent must file a notice of the company's discontinuance in the approved form (Section 184(3)). If the registrar is satisfied that the requirements of the Companies Act for the continuation of the company under the laws of a foreign jurisdiction have been complied with, he will issue a certificate of discontinuance, strike the name of the company off the register of companies with effect from the date of the certificate of discontinuance and publish the striking-off of the company in the *Gazette* (Section 184(4)).

A continuation out of the BVI will not release or impair any conviction, judgment, ruling, order, claim, debt, liability, obligation or cause existing against a company or any member, director, officer or agent thereof or result in the discontinuation or abatement of any civil or criminal proceedings that are pending at the time of the continuation or discontinuation (Section 184(5)).

5. Management and administration

5.1 Registered office and registered agent

Every company must have a registered office in the BVI (Section 90(1)), which must be a 'physical address' (ie it cannot be a post office box (Section 90(3)). The company can change its registered office at any time, but the registrar must be notified of such a change (Section 90(2)).

A BVI company must also have a registered agent in the BVI (Section 91(1)). A registered agent must be licensed to act as such under either the Company Management Act or the Banks and Trust Companies Act (Section 91(3)) and he must also have obtained the approval of the BVI Financial Services Commission (the

Commission) to provide registered agent services. Failure to obtain such a licence and approval means he will cease to be eligible to act as a registered agent (Section 94).

The company may change its registered agent at any time, but the registrar must be notified of such a change (Section 91(2)). The registered office of the company may also be the office of its registered agent (Section 91(3)(b)). A company that does not have a registered agent is liable on summary conviction to a fine of $10,000 (Section 91(6)). Failure on the part of a company to appoint a new registered agent may make it liable to be struck off the register of companies.

A resolution by the members of the company is required in order to change the location of a company's registered office or to change a company's registered agent; however, the company's directors may resolve as such if authorised by the memorandum or articles (Section 92(1)). As noted above, the registrar must be notified of a change of registered office, but only the registered agent or a legal practitioner in the BVI may act on behalf of the company for the purposes of filing the notice (Section 92(4)). A notice of change of registered agent must be endorsed by the new registered agent with his agreement to act as registered agent (Section 92(3)). A change of registered office or registered agent will take effect upon the registration by the registrar (Section 92(6)).

A registered agent may only resign in accordance with the provisions of the act (Section 93(1)). A person wishing to resign as the registered agent of a company must give not less than 90 days written notice of his intention to resign; and, together with the written notice, he must provide a list of all approved registered agents in the BVI with their names and addresses (Section 93(2)), and send both the notice and the list of approved registered agents to a director of the company's last known address (Section 93(3)) and copies to the registrar (Section 93(2)(c)).

The Financial Services Commission maintains a register of approved registered agents where the following information will be recorded (Section 95(1)):

- the name of the approved registered agent;
- the address of the approved registered agent;
- the names of the individuals authorised to sign on behalf of any firm or company that is an approved registered agent;
- the date when the registered agent was issued with the requisite licence (as discussed above) and approval was obtained by the Commission to provide registered agent services; and
- where a person ceases to be an approved registered agent, the date on which the person ceased to be so approved and the reason for him ceasing to be so approved.

A registered agent must send notification to the Commission of any changes in the details contained in the register (Section 95(3)).

5.2   Articles of association

The articles of association of a company govern its internal organisation, management and administration. The rights and duties of the members as against the company, and as between the members themselves, are set out in the articles, which constitute a contract between these parties. They are a private document, subject neither to governmental review nor to public inspection. A company's articles are subject to the same provisions of the act that apply to a company's memorandum.

The act is silent as to the content of a company's articles. Accordingly, a company's articles can be tailor-made to suit its needs. The reader should therefore pay special attention to a company's articles as they may well differ from company to company. In addition, there is considerable scope for overlap between the procedures set out in the act and those that may also be contained in the company's articles (eg a company can always provide in its articles to adopt a procedure that is more onerous than that contained in the Companies Act).

5.3   Requirements for officers or representatives in the BVI

As stated at section 5.1 above, a BVI company must have a registered agent in the BVI at all times, who is responsible for incorporating the company and appointing the first directors of the company, amongst other things. The directors of the company, however, manage its business and affairs (Section 109(1)).

5.4   Directors

Subject to the company's articles, the act provides that "the directors of a company have all the powers necessary for managing, directing and supervising, the business and affairs of the company" (Section 109(2)). There is no requirement under the act for any of the directors to be actual residents of the BVI.

The number of directors may be fixed by the articles (Section 109(5)). Apart from the time between the incorporation of the company and the appointment of the first directors by the registered agent, a company must have at least one director (Sections 109(4) and (4A)). If a company does not have a director for any period of time, then the person who manages (or supervises the management of) the company is deemed to be a director for the purposes of the act (Section 109(6)).

The directors also have the power, subject to the memorandum and articles, to designate a committee of directors and to delegate their powers, including the power to affix the common seal of the company, to that committee (Section 110(1)). Notwithstanding anything in the company's memorandum or articles, a committee does not have the power to amend the memorandum or articles; to designate further committees of directors or to delegate powers to them (though sub-committees are permitted (Section 110(3)); to appoint or remove directors or agents; to approve a plan, merger, consolidation or arrangement; or to make declarations regarding the company's (in)solvency (Section 110(2)). Where the directors delegate as such, they remain responsible for the exercise of that power by the committee, unless they believed on reasonable grounds that the committee would exercise its power in conformity with the duties imposed on directors by the act (Section 110(4)).

A director may, subject to the company's memorandum or articles, appoint an alternate. This person need not be a director at the time. In the absence of the director, an alternate is entitled to attend meetings and to vote in place of the director (Section 130)).

The act also introduces the concept of 'reserve director'. Under the Act, where a company has only one member who is also the director of the company, the sole member/director may appoint a person as a reserve director of the company to act as sole director in the event that the appointing director dies (Section 113(7)). This provides a very useful succession mechanism for sole member/directors.

(a) Directors' duties

The main duties of directors are contained in Sections 120 to 123 of the act. The statutory duties of directors under the act to a large extent codify the equitable and common-law duties of directors, but they do not replace the common law.

For example, a director can still be liable to the company under common-law principles relating to negligence. Under the common law, however, directors can only be liable in this regard if "no man with any degree of prudence", acting on his own behalf, would have acted or failed to act in the way that the director did under the particular circumstances.

The main statutory duty of directors is to act honestly, in good faith and in what the director believes to be in the best interests of the company (Section 120(1)). Other statutory duties of directors include exercising their powers for a proper purpose. This includes not acting or agreeing to act in a manner that contravenes the act and the memorandum or articles of the company (Section 121), and a duty to exercise their powers and perform their duties with a level of care, diligence and skill that a reasonable director would exercise in the circumstances, taking into account (amongst other things) the nature of the company, the nature of the decision and the position of the director and the responsibilities undertaken by the director (Section 122).

The act expressly provides that directors, when exercising their powers and performing their duties, are entitled to rely upon the register of members and books, records, financial statements and other information supplied and/or professional or expert advice given by: (a) an employee of the company, but only where the director believes on reasonable grounds that the employee is reliable and competent; (b) a professional adviser or expert, where the director believes the matter is within their professional or expert competence; and (c) another director, or a committee of directors in which the director did not serve, in relation to matters within the director's or committee's designated authority.

The act states that directors may only act upon such information or advice where they: (a) act in good faith; (b) make proper inquiry where the need for such an inquiry is indicated by the circumstances; and (c) have no knowledge that such reliance is not warranted (Section 123(2)). The act does not provide, however, that the director will satisfy his or her statutory or common-law duties when relying upon such information or advice.

The above duties work together to comprise the standard of care expected of a director of a BVI company.

The act also responds to the potential for conflict confronting directors in group company structures and joint-venture scenarios. In doing so, the act has extended the duties of directors beyond the traditional principle that fiduciary duties are owed only to the company. The act (Section 120(2)–(4)) provides that, so long as the company's memorandum or articles expressly permit, directors may act in the best interests of:

- the company's holding company where the company is wholly owned, despite the fact that the action may not be in the best interests of the wholly owned company;
- the company's holding company where the company is not wholly owned, despite the fact that the action may not be in the best interests of the company – provided that prior agreement of all shareholders (other than the holding company) has been obtained;
- the member(s) (who appointed the director) in circumstances where the company is carrying out a joint venture between the members, despite the fact that the action may not be in the best interests of the company.

It is important to note that the duties of directors at both common law and under the act are owed to the company as a whole, not to individual shareholders. There are, however, 'special circumstances' where the common law holds that a director may owe a fiduciary duty to shareholders. In terms of understanding the common-law duties of directors in the BVI, reference is usually made to the decisions of English courts and courts in Commonwealth jurisdictions, as the BVI presently does not have a formal system of law reporting in place.

(b)   *Directors' interests*

The act completely redrafted and tightened the provisions dealing with the disclosure of directors' interests. It now includes a comprehensive regime dealing with disclosure (see Sections 124 and 125). The main aspects of this regime are as follows:

- **Circumstances where disclosure is required:** Under the act, directors are required to disclose to every other director on the board any 'interest' in a transaction entered into or to be entered into by the company, as soon as they become aware of that fact (Section 124(1)). The act facilitates the making of regulations to prescribe the circumstances in which a director is 'interested' in a transaction (Section 124(2)). No regulations have been made up to now. The director is not required to disclose this interest if:
  - the transaction is between the director and the company; and
  - the transaction is or is to be entered into in the 'ordinary course of the company's business' and on 'usual terms and conditions' (Section 124(3)) Interestingly, the act does not define what is in the 'ordinary course of the company's business' or what are 'usual terms and conditions', and accordingly this is a matter for the directors' personal judgement.

  It is an offence if a director fails to make appropriate disclosure where required under the act (Section 124(7)).
- **Voidable transactions:** A transaction entered into by the company where a director is 'interested' is voidable at the option of the company where the director does not, prior to the company entering into the transaction, disclose his interest unless:

- the material facts of the director's interest are known to those members entitled to vote at a meeting of members, and the transaction is approved or ratified by a resolution of members (Section 125(2))(a)); or
- the company received 'fair value' for the transaction (Section 125(2)(b)). What is 'fair value' for the transaction is to be determined based on information known to the company and the interested director at the time the transaction was entered into (Section 125(3)).

Importantly, any avoidance of a transaction arising from this disclosure regime does not affect another person's interest in property if the property was acquired: (i) from a person other than the company ('the transferor'); (ii) for valuable consideration; and (iii) without any knowledge of the circumstances of the transaction whereby the transferor acquired the property from the company (Section 125(5)).

This disclosure regime has important implications for financial institutions that lend to, or take security from, BVI companies. To respond to the risk that a transaction may be voidable at the company's option, financial institutions should ensure that where a director has an interest in the transaction, shareholders of the company have approved the transaction. Where it is considered by the company that 'fair value' has been received for the transaction, lenders should ensure that the board's considerations pertaining to fair value are minuted and substantiated.

Members of the company who did not vote in favour of the resolution, or creditors of the company, can invalidate the transaction if they can prove it was 'unfairly prejudicial' to them.

(c) *Indemnities and insurance*

A company may, unless its memorandum or articles state otherwise, indemnify against all expenses, including legal fees and all judgments, fines and amounts incurred, any person who is or was a director of the company or is or was, at the request of the company, serving in a similar capacity for another company or a partnership, joint venture, trust or other enterprise (Section 132(1)). This indemnity is permitted only where the director acted honestly and in good faith and in what the director believes to be the best interests of the company and, in the case of criminal proceedings, where the director had no reasonable cause to believe that his conduct was unlawful (Section 132(2)).

A company may purchase and maintain insurance in relation to any person who is or was a director of the company, or who at the request of the company is or was serving in a similar capacity for another company or a partnership, joint venture, trust or other enterprise, against any liability asserted against the person and incurred by the person in that capacity, whether or not the company has or would have had the power to indemnify the person under the act (Section 133).

5.5 Board meetings

The act provides that, subject to the company's memorandum or articles, the directors of the company may meet at such times and in such manner and places (either within or outside the BVI) as the directors deem necessary or desirable (Section 126(1)). A director can attend the meeting by way of telephone or other electronic means, provided that all directors participating in the meeting are able to hear each other (Section 126(2)).

Subject to the company's memorandum and articles, one or more directors of the company may convene a board meeting (Section 126(1A)). A director is to be provided with reasonable notice of a meeting of directors. What is 'reasonable notice' is subject to any requirements regarding notice contained in the company's memorandum or articles (Section 127(1)). The requirement for reasonable notice can be waived by all of the directors entitled to vote (or the majority requirement specified in the company's articles or memorandum) (Section 127(2)).

In order for resolutions to be implemented at a board meeting, there must be a quorum. The act provides that the quorum for a board meeting is that fixed by the memorandum or articles; however, if the memorandum or articles does not deal with quorum, a board meeting is considered to be properly constituted if at the commencement of the meeting one half of the total number of directors are present (Section 128).

As an alternative to physically meeting in person, any action that may be taken by the directors at a board meeting (or a meeting of a committee of directors) may be taken by a resolution of directors (or committee of directors) consented to in writing or by telex, telegram, cable or other written electronic communication (Section 129(1)).

5.6   General meetings

The act does not require companies to hold an annual general meeting of its members. The company's memorandum or articles may, however, provide a requirement for a meeting of members in certain circumstances, and in which case the memorandum or articles will set out the rules and procedures relating to these meetings.

The act contains some general provisions dealing with meetings of members and voting by members (see Sections 81 to 84), all of which are subject to any contrary or varying provisions in the company's memorandum or articles. Accordingly, the act is only to be consulted if there are no relevant provisions in the company's memorandum or articles.

(a)   Convening of a special general meeting on requisition

The act provides that the directors of a company are required to call a meeting of members if requested by members who are entitled to exercise at least 30% of the voting rights in relation to a matter in which a meeting is requested (Section 82(2)). This is subject to the company's memorandum and articles, which may specify that a lesser percentage of shareholders is required to requisition a meeting.

A meeting of the company's members may be held at such time and in such place (either within or outside the BVI) as the convenor of the meeting considers appropriate (Section 82(3)). A person convening a meeting of members is required, subject to the company's memorandum or articles, to give not less than seven days' notice of the meeting to those persons who appear in the company's register of members and are entitled to vote at the meeting (Section 83(2)). This notice requirement can be waived by members holding a 90% majority (or a lesser majority specified in the company's memorandum or articles) of the total voting rights on all matters to be considered at the meeting.

(b) *Voting*

Where member approval is required under the Act, and there is no specific reference to what percentage of members is required for approval in the company's memorandum or articles or pursuant to any other source (such as stock exchange listing rules, where relevant), a resolution is considered to be passed if approved by a majority in excess of 50% (or where the memorandum or articles requires a higher majority, that higher majority) of the votes of members entitled to vote and voting on the resolution: Section 81(2). The votes of shareholders are counted according to the votes attached to the shares held by the voting shareholder (Section 81(3)).

Unless the memorandum or articles of the company state otherwise, the exercise by the members of a company of a power provided to them under the act, or under the company's memorandum or articles, can be by a resolution passed at a duly convened meeting of members, or one proposed (without the need for any notice) and consented to in writing or by telex, telegram, cable or other written electronic communication.

5.7 Auditors

There are no provisions in the act either for an annual audit or for the appointment of auditors. Companies registered in the BVI may, however, provide for the appointment of an auditor in their memorandum or articles.

5.8 Records and financial statements

The act requires a company to keep a number of essential documents (the memorandum and articles of the company, the register of members (or a copy thereof), the register of directors (or a copy thereof) and copies of all notices and other documents filed by the company in the previous 10 years) at the office of the registered agent (Section 96(1)). A company must, within 15 days, notify the registered agent, in writing, of any change in the register of directors or register of members (Section 96(2)(a)). A company that fails to provide such notification is liable to a fine of $10,000.

The act also requires that other records of the company be maintained, either at the office of the company's registered agent, or such other place(s) either within or outside the BVI as the directors decide. These records are minutes of meetings and resolutions of members and of classes of members, and minutes of meetings and resolutions of directors and committees of directors (Section 97(1)). Where any of these records are kept at a place other than the office of the company's registered agent, the company is required to provide the registered agent with a written record of the physical address of the place(s) at which the records are kept (Section 97(2)), and also to notify the registered agent of any change in the physical address of the records within 14 days of the change of location (Section 97(3)). A company must have a common seal and an imprint of the seal needs to be kept at the office of the company's registered agent (Section 102(2)).

A BVI company is also required to keep financial records. A company is required to keep records that are sufficient to show and explain the company's transactions and that will, at any time, enable the financial position of the company to be determined with reasonable accuracy.

Section 100(1) of the act also provides directors and members with a right to inspect the company's records. A director of a company is entitled, on giving reasonable notice and at a reasonable time specified by the director, to inspect the documents and records of the company without charge, and to make copies of, or take extracts from, the documents and records. A member of the company is entitled, once written notice has been given, to inspect the company's memorandum and articles, the register of members, the register of directors, and minutes of meetings and resolutions of members and classes of members of which he is a member, and to make copies or take extracts from the documents and records (Section 100(2)). The directors can refuse to allow this, or can limit the inspection, if the directors are satisfied that such inspections would be contrary to the company's interests (Section 100(3)). The member then has the right to apply for a court order that allows the member to inspect the documents without limitation (Section 100(5)).

5.9 Employment of personnel

Although the majority of BVI companies have no employees in the BVI, many have their own offices and some staff. All persons other than those who reside in the BVI require the permission of the Labour Office to seek or take up employment in the BVI. The Labour Office will allow the employment of skilled and experienced non-resident personnel where it can be demonstrated that there are no residents available or suitable for the job.

5.10 Investments

A BVI business company is free to acquire, hold and deal in all types of investments. The act provides that, subject to any other enactment and its memorandum and articles, a company has full capacity to carry on or undertake any business or activity, do any act or enter into any transaction (Section 28(1)).

5.11 Registration of charges

The act introduced an entirely new regime for the registration of charges at the Registry of Corporate Affairs, with the previous regime widely acknowledged to have been unsatisfactory.

A company must maintain at its registered office or the office of its registered agent a register of charges (Section 162). This must include details of each charge entered into by the company, including the liability secured, a description of the property charged, the name and address of the charge (or trustee), the date of creation of the charge and details of any restriction on the power of the company to create any future charge ranking in priority to, or equally with, the charge.

The company or a chargee may now choose to submit a charge for registration with the registrar (Section 163(1)). The registrar keeps a register of registered charges for each company (Section 163(3)). In the event that questions of priority fall to be determined by reference to BVI law, any charge registered pursuant to the act will take priority over any other charge that is registered subsequently in regard to the same assets, and over all other charges created over such assets after January 1 2005 (or, in the case of a former BVI International Business Corporation (IBC), the date on which the IBC re-registered or was deemed to have re-registered pursuant to the act), which are not registered (Section 166). Charges created before January 1 2005 (or, in the case of a former BVI IBC, the date on which the IBC re-registered or was deemed to have been re-registered pursuant to the act) maintain their original priority (Section 167).

The regime introduced under the act is considered to be particularly important for financial institutions by providing for greater certainty because, prior to the introduction of the new regime, there was no central registry of charges.

5.12   Contracts

A company may enter into valid and binding contracts in writing under the common seal of the company (or in some cases without a common seal) and signed on behalf of the company by a person acting under the express or implied authority of the company, or orally by or on behalf of the company by a person acting under the express or implied authority of the company (Section 103).

Persons who enter into a contract in the name of, or on behalf of, a company before it has been incorporated under the act are personally liable under the contract unless the contract specifically provides otherwise, or the company, within a reasonable time after incorporation, expressly or impliedly adopts the contract (Section 104(1) and (2)). If a company adopts a contract in this manner after incorporation, it is deemed to be bound by, and is entitled to, the benefits of the contract as if it had been in existence at the date of the agreement and had been a party to it (Section 104(3)).

5.13   Electronic records

The financial and other records of the company that are required to be kept under the act may be kept in either written form, or either wholly or partly in electronic form (complying with the requirements of the Electronic Transactions Act) (Section 99).

6.   Taxation

6.1   Income tax, stamp duty and registration of documents

Companies incorporated under the act are exempt from all provisions of the BVI Income Tax Act, CAP 206 (the Income Tax Act). All dividends, interest, rents, royalties, compensations and other amounts paid by a company to persons who are not resident in the BVI, and capital gains realised with respect to any shares, debt obligations or other securities of such a company by persons who are not resident in the BVI, are exempt from the provisions of the Income Tax Act. No estate, inheritance, succession or gift tax, rate, duty, levy or other charge is payable by persons who are not resident in the BVI with respect to any shares, debt obligations or other securities of a company. All instruments relating to transfers of property to or by a company and transactions in respect of the shares, debt obligations or other securities of a company are exempt from the payment of stamp duty. Further, transfers of property to or by a company, transactions in respect of the shares, debt obligations or other securities of a company and other transactions relating to the business of a company are exempt from the provisions of the Registration and Records Act.

6.2   Government fees

The Business Companies Act sets out the fees payable to the registrar on the incorporation of a company or amendments to its memorandum and articles, searching the records and registers maintained by the registrar or obtaining certificates and copies of documents from the registrar. A company is also required to pay an annual fee to the registrar on or before May 31 of each year if it was incorporated in the first six months of the year, or on or before November 30 of each year if it was incorporated in the second half of the year.

7.   Share capital and debentures

7.1   Exchange control

There are no laws or regulations governing exchange control in the BVI.

This means that a company registered in the BVI is free to deal in any currency (eg the currency in which the company's shares will be issued (see Section 37(1)(b) with respect to a share with a par value) of their choosing, other than the local currency, which is US dollars.

7.2   Share capital

The Business Companies Act abolished the concept of authorised share capital to accord with companies' legislation in Commonwealth jurisdictions such as Australia and Canada (however, the concept continues to apply for some previous IBCs that were automatically re-registered on January 1 2007, rather than voluntarily re-registering). Under the act, a company can either authorise to issue shares up to a maximum number or authorised to issue an unlimited number of shares.

Under the act, no minimum share capital is prescribed for a company. A company may issue shares with par value, with no par value or a combination thereof. The company may also issue fractional shares. A share is deemed to be issued when the name of the shareholder is entered in the company's register of members (Section 50).

Shares may be issued fully paid, partly paid or nil paid. The consideration for shares may be money, services rendered, personal property, real property, a promissory note or other binding obligation to contribute money or property to the company or any combination thereof (Section 47(1)). Subject to its memorandum or articles, a company may issue its shares for such amount as may be determined from time to time by the directors, save that where the shares have a par value the consideration payable for such shares may not be less than the par value (Section 47(2)).

Save as otherwise stated in its memorandum or articles, a company may increase or reduce the maximum number of shares that it is authorised to issue. The company must inform the registrar in writing of any such change to the maximum number of shares that it may issue and it must file an amendment to the memorandum.

7.3   Redemption or purchase of shares by a company

The act provides that the directors of a company may make an offer to purchase, redeem or otherwise acquire a company's shares, if the offer is to:

- **all shareholders** to purchase, redeem or otherwise acquire shares issued by the company that would, if accepted, leave unaffected the relative voting and distribution rights of the shareholders and provides each shareholder with a reasonable opportunity to accept the offer (Section 60(1)(a)(ii)); or
- **one or more of the company's shareholders** in which all shareholders have consented in writing, or it is permitted by the company's memorandum or articles and the directors have passed a resolution stating that, in their opinion, the purchase, redemption or other acquisition is to the benefit of the remaining shareholders, and the terms of the offer are fair and reasonable to the company and to the remaining shareholders (Section 60(1)(b) and Section 61)).

Shares can also be redeemed otherwise than at the option of the company. First, if a share is redeemable at the option of the shareholder and that shareholder gives notice of their intention to redeem the share, the company shall redeem the share on the date specified in the notice (or the date of the receipt of the notice, if no date is specified) and the share is cancelled unless held as a treasury share (Section 62(1)). (Treasury shares are discussed in section 6.5 below.) Second, if a share is redeemable on a specified date, the company shall redeem the share on that date, and the share is deemed to be cancelled unless held as a treasury share (Section 62((2)).

A company may, alternatively, purchase, redeem or otherwise acquire its own shares in accordance with a process specified in its memorandum or articles. The provisions of the act dealing with redemption or purchase of shares by a company are negated to the extent that they are inconsistent with the provisions of the company's memorandum or articles dealing with purchase, redemption or acquisition (Section 59(2)).

A company may purchase, redeem or otherwise acquire its own shares, provided that, immediately after doing so, the company is solvent (ie the value of the company's assets exceeds its liabilities, and the company is able to pay its debts as they fall due), and the directors believe on reasonable grounds that the company will be solvent after the purchase, redemption or other acquisition (Section 59(1) and Section 57).

7.4   Bearer shares

Shares in a BVI company can either be in registered or bearer form (the latter not being registered on the company's books and thus rights attaching to the share, including dividends, belong to whoever possesses the share at any one time).

A company can only issue bearer shares if authorised to do so by the terms of its memorandum of association (Section 38(1)). A company can, however, convert a bearer share to a registered share at any time, notwithstanding any contrary provisions in its memorandum or articles.

Bearer shares must be delivered into the custody of a custodian (Section 69(2)). There are two types of custodians: authorised and recognised. An authorised custodian is a BVI licensed financial institution or a foreign company that is acceptable to the BVI Financial Services Commission. A recognised custodian is an investment exchange or a securities clearing organisation that carries on business in a Financial Action Task Force member jurisdiction and is recognised by the Commission (Section 67). Custodians are required to maintain information on the beneficial ownership of bearer shares in their custody and the names of any persons having an interest in the shares, whether by virtue of a charge or otherwise (Section 72).

Where a bearer share certificate is delivered to an authorised custodian, it must be accompanied by a notice containing prescribed information concerning beneficial ownership, which must be kept at the authorised custodian's principal office in the BVI or such other office as the Commission may approve (Section 71(1)). Where a bearer share certificate is delivered to a recognised custodian, notice of the delivery and the prescribed information concerning beneficial ownership must be sent to the registered agent of the company (Section 71(3)). Any change in the beneficial ownership of a bearer share will not be effective unless the authorised custodian or, in the case of a recognised custodian, the registered agent, has been notified of the change (Section 75(1)). An authorised custodian of a bearer share must send notification to the registered agent of the company that it is the custodian of the share (Section 72(1)).

Registered shares are transferable by an instrument in writing signed by the transferor and containing the name and address of the transferee (Section 54). Bearer shares are transferable by delivery of the share certificates (Section 55), but an authorised custodian may deliver bearer shares only to another authorised custodian who has agreed to hold the certificates, to the company for purposes of an exchange of the certificate for a registered share or redemption, or to the registered agent for onward transfer to another custodian (Section 73(1)). The registered agent of the company must be notified each time the possession of a bearer share certificate is transferred by an authorised custodian (Section 73(3)). Recognised custodians may only transfer possession of a bearer share certificate to the registered agent of the company for onward transfer to another custodian, or to the company to exchange it for a registered share or redemption (Section 73(4)). Where the possession of a bearer share certificate is transferred by a recognised custodian to the company, the company must notify its registered agent of the receipt of the certificate (Section 73(6)).

7.5 Treasury shares

The concept of 'treasury share' encompasses both authorised but non-issued shares of the company and shares previously issued by a company that have been reacquired but not cancelled.

Unlike some other leading financial jurisdictions (eg the Cayman Islands), the BVI enables companies to hold treasury shares (subject to provisions to the contrary in the company's memorandum or articles). The act provides that a BVI company may hold as treasury shares those shares that have been purchased, deemed or otherwise acquired under the act, if the memorandum or articles of the company do not prohibit it from holding treasury shares; the company's directors resolve that the acquired shares will be held as treasury shares and the aggregate number of treasury shares of the class of shares concerned will not exceed 50% of the share class after the shares have been purchased, redeemed or otherwise acquired (excluding shares that have been cancelled) (Section 64(1)).

The rights and obligations attaching to a treasury share are suspended, and cannot be exercised by or against the company, whilst the shares are held as treasury shares by the company (Section 64(2)). Treasury shares can be transferred in the same way as registered shares (ie by a written instrument of transfer signed by the transferor and containing the name and address of the transferee) (Sections 54(1) and 65).

7.6 Register of members

Every company must keep a register of its members in the BVI (Section 41(1)). The register of members must detail (Section 41(1)):

- the names and addresses of the members holding registered shares in the company;
- the number of each class of shares held by each member;
- the names and addresses of the persons (if any) who are guarantee members or unlimited members of the company;
- if a company has issued bearer shares, the total number of each class and series of bearer shares held by the member;
- if a company has issued bearer shares, with respect to each bearer share certificate: the identifying number of the certificate; the number of each class or series of bearer shares specified in the certificate; the date of issue of the certificate; and the name and address of the custodian of the certificate;
- the date in which each person was entered in the register of members; and
- the date in which any person ceased to be a member.

The act provides that the register of members may be in such form as the directors approve; however, if the register is kept in magnetic, electronic or other data-storage form, the company must be able to produce legible evidence of its contents (Section 41(2)).

Entry of a person's name in the register of members as a holder of a share in a company is considered prima facie evidence that legal title in the share vests in that member (Section 42(1)). Accordingly, a company can treat the holder of a registered share as the only person entitled to: exercise any voting rights attaching to the share; receive notices; receive a 'distribution' (as defined in Section 56(b) of the act) for the share; and exercise other rights and powers attaching to the share (Section 42(2)).

7.7 Prospectuses and public offers

The act does not require a company to prepare, file or distribute a prospectus or any other form of offer document when offering shares to the public. However, if a company decides to list on a stock exchange, the rules of that stock exchange should be consulted as they will typically require the preparation and distribution of a prospectus or some other form of offer document.

7.8 Stock exchange listing of a BVI company

There is presently no stock exchange operating in the BVI. Whilst both the Cayman Islands and Bermuda have a well-established stock exchange, in practice most BVI companies that decide to list on a stock exchange (mainly for the purpose of raising funds more easily) tend to list on the London Stock Exchange (both the Main Market and AIM), and on the New York Stock Exchange or NASDAQ.

However a number of BVI companies do list on the Bermuda Stock Exchange (BSX) and the BSX will normally fast-track BVI companies seeking a listing.

7.9 Securities clearance

Unlike some other jurisdictions (eg Bermuda) the issue or transfer of shares in a BVI company does not require the specific permission of the Financial Services Commission – the BVI companies' regulator.

7.10 Distributions

The Companies Act 2004 introduced a wider concept of 'distribution'. The concept is now no longer limited to dividends. Under the act, a 'distribution', in relation to a distribution by a company to a member, means (Section 56):

- the direct or indirect transfer of an asset, other than the company's own shares, to or for the benefit of the member;
- the incurring of a debt to or for the benefit of a member; or,
- the purchase, redemption or other acquisition of shares, a transfer of indebtedness or otherwise in relation to shares held by the shareholder (this includes a dividend), or to the entitlement to distributions of a member who is not a shareholder, and whether by means of the purchase of an asset.

The directors of a BVI company may, subject to the memorandum and articles of the company, authorise (by passing a resolution) a 'distribution' by the company to members at such a time and for an amount that they think reasonable, provided they are satisfied that the company will, immediately after the distribution, satisfy the 'solvency test' (Section 57(1)). A resolution of the directors authorising the distribution must contain a statement that the company will, immediately after the distribution, satisfy this solvency test.

The act provides that a BVI company satisfies the solvency test if: (i) the value of the company's assets exceeds its liabilities, and (ii) the company is able to pay its debts as they fall due (Section 56(a)).

A company may recover a distribution made to a member when the company did not satisfy the solvency test immediately after the distribution, unless the member:

- received the distribution in good faith and without knowledge of the company's failure to satisfy the solvency test; or
- has altered his position in reliance on the validity of the distribution, and it would be unfair to require payment in full or at all (Section 58(1)).

A director is deemed to be personally liable to repay to the company as much of the distribution as cannot be recovered from members, where the director ceased to be satisfied, after authorising the distribution but before making it, that there were reasonable grounds to believe that the company would satisfy the solvency test immediately after the distribution was made, and failed to take reasonable steps to prevent the distribution being made (Section 58(2)).

7.11 Protection of members' rights

The act puts two key mechanisms in place to protect the rights of members: the investigation procedure, and a series of members' remedies.

(a) Investigation

The act allows members of a BVI company, along with the registrar of corporate affairs, to apply to the High Court of Justice, either without notice being given to the company or with whatever form of notice that the court may require, for an order that allows the company and any of its affiliated companies to be investigated (Section 223(1)).

The court may make any order it thinks fit in relation to the investigation of the company (and any of its affiliated companies) if it appears that (Section 223(2)):

- the business of the company (or any of its affiliates) is or has been carried on with intent to defraud;
- the company (or any of its affiliates) was formed for a fraudulent or unlawful purpose or is to be dissolved for a fraudulent or unlawful purpose; or
- persons concerned with the incorporation, business or affairs of the company (or any of its affiliates) have in connection with this acted fraudulently or dishonestly.

If the court believes an investigation is warranted, an inspector will be appointed. The court will set out the inspector's powers in the order (Sections 224 and 225).

The court may at any time make any orders it considers appropriate in relation to the investigation, including (Section 224(2)):

- authorising the inspector to enter any premises where the court is satisfied that there might be relevant information, and to examine anything, and to make copies of any documents or records, found on the premises;
- requiring any person to produce documents or records to the inspector;
- authorising the inspector to conduct a hearing, administer oaths or

affirmations and examine any person upon oath or affirmation, and prescribe rules for the conduct of the hearing;

- requiring any person to attend a hearing conducted by the inspector and to give evidence on oath or affirmation, requiring an inspector to discontinue an investigation, and requiring the company to pay the costs of the investigation in part or in full.

An application for an investigation, and any subsequent proceedings relating to an investigation, are to be conducted privately unless the court orders otherwise: Section 226(1). A person who is subject to an investigation may appear in person at any hearing, and has the right to be represented by a legal practitioner (Section 226(2)).

(b)   Members' remedies
The act sets in place a number of general remedies for members of a BVI company (there are also specific members' remedies that arise in the context of a change-of-control transaction). These include those set out next.

(i)   Restraining or compliance order
This remedy is available to members and directors of a BVI company by way of applying to the High Court of Justice. If the court is satisfied that the company or a director is engaging, has engaged or proposes to engage in conduct that contravenes the act or the memorandum or articles of the company, it may order the company or its director to comply with, or restrain from engaging in, conduct that contravenes the act, or the company's memorandum or articles, as well as any consequential relief it thinks fit (Sections 184B(1) and (2)).

(ii)   Derivative actions
Upon the application of a member of the company, the court may grant leave to bring proceedings in the name and on behalf of that company, or intervene in proceedings to which the company is a party, with the purpose of continuing, defending or discontinuing the proceedings on the company's behalf (Section 184C(1)). Unless the court orders otherwise, not less than 28 days' notice must be served, with the company being entitled to appear and be heard at the hearing of the application (Section 184C(4)).

In determining whether to grant leave for such a derivative action, Section 184C(2) of the act expressly states that the court must take into account five matters:

- whether the member is acting in good faith;
- whether the derivative action is in the interests of the company, taking into account the views of the company's directors on commercial matters;
- whether the proceedings are likely to succeed;
- the costs of the proceedings in relation to the relief likely to be obtained; and
- whether an alternative remedy to the derivative action is available.

Further leave to bring or intervene in proceedings may only be granted if the court is satisfied that the company does not intend to bring, diligently continue or defend, or discontinue the proceedings (as the case may be), or it is in the interests of the company that the conduct of the proceedings should not be left to the directors or to the determination of the members as a whole (Section 184C(3)).

Where a court grants leave to a member to bring or intervene in proceedings on behalf of the company, upon application by the member the court may order that the whole of the reasonable costs of bringing or intervening in the proceedings must be met by the company (Section 184D(1)). The court will not do this if it considers that it would be unjust or inequitable for the company to bear those costs. The court can order that the company must pay a proportion of the costs that it considers to be reasonable, or order that it not bear any costs (Section 184D(2)).

No derivative proceedings may be settled, compromised or discontinued without the leave of the court (Section 184F).

(iii) *Personal and representative actions*
The act confirms that a member of a company can bring an action against the company for breach of a duty owed to the person in their capacity as a member (Section 184G).

If a member brings proceedings against the company, and there are other members with the same or substantially the same interest in the proceedings, the court may appoint that member to represent all or some of the other members. In doing so, the court may make an order as to the control, conduct and costs of the proceedings; and direct the distribution of any amount ordered to be paid by a defendant in the proceedings among the members represented (Section 184H).

(iv) *Oppressive conduct*
A member of a company may apply to the court if they consider that the affairs of the company have been, or are likely to be, conducted in a manner that is oppressive, unfairly discriminatory or unfairly prejudicial to the member (Section 184I).

If the court agrees, it may make an order:
- requiring the company or any other person to acquire the member's shares;
- requiring the company or any other person to pay compensation to the member;
- regulating the future conduct of the company's affairs;
- amending the memorandum or articles of the company;
- appointing a receiver or liquidator of the company;
- directing the rectification of the records of the company; and/or
- setting aside any decision made or action taken by the company or its directors in breach of the act or the company's memorandum or articles.

8. Arrangements, mergers, dispositions, squeeze-outs and redemptions

8.1 Arrangements
The act sets in place a procedure whereby a BVI company can apply to the BVI High Court of Justice for approval of an 'arrangement', even where the proposed arrangement may be authorised or permitted by another provision of the act

(Section 177(2)). Before applying to the court to have the arrangement approved, the directors of the company first need to determine that the arrangement is in the best interests of the company (or the creditors or members thereof), and approve a 'plan of arrangement' that contains details of the proposed arrangement (Section 177(2)).

The term 'arrangement' is given (and is intended to have) a very wide meaning for the purposes of this part of the act. An 'arrangement' includes (Section 177(1)):

- an amendment to the company's memorandum or articles;
- a reorganisation or reconstruction of a company;
- a merger or consolidation of one or more companies registered under the act with another company, if the consolidated or surviving company is a company incorporated under the act;
- a separation of two or more businesses carried on by a company;
- any sale, transfer, exchange or other disposition of any part of the company's business to any person in exchange for shares, debt obligations or other securities (or money or other property) of that person;
- any sale, transfer, exchange or other disposition of shares, debt obligations or other securities in a company in exchange for shares, debt obligations or other securities of the company, or money or other property;
- a dissolution of a company; and
- any combination of these arrangements.

In hearing an application for approval of an arrangement, the court may, under Section 177(4) of the act:

- determine what notice (if any) is to be given to any person of the proposed arrangement;
- determine whether approval of the proposed arrangement by any person (eg affected members) should be obtained and the manner in which it should be approved;
- determine whether any holders of shares, debt obligations or other securities in the company may dissent from the proposed arrangement and receive payment of the fair value of their shares, debt obligations or other securities;
- conduct a hearing and permit any interested person to appear; and approve or reject the plan of arrangement either as proposed or with amendments.

If the court makes an order approving the plan of arrangement, the company's directors must then confirm the plan of arrangement if they still want to proceed (Section 177(5)). The directors must notify them and submit the plan of arrangement for their approval (Section 177(6)).

Once the plan of arrangement has received the approvals, if any, required by the court, the company must execute 'articles of arrangement'. These must contain the plan of arrangement, the court's order approving the plan, and the manner in which the plan was approved (if approval was required by the court) (Section 177(7)). Once executed, the articles of arrangement are filed with the BVI registrar of companies, and the registrar shall then issue a certificate certifying that the articles of arrangement have been registered (Section 177(8)). An arrangement becomes effective on the date that the articles of arrangement are registered by the registrar, or on a subsequent date (not exceeding 30 days after registration) that is specified in the articles of arrangement (Section 177(11)).

8.2 Schemes of arrangement

In addition to the procedure for arrangements discussed above, the act also provides for 'schemes of arrangement', which are a court-sanctioned arrangement (Section 179A). However, this follows a different process from the arrangements discussed above.

Schemes can be used for a wide range of things, including the merger or consolidation of companies and the reconstruction/reorganisation of companies. While these schemes are wide-ranging, because of the binding effect of a court-sanctioned order approving the scheme they are rarely used in practice.

Under the act, there is a three-stage process that needs to be followed before the scheme can be implemented. First, where a compromise or arrangement is proposed between a company and its creditors (or class of creditors), or between a company and its members (or class of members), the court may order that a meeting of the creditors (or class of creditors) or of members (or class of members) be convened, on such terms as the court thinks fit (Section 179A(1)). An application for the court to order the meeting can be made under Section 179A(2) of the act by:

- the company;
- a creditor of the company;
- a member of the company;
- the company's administrator (if the company is in administration);
- the voluntary liquidator (if the company is in voluntary liquidation); or
- the company's liquidator (if a liquidator has been appointed under the Insolvency Act).

The second stage is the meeting of members or creditors, or the class of members or creditors (as the case may be). If a 75% majority of those present in person or by proxy at the meeting agree to the compromise or arrangement, then the scheme returns to court. If the scheme is sanctioned by the court, it becomes binding on all the creditors or classes of creditors, or on all the members or classes of members to which the scheme relates. It also becomes binding on the company or, if the company is in voluntary liquidation or liquidation under the Insolvency Act, on the liquidator as well as each person liable to contribute to the company's assets in the event of liquidation (Section 179A(3)). An order of the court sanctioning the scheme has no effect until a copy of the order is filed with the registrar (Section 179A(4)). A copy of the court order must be annexed to every company memorandum issued after the order has been made (Section 179A(5)).

8.3 Mergers and consolidations

There is no separate code dealing with mergers and consolidations in the BVI (eg similar to the City Takeover Code in the UK), nor is there a separate Takeovers Panel, or a distinction between public and private companies when dealing with the law and procedure pertaining to mergers and consolidations.

In the BVI, a merger of companies is defined in the act as the merging of two or more constituent companies into one constituent company (known as the surviving company). A consolidation occurs when two or more constituent companies are united into one new company. A 'constituent company' means an existing BVI-registered company that is participating in a merger or consolidation with one or more existing BVI companies (Section 169). A company incorporated under the act may also, subject to and in compliance with the law in the foreign jurisdiction where a foreign company is domiciled, merge or consolidate with a foreign company and, in turn, continue as a BVI-registered company or as a foreign company (which may or may not conduct business in the BVI) (Section 174).

Where a merger or consolidation is proposed, the directors of each company must approve a written plan of merger or consolidation that sets out, amongst other things, the name of the surviving or consolidated company, the terms and conditions of the proposed merger or consolidation, a statement of any amendment to the memorandum or articles of the surviving company to be brought about by the company, and the manner and basis of cancelling, reclassifying or converting shares of each constituent company (Section 170(2)). The plan of merger or consolidation must be circulated to all members of the company (whether or not they are entitled to vote on the merger or consolidation) and approval obtained, by resolution, of a majority of the members entitled to vote (unless the memorandum or articles set down a different requirement) (Section 170(5)).

After the plan has been approved by the directors and members, the company must submit articles of merger or consolidation to the registrar. This contains the plan of merger or consolidation, the date on which the memorandum and articles of each constituent company were registered, the manner in which the merger or consolidation was authorised with respect to each constituent company, and details of any resolution to amend the company's memorandum or articles (in the case of a merger), or, where there is a consolidation, details of the memorandum and articles for the consolidated company (Section 171(1) and (2)). If satisfied that the requirements of the act have been complied with, the registrar will retain and register the articles of merger or consolidation, and he will issue a certificate of merger or consolidation (and a certificate of incorporation for a consolidated company) (Section 171(3)). A simplified procedure (where authorisation for the merger or consolidation by the members of the company is not required) is provided for mergers and consolidations between parent companies and subsidiaries, where the parent company owns at least 90% of the outstanding shares in the subsidiary (Section 172).

A merger or consolidation is deemed to be effective on the date on which the articles of merger or consolidation are registered by the registrar, or such other date not exceeding 30 days subsequent thereto as specified in the articles of merger or consolidation (Section 173(1)). The effect of a merger or consolidation is that the surviving company or the consolidated company (in so far as is consistent with its memorandum and articles) has all the rights, privileges, immunities, powers, objects and purposes of each of the constituent companies. In the case of a merger, the memorandum and articles of the surviving company are automatically amended. In the case of a consolidation, the memorandum and articles filed are the memorandum and articles of the consolidated company. All property of each of the constituent companies immediately vests in the surviving company or the consolidated company (as applicable) and the surviving or consolidated company is liable for all claims, debts, liabilities and obligations of each of the constituent companies (Section 173(2)).

A merger or consolidation will not release or impair any conviction, judgment, ruling, order, claim, debt, liability, obligation or cause existing against a constituent company or any member, director, officer or agent. Any civil or criminal proceedings that are pending at the time of the merger or consolidation by or against a constituent company or any member, director, officer or agent will continue (Section 173(3)).

8.4 Disposition of assets

If there is a sale, transfer, lease, exchange or other disposition (other than a mortgage, charge or other encumbrance or the enforcement thereof) of more than 50% in the value of the assets of the company, and this is not carried on by the company in the usual or regular course of the business, then the sale, transfer, lease, exchange or other disposition will be approved by the directors. On approval of the sale, transfer, lease or other disposition, the directors shall then submit details of the disposition for it to be approved by the members; if there is to be a meeting of members, then a notice of the meeting, accompanied by an outline of the disposition, needs to be given to each member (whether or not they can vote on the transaction); and if the written consent of members is to be obtained, an outline of the disposition is to be given to each member (whether or not the member can consent to the transaction) (Section 175).

8.5 Compulsory buy-out of dissenting members – the 'squeeze out'

The act has introduced a unique and highly sophisticated procedure to deal with the rights of members dissenting from a reorganisation of the company in which they are members. This so-called 'squeeze out' procedure is found in other developed jurisdictions. However, it is substantially different in the BVI. The squeeze-out procedure in essence provides a mechanism for members to be paid 'fair value' for the acquisition of their shares in the company (Section 179(1)).

Under the act, the squeeze-out provisions can be utilised when a member dissents from: a merger (if the company is registered in the BVI, but not if the company is the surviving company and the member continues to hold the same or similar shares); a consolidation (if the company is registered in the BVI); a sale, transfer, lease, exchange or other disposition of more than 50% in value of the assets or business of the company, if not made in the usual or regular course of the business carried on by the company (with some exceptions); a redemption of shares pursuant to the act; or an arrangement sanctioned by the act (Section 179(1)). A member who wishes to utilise the act's squeeze-out procedure needs to have provided a written objection to the company's action before the members meeting, unless the member was not given notice of the meeting or the proposed action was authorised by members without a vote (Section 179(2)).

Within 20 days following the date of the members meeting authorising the company's action (or the date in which written consent of members without a meeting was obtained), the company shall give written notice of the consent to each member who provided a written objection, or from whom a written objection was not required (Section 179(4)). If, on receiving this notice, a member elects to dissent, that member has up to 20 days immediately following the date on which the company's notice was given (or, if the member is dissenting from a merger, up to 20 days following the date in which the plan of merger was given to the member) to provide the company with written notice of their decision (Section 179(5)). Once a member provides a notice of dissent, they automatically cease to have any members' rights (except the right to be paid 'fair value' for their shares) (Section 179(7)).

Following this, within seven days of the expiration of the period in which members may provide their notice of election to dissent, or within seven days following the date in which the company's proposed action is put into effect (whichever is later), the company (or the surviving company or consolidated company) must make a written offer to each dissenting member to purchase their shares at a price the company deems to be 'fair value'. If, within 30 days of this offer being made, the company and the dissenting member agree a price, the company will pay this to the member in exchange for their share certificates (Section 179(8)). If, however, the company and a dissenting member fail to agree a price within this 30-day period, then within 20 days the following procedure applies (Section 179(9)):

- the company and the dissenting member each designate an 'appraiser';
- the two designated appraisers then designate a third appraiser;
- the three appraisers fix the fair value of the shares owned by the dissenting member as at the close of business the day before the vote of members authorising the shares was taken (or the date on which the written consent of members without a meeting was obtained). This price excludes any appreciation or depreciation resulting from the action (or its proposal); and
- the company pays the member the fair value in money in exchange for the member's share certificates.

8.6 Redemption of minority shares

The act provides that, subject to the company's memorandum or articles, members of the company holding 90% of the votes of the outstanding shares entitled to vote (or 90% of the votes of the outstanding shares of each class of shares entitled to vote as a class) can give the company a written instruction directing it to redeem the shares held by the remaining shareholders (Section 176(1)). Once this written instruction has been received, the company must redeem the shares specified in the instruction regardless of whether or not they are redeemable (Section 176(2)). The company must give written notice to each member stating the redemption price and the manner by which the redemption is to be effected (Section 176(3)).

9. General information

9.1 Banking facilities

There are a number of major retail banks operating in the BVI, including Banco Popular, ScotiaBank and the First Caribbean International Bank. Most of the major retail banks have subsidiaries, affiliates and correspondent relationships throughout the world.

The incorporation of companies that propose to engage in 'banking business' is dealt with under the Banks and Trust Companies Act 1990.

9.2 Accountants

There are many firms of accountants in the BVI available to provide accounting and consultancy services to exempted undertakings. Many of the leading international firms have local affiliates.

9.3 Mutual and mutual fund companies

Mutual funds are regulated separately in the BVI under the Mutual Funds Act 1996.

A 'mutual fund' is defined under BVI law to mean a company incorporated, a partnership formed, a unit trust organised, or other similar body formed or organised under the laws of the BVI (or any other country or jurisdiction) that: (a) collects and pools investor funds for the purpose of collective investment; and (b) issues shares that entitle the holder to receive on demand (or shortly thereafter) an amount calculated by reference to the value of a proportionate interest in the whole or in part of the net assets of the company, the partnership, the unit trust or other body (Section 2 of the Mutual Funds Act 1996).

9.4 Registers and inspection

(a) Registers

The act provides for a registrar of corporate affairs, who is to maintain a register of companies incorporated or continued under the act; a register of foreign companies; and a register of charges (Section 230(1)). The registers, maintained by the registrar, and the information contained in any filed document can be kept in any manner that the registrar considers fit, including (either wholly or partly) through a device or facility that records or stores information magnetically, electronically or by other means; and that permits the information recorded or stored to be inspected and reproduced in legible and usable form (Section 230(2)).

The registrar is required to retain every 'qualifying document' filed with it. A document is a qualifying document if the act (or the regulations, or another enactment) requires or permits the document to be filed, and the document complies with the act (or the regulations or other enactment) that requires or permits the document to be filed (Section 230(5)).

A document that is required or permitted to be filed by a company under the act must (except where otherwise permitted in the act or regulations) only be filed by the company's registered agent, or a liquidator under the Insolvency Act if one has been appointed by the company (Section 232).

Under the act, companies may elect to file, for registration by the registrar, a copy of its register of members and register of directors (Section 231).

(b) Inspection

Except where otherwise provided in the act, the regulations or any other enactment, under Section 233(1) a person may:

- inspect the register of companies, foreign companies and/or charges maintained by the registrar;
- inspect any document that is filed by a company and retained by the registrar; and
- require the registrar to provide a certified or uncertified copy or extract certificate of incorporation, merger, consolidation, arrangement, continuation, discontinuance, dissolution or good standing of a company, or a copy or an extract of any document that the person has in their possession to be certified by the registrar.

A document (or the copy of an extract of a document or part of that document) that is certified by the registrar is admissible in evidence in any proceedings as though it were an original document (Section 233(2)).

9.5 Voluntary liquidation

The 2004 Act introduced new provisions dealing with voluntary liquidation. A company can enter into voluntary liquidation to wind itself up if the directors resolve that the company remains solvent (Part XII, Division 1). Under the act, a voluntary liquidator appointed by the company does not need to be a licensed insolvency practitioner but must be an individual. If it is subsequently found that the company is insolvent, liquidation must immediately be dealt with under the BVI Insolvency Act.

Bulgaria

Violetta Kunze

Djingov, Gouginski, Kyutchukov & Velichkov

---

1. Types of limited liability company and applicable legislation

A company of limited liability may be incorporated in one of the following legal forms:

- limited liability company;
- joint stock company; and
- partnership limited by shares.

Experience throughout the last ten years has shown that the legal forms of limited liability corporate structures that are preferably used by foreign investors in Bulgaria are the limited liability company (Дружество с ограничена отговорност, abbreviated as ООД (OOD)), and the joint-stock company (Акционерно дружество and abbreviated as АД (AD)). This chapter provides an overview of the law and regulations relating to these two legal forms of incorporation.

The Law on Commerce is the major legal act governing the incorporation, corporate governance, company reorganisation, liquidation, and bankruptcy proceedings of limited liability and joint stock companies.

The Law on Commerce allows each type of company to be a sole owner company, the sole owner being a natural person or a legal entity. Should this be the case, the company is named Еднолично дружество с ограничена отговорност (ЕООД) (EOOD) and Еднолично акционерно дружество (ЕАД) (EAD).

A limited liability company cannot be a publicly listed (traded) company. A joint-stock company can only be publicly listed or traded. All financial institutions must be incorporated in the form of a joint-stock company.

The law does not differentiate between Bulgarian and non-Bulgarian investors in the requirements that apply to shareholders, general managers and directors of limited liability companies.

2. Incorporation procedure

2.1 Proceedings prior to incorporation

A limited liability company must be incorporated by its founding shareholders and be registered on the commercial register before it comes into existence.

In 2008 the commercial register in Bulgaria became a centralised and uniform electronic database administered by the Bulgarian Registry Agency and the Ministry of Justice. It can be accessed via the internet.

In the interval between the decision to incorporate the company and it being registered on the commercial register, the company is known as a 'company in the process of incorporation'. A limited liability company in the process of incorporation can start to trade. Even though any rights and obligations would automatically transfer to the company on registration, the shareholders usually wait until the company has been registered as they are personally and jointly liable for any transactions undertaken at this time.

The law does not recognise the concept of a shelf company.

The start-up of a limited liability company takes at least five business days. The start-up of a limited liability company by a foreign investor would usually take between 15 and 20 business days depending on how quickly the foreign investors obtain the required corporate resolutions and documents issued by foreign state authorities. Registration in the commercial register would usually take between two and four business days after the date of documents were filed.

The statutory fees related to the registration of a limited liability company in the commercial register currently (2009) amount to BGN210.

(a) *Corporate name*

The name of a company must be unique. It must not be misleading in respect of the company's business and must not contradict public order and accepted moral rules.

The abbreviations OOD and EOOD must form part of the company name, as they give a clear indication of the company's legal form of incorporation.

The commercial register electronic database can be easily checked to see whether a specific company name is available. A name can be reserved for a three-month period, so a company should reserve the name before passing any corporate resolutions on the company's incorporation.

(b) *Corporate resolutions approving the incorporation of the company*

The incorporation of the company must be evidenced in writing. The corporate resolutions of the founding meeting of the shareholders (or of the sole owner, in the case of an EOOD) must:

- determine at least the following in respect of the limited liability company:
  - the company name, principal place of business and registered office address;
  - the scope of activities and the term of existence;
  - the amount of the registered share capital and its distribution in shares; and
  - the number, names and representative powers of the appointed managers; and
- approve the articles of incorporation of the company.

In the case of an OOD, the first meeting of the shareholders must unanimously pass the corporate resolutions on the above matters. For an EOOD, the corporate body of the sole owner that is competent to resolve on the incorporation of subsidiaries as provided for in the bylaws or other applicable corporate regulations must decide on these matters.

(c) *Articles of incorporation*

The articles of incorporation of the limited liability company must be in a simple written form. No notarisation is required. All founding shareholders must sign the articles of incorporation upon the company's incorporation. These are usually attached to the protocol for resolutions or minutes of the meeting relating to the incorporation of the company.

The articles of incorporation must provide the following:

- company name, seat and registered office address;
- scope of the company's activity and the validity term of the articles;
- name and identification details of the shareholders in the company;
- amount of the registered share capital, and if this amount is not fully paid up on the company's incorporation, the time period within which the outstanding balance must be paid;
- registered value of the shareholders' shares in the company's registered share capital;
- management and representation arrangements in the company;
- options and privileges to shareholders, if agreed; and
- the rights and responsibilities of shareholders.

(d) *Capital contributions*

The minimum share capital required for the incorporation of a limited liability company is BGN5,000. The share capital must be distributed in shares of a minimum registered value of no less than BGN10.

All issued shares must be subscribed by the registered shareholders or by the sole owner, if the company is a sole-owner limited liability company.

Shares in a limited liability company, unlike shares in a joint stock company, are not securities. Although the law provides for the issuance of share certificates and for keeping corporate records and books, in practice no share certificates are issued for the rights incorporated in the shares of a limited liability company. The shareholding in a limited liability company is usually established by obtaining relevant information from the commercial register, which is in the public domain.

On incorporation and as a condition precedent to the company's registration in the commercial register, the founding shareholders must pay at least 70% of the registered share capital of the company into a Bulgarian bank account, whereby each founding shareholder must pay at least one-third of his shareholding (but not less than BGN10); in the event the registered share capital of the company is not fully (100%) paid up at the time the company is registered, the outstanding balance must be paid within a term defined in the company's articles of incorporation, but not later than two years after the company's initial registration in the commercial register.

The law also permits share capital in a limited liability company to be subscribed for an in-kind contribution, such as property rights over real estate, movables, receivables etc. Should this be the case, the in-kind contribution is subject to an independent valuation by an expert valuer appointed by the Bulgarian Registry Agency, which is the state authority administering the commercial register. The valuation of the in-kind contribution must be completed prior to the subscription of the shares by the respective contributing shareholder and the value at which the contributing shareholder agrees to obtain his respective shareholding in the company must not exceed the value of the in-kind contribution provided by the expert valuers in their independent valuation report. Should the contributing shareholder disagree with the value stated in the independent valuation report, he may subscribe to shares for a monetary contribution or refuse to invest in the company.

(e) ***Appointment of the general manager***

Upon its incorporation, the limited liability company must have one or more appointed general managers.

The company usually contracts the general manager under a management agreement. This agreement is not a condition precedent for the registration of the company on the commercial register.

2.2 Registration in the commercial register

Registering a company on the commercial register serves all commercial, tax, social security and statistical purposes. Once the registration procedure has been completed, the limited liability company is given a uniform identification code and this identifies the company for all state purposes before all state authorities and private third parties throughout its existence.

An application for registration in the commercial register is standard and requires notary certification of the signatory's signature. The general manager of the company or a lawyer specifically authorised to do so by the legal representative of the company can apply. The general manager must also submit the application in person or expressly authorise another person to submit the application.

The following documents must be enclosed with the application:

- minutes of the founding shareholders' meeting or a protocol for shareholder resolutions showing the corporate resolution on incorporation;
- the articles of incorporation of the company;
- a certificate issued by a bank in Bulgaria certifying that the minimum of shareholder contribution for the subscribed shares in the company has been paid into a bank account of the company (for in-kind contributions, the independent valuation report and the consent of the contributing shareholder with the value determined therein must be enclosed);
- a certificate of company's name issued by the Bulgarian Registry Agency;
- a statement of consent and specimen signature in written form with a notary certification of the signature of each appointed general manager;
- a standard non-compete affidavit in simple written form by each appointed general manager;
- an official excerpt from the commercial register and officially certified articles of incorporation (bylaws) for each shareholder who is a legal entity; and
- a power of attorney for the proxy who has signed and/or submitted the application.

Any document that is not in Bulgarian must be accompanied by a certified translation. Documents issued by foreign authorities or bearing notarisations carried out in a foreign jurisdiction are subject to legalisation in accordance with Bulgarian law (where the foreign jurisdiction is a party to the 1961 Hague Convention, this means that an apostille stamp must be affixed to the relevant document by the competent authority of such foreign jurisdiction).

The fact that the company is duly registered on the commercial register is shown by a certificate of legal standing issued and stamped by the Bulgarian registry agency. The information on the certificate is available on the website of the Bulgarian registry agency[1] under the company's identification code.

3.   Corporate governance (administration) of the limited liability company

The governing bodies of a limited liability company are

- the general meeting of the shareholders; and
- one or more general managers.

3.1   Shareholders' rights

A shareholding in a limited liability company entitles the respective shareholder to:

- participate in the management of the company;
- receive dividends;
- obtain information on the company's activities and access the company's corporate books; and
- in a case of winding-up, receive a liquidation quota of the company's property after the settlement of receivables from all the company's creditors.

Shareholder receivables from dividends and any liquidation quota are freely transferable abroad.

3.2   General meeting of the shareholders

(a)   Composition

All shareholders in the company form the general meeting of the shareholders, which is the supreme governing body of the company. Shareholders' votes are proportionate to their share capital, unless the articles of incorporation of the company provide otherwise. Shareholders can participate in any resolutions of the shareholders' general meeting either in person or by using their legal representative, should the shareholder be a legal entity or a proxy duly authorised in writing.

If the limited liability company has more than 50 employees, they are entitled to have a designated representative who can take part in the shareholders' meeting with a consultative vote.

---

1   www.brra.bg.

(b) **Powers**

The general meeting of the shareholders is competent to resolve on the following matters:

- amendments to the articles of incorporation or adoption of new articles of incorporation;
- acceptance of a new shareholder, expulsion of a shareholder, and transfer of shares to a third party;
- approval of the annual financial statements, distribution of profits and payment of dividends;
- share capital increase and decrease;
- appointment and dismissal of the general manager(s) and determination of the general manager's compensation;
- opening and closing of branches and acquisition and transfer of shareholding(s) or interest in other corporate entities;
- acquisition and disposal of real estates and other property rights thereon;
- bringing a claim on behalf of the company against a general manager or compliance officer of the company and authorisation of a proxy of the company for the purposes of the company's representation in a civil case thereto; and
- supplementary monetary contributions.

The articles of incorporation of the company may provide for any other matter falling within the exclusive competence of the general meeting of the shareholders.

In case of an EOOD, the powers of the general meeting of the shareholders fall within the competence of the sole owner, the latter being the supreme governing body of the company.

(c) **Meetings and resolutions**

The general meeting of the shareholders is convened by the general manager of the company acting upon his own initiative or upon the initiative of the shareholder(s) holding at least 10% of the registered share capital of the company. The general meeting can further be convened by a written invitation to all shareholders received at least seven days before the scheduled date of the meeting and providing the agenda, draft resolutions and all relevant written materials and data for the items on the agenda.

There are no quorum requirements under the law, but the articles of incorporation of the company may set this out.

The majority required under the law for the approval of the resolutions of the general meeting of the shareholders is as follows:

- unanimity for resolutions relating to an increase or decrease in share capital;
- a qualified majority of more than three-quarters of the registered share capital for resolutions relating to amendment of the articles of incorporation or the adoption of new articles of incorporation; acceptance of a new shareholder, expulsion of a shareholder, and transfer of shares to a third party; supplementary monetary contributions; merger, acquisition or other

form of reorganisation of the company; and
* a simple majority for all other resolutions.

The articles of incorporation of the company may provide for stricter requirements to voting majority.

The general meeting of the shareholders may also pass resolutions *in absentia*. In this case the approved resolutions must be recorded in a written protocol and this must be signed by all shareholders.

3.3 General manager

(a) *Requirements, appointment and dismissal*

A limited liability company can have one or more general managers. A general manager must be a person, not a legal entity. He or she may be a Bulgarian national or a foreigner.

The general meeting of the shareholders appoints, dismisses and determines the compensation of each general manager. The general meeting of the shareholders may dismiss the general manager at any time.

Each general manager is charged with a non-compete duty concerning the activity of the company. Only the general meeting of the shareholders can discharge him from such duty.

(b) *Powers*

The general manager or the company must organise and manage the activity of the company in accordance with the law and the resolutions of the general meeting of the shareholders. The general manager is also the legal representative of the company.

The general manager must exercise his powers and fulfil his duties with due care and under no conflict of interest.

(c) *No board of directors in case of two or more general managers*

Provided that there is more than one general manager, each manager is considered competent to represent and manage the company severally and independently, unless the articles of incorporation of the company state otherwise (ie for a joint representation to be established in an OOD, this arrangement must be expressly provided for in the articles of incorporation of the company and registered in the commercial register). Other restrictions of the signatory powers may not be invoked against third parties.

If there are two or more general managers in an OOD, they do not form a board of directors but represent the company severally or jointly, as the case may be.

An EOOD may have no general manager and may be managed and represented by the sole owner.

(d) *General manager's liability*

The general manager is liable for any wilful or negligent damages caused to the company.

The general manager is also subject to administrative liability. Under the Tax and Social Security Procedure Code the general manager is liable for any taxes, social security contributions or other public revenues due by the company, when these have been wilfully misrepresented by the general manager in a tax return or otherwise to the competent revenue authorities, so that revenues owed may not be effectively collected by the state. Here, the general manager is jointly liable with the company. The general manager is charged with the same administrative liability if he/she wilfully fails to pay tax or any other mandatory contribution due to the state budget, when this has been collected by the manager but has not been paid to the state.

Embezzlement, misappropriation, malpractice and the abeyance of company property are all recognised crimes and, if committed by the general manager, would constitute qualified grounds for criminal liability and will result in a prison term of between five and eight years.

3.4 Transfer of shares

Transfer of shares between the shareholders of the company is free. The transfer of shares between a shareholder and a third party is subject to preliminary approval by the general meeting of the shareholders. The transfer must be formalised in a share transfer agreement executed in writing and with notary certification of the signatories' signatures thereon, and be registered with the commercial register.

The articles of incorporation of the company may provide for any additional share transfer restrictions.

4. Incorporation of a joint-stock company

The existence of a joint-stock company as a separate legal entity starts on the date of registration on the commercial register. Registration is normally obtained within five business days of filing the package of required documents with the commercial register. However, the process of assembling all the required documents (see section 4.2 below) may take as long as four to eight weeks, especially where a legal entity established under the laws of a foreign jurisdiction is involved as a founding shareholder. The reason for this is that a number of documents relating to the foreign entity and issued and certified by foreign authorities must be obtained.

Any actions and transactions completed by the company's founders from its incorporation until its registration on the commercial register are subject to the same rules as a limited liability company (see section 2.1).

4.1 Registration requirements

(a) Company name

The company name of a joint-stock company must include the abbreviation AD or EAD depending on whether it has several shareholders (AD) or a single shareholder (EAD). The rules for the selection of a company name do not otherwise differ from those described in section 2.1(a).

(b) Resolutions approving the incorporation

The resolutions approving the incorporation of the company must be passed at a constituent meeting attended by all the persons/entities that are to subscribe shares in the new company. A founding shareholder may be represented at the constituent meeting by proxy using a notarised power of attorney specifically issued for that purpose.

The constituent meeting must pass resolutions (to be reflected in a written record of proceedings) on the following matters:

- a formal decision to incorporate the new company (including indications of the company name, scope of the company's operations, principal place of business and registered office of the company, amount of the registered capital and number and type of shares, the identification details of the persons/entities subscribing shares together with the number of shares subscribed by each of them, the type of corporate governance system (two-tier or one-tier), and the manner of exercising signatory powers by the relevant signatories);
- adoption of the articles of association (also referred to as the bylaws); and
- the appointment of the first supervisory board (under the two-tier corporate governance system) or board of directors (under the one-tier corporate governance system), as the case may be.

The written record of proceedings need not be notarised.

Resolutions approving the formal decision to incorporate the new company and the bylaws must be passed with the affirmative vote of all founding shareholders.

In the event that the new company is being incorporated by a single founding shareholder, a deed of incorporation must be executed by such shareholder (and if this shareholder is a legal entity, the deed must be executed by the person having the requisite signatory powers under the constitutive documents).

(c) Articles of association (bylaws)

The bylaws of a joint-stock company must be established in plain written form; no notarisation is required. The mandatory features of the bylaws of a joint-stock company include:

- the company name, principal place of business and registered office;
- the scope of corporate operations and term (if any);
- the amount of the registered capital, the portion thereof that must be paid upon incorporation, the type and number of shares, the rights attaching to the different classes of shares, share transfer restrictions (if any) and the nominal value of each share;
- the corporate bodies, the number of members thereof and their terms of office;
- the type and value of in-kind contributions (if any), the persons/entities making these contributions and the number and nominal value of shares issued for the in-kind contributions;
- the preferences retained by each founding shareholder (if any);

- the terms and procedures applicable to the issuance of redeemable shares (if any);
- the manner of distributing profits;
- the manner of convening shareholders meetings; and
- any other clauses of relevance to the establishment, existence and winding-up of the company.

The bylaws may deviate from the provisions of the law on commerce and other applicable legislation only in so far as expressly permitted, or where these provisions may otherwise be deemed non-mandatory.

(d)   *Registered capital*

The minimum amount of the registered capital for a joint-stock company is BGN50,000 (approximately €25,000). The registered capital is distributed into shares. The minimum nominal value of a share is BGN1.00 (roughly €0.50) and any greater nominal value of a share must be a multiple of BGN1.00 (ie BGN2.00, 3.00, 4.00, etc). The issuance value of the shares may not be below the nominal value thereof but shares may be subscribed to in consideration of a subscription price per share that is higher than the nominal value. The amount of the registered capital is equal to the aggregate nominal value of all outstanding shares (ie the difference between the issuance value and the nominal value is not counted as part of the registered capital, but it is allocated to the company's reserves).

All shares must be subscribed to upon incorporation. Such portion (but not less than 25%) of the nominal value or issue value of the shares, as the case may be, as is set out in the bylaws must have been paid prior to the registration of the company. Evidence that the required portion has been paid up forms part of the package of documents to be filed with the commercial register for the purposes of registration of the new company. The remaining part of the value of the shares is to be paid in within the time limits set out in the bylaws – always provided, however, that such time limits may not exceed two years from the date of registration with the commercial register of the company or the corresponding capital increase, as the case may be.

Contributions owing for the shares subscribed to by the relevant shareholder may be made in cash or in kind. The rules applicable to in-kind contributions do not differ from those already discussed in section 2.1(d) above.

(e)   *Shares*

Shares in a joint stock company are negotiable instruments and may be issued as either materialised or dematerialised (book-entry form) shares. Different rules apply to share transfers depending on whether the shares being transferred are materialised or dematerialised (see section 5.6 below).

Shareholders receive paper-based share certificates issued by the joint stock company in consideration of the contributions made for the materialised shares that they have subscribed to. Holders of materialised shares are referenced in the company's shareholders book.

The ownership in dematerialised shares is subject to registration with the Central Depository, which is a sort of centralised registration and clearing house in respect of the issuance of and transactions with dematerialised shares. The Central Depository issues depository receipts to the owners of dematerialised shares. However, these receipts are merely evidentiary documents, not negotiable securities. The Central Depository is in charge of maintaining the shareholders book of companies with dematerialised shares.

A further distinction, of relevance to materialised shares only, is made between registered shares and bearer shares.

(f) Appointment of corporate bodies

As indicated above, the constituent meeting of the joint stock company being incorporated must appoint the first supervisory board (under the two-tier corporate governance system) or board of directors (under the one-tier system).

Where a two-tier joint stock company is to be registered, the supervisory board must appoint the first management board as a condition precedent to registration of the new company with the commercial register.

4.2 Application for registration

The standard application form for registration of a joint stock company must bear the notarised signature of the lawful signatory for the new company (typically the executive director) or a lawyer who has been specifically authorised to do so under a notarised power of attorney executed by such lawful signatory.

The following documents must be attached to the standard application form:

- record of proceedings of the constituent meeting;
- copy of the bylaws certified as true and accurate by the lawful signatory for the new company;
- where a founding shareholder is a legal entity, the resolution for each such founding shareholder to participate in the incorporation of the new company (and if the founding shareholder in question is a legal entity established under the laws of a foreign jurisdiction, relevant documents must be submitted to evidence the good standing of such legal entity and the signatory powers of the persons that have executed the resolution on its behalf);
- the resolution of the supervisory board approving the appointment of the management board (only applicable under the two-tier corporate governance system);
- where the bylaws permit the appointment of a legal entity as a board member, the corporate resolution of such legal entity whereby a natural person is appointed to represent the legal entity on the board (and if the legal entity in question is established under the laws of a foreign jurisdiction, relevant documents must be submitted to evidence the good standing of such legal entity and the signatory powers of the persons that have executed the resolution on its behalf);
- as the case may be, the resolution of the management board with the consent

of the supervisory board, or the resolution of the board of directors, whereby one or more members of the management board/board of directors are authorised to bind the company by their signatures;

- a list (certified as true and accurate by the management board/board of directors) of the persons/entities that have subscribed shares at the constituent meeting;

- an affidavit signed by each founding shareholder whereby it declares that it has not been adjudicated bankrupt;

- the notarised consent and affidavit by each board member declaring that he/she agrees to sit on the relevant board and that there are no impediments to his/her membership under applicable law or the bylaws;

- a notarised specimen signature for each member of the management board/board of directors authorised to bind the company by its signature;

- any other such documents as may be required under special legislation (notably a copy of the relevant license where the operations of the new company are subject to licensing, as in the case of banks, insurance companies, etc);

- bank certificate(s) showing that the relevant cash contributions with respect of the subscribed shares have been duly made by the corresponding founding shareholders;

- in case of in-kind contributions, the independent valuation report and the notarised consent of the contributing shareholder, including a description of the contribution; and

- a power of attorney for the proxy who has signed and/or submitted the application.

All documents submitted to the commercial register must be in the Bulgarian language and any certifications by foreign public authorities must be duly legalised under Bulgarian law (see section 2.2 above).

5. Corporate governance of a joint stock company

5.1 Systems under Bulgarian law

The governance system of joint stock companies under Bulgarian law may be two-tier or one-tier depending on the choice of the shareholders.

Under the two-tier system, a joint stock company has a shareholders' meeting, a supervisory board appointed by the shareholders' meeting, and a management board appointed by the supervisory board.

The one-tier system consists of a shareholders' meeting and a board of directors appointed by the shareholders' meeting.

5.2 Shareholders' meeting

The shareholders' meeting is composed of all shareholders with voting shares. Normally, one vote attaches to each voting share. Listed companies may not issue preference shares with more than one vote attached. However, such preferences may attach to shares issued by unlisted companies. If the joint-stock company has more than 50 employees, they are entitled to have a representative at the shareholders meeting with a consultative vote.

The standard powers of the shareholders' meeting of a joint-stock company include the following:

- adoption of and amendments to the bylaws;
- capital increases and decreases;
- reorganisation (merger, split-up, etc) and dissolution of the company (voluntary winding-up);
- appointment and removal of members of the supervisory board/board of directors;
- determination of the remuneration of supervisory board members or non-executive members of the board of directors, as the case may be;
- appointment of registered auditors with a view to the independent audit of the company's financial statements;
- approval of the annual financial statements after an independent audit by appointed registered auditors;
- discharging board members of liability towards the company;
- appointment of liquidators in the event of voluntary winding-up;
- approval of resolutions concerning the allocation of distributable profits and dividend payouts;
- issue of corporate bonds; and
- any other matter vested in the powers of the shareholders meeting by virtue of applicable law or the bylaws.

The shareholders' meeting is also required to authorise transactions exceeding certain thresholds (eg disposal of the entire business of the company or disposal of assets the value of which exceeds 50% of the aggregate value of the company's assets). The bylaws may delegate the authorisation of such transactions to the management board/board of directors. In any event, failure to obtain such authorisations does not invalidate the corresponding transaction but merely entitles the company to seek compensation for damages from the relevant signatory.

For listed companies, transactions crossing certain thresholds (further detailed in Article 114 of the Bulgarian Law on Public Offering of Securities) must be specifically authorised by the shareholders' meeting or the management board/board of directors, as the case may be, failing which such transactions are null and void.

Shareholders meetings may be convened by the management board or board of directors. The supervisory board can also call a shareholders' meeting under the two-tier corporate governance system. A meeting may also be required by shareholders who have been holding shares representing at least 5% of the registered capital for more than three months. This is done by public invitation by submission to the commercial register. If the company has no outstanding bearer shares, the bylaws may provide that the convocation is to be carried out by dispatching a written invitation to each shareholder, avoiding the need to publicise the invitation. Nevertheless, listed companies must always publicise the invitation through the commercial register. Each time the shareholders meeting is convened by an invitation in the commercial register, at least 30 days must elapse between the date of the publication and the date of the shareholders' meeting. Any matters to be discussed and voted on at the shareholders' meeting must be detailed in the invitation.

Applicable law requires that at least 50% of shareholders must attend or be represented, if the shareholders' meeting is to deliberate on issues involving amendments to the bylaws, capital increases/decreases or corporate reorganisations and dissolutions. No other quorum requirements apply, unless expressly stated in the bylaws.

As a general rule, resolutions of the shareholders' meeting require the affirmative vote of more than half the attending or represented shares. Higher majority requirements apply if they are provided for by applicable law or the bylaws. Amendments to the bylaws, capital increases/decreases and dissolutions require the vote of at least two-thirds of attending or represented shares, in accordance with applicable Bulgarian law. The approval of a corporate reorganisation requires the affirmative vote of at least 75% of attending or represented shareholders.

5.3   Management and representation

(a)   *Two-tier corporate governance system*

Under the two-tier corporate governance system, the company is managed by a board composed of not less than three and not more than nine members appointed by the supervisory board for a term not exceeding five years (three years for the first management board). The supervisory board can replace a management board member at any time. The management board (with the approval of the supervisory board) usually delegates signatory powers to one or more of its members (each member being referred to as a 'lawful signatory for the company').

The supervisory board is composed of not less than three and not more than seven members appointed by the shareholders' meeting for a term not exceeding five years (three years for the first supervisory board). The shareholders' meeting can replace board members at any time. The supervisory board does not take part in the management of the company; it represents the company in its relations with the management board.

The bylaws may state that the management board can make decisions about capital increases and the issuing of corporate bonds, matters otherwise reserved for the shareholders' meeting.

(b)   *One-tier corporate governance system*

Under the one-tier corporate governance system, the management of the company is vested in a board of directors composed of not less than three and not more than nine members appointed by the shareholders' meeting for a term not exceeding five years (three years for the first board of directors). The shareholders' meeting can remove or replace members of the board of directors at any time. The board of directors may assign the management of the company to one or more of its members (executive directors) and usually delegates signatory powers to these members (making them a 'lawful signatory for the company'). The number of executive directors must be fewer than the number of non-executive members.

The board of directors can only deal with capital increases and the issue of corporate bonds if this is stated in the bylaws.

5.4 Limitation of the signatory powers of lawful signatories

Signatory powers delegated to certain members of the management board/board of directors may be exercised individually (ie by each member independently from other members with signatory powers) or collectively (eg jointly by all the board members with signatory powers, jointly or by any combination of board members with signatory powers). The way in which these signatory powers are exercised is to be determined by the management board/board of directors. If these restrictions are registered with the commercial register, they are binding upon third parties. Other restrictions of the signatory powers cannot be invoked against third parties.

5.5 Liability of board members

Board members are jointly liable for damages resulting from their negligent or intentional misconduct. A board member can be discharged from such joint liability if it is established that their conduct was neither negligent nor intentional, or that their conduct does not stand in direct causal relation to the damages incurred by the company.

Shareholders with at least 10% of the registered capital can file lawsuits against individual board members with a view to obtaining compensation for the company for damages incurred by the latter as a result of such board member's misconduct.

The administrative and criminal liability of board members is dealt with in the same way as that of general managers of limited liability companies (see section 3.3(d)).

5.6 Share transfers

(a) Materialised shares

Bearer shares may be transferred by surrendering the share certificates representing such shares. Registered shares may be transferred by an endorsement on the back of the share certificate coupled with its surrender. Any transfer of registered shares must be entered in the shareholders' book of the company to render it binding on the company.

(b) Dematerialised shares

Transfers of dematerialised shares must be registered with the Central Depository to become effective. The transfers are normally registered with the Central Depository at the request of investment intermediaries that are members of the Central Depository (ie transferors and transferees must use the services of an investment intermediary, which is a member of the Central Depository).

(c) Share transfer restrictions

The transfer of shares may be restricted by law (eg the acquisition of equity participation beyond certain thresholds in companies falling within the scope of regulated industries is often subject to regulatory approval). Also, the bylaws may include clauses that restrict the transfer of registered shares. Restrictions set out in the bylaws often appear as a right of first refusal, or need the approval of a corporate body prior to the share transfer.

6. Taxes

6.1 Types of taxes

Companies are subject to state taxes on any business profits. They will only pay local taxes and fees provided they hold property rights in real estate and some precious movables, such as motor vehicles, or they receive a donation.

All companies registered in Bulgaria are subject to a corporate income tax currently at the rate of 10%. The tax is due annually.

Currently, the VAT rate is 20%. Companies are subject to mandatory VAT registration when they reach the statutory threshold of BGN50,000, realised from chargeable supplies with a place of performance in the country over a period of 12 consecutive months. Companies registered for VAT are obliged to charge VAT on goods or services supplied by them and are entitled to VAT credit for the input VAT on meeting all statutory requirements. Companies are also free to register for VAT voluntarily (ie free from any minimum turnover as a registration threshold).

Dividends and liquidation quotas paid by companies to non-Bulgarian legal entities, other than EU tax residents, are subject to a tax at the rate of 5%. For EU tax residents, a rate of 0% applies. For a Bulgarian commercial company tax resident, the same rate of 0% applies in respect of dividends but these proceeds are also treated as pass-through income. Profits received from purchase price payment under a sale of shares, should the beneficiary be a non-Bulgarian legal entity, are chargeable for capital gains tax, but at the rate of 10%. The same rate applies to interest paid on shareholder loans, royalties, rentals, management fees, etc. In any of these cases the tax is a one-time tax and is collected by the company payor of the respective income, except for capital gains, for which only the recipient is liable. The tax obligor may be released from tax provided a double-taxation treaty applies and the tax obligor obtains tax clearance from the national tax authorities.

6.2 Tax registration

As of January 1 2008, companies are identified by their uniform identification code received when they are registered on the commercial register. VAT registration with national tax authorities is the only secondary registration.

7. Annual financial statements

Under the Bulgarian Law on Accountancy, each company must prepare an annual financial statement. This must be prepared by persons who meet the educational and professional requirements set out in Article 35 of the Law on Accountancy.

A limited liability company must have its annual financial statements independently audited by a registered auditor, provided that it has met during the current or preceding year a combination of any two of the following criteria:

- book value of assets as of December 31 in excess of BGN1.5 million (roughly €750,000);
- net revenues from sales in excess of BGN2.5 million (roughly €1.25 million); and
- more than 50 employees.

Joint stock companies must have their annual financial statements independently audited by a registered auditor regardless of whether they meet the criteria described above.

Where an independent audit is required, a registered auditor must be appointed by the shareholders' meeting.

In so far as an independent audit of the annual financial statements by a registered auditor is required, the shareholders can only approve the annual financial statements after the independent audit has been completed.

Once the annual financial statements are drafted and after the independent audit has been completed, financial statements are submitted to the shareholders for consideration and approval. For joint stock companies, the financial statements and the registered auditor's report are reviewed by the management board and the supervisory board or the board of directors, before the documents are submitted for the shareholders' consideration and approval.

The annual financial statements approved by the shareholders (together with the registered auditor's report, where applicable) must be made public by way of submission to the commercial register not later than June 30 following the end of the corresponding fiscal year (which coincides with the calendar year).

8.   Declaration of foreign investment

No such declaration is required in Bulgaria.

9.   Company reorganisation

Chapter XVI of the Law on Commerce is the major legislation governing corporate reorganisations. Additional legal provisions may be relevant depending on whether the company is involved in a corporate reorganisation falling within the scope of regulated industries (banking, insurance, financial services, etc).

9.1   Merger

A merger is a type of reorganisation, which may be effected in one of two ways:

- all assets (ie rights, obligations and factual status) of one or several companies (the 'merging companies') are transferred to one existing company, which becomes the universal successor in title of the merging companies while the latter are wound up without liquidation; or
- all assets of two or several companies (the 'merging companies') are transferred to one newly established company, which becomes the universal successor in title of the merging companies while the merging companies are wound up without liquidation.

9.2 Split-up

This is a type of reorganisation, which may be effected in one of two ways:

- all assets of one company (the 'company in reorganisation') are transferred to two or more existing or newly established companies, which become the universal successors in title of the company in reorganisation for corresponding portions of the assets being transferred, while the company in reorganisation is wound up without liquidation; or
- a portion of the assets of one company (the 'company in reorganisation') is transferred to one or several existing or newly established companies, which become the universal successors in title of the company in reorganisation for the portion of assets being transferred, while the company in reorganisation continues to operate with the remaining assets.

A specific instance of split-up occurs where a portion of the assets of the company in reorganisation is transferred to one or several newly established limited liability and/or joint-stock companies, each of which becomes a wholly owned subsidiary of the company in reorganisation, while the company in reorganisation continues to operate.

9.3 Conversion

Conversion is a type of reorganisation whereby an existing company (the 'company in reorganisation') is converted into a newly established company of a different type (eg a limited liability company is converted into a joint stock company). The newly established company becomes the universal successor in title of the company in reorganisation, which is wound up without liquidation.

9.4 Reorganisation terms and procedures

A number of terms and procedures must be complied with in the context of any corporate reorganisation. The main ones are set out next.

The shareholders in a merging company or company in reorganisation must obtain an equity participation in the companies resulting from the reorganisation that is equivalent to the fair value of their shares in the merging company or the company in reorganisation, as the case may be. As part of the reorganisation procedure, a registered auditor must confirm that the applicable share-exchange ratio is adequate and reasonable.

A reorganisation contract with notarised signature must be concluded among the companies involved in the reorganisation. (In split-up scenarios, a reorganisation plan is prepared by the company in reorganisation instead.)

The reorganisation must be approved by the shareholders of each company participating in the reorganisation.

The reorganisation is subject to registration in the commercial register and becomes effective on registration.

9.5 Protection of creditors

Regardless of the type of reorganisation, the personal liability of shareholders in the merging company or company in reorganisation, as the case may be, remains unaffected after the reorganisation in so far as liabilities that have arisen prior to the reorganisation are concerned. Other protection rules applicable to specific types of reorganisation are detailed below.

(a)   *Merger*

Any company acquiring assets as a result of a merger must administer them separately for six months after the date the merger was registered in the commercial register (the 'non-commingling period'). During this period any creditor of a company participating in the merger may seek performance or collateral, if its claims are not secured and have arisen prior to the merger. If the creditors' demands are not satisfied, they have a preferential claim on any assets that were the property of the debtor prior to the merger.

(b)   *Split-up*

All companies participating in the split-up (except those that are wound up in the process) remain jointly liable for any liabilities that have arisen prior to the split-up. The liability of each company is limited to the amount of assets it has received as a result of the split-up (except for the company that has been allocated the liabilities in question under the reorganisation contract/plan, which remains liable with all its available assets).

In addition, where a portion of the assets of the company in reorganisation has been transferred to one or several existing companies, the rules relating to the non-commingling period (see Section 9.5(a) above) apply to each company.

10.   Liquidation

When a company winds up voluntarily (ie on the grounds of a corporate resolution) it goes through a liquidation procedure. The company's winding-up, the period of the liquidation and the appointed liquidator(s) must all be approved by a resolution of the general meeting of the shareholders passed by a qualified majority of three-quarters of the registered share capital.

The incumbent legal representative(s) or any third party may be appointed as liquidator(s) of the company. The liquidator is responsible for the winding-up of the company and for the period of the liquidation procedure.

After registration in the commercial register of the appointed liquidator, the liquidation procedure has the following four phases:

- invitation to the company's creditors to claim their receivables against the company;
- establishment of company property, collection of company receivables and settlement of any obligations to creditors;
- distribution of liquidation quotas, if any; and
- deregistration of the company from the commercial register.

The company is not permitted to deregister if it has any unsettled claims. The company terminates its existence on the date of deregistration from the commercial register.

11.   Bankruptcy proceedings

In general, any creditor with claims that have remained unpaid and overdue for a certain period of time can file for the commencement of bankruptcy proceedings against the company. Proceedings would start if the court establishes that the debtor is insolvent or over-indebted.

A company is required to file for bankruptcy if it is insolvent (ie actually unable to meet its current payment obligations or simply suspending payments for a certain period of time) or over-indebted (ie the company's debts exceed its assets). Insolvency should be presumed upon suspension of payments for 30 days.

A debtor-company operating under an approved reorganisation plan must carry out its activities in accordance with the reorganisation plan.

A company undergoing bankruptcy proceedings is not allowed to reject or disclaim any contract other than on grounds provided for in the respective contract itself. Contracts can be disavowed, but only by the bankruptcy trustee, who is empowered to terminate any contract provided it has not been fulfilled wholly or in part. The party to a terminated contract would become a creditor in the bankruptcy.

Upon commencement of bankruptcy proceedings, as a general rule all court or arbitral proceedings of civil or commercial nature or enforcement proceedings against the company are suspended. Commencement of new court or arbitration proceedings against the company is inadmissible, except for labour disputes and claims for protection of the interests of third-party owners of movables placed in the bankruptcy estate. No injunction orders can be imposed after the bankruptcy proceedings have commenced.

Distribution to the creditors to satisfy their claims is made out of the proceeds from the sale of the debtor's assets, in accordance with the creditors' priority ranking. There are no claims that precede the secured claims. The major priority classes are as follows:

- secured claims (mortgages, pledges);
- employment-related claims;
- public-liability claims (tax, social security, and the like);
- claims arising after the commencement of the bankruptcy, to the extent they have not been satisfied at maturity during bankruptcy;
- other unsecured claims; and
- claims under shareholder loans etc.

If proceeds are insufficient to satisfy the creditors of a given class, the funds available to that class will be distributed within the class on a pro-rata basis.

Canada

Tammy Shulman
Borden Ladner Gervais LLP

1. Types of company with limited liability and applicable legislation

In Canada, the most frequently used corporate vehicle is the corporation (also referred to as a company), which is a limited liability entity. Its most notable features are as follows:

- limited liability of shareholders;
- no minimum capitalisation required;
- flexible share capital structure;
- possibility for one individual to act as sole shareholder, director and officer;
- no formalities (eg notarisation) for legalisation of documents and corporate records;
- no residency requirements for directors (depending on the jurisdiction of incorporation); and
- possibility to enter into unanimous shareholder agreements, which allow shareholders to limit the power of directors.

Canada's governmental framework and legal system (which combines English common law and French civil law) is based on a federal structure, which divides constitutional powers between the federal government and the provinces. In some areas, such as trade and commerce and taxation, there is overlap, and both the federal government and the provinces may legislate.

The result is that each Canadian jurisdiction has its own corporate legislation. There are 14 in all:

- Canada (ie federal);
- the provinces of Alberta, British Columbia, Manitoba, New Brunswick, Newfoundland & Labrador, Nova Scotia, Ontario, Prince Edward Island, Quebec and Saskatchewan; and
- the Northwest Territories, Nunavut territory and the Yukon Territory.

Despite the variety of choices, incorporated entities in Canada bear a strong similarity to each other. Moreover, all corporations – whether federally or provincially incorporated – may, as a matter of right, carry on business anywhere in Canada, provided that they comply with applicable provincial filing requirements. Consequently, the decision whether to incorporate under federal or a particular provincial jurisdiction will in part be driven by the type of business to be carried on by the corporation.

In general, legislation concerning the carrying on of a business is within the jurisdiction of the provinces unless an area is specifically reserved for the federal government (eg such as inter-provincial transportation and telecommunications). The provincial laws do not vary greatly from province to province; however, discrepancies do exist between the provinces, so the applicable laws of each province in which the corporation will conduct business should be examined.

With regard to matters concerning Canada's involvement in international trade and commerce, the Canadian federal government is generally responsible for Canada's trade policies and laws. The Customs Act (Canada) regulates the valuation of goods for the purpose of calculating the duties that may be payable upon the importation of such goods to Canada, and that act also provides for exemptions from the payment of such duties. Canada is also a party to a number of bilateral trade agreements under which preferential benefits may be extended to goods from countries that are parties to such trade agreements, notably the North America Free Trade Agreement (NAFTA) and the Agreement Establishing the World Trade Organisation. In addition, Canada actively participates in many international organisations, including the United Nations and its specialised agencies, the World Trade Organisation and the Organisation for Economic Cooperation and Development. Due to Canada's interest and involvement in international matters, many of Canada's laws and governmental policies reflect internationally accepted norms.

This chapter focuses on corporations under the federal Canada Business Corporations Act, although what is discussed generally applies to corporations incorporated under provincial and territorial legislation. Differences between the various specific jurisdictions that may affect or be of interest to foreign investors are highlighted.

The creation of partnerships, trusts and other types of business entities is within the exclusive jurisdiction of the provinces, and although available throughout the country they are not discussed in this chapter since they afford limited liability only when elaborately structured.

1.1 Rights, powers and privileges of corporations

A corporation is a legal entity that is separate and distinct from the shareholders who contribute to its capital, meaning that the death of an individual shareholder or the dissolution of a corporate shareholder does not affect its existence. Corporations have capacity and generally enjoy the same rights, powers and privileges, and are subject to the same obligations, as natural persons.

1.2 Limited liability

Shareholders benefit from limited liability, unlike individuals who have unlimited liability for debts and obligations contracted while carrying on business. The liability of a shareholder is limited to the amount he has contributed to the corporation. Exceptions to the general principle of limited liability include the following:

- where the shareholder personally guarantees payment of the corporation's debts or liabilities to its creditors;

- where the shareholders adopt a unanimous shareholder agreement (see section 4.2(c)) that restricts the powers of the directors to manage the corporation;
- where a shareholder receives funds from the corporation upon a reduction of capital in violation of applicable solvency tests or pursuant to an improper issuance of shares, in which case it may be liable to restore such amounts to the corporation; and
- in the event of dissolution, in which case the shareholder may be liable to satisfy the claims of a creditor (see section 7.1).

The provinces of Nova Scotia, British Columbia and Alberta have legislation providing for 'unlimited liability corporations' (ULCs). Some of the principal differences between the rules governing ULCs in these three jurisdictions include: (i) when and under what circumstances shareholder liability attaches; (ii) director residency requirements; and (iii) incorporation fees. Except for the lack of limited liability, the characteristics of ULCs generally do not differ to any great extent from other Canadian limited liability corporations. To an investor from the United States, however, the use of ULCs could be attractive from a tax perspective given that, assuming various conditions are met, the US investor may elect to have the income from the Canadian ULC treated as partnership income for US tax purposes. In addition, if a ULC is properly structured, its shareholders may benefit from limited liability not unlike that discussed above.

However, in December 2008 the United States ratified the Fifth Protocol to the Canada–US Income Tax Convention the provisions of which, together with the provisions of the Technical Explanation of the Fifth Protocol, will no longer recognise certain of the tax attributes associated with ULCs that are attractive to US investors. Therefore, the provisions of the Convention currently provide that the tax benefits associated with Canadian ULCs will be eliminated as of January 1 2010.

2.   Incorporation procedure

2.1   Proceedings prior to incorporation

(a)   Foreign investment
The federal Investment Canada Act requires that notice be filed with the minister of industry within 30 days of completion of an investment where a non-Canadian, directly or through a Canadian corporation, establishes a new business in Canada or acquires control (by the purchase of shares or assets) of an existing Canadian business.

In certain cases the non-Canadian investor must file an application for review, which must be approved by the minister of industry prior to implementation of the proposed investment, including where the investment:
- exceeds C$295 million (for 2008) and is made by an investor from a country that is a member of the World Trade Organisation (WTO);
- exceeds C$5 million for a direct acquisition or C$50 million for an indirect

acquisition and is made by an investor from a non-WTO country; or

- relates to an area of Canadian cultural heritage (eg book or magazine publishing, film or sound recordings).

There are generally few restrictions on foreign investment in Canada, although some sectors are subject to special rules or limits at the federal or provincial level, and all foreign investment over the above-mentioned financial thresholds is subject to the federally administered investment review process. Two federal government departments, Industry Canada and Heritage Canada, administer the Investment Canada Act, which has the twofold function of promoting foreign investment and reviewing significant investments to ensure that they are of 'net benefit to Canada'. However, since the enactment of the Investment Canada Act some 23 years ago, Industry Canada has only once (in 2008) prevented the proposed foreign takeover of a Canadian business on the basis that it failed to meet the 'net benefit' requirement. The proposed transaction involved the sale of a prominent Canadian space satellite and robotic technology firm that had received Canadian taxpayer funding for its activities and whose acquisition by foreign interests raised issues of national security. The prevailing opinion is that the refusal by Industry Canada to approve the transaction arose from the exceptional nature of the business of the proposed target of the foreign investment, and it does not signal a change in the overall policy of the government.

There are also corporate ownership restrictions in certain strategic or sensitive industries, such as banking, telecommunications and air transportation, which are matters of constant public debate and may be liberalised in the coming years.

(b)   *Competition Act*

The Competition Act, which is Canada's antitrust legislation, is designed to maintain and encourage competition in Canada by preventing anti-competitive practices in the marketplace. In Canada, pre-merger notification filings are required under the federal Competition Act in respect of proposed acquisitions where:

- the parties to a transaction, together with their affiliates, have combined assets in Canada or annual gross revenues from sales in, from or into Canada of more than C$400 million; and
- the value of the Canadian business to be acquired is greater than C$50 million, or C$70 million in some cases.

The proposed acquisition cannot be implemented until the Competition Bureau has reviewed and approved it.

Where a merger substantially lessens or prevents competition in any relevant market (whether or not it meets the above pre-merger notification requirements), the Competition Tribunal may, prior to or within three years of completion of the merger, on application by the commissioner of competition, issue a remedy in respect of the merger that may result in an order preventing the merger or requiring the purchaser to divest all or part of the assets purchased.

(c) **Corporate name**

A corporate name is not obligatory; if one is not requested, the corporation will be incorporated using a designated number followed by the word 'Canada' and a permitted legal ending (eg '123456 Canada Inc'). Provincial corporations substitute the word 'Canada' for the name of the province.

However, if a name is desired, the applicant must conduct a name search prior to incorporation to ensure that the proposed corporate name is available and is not substantially similar to that of another corporation so as to cause confusion in the marketplace. Names may be reserved for successive 90-day periods. Obtaining a name reservation does not give the corporation any proprietary interest in the corporate name, although it does afford some practical protection since the federal and provincial authorities will usually refuse to incorporate a corporation under a name that is identical or substantially similar to that of an existing corporation.

The Canada Business Corporations Act and most provincial statutes permit incorporation under an English and/or a French corporate name. Most also permit a name in any other language for use outside Canada. Quebec, which has special legislation regulating the use of French as the official language of the province, requires a French name but also permits a version of the corporate name in another language. Other provinces (eg Ontario, Nova Scotia, Manitoba and Newfoundland & Labrador) permit corporate names in any language, provided that they have a version in English and/or French.

Corporate legislation contains guidelines regulating the form of a corporate name and restricting the use of certain words and symbols. Generally, a corporate name must contain a distinctive and descriptive element and a legal ending such as 'Incorporated', 'Limited', 'Corporation' or their abbreviations. It is recommended to engage an authorised agent to conduct the name search and obtain the appropriate reservation to ensure that the name complies with applicable laws.

Protection of a name may be further enhanced by its registration under federal trademark legislation.

2.2   Incorporation

(a)   *Articles of incorporation*

(i)   *Form*

Federal and most provincial corporations (except for Nova Scotia and Prince Edward Island) are incorporated by filing articles of incorporation, the form of which is prescribed by law. Generally the articles are contained in a pre-printed government form, which is filed with the federal director of corporations or the equivalent provincial authority.

The articles of incorporation are signed by one or more incorporators, which may be incorporated entities or qualified individuals. No formalities are required (eg witnesses or notarisation). There is also no prohibition against the incorporator subsequently becoming a shareholder of the corporation.

Provided that the form of the articles meets the minimum legal requirements, upon receipt of the articles with the appropriate fee (C$200 federally) the director of corporations is required to issue a certificate of incorporation pursuant to which the corporation comes into existence. Incorporation is a matter of right and is no longer a privilege granted pursuant to government prerogative. The certificate and articles of incorporation are public documents and are available for review by any interested party upon request to the director of corporations.

(ii) *Bylaws*

Generally, it is not necessary to pass a bylaw to confer any particular powers on the corporation or its directors. However, although it is still common for corporations to adopt general bylaws, most corporate legislation contains comprehensive default provisions governing the manner in which the affairs of the corporation are to be conducted. Consequently, with very few exceptions, bylaws do not form part of the articles of incorporation and are not permitted to be filed with the governmental authorities.

(iii) *Content*

The following documents must be filed with the director of corporations in order to incorporate:

- articles of incorporation –
  - Article 1 – corporate name (see section 2.1(c));
  - Article 2 – place in Canada where the registered office is to be located. One of the provinces or territories in Canada must be specified as the place within which the registered (or head) office must be located. This is the corporation's domicile. The articles require amendment if the corporation moves its registered office to another province or territory. Provincial statutes require that the place where the registered office is to be located be a city or other similar place within that province;
  - Article 3 – the classes and any maximum number of shares that the corporation is authorised to issue (see section 3);
  - Article 4 – restrictions on the transfer of shares (see section 3.3(a));
  - Article 5 – number of directors. There must be a fixed number of one or more directors, or a range (a minimum and maximum) (see section 4.2(a));
  - Article 6 – restrictions on the activities of the corporation. The requirement to state the corporate purpose of a corporation has been abolished (this is generally true for all provinces) and therefore this section is commonly left incomplete; and
  - Article 7 – other provisions. Any provisions permitted by the corporate legislation or by law to be set out in the bylaws of the corporation may be included;
- notice of registered office – the address of the registered office; and
- notice of directors – the names and addresses of the first directors of the corporation.

Once the corporation is incorporated, the director of corporations assigns it a corporate number, which is used by both federal and provincial government departments to identify the corporation for administrative purposes.

(b)   Business and tax registrations

The corporation must register in the provinces where it will carry on business. Business registration is a formality that generally involves completing a form and filing it together with the applicable fee. The corporation may also register to carry on business under a trade name that is different from its corporate name. This name usually cannot be reserved, but its use and registration are subject to rules similar to those applicable to corporate names (see section 2.1(c)).

Depending on its places of business and its activities, the corporation must obtain various tax registrations for income, payroll, capital and sales tax purposes. Each of the federal and provincial governments has the power to tax and registration requirements vary from jurisdiction to jurisdiction. (Please see section 5.2 for details regarding the payment of taxes.)

Merely being a director or shareholder (whether Canadian or foreign) of a Canadian federal or provincial corporation does not in and of itself require registration for tax and business purposes of such director or shareholder.

Canadian tax legislation contains no provisions regarding a tax number for international value-added tax purposes.

(c)   Corporate records

A corporation must maintain records at its registered office, or any other place in Canada designated by the directors (or outside Canada, provided that the records are available for inspection in Canada by means of computer or other technology), containing the following:

- the articles and bylaws, any amendments thereto and a copy of any unanimous shareholder agreement;
- minutes of meetings and resolutions of the directors and shareholders;
- copies of all notices of directors;
- a securities register recording the securities issued by the corporation, showing the name and address of each present and former shareholder, the number and class of shares held by such shareholder, and the date and particulars of the issue and transfer of each share; and
- accounting records.

No formalities are required in connection with the form of the registers and other corporate records, and such records may be maintained in writing or recorded electronically, provided that any required information may be reproduced in intelligible written form within a reasonable time. The corporation must take reasonable precautions to prevent the loss, destruction or falsification of the records.

A corporate seal is permitted, but no longer required under the Canada Business Corporations Act and most provincial statutes; the mere absence of a corporate seal does not invalidate a document executed on behalf of a corporation.

Subject to the requirements of other applicable legislation (eg tax laws), corporate records must be retained for six years following the end of the financial year to which they relate.

3.   Capitalisation

3.1   Share capital structure

(a)   *Characteristics*

The Canada Business Corporations Act contains few mandatory requirements regarding the characteristics of the share capital of the corporation. 'Par value' shares are not permitted under the act and the following three characteristics must attach to at least one class of shares, although all such rights are not required to attach to the same class:

- the right to vote;
- the right to receive dividends as and when declared by the corporation; and
- the right to receive the remaining property of the corporation upon its dissolution.

These characteristics may be shared by more than one class of shares, and there exist many other characteristics that may be added, thereby permitting the separation of capital contributions from control and participation in future profits. For example, shares may:

- be voting or non-voting;
- entitle their holders to fixed, preferential or cumulative dividends or limited or unlimited participation in equity; and
- be issued in series or made redeemable for a fixed price at the option of the corporation or the holder.

Canada does not have a federal or central securities regulator, although the federal government is currently in discussions with the provinces and territories to implement a single securities regulator. The regulation of securities is a provincial matter and it varies by province, as each province has its own set of laws, regulations, rules and policies governing the trade of securities. However, the various provincial regulators work together through the Canadian Securities Administrators organisation in an effort to encourage the uniform application of securities regulation across Canada.

(b)   *Amount of contribution: debt versus equity*

The Canada Business Corporations Act requires no minimum investment by way of share capital; nor is a maximum required to be stated in the articles of the corporation in terms of either a dollar amount or number of shares (although permitted). It is common to see 'unlimited' in the share capital description, thereby avoiding amendments to the articles if the capital is increased. The only requirement is that at least one share be issued following incorporation. Federal and provincial incorporation or registration fees are generally unaffected by the amount of authorised or issued capital of a corporation.

Therefore, the capitalisation of the corporation is usually driven by factors other than the requirements of corporate legislation. Although it is not uncommon to see one share issued for C$1, on a practical level this would oblige the corporation to raise funds through debt financing by issuing debt instruments (which may be convertible) or contracting for loans. However, since financial institutions are generally reluctant to provide credit in the absence of a reasonable capital contribution by the shareholders, it is likely that the shareholders or ultimate parent would be required to guarantee the obligations of the corporation.

The capitalisation of foreign-controlled corporations may also be influenced by Canadian tax rules, such as the non-deductibility of interest paid by the corporation to its foreign parent if certain debt–equity ratios are not met (the 'thin capitalisation' rules). Accordingly, although great flexibility is permitted in the capitalisation of Canadian corporations, professional advice should be obtained before a corporation is established and capitalised, to avoid adverse tax implications.

With regard to debt financing, Canada possesses an extensive, sophisticated and highly regulated banking system that, in 2008, in the midst of global economic turmoil, was ranked by the World Economic Forum as the soundest in the world. All Canadian banks offer the standard range of services including retails savings and chequing accounts, secured and unsecured loans, financial leasing and a variety of instruments used to finance international trade.

In addition to banks, businesses may obtain financing from other Canadian financial institutions such as trust and loan companies, credit unions, 'caisses populaires' and, in some instances, insurance companies. Additionally, the federal and most provincial governments in Canada have established government assistance and/or incentive programmes.

(c) *Nature of contributions*

The shares of federal corporations must be without nominal or par value and cannot be issued until fully paid. The directors of the corporation determine when and to whom shares are issued and the price or consideration for which the shares are issued. The consideration may include property (except a promissory note payable by the person or a related party to whom the shares are being issued) or past services that are valued at not less than the fair equivalent of money that the corporation would have received had the shares been issued for money (see section 4.2(g)(iii)).

Par value shares are still permitted in British Columbia, New Brunswick, Nova Scotia, Prince Edward Island and Quebec; and in Nova Scotia, Prince Edward Island and Quebec shares can be partially paid and are therefore subject to the rules governing subscriptions and calls.

Shares are non-assessable, generally limiting the liability of the shareholder to the amount paid for such shares, save as set out in section 1.2.

3.2 Representation of shares

Shares may be represented by one or more share certificates or may be uncertificated securities. Shares represented by share certificates must be in registered form, specifying the shareholder's name or bearing a statement that the share is in registered form. Every shareholder of such shares is entitled to either a certificate or a non-transferable written acknowledgement of its right to obtain such a certificate.

In addition, the share certificate must also bear the following information:

- the name of the corporation;
- the name of the corporate legislation pursuant to which the corporation was incorporated; and
- the number and class of shares that the certificate represents.

Any restriction on transfer, charge in favour of the corporation, unanimous shareholder agreement or endorsement to which the shares are subject must also be referenced on the share certificate in order to be effective against subsequent transferees without knowledge thereof.

In some provinces, the above-mentioned information is required to be included in a notice that must be sent to the registered owner of uncertificated securities. Failure to give such notice may, among other things, have the result that a restriction on the transfer of uncertificated securities imposed by the issuer will be ineffective against a person without knowledge of the restriction.

3.3   Transfer of shares

(a)   Restrictions

Corporate law does not require restrictions on the transferability of shares or other securities of a corporation. However, Canadian securities regulators distinguish between public corporations, which distribute their securities to the public, and closely held or private corporations, which restrict the number of shareholders and/or the transferability of shares in some manner. To avoid the strict regulatory regimes established by the provincial securities commissions and applicable to publicly traded corporations, the corporation typically includes provisions restricting the transferability of its securities in its articles, namely that the securities cannot be transferred without the approval of a majority of the directors or shareholders.

The Canada Business Corporations Act and most provincial laws prohibit a corporation from holding shares in itself; therefore, if shares are transferred to the corporation they must (except in limited cases) be cancelled. Corporations are also generally prohibited from holding shares in their parent (with Nova Scotia being a notable exception).

(b)   Formalities

Most provinces regulate the transfer of shares by provincially enacted securities-transfer legislation. Securities transfer legislation is considered to be legislation governing the transfer of property rather than securities regulatory law. Its purpose is to codify the rights and obligations of persons involved in the transfer and pledging of securities, regardless of whether the security is represented by a paper certificate or by an entry in a computer database.

Securities transfer legislation contains provisions that determine when an investor (or a person acting on behalf of the investor) is considered to have taken possession of securities, based on whether the securities are certificated or uncertificated, and whether such securities are considered to be directly or indirectly held by the investor.

The effect of the provisions of securities transfer legislation may be varied by contractual agreement, subject to certain mandatory provisions of the legislation that may not be varied. For example, the obligations of good faith, diligence, reasonableness and care imposed by securities transfer legislation may not be disclaimed by agreement, but the parties may by agreement determine the standards by which the performance of such obligations is to be measured, so long as such standards are not manifestly unreasonable.

4.   Administration

4.1   Shareholders
The shareholders own the corporation, and as such have certain rights and liabilities. They appoint the directors, who manage the corporation, while retaining some significant rights to control major decisions affecting the corporation (see section 4.1(b)). A corporation requires only one shareholder, who may also be the director and officer of the corporation.

(a)   Shareholders' meeting
Generally, the directors determine the place in Canada where the shareholders' meetings are held. Meetings may also be held outside Canada, subject to certain conditions. Generally, notice must be sent to the shareholders not more than 60 and not less than 21 days prior to the date of the meeting; however, if the corporation is not publicly traded, the articles or bylaws may provide for a shorter notice period. The notice must:

- state the nature of any special business to be transacted at the meeting in sufficient detail to permit the shareholder to form a reasoned judgement thereon; and
- contain the text of any special resolution that will be submitted (which includes all business other than the consideration of the annual financial statements, the election of directors and the appointment of auditors at the annual meeting).

Shareholders are permitted to waive notice of a meeting and may requisition a meeting provided certain conditions are met.

There is a quorum where the holders of a majority of the voting shares are present in person or by proxy, unless the bylaws provide otherwise. The bylaws commonly provide that two shareholders present in person or representing a certain percentage of the outstanding shares constitute a quorum. Where there is only one shareholder, that shareholder, present either in person or by proxy, constitutes the meeting.

A shareholders' meeting may be held by telephone conference call or other electronic means, provided that all participants can communicate adequately with each other during the meeting. In lieu of a meeting, the shareholders may adopt a resolution in writing; to be valid, it must be signed by all of the shareholders entitled to vote on that resolution at a shareholders' meeting.

Unless the articles provide otherwise, each share of the corporation entitles the holder to one vote at the shareholders' meeting and voting takes place by show of hands, unless a shareholder demands a ballot. Electronic voting is permitted.

(b)   *Shareholder rights*
The Canada Business Corporations Act grants shareholders the following rights:
- the right to limited liability, subject to certain exceptions (see Section 1.2);
- the right to access corporate records;
- the right to attend annual shareholders' meetings;
- the right to receive dividends and other distributions made by the corporation;
- the right to submit proposals to be considered at a shareholders' meeting;
- the right to dissent and seek relief from oppressive action;
- the right to receive annual financial statements;
- the right to elect directors;
- the right to appoint an auditor;
- the right to adopt bylaws;
- the right to approve fundamental changes, including amendment of the articles, amalgamation, continuance and dissolution of the corporation; and
- the right to receive the remaining property of the corporation upon its dissolution.

Shareholder approval is generally by majority (approval by ordinary resolution). However, in cases such as the amendment of the articles, amalgamation and continuance, as well as for the sale of all or substantially all of the property of the corporation, the Canada Business Corporations Act requires a higher standard of 66.66% of the votes (approval by special resolution), and in some cases the special resolution must be adopted by the holders of each class of shares (both voting and non-voting). Shareholders may, by way of bylaws or a unanimous shareholder agreement, require an even higher standard. The Canada Business Corporations Act provides that shareholder approval must be unanimous in order to waive the appointment of an auditor (see section 5.4).

(c)   *Eventual partner separation – shareholder remedies*
Where shareholder approval by special resolution is required, a shareholder who does not agree with the proposed action and wishes to exit from the corporation may exercise his right of dissent. This is a remedy granted to shareholders by the Canada Business Corporations Act, pursuant to which the corporation (once the shareholder has notified the corporation of its dissent) must purchase the shareholder's shares for their fair value. The act also provides for what is commonly referred to as an 'oppression remedy', pursuant to which a shareholder (as well as a director, officer or

other interested person) may apply to a court for relief if it claims that the corporation or its directors have acted in an oppressive or unfairly prejudicial manner. The court has very broad powers to grant relief in such cases, including awarding damages, ordering specific performance, ordering the purchase of the shareholder's shares for fair value or even ordering the liquidation and dissolution of the corporation.

Most provinces grant similar rights and remedies to shareholders. For these reasons, the federal and most provincial laws are considered to be minority-shareholder-friendly statutes. Although Quebec and Prince Edward Island lack specific statutory protections, the courts in those provinces recognise that the general laws applicable in such provinces provide shareholders with legal remedies to which they may be entitled.

4.2 Directors

Subject to any unanimous shareholder agreement (see section 4.2(c)), the directors manage, or supervise the management of, the business and affairs of the corporation.

The directors are elected or appointed by the shareholders, usually for a term of one year, but in any event for not longer than a term expiring after the close of the third annual shareholders' meeting following such election. Staggered terms are permitted and directors, notwithstanding the length of their term, remain in office until they resign, are removed or their successor is elected.

A director may be removed by resolution adopted by a majority of the voting shareholders.

(a) Number of directors and their qualifications

A corporation must have at least one director – except for publicly traded corporations, which must have at least three. To be qualified to be a director, an individual:

- must be at least 18 years of age;
- must not be found by a court to be of unsound mind;
- must not be a 'bankrupt';
- is not required to hold shares in the corporation; and
- subject to the discussion below, must meet Canadian residency requirements.

Canadian corporate law does not recognise the concept of alternate directors or corporate directors, and the powers of a director cannot be exercised by proxy.

(b) Residency requirements

At least 25% of the directors of a federal corporation and some provincial corporations must be resident Canadians. A 'resident Canadian' is someone who is either a Canadian citizen or a permanent resident under applicable federal immigration legislation. In certain exceptional cases, the residency requirement for directors may be higher. If the corporation has fewer than four directors, at least one must be a resident Canadian.

Canadian residency requirements may be legitimately avoided by incorporating in a province or territory that has no residency requirements, such as British Columbia, New Brunswick, Nova Scotia, Prince Edward Island, Quebec, the Northwest Territories, Nunavut or the Yukon Territory. It is also possible for shareholders to alleviate the practical impact of the requirement of Canadian residency by adopting a unanimous shareholder agreement as discussed in Section 4.2(c) below.

Alternatively, non-Canadian directors may become Canadian residents by immigrating to Canada. Canada's immigration legislation and programmes are aimed at assisting the entry into Canada of experienced business people or skilled workers. As a general rule, no person, other than a Canadian citizen or permanent resident, may work in Canada without a valid work permit. The categories for which work permits may be obtained include: (i) intra-company transferees; (ii) entry under trade agreements; and (iii) a confirmed job offer. A work permit generally allows a spouse (legal or common-law, in each case including same-sex arrangements) and children to accompany the person authorised to work in Canada.

Furthermore, a person may enter Canada as a business visitor without the need for a work permit if that person seeks to engage in international business activities in Canada without directly entering the Canadian labour market. There are numerous permissible activities encompassed by the business visitor status for entry into Canada without a work permit. It represents the most often used exemption to the work permit requirement.

(c) Unanimous shareholder agreement

A unanimous shareholder agreement is a method by which, among other things, a foreign corporation may limit the powers of the resident Canadian directors over the operation of the subsidiary where these directors are outsiders who were appointed primarily to fulfil residency requirements.

A unanimous shareholder agreement is generally defined as a written agreement among all of the shareholders of the corporation that restricts, in whole or in part, the powers of directors to manage or supervise management of the business and affairs of the corporation. Where there is only one shareholder, a written declaration to the same effect by the sole shareholder is deemed to be a unanimous shareholder agreement.

To the extent that the unanimous shareholder agreement transfers the powers of the directors to the shareholders, the directors are relieved of the liability associated with such powers and such liability is assumed by the shareholders. Such transfer of powers may also give rise to issues of who controls the corporation and the location of the 'mind and management' of the corporation, which may have tax implications. Therefore, professional legal and tax advice should be obtained prior to the adoption of a unanimous shareholder agreement.

(d) Powers of directors

The powers of the directors to manage, or supervise the management of, the business and affairs of the corporation include (subject to the articles, bylaws and any unanimous shareholder agreement) the power:

- and the obligation to organise the corporation after its incorporation and issue shares to the shareholders;

- to make, amend and repeal bylaws, subject to confirmation by the shareholders;
- and the obligation to call annual general meetings of shareholders and such other special meetings as may be required;
- and the obligation to prepare and place before the shareholders at each annual meeting the annual financial statements of the corporation and comply with financial disclosure obligations;
- to adopt forms of security certificates and corporate records, and the obligation to maintain such records;
- to authorise the issue, redemption or purchase for cancellation of shares of the corporation, declarations of dividends and other distributions;
- to appoint officers. While the Canada Business Corporations Act does not require the appointment of officers (unlike some provincial statutes), it is common for at least a president and a secretary to be appointed. There is no prohibition against a director holding one or more offices;
- to fix the remuneration of the directors and officers of the corporation;
- to fill any vacancy on the board of directors if the shareholders fail to elect the minimum number required by the articles;
- to appoint an auditor to hold office until the first annual meeting of the shareholders and subsequently to appoint accountants if the shareholders waive their right to appoint an auditor;
- to delegate their powers to a committee of directors or a resident Canadian managing director, subject to certain limitations provided by the legislation;
- to fix the financial year of the corporation (which must be 12 months but need not follow the calendar year);
- to make banking arrangements and obtain financing; and
- to transact any other business.

(e) Directors' meetings

Subject to the articles or bylaws of the corporation, the directors may meet at such times, upon such notice and in such places as they determine. The quorum for such meetings is a majority of the directors in office, provided that the required number of Canadian-resident directors are present or approve in writing the business transacted at the meeting.

Where there is only one director, that director constitutes the meeting.

Directors may hold their meetings by telephone conference call or other electronic means, provided that all participants can communicate adequately with each other during the meeting. In lieu of a meeting, the directors may adopt a resolution in writing; to be valid, the written resolution must be signed by all of the directors entitled to vote on that resolution at a meeting.

(f) Authority of directors, officers and agents

Generally, corporations in Canada are subject to the 'indoor management' rule, pursuant to which the corporation is bound to any agreement or other obligation entered into on its behalf if such person was held out by the corporation to be a director, officer or agent of the corporation, even if such person was not duly appointed to such office or if the articles, bylaws and any unanimous shareholder agreement were not complied with.

(g) *Duties and liabilities of directors*

Directors must fulfil duties arising from provincial and federal legislation as well as from common law; failure to do so may result in the personal liability of the director. Because of the various federal and provincial governmental authorities in Canada, the liability of directors varies according to the corporate legislation under which the corporation was incorporated as well as the provinces where the corporation carries on business. However, there are certain similarities between the various jurisdictions as outlined below.

(i) *Fiduciary duty*

Directors owe a fiduciary duty to the corporation to act honestly and in good faith with a view to the best interests of the corporation. They must avoid conflicts of interest, which result when a director's duty to the corporation conflicts with his self-interest. Directors are bound to disclose any personal interest in a material contract with the corporation, and to refrain from voting on any resolution that places them in a conflict of interest and from using corporate information or property in their control for personal benefit (which includes the duty not to disclose confidential information or compete). The province of Ontario takes this duty one step further by prohibiting a director from attending any part of a meeting of the board of directors during which the contract or transaction, relating to his conflict of interest, will be discussed.

(ii) *Duty of care*

Directors also owe what is generally described as 'a duty to exercise the care, diligence and skill that a reasonably prudent person would exercise in comparable circumstances'. A director must apply his knowledge, experience, skills and best judgement when acting as a director. Where the provincial statute does not define 'duty of care', the common-law definition is "to exercise the care, diligence and skill of a person possessing the knowledge and experience of that director". Therefore, a director who possesses greater knowledge or skill (eg one holding a management position in the corporation) may be expected to meet a higher standard of care. The court will examine the process by which the director's decision was made. Simply being absent from the meeting at which the decision was made does not provide relief from liability, unless the director properly registered his dissent to the decision.

(iii) *Payment of dividends, etc*

Directors will be jointly and severally liable for amounts paid where they authorise payments relating to the purchase, redemption or other acquisition of shares by the corporation or to a commission, a dividend or an indemnity, in cases where the corporation would not, after such payment, meet the solvency tests provided by the legislation. Directors who authorise the issue of shares for consideration other than money are jointly and severally liable for amounts by which the consideration received is less than the fair equivalent of money that the corporation would have received had the share been issued for money. Such liabilities may be avoided if the director can show that he exercised his duty of care.

(iv)   *Wages and pensions*
Under the various federal and provincial statutes relating to employment (as well as under the Canada Business Corporations Act and other corporate legislation), directors can be held jointly and severally liable to the corporation's employees for unpaid wages and vacation pay earned by the employees during their directorship. Moreover, where a corporation is found to have committed an offence under provincial pension benefits legislation, a director who participated in such offence may be held personally liable.

(v)   *Taxes*
A director may be held personally liable for income, excise and certain other taxes where the corporation fails to withhold, deduct or remit as required, or commits an offence under federal or provincial tax legislation.

(vi)   *Environmental legislation*
Where a corporation commits an offence under certain environmental legislation, directors may be held liable even if they were not actively involved in committing the offence, since directors are deemed to have control of the corporation and its employees.

(vii)   *Publicly traded corporations*
Directors of publicly traded corporations are subject to additional duties, such as the duty to ensure that the corporation has complied with the various filing, disclosure and reporting requirements and restrictions arising from applicable securities legislation.

(viii)   *Other duties*
Directors can be subject to a number of other duties and liabilities, including those arising from bankruptcy and insolvency legislation, pension benefits legislation and legislation governing financial institutions, as well as those related to specific legislation governing the activities of the corporation.

(h)   **Indemnification of directors**
The corporation may indemnify a director or officer, or a person who acts on his behalf, against all costs, charges and expenses incurred in respect of any civil, criminal, administrative, investigative or other proceeding in which he is involved because of his association with the corporation if:
- such person acted honestly and in good faith with a view to the best interests of corporation; and
- in the case of a criminal or administrative action or proceeding that is

enforced by a monetary penalty, such person had reasonable grounds to believe that his conduct was lawful.

It is also common for the corporation to purchase directors' and officers' liability insurance.

5.   Financial disclosure

5.1   Annual financial statements
The directors must place before the shareholders at each annual meeting:
- comparative financial statements in the prescribed form which have been approved by, and signed by one or more of, the directors;
- the auditors' report, if any; and
- any further information regarding the financial position of the corporation required by the articles, bylaws or any unanimous shareholder agreement.

Not less than 21 days before each annual meeting, such financial documents must be sent to each shareholder, except to a shareholder who has informed the corporation in writing that he or she does not want a copy.

Publicly traded corporations must also, pursuant to the provincial securities legislation applicable to them, send a copy of such financial statements to the director of the provincial securities commission(s) and comply with the financial disclosure obligations found in such applicable provincial securities legislation.

Canada shall, as of January 1 2010, begin its transition towards the adoption of the International Financial Reporting Standards (IFRS) for all Canadian publicly accountable entities. The IFRS, as a single set of global accounting standards, have been accepted or are required in more than 100 jurisdictions around the world.

5.2   Company tax
In general, a corporation must prepare its annual financial statements and file its federal corporate income tax return within six months of its financial year end. Provincial filing requirements and corporate income-tax rates vary from jurisdiction to jurisdiction; however, a typical combined federal and provincial income-tax rate may range from 30% to 36%. Corporations may also be subject to a tax on the value of their capital assets, as well as capital gains tax in the event that such assets are sold for more than their cost. Corporations that are foreign owned are not entitled to benefit from the lower tax rates available to qualifying Canadian-controlled private corporations. Please see section 5.3 below regarding taxes payable by shareholders.

Most corporations must pay federal goods and services tax (GST), which is currently a 5% tax on a wide range of goods and services. GST is a 'flow-through' tax for corporations (in some respects similar to value added tax (VAT)) and if properly administered a corporation will, upon the filing of its GST returns, obtain refunds equal to the GST paid. GST returns must be filed on a monthly, quarterly or annual basis, depending on the revenue of the corporation.

Most provinces also have a provincial sales tax, which is often levied on the aggregate of the price of the goods or services and the GST. Provincial sales tax, how it is calculated, its rates and how or whether it is refunded vary from jurisdiction to jurisdiction.

5.3 Distribution of profits

The Canada Business Corporations Act does not expressly state that profits are distributed to shareholders by way of the declaration and payment of dividends; instead it provides for a solvency test, which must be met each time dividends are declared and paid. Therefore, subject to the articles of the corporation, dividends may be declared at any time and the corporation need not necessarily wait until approval of the annual financial statements. The solvency test provides that a corporation shall not declare or pay a dividend if there are reasonable grounds to believe that:

- the corporation is, or after the payment would be, unable to pay its liabilities as they become due; or
- the realisable value of the corporation's assets would thereby be less than the aggregate of its liabilities and stated capital of all classes.

Corporations may pay dividends in money or property, or by issuing fully paid shares.

Similar solvency tests apply to other types of distributions made by the corporation, such as those made by way of the redemption of shares or reduction of stated capital.

Dividends received from a resident Canadian corporation by a resident Canadian corporate shareholder are generally tax free, while dividends received by an individual who is a resident Canadian are taxed as income in the hands of the individual at a combined federal-provincial rate that varies from jurisdiction to jurisdiction but that could exceed 30%. Dividends paid to non-resident individuals or corporate shareholders are subject to a 25% withholding tax, which may be reduced by a tax treaty between Canada and the shareholder's country of residence. A similar withholding tax is applicable to the sale of shares of a Canadian corporation by a non-resident shareholder. However, Canada is a party to many bilateral tax treaties that reduce or eliminate withholding tax rates and provide further tax exemptions. Additionally, for dispositions after 2008 new measures under Canadian tax legislation may provide relief from withholding tax in certain circumstances where a non-resident shareholder sells shares of a Canadian corporation.

5.4 Auditor

An auditor is appointed by the shareholders at each annual meeting for the succeeding financial year, unless all of the shareholders (both voting and non-voting) unanimously dispense with such appointment. The Canada Business Corporations Act and provincial securities legislation impose various duties on the auditor to ensure proper financial reporting.

6.   Corporate reorganisation

6.1   Amalgamation

Under Canadian corporate law, two or more corporations may amalgamate and continue as one corporation. The amalgamated corporation is not considered to be a new corporation and is possessed of all the assets and liabilities of the amalgamating corporations. (However, various government agencies treat the amalgamated corporation as a new corporation for administrative purposes, thus requiring re-registration and so on, in certain cases.)

6.2   Continuance (import and export)

A company incorporated under the laws of another jurisdiction may apply to be continued under the Canada Business Corporations Act as if it had been incorporated under the act (import continuance). The director of corporations will issue a certificate of continuance if certain conditions are met and it is satisfied that the continuance will not adversely affect the creditors or shareholders of the corporation.

A corporation incorporated under the Canada Business Corporations Act may apply to the appropriate authority of another jurisdiction to be continued as if it had been incorporated under laws of that other jurisdiction (export continuance). The director of corporations will issue a certificate of discontinuance if certain conditions are met and it is satisfied that the discontinuance will not adversely affect the creditors or shareholders of the corporation.

The Canada Business Corporations Act and most provincial statutes allow continuance and therefore corporations may 'continue' from one jurisdiction to another (including foreign jurisdictions, in some cases). This is particularly useful where corporations wishing to amalgamate are organised under the laws of different jurisdictions. They may first continue under the same corporate legislation, thus permitting the amalgamation to take place.

A notable exception to the above is the province of Quebec, which permits neither import nor export continuance.

6.3   Split-off

If a corporation wishes to split off or incorporate part of its business, it may transfer business assets to another corporation in exchange for money or shares. Canadian tax legislation provides mechanisms to defer tax arising from the transfer.

6.4   Reorganisation or arrangement

The Canada Business Corporations Act contains provisions permitting a corporation to reorganise where it is subject to a court order affecting the rights of the corporation, its shareholders and creditors, or where it wishes to engage in a transaction or corporate act that is not provided for in, or where the act as contemplated does not meet the requirements of, the Canada Business Corporations Act.

6.5 Merger and consolidation

As mentioned in section 6.1 above, two or more corporations who wish to merge and become one corporate entity may amalgamate. Other options available include: (i) in the case of a parent corporation and its wholly-owned subsidiary, the liquidation of the subsidiary and its subsequent dissolution, pursuant to which the subsidiary transfers all of its assets to its parent (see section 7 below); or (ii) the transfer by one corporation of its business assets to another corporation in exchange for money or shares. Canadian tax legislation provides that such mergers may in some cases be made on a tax-deferred basis. A tax professional should be consulted to ensure that such a deferral is available.

7. Liquidation, dissolution and revival

7.1 Liquidation and dissolution

The Canada Business Corporations Act contains various methods to liquidate and dissolve a corporation that is not insolvent within the meaning of Canadian bankruptcy legislation.

Shareholders may voluntarily resolve to dissolve the corporation where:
- the corporation has no property or liabilities; or
- the directors have distributed any property and discharged any liabilities prior to filing the articles of dissolution.

No other formalities are required.

To liquidate an active business, the Canada Business Corporations Act provides a more complex procedure involving:
- appointment of a liquidator;
- filing of a statement of intent to dissolve;
- publication of notices to creditors;
- payment of liabilities; and
- distribution of any remaining assets prior to filing of the articles of dissolution.

Upon filing the articles of dissolution, a certificate of dissolution is issued and the corporation ceases to exist as of the date on such certificate. The shareholders remain liable to creditors of the dissolved corporation for debts up to the amount that they received upon liquidation, provided that such creditor brings action within two years of the date of dissolution.

The director of corporations may also dissolve a corporation *ex officio* in certain prescribed circumstances.

7.2 Revival

In certain instances, provided that the director of corporations is satisfied that such revival is warranted, a dissolved corporation may be revived by filing articles of revival. Upon the issuance of a certificate of revival, the corporation is restored to its previous existence in the same manner and to the same extent as if it had not been dissolved. However, some provincial jurisdictions subject a corporation's revival to specific time limits or conditions.

8. Branches

Federal and provincial laws do not normally require Canadian incorporation as a condition of doing business in Canada, so long as the foreign corporation complies with the applicable registration requirements of each Canadian province or territory in which it wishes to conduct business. A foreign corporation wishing to carry on business in Canada through a branch office must comply with the same registration requirements as Canadian corporations described in this chapter.

As such, a foreign investor is free to choose between conducting business in Canada directly as a branch of the foreign entity or establishing a Canadian subsidiary. However, Canadian federal and provincial laws treat branches of foreign corporations and Canadian corporations very differently. The use of a Canadian subsidiary is more convenient for administrative purposes. For example, a Canadian subsidiary facilitates the process of executing documents and can, in some cases, reduce Canadian withholding tax requirements in respect of payments made by the subsidiary. In addition, if the foreign corporation carries on business through a branch, its books and records relating to its non-Canadian operations may be opened to inspection and audit by the Canadian taxation authorities.

By using a Canadian corporation, a foreign investor may limit its liability to the amount of its investment in the Canadian subsidiary. By contrast, the foreign investor directly exposes itself to all of the liabilities of its Canadian operations if it conducts its business through a branch office. Branch offices of Canadian corporations have no separate legal personality or limited liability apart from the corporation itself; therefore, to obtain limited liability protection for 'branch office' activities, these activities should be carried on through another corporation.

China

Paul Thaler
Wenfei Attorneys-at-Law Ltd

---

1. Types of company with limited liability and applicable legislation

Foreign investors wishing to incorporate a company in China have several options. First, they may decide to establish a wholly foreign-owned enterprise (WFOE). Previously available only under various restrictions, this form of company can now participate in a wide range of economic sectors in line with China's commitments to the World Trade Organisation. In practice, a WFOE always takes the form of a limited liability company, although other company forms are theoretically possible with the approval of the competent authorities.

While WFOEs are becoming increasingly popular, many foreign investors still follow the traditional route of entering into a joint venture with a Chinese partner. Joint ventures between foreign and Chinese partners can take three forms:

- equity joint venture;
- cooperative joint venture; and
- joint venture company limited by shares.

An equity joint venture must take the form of a limited liability company, while a cooperative joint venture can be with or without Chinese legal person status. As its name indicates, a joint venture company limited by shares must be a joint stock limited company.

Finally, investment companies represent a further option to foreign investors wishing to enter the Chinese market. However, this type of company is an option only for companies with subsidiaries in China. A holding company must take the form of a limited liability company.

This chapter focuses on the two types of company with limited liability that foreign investors can establish in China: the limited liability company and the joint stock limited company.

A joint stock limited company may be established either by promotion or through a share offer. Establishment through promotion is undertaken by direct subscription by the initial shareholders of all shares to be issued by the company. In contrast, where a company is established through a share offer, the promoters subscribe only a portion of the shares, while the remaining shares are purchased by the general public, generally on stock exchanges.

At present, in virtually all cases, foreign investors establish limited liability companies. Probably the most important reason why foreign companies choose to establish a limited liability company is that the minimum capital requirement is lowei. The incorporation of a joint stock limited company, by contrast, may offer some advantages if the investors plan to list the company in the short or medium term. Nonetheless, the burdensome approval and listing procedures, as well as the relative immaturity of the Chinese capital markets, may militate against the establishment of a joint stock limited company.

The main applicable legislation is as follows:

- the Company Law (December 29 1993, last amended October 27 2005);
- the Law on Chinese-Foreign Equity Joint Ventures (March 15 2001);
- the Law on Chinese-Foreign Cooperative Joint Ventures (October 31 2000);
- the Law on Foreign-Owned Enterprises (October 31 2000);
- Interim Provisions Concerning Some Issues on the Establishment of Joint Stock Limited Companies with Foreign Investment (January 10 1995);
- Foreign Investment Issues Relating to Listed Companies – Several Opinions (November 5 2001); and
- Regulations on Company Registration (June 24 1994, last amended December 2005).

2.   Incorporation procedures

2.1   Proceedings prior to incorporation

(a)   *Name registration*

Registration of the company name is not only necessary but also one of the first tasks to be performed by an investor interested in establishing a company in China.

The establishment of a company, along with the substantial modification of existing business activities, is subject to approval by the competent government authorities. Before the investors intending to establish a company file a corresponding request with the authorities, an application for pre-approval of the company name must be filed with the Administration of Industry and Commerce (AIC).

The AIC must decide whether the requested company name can be reserved within 10 days of receipt of the request. In principle, if the name has not already been registered, the AIC will accept the application and issue a reservation certificate. The company name is thereby reserved, preventing other companies from registering the same name. The reservation period lasts for six months. During this period the applicant may not use the reserved company name to conduct business activities or transfer the reserved name to another company. If the company is not established during this six-month period, the reservation will be cancelled automatically. (In practice, however, it may be possible to obtain a six-month extension.)

(b)   *Capital contributions*

See section 7.2 later in this chapter.

(c)   *Declaration of foreign investment*

In China, the establishment of a foreign-invested company cannot be reduced to simple registration with the mercantile registry. On the contrary, an investor must obtain formal authorisation from the competent authorities to establish a company. The authorities must also approve the business scope of the company. Although the formal requirements for government approval were recently relaxed, the authorities still have a far-reaching involvement in the incorporation process.

The establishment of a foreign-invested company involves a process of examination and approval by the competent government authorities – usually the Ministry of Commerce or the equivalent body at the local level. The investors wishing to establish a company must submit a series of documents, such as the joint venture agreement, the shareholders' contract and the articles of association of the new company. The authorities extensively examine such documents.

Further, in certain sectors that the Chinese government considers strategic, establishing foreign-invested companies is subject to specific rules. Aside from the Ministry of Commerce, which is generally in charge of examining foreign investment, additional governmental bodies may be involved. For example, foreign investors in the securities, banking and insurance sectors must file additional registrations with the respective watchdogs: the China Securities Regulatory Commission, the China Banking Regulatory Commission and the China Insurance Regulatory Commission. Deals concerning state-owned assets are subject to authorisation by the State-Owned Assets Supervision and Administration Commission.

Once the investors have obtained authorisation from the Ministry of Commerce, and, if necessary, other government authorities, the relevant authorities must approve the proposed business scope of the company. For this purpose, an application to obtain an administrative licence must be filed with the authorities – generally the Ministry of Commerce, the State Administration for Industry and Commerce (SAIC) or their equivalent bodies at the local level, depending on the circumstances.

Where a foreign-invested joint stock limited company is set up through a share offer, the approval of the China Securities Regulatory Commission is also required.

(d)   *Tax identification number for foreign shareholders/directors*
Foreign shareholders need not undergo special tax registration in China as long as their China source income is passive (eg obtaining dividends or royalties from the company in which they hold shares). However, before this income can be transferred abroad, a withholding tax may be imposed. If foreign shareholders derive active income in China, registration with the national tax administration where the income originates is required. Local registration requirements must then be considered.

Foreign directors who work in China must register with the respective local tax administration and file a monthly tax return. The formal requirements of local tax administrations vary from place to place.

2.2   Incorporation

(a)   Bylaws

(i)   Essential clauses

The essential clauses in the bylaws vary slightly for limited liability companies and joint stock limited companies (and also within the category of limited liability companies). By way of example, the following clauses are mandatory for a joint stock limited company:

- the company name and domicile;
- the scope of business;
- the method of establishment;
- the total number of shares, the amount of each share and the registered capital;
- the names and number of shares subscribed for by the promoters;
- the rights and obligations of shareholders;
- the composition, functions, powers, term and rules of procedure of the board of directors;
- the legal representative;
- the composition, functions, powers, term and rules of procedure of the supervisory board;
- the method for distributing company profit;
- the grounds for dissolution and method of liquidation;
- methods for notices and announcements; and
- other matters that the shareholders' general meeting considers.

(ii)   Clauses not foreseen by law

Optional clauses may be formulated in the bylaws at the discretion of the company, as long as they are not contrary to law.

Optional clauses included in the bylaws are recorded by the competent registration authority. The effect of such registration is that they are enforceable not only among the shareholders but also in respect of third parties.

(b)   Execution of public deed

The most important documents for the establishment of a joint stock limited company or limited liability company, including the company contract, must be reviewed and approved by the relevant authorities. As a general rule, it is sufficient if the documents submitted are private documents.

(c)   Tax identification number

Within 30 days of obtaining the business licence, the company must register with both the national tax administration and the local tax administration to obtain certificates that include the company's tax identification number.

(d)   Indirect taxes, incorporation fees and other levies

Indirect taxes: Foreign-invested companies in the form of limited liability companies or joint stock limited companies are mainly subject to the following indirect taxes in China:

- value added tax (VAT);
- consumption tax; and
- business tax.

VAT is imposed on the supply of tangible goods and certain specified services. The standard rate is currently (2009) 17%, except for food grains, edible vegetable oils, tap water, heating, air conditioning, hot water, coal gas, liquefied petroleum gas, natural gas, methane gas, coal/charcoal products for household use; books, newspapers, magazines, fees, chemical fertilizer, agricultural chemicals, agricultural machinery and covering plastic film for farming and other goods as regulated by the State Council, where a reduced rate of 13% applies.

In addition to VAT, a consumption tax is imposed on manufacturers and importers of certain luxury goods, including tobacco and alcoholic beverages. Tax rates vary from 3% to 45%.

Business tax is a local tax on business activities, including services not covered by VAT, the transfer of immovable property not covered by VAT and the transfer of intangible property within China. The tax rate ranges between 3% and 5%, except for entertainment businesses, where the rate reaches 20%.

Stamp duty of 0.05% of the registered capital of limited liability companies and joint stock limited companies must be paid on incorporation. Further, the registration and approval procedures with the various government authorities involved require the payment of certain other fees. The exact amount of these fees depends on the particular circumstances of the procedure and on the location of the authority. In Beijing, for example, the most important fees are the fee for the procedure before the local AIC and the payment to be made to the capital verification institution – which is responsible for examining whether the contributions are made in full – in an amount of 2% of the paid-in contributions. Generally, no fee is necessary for the procedure relating to the Ministry of Commerce. For other procedures, additional fees of approximately RMB2,000 (approximately $290) may be levied.

(e)   ***Registration with the Mercantile Registry***
There is no mercantile register in China. That said, however, most relevant company information is registered with the AIC during the procedure for obtaining the business licence. As it may be possible to request the AIC to grant access to the files, AIC registration may be seen as performing a similar function to a mercantile register.

(f)   ***Legalisation of official books***
See section 2.2(e).

(f)   ***Declaration of start date and other tax declarations***
A foreign-invested company must first obtain the approval of the relevant authorities and then obtain a business licence to confirm its establishment. Once the company has

obtained the business licence, it may commence business activities. However, to carry out business activities a series of other registrations must be conducted. These include foreign exchange registration, the opening of a bank account, national and local tax registration, customs registration and registration with the Public Security Bureau.

Expatriates who are already in China and who intend to work for a foreign-invested company must go through a number of procedures to acquire a work permit and a residence certificate. Where expatriates are dispatched from a foreign country to work in the foreign-invested company in China, a foreigner working licence and a working visa must be obtained before the work permit and a residence certificate can be applied for.

3.   Number of shareholders

A limited liability company can have no more than 50 shareholders. Recent changes in the law have made it possible to establish a one-person limited liability company, with a minimum registered capital of RMB100,000 to be paid in a lump sum.

Chinese law requires that there are between two to 200 promoters of a joint stock limited company. For a joint stock limited company with foreign participation, one foreign promoter is sufficient. Nonetheless, Chinese law requires that foreign shareholders must hold at least 25% of the total shares. If there are several foreign shareholders, the overall foreign participation is assessed for this purpose. If the joint stock limited company is listed on a Chinese stock exchange, the minimum percentage of shares held by foreigners is 10%.

While the law does not stipulate a maximum percentage of a foreign shareholder's participation, two restrictions apply:

- A joint stock limited company with foreign participation must have at least one Chinese shareholder, although his stake in the company can be minimal and need not represent a minimum percentage of shares; and
- While it seems possible to establish a foreign-funded joint stock limited company with one Chinese party, Chinese law still requires that more than half of the promoters (ie initial shareholders), including foreign promoters, are resident in China. Thus, a purely foreign joint stock limited company is not permitted.

4.   Corporate name – limitations

For both limited liability companies and joint stock limited companies, there are two relevant types of company name under Chinese law:

- the strict company name, registered as such by the authorities; and
- the business name, which is how the company is usually known to other traders and clients.

The business name is generally shorter than the company name.

A company name must be in Chinese characters. It cannot contain the Chinese *pinyin* alphabet, foreign letters or Arabic numerals. As a general rule, a company name must be composed of the following elements, in the following order:

- the administrative division indicator (eg 'Beijing' or 'Shanghai');

- the business name;
- the industry sector; and
- the form of organisation. Thus, a limited liability company must include the words 'limited liability company' or 'limited company' in its name, while a joint stock limited company must feature the words 'joint stock limited company' or 'joint stock company' in its company name.

Finally, the name of another company cannot be included in the company name unless approved by the SAIC.

5. Corporate domicile

The domicile of both limited liability companies and joint stock limited companies is the location of the main office. A company may have only one domicile, which in China is referred to as the 'registered legal seat'. This should be located in the jurisdiction of the registration authorities (ie the SAIC and its local bodies) with which the establishment of the company is registered. In practice, there may be a division between the actual headquarters and the registered legal seat, although such arrangements require the consent of the relevant authorities (eg the state shareholder, or the tax authorities).

A change in domicile must be filed with the competent authorities, and the company must apply for the renewal of its certificate of approval, business licence and suchlike.

6. Corporate purpose

The fundamental object of a company, including limited liability companies and joint stock limited companies, is to pursue economic goals and to make a profit. From this starting point, any company can pursue the object intended and specified by its shareholders.

The object of the company must be stated as the company's business scope. The business scope should be defined in the bylaws, registered and approved by the competent authorities, and included in the business licence. Unlike in most Western jurisdictions, a company can perform only the activities indicated in the approved business licence. To obtain an extension of these activities, the company must file a further application with the authorities.

7. Capital stock

7.1 Minimum capital requirement

For limited liability companies other than foreign-invested companies, the minimum amount of registered capital is RMB30,000 (approximately $4,300). The laws impose no minimum capital requirement. In practice, this may depend to a large extent on the policy of the local authorities at the company's domicile.

As regards joint stock limited companies, while Chinese law was recently amended to lower the general threshold for the minimum registered capital, joint stock limited companies with foreign participation are subject to a different threshold of RMB30 million (approximatcly $4.3 million). Therefore, as there must be at least 25% foreign participation, the (individual or aggregate) foreign contribution is at least RMB7.5 million (approximately $1,100,000). If the promoters wish to enable the general public to purchase shares of the joint stock limited company (ie in the event of a share offer), the promoters' participation cannot be less than 35% of the total shares.

Depending on the sector in which the established limited liability company or joint stock limited company plans to operate, the minimum thresholds may be higher.

7.2   Nature of contributions

Shareholders of limited liability companies and joint stock companies can pay in their investments in cash or in kind (eg by contributing industrial property rights, non-patented technology or land use rights).

If the contribution is made through the provision of industrial property rights or proprietary technology, in the case of a WFOE the value of these rights cannot exceed 20% of the total investment amount.

If the contribution consists of land-use rights, their value must be assessed by a qualified asset evaluation institution.

Subsequently, a qualified capital verification institution must be appointed to carry out an examination of whether full payment has been made.

Whether explicitly or implicitly, Chinese law attempts to protect the Chinese shareholders in a Chinese-foreign joint venture. In this context, Chinese law requires that assets be "correctly" valued. This means that the economic value of a foreign party's contribution to a joint venture will be assessed by the authorities (and may be rejected).

7.3   Partial payments

For limited liability companies, it is possible to divide payment of the contribution into fractions. Shareholders of a limited liability company must pay in their investment within the timeframe stipulated in the shareholders' contract. If a foreign-invested limited liability company is wholly foreign owned, the overall contribution must be completed within three years of the company's establishment. For all foreign-invested limited liability companies, the first instalment cannot be less than 15% of the subscribed amount and is due within 90 days of establishment of the company.

In the case of joint stock limited companies, partial payments are not possible. Each promoter is obliged to make his contribution within 90 days of the certification of approval being issued.

7.4   Representation of shares

Shares of a joint stock limited company take the form of signed share certificates, in paper or other forms approved by the China Securities Regulatory Commission. The share certificates must set out:

- the name of the company;
- the date of registration and establishment of the company;

- the class of share certificate, the par value and the number of shares represented by the share certificate; and
- the serial number of the share certificate.

The share certificates should be signed by the company's legal representative and marked with the company stamp. Shares subscribed by the promoters should indicate that they are promoter shares.

As a general rule, the share certificates must be registered and bear the names of the holders. The company, for its part, is obliged to keep a list of shareholders.

Unlike in many Western countries, Chinese law requires that the capital be divided into shares of equal value, and that all shares have the same rights and benefits. Thus, it is not possible to issue privileged shares. Further, the law requires that shares issued at the same time have the same price and conditions.

A further restriction to the issuance of shares is that shares cannot be issued below the par value.

7.5   Transfer of shares

(a)   *Restrictions*

The transfer of stock rights of a limited liability company is subject to the provisions of the bylaws. Where the bylaws fail to include such provisions, the stock rights of the shareholders may be freely transferred among the shareholders. However, where a shareholder intends to transfer his stock rights to a non-shareholder, the transfer is subject to the consent of more than half of the other shareholders. The sale of shares to non-shareholders can be avoided if current shareholders themselves buy the shares offered. This is in line with the more general rule that current shareholders have a pre-emptive right to purchase shares to be transferred.

With regards to joint stock limited companies, a significant restriction under Chinese law is that a promoter cannot sell its shares until one year after the establishment of the company. If the company is established through a share offer, the promoters' shares acquired prior to public listing cannot be transferred until one year after the public listing takes place.

The law further states that the transfer of shares must be conducted through legally established stock exchanges or in other manners provided by the authorities. Although it is theoretically possible for shareholders of a joint stock limited company to transfer shares in other forms than through stock exchanges, in practice it remains unclear how this could be done. As a result, most of the share transfers of joint stock limited companies take place on stock exchanges.

Each year, the directors, supervisors or senior managers of a joint stock limited company cannot transfer more than 25% of their shares. These persons are further prohibited from transferring their shares within one year of public listing and within six months of resignation from their positions. The bylaws may establish further restrictions.

One restriction exclusively concerning foreign shareholders is that the overall percentage of shares of a joint stock limited company held by foreigners cannot fall below the 25% threshold. While this requirement does not prohibit foreign shareholders from selling their shares, the provision has restrictive effects in so far as it limits the group of potential buyers to foreign candidates. If the foreign-invested joint stock limited company is listed on a Chinese stock exchange, the shares held by foreigners cannot be less than 10% of the total shares.

Another restriction regarding the identity of the buyer is that, as a general rule, shares cannot be sold to the company itself. In other words, a company cannot buy its own shares.

(b) *Formalities*

Chinese law provides that a valid share transfer requires the approval of the same authorities that examined and authorised the establishment of the company.

For limited liability companies, there are no formal requirements other than an amendment of the shareholder register. The registered shares of joint stock limited companies are assigned by way of endorsement or through other means as specified in laws and regulations. Non-registered shares are to be transferred on stock exchanges.

Finally, there are certain procedural requirements accompanying the transfer of shares of a joint stock limited company. As such, less than 20 days before the general shareholders' meeting or less than five days before the distribution of dividends, changes in the registration of shares are no longer possible. Also, within its general obligation to keep a list of shareholders, the company must record a transfer of registered share certificates.

8. Equity

8.1 Equity–capital ratio

Chinese law does not explicitly stipulate a ratio between registered capital and debt. However, it does establish a ratio between registered capital and total investment (which is identical for foreign-invested limited liability companies and joint stock limited companies), as outlined in the table below.

Total investment ($)	Ratio of registered capital to total investment	Minimum equity contribution ($)
Up to $3 million	7:10	See section 7.1
$3 million – $10 million	1:2	$2 million if total investment is less than$4.2 million
$10 million – $30 million	2:5	$5 million if total investment is less than $12.5 million
More than $30 million	1:3	$12 million if total investment is less than $36 million

8.2 Convertible bonds

Listed joint stock limited companies are allowed to issue convertible bonds, while limited liability companies do not have this option.

The shareholders' meeting of a listed joint stock limited company can decide to issue company bonds convertible into shares. The method of conversion must be specified in the offer of the company bonds. Before the offer is released, the approval of the China Securities Regulatory Commission must be obtained.

When issuing convertible bonds, it is necessary to indicate clearly the words 'convertible company bond' on the bonds. The amount of convertible company bonds must be recorded by the company.

A company that issues convertible bonds must issue shares in exchange for such bonds to the bondholders following the announced conversion method. Bondholders, for their part, have the option to decide whether to convert their bonds into shares.

9. Administration

The shareholders' meeting of limited liability companies and joint stock limited companies is where basic business decisions are taken. The board of directors is the fundamental administrative organ of both limited liability companies and joint stock limited companies, which determines important issues according to the bylaws. Certain management and representative powers are vested in the board of directors. The implementation of corporate policies and day-to-day management are generally performed by a dedicated management. The administrative structure of a company incorporated in China is completed by the board of supervisors, whose task is to supervise the behaviour of directors and senior managers.

9.1 General shareholders' meeting

For wholly foreign-owned limited liability companies, the first general shareholders' meeting following establishment of the company is convened and presided over by the shareholder with the largest shareholding. Subsequently, the procedure established in the bylaws is followed. Foreign-invested limited liability companies in the form of joint ventures do not have shareholders' meetings. Their main decision-making body is the board of directors.

The general shareholders' meeting of a joint stock limited company is to be convened by the board of directors and should take place at least once a year. The chairman of the board (or an appointed substitute) presides over the meeting.

For the foreign-invested companies that had been established before January 1 2006, they can choose whether to make revisions on their articles of association according to the above-mentioned regulations.

(a) Quorum requirements

(i) Attendance

The necessary quorum for attendance at a shareholders' meeting of a limited liability company or a general shareholders' meeting of a joint stock limited company is not regulated in Chinese law and is thus left to the bylaws.

(ii) *Voting*

Limited liability company: The quorum for the valid adoption of resolutions of the shareholders' meeting and of the board of directors should be specified in the bylaws. For certain decisions, the quorum is imposed by law – resolutions on the following issues require a quorum of two-thirds of the voting rights:

- amendment of the bylaws;
- increase or reduction in registered capital;
- merger, split-off or dissolution; and
- transformation of the company.

Joint stock limited company: To be valid, a resolution of the shareholders' meeting must be adopted by half or more of the voting rights present at the meeting, except in the case of resolutions regarding amendment of the bylaws, an increase or reduction in registered capital, merger, and division or dissolution of the company. In such cases a qualified majority of shareholders representing at least two-thirds of the voting rights present at the shareholders' meeting is required.

(b) *Challenging resolutions*

For both limited liability companies and joint stock limited companies, resolutions that are contrary to laws or administrative regulations are void. Any shareholder can lodge a claim before a court requesting the revocation of a resolution if the voting or other procedures leading to the resolution were carried out in breach of laws, administrative regulations or the bylaws, or if the content of the resolution is contrary to the bylaws.

9.2 Administrative body

(a) *Different systems of administration*

Board of directors: For limited liability companies, the board of directors is a mandatory company organ, except for companies with a small number of shareholders or with small operations, which may have an executive director instead. The chairman of the board of directors is entitled to convene and preside over the meetings.

A joint stock limited company must have a board of directors. The quorum for attendance at meetings of the board is at least half of all board members. A director unable to attend the board meeting may appoint a proxy to represent him at the meeting. Resolutions of the board of directors must be adopted by majority of the directors present. The board of directors must meet at least twice a year.

Management: The management system imposed by Chinese law envisages a general manager and several deputy managers. The system for limited liability companies and joint stock limited companies is equivalent. The board of directors decides on the general manager's appointment and dismissal. The general manager is in charge of the day-to-day management and of implementing company policies. He is responsible to the board.

Apart from this basic structure required by law, the general manager enjoys a certain degree of discretion when it comes to devising the company's management structure. The general manager has the power to formulate the internal organisation plan and draw up the basic management system of the company. However, while the general manager of a limited liability company or a joint stock limited company can appoint and dismiss staff members, he is not entitled to appoint the deputy managers and the financial officers. This task falls to the board of directors.

(b) ***Term of office, resignation and removal of directors***

Board of directors: For a foreign-invested limited liability company, members of the board of directors are appointed by the investors and can serve a term of four years (or longer if reappointed). No fixed term for the tenure of board members of a joint stock limited company is required by law, but this may be established in the bylaws or decided by the board in its resolution of appointment.

The resignation of a director of a limited liability company or a joint stock limited company must comply with the terms of the bylaws.

Finally, as regards the removal of directors, on the one hand the shareholders' meeting of a limited liability company or a joint stock limited company can dismiss a director before the expiry of his term of office only if it has justifiable reasons to do so; on the other hand, Chinese law sets conditions for the qualification of directors and establishes a system of incompatibilities. Further incompatibilities may be established in the bylaws. If the conditions of incompatibility are met, the director is under a duty to resign. Failing that, he may be removed by the general shareholders' meeting.

Management: The term of office and the financial and other conditions for the members of senior management of a limited liability company or joint stock limited company can be established in the bylaws or determined by the board of directors.

The resignation of managers must comply with the law, the bylaws and their contractual obligations. Similar to the regime applicable to directors, senior managers are subject to a system of incompatibilities imposed by Chinese law.

The boards of limited liability companies and joint stock limited companies have the power to appoint and dismiss the general manager, the deputy managers and the financial officers.

(c) ***Administrators' liability to third parties***

Under Chinese law, as a general rule, the directors and managers of a company are not subject to liability with respect to third parties for claims under civil law. Nonetheless, if a director or manager commits a criminal offence, he may be held liable towards third parties. This may lead to the compensation of damages suffered by a third party as a result of the manager's wrongful action.

(d) ***Non-competition***

For both limited liability companies and joint stock limited companies, Chinese law prohibits managers and directors from engaging in any businesses that have the same or similar scope as the company. More generally, the manager is under an obligation not to pursue activities that are harmful to the company.

Furthermore, agreements to extend the non-competition obligation to the period after the manager leaves the company are also permissible. Depending on the locality, the maximum period for a post-employment non-competition agreement varies. In Beijing, for example, the maximum period is three years and the validity of the agreement is subject to the granting of an adequate compensation package to the manager.

(e)   *Special duties of secrecy and loyalty*

Chinese law provides that directors and senior managers have a duty of diligence and loyalty. The law obliges managers to "faithfully perform their duties". This duty includes the obligation to protect the company's interests and refrain from activities that harm the company. Chinese law contains a series of provisions aimed at ensuring that the manager does not exploit his position in the company for personal gain.

Pursuant to the law, directors and managers are under a general obligation not to divulge company secrets, except with the consent of the shareholders' meeting. Special duties of secrecy and loyalty can further be extended in the employment or cooperation contracts. Duties of secrecy may last beyond the term of office or period of employment.

(f)   *Civil and criminal liability*

Civil liability: Resolutions of the shareholders' meeting or of the board of directors adopted in violation of the law or regulations are void. In such cases, and where resolutions encroach on the legitimate rights of shareholders, any shareholder can bring an action before the courts to demand that the infringement be stopped.

While a director or manager generally cannot be held liable towards third parties, the company can hold him responsible and seek compensation for any damage caused. The company itself bears civil liability with respect to third parties. Private parties may seek compensation for damages, and public authorities may impose fines and other penalties.

Criminal liability: The provisions of criminal law are manifold, and are even set out in the main texts of Chinese corporate legislation.

Some of the provisions of criminal law apply directly to Chinese companies, whether limited liability companies or joint stock limited companies, while others are targeted at the individuals in charge of the company at the time of infringement.

9.3   Others

(a)   *Attorneys*

For both limited liability companies and joint stock limited companies, the chairman of the board of directors is the legal representative of the company. The appointment of additional legal representatives may be established in the bylaws or determined on a case-by-case basis. In such cases the chairman of the board can draft a power of attorney bearing the company stamp.

(b)   *Internal controllers and auditors*

While this is not legally required, larger companies can appoint internal controllers and/or auditors. Generally, the individuals hired for these positions are certified public accountants.

The main accounting principles apply to both limited liability companies and joint stock limited companies. However, the financial statements of listed joint stock limited companies must be publicly disclosed, whereas those of limited liability companies and non-listed joint stock limited companies need only be delivered to the shareholders.

As its name indicates, the board of supervisors fulfils certain supervisory functions. All companies incorporated in China are obliged to establish one, except for limited liability companies with a small number of shareholders or with small operations, which may have one to two supervisors instead. The board of supervisors is responsible for inspecting and supervising the board of directors and senior managers, and can bring legal actions against these persons.

10.   Fiscal year, commencement of activities

Chinese law requires that the fiscal year of any company, including foreign-invested companies, coincide with the calendar year.

The company's start date of activities is the date of issuance of the business licence.

11.   Financial statements

11.1   Company tax

The income tax on foreign-invested enterprises is computed on the taxable income, currently at a rate of 25%.

The income tax on enterprises shall be prepaid on a monthly or quarterly basis, the specific measures for which shall be subject to the assessment of the tax authorities. Payments must be made within 15 days of the end of each month or quarter. The final payment is due within five months of the end of the tax year.

In order to attract foreign investors, Chinese tax law used to offer substantial tax incentives for foreign-invested enterprises, including the following:

- The income tax on foreign-invested enterprises established in certain areas recognised as special economic zones or economic and technological development zones was reduced to 15%. Similarly, income tax at 24% applied to foreign-invested production companies located in coastal economic open zones or in the old urban districts of cities near the special economic zones or the economic and technological development zones;
- A foreign-invested company engaged in the production of goods was exempt from income tax in the first and second year it made a profit, provided that its term of existence was at least 10 years. From the third to the fifth year, the income tax due was reduced by 50%. If a company's term of existence proved to be shorter than the registered minimum 10 years, the company was obliged to repay the tax benefits enjoyed.

However, after the latest round of taxation reform took place at the beginning of 2008, the above-mentioned tax incentives have been abolished. Therefore, the foreign-invested enterprises are taxed in the same way as a Chinese company. But this recent reform does not mean foreign investments will be unable to benefit from any kind of reductions in, or even exemptions from, tax. If the foreign-invested enterprises invest in projects, sectors or areas particularly encouraged by the Chinese government, they may still benefit from reductions in, or even exemptions from, tax at the discretion of the competent authorities at national or local level.

In addition, the enterprises that are established upon registration at the Administrative Department for Industry and Commerce before March 16 2007 will be regarded as enterprises established before the promulgation of the new Enterprise Income Tax Law. According to the new Enterprise Income Tax Law, if these enterprises enjoyed lower tax rates according to the provisions of the previous tax laws and administrative regulations, their income tax rates shall, according to the provisions of the State Council, gradually be transferred to the tax rate provided in the new Enterprise Income Tax Law within five years after the Law is promulgated. Enterprises that have enjoyed the preferential treatment of tax exemption for a fixed term may, according to the provisions of the State Council, continue to enjoy such treatment after the promulgation of the new Enterprise Income Tax Law until the fixed term expires. However, for those that have failed to enjoy the preferential treatment due to lack of profits, the term of preferential treatment may be counted as ending in the year when the new Enterprise Income Tax Law is promulgated.

11.2 Annual accounts

(a) Documents
At the end of each fiscal year, a limited liability company must produce a financial and accounting report, examined by a recognised auditor. Financial and accounting statements include:
- balance sheets;
- profit and loss statements;
- statements of financial changes;
- statements of the company's financial situation; and
- statements on profit distribution.

A joint stock limited company has equivalent obligations, although further, more stringent conditions are imposed on listed companies.

(b) Auditor's report
Each year, a company must submit an auditor's report, signed by a certified public accountant registered in China, together with the company's final accounting statements.

Regardless of whether they made a profit in the relevant fiscal year, foreign-invested companies should file their income tax returns and final accounting statements with the local tax authorities within five months of the end of each calendar year.

(c)   *Approval and distribution of profits*

When distributing after-tax profits, both limited liability companies and joint stock limited companies are required by law to set aside 10% of the profits for the company's reserve fund and 5% to 10% for the company's public welfare fund. However, if the money deposited in these funds exceeds 50% of the registered capital, the company is no longer required to transfer money into the two funds.

These funds have the object of forcing the company to put aside money for the compensation of losses in coming years, if needs be, and to guarantee future welfare payments to its employees. With regard to the compensation of losses, if the aggregate balance of the reserve and public welfare funds is not sufficient to make up for losses sustained in the previous year, the current-year profits must be used to compensate for those losses.

After the compensation of losses sustained in previous exercises and the topping-up of reserve and public welfare funds, the remaining profits can be distributed to shareholders in proportion to their capital contributions.

Dividends paid from foreign-invested limited liability companies and joint stock limited companies to investors located abroad are not subject to Chinese income tax or any withholding tax.

(d)   *Deposit and publication*

All documents forming part of the annual accounts, including the annual audit report, must be deposited with the competent tax authorities.

Only listed joint stock limited companies are obliged to publish their annual accounts in newspapers and on websites designated by the authorities. Limited liability companies and non-listed joint stock limited companies are merely required to send their annual accounts to their shareholders.

Both joint stock limited companies and limited liability companies are required to grant access to the audit report at the request of shareholders.

12.   Company reorganisation

12.1   Transformation

As a general rule, Chinese law allows for the transformation of the company into another type of company if the mandatory requirements of the new company form are met. Chinese law provides detailed provisions on the conversion of a foreign-invested limited liability company into a joint stock limited company.

All assets and liabilities of the former company are taken over by the new company.

12.2   Merger

The decision to merge with another company must be approved by the general shareholders' meeting of a limited liability company or joint stock limited company. Furthermore, the merger must have the approval of the Ministry of Commerce or the competent authorities at the local level.

After the merger agreement is signed, the balance sheets and lists of assets of the participants must be compiled, and their creditors must be notified within 10 days of adoption of the resolutions to merge. The participants must also make at least three series of public announcements of the merger.

Creditors have the right to demand that the participants clear their debts or provide corresponding guarantees; if the participants fail to do so, the merger cannot be carried out. The company resulting from the merger will then assume all assets and liabilities of the participants in the merger.

12.3 Split-off

As in the case of a merger, the general shareholders' meeting has the power to decide on split-off. The Ministry of Commerce or the competent authorities at the local level must give their authorisation.

The same procedure as for a merger applies, involving preparation of the balance sheets, public announcements and debt clearing. The companies resulting from the split-off are jointly and severally liable for the liabilities of the predecessor companies, unless the creditors and the company agree otherwise.

13. Eventual shareholder separation

In principle, any shareholder of a limited liability company or a joint stock limited company is free to sell his stake in the company, subject to the restrictions on the transfer of shares.

For limited liability companies, a special mechanism for shareholder withdrawal is provided by law. A shareholder who votes against resolutions on the following matters at the shareholders' meeting may request the company to purchase his shares at a reasonable price:

- a decision not to distribute profits if, despite having made a profit in the last five years, the company has not distributed any profits to the shareholders during this period;
- a decision to merge, split off or transfer the main assets of the company; or
- a decision to prolong the company's existence where the business term expires or other causes for dissolution as prescribed in the bylaws occur.

More detailed conditions for the separation of shareholders of limited liability companies and joint stock limited companies may be established in the bylaws.

14. Dissolution and liquidation

Chinese law on the dissolution and liquidation of a company is relatively undeveloped. This means that clear provisions should be included in the bylaws.

Both limited liability companies and joint stock limited companies can be dissolved for the following reasons:

- expiry of the term or the occurrence of the causes for dissolution specified in the bylaws;
- merger or split-off;
- as a result of an administrative penalty (eg revocation of the business licence or an order to close down);

- following a resolution on dissolution adopted at the general shareholders' meeting; or
- following a judgment of a competent court.

To proceed to liquidation, a company must form a liquidation committee. If the shareholders fail to form a liquidation committee, the creditors can apply to the court to appoint the members of the committee.

As a general rule, recourse to the judge is also sought where a company should be declared bankrupt as a result of its inability to serve debt payments. The judge is then called upon to appoint a liquidation group composed of selected shareholders of the company, representatives of relevant government authorities and other specialised personnel, such as lawyers and accountants. The liquidation is then guided and organised by the liquidation group.

15. Branches

In line with many Western jurisdictions, a branch is an accessory to the parent company and cannot have an independent legal personality. The parent company remains liable for the debts of the branch.

Specific provisions relating to foreign companies ensure that this rule applies where foreign incorporated companies establish a branch in China. The law clearly stipulates that a foreign company bears civil responsibility for the operational activities of its branch in China.

Colombia

Álvaro Ivan Cala
Laura Carreño
María Andrea Duque
Brigard & Urrutia Abogados SA

1.   Branch of foreign company

Under Colombian law, a branch of a foreign company shares the legal personality of its parent company. The branch does not have its own partners or shareholders, as it is merely an extension of the parent company, which has given it:

- an assigned capital;
- a defined corporate purpose; and
- its own officers and statutory auditors.

A branch is created through the execution of a public deed before a local notary public. The deed must include copies of:

- the parent company's founding charter;
- the parent company's bylaws;
- a resolution of the parent company approving the incorporation of the branch in the Colombian territory;
- a certificate of incorporation of the parent company; and
- a standing certificate of the parent company.

The local notary public will issue copies of the public deed containing these documents. One copy of the deed must be registered with the local chamber of commerce, which acts as the registrar of companies in Colombia. At the request of any individual or entity, the local chamber of commerce will issue certificates evidencing the organisation and good standing of the branch, including reference to its name, corporate purpose, domicile and assigned capital, and the names of its officers and statutory auditors.

All documents to be filed with the local notary public must be either originals or certified copies. The signatures on each document must be authenticated by a notary public or another competent authority in the country of origin of the parent company. If the country of origin is a party to the Hague Convention 1961, these signatures must be endorsed by apostille.

If the country of origin is not a party to the Hague Convention, the signature of the competent authority must be certified by the Colombian consulate with jurisdiction in the domicile of the parent company. The consulate must additionally issue a certificate stating that the company exists and that it is in good standing in accordance with the laws of its jurisdiction. The certificate must also show that the individuals who executed the documents have the power and authority to act on behalf of the company.

Finally, the company must register with the Colombian Tax Administration using its Unique Tax Registration (UTR) and will be assigned a tax identification number.

Once these steps have been completed, the branch may start trading.

2.   Subsidiary of foreign company

Different options are available with respect to the incorporation of a subsidiary in Colombia. Entities and individuals can choose the option that suits them best, depending on the purpose of their business.

2.1   Limited liability company

The main characteristics of a limited liability company (*Sociedad de Responsabilidad Limitada*) are outlined below.

(a)   *Partners*

The limited liability company must have at least two partners but no more than 25.

(b)   *Capital*

The capital of a limited liability company is divided into quotas that, in general, can be transferred only with the consent of those holding at least 70% of the outstanding quotas. The transfer of quotas represents an amendment to the bylaws of the company and must be executed in the form of a public deed before a local notary public. This must be registered with the local chamber of commerce.

(c)   *Board of directors*

A limited liability company does not require a board of directors. It is managed directly by the partners, although they can delegate their authority to general managers appointed by the board of partners. Nonetheless, applicable regulations allow for a limited liability company to have a board of directors if the partners agree.

(d)   *Statutory auditors*

In general, a limited liability company does not require statutory auditors until it reaches a defined level of net worth or income, at which point it must appoint statutory auditors.

(e)   *Liability*

In principle, the partners are liable only to the extent of their equity contributions, with the exception of: (i) amounts owed for tax; and (ii) some labour charges. Limited partners are jointly liable with the company for any outstanding sums. However, the liability for tax does not include fines and interest; it only includes capital not paid to the tax administration.

2.2 Corporation

(a) *Shareholders*

A corporation (*Sociedad Anónima*) requires at least five shareholders, none of whom can directly own 95% or more of the outstanding shares of the corporation. There is no limit to the number of shareholders.

(b) *Capital*

The capital of a corporation is divided into shares that are, in general, freely negotiable by endorsement, unless the bylaws provide for rights of first refusal in favour of the shareholders.

(c) *Board of directors*

Corporations require a board of directors formed of at least three principal members and their respective alternates, both appointed by the shareholders assembly. The powers of the board of directors typically include:

- the appointment of general managers and officers of the corporation;
- the authority to issue shares that would be subject to pre-emptive rights in favour of the shareholders; and
- the power to approve certain acts of the general managers as provided for in the bylaws.

(d) *Statutory auditors*

The corporation requires statutory auditors, appointed by the shareholders' meeting.

(e) *Liability*

The shareholders are, in principle, liable to the extent of their contributions.

2.3 Stock-issuing limited partnership

(a) *Partners*

The stock-issuing limited partnership (*Sociedad en Comandita por Acciones*) must have at least five shareholders, none of whom can directly own 95% or more of the outstanding shares of the company (limited partners). It must have at least one partner who is in charge of, and jointly and severally liable for, the management of the company (a general partner). The general partner is appointed in the deed of incorporation and may be an individual or a legal entity. There is no maximum limit as to the number of shareholders.

(b) *Capital*

A stock-issuing limited partnership is similar to a US general partnership, as its capital is divided into shares that are freely negotiable by endorsement, unless the bylaws provide for the right of first refusal in favour of the shareholders.

(c)   **Board of directors**

The stock-issuing limited partnership does not need a board of directors, as it is deemed to be managed directly by the general partner(s); they can delegate the management of the company to their co-general partners or third parties. Moreover, regulation allows for a stock-issuing limited partnership to have a board of directors if the partners deem it necessary.

(d)   **Statutory auditors**

The stock-issuing limited partnership requires statutory auditors. These are appointed by the shareholders' assembly.

(e)   **Liability**

The shareholders are, in principle, liable only to the extent of their equity contributions, with the exception of monies owed for tax; here the shareholders are jointly liable with the company for sums not paid by the latter. However, the general partner of the stock-issuing limited partnership is jointly and severally liable for the management of the company. This liability is unlimited.

2.4   Simple limited partnership

(a)   **Partners**

Like the stock-issuing limited partnership, the simple limited partnership (*Sociedad en Comandita Simple*) must have at least one partner who is in charge of and jointly and severally liable for the management of the company (general partner). It must have one or more partners whose liability is limited to their own contributions (limited partners). The simple limited partnership cannot have more than 25 limited partners. The general partner is appointed by the deed of incorporation and may be a natural or legal person.

(b)   **Capital**

The capital of a simple limited partnership is divided into quotas. The transfer of quotas requires the unanimous vote of the remaining limited partners, while the transfer of quotas of the general partner(s) requires the express approval of the co-partners. The transfer of quotas requires amendment of the bylaws and must be executed by means of a public deed before a local notary public.

(c)   **Board of directors**

The simple limited partnership does not require a board of directors, as it is deemed to be managed directly by the general partners, who may delegate the management of the company to their co-general partners or third parties.

(d)   **Statutory auditors**

A simple limited partnership does not require statutory auditors until it reaches a defined level of net worth or income, at which point the partners must appoint statutory auditors.

(e)   *Liability*
The limited partners are, in principle, liable only to the extent of their equity contributions, with the exception of monies owed on account of taxes and labour charges, in which case they are jointly liable with the company for sums not paid by the latter. Moreover, the general partner is jointly and severally liable for the management of the company. This liability is deemed to be unlimited.

2.5   General partnership

(a)   *Partners*
A general partnership (*Sociedad Colectiva*) requires at least two partners. There is no maximum limit as to the number of shareholders.

(b)   *Capital*
The capital of a general partnership is divided into parts of interest. The transfer of the parts of interest requires:
* the unanimous vote of the partners, if not otherwise provided in the bylaws; and
* amendment of the bylaws, which must be executed in the form of a public deed before a local notary public.

Each partner is entitled to one vote.

(c)   *Board of directors*
The general partnership does not require a board of directors. The administration of the company is the responsibility of all partners, who may delegate it to their co-partners or third parties. If the bylaws do not allow for delegation, this should be done in accordance with the formalities for amendment of the bylaws.

(d)   *Statutory auditors*
The general partnership does not require statutory auditors until it reaches a defined level of net worth or income, at which point the partners must appoint statutory auditors.

(e)   *Liability*
The partners of the general partnership are jointly and severally liable for the management of the company, and have unlimited liability.

2.6   Sole proprietorship enterprise

(a)   *Owner*
The sole proprietorship enterprise (*Empresa Unipersonal*) is formed by one partner (whether a natural or legal person) and is considered a different entity from the owner.

(b) *Capital*

The capital of a sole proprietorship enterprise is divided into quotas, which may be transferred by means of a public deed. The transfer of quotas requires amendment of the bylaws and, if the transfer results in more than one owner, the public deed must show the alteration of the corporate structure. Colombian law requires the entity to adopt the structure of a company.

(c) *Board of directors*

The sole proprietorship enterprise does not require a board of directors, as it is deemed to be managed directly by the owner. However, the owner is entitled to delegate his authority to a general manager. Moreover, regulation allows for a sole proprietorship enterprise to have a board of directors if the owner deems it convenient.

(d) *Statutory auditors*

A sole proprietorship enterprise does not require statutory auditors until it reaches a defined level of net worth or income, at which point the owner must appoint statutory auditors.

(e) *Liability*

In general, the owner is liable only to the extent of his equity contribution to the company, with the exception of:

- unpaid taxes, for which he is jointly liable with the company; and
- salaries, benefits and indemnities owed to employees and not paid by the sole proprietorship enterprise, for which he is liable.

(f) *Restrictions*

The sole proprietorship enterprise may not enter into agreements with its owner.

2.7 Simplified stock company

(a) *Shareholders*

A simplified stock company (*Sociedad por Acciones Simplificada*) can be formed by one or more shareholders and is considered a different entity from the owner. There is no maximum limit as to the number of shareholders.

(b) *Capital*

The capital of a simplified stock company is divided into shares that are, in general, freely negotiable by endorsement, unless the bylaws provide for rights of first refusal in favour of the shareholder(s). The shareholder(s) may not allow any purchase of shares for a 10-year period.

(c) *Board of directors*

Simplified stock companies do not require a board of directors. Nonetheless, the shareholder(s) may create this corporate body in the bylaws of the company. The board of directors may be formed by any number of individuals with or without alternates, appointed by the shareholders' assembly or the unique shareholder. The powers of the board of directors should be provided by the shareholder(s) in the bylaws or remitted to the regulation of the code of commerce.

(d) ***Statutory auditors***

Although the law is not completely clear, pursuant to the doctrine from the Superintendence of Companies the simplified stock company is in principle not obliged to appoint fiscal auditors unless the gross assets (*activos brutos*) of the company are equal to or more than 5,000 minimum legal monthly salaries as of December 31 of the last fiscal year and/or the gross income (*ingresos brutos*) of the company is equal to or exceeds 3,000 minimum legal monthly salaries as of December 31 of the previous fiscal year. In the event, the shareholders' assembly should appoint fiscal auditors, whose duties and functions are set out in Colombian law.

(e) ***Liability***

The shareholder(s) is (are) liable to the extent of their contribution.

3. Incorporation

Once the future shareholders or partners of a company have decided on the type of company they want to incorporate, they must appear before a local notary public to execute the founding charter. A simplified stock company may be incorporated by means of a private document, in which the signature of the shareholder(s) must be recognised before a notary public.

The founding charter must contain the bylaws of the company and include at least the following information:

- the names and domicile of the shareholders or partners;
- the type of company being incorporated;
- the corporate domicile: If the shareholders establish different branch offices by means of the same public deed, the domiciles of the branch offices must also be included;
- the corporate purpose: This must clearly indicate the main activities that the company will carry out and binds the legal capacity of the company. Companies cannot have an undetermined purpose under Colombian law, but a simplified stock company can establish that its corporate purpose is to execute or undertake any activity permitted by law;
- the company's capital and the portion subscribed and paid in by each partner or shareholder at the time of incorporation. In stock companies (simplified stock companies, corporations and stock-issuing limited partnerships) the bylaws must also indicate the class and nominal value of representative stock, and the form and terms of payment of outstanding instalments to the capital, which may not exceed one year;
- how the company's operations will be managed, as well as any limitations on the managers' powers and authority;

- the dates and procedure for convening both ordinary and extraordinary assemblies or partners' meetings, as well as the decision-making system and the procedure for the adoption of relevant motions;
- the dates on which inventories and general balance sheets must be drawn up;
- the procedure for distribution of profits or income in each fiscal term, with an indication of reserves to be made;
- the exact duration of the company and the grounds for early dissolution (although simplified stock companies may be incorporated for an indefinite term);
- the applicable dispute resolution mechanisms in the event of disagreements between the partners or shareholders, or with the association. Where the shareholders or partners decide to submit their disputes to arbitration or referee's decision, the bylaws must indicate how the arbitrators will be appointed;
- the name and domicile of the person or persons who legally represent the company, where this does not correspond by law or by contract to all or some of the partners or shareholders. The bylaws must clearly indicate the powers and duties of the legal representatives; and
- the powers and duties of the statutory auditors, where their appointment is required by law or the bylaws;

The founding partners or shareholders must appear before the notary public either in person or through an individual who has a power of attorney which, in the case of foreign individuals or companies, has been properly certified by a notary public in its country of origin and legalised in accordance with the formalities of the Hague Convention. If the country is not party to the Hague Convention, the signature of the notary public should be legalised before the nearest Colombian consulate.

The power of attorney must grant sufficient authority for the attorney to:
- incorporate the new company;
- execute the founding deed or private document for the simplified stock companies;
- obtain a tax identification number from the tax administration for the partners or shareholders, if necessary; and
- register the investment before the Central Bank, if necessary.

Once the public deed has been granted, the notary public will issue the relevant copies of the founding deed, which must subsequently be registered at the chamber of commerce of the principal domicile of the company. At the request of interested parties, the local chamber of commerce will issue a certificate evidencing the due organisation and good standing of the company and the names of its officers and statutory auditors.

3.1 Specifics for certain types of company

The incorporation of a stock-issuing limited partnership and simple limited partnership does not require the intervention of the limited partners. Nonetheless, the relevant public deed must always list the name, domicile, number and nationality of each partner, the number of shares subscribed and their nominal value, and the amounts paid in.

A simplified stock company may be incorporated by means of a private document, which need not be formalised as a public deed; it only needs to be registered before the local chamber of commerce.

3.2 Incorporation fees and other levies

The incorporation of a company is subject to:

- a registration tax at a rate of 0.7% of the amount of the capital initially subscribed by the partners or shareholders, payable to the local chamber of commerce;
- a fee depending on the assets of the company – equivalent to a minimum of US$10 and a maximum of US$521, depending on the exchange rate – also payable to the chamber of commerce; and
- notary fees, applicable at a rate of 0.27% to 0.29% of the capital initially subscribed by the partners or shareholders. VAT also applies to the notary fees.

These are not tax deductible.

3.3 Tax identification number

The legal representative, or the attorney empowered by the shareholders or partners to carry out the necessary steps to incorporate the company, must register the company in the Unique Tax Registration (UTR) within the tax administration to obtain a tax identification number for the company. The relevant form must be filed online and with the chamber of commerce, together with the public deed containing the bylaws. Once the chamber of commerce issues the certificate showing the due organisation and good standing of the company, a copy of this certificate must be filed with the tax administration to obtain the definitive tax identification number for the company. The chamber of commerce will not proceed with the registration of the public deed of incorporation of the company unless it is accompanied by the tax form.

4. Liability

4.1 Liability of managers and directors

The managers and directors have different types of liability.

(a) Commercial liability

The code of commerce sets out the following rules pertaining to the commercial liability of managers and directors of companies incorporated in Colombia:

- Managers and directors are jointly and severally liable to the company, the shareholders and third parties for damages resulting from their wilful misconduct or gross negligence. Gross negligence is presumed in the event of violation of the law or the bylaws, and in the event of a distribution of profits in breach of the requirements set out in the applicable legislation.

- However, such liability does not apply to managers and directors – especially members of the board of directors – who had no knowledge of the relevant action or omission, or who voted against such act or omission, provided that they did not in fact carry out any such action or omission.
- Where the manager or a director is a legal entity, that legal entity and its legal representative will be considered liable as outlined above.
- The liability of the managers and directors may not be limited or waived in the bylaws.
- The managers and directors are not entitled to file claims against the company for damages or to recover the amounts paid as a result of sanctions or penalties imposed on them for breach of their duties.

(b) *Criminal liability*

Managers and directors of a company may be subject to criminal liability in the following cases:

- The managers and directors may be found guilty of forgery where they:
  - order, tolerate, perform or cover up alterations to the financial statements of the company;
  - issue false certificates or provide false information to the competent authorities; or
  - falsely represent the names of shareholders or administrators of the company to induce the subscription of shares by third parties.
- The managers and directors may be found guilty of the use of privileged information if they use such information for their own benefit or for the inappropriate benefit of a third party.
- In the above cases, the managers and directors cannot file claims against the company for damages or for the recovery of amounts paid as a result of sanctions or penalties imposed upon them in connection with their criminal liability.
- Criminal liability also results in liability for damages to third parties.

Under fiscal rules there are three main instances of criminal liability:

- non-payment of income taxes withheld from third parties within two months of withholding, or incorrect issuance of withholding tax certificates to third parties (however, the legal representative will not be liable if another individual in the company has been expressly appointed as liable for withholding tax before the tax administration);
- non-payment of value added tax charged to third parties within one month of the corresponding two-month period; and
- introduction of merchandise valued in excess of 100 legal minimum monthly wages (approximately US$20,062) in unauthorised places, or concealment of such merchandise from the customs authorities.

4.2 Liability of the controlling company

In general terms, whenever a person has a dominant influence on the decisions of a company by virtue of shareholding or administrative control, or by virtue of any act or business, this person is deemed to be the controlling entity of the company. Regulation establishes a presumption of the controlling company's liability concerning its subordinate companies.

This provision applies in the context of insolvencies only where:

- the assets of the subordinate company are insufficient to pay the value of the registered liabilities (or contingencies) of the company; and
- the insolvency of the subordinate company is attributable to actions of the controlling company by virtue of the subordination and in the interest of the parent company or of its subordinates, and against the company being insolvent.

The liability of the controlling company must be declared before a competent court. Despite the fact that the law shifts the burden of proof to the controlling company, judicial proceedings should be commenced before the competent courts. The defendant has the right to prove that any damage suffered by the company in liquidation was not due to the controlling company.

5. Foreign investment regime

Foreign exchange control regulations, including foreign investment matters, are important aspects to consider when incorporating a company in Colombia. The Central Bank continually strives to make this easier. To this end, it has made an effort to provide all relevant information, forms and instructions online.

Article 3 of Decree 2080 of 2000 states that any contributions and/or participation in the capital of a Colombian company, provisional investments in trusts, acquisition of real estate, contributions in kind, initial or supplementary investment in the assigned capital of a local branch of a foreign company, among others, qualifies as a direct foreign investment (DFI).

A DFI can be formalised by transferring the funds either to Colombia or to a so-called 'compensation account'. Compensation accounts are mechanisms provided to Colombian residents to handle their foreign exchange transactions (eg imports and exports, foreign indebtedness, DFI, derivatives and international guarantees) and free-market transactions (eg other types of transactions) without the need to report to the *Intermediarios del Mercado Cambiario* (IMC).

If the funds are transferred to Colombia, they must be converted into Colombian pesos. This conversion must be made through IMCs. These banks and other financial institutions are authorised to buy and sell foreign currencies.

Accordingly, foreign investors in Colombia have the obligations set out next.

5.1 Registration of initial investment

Foreign investors must register their initial investment. The general rule is that the foreign investment is automatically registered with the submission of an exchange declaration for international investment (Form 4 of the Central Bank). Non-compliance with this obligation will incur penalties for unregistered foreign investment or for the remittance of foreign currency derived from foreign investment in breach of the rules of the exchange market.

5.2 Registration of amendments

When foreign investment derives from the capitalisation of profits from previously registered investments, or from the substitution of foreign investors, the company must file a petition to register the transaction with the Central Bank. The registration, or amendment to the initial registration, must be completed before March 31 of the year following that in which the transaction is completed.

5.3 Registration of updates

Information regarding foreign registration must be updated annually. Local companies must file Form 15 with the Central Bank before June 30 in the relevant year in order to update any foreign investment registrations they have.

5.4 Cancellation of foreign investment

Where a foreign investment registration is cancelled due to the liquidation of a local company or the transfer of shares to a resident, the company must file a petition to cancel the foreign investment with the Central Bank before March 31 of the year following the date on which the transaction was completed.

Foreign investors may be subject to penalties imposed by the Superintendence of Companies if they do not:

- register foreign investment before the Central Bank;
- update such registrations annually; or
- register any modifications to the investment on time.

The Superintendence of Companies – the entity responsible for enforcing compliance with these obligations – is entitled to impose penalties amounting to as much as 200% of the unregistered amount. However, the penalties normally do not exceed 2%.

5.5 Rights and benefits of a registered DFI

Pursuant to Article 10 of Decree 2080 of 2000, the rights and benefits of registering a DFI before the Colombian Central Bank are:

- to remit abroad or repatriate proven net profits generated by the investment;
- to reinvest profits or retain them as surplus undistributed profits;
- to capitalise amounts with remittance rights and further remit them abroad; and
- to remit any income received from the investment in Colombia, from liquidating the company receiving the investment, or from reducing its capital.

6. Capital stock

6.1 Minimum capital requirement

There are no minimum capital requirements for companies, but the requirements tend to be determined on an individual basis. However, there might be additional requirements depending on the company's activities (eg telecommunications regulations require that operators have capital for the granting of a licence). Financial institutions and airlines must also comply with certain legal requirements.

6.2 Nature of contributions

Contributions may be made in cash, in kind or in services. This provides the necessary flexibility for partners or shareholders to participate in the incorporation of a company without having to contribute sums of money.

Contributions may be classified as follows:

- **Capital contributions:** partners or shareholders may agree to make in-kind contributions or contribute specified sums of money. The shareholders or partners must determine the value of any in-kind contribution to quantify the contribution of the partner or shareholder. The shareholders or partners are deemed liable for the value attributed to the in-kind contribution.
- **Contributions of personal work:** shareholders or partners may contribute their work in the incorporation of a company. Consequently, they may commit to carry out certain activities for the benefit of the company during a certain period of time.

7. Equity

7.1 Equity–capital ratio

Colombian regulations do not include specific provisions on the balance between capital and the company's own resources. However, a company will be dissolved if it incurs losses that reduce its net worth to less than 50% of its equity.

7.2 Convertible bonds

Pursuant to commercial regulations, Colombian companies may issue convertible bonds. The bonds may be converted into a predetermined number of shares, usually at the discretion of the bondholder. Bondholders are treated as creditors of the company in so far as their bonds have not been converted into shares.

8. Management

The management of the company may vary, depending on the type of company chosen.

The corporation requires a board of directors formed of at least three principal members and their respective alternates. In general, the powers of the board of directors typically include:

- the appointment of general managers and officers of the company;
- the authority to issue shares subject to pre-emptive rights in favour of the

remaining shareholders; and
- the power to approve certain acts of the general managers as provided for in the bylaws.

Nevertheless, the most important decisions – such as the distribution of profits and any waiver of pre-emptive rights – always remain with the shareholders' assembly. These powers cannot be assigned to the board of directors.

Limited liability companies do not require a board of directors. The limited liability company is deemed to be managed directly by the partners, although they are entitled to delegate their authority to general managers. The powers of the board of directors must be listed in the bylaws.

8.1 General meeting of partners/shareholders

(a) Ordinary meeting

The corporate bodies of the company must meet at least annually in an ordinary meeting. This usually takes place in the first quarter of the year.

In the ordinary meeting, the shareholders' assembly or board of partners, as the case may be, takes all decisions within its legal and statutory powers. In particular, the shareholders or partners will:
- evaluate the company's situation;
- appoint managers or directors;
- approve or reject the financial statements of the company; and
- decide on the distribution of profits.

The management of the company must submit the following documents to the corporate bodies for these purposes:
- the annual report;
- the audited financial statements; and
- the plan for distribution of profits.

The shareholders or partners can attend the meeting either in person or by means of a duly empowered attorney-in-fact. Further, following certain regulations, meetings can be held by telephone, fax or in any other way that allows the parties to discuss and decide on the proposed issues.

Partners or shareholders must define the specific rules for the convening of meetings and the required majorities to take decisions in the bylaws.

(b) Extraordinary meetings

The corporate bodies can meet at any time. The managers, fiscal auditors and/or competent authorities, where applicable, may convene extraordinary meetings at any time to discuss issues related to the company. The bylaws must set out the rules on convening, the decision-making process and the formalities of extraordinary meetings.

(c)   *Quorums*

(i)   *Attendance*

With certain limitations and exceptions, the attendance quorums may be freely agreed by the partners or shareholders in the bylaws. If there is no provision in the bylaws, Colombian law provides that the quorum for attendance at meetings shall be 50% plus 1 of the shares or quotas subscribed.

(ii)   *Voting*

With certain limitations and exceptions, resolutions may be adopted by the majority of the votes present at the meeting.

There are three exceptions to this rule:

- the distribution of less than 50% of the profits must be approved by a majority of 78% of the shares or quotas at the meeting. Shareholders or partners may specify a higher majority in the bylaws.
- the waiver of the pre-emptive rights of shareholders in the issuance of shares of the company must be approved by a majority of 70% of the shares at a meeting.
- the payment of dividends with shares of the company must be approved by a majority of 80% of the shares present at a meeting.

(d)   *Challenging resolutions*

Any decisions taken by the shareholders' assembly or board of partners meetings that do not comply with the applicable regulation or the bylaws can be challenged by the shareholders or partners, the managers and the fiscal auditors within two months of:

- the meeting at which the resolution was adopted by the shareholders or partners, if the resolution need not be registered with the local chamber of commerce; or
- registration of the resolution with the local chamber of commerce, where this is necessary.

9.   Fiscal year

According to commercial law, the fiscal year for all companies in Colombia must start on January 1 and end on December 31. A company can also have other individual deadlines (eg dates for quarterly accounts). These must be approved by the shareholders assembly or board of partners meetings (see section 8.1 above).

10.   Financial statements

Colombian companies must prepare and approve their annual financial statements within three months following the fiscal year (or after the close of each period agreed by the shareholders or partners, where there is more than one per year). In general, companies and branches of foreign companies established in Colombia must submit their annual financial information to the Superintendence of Companies, as well as intermediate financial information during the months of March, June and September.

10.1 Company tax and tax on dividends

Companies in Colombia are subject to income tax on their worldwide income (branches only on their Colombian-source income), currently (2009) at the rate of 33%.

The tax base for the annual income-tax calculation is the highest between ordinary taxable income and 'presumptive income'.

Ordinary taxable income is calculated by subtracting deductible costs and expenses from net revenues (taxed revenues minus rebates and discounts). If this results in a net operating loss, it may be carried forward.

Presumptive income is calculated as 3% of the prior tax year's net tax equity (tax assets minus tax liabilities). Some assets may be excluded from the taxable basis. The excess of presumptive income over ordinary income may be carried forward for five years to offset the net taxable income result of those years.

Dividend withholding-tax leakage exists in Colombia as follows:

- Cash dividends paid to non-residents that correspond to profits that were already taxed at the company's level will not be taxed when they are distributed to shareholders; and
- Cash dividends paid to non-residents that were not taxed at the company's level (eg if profits are generated through activities that are exempt from income tax or if the company has deducted, for tax purposes, a greater amount of depreciation compared with book depreciation) are subject to a 33% income tax withholding on the amount paid.

10.2 Annual accounts

Colombian companies must annually prepare financial statements, as well as a management report on the results of the company (see sections 9, 10 and 11).

10.3 Deposit and publication

According to Colombian commercial regulations, a copy of the financial statements of the company must be filed with the chamber of commerce at the place of the corporate domicile within one month of approval by the corporate body.

11. Company reorganisation

Pursuant to Colombian law, companies may undergo reorganisation either through conversion into another type of company, or through merger or split-off.

11.1 Conversion

The procedure for conversion is outlined below.

(a) Approval by corporate bodies

The partners or shareholders must draft the new bylaws of the company. Within the conversion process, the partners or shareholders are entitled to exercise their right of withdrawal if their liability is to be increased in the new company or if the conversion will result in a reduction in their economic interests. The company must grant the partners the opportunity to exercise their right of withdrawal.

The draft of the new bylaws must be available for review by the partners or shareholders at least 15 days prior to the meeting. The notice convening the meeting must mention the possibility of exercising the right of withdrawal during the eight days following the approval of the conversion by the partners or shareholders.

The company must also prepare a balance sheet, the end period of which may not be 30 days before the date of the partners' or shareholders' meeting.

(b)   *Compliance with legal requirements for new type of company*
The new company must comply with all corporate requirements established for the new structure. This may mean an increase in the number of shareholders.

(c)   *Formalisation and registration of the amended bylaws*
The legal representative of the company must execute a public deed containing the new bylaws of the company and register it before the chamber of commerce. On formalisation, the company must send several notifications to the relevant tax authorities, the customs authorities, the Central Bank and the Superintendence of Companies, as well as creditors, suppliers and customers.

11.2   Merger
The merger procedure is as follows.

(a)   *Special purpose financial statements*
Each company participating in the merger must prepare consolidated financial statements, which must be examined and approved by an independent fiscal auditor.

(b)   *Merger agreement*
A merger agreement must be prepared and made available to all shareholders or partners for review 15 business days prior to the date on which the merger is to be considered. The merger agreement must be made available to shareholders or partners in the main offices of each participating company. The agreement must include the following items:
- the reasons for and conditions pursuant to which the merger will take place;
- accounting information on which the conditions for the merger were determined;
- a detailed pricing report of all assets and liabilities of the participating companies;
- an explanation of the pricing method used to set the price of the companies and the share swap to occur as a result of the merger; and
- financial statements of each participating company and consolidated financial statements.

(c)   *Shareholders' assembly and notification*
A shareholders' assembly of each participating company must be summoned with at least 15 business days' notice.

A merger notice must also be published in a national newspaper.

(d)   Compliance with antitrust regulations

All entities that are devoted to the same manufacturing, distribution or consumption activity of a certain product, raw material, goods or services must file a report with the Superintendence of Industry and Commerce (SIC) in connection with any merger, consolidation, acquisition of control or economic integration.

The SIC has indicated that an economic integration is any kind of legal agreement or economic transaction that results two or more business units combining under a common interest. This may take place in a merger, consolidation or acquisition of control.

Authorisation to proceed can come in two forms, as described next.

(i)   Automatic authorisation

This is given to integration transactions where the following two conditions are met:

- integrations where the annual consolidated operational income (ie of all companies involved in the transaction, as well as of all other related companies within the Colombian territory) as of the year prior to that in which the transaction is to take place is less than 100,000 legal minimum monthly wages (approximately US$20 million); and
- integrations where the total value of consolidated assets as of the year prior to that in which the transaction is to take place is less than 100.000 legal minimum monthly wages (approximately US$20 million).

Only local income and assets need be taken into account for the purposes of determining both the consolidated operational income and the total value of consolidated assets.

Where these two conditions are met, execution of the integration transaction will only be subject to the approval of the shareholders assembly and/or board of partners of the companies involved in the transaction regarding their compliance with these thresholds.

(ii)   Mandatory authorisation

A mandatory authorisation request must be filed before the SIC if any or both of these thresholds are not met prior to the completion of the proposed integration.

Broadly speaking, authorisation will be granted where market conditions are not affected and fair competition is not restricted.

The mandatory authorisation request must comply with several formal requirements. It must provide a wide range of information from all of the parties involved in the transactions along with information on the industry in which the parties operate.

Once the request for clearance has been filed, the SIC has 30 business days to clear the transaction or to request additional information. After the parties have submitted this information, the SIC has 30 business days to issue a decision. If there is no response from the SIC, the transaction is deemed to have been approved.

If there is any objection, or conditions have been imposed, the petitioner will be notified. An appeal may be filed within five business days. If the decision is not reversed, the petitioner may initiate nullification proceedings within four months.

If no authorisation is requested, two material consequences may arise:

- fines of up to 2,000 legal minimum monthly wages (equal to approximately US$520,000) may be imposed upon the parties involved in the transaction, as well as fines of up to 300 legal minimum monthly wages (equal to approximately US$78,500) that may be imposed upon the company's directors, officers and/or administrators; and
- annulment of the sale/purchase transaction.

Under Colombian antitrust laws the sale/purchase transaction might be found to have affected market conditions or restrict free trade. The SIC is entitled to reverse the transaction where appropriate.

If market conditions have been affected or there has been a restriction of free trade, the sale/purchase transaction will be deemed to have an illicit object (*objeto ilícito*). It cannot be ratified by the parties, and it may be declared null and void on formal solicitation to a court by either the sellers, the Office of the General Attorney (*Procuraduría General de la República*) upon request of the SIC, or a third party,.

Likewise, third parties may initiate lawsuits if they feel that a merger unduly restricts free competition (ie an unfaithful competition lawsuit (*Demandas de Competencia Desleal*)). The infringers would have to pay damages to the affected parties.

11.3   Split-off

The procedure for split-off is as follows.

(a)   *Split-off plan*

The corporate body of the company must approve the split-off. If the process involves existing companies, their corporate bodies must also give their approval. The split-off plan must include the following information:

- the reasons for the split-off and the conditions under which it will be carried out;
- the names of the companies that will participate;
- where new companies are to be incorporated, the bylaws of the latter;
- a valuation of all assets and liabilities of the beneficiary companies;
- an explanation of the pricing method used, as well as a description of how the shares of the beneficiary companies will be allocated to the partners or shareholders of the company undergoing the split off;
- the options offered to bondholders; and
- special purpose financial statements of the participating companies.

(b)   *Notification*

A split-off notice must be published in a national newspaper and sent to the company's creditors.

Pursuant to commercial regulations, the creditors of the company undergoing a split-off may request additional and sufficient guarantees for the payment of their debts in the 30 days following publication of this notice.

(c) **Execution of public deed**

Once all steps have been completed and the legal representatives of the company have executed the relevant public deed, the assets and liabilities of the company undergoing the split-off will be transferred to the beneficiary companies in their entirety.

12. Liquidation

Voluntary liquidations arise:

- as a result of the expiration of the company's term of duration as specified in the bylaws;
- by virtue of a decision of the partners or shareholders to dissolve and liquidate the company; or
- as a result of an event that constitutes grounds for dissolution of the company pursuant to the code of commerce (this depends on the type of company).

The ability to liquidate the company voluntarily depends on whether the company has sufficient assets to pays its debts; here the liquidation does not require the protection afforded by the mandatory liquidation proceedings. Accordingly, in a voluntary liquidation the focus is on selling corporate assets to pay the company's liabilities. The process is outlined below.

12.1 Notification to third parties

The liquidator must inform the tax administration and creditors of the liquidation by sending a notice to the tax administration and publishing a notice in a national newspaper.

12.2 Inventory of corporate assets

The liquidator must prepare an inventory that is subsequently authorised by the auditor of the company. The inventory must include a detailed list of all assets owned by the company and all its obligations, specifying their preference and payment priority. If the company is under the supervision of the Superintendence of Companies, the inventory must be submitted for its approval. The inventory forms the basis of the liquidation process.

12.3 Approval of final liquidation account

After completing the sale of the assets and paying the company's liabilities, the liquidator must prepare a final liquidation account, together with a report, which is subject to the approval of the equity holders.

12.4 Distribution of the balance of the proceeds

To conclude the liquidation, the liquidator must distribute the balance of the proceeds from the liquidation among the equity holders. The liquidator's final report and the minutes evidencing the distribution must be approved by the shareholders' assembly or a board of partners meeting. These documents must then be registered with the local chamber of commerce where the company is registered.

12.5 Formalisation of liquidation

Finally, the liquidator must file the documents related to the liquidation process, including the approval of the inventory, the final liquidation report and the minutes of the distribution of proceeds to the equity holders before a notary public.

The most important difference between voluntary and mandatory liquidation is that in voluntary liquidations the company's equity holders appoint the liquidator directly and have control of the process.

12.6 Involvement of state authorities

The Superintendence of Companies has the power to approve the inventory and ensure that the rights of all creditors are adequately protected. To this end, the Superintendence of Companies will verify that the liquidator has correctly established the priority of claims owed by the company and the order in which they must be paid. In addition, the Superintendence of Companies will verify that the creditors have access to the necessary information concerning the amount and nature of their claims and can raise objections concerning their own claims or those of other creditors.

Finally, the Superintendence of Companies can change a voluntary liquidation into a mandatory liquidation.

Costa Rica

John Aguilar Jr
Marco Solano Gómez
Aguilar Castillo Love

1. Types of company with limited liability and applicable legislation

The civil and commercial entities that can be incorporated in accordance with the laws of the Republic of Costa Rica are: limited partnerships (*Sociedad en Comandita Simple*), general partnerships (*Sociedad en Nombre Colectivo*),[1] limited liability companies (*Sociedad de Responsabilidad Limitada*) and corporations (*Sociedad Anónima*). The most popular and widely used are corporations and limited liability companies (from now on referred to as 'entities'). Both have limited liability which means that shareholders (in the case of the corporations) and quotaholders (in the case of the limited liability companies) are only liable for the amount of their investment. To register an entity, the partners must execute a public deed before a notary public, register the deed at the Mercantile Registry[2] and publish a notice of incorporation in the *Official Gazette*. A municipal licence from the local government where the entity is domiciled must also be obtained. The licence involves the payment of a tax during the company's existence.

The legal entities that can be incorporated in Costa Rica are mainly governed by the following legislation:

- the Commercial Code, Decree 3284 of April 30 1964; and
- the Civil Code, Decree 30 of April 19 1886.

2. Incorporation procedure

2.1 Incorporation

(a) Bylaws

(i) Essential clauses

A company's regime and operating system is set out in its articles of incorporation and bylaws (which are submitted as one document). This must contain, at a minimum, the following information:

- place and date of the incorporation agreement;

---

1 Both limited partnerships and general partnerships are recognised as entities where capital is not the central organising factor. The partners' capital contribution does not necessarily entail greater control over the direction of the entity and the partners may be jointly and severally liable for the consequences of the activities of the entity.

2 Information from the Mercantile Registry can be accessed at: www.registronacional.go.cr

- name, nationality, occupation, marital status and domicile of the incorporators;
- the name of the entity;
- its corporate purpose, with an indication of the activity or activities to be carried out;
- its duration;
- the capital stock and how it is to be paid;
- the social domicile of the entity within Costa Rica;
- the structure of the administrative body (board of directors for corporations and manager for a limited liability company), as well as the number of administrators (at least three for a corporation: president, secretary and treasurer and at least one manager for a limited liability company) and their terms of office (it can be for an open term);
- the details of appointment of a resident agent if the agents or representatives of the entity are not domiciled in Costa Rica;
- how profits and losses will be divided among the investors; and
- situations in which the entity will be dissolved.

(ii) *Optional clauses governed by law*

The bylaws are the internal rules governing the company. Although the law sets out specific minimum legal requirements that must be included in the bylaws (as detailed above) the shareholders and quotaholders can also establish other clauses as long as these are not against the law. It is important to include these optional clauses, because if they are set out in the bylaws and registered with the Mercantile Registry they are enforceable not only among the shareholders and quotaholders, but also among any related third parties.

(iii) *Optional clauses governed by the bylaws*

In some cases the regime set out by law can be amended by the bylaws. For example, a limited liability company is a more basic entity, intended to be used by small businesses. However, it can be quite flexible with regard to the weight granted to the will of the quotaholders as set out in the bylaws.

(b) **Execution of public deed and registration**

Corporations and limited liability companies are incorporated by means of a public deed, executed and granted before a notary public. The articles of incorporation are executed by all founding shareholders and quotaholders, present or represented. The deed contains the bylaws, all essential clauses, as well as the covenants and provisions deemed appropriate, provided they are not against law or the principles governing the entity.

In order to legally exist, the public deed must be registered with the Mercantile Registry; no de facto corporation or limited liability company is legally acknowledged or recognised. Once the registration process is complete at the Mercantile Registry, a corporate identification number (or *Cédula Jurídica*) will be assigned to the entity, which will serve to identify it for all legal purposes.

(c) **Tax identification number**

Once the corporation or limited liability company has been registered with the Mercantile Registry, it must register with the tax authority (*Dirección General de Tributación Directa*[3]) before it can start trading. The corporation or limited liability company is identified by the corporate identification number issued by the Mercantile Registry for all tax-related purposes.

(d) **Corporate books**

The tax authority is also in charge of the legalisation of the books for both corporations and limited liability companies. These are bound books that are used to record both corporate minutes and accounting records.

There are books for:

- a journal (*Diario*);
- inventory and balances (*Inventarios y Balances*);
- accounts (*Mayor*);
- the minutes of general meetings (*Actas de Asamblea General*);
- registered shares or quotas record (*Registro de Accionistas*);
- the minutes of the board of directors (*Actas de Junta Directiva*). This is only used for corporations.

(e) **Municipal registration, local taxes and other levies**

A municipal permit (*Patente*) is necessary before the entity can start to operate. An application must be submitted to the entity's local municipality (the local city council). The permit analyses the entity's activity and determines whether it conforms to urban planning and municipal regulations. If the entity owns any real estate, municipal taxes will be charged based on the land value. Taxes for land-related services will also be charged, usually on a quarterly basis.

Due to municipal autonomy, the forms and requirements to obtain a licence may vary due to differences in their legislation and administrative dispositions. Nonetheless it is common for the municipalities to ask for:

- an incumbency certificate showing who represents or acts on behalf of the entity and that it is in good standing;
- a copy of the sanitary operation certificate[4] (*Permiso Sanitario de Funcionamiento*) approved by the Ministry of Health, where applicable, pursuant to the granting of such a certificate;
- employees' risk insurance policy and the receipt of payment, if applicable.
- a use-of-land certificate (*Certificado de Uso de Suelo*), pursuant to Article 28 of the Urban Planning and Municipal Code, granted by the same municipality; and
- proof that the applicant and owner of the property have paid all municipal taxes owed to date – usually the respective certifications are requested.

---

3   Information from the Tax Authority can be accessed at http://dgt.hacienda.go.cr
4   The permit analyses the health-related issues associated with the activity and its compliance with risk-mitigating procedures.

(f) Employment-related matters

The entity must:

- register with the social security system (*Caja Costarricense de Seguro Social*);
- take out an insurance policy to cover risks deriving from occupational accidents and illnesses;
- register employees with the social security system; and
- cover all social charges.[5]

3. Administration

3.1 Corporations

In corporations, there must be a minimum of two founding partners (after registration, the number of shareholders can be reduced to a sole partner by the assignment of shares). There are no minimum capital requirements, but at least 25% of the subscribed capital must be paid on formation.

Shares are indivisible but must be nominative and transferable by nominative

---

5   Social charges currently add up to approximately 27% of monthly gross salaries, distributed as indicated:

Concept:	Employer's contribution to *Banco Popular*.
Amount:	0.25% of the monthly gross salaries.
Legal reference:	Art 5 of the Organic Law of the Popular and Community Development Bank.

Concept:	Employer's contribution to *Asignaciones Familiares*.
Amount:	5% of the monthly gross salaries.
Legal reference:	Art 15 of the Social Development and Family Aid Program Law

Concept:	Employer's contribution to the *Instituto Nacional de Aprendizaje* (INA).
Amount:	1.50% of the monthly gross salaries.
Legal reference:	Art 15 of the Organic Law of the National Learning Institute.

Concept:	Employer's contribution the *Instituto Mixto de Ayuda Social* (IMAS).
Amount:	0.50% of the monthly gross salaries.
Legal reference:	Art 14 of the Establishment Law from Mixed Social Aid Institute.

Concept:	Employer's contribution to the Capitalisation Labour Fund.
Amount:	3% of the monthly gross salaries.
Legal reference:	Art 3 of the Worker Protection Law.

Concept:	Employer's contribution to the Obligatory Complementary Pension Fund.
Amounts:	0.25% of the monthly gross salaries that were assigned to the Popular and Community Development Bank; 0.50% of the monthly gross salaries that were assigned to the National Learning Institute and 1% of the monthly gross salaries that were paid for premium payment of the Insurance Policy of Labour Risks.
Legal reference:	Art 8 of the Worker Protection Law.

Concept:	Premium Payment for the Insurance Policy of Labour Risk
Amount:	1% of the monthly gross salaries.
Legal reference:	Art 208 of the Labour Code.

Concept:	Employer's contribution to the *Caja Costarricense de Seguro Social* (CCSS) regarding illness and maternity.
Amount:	9.25% of the monthly gross salaries.
Legal reference:	Art 62 of the Social Security Bylaws.

Concept:	Employer's contribution to the Handicapped, Elder and Death Regime (CCSS).
Amount:	4.75% of the monthly gross salaries.
Legal reference:	Art 33 of the Handicapped, Elder and Death Regime Bylaws.

endorsement. The nominative endorsement has to be inserted on the titles or certificates of shares, and annotated in the shareholders registry book. Ownership is evidenced by the existence of the titles or certificates of shares and by the annotation in the shareholders registry book. The express consent of all the shareholders is not required for transfers to third parties and neither is the express consent of the board of directors. However, the bylaws can provide that the transfers must be approved by the board of directors or that a reasonable right of first priority exists for the shareholders to acquire the shares. The restriction must be inserted in the text of the titles or certificates of shares. These must contain:

- the name of the company, domicile, and duration;
- the date of the incorporation deed, the name of the notary authorising it, and other information regarding its registration in the Mercantile Registry;
- the name of the shareholders;
- the amount of social capital authorised or paid and the total number and the nominal value of shares;
- series, number, and type of titles or certificates of shares, indicating the total number of shares covered, if applicable; and
- the signature of the directors as set out in the articles or bylaws.

The shareholders registry book must contain:
- the name, nationality, and domicile of shareholders, as well as the number of shares belonging to them, indicating their number, series, types, and other related aspects;
- share transfers; and
- the liens affecting the shares.

Shareholders may be individuals or entities, foreign or national citizens. Corporations are managed by a board of directors of no less than the following three members: the president (who is usually the managing director with full powers of attorney), the secretary and a treasurer. The members of the board need not be shareholders. Additional members can be appointed depending on the needs and structure of the corporation. The members of the board of directors need not be shareholders. Members may be national or foreign, and are not required to be domiciled in Costa Rica, or present at the moment of the incorporation.

A controller must also be appointed by the shareholders. The controller will report on yearly balance sheets and will regulate and review the activity of the board of directors. Unless indicated otherwise, the controller's appointment will be for one year. More than one controller can be appointed, but they cannot hold any other position in the corporation or be a spouse or blood relative of a member of the board of directors.

A resident attorney or agent will be necessary if no agent or representative of the company resides in Costa Rica. He will serve as a local representative of the corporation and must have the facilities to deal with any communication addressed to the corporation.

3.2 Limited liability companies

These have many of the same attributes as corporations.

The social capital has to be represented by nominative quotas. As a contract, the assignment implies the express acceptance of the assignor and the assignee, and it must be inserted in the corporate books, or be notarised. Ownership is evidenced by the quotaholders registry book. The express consent of all the quotaholders is legally required for any transfer to third parties.

The partners must hold a general ordinary meeting at least once a year, within the three months following the closing of the fiscal year, to appoint managers (when necessary), discuss the balance sheet and address any issues for the proper operation of the entity. The manager will call the meeting with at least eight days' notice. No minimum quorum exists.

The basic difference is that limited liability companies are managed by one or more individual managers, who need not be members and who have either general powers of attorney or administrative powers of attorney. A limited liability company does not require a controller, but it can create this position by including it in the articles of incorporation and/or bylaws.

Unlike a corporation, the limited liability company cannot issue commercial paper or bonds; it must therefore rely only on self-finance or banking facilities for credit alternatives. This limitation is compensated by the flexibility of its structure, which allows it to be more freely arranged by its members given that there are no shareholders.

The limited liability company is intended for smaller enterprises, usually a family business or closely held operations. Because the Internal Revenue Service of the United States sees it as a pass-through entity, its use as a business vehicle has not declined.

4. Company tax

Costa Rica only taxes income generated within the national territory. All entities with a permanent establishment in the country are subject to income tax. Corporations and limited liability companies are currently (2009) taxed at 30% for net income over a minimum amount that is set annually by the tax authority (with the fiscal year running from October 1 to September 30).

Remittance tax is a withholding tax on income sourced in Costa Rica that will be remitted to a foreign country. Tax rates vary depending on profit distributions, royalties and services, salaries, etc. Only interest payments to foreign companies, financial entities and banks recognised by the Central Bank of Costa Rica are exempt from this tax.

Subsidiaries of foreign companies may deduct as expenses (up to a 10% of gross sales) the payments to their parent company for technical and financial assistance, patents, trademarks, etc. Capital gains are excluded from gross income. Distributions to owners of a Costa Rican entity are excluded, although they may be subject to a tax on remittance abroad. Taxpaying entities may carry forward up to three years of operating losses for most activities and up to five years for agricultural activities.

A sales tax of 13% applies to all imports and sales of goods, and to all levels of the supply chain. Additionally, some imported goods may be subject to a selective consumption tax. Finally, entities wishing to operate in Costa Rica must pay an active-specific licence tax to the local municipality.

5. Dissolution and liquidation

5.1 Dissolution

Dissolution will occur by operation of law when:

- the duration of the entity has expired;
- the entity cannot achieve its corporate purpose;
- 50% of the social capital has been lost, unless the shareholders reinvest or agree to its reduction; and
- the shareholders agree.

Except for the expiration of the duration, all other grounds must be filed with the Mercantile Registry, stating the reasons for the dissolution. A notice must be published in the *Official Gazette*. Any affected party can object to the dissolution within 30 days.

5.2 Liquidation

Once the entity has been dissolved, it will enter into a liquidation process that will be headed by one or more liquidators, who will manage and administer the entity. An inventory of all assets must be made by the entity administrators and everything (including the corporate books) must be passed on to the liquidators.

The liquidators will be in charge of:

- winding up the social operations that might have been pending at the time of the dissolution;
- requesting payment of all debts owed to the entity and comply with all entity obligations;
- selling the assets;
- preparing the final balance statement and submitting this to the investors for review and approval; and
- distributing any outstanding money among the investors.

6. Branches

According to Article 226 of the Commercial Code, the creation of a branch will necessarily imply the designation and appointment of a representative with full powers according to Costa Rican law. A branch has no independent legal status; it is just an extension of the foreign parent company.

The power of attorney[6] must set out:

---

6   Costa Rican law distinguishes between three basic types of powers of attorney: special, general and universal, all of which may be limited in kind, time and/or amount. They are summarised as follows:
    • **Full universal power of attorney**: This allows purchase, sale, mortgage, etc of any goods that the corporation may have. It also empowers to sign cheques, pay invoices, contract with suppliers, etc. It
continued overleaf

- the business purpose of the branch and the capital assigned;
- the purpose, capital, names of officers, board members and duration of the foreign entity;
- a declaration that the representatives and the branch submit to the laws and courts of Costa Rica with respect to acts or contracts that they enter into or that are to be executed in the country, and that they renounce the protection of the laws of their domicile; and
- evidence that the grantor of the power has sufficient authority to make the grant is mandatory.

---

can be limited, both in the type of acts that are permitted and prohibited, as well as in amount of the acts or contracts.

- **General power of attorney:** This is solely intended to be used for administrative purposes, such as contracting of personnel for business purposes, signing invoices and, in general, any other document that is strictly related to the company's scope of activity. It can be also limited in the number of times it can be used.
- **Special power of attorney:** This is for a specific act that must be clearly defined in the document of empowerment. It entitles the representative to execute one or more specific acts, whether of administration or disposition. One special characteristic of this power of attorney is that, in contrast with the two previously explained, it does not need to be recorded in the Mercantile Section of the Public Registry.

Czech Republic

Vojtech Triska
Triska & Zak

1. Types of company with limited liability and applicable legislation

Two types of company with limited liability are recognised under Czech law: the limited liability company (SRO) and the joint stock company (AS). There is no real economic difference between the two in terms of either members/shareholders and their rights and obligations, or the kinds of activity that they may carry out. However, certain kinds of business may be carried out by joint stock companies only (eg banking business, insurance business). This is because a stricter regulatory regime applies to joint stock companies, in particular as regards the convening of general meetings and the adoption of resolutions, and the obligatory formation of a supervisory board and a board of directors. The regime governing limited liability companies is more flexible: more issues may be regulated by the memorandum of association and the overall operating costs are lower than those for a joint stock company.

The members/shareholders of both types of company are bound to contribute to the registered capital. The minimum registered capital of a limited liability company is 10 times lower than that of a joint stock company. However, one advantage of joint stock companies is that it is generally easier to transfer shares, as shares must be issued in the form of securities and certificated bearer shares are still permitted. In contrast, the members of a limited liability company are publicly registered in the Commercial Register, no securities are issued, and the transfer of shares requires a special form and (usually) an agreement of the general meeting; the memorandum of association may restrict share transfers to third parties even further.

Overall, most companies in the Czech Republic, both existing and newly established (including those established/owned by foreign investors), take the form of a limited liability company.

Both joint stock companies and limited liability companies are regulated by the Commercial Code (513/1991 Sb, as amended).

2. Incorporation procedure

The process of setting up a new company begins with its foundation – that is, with the execution of a contract among the founders in the form of a notarial deed. Upon execution of this deed, the founders can start to fulfil the obligations necessary to incorporate the company, which comes into being on the date it is entered in the Commercial Register.

2.1 Proceedings prior to incorporation

The first step is the adoption of the memorandum of association (the deed of association) – or, where the company is founded by a sole member, the founder's deed – in the form of a notarial deed.

(a) Name registration

The corporate name is the name under which the company is recorded in the Commercial Register. The name must not be capable of creating confusion with the commercial name of another enterprise, and must not be misleading.

There is no separate procedure for registration of the corporate name, which is registered with the Commercial Register upon registration of the company. Nevertheless, the name of the company must be determined at the time of its foundation. Therefore, close attention should be paid when deciding on the corporate name: if a court subsequently holds that the name is contrary to law, the company will be refused registration in the Commercial Register. Potential confusion with the names of other companies may be checked online at the website of the Ministry of Justice (where other important information on Czech companies is also publicly available), but some uncertainty still remains.

(b) Capital contributions

Both limited liability companies and joint stock companies must have a registered capital to which each member of the company contributes. Contributions may be made in cash or in kind; however, in-kind contributions must be assets with an ascertainable economic value that the company can utilise in its business activities. Contributions in the form of an undertaking to perform work or provide services are prohibited.

In-kind contributions must be provided before the amount of registered capital is entered in the Commercial Register. The value of an in-kind contribution must be stated in the memorandum of association or the founder's deed, based on an opinion drawn up by a court-appointed expert who is independent of the company.

Before filing a petition for the entry of a company in the Commercial Register, the full issue premium and at least 30% of each contribution and the full value of in-kind contributions must be paid in. Cash contributions must be paid into a special account opened with a bank.

In the case of limited liability companies, the total paid-in contributions and the value of in-kind contributions must amount to at least Kr100,000 (approximately €3,800) before a petition for registration of the company in the Commercial Register is filed. Where the limited liability company is established by a single founder, it may be registered in the Commercial Register only once its registered capital has been fully paid in.

(c) Declaration of foreign investment

Such a declaration is not applicable in the Czech Republic.

(d) Tax number for foreign partners/directors

This is not applicable in the Czech Republic, but see section 2.2(c) below.

(e) **Trade licences**

If the business activities to be pursued by the company are regulated by a Trade Licensing Act or other legislation, the company must obtain the relevant trade licence before filing the petition for registration in the Commercial Register. The trade licence is obtained from the Trade Licensing Office (or another authority); the conditions for grant depend on the proposed business activities (eg the need for special education or experience for the responsible business representative for certain business activities).

(f) **The use of premises**

The company must provide documentary evidence of its legal right to use the premises proposed as the seat of the company or its place of business. Such documentation (eg written consent of the premises owner or a lease contract) must be attached to the petition for entry in the Commercial Register.

2.2 Incorporation

A limited liability company is founded upon execution of the memorandum of association if the company is formed by two or more founders, or of the founder's deed where the company is formed by a sole founder. Bylaws are not obligatory for limited liability companies.

(a) **Bylaws**

(i) *Essential clauses*

Limited liability company: The memorandum of association must contain the following information, at a minimum:

- the corporate name of the company;
- the seat of the company;
- identification of the company's members – in the case of a legal entity, its commercial name and seat, and in the case of an individual, his full name and home address;
- its corporate purpose;
- the amount of registered capital and the amount of each member's contribution, including the method and timeframes for payment;
- the names and addresses of the company's first directors and the method by which they will act in the name of the company;
- the names and addresses of the members of the first supervisory board, if any (the establishment of a supervisory board is not obligatory for limited liability companies); and
- the determination of the manager of the contributions.

Joint stock company: The bylaws must contain the following information, at a minimum:

- the corporate name and seat of the company;
- its corporate purpose;

- the amount of its registered capital and the method for paying the issue price of shares;
- the number and nominal value of shares, their form and whether they are registered or bearer, together with the number of registered shares and bearer shares;
- the number of votes attaching to one share, the method of voting at general meetings and, where the company will issue shares of different nominal values, the number of votes attaching to each share of a particular nominal value;
- the procedure for convening the general meeting, its powers and the rules governing the adoption of resolutions;
- the number of members of the board of directors, the supervisory board and any other bodies of the company, their tenure, their powers and the rules governing the adoption of decisions;
- the method for creating a reserve fund and the level at which it must be maintained, together with the method for topping it up;
- the method for distributing profits and compensating losses;
- the consequences of breach of the duty to pay for subscribed shares on time;
- the method of increasing or reducing the registered capital (in particular, the possibility to reduce the registered capital by withdrawing shares from circulation on the basis of drawing lots); and
- the procedure for supplementing and altering the bylaws.

(ii)   *Clauses not foreseen by law; optional clauses governed by law*
The memorandum of association/bylaws may regulate any other issue that is not regulated by law or that the law allows to be regulated in another manner. Such modifications are more usual in limited liability companies where the conditions for share transfers are often modified or directors' powers limited in favour of the general meeting. A higher quorum for adopting resolutions of the general meeting is also common in limited liability companies.

The bylaws of joint stock companies may also regulate issues such as:
- a higher quorum for the adoption of resolutions by the general meeting;
- restrictions on the transfer of shares;
- conditions under which company employees may acquire shares of the company under advantageous terms;
- the issue of priority shares; and
- the issue of convertible or preferable bonds (debentures).

(b)   ***Execution of public deed***
The memorandum of association must be adopted in the form of a notarial deed and signed by all founders. A representative may sign on behalf of a founder, but in such case a specific power of attorney with an authenticated signature is required. Where a joint stock company is founded by an initial public offering of shares, a constituent general meeting must be held to approve the foundation of the company.

(c)   *Tax identification number*

All companies must register for tax purposes with the appropriate tax office within 30 days of registration in the Commercial Register. The tax number consists of the company's identification number received on the day of incorporation, together with the prefix 'CZ'.

(d)   *Payment of indirect taxes*

The foundation of companies and cash contributions to the capital are generally not subject to tax; however, a real-estate transfer tax may be levied in certain cases where real estate is contributed.

The following fees must be paid when setting up a Czech company:

- Notary fees – these are based primarily on the amount of the registered capital, starting at around Kr4,000 (approximately €150) for a limited liability company with a registered capital of Kr200,000 and around Kr25,000 (approximately €1,000) for a joint stock company with a registered capital of Kr2 million.
- Court fees – the fee for registering a company in the Commercial Register is Kr5,000 (approximately €200).
- Administrative fees for trade licences – a fee of Kr1,000 (approximately €40) is levied for the issue of a standard trade licence, although higher fees are levied for certain types of trade licence.
- Other costs (eg for translation, verification) – these usually do not exceed a couple of hundred euros.

(e)   *Registration with the Commercial Registry*

A company officially comes into being on the date it is registered in the Commercial Register by a regional court. The petition for registration in the Commercial Register must be filed with the court within 90 days of the company's foundation or of the date on which a trade or similar business licence is issued.

The petition must be filed on a specific form and signed by all directors of the company. The information to be entered in the Commercial Register must be proved in the manner specified by law and the required documentation must be attached to the petition (eg the memorandum of association, the bylaws, the trade licence, documentary proof of legal title to the premises where the company will have its seat, the sample signatures of the directors, and a statement confirming that the directors/members of the supervisory board meet all legal requirements for office).

(f)   *Legalisation of official books*

No legalisation is required under Czech law.

(g)   *Declaration of start date and other tax declarations*

The company may commence business activities as of the date on which it is registered in the Commercial Register.

The company must register for corporate income tax within 30 days of incorporation, and it must register for other taxes once the conditions for such taxation are met.

3. **Number of partners**

A limited liability company can be formed by one or more natural or legal persons; the maximum number of members is 50. All members are entered in the Commercial Register. An individual may be the sole member of up to three limited liability companies. A single-member limited liability company may not be the sole founder or sole member of another limited liability company.

A joint stock company may be founded by only one person where the founder is a legal entity, or by two or more natural and legal persons. An individual may become the sole shareholder of the company after its incorporation (eg by purchasing or otherwise acquiring all shares of the company). The sole shareholder of a joint stock company must be recorded in the Commercial Register.

4. **Corporate name – limitations**

See section 2.1(a) above.

5. **Domicile**

The seat (a city at least) of the company must be stated in the memorandum of association/bylaws. The petition for registration in the Commercial Register must be accompanied by documentary proof of legal title to the premises where the company will have its seat.

Relocation of the corporate seat from the Czech Republic to a foreign country is admissible under terms laid down in EU law or where an international treaty to which the Czech Republic is a signatory so provides.

6. **Corporate purpose**

The corporate purpose of the company must be stated in the memorandum of association/bylaws. The corporate purpose may be changed by decision of the general meeting in the same way that the memorandum of association/bylaws may be changed.

Both limited liability companies and joint stock companies can be set up for purposes other than carrying on business activities.

If the business activity is regulated by a Trade Licensing Act, the company must obtain the relevant trade licence before it is registered in the Commercial Register.

7. **Capital stock**

7.1 **Minimum capital requirement**

A limited liability company must have a minimum registered capital of Kr200,000 (approximately €7,500). Each member of the company must contribute to the registered capital. The minimum amount of a member's contribution is Kr20,000 (approximately €750). The contributions of individual members may be established at different amounts, in multiples of thousands. The aggregate of all contributions to the registered capital must be equal to the registered capital of the company.

A joint stock company must create its registered capital. Where a company intends to offer its shares to the public, the registered capital must amount to at least

Kr20 million (approximately €800,000). The registered capital of a joint stock company which does not intend to offer its shares to the public must be at least Kr2 million (approximately €80,000).

7.2 Nature of contributions
See section 2.1(b) above.

7.3 Partial payments
Before filing a petition for registration in the Commercial Register, the full issue premium and at least 30% of each contribution, together with the value of all in-kind contributions, must be paid in. The total paid-in contributions and the value of in-kind contributions must amount to at least Kr100,000 (approximately €4,000) in the case of a limited liability company Where a limited liability company is established by a single founder, it may be entered in the Commercial Register only once its registered capital has been fully paid.

Each member of the company must pay his contribution under the terms and within the timeframe specified in the memorandum of association, but no later than five years (in the case of a limited liability company) or one year (in the case of a joint stock company) after the company's incorporation.

When all business shares in a limited liability company fall into the possession of a single member, this member must pay in all contributions within three months of the concentration.

7.4 Representation of shares
A share in a joint stock company is a security to which the rights of the shareholder are attached. The shares may be issued either as certificated shares (ie in physical form) or as uncertified shares (ie book-entry shares). Shares may be issued as registered shares (ie registered in the shareholder's name) or as bearer shares.

Each member of a limited liability company can have only one share; however, this may change over time. The share may not take the form of a security.

7.5 Transfer of shares

(a) Restrictions
Unless the memorandum of association provides otherwise, a member of a limited liability company may, with the approval of the general meeting, transfer his share to another member. Where the memorandum of association so allows, a member may transfer his business share to a third party. The memorandum of association may make such a transfer conditional on the approval of the general meeting.

Where a limited liability company has one member, the business share is always transferable to third parties.

The bylaws of a joint stock company may restrict, but cannot exclude altogether, the transfer of registered shares. If the conditions laid down in the bylaws are not fulfilled, a contract for the transfer of shares is void, unless the acquirer acted in good faith. Where the transfer of shares is conditional on the approval of the corporate body, the contract does not take effect until the corporate body has approved it. The bylaws may also specify the conditions under which the corporate body will approve or deny the transfer.

The transferability of bearer shares is unrestricted.

Other restrictions apply to a joint stock company's acquisition of its own shares or the acquisition of the shares of a parent or subsidiary.

(b)   *Formalities*

In the case of limited liability companies, business shares may be transferred on the basis of a written contract. If the acquirer is not a member of the company, he must state in the contract that he accedes to the memorandum of association and, where appropriate, the statutes. The signatures to the contract must be officially authenticated. The change in members must be recorded in the list of company members held by the company and in the Commercial Register; however, such registration has no impact on the validity of the transfer.

In the case of joint stock companies, certified registered shares are transferable by endorsement and delivery. The endorsement must state the commercial name or designation and the seat of the legal entity to which, or the name and home address of the individual to whom, the shares are transferred, and the date of the transfer.

A (certificated) bearer share is transferred on being physically handed over, unless the contract states otherwise. No special contractual form is required; however, in the case of uncertified bearer shares the book-entry rules may apply.

8.   Equity

8.1   Equity–capital ratio

The board of directors of a joint stock company must convene a general meeting without undue delay where it determines that settlement of a loss (as shown in any of the company's financial statements) from the company's disposable funds would still leave an outstanding amount representing half of the company's registered capital, or where this fact may be anticipated taking into account all the circumstances, or if the board establishes that the company has become insolvent. In such case the board of directors will recommend that the general meeting wind up the company or adopt other measures as appropriate.

A company may not distribute profits or other own resources among the shareholders when its equity capital, as shown in the ordinary financial statements, is (or, following the distribution of profits, would be) less than the amount of the registered capital.

Similar rules apply to limited liability companies.

8.2   Convertible bonds

Where the bylaws so allow, a joint stock company may, on the basis of a resolution of the general meeting, issue bonds (debentures) that entitle the holder to exchange them for shares in the company, provided that the general meeting decides at the same time conditionally to increase the company's registered capital. The decision of the general meeting must be passed by two-thirds of the shareholders in attendance (unless the bylaws require a higher majority) and must specify:

- the nominal value of the bonds;
- the determination of the yield per bond;
- the number of bonds;
- the place and time limit for exercising the right derived from a convertible bond;
- the class, type, form, nominal value and number of shares that can be exchanged or subscribed for one bond; and
- the issue price of the bonds.

9. Administration

The mandatory bodies of a joint stock company are the general meeting, the board of directors and the supervisory board.

The mandatory bodies of a limited liability company are the general meeting and one or more directors.

9.1 General meeting of members/shareholders

The general meeting of a company's members/shareholders is the supreme body of the company. The members/shareholders may participate in the general meeting either in person or through a representative holding a written power of attorney. A shareholder may not be represented by a member of the board of directors or supervisory board. A general meeting must be held at least once a year, no later than six months from the last day of the accounting period (fiscal year).

The general meeting of a limited liability company may reserve the right to decide on any other matters falling within the competence of other bodies of the company. In contrast, the general meeting of a joint stock company may not decide on matters that are not within its competence under either the law or the bylaws.

(a) Quorum requirements

(i) Attendance

In the case of limited liability companies, there is a quorum when members holding at least half of the votes are in attendance, unless the memorandum of association requires a higher quorum.

Company members may also take decisions outside the general meeting. In such circumstances, a person who is otherwise authorised to convene the general meeting submits a draft resolution to the members with a request that they submit their written comments within a fixed period. A majority is determined on the basis of the overall number of votes available to all members. The member of the company who does not execute the resolution is considered not to agree with the resolution.

In the case of joint stock companies, there is a quorum when shareholders representing at least 30% of the registered capital are in attendance, unless the bylaws require a higher number of votes. If a general meeting falls short of a quorum, the board of directors will convene a substitute general meeting with the same agenda; this meeting will constitute a quorum irrespective of attendance.

(ii)   *Voting*

The general meeting passes resolutions by majority vote of the attending shareholders, unless the Commercial Code or memorandum of association/bylaws requires a higher majority.

Such a higher majority might include:

- two-thirds of the attending shareholders (eg changes to the bylaws, liquidation or an increase or reduction in registered capital, in the case of a joint stock company);
- two-thirds of all members (eg some changes to the memorandum of association, liquidation or an increase or reduction in the registered capital, in the case of a limited liability company);
- three-quarters of the attending shareholders (eg merger, demerger (division), approval of a controlling agreement, profit transfer agreement or an increase in registered capital by in-kind contributions);
- 90% of all shareholders/members (certain types of transformation); or
- a majority of all members of a limited liability company (certain changes to the memorandum of association).

(b)   **Challenging resolutions**

Any company member/shareholder and any executive officer, liquidator, bankruptcy trustee, composition administrator or member of the supervisory board may petition the competent court to nullify a resolution of the general meeting, where such resolution contravenes the statutory provisions, the memorandum of association or the bylaws.

9.2   Administrative body

(a)   *Different systems of administration*

The statutory body of a limited liability company is one or more executive officers (directors) appointed by the general meeting from among the company's members or other individuals. Each executive officer has the right to act independently in the name of the company, unless the memorandum of association or the statutes provide otherwise. An executive officer's authority to act in the name of the company may be restricted only by the memorandum of association, the statutes or a general meeting. However, such restrictions are ineffective against third parties.

The statutory body of a joint stock company is the board of directors, which manages the company's activities and acts in its name. It takes decisions on all company matters unless they fall within the powers of the general meeting or the supervisory board. Unless the bylaws provide otherwise, any member of the board of directors may act in the name of the company in relation to third parties. The bylaws, decisions of the general meeting and supervisory board decisions may restrict the right of the board of directors to act in the company's name. However, such restrictions are ineffective against third parties.

The board of directors must have at least three members (unless the company has a sole shareholder). The board members elect the chairman from among themselves.

The board takes decisions by majority vote of its members, with the majority being specified in the bylaws, or else by simple majority of all board members, with each member having one vote.

Members of the board of directors are generally elected and recalled by the general meeting. However, the bylaws may provide that the members of the board of directors be elected and recalled by the supervisory board in a manner specified therein.

(b)   ***Term of office, resignation and removal of directors***
The directors of a limited liability company are appointed for an indefinite period, unless the memorandum of association states otherwise.

In joint stock companies, the term of office of each individual member of the board of directors is five years, unless the bylaws provide otherwise.

(c)   ***Directors' liability***
Officers must exercise their powers with due managerial care, and must not disclose confidential information and facts to third parties if such disclosure might be detrimental to the company. In the case of a dispute as to whether a particular officer exercised due managerial care, the burden of proof rests with that officer.

Officers who cause harm to the company by breaching their duties in exercising their powers will be held jointly and severally liable for such harm. A contract between the company and the officer, or a provision in the bylaws, which excludes or limits the liability of an officer is null and void. Officers are liable for harm caused by their execution of a specific instruction of the general meeting if this instruction was contrary to the statutory provisions.

The company is always liable against third parties.

(d)   ***Non-competition***
A director may not:
- carry out business activities in an identical or similar line of business as the company, or enter into business dealings with the company;
- act as an intermediary for other persons in transactions with the company;
- participate in the business activity of another entity as a partner with unlimited liability, or as a person controlling other persons engaged in an identical or similar line of business activity; or
- act as, or be a member of, the statutory body of another legal entity engaged in an identical or similar line of business as the company, except where it is a holding-type group.

The bylaws (memorandum of association) or a resolution of the general meeting may impose further restrictions in this regard.

Where a director violates this prohibition, the company may demand that he surrender to the company any benefit gained from the relevant transaction or transfer the corresponding rights to the company. This does not affect the right of the company to claim damages.

(e)   ***Special duties of secrecy and loyalty***
See section 9.2(c) above.

(f)   ***Civil and criminal liability***
Civil liability is discussed in section 9.2(c).

Only individuals may be held liable for criminal offences. As a rule, all legal acts of the directors and officers against third parties are binding on the company, even where they constitute a criminal offence, as long as they were executed in good faith of the third party. Nevertheless, the company has the right to seek damages from the person responsible.

The Criminal Code recognises a wide range of commercial and business-related crimes, such as the misinterpretation of data on financial results and assets, the breach of duties in relation to the management of assets, the misuse of information in business relations, and fraud.

9.3   Others

(a)   ***Attorneys***
There are generally no limits on the individuals to whom the company can grant power of attorney and the scope of these powers. The law stipulates when this power of attorney must be specific for certain transactions or must be issued in a specific form (eg written, or written with authenticated signatures).

The law also provides for different kinds of representation as follows:

- Procuration authorises the holder to perform all legal acts involved in operating the company, even where a special power of attorney might otherwise be required. Procuration may be granted to individuals only. It does not authorise the procurator to sell or encumber real estate unless this is expressly stated in the procuration;
- A person who has been entrusted to perform a certain activity in the company's operation is authorised to undertake all acts usually involved in the course of such activity; and
- A company is also bound by a transaction entered into by another individual within the company if the counterparty could not have been aware that the individual was not authorised to engage in such transaction.

(b)   ***Controllers and internal auditors***
Except for certain types of business activities (eg bank), there are no provisions on in-house controllers or auditors.

10.   Fiscal year, commencement of operations
The fiscal year can be either a calendar year or, with prior notification to the tax authority, any 12-month period starting on the first day of any month except January.

The company is allowed to carry out activities from the date on which it is registered in the Commercial Register for an indefinite period, unless the bylaws (or memorandum of association) state that the company is to be set up for a specific purpose or a specific period of time.

11. Financial statements

11.1 Company tax

Companies must file a corporate income tax return within three months (or six months if the financial statements are audited or the tax return is prepared by a tax adviser) of the end of the fiscal year.

The corporate income tax rate in the Czech Republic is 21% from January 1 2008, 20% from January 1 2009 and 19% from January 1 2010.

11.2 Annual accounts

(a) Documents

All companies must produce financial statements (a balance sheet and profit and loss statement, together with appendices) by the last day of the fiscal year. The financial statements may also include a cash-flow statement and a statement on changes in equity. Moreover, where an audit is mandatory the company must also prepare, as part of its financial statement, an annual report containing complex, true and balanced information on its activities and its economic situation.

The financial statements (including the audit report, where applicable) are to be approved by the general meeting.

(b) Audit report

Joint stock companies must have their financial statements audited by an external auditor where at least one of the following criteria is met:

- the total assets exceed Kr40 million (approximately €1.5 million);
- the net annual turnover exceeds Kr80 million (approximately €3 million); and
- the average number of employees exceeds 50.

Limited liability companies must have their financial statements audited where at least two of the above criteria are met.

(c) Approval and distribution of profits

The financial statements are to be approved by the general meeting, which also approves the distribution of profits or the manner in which losses will be settled. A company may not distribute profits or other own resources among the shareholders if its equity capital, as shown in the ordinary financial statements, is or will consequently fall below the amount of the registered capital.

Withholding tax at a rate of 15% is levied on dividends distributed by a Czech company to a non-resident company. This rate may be reduced by an applicable double-taxation treaty. If an exemption under the EU Parent-Subsidiary Directive applies, no withholding tax will be levied.

(d)   *Deposit and publication*

The financial statements must be filed with the Commercial Register and are publicly available (including on the internet).

12.   Company reorganisation

Companies with their seat in the Czech Republic may be transformed by:

- merger;
- transfer of business assets to a sole member;
- division (split-off); or
- change of a corporate form.

A merger may be effected through the acquisition of another company (takeover) or through the formation of a new company. In a merger by takeover, one or more companies are wound up (without going into liquidation); they cease to exist and their assets pass to another company. The members/shareholders in the original companies become members/shareholders of the successor, unless the law provides otherwise.

In a merger effected through the formation of a new company, two or more companies are wound up (without going into liquidation); they cease to exist and their assets pass to a newly formed company. Members/shareholders of the merging companies become members/shareholders of the successor company, unless the law provides otherwise.

The assets may also be transferred to a sole member of the company – in such cases the company is wound up (without going into liquidation) and the assets are assumed by one member/shareholder which has its seat in the Czech Republic. The decision must be approved by 90% of all members. Minority shareholders whose membership in the company will cease to exist have the right to appropriate consideration.

Upon division, the company being divided is wound up (without going into liquidation); the company ceases to exist and its assets pass to the successor companies. Members of the company being divided become members of the successor companies, unless the law provides otherwise. A division may be effected by the formation of new companies or by acquisition, or by a combination of the two methods.

In the case of a change in corporate form, the company does not cease to exist and its assets do not pass to a successor; only the company's internal relationships and the legal status of its members change. A company may convert into another corporate form (partnership) or into a cooperative.

13.   Eventual partner separation

A member of a limited liability company who fails to pay his contribution may be expelled from the company by resolution of the general meeting.

A limited liability company may also petition the court to order the expulsion of a company member who has seriously breached his duties even though he was requested to discharge them and was notified in writing of the possibility of expulsion. The filing of this petition is subject to approval by members representing at least half of the registered capital.

A member of a limited liability company may not withdraw from the company upon his own initiative, unless he is the sole member. However, a member may petition the court for termination of his participation if he cannot reasonably be required to remain in the company any longer.

A shareholder owning securities in a particular joint stock company whose total value is equal to at least 90% of the registered capital, and which represent at least 90% of the voting rights, can request the board of directors to convene a general meeting in order to adopt a resolution on the transfer of all outstanding participating securities to him. The resolution must be passed by at least 90% of all shareholders. Minority shareholders whose membership in the company will cease to exist are entitled to appropriate consideration.

14. Dissolution and liquidation

The liquidation of a company is divided into two steps:

- the decision on winding-up; and
- the deletion of the company from the Commercial Register once the company ceases to exist.

A company is wound up:

- upon expiry of the period for which it was established;
- upon achievement of the purpose for which it was established;
- on the date specified in a resolution adopted by the members/shareholders as the date on which the company will be wound up; otherwise, on the date such a resolution is adopted, if the winding-up is connected with going into liquidation;
- on the date specified in a court ruling on the winding-up; otherwise, on the date such a ruling comes into force;
- on the date stated in a resolution adopted by the members/shareholders or the competent corporate body if the company is dissolved due to transformation;
- upon termination of a bankruptcy order following implementation of the distribution plan, or upon cancellation of a bankruptcy order because the bankruptcy estate is insufficient to cover the costs of the bankruptcy proceedings; or
- upon dismissal of a bankruptcy petition due to the company's lack of assets.

The court may rule on the winding-up of a company and its entry into liquidation on the basis of a motion by a state authority, or a party with a legal interest, in the following circumstances:

- if no general meeting has been held for two years, or if statutory bodies whose term of office terminated more than one year ago were not elected in the following year, or if the company undertook no activities in the last two years;

- if the company is no longer authorised to undertake business activities;
- if legal prerequisites for the incorporation of the company are no longer satisfied, or if the company is unable to carry out activities due to irreconcilable differences between the members;
- if the company has breached its duty to create a reserve fund;
- if the company does not carry out business activities through authorised persons;
- if the company has failed to fulfil a duty to divest part of its enterprise or divide as required by the Office for the Protection of Economic Competition pursuant to other statutory provisions.

The company goes into liquidation on the day it is wound up; this fact must be entered in the Commercial Register. The powers of the statutory body to act on behalf of the company pass to the liquidator upon his appointment. The liquidator is appointed by the statutory body unless the law, the bylaws or the memorandum of association stipulate otherwise. If the liquidator is not appointed without undue delay, he will be appointed by the court. The court will also appoint the liquidator if the liquidation is based on a court order.

After completion of all the legal acts necessary to execute the liquidation, the liquidator will draw up a report on the course of the liquidation, which must include a proposal on how to distribute any assets remaining after liquidation among the company's members. Liquidation is completed by:

- distribution of the remaining assets;
- use of the proceeds from the sale of assets to satisfy creditors' claims; or
- creditors' appropriation of certain property in settlement of their claims.

Within 30 days of completion of the liquidation, the liquidator must file a petition for deletion of the company from the Commercial Register. The company ceases to exist as of the day it is deleted from the Commercial Register.

15. Branches

As a branch is merely an organisational component of the company, it has no independent legal status and has no liability separate from the company. A company setting up a branch is liable for all obligations incurred through the operation of that branch.

Denmark

Christian Bredtoft Guldmann
Simon Krogh
Niels Walther-Rasmussen
Kromann Reumert

1. Types of company with limited liability and applicable legislation

Danish company law is, as a theoretical starting point, based on a general principle of freedom of contract (ie the right to incorporate any type of company of the incorporator's choice). This principle applies – to a certain extent – to some types of companies, in particular to partnerships and private limited liability companies (see below). As a practical matter, however, it is not possible to obtain a legal entity with separate legal personality from the shareholders and limited liability for the shareholders without complying with the rather strict and detailed regulation of the establishment, structuring and operation of limited liability companies. Thus, there is a very limited access to incorporate limited liability companies not covered by the acts mentioned below.

The most commonly used corporate forms are two types of limited liability company:

- the public limited liability company (*Aktieselskaber*); and
- the private limited liability company (*Anpartsselskaber*).

This chapter focuses on the above types of company. Other fairly common corporate forms include limited partnerships (*Kommanditselskab*), limited partnership companies (*Kommanditaktieselskab*) and cooperative companies (*Andelsselskaber*). As of October 8 2004, companies have also had the option of forming a European company (*SE-selskab*) on the basis of EU Council Regulation 2157/2001 on the statute for a European company.

The main legislation within Danish company law is the Public Limited Liability Companies Act (Consolidated Act 649 of June 15 2006 as latest amended by Act 510 of June 17 2008) and the Private Limited Liability Companies Act (Consolidated Act 650 of June 15 2006 as latest amended by Act 468 of June 172008).

The Private Companies Act generally provides for a more flexible regulation of private limited liability companies compared to that of public limited liability companies, with respect to, for example, governing structure and protection of share capital. However, the most important features of both types of company (ie separate legal personality, a limitation of liability for shareholders and tax treatment) are generally identical.

Private limited liability companies are primarily used for smaller businesses, and particularly as a way to incorporate personally owned businesses; but they have also been used by large international entities because they are treated differently from public limited liability companies for tax purposes in some foreign jurisdictions (in particular, the United States). In Denmark, a private limited liability company will generally be viewed as a less solid and professional player in a given market compared to a public limited liability company.

2. Incorporation procedure

2.1 Proceedings prior to incorporation

(a) Name registration
See section 4 below.

(b) Capital contributions
The minimum share capital of a public limited liability company is DKK500,000, whereas the minimum share capital of a private limited liability company is DKK125,000. Incorporations may also take place in euros. Further, the Danish Commerce and Companies Agency (DCCA) may, by executive order, allow the share capital to be stated in other currencies.

Shares may be subscribed for by way of cash or in-kind contributions. Where in-kind contributions are made, an auditor must prepare a valuation report on the consideration. Similarly, a valuation report is required if the company is to acquire assets from the promoters, shareholders or others in relation to its formation.

Where the company takes over an existing business, the valuation report must also include an opening balance sheet for the company together with an unqualified auditor's report.

In-kind contributions cannot take the form of obligations to perform work or render services, or claims against the promoters or subscribers (irrespective of whether collateral security is provided for such claims).

(c) Declaration of foreign investment
No requirements with respect to the declaration of foreign investments apply. However, for statistical purposes, the Danish Central Bank (*Danmarks Nationalbank*) may impose a reporting obligation on public limited liability companies and private limited liability companies that handle a significant number of cross-border money transfers.

(d) Tax number for foreign partners/directors
A foreign company that acts as the promoter of a public limited liability company or private limited liability company must provide the DCCA with documentation in the form of a translated transcript from the corresponding regulatory authority of the country in which it is registered. Foreign individuals who act as promoters must submit a copy of their passports to the DCCA.

2.2   Incorporation

(a)   *Articles of association*

(i)   *Essential clauses*

According to Section 4 of the Public Companies Act and Section 5 of the Private Companies Act, the articles of association must include provisions on:

- the name and any secondary names of the company;
- the municipality in Denmark in which the company is to have its registered office;
- the corporate purpose;
- the amount of the nominal share capital;
- the nominal value of the shares and the shareholders' voting rights;
- the number, or the minimum and maximum number, of members of the board of directors and any alternates for such members, as well as their term of office (however, a private limited liability company is not obliged to establish a board of directors – see Section 9.2(a));
- the number, or the maximum and minimum number, of auditors as well as their term of office;
- notices to convene general meetings;
- the business to be transacted at annual general meetings;
- the financial year of the company;
- whether the shares are to be nominative shares or bearer shares; and
- whether the shares are to be non-negotiable instruments.

The articles of association must include any decisions made in respect of:
- special rights conferred on some shares;
- restrictions on the transfer of shares;
- the shareholders' obligation to allow the company or others to redeem their shareholdings in whole or in part;
- the shareholders' right to access the share register;
- a management board of more than three members;
- limitations on the right of the members of the board of directors and the members of the management board to sign for the company;
- electronic participation in general meetings; or
- use of electronic documents and email instead of paper-based documents in communications between the company and the shareholders (electronic communication).

(ii)   *Clauses not foreseen by law*

Danish company law is largely based on principles of freedom, which allows the shareholders to organise their company as they see fit. Consequently, the shareholders can include clauses relating to other issues than those listed above in the articles of association, provided that these comply with the Public Limited Liability Companies Act or the Private Limited Liability Companies Act, as applicable. In addition to the relatively detailed requirements for the modeling of the articles of association, it should be noted that the articles of association are disclosed to the public due to the filing with the DCCA. Thus, it is fairly common to apply standard terms to the articles of association and regulate the relationship between the shareholders in a more detailed and tailor-mode shareholders' agreement, which is not subject to a public disclosure requirement.

(iii)   Optional clauses governed by law

The company legislation imposes some limitations on the provisions that shareholders can include in the articles of association and the amendments that they can make to clauses stipulated in the Public Limited Liability Companies Act and the Private Limited Liability Companies Act. Generally, the shareholders of private limited liability companies are subject to more flexible rules on which provisions they can include in the articles of association than the shareholders of public limited liability companies.

(b)   Execution of public deed

Public limited liability companies and private limited liability companies acquire separate legal personality upon registration of the various company documents with the DCCA, including:

- the memorandum of association;
- the articles of association;
- the minutes of the statutory general meeting; and
- evidence that the entire share capital, including any premium, has been paid in full.

The company cannot be registered unless the nominal value of the shares, in addition to any premiums, has been fully paid up.

The board of directors of a public limited liability company must deliver the company's particulars for registration within six months of the date of the memorandum of association. For private limited liability companies, an eight-week time limit applies.

The memorandum of association is a private agreement and no notary intervention is required in order for the memorandum of association to be an enforceable instrument.

(c)   Tax number for the company

The tax number of a public limited liability company or a private limited liability company is generally the same as the company registration number. However, companies that keep separate accounts for individual divisions can apply for separate tax numbers for each of their divisions. In such cases, each division must prepare a monthly value added tax (VAT) return.

(d)   Indirect taxes, incorporation fees and other levies

To a large extent, the Danish tax regime relies on direct, rather than indirect, taxes (save for VAT).

The incorporation of a public limited liability company or a private limited liability company does not trigger any fee or indirect tax. However, if a company is incorporated by means of in-kind contributions, any capital gain by the promoters may be subject to taxation. Registration fees may also be payable in certain cases (eg real estate, where a registration fee of DKK1,400 is charged).

(e) **Registration with the Mercantile Registry**
Public limited liability companies and private limited liability companies are only required to register with the DCCA (see section 2.2(b)).

(f) **Legalisation of official books**
Public limited liability companies and private limited liability companies are required to keep the following books:

- a shareholder register;
- an audit report book (to be kept by the accountant);
- a register of shareholders holding at least 5% of the share capital (public limited liability companies only);
- a minute book of board meetings;
- a minute book of the general meeting; and
- a register of the shareholdings of board members and managers in the company and other group companies (public limited liability companies only).

None of these books are subject to legislation requirements.

Please note that it is possible (with a few exceptions) to carry out registrations electronically on the DCCA's website (www.webreg.dk). Therefore, it is possible to establish and register private limited liability companies and public limited liability companies (using standard documentation) within two or three hours.

(g) **Declaration of start date and other tax declarations**
In addition to filing the company documents mentioned in section 2.2(b) above, the company must file a registration form with the DCCA.

Any public limited liability company or private limited liability company that intends to conduct business for profit must, prior to doing so, additionally file a registration form with the Central Customs and Tax Administration. To the extent relevant, this must include information on:

- VAT registration;
- labour market contribution;
- registration for import and/or export from/to non-EU countries;
- pay-as-you-earn tax (the employer is obliged to withhold income tax on behalf of the tax authorities when paying out employee salaries);
- payroll tax;
- registration for mandatory payments to the Labour Market Supplementary Pension Fund; and
- registration of employees.

Further, within certain areas of business (eg the insurance and banking industry, the pharmaceutical industry), a licence must be obtained from the ministry or agency overseeing that particular industry in order to conduct business within the set boundaries of that business.

3. Number of shareholders

There are no requirements with respect to the number of shareholders in a public limited liability company or a private limited liability company. Further, companies with a single shareholder are not subject to special provisions under the Public Limited Liability Companies Act or the Private Limited Liability Companies Act.

4. Corporate name

The name and any secondary names of a public limited liability company or a private limited liability company must be stated in the articles of association.

Public limited liability companies and private limited liability companies have an obligation and an exclusive right to use the words '*aktieselskab*' and '*anpartsselskab*' respectively, or their abbreviations (A/S and ApS), in their corporate names.

The name of a public limited liability company or a private limited liability company must differ clearly from the names of other companies registered with the DCCA (all registered company names can be found at the Central Business Register's website, www.cvr.dk). The name must not include surnames, firm names, specific names of real property, trademarks, logos and so on that do not belong to the company, nor anything that may be confused therewith.

The name of a public limited liability company or a private limited liability company must not be likely to mislead the public. It must not include any specification of undertakings that have no connection with the company's corporate purpose.

5. Corporate domicile

The registered office of a public limited liability company or a private limited liability company must be located in Denmark, and the municipality in which the registered office is located must be stated in the articles of association. The DCCA must be notified of the address of the registered office, including any changes thereto.

The actual management of the company must take place at the registered office. In practice, however, the consequences of non-compliance with this requirement are unclear.

The board of directors can decide to move the registered office within the municipality stated in the articles of association, but any decision to move the registered office to another municipality must be made by the general meeting and approved by the majority required to alter the articles of association (see section 9.1(b)).

6. Corporate purpose

The purpose for which a public limited liability company or a private limited liability company is to conduct its business must be stated in the articles of association. Fairly broad descriptions of the corporate purpose are accepted by the DCCA.

7. Capital stock

7.1 Minimum capital requirements

For a public limited liability company the minimum share capital is DKK500,000 whereas the minimum share capital of a private limited liability company is DKK125,000.

7.2 Nature of contributions

Payment for shares in a public limited liability company may be made either in cash or in kind. The incorporation, or a subsequent increase in share capital, cannot be registered with the DCCA until the subscribed capital (together with any premium) has been paid in full.

In-kind contributions must have a value that can be expressed in monetary terms. Such contributions cannot consist of an obligation to perform work or render services. Claims of promoters or subscribers cannot be contributed, irrespective of whether collateral security is provided for such claims.

If the promoters or others are to contribute assets as consideration for subscribed shares, a valuation report must be attached to the memorandum of association. The valuation report must include:

- a description of each contribution or acquisition;
- details of the valuation procedure utilised;
- a specification of the consideration fixed for the contribution or acquisition; and
- a statement to the effect that the assessed value corresponds with the agreed consideration as a minimum, including both the nominal value of the shares that are to be issued and any additional premium.

If, in connection with incorporation, the company takes over an existing business, the valuation report must also include an opening balance sheet for the company together with an unqualified auditor's report. The opening balance sheet must be prepared in accordance with Denmark's Financial Statements Act.

7.3 Partial payments

The share capital of public limited liability companies and private limited liability companies must be fully paid up at the time of incorporation.

7.4 Representation of shares

The articles of association of a public limited liability company must contain information on whether the shares are to be nominative shares or bearer shares, and whether they are to be non-negotiable instruments. These choices will affect the measures to be observed by a shareholder in order to protect his rights against third parties, and also to determine whether share certificates must be issued. The same requirement does not apply to private limited liability companies.

The board of directors of a public limited liability company or a private limited liability company must keep a register of all shares of the company. Any transfer or pledge of shares must be entered in the share register.

The board of directors of a public limited liability company may choose to issue share certificates, but is not obliged to unless:

- shareholders representing at least 10% of the share capital require the company to do so;
- the shares are negotiable instruments; or
- the shares are bearer shares.

Irrespective of the above, share certificates cannot be issued if the shares are listed on a stock exchange or on an authorised or alternative marketplace.

Further, if there are any restrictions on the transfer of shares of a public limited liability company, or if the shareholders are under an obligation to allow their shares to be redeemed, the share certificates cannot be issued to bearer, and any transfer of shares to bearer will not be binding upon the company.

Share certificates may not be issued until the subscription has been registered by the DCCA. Shares made out to a named holder may be issued only to shareholders recorded in the register of shareholders.

Share certificates cannot be issued to the shareholders of a private limited liability company. The shareholders of a private limited liability company have a right to receive confirmation that their shareholding has been entered in the share register, but such confirmation does not constitute a legal instrument and no rights attach to it.

7.5   Transfer of shares

(a)   Restrictions

As a general rule, shares of a public limited liability company or a private limited liability company are freely transferable. However, the articles of association may impose restrictions on the transfer of nominative shares. The most common restriction in privately held companies is that a transfer requires the consent of the board of directors.

The articles of association can also contain a provision according to which, for example, a right of first refusal in favour of the other shareholders applies when transferring shares.

Further, the articles of association may prescribe that no shareholder can hold shares exceeding a certain amount of the share capital.

Restrictions on the transfer of shares are often included in a shareholders' agreement. The main reason for this is that a shareholders' agreement, as mentioned above, need not be filed with the DCCA. Restrictions on the transfer of shares that are included in a shareholder agreement apply between the parties to the agreement, whereas similar restrictions apply to third parties if they are included in the articles of association.

(b)   Formalities

As a general rule, no formalities apply when transferring shares in public limited liability companies or private limited liability companies, except where restrictions such as those described above apply.

However, for the purchaser to obtain protection against any third-party interest in the transferred shares, an act of security must be observed. When transferring shares in a public limited liability company that are not issued through the Danish Securities Centre or for which share certificates have not been issued, this act of security is observed when either the seller or the purchaser notifies the person responsible for the share register of the transfer.

Since shares in a private limited liability company cannot be issued through the Danish Securities Centre or by means of share certificates, notification of the person responsible for the share register constitutes the relevant act of security when transferring such shares.

When transferring shares in a public limited liability company for which share certificates have been issued, the act of security is observed when the seller is deprived of his right to dispose of the shares, unless the share certificates and the articles of association clearly state that the shares are non-negotiable, in which case notification of the person responsible for the share register is the relevant act of security.

When transferring shares issued through the Danish Securities Centre, the act of security is electronic registration by the Danish Securities Centre.

8. Equity

8.1 Equity–capital ratio
Shares in a public limited liability company or a private limited liability company cannot be subscribed at a price lower than par value.

If a private limited liability company or a public limited liability company's equity at any point corresponds with only half of its share capital, the board of directors must call a general meeting, at which it must account for the company's financial situation and submit proposals on any necessary measures to be taken, including the dissolution of the company.

8.2 Convertible bonds and other debentures
The general meeting of public limited liability companies can decide to issue convertible bonds or other debentures. The decision must include the terms of the loan and potential conversion of the loan into shares in the company. The decision must be adopted in the articles of association.

Further, the general meeting of a public limited liability company can authorise the board of directors to decide on whether to issue convertible bonds or other debentures, provided that authorisation to increase the share capital is granted at the same time. The authorisation must expire after five years, at which point the general meeting is entitled to grant a new authorisation. The authorisation must be limited to convertible debentures amounting to half the share capital and must be adopted in the articles of association.

The Private Limited Liability Companies Act does not contain similar rules on convertible bonds or other debentures. However, it is generally accepted among legal scholars that the legislators did not intend to prevent a private limited liability company from issuing convertible debentures, provided that the rules on increase of the share capital and the other provisions in the Private Limited Liability Companies Act are complied with.

9. Governance

9.1 General meeting

(a) *Quorum requirements*

(i) *Attendance*

The Public Limited Liability Companies Act and the Private Limited Liability Companies Act include no general quorum requirement.

(ii) *Voting*

As a general rule, all business transacted at general meetings shall be determined by a simple majority of votes cast, in the absence of any provision to the contrary in the articles of association or the relevant act.

In order to adopt a resolution to amend a public limited liability company's articles of association, at least two-thirds of the votes cast and not less than two-thirds of the share capital represented at the general meeting and entitled to vote must vote in favour of the resolution. In certain circumstances, in order to protect minority shareholders, a majority of at least 90% of the votes cast and not less than 90% of the share capital represented at the general meeting and entitled to vote is required (eg where the shareholders' right to receive dividends or asset distributions is curtailed to the benefit of third parties). Further, certain decisions that are particularly burdensome or intrusive to individual shareholders require unanimous approval by the shareholders (eg a decision to change the legal rights between shareholders who would otherwise have the same rights).

The qualified-majority rules for private limited liability companies are slightly different. In order to adopt a resolution to amend a private limited liability company's articles of association, a majority of at least two-thirds of the votes cast must vote in its favour. In certain circumstances, the consent of all shareholders is required in order to protect minority shareholders.

(b) *Challenging resolutions*

The general meeting of a public limited liability company or a private limited liability company may not pass resolutions that are clearly likely to confer undue advantages on certain shareholders, or other parties, over other shareholders or over the company.

In such events, shareholders, members of the board of directors and members of the management board may commence legal proceedings. If a resolution passed by the general meeting is contrary either to law or to the articles of association, the court can either declare the resolution null and void and/or award the claimant financial compensation. The same provision applies to private limited liability companies (with the modification that a private limited liability company is not required to have both a board of directors and a management board, as outlined in section 9.2(a) below).

As a general rule, if legal proceedings are not instituted within three months of the passing of the resolution, the resolution is considered to be valid. In the following situations, however, the resolution remains invalid even where legal proceedings are not instituted within three months:

- where the resolution could not lawfully be passed even with the consent of all shareholders;
- where, under the law or the articles of association, all or certain shareholders are required to consent to the resolution and such consent has not been given;
- where the general meeting has not been duly convened or the rules applicable to the notice convening the general meeting have been neglected; or
- where the shareholder who instituted the proceedings after the expiry of the time limit had reasonable grounds for the delay and the court, for this reason and in consideration of the circumstances in general, finds that the application of the time limit would lead to obvious injustice, provided that the proceedings have been instituted no later than 24 months after the resolution was passed.

9.2   Management bodies

(a)   Different governance systems

The management boards of public limited liability companies, consisting of one or more managers, is responsible for the day-to-day business, while the board of directors has the overall responsibility for the company's business as well as a duty to supervise the management board.

A private limited liability company may be managed by a board of directors, a management board or a combination of the two. If the company establishes only one of these bodies, that body shall also perform the duties otherwise incumbent on the other management body according to the Private Limited Liability Companies Act.

No nationality or residence requirements apply to the directors or managers of public limited liability companies or private limited liability companies.

(b)   Term of office, resignation and removal of directors

The board of directors of a public limited liability company must consist of at least three persons elected by the general meeting. A company as such cannot be a member of the board of directors. The majority of the members of the board of directors may not be managers of the company. A member of the management board may not be chairman of the board of directors.

Rules on employee representation on the board of directors apply to public limited liability companies and private limited liability companies that have employed at least 35 employees on average over the most recent three years. Where applicable, the employees can nominate half of the number of board members elected by the general meeting (rounded up if necessary).

The term of the board members elected by the general meeting is determined in the articles of association. However, the term for board members of a public limited liability company cannot exceed four years. Board members may be re-elected.

There are no statutory limitations on the term of the board members of a private limited liability company.

The term of board members in both public limited liability companies and private limited liability companies who are elected after nomination by the employees is four years, irrespective of any provisions in the articles of association.

A board member of a public limited liability or a private limited liability company can choose to resign from the board at any time. Further, the board members can at any time be removed by those who elected them (typically, the general meeting).

(c)   *Directors' liability*

Members of the board of directors of public limited liability companies and private limited liability companies who, in the performance of their duties, act negligently or are guilty of wilful misconduct may be held liable for losses caused by their acts or omissions.

Where the company has suffered a loss, the company has the primary right of action.

The decision to bring an action against board members on behalf of the company is taken at the general meeting. If the general meeting of a public limited liability company decides not to bring an action on behalf of the company, a dissenting minority of 10% of the share capital are entitled to file individual suits on behalf of the company. This rule does not apply to private limited liability companies.

Board members may also be liable where damage is inflicted on shareholders, creditors or any third party by a violation of law or of the articles of association by the board members. In such cases, where only the shareholders have incurred a loss and not the company, the right of action lies with the shareholders, creditors or third parties, respectively.

The acts and omissions of board members are generally assessed under the ordinary negligence standard applicable as defined in case law under Danish law. The board members' liability is individual, and accordingly they cannot be held liable for acts or omissions that occurred before they became board members or for acts or omissions from which they have dissented. The board members who are responsible are jointly and severally liable.

It is still customary for some public limited liability companies to provide the board of directors with a *décharge* (ie a release from liability) at the annual general meeting. Although the shareholders of a private limited liability company are entitled to provide the board of directors with a *décharge*, this is rare. A *décharge* will protect the board members from any claim for damages by the company. However, if the *décharge* has been provided on the basis of false or incomplete information in the annual report, the *décharge* is without any effect. The *décharge* does not prevent shareholders from bringing individual actions against the board members.

(d)   *Non-competition*
The Public Limited Liability Companies Act and the Private Limited Liability Companies Act do not expressly regulate whether board members may engage in activities that compete with or are similar to those of the company they manage, or whether they may serve on the management board or board of directors of competing companies.

However, board members and managers have a general duty of loyalty towards their company, which may restrict their ability to accept such other positions. Board members also have a duty to inform on any management position they hold in other Danish companies, in order to prevent any potential conflict of interest.

Further, the general meeting may dismiss members of the board of directors at its discretion (eg where they have been disloyal to the company).

(e)   *Special duties of non-disclosure and loyalty*
Members of the board of directors of a public limited liability company and of a private limited liability company, and their alternates, are not allowed to pass on or to make unauthorised use of confidential information acquired in the performance of their office or duties.

This duty of confidentiality does not prevent the board of directors and, depending on the matter, the individual board members from seeking advice from an attorney-at-law or other counsel who is subject to a professional confidentiality obligation.

The board members have a duty of loyalty towards the company. This means that board members appointed by a specific shareholder primarily shall act in the interest of the company, and not take the special interests of that shareholder into account if that interest is contrary to the interests of the company.

(f)   *Criminal liability of board members*
Grossly negligent violation of certain provisions of the Public Limited Liability Companies Act or the Private Limited Liability Companies Act may result in a financial penalty. A prison sentence may be imposed on board members in more severe circumstances, if the act or omission can be classified as wilful criminal behaviour under the Criminal Act.

9.3   Others

(a)   *Holders of power of attorney*
Those authorised in the articles of association to sign on behalf of a public limited liability company or a private limited liability company are entitled to grant power of attorney to bind the company, provided that the power of attorney is limited with

respect to duration and the commercial areas in which the holder can act on behalf of the company.

Further, the board of directors can grant procuration according to the Public Limited Liability Companies Act and the Private Limited Liability Companies Act with respect to day-to-day business affairs. Procuration is rarely used outside the financial sector.

(b)   *Internal controllers and auditors*

Danish law does not require or regulate use of internal controllers and internal accountants.

Public limited liability companies and private limited liability companies must appoint a state-authorised chartered accountant or a registered chartered accountant at the annual general meeting. However, companies that have not exceeded two of the following thresholds during the most recent two years can choose not to have the annual report audited:

- balance sheet total of DKK1.5 million;
- net turnover of DKK3 million;
- 12 employees on average.

10.   Financial year, duration, commencement of activities

10.1   Financial year

The first and last day of the financial year of public limited liability companies and private limited liability companies must be set out in the articles of association.

The first financial year of a public limited liability company can be up to 18 months. Thereafter, the financial year must be 12 months. Alteration of the financial year of a public limited liability company requires a decision of the general meeting by the majority required to amend the articles of association. Group companies are required to have identical financial years. If alteration of the financial year becomes necessary due to the establishment of a group structure, a merger or similar, the reorganisation period can be up to 18 months.

Most Danish companies have chosen the calendar year as their financial year.

10.2   Duration

The duration of public limited liability companies and private limited liability companies may be limited, although typically they are established for an indefinite period of time.

10.3   Commencement of activities

A public limited liability company or a private limited liability company does not acquire legal personality until it has been validly incorporated and registered by the DCCA. Public limited liability companies and private limited liability companies can commence activities as of the signing of the memorandum of association and the articles of association. During the period from signing of the memorandum and the articles of association until the statutory general meeting, the promoters and the company under formation are severally liable for any obligations arising out of activities performed on behalf of the company under formation. The company under formation assumes such obligations only if they are stated in the memorandum of association.

A public limited liability company or private limited liability company automatically assumes any obligation that arises during the period between the statutory general meeting and registration of the company by the DCCA. However, often public limited liability companies and private limited liability companies are purchased as shelf companies in order to commence activities immediately.

11. Financial statements

11.1 Company tax

The rate of Danish corporate income tax is currently (2009) 25%. According to the Company Taxation Act (Consolidated Act 1037 of August 24 2007), corporate income tax is to be paid as a tax on account equivalent to 50% of the average corporate income tax for the three preceding fiscal years. The tax on account is to be paid in two equal instalments on March 20 and November 20 in the relevant year.

11.2 Annual accounts

(a) Documents

Danish companies are required to prepare an annual report, in accordance with the Financial Statements Act. The annual report should provide a true and fair view of the company's (or group's) profit or loss, balance sheet, financial position and cash flow.

(b) Audit report

The annual report must be audited by an independent auditor, who must issue a written opinion that is then included in the company's annual report. However, small companies with key figures below certain thresholds are not required to have the annual report audited.

The auditor, if any, is appointed by the shareholders at the general meeting.

(c) Approval and distribution of profits

The shareholders approve the annual report and decide how the profit or loss shall be allocated at the annual general meeting. Distribution of dividends to the shareholders cannot exceed the amount approved by the board of directors.

According to the Personal Income Tax Act (Consolidated Act 959 of September 19 2006), dividend distributions to individual Danish shareholders that do not exceed DKK46,700 (in 2008 – adjusted annually) are taxed at a rate of 28%. Dividends exceeding this amount are taxed at a rate of 43%.

Dividends distributed to foreign individual shareholders are subject to withholding tax at a rate of 28%.

Dividend distributions to Danish companies are subject to corporate tax (25%). However, if the company holds at least 10% (15% in 2008) of the shares, the dividend distribution is exempted from tax. This also applies to companies located in EU or EEA (European Economic Area) countries holding at least 10% (15% in 2008) of the shares.

Double-taxation treaties may also have an impact on the taxation.

(d)   *Deposit and publication*

The annual report must be filed with the DCCA no later than four months (listed companies) or five months (non-listed companies) after the end of the financial year.

12.   Company reorganisations

12.1   Merger

A merger basically includes the following main steps:

- preparation of a joint merger plan by the board of directors of the merging companies;
- preparation by the board of directors of each company of a written statement explaining and substantiating the reasons for the plan to merge;
- issue of a written opinion on the merger plan, including a creditor statement, by an independent appraiser;
- decision to merge in each of the participating companies; and
- registration of the merger with the DCCA and filing of the merger documents with the DCCA.

The resolution to merge is made by the discontinuing company at a general meeting. The resolution to merge must be approved by not less than two-thirds of the votes cast and by not less than two-thirds of the share capital represented at the general meeting and entitled to vote, or a higher majority if required by the articles of association.

The resolution to merge by the continuing company must be made at a general meeting if the merger requires amendments to the articles of association (eg due to a capital increase to compensate the shareholders in the discontinuing company); if no amendments are required, the decision can be made by the board of directors unless a minority of at least 5% of the share capital requests that a general meeting be convened. If the merger requires amendments to the articles of association, the resolution to merge must be approved by not less than two-thirds of the votes cast and by not less than two-thirds of the share capital represented at the general meeting and entitled to vote, or a higher majority if required by the articles of association.

The resolution to merge cannot be adopted earlier than four weeks after publication by the DCCA of receipt of the joint merger plan and a creditor statement. The merger documents of each participating company must be filed with the DCCA no later than two weeks after the resolution to merge has been adopted in all the participating companies.

All assets and liabilities in the discontinuing companies are transferred to the continuing company by way of universal succession.

12.2   De-merger

The de-merger of a company may be total (ie the divided company is wound up and all assets and liabilities are transferred to two or more companies) or partial (ie part of the company, normally an independent undertaking, is transferred to one or more other companies).

The de-merger procedure is very similar to the merger procedure. A joint de-merger plan and a de-merger statement for each participating company must be prepared and an independent appraiser must issue an opinion on the merger plan. Specifically, the appraiser must verify that the compensation to the shareholders is reasonable and that the creditors are secured after the de-merger. When the DCCA receives the said documents, it announces publicly through the Central Business Register the filing of the documents and the documents may subsequently be requested by the public from the Central Business Register. The decision to de-merge is made by the shareholders at the general meeting and requires a qualified majority (ie not less than two-thirds of the votes cast and by not less than two-thirds of the share capital represented at the general meeting and entitled to vote) or a higher majority if required by the articles of association.

All companies participating in the de-merger are jointly and severally liable for claims that are not fulfilled by the company primarily liable for the claim. This applies to claims that arose before the filing of the de-merger plan was made public. However, the joint liability is limited to the net value of the assets transferred to the receiving company and to the remainder of the net value according to the de-merger plan.

12.3   Transformation

The decision to transform a public limited liability company into a private limited liability company or the decision to transform a private limited liability company into a public limited liability company can be made by the shareholders and requires a qualified majority (ie not less than two-thirds of the votes cast and by not less than two-thirds of the share capital represented at the general meeting and entitled to vote) or a higher majority if required by the articles of association.

Transformation of a private limited liability company into a public limited liability company additionally requires the preparation of a valuation report by an auditor, to ensure that the minimum share capital requirement for public limited liability companies is met.

When a decision to transform a private limited liability company into a public limited liability company or a decision to transform a public limited liability company into a private limited liability company is taken, the articles of association must be amended accordingly. Thereafter, the decision is notified to the DCCA, and the transformation takes effect from the date of the registration and publication by the DCCA.

13.   Eventual partner separation

Neither the Public Limited Liability Companies Act nor the Private Limited Liability Companies Act regulates the eventual separation of shareholders. However, shareholders in these companies typically enter into shareholder agreements in order to regulate their cooperation and the management and control of the company, and to provide for an orderly separation of shareholders by regulating issues such as:

- dispute resolution;
- transfer and sale of shares;
- tag-along and drag-along provisions;
- right of co-sale;
- right of first refusal; and
- put and call options.

14. Dissolution and liquidation

The decision to wind up a company voluntarily is taken by the shareholders at the general meeting and requires a qualified majority (ie not less than two-thirds of the votes cast and by not less than two-thirds of the share capital represented at the general meeting and entitled to vote) or a higher majority if required by the articles of association.

One or more liquidators must be appointed. The liquidators take over the management of the company from the previous management (the board of directors and the board of management) and the company thus shifts to a one-tier management structure. The liquidators are chosen by the shareholders at a general meeting. A minority of shareholders with at least 25% of the capital can appoint a joint liquidator to join the liquidators appointed by the majority. The liquidators are subject to the same rules and responsibilities as the board of directors.

The liquidation aims to realise the company's assets and ensure that the company's debts are settled.

The company's creditors must be notified of the winding-up. Once the creditors have been paid, any surplus can be distributed to the shareholders and a final report is then filed with the DCCA. The company is then removed from the company register and ceases to exist.

15. Branches

Public limited liability companies, private limited liability companies and limited partnerships domiciled in other EU member states, the United States or other countries that afford reciprocal treatment to Danish companies may establish a branch in Denmark. A branch is not considered a separate legal entity but viewed as part of the parent company. The parent company is therefore fully and directly liable for any claim against the branch.

Dominican Republic

Georges Santoni-Recio
Mónica Villafaña Aquino
Russin, Vecchi & Heredia Bonetti

---

1.   Incorporating a Dominican company

For the purposes of this chapter, the term 'company' refers to a Dominican company or corporation divided by shares. A Dominican company divided by shares is variously known as a *Compañía por Acciones*, a *Compañía Anónima* or a *Sociedad Anónima*; however, the legal structure and requirements are identical. The founders of a company are free to select one of these titles, which must then become part of the company's legal name (eg 'XYZ, SA'). The most popular titles are *Sociedad Anónima* and *Compañía por Acciones*. Law 5546/1961 allows these terms to be used in a non-discriminatory sense.

1.1   General characteristics of a Dominican share company

Ownership of a company is divided among the shareholders, who participate in the profits and losses in proportion to their respective shareholdings. In the absence of fraud or deceptive practice, the shareholders are not personally liable for the company's obligations and a shareholder's liability is limited to the extent of his investment. The company has separate legal personality and can sue or be sued in its own name.

1.2   Preliminary considerations

(a)   Corporate name

Before incorporating a company, it must first be determined whether an identical or similar company name to that chosen by the founder(s) has already been registered with the Ministry of Industry and Commerce. Once it is confirmed that the company name is available, and there is no chance that two different companies might be incorporated under the same name, the chosen company name can be registered in the Book of Names and a formal registration of company name can be obtained.

(b)   Minimum number of shareholders

At least seven shareholders are required to incorporate a Dominican company; this minimum number of shareholders must be maintained throughout the life of the company. Six of the shareholders may hold just one share each. The shareholders may be natural or legal persons. When two shareholders in the same company are married, and the community property marital regime applies, both spouses will be considered to be one person, in the sense that the community is regarded as the owner of the shares.

(c)   *Nationality of shareholders*

There are no requirements regarding the nationality of shareholders, except where the company is engaged in special activities (ie insurance, public concessions), which requires that a percentage of the shares be retained in the hands of Dominican citizens or legal entities.

(d)   *Face value of shares*

According to the Commercial Code, the face value of each share cannot be less than five Dominican pesos (RD$5). However, the company usually sets it at 100 Dominican pesos (RD$100).

(e)   *Paid-in capital*

A minimum of 10% of the authorised capital must be subscribed and paid in prior to incorporation. Any subscribed capital beyond this minimum must also be paid in.

(f)   *In-kind contributions*

If shares are issued in exchange for assets other than cash, the first general constitutive assembly must order a valuation of those assets. The valuation report must be made available to the shareholders at least five days prior to a second general constitutive assembly, which must be convened to approve the valuation. Those shareholders whose contributions are being valued cannot vote on the resolution to approve their contributions.

(g)   *Management body*

The management of the company must be entrusted to one or more administrators, appointed by the bylaws or by the general constitutive assembly for a set period of time. They may or may not be salaried. The administrators must prepare a half-yearly statement of profits and losses, to be reviewed by the account comptroller (*Comisario de Cuentas*). The account comptroller must present a report on the financial condition of the company at each annual shareholder's assembly, which is submitted to the shareholders for approval along with the administrators' financial report.

(h)   *Legal reserve*

A minimum of 5% of the gross profits must be contributed to a general reserve fund before dividends are distributed. Once the legal reserve reaches 10% of the paid-up capital, contributions are no longer necessary.

(i)   *Certified financial statements*

A company must present its financial statements on an annual basis. These must be verified and accompanied by a ruling issued by an independent authorised public accountant, or by an authorised auditor's firm.

(j)   *Corporate books*

In addition to any other records they may have, companies must maintain a daily book and a balance book. The law prescribes certain procedures for the maintenance of these books, which include the use of special paper. The books must be inspected and stamped by legal officials once a year. In practice, the requirement to maintain a daily book may be satisfied by a summary of the regular accounting operations of the company. These books, together with all company correspondence, must be preserved for 10 years pursuant to the Commercial Code.

(k) Financial year

All companies must establish the close of their financial year when they are incorporated. They may choose from among the following dates:
- December 31;
- March 31;
- June 30; and
- September 30.

The corresponding sworn declaration must be submitted to the Tax Agency within 120 days of the end of the financial year.

(l) Taxation of company revenue

According to the Tax Code, companies settled in the Dominican Republic are subject to tax on their net income in both Dominican currency and any external currency at a rate (as at 2009) of 25%. A company is considered to be settled in the Dominican Republic when it is incorporated according to Dominican law or when it establishes its headquarters in the country.

1.3 Bylaws

The bylaws set out the rules for the operation of a Dominican share company, tailored to the needs of the individual company and the wishes of its founders. It is the basic constitutional charter of a share company, and it is roughly equivalent to a combination of the articles of incorporation and bylaws of a company incorporated in the United States.

(a) Essential clauses

The following information, at a minimum, must be included in the bylaws:
- the full name of each founder and general personal credentials (ie nationality, legal and marital status, profession, domicile and identification number). In the case of foreigners who do not have a Dominican identification document, a social security number or passport number will suffice. If one or more of the founders is a company, the general credentials of its representative must be provided;
- the company name, followed by the abbreviation 'SA', 'C por A' or 'CxA';
- the corporate domicile, which must be located in the Dominican Republic (the administrative body can decide to change the corporate domicile at any time within the Dominican territory);
- the corporate purpose, described in general terms;
- the duration of the company (this may be fixed or indefinite);

- the authorised capital, the face value of the shares (which must be at least RD$5), the types of shares (bearer, nominative or to order), and the rights and obligations that they carry;
- the capitalisation taxes, which are paid to the Tax Agency at the moment of incorporation and subsequently where a company increases its authorised capital;
- the duties and quorum requirements of the shareholders' meeting, and the time and place at which shareholders' meetings will be held (the shareholders must meet at least once a year in order to verify the accounts of the operations of the company);
- the management body and its duties. The corporate governing bodies are the general shareholders' meeting, which elaborates and makes the major corporate decisions, and the board of directors, vested with the management and representation of the company;
- the fiscal year chosen by the company, in accordance with the four dates described above, established by the Dominican Tax Code;
- the reserve fund; and
- the procedures for utilisation of profits and distribution of dividends.

(b) Structuring rules

(i) Board of directors vs president-manager

The founders can choose to entrust the management either to a single person or to a board of directors. A sole manager or president-manager may be preferable where one shareholder dominates or where the shareholders are members of one family. A single executive officer is the most efficient option to operate the company.

On the other hand, where two or more persons have significant holdings in the company, they generally prefer to use a board of directors. An odd number of directors is recommended, as this avoids tied votes. The bylaws must specify:

- whether the members of the board must be shareholders or not;
- how board meetings are to be convened;
- quorum requirements;
- proxy provisions;
- the majority required for the adoption of resolutions; and
- the preparation of a board meeting minutes book.

(ii) Officers and liabilities

The simplest and most efficient company structure is the president-manager model, whereby the president-manager is the sole executive officer together with the account comptroller (a special officer). However, it is common to have a more complex structure, with four officers in addition to the account comptroller: a president, vice president, treasurer and secretary. Two or more of these posts can be held by one person (ie president-treasurer). The bylaws can also restrict the president's powers by requiring that significant contracts be approved by the shareholders' meeting or the full board of directors.

In the absence of fraud or deceptive practices, the shareholders or directors have no personal liability for the company's obligations, and a shareholder's liability is limited to the extent of his investment. The company has separate legal personality and can sue or be sued in its own name. Debtors of the company have no recourse to the personal assets of its shareholders.

(iii) *Shareholders' meetings*

The shareholders must gather at least once a year to approve the following matters:

- the financial statements;
- the reports of the board of directors and the account comptroller on the previous fiscal period;
- the appointment of the members of the board of directors for the forthcoming period;
- the appointment of the account comptroller; and,
- if proceeds are available, the distribution of dividends.

For fiscal reasons, this meeting customarily takes place in the three months following the close of the financial year.

Decisions are usually approved by majority vote. The bylaws must be clear on whether this refers to a simple majority (ie half the shares represented at the meeting plus one) or to an absolute majority (ie half of all shares issued plus one). A greater majority is often required for amendment of the bylaws at extraordinary general meetings. Where two people or groups in a company hold the same number of votes, the bylaws should include measures to address any problems that might arise, including a mechanism for the resolution of disputes.

If one of the shareholders holds a majority of the shares, the minority shareholders may wish to appoint a representative to the board of directors in order to ensure they remain well informed and to guard against majority abuse. In case of abuse of any kind, a voting formula should be established in order to guarantee the proportional representation of the minority; otherwise, the majority shareholder could exercise his power to select every member of the board. An appropriate formula to adopt would grant each shareholder a number of votes equal to the number of shares owned multiplied by the number of directors to be elected (the typical cumulative voting procedure).

(c) *Authorised capital, and subscribed and paid-in capital*

The authorised capital is the maximum limit for the subscribed and paid-in capital. Upon incorporation, taxes are paid on the basis of the authorised capital. Within the limit of the authorised capital, the subscribed and paid-in capital can vary, depending on shareholder contributions and withdrawals, reinvestment, company losses and reserve-fund contributions. The bylaws must specify who has the power to decide on a change to the subscribed and paid-in capital (eg the president, the board of directors or the shareholders' meeting). If another body is to decide on changes to the subscribed and paid-in capital, the general shareholders' meeting must recognise the change within six months.

(d)   *Types of shares*

According to the bylaws, shares may be nominative, bearer or to order.

If the shares are nominative, the company must keep a book in which the shareholders' names and addresses are recorded. The holders of nominative shares are entitled to be notified in writing and to receive dividends without having to show the corresponding certificates. Nominative shares are transferred by way of endorsement of the certificates and delivery to the purchaser, who in turn must return the old certificates to the company for cancellation and the issuance of new certificates in his name. The transfer is then recorded in the company registry book, which renders the transfer final and enforceable. The company secretary will enter the name and address of the new shareholder in the shareholder book.

Shares to order are also transferred through endorsement, but the company does not issue a new certificate or amend the shareholder book.

Bearer shares are transferred through simple delivery.

Both ordinary and preference shares may be issued, subject to certain regulatory procedures. Preference shares grant the right to a priority dividend payment and may also give the holder a preferred position upon dissolution of the company. In addition, the voting rights attached to preference shares are different from those of ordinary shares.

The bylaws may reserve for existing shareholders a preferential right to purchase new shares – either to conserve their respective percentage of the company capital or to buy new shares at less than market price. The issue price may be established either as the nominal share value or as a certain percentage below the price offered to third parties, so that third parties must pay an issuance premium in addition to the nominal value of the shares.

(e)   *Dividends*

The decision to distribute or reinvest company profits is customarily taken by the shareholders' meeting, although this can also be left up to the board of directors. In the event of reinvestment of profits, the subscribed and paid-up capital is increased and the corresponding shares are issued. According to the Tax Code, companies settled in the Dominican Republic are subject to tax on their net income in both Dominican currency and any foreign currency at a current rate of 25%. In addition, dividends paid in cash to shareholders are taxed, but dividends paid in shares are tax exempt. Companies that pay or credit dividends in Dominican currency must withhold tax at a rate of 25%. In order to eliminate double taxation of dividend payments (which would be the case upon retention, since the company has already paid corporate tax on the distributed profits), the Tax Code allows for the deduction of the sums withheld from the company's tax base for the same year.

1.4   Incorporation procedure

(a)   *Availability and registration of company name*

Before incorporating a company, it must first be determined whether an identical or similar company name to that chosen by the founder(s) has already been registered with the Ministry of Industry and Commerce. Once it is confirmed that the company name is available, and that there is no chance that two different companies might be incorporated under the same name, the chosen company name may be registered in the Book of Names and a formal registration of company name may be obtained.

(b)   *Preparation and signature of bylaws*
The bylaws must be prepared and signed by the founders; at least seven original documents must be signed.

(c)   *List of shareholders and statement of payment of shares*
A list of subscribers or founding shareholders is prepared, indicating their personal credentials, the value of their contributions and their respective shareholdings. A description of inventory of any in-kind contributions must be included.

(d)   *Payment of capitalisation tax*
To incorporate a Dominican company, constitution or capitalisation tax must be paid to the local revenue inspector based on the authorised capital. There is a 1% tax on the authorised capital, regardless of the value authorised.

(e)   *Notary statement*
Prior to the general constitutive meeting, the recipient of any cash contributions must make a statement before a notary. The notary must be provided with a copy of the bylaws, a list of shareholders and the statement of payment of shares, as well as receipt of payment of the capitalisation tax.

The notary fee for preparation of the statement of subscription and payment of shares currently ranges from RD$1,000 to RD$5,000.

(f)   *General constitutive meeting*
Once these requirements have been met, the first shareholders' meeting – called the general constitutive meeting – is held. A list is made of the shareholders present and represented, setting out their personal credentials, their respective shareholdings and the number of voting rights they hold. Regardless of the number of shares owned, no shareholder can have more than 10 votes at the general constitutive meeting.

This meeting formally:
- approves the bylaws;
- approves the statement prepared before the notary;
- elects the first managers and the first account comptroller; and
- authorises the formal incorporation of the company.

A second constitutive meeting is necessary to approve any in-kind contributions. The first meeting approves the statement made before a notary and appoints an expert to verify the estimated value of the contributions. This should be submitted at least five days prior to the second constitutive meeting, which will approve the expert's report and then appoint the first managers and the account comptroller.

(g) Registration of documents

The bylaws, the list of shareholders and the minutes of the constitutive meeting(s) must be registered with the Chamber of Commerce and Production. Proof that the capitalisation tax has been paid will be required.

The fee for registration with the Chamber of Commerce and Production is paid upon registration of the incorporation documents. A charge of RD$100 is levied for each original document and RD$50 for any copies. However, when a company is first registered at the Chamber of Commerce, the original and one copy of all the requested documentation are exempt. The collector's receipt must be presented as proof of payment of the capitalisation tax.

A standard fee must be paid, depending on the amount of the authorised capital, in order to obtain a certificate of registration with the Mercantile Registry, as outlined in the table below.

Amount of authorised capital	Mercantile Registry fee (RD$)
From RD$1 to 100,000	1,200
From RD$100,001 to 150,000	1,500
From RD$150,001 to 200,000	2,000
From RD$200,001 to 500,000	3,000
From RD$500,001 to 1,000,000	4,000
From RD$1,000,001 to 1,500,000	5,000
From RD$1,500,001 to 2,500,000	6,000
From RD$2,500,001 to 3,500,000	7,000
From RD$3,500,001 to 5,000,000	8,000
From RD$5,000,001 to 7,000,000	9,000
From RD$7,000,001 to 10,000,000	10,000
From RD$10,000,001 to 25,000,000	12,000
From RD$25,000,001 to 50,000,000	14,000
From RD$50,000,001 to 75,000,000	16,000
From RD$75,000,001 to 100,000,000	18,000
From RD$100,000,001 to 125,000,000	19,000
From RD$125,000,001 to 150,000,000	21,000
From RD$150,000,001 to 250,000,000	23,000
From RD$250,000,001 upwards	25,000

(h) Filing with the Mercantile Registry

The Mercantile Registry Law (3–02) establishes a new system for the registration and recording of all industrial, commercial and service activities carried out by companies. All company documents must be filed with the Chamber of Commerce and Production. Registration must be renewed every two years through payment of a fixed fee that will be amended from time to time by the Chamber of Commerce and Production. The registration process is mandatory and all information contained in registered documents is effective towards third parties.

The Mercantile Registry Law has superseded the publication requirements of the Commercial Code of Commerce (civil registration, deposit of documents with the corresponding courts and publication in a national newspaper).

To ensure compliance with the law, the Chamber of Commerce and Production will request delivery of the following documents:

- information on the company's financial and commercial references;
- the number of male and female employees;
- a copy of the incorporation documents;
- where the main shareholders are themselves corporations, their own incorporation documents, duly translated into Spanish and legalised by the nearest Dominican consulate, if necessary; and
- a copy of the personal identification document or passport of the members of the board of directors, shareholders and representatives of the company.

(i) *Taxpayer identification card*

Law 53/1970 requires that all companies and persons who undertake commercial activities obtain a national taxpayer identification registration card.

(j) *Timeframe for incorporation*

The approximate timeframe for incorporation of a Dominican company is two months. For this reason, some law firms in the Dominican Republic maintain a list of 'shelf' companies, so they can offer their clients the opportunity to acquire a company that has already been incorporated and is immediately available. The main difference between the two types of company is the timeframe for delivery: a shelf company can be delivered in 24 hours, which is how long it takes to transfer all shares to the new owners.

A shelf company can be adapted to any legal requirement that a client may propose (eg new name, change in administrative structure, increase in authorised capital or in-kind contributions).

2. Financial statements

2.1 Audited financial statements and sworn declaration

If a company has social capital of more than RD$50,000, it must prepare audited financial statements regardless of the commercial activities it carries out. A copy of these statements must be deposited with the Tax Agency, along with a sworn declaration of the tax payment. The agency will duly issue certification confirming that the company in question has met its tax obligations.

If the company has not started to trade, the Tax Agency will issue a certificate to this effect and stating that it is exempt from tax. The agency nonetheless requires that such companies file informative sworn declarations, so it can keep a record of non-operative companies.

2.2 Annual inventory

Each year, Dominican companies should prepare an inventory setting out the value of immovable assets and all active debts. This inventory should be provided to the account comptroller, along with the balance sheet and profit and loss account, at least 40 days before the date of the general meeting at which they will be presented. The documents should also be made available for shareholder review at least 15 days before the general meeting.

2.3 Summary statement of financial situation

A company must prepare a summary statement of its financial situation every six months,. This statement, along with the other books and records, will be placed at the disposal of the account comptroller, who is entitled to verify them by inspecting the company's operations as often as he deems necessary.

3. Maintenance of a Dominican company

Once the Dominican company has been incorporated, there are a number of legal requirements it must satisfy to keep its corporate status and its relationship with the Dominican tax and mercantile administration in order.

3.1 Annual general meeting

Each year the company must hold a general shareholders' meeting on a date fixed in the bylaws. The agenda is as follows:

- review of the board of directors' report for the financial year;
- review of the account comptroller's report on the company's overall situation and the balance sheet and accounts presented by the administrators. this report must necessarily include deliberation and approval of the account balances;
- release of the directors and account comptroller from their duties;
- allocation of sums to the reserve fund and declaration of profits or losses;
- appointment of the board of directors (unless it has been elected for a period of more than one year); and
- appointment of the account comptroller for the following financial year.

The meeting is completely independent of the company's commercial affairs: even non-operative companies are obliged to hold an annual meeting. In such cases the minutes must still mention the above points even though no activity has in fact taken place.

The quorum requirements are specified in the bylaws.

Once the meeting is held, it must be registered with the Chamber of Commerce and Production. Where appropriate, the Mercantile Registry certificate must also be modified to reflect any changes made at the general meeting.

3.2 Audited financial statements and sworn declaration

All the company's financial statements must be verified and accompanied by the ruling issued by an independent authorised public accountant, or by an authorised auditor's firm.

3.3   Annual inventory

Each year, the company must prepare an inventory setting out the value of its immovable assets and its active debts.

3.4   Biannual general assembly

Every six months, a general biannual assembly must be held to record the subscription and payment of new shares, if any. To be valid, the meeting must be attended by shareholders representing at least one-quarter of the corporate capital; decisions are taken by majority vote. However, the bylaws may stipulate alternative quorum requirements for attendance and voting.

4.   Establishing a branch

A foreign company that wishes to establish a branch in the Dominican Republic should to obtain authorised domicile so that the branch can enjoy the same rights as an incorporated company.

Branches are not obliged to obtain authorised domicile under Dominican law, and some companies have established branches without doing so. However, in such cases the branch cannot obtain a taxpayer identification card for payment of its tax obligations and runs the risk of having to pay a *judicatum solvi* bond under Article 16 of the Civil Code and Articles 166 and 167 of the Civil Procedure Code.

The main advantage of having authorised domicile is the ability to undertake commercial and usual operational activities in the Dominican Republic. In this way, the government offices can confirm the legitimacy and capacity of the foreign company to deal with commercial issues in the Dominican Republic.

Authorised domicile for the Dominican branch of a foreign company is obtained by submitting a written petition to the Dominican president. The request is processed through the Ministry of Interior and Police. The request may be undersigned by a company official or by a local representative with the power of attorney to do so.

The foreign company must obtain a certificate of good standing from the corresponding government agency in its home state, confirming that it is properly registered and authorised to do business. A Dominican consul must verify the signature of the government official who signs the certificate, and the Dominican Ministry of International Relations must in turn verify the consul's signature.

A copy of the bylaws filed before the authorities of the foreign company's home state must be provided. This document must be verified as an exact copy of the original by the appropriate public official; again, the Dominican consul must authenticate the public official's signature, and the Dominican Ministry of International Relations must in turn certify the consul's signature.

A company should state its intention to set up a domicile in the Dominican Republic and designate a local representative who will deposit the authorised residency request with the Dominican officials for due processing. The request must include a copy of the resolution of the board of directors or another body with the capacity to authorise the move into the Dominican Republic. Again, the corresponding authorities (ie the Dominican consul and the Ministry of International Relations) must certify this document.

If any of the above documents is drafted in another language, it must be translated into Spanish by a judicial translator.

As branches do not have separate legal personality, debtors must make any claims against the parent company. Where a claim is brought against a branch, the parent company is fully liable. Foreign companies with branches in the Dominican Republic are obliged to file their annual accounts and sworn declarations, as well as any other tax filing required for Dominican companies, with the Tax Agency.

5. Company reorganisation

Article 323 of the Tax Code defines 'reorganisation' as:

- the merger of two or more existing companies into a new or existing company;
- the split or division of a company into other companies that jointly continue the operations of the first company; or
- the sale and transfer of one entity to another that, despite being legally independent, jointly constitutes an economic group.

In the same sense, Article 325 of the Tax Code establishes that, in the case of cessation of the business or termination of operations through sale, liquidation, trade or other cause, the current fiscal period shall be considered to have ended. Companies in liquidation will continue to be subject to the provisions of the code and its supplementary regulations. Following the final distribution of the liquidation proceeds, the terms of Article 325 are deemed fulfilled.

6. Dissolution and liquidation

The dissolution of a company is effected through liquidation. Article 57 of the Commercial Code identifies one of the causes of dissolution as "the will of the shareholders". In such cases the process is initiated by convening an extraordinary general meeting, which will decide on the following issues:

- the reports presented by the board of directors and the account comptroller on the results of the fiscal period up until the date of dissolution, and release of these officials from their duties;
- dissolution of the company;
- cessation of the functions of the directors and officers; and
- the appointment of a liquidator to perform the pertinent operations for the dissolution and liquidation of the company.

The liquidator doesn't have be a shareholder of the company. He is charged with performing all necessary operations with regard to the dissolution and liquidation, and he has the power to make and receive payments in the name and as the representative of the company.

The shareholders' meeting may also set dates for subsequent meetings at which the liquidator's reports will be examined and the company's final dissolution decided.

Once these minutes of the shareholders' meeting have been signed, a copy must be sent to the Chamber of Commerce and Production, which will register them accordingly and issue a certificate of dissolution.

The company is considered dissolved from the moment that the shareholders decide on dissolution in general meeting. Nevertheless, it can continue to operate for liquidation purposes.

Once the Tax Agency has approved the dissolution and all publication requirements have been fulfilled, it is recommended that a public notice of dissolution be placed in a national newspaper. This notice of dissolution has the purpose of:

- providing public notification of the decisions of the extraordinary general shareholders' meeting;
- inviting creditors who do not have registered guarantees, securities or mortgages to communicate with the liquidator, so he can make a list of all pending claims against the company and satisfy them *pro rata*; and
- indicating to creditors that the liquidator will make and receive payments on behalf of the company, as the only person with capacity to grant formal receipt of discharge and settlement on behalf of the company.

In the same sense, liquidation is the process by which operations are wound up, debts are recouped, assets are realised, liabilities are balanced and any surplus remaining is distributed to the shareholders in proportion to their contributions. During the liquidation process, the company is represented solely by the liquidator.

Once the liquidation process has ended, an extraordinary general meeting must be convened in order to:

- review the liquidator's report;
- release the liquidator from his duties;
- declare the definite dissolution and liquidation of the company; and
- authorise the liquidator to perform all necessary acts to satisfy the publication requirements.

The Tax Code provides that in a case of dissolution the fiscal period will be considered to have ended, and the company has 60 days from the date of dissolution to submit the corresponding sworn declaration to the Tax Agency and pay any outstanding taxes.

Note: At the time of writing, the Dominican Congress had recently passed a new statute for Dominican corporations and other types of corporate legal entities. This new law will make a number of changes to the material in this chapter. Nevertheless this Law (Ley de Sociedades Comerciales y Empresas Individuales de Responsabilidad Limitada) will only take effect within 190 days of commencement by the Executive office in June 2009.

Egypt

Amr ZA Motaal
Abdel Motaal, Moharram & Heiza Law Firm

1. Introduction

1.1 The Egyptian legal system

Egypt is a unitary state, a republic with constitutional traditions. The current legal system is a hybrid system. It is essentially a civil law country with some roots in Sharia law and some features of modern Anglo-American law especially in its business law. The laws are issued by the People's Council (the Parliament) and are enacted and published by presidential decrees in the Egyptian *Official Gazette*.

The Egyptian constitution, which was published in 1971, is the core of Egyptian law. The sources of the law in Egypt are the legislation, customs, Sharia law and the principles of natural law and equity. Judicial precedents and jurisprudence are respected in the interpretation of the law. The official language and the language of the legislation is Arabic. The major laws are codified. Civil, commercial, procedural and criminal codes have been enforced since the nineteenth century (these are amended from time to time). Specific legislation governs different topics.

Ministerial decrees and regulations are issued to implement and/or clarify the legislation; they should not contravene the legislation or the constitution. Disputes are settled using the courts system (civil, criminal or administrative). The specialised circuits are the first Degree Courts, the Courts of Appeal or the Court of Cassation. The Supreme Constitutional Court rules on matters concerning the constitutional validity of the legislation and regulations. Disputes can also be settled by arbitration, by amicable means or by using alternative dispute resolution (ADR), according to the arbitration and conciliation law. Foreign judgments or arbitral awards are enforced by the Egyptian judiciary if they do not contravene Egyptian law in relation to public order.

1.2 Partnerships and companies in Egypt

Partnerships and companies are organised under various Codes. The formation, management, company entailments, methods for company expiry and dissolution are dealt with under Egyptian Civil Code 131/1948. The old code of commerce (dated November 13 1883) included commercial companies and partnerships and contained the rules governing the establishment, management and dissolution of commandites, partnerships in commendam and joint stock companies. It stated that the general principles as expressed in the civil law and the conditions agreed between partners should apply. Law 26/1954 modernised the laws governing joint stock and limited liability companies. Law 159/1981 (and its consecutive amendments) applied to joint stock companies, partnerships in commendam limited by shares and limited liability companies. Despite several amendments, this law is still the principal law governing this type of company in Egypt.

Egypt adopted capitalism until the beginning of the 1960s, whereupon the country adopted socialism (its essence was state capitalism) under which the state nationalised many corporations. Heavy and medium-sized industry, banks and insurance companies were owned and managed by the public sector. Smaller businesses were allowed to remain in the private sector. At the beginning of the 1970s, Egypt reverted to a market economy. Most of the public sector companies were privatised, although some companies and banks remained in the public sector. New laws were enacted. These include:

- investment law;
- laws designed to attract foreign investments, including Law 43/1979 and Law No 8/1997 that grant investment guarantees and incentives regulating companies;
- Law 8/1997 exempting said companies from paying tax for a set number of years (according to its type of activity); and
- Law No 91/2005, which reformed and unified the tax system for all companies with some exceptions or acquired rights for those companies that were established under Law 8/1997 or that were in the gas and oil sector.

The maximum tax imposed on the profits of companies and partnership is currently (2009) 20% after all expenses have been deducted. Companies are usually established under Law 159/1981 or Law 8/1997 as well as civil and commercial law. The payment of income tax has become unified for all companies. After the modernisation of the money, banking and credit laws, the principle of free foreign capital and profit transfer for foreign and national shareholders using the free money markets has been applied. Egypt is about to enact a new unified law governing companies and partnerships under one law.

2. Types of limited liability companies and applicable legislation

Under Egyptian Law, there is one type of company: the limited liability company. However, there are several types of company and partnerships, where the liability of the partners or shareholders is limited to the value of their contribution or to their role in the management of the company. These are:

- *société en commandite simple*/partnership in commendam;
- *société en participation*/copartners;
- *société par action*/joint stock company;
- *société à responsabilité limitée*/limited liability company; and
- *société en commandite par actions*/partnership in commendam by shares.

2.1 The tax treatment of net profits generated by companies, partnerships and corporations

On June 9 2005, Tax Law 91/2005 came into force and was published in issue number 23*bis* of the Egyptian *Official Gazette*. The tax rates for net income are as follows:

- E£5,000 to E£20,000 – 10%;
- E£20,000 to E£40,000 – 15%; and
- more than E£40,000 – 20%.

Accordingly the maximum ceiling of the tax on net income (individual or corporate) is now 20%. This applies to net company profits. Tax is not payable on dividends distributed and transferred to foreign non-resident shareholders or partners.

2.2 Company registration

Law 34/1976 (as amended) governs the registration of trader 'merchants' (defined as physical or moral persons, including partnerships and corporations) in the commercial registry. The main stipulations are:

- a Commercial Registry should be set up to register traders (merchants) in each region or city;
- individuals (those involved in commerce, partnerships, joint stock companies, partnerships with shares and limited liability companies) must be registered;
- the main headquarters, branch, or agency of a trader (merchant) should be registered within the geographical jurisdiction of their local commercial trade registry office;
- the company name, any regional information about the trade registration office where the company is registered and the company's registration number must appear on all company stationery and documents;
- any change to the data in the register should registered within one month;.
- the company's registration must be renewed every five years;
- any court order or ruling pertaining to bankruptcy judicial seizure or concordat must be sent to the appropriate registry office within one month;
- any request for registration, or modification of registration, must be presented at the Commercial Registry, along with the necessary documents. The office can refuse this request, but the decision can be challenged before the Administrative Court;
- any official document can be requested from the appropriate commercial registration;
- the Ministry of Trade will publish the trader's registration information in the *Commercial Trade Names Gazette*;
- a company cannot legally trade unless it is registered;
- Commercial Registry fees must be paid for renewal or registration; fees are also due if the registration data has been amended; and
- annual accounts are required, but they are not deposited with the Commercial Registry unless the company's capital has been amended.

3. General rules and principles for partnerships

3.1 The definition of partnership

A partnership is a contract by which two or more persons commit to a financial enterprise by offering a share of money or work and a share in any profit or loss.

3.2 The Partnership's Juridical Personality

The Partnership, upon its institution, shall be considered a juridical person, but this personality shall not be used against a third party except after fulfilling the procedures of publication as described by the Law.

3.3 The contract

A partnership contract must be set out in writing; otherwise it is null and void. Any modifications must also be in writing.

3.4 Shares

Partners hold equal shares. They shall be connected to the ownership of the whole partnership, unless otherwise prescribed by agreement or usage.

If a partner's share is a title of property, or any other real right, the sale provisions will guarantee the price of that share.

If the share is beneficial, lease provisions apply.

If a partner undertakes to contribute to the partnership in the form of work, he shall undertake to carry out the work and submit an account detailing any profit he has made. However, he does not need to account for anything he might have acquired from the right of invention, unless this is in the company agreement.

If the share contributed by the partner consists of debts payable to him by third parties, his obligation toward the partnership will not terminate unless the debts are paid.

If it is decided that one of the partners will no longer contribute to the profit and loss of the company, the articles of incorporation will be null and void.

3.5 Management of the partnership

A partner elected as a director by virtue of a special provision in the articles of incorporation may, despite the objection of the rest of partners, undertake administrative tasks and carry out any disposals due within the partnership, A partner cannot be removed from the management team as long as the partnership remains intact.

If a partner was made a director after the partnership had been disbanded, the decision will be retracted.

Directors other than partners are always subject to removal.

If several parties are made directors without their powers being defined and without a provision in their contracts that none of them will take on management responsibilities, each director can make decisions as long as the remaining partners can object. Where the two sides are equal in a dispute, the right to refuse an objection is vested in the majority of all partners. However, if the directors' decisions are taken unanimously or by a majority, no one can depart from that provision, unless it will result in a loss that cannot be offset by the partnership.

If a decision is to be taken by a majority, the numerical majority will apply unless otherwise agreed.

Partners who are not directors cannot undertake management duties; however, they have access to all company books and documents. If there is no special provision on the method of management, all partners are responsible for managing the partnership on an equal basis.

Unless otherwise stated, if the partnership's funds are inadequate to settle its debts, the partners are responsible for the debts out of their personal funds and property, in proportion to their share in the partnership's losses.

Partners shall not be jointly liable for the company's debt. However, if a partner becomes insolvent, his share of the debt will be divided among the rest of partners.

The partnership shall either terminate on the date determined in its articles, or when the work for which it has been established has been completed. If the partners continue the business after this date, their will continue under the same terms and conditions. Any creditor can object to such an extension; in this situation any benefit resulting from the extension will not apply.

3.6   Expiration and termination

The partnership will expire if its property is destroyed.

If a partner has undertaken to contribute his share in kind and this perishes before he could submit it, the partnership will be dissolved.

If a partner dies, becomes insolvent or bankrupt, or withdraws, the partnership will still exist between the remaining partners according to the provisions of the company articles. The partnership terminates if one of the partners withdraws from the company, or the partners unanimously agree to dissolve it.

The court may dissolve the partnership at the request of one of the partners, if another partner fails to honour his commitments or for any another reason. Any agreement providing otherwise shall be null and void.

Any partner can ask the court to dismiss a partner whose behaviour justifies the dissolution of the partnership, provided the partnership continues to exist among the rest of the partners.

If the partnership has a defined duration, any partner can ask the court to release him from the partnership if he gives an acceptable reason. The partnership will then be dissolved unless the remaining partners agree to continue.

3.7   Liquidation

Any property and funds will be liquidated and divided as prescribed in the articles of association. If the contract does not contain any special provisions, the following apply:

- On dissolving the partnership, the power and authority of the directors expires. However, its personality shall continue as long as is required for dissolution;
- Liquidation is carried out either by all the partners, or by one or more

liquidators to be appointed by the majority of partners;

- If the partners cannot agree on the appointment of a liquidator, a judge will appoint one;
- The liquidator cannot authorise any new activities, unless they are necessary to complete previous works;
- The liquidator can sell property, movables or real estate, whether by auction or by private agreement, unless his appointment order restricts this power;
- Property will be divided among all the partners after the creditors have been paid, all debts have been settled and when the expenses or loans that any partner might have incurred in the interests of the partnership have been refunded;
- Every partner will receive an amount equal to the value of his share capital, as indicated in the contract (or the value of that share). If anything remains, it can be divided among the partners as a proportion of their shares in the profits; and
- If the capital of the partnership is not enough to settle the partners' shares, the loss must be shared. The shares will be divided according to the rules dealing with the division of common property.

3.8 Other general principles governing partnerships

Companies and partnerships should comply with the general rules set out in civil law, or as agreed by the partners.

A partnership is a legal entity formed by two or more partners to carry out business under a specific company name. The name of one or more of the partners shall be the trade name (style) of the partnership.

Partners in a partnership shall jointly and severally guarantee all its undertakings even though the right of signature is vested in one of the partners who signs in the name of the company.

A partnership can also be an association between one or several partners who are jointly and severally liable and other partners who contribute to the capital, but do not take part in the management of the company (sleeping partners).This type of partnership will be managed under a trade name that will include the names of one or more of the jointly liable partners.

If there are several jointly liable partners, the association will be deemed a private company in relation to the active partners and a partnership in relation to the sleeping partners.

The partnership trade name does not include the name of any of the sleeping partners or of businesspeople not concerned with management. Sleeping partners are only liable for losses within the limited capital they have contributed or have undertaken to contribute to the partnership. They cannot act in a managerial capacity even through power of proxy.

If one of the sleeping partners agrees to include his name in the trade name of the partnership, he shall be jointly liable for all debts and commitments of the partnership.

If a sleeping partner carries out any management work, he shall become jointly liable for the debts and commitments of the partnership resulting from his action and may be jointly liable for all or part of the commitments of the partnership depending on the frequency and scope of his action according to how much trust was placed in him by third parties.

If a sleeping partner offers advice or carries out an inspection, he will not incur any liability.

4. Incorporation for three types of company

There are three types of company relevant to this chapter and as set out in Law 159/1981. These are outlined in the remainder if this section, including aspects of incorporation, and more details are given for each of the three types of company in sections 5, 6 and 7 following.

4.1 Definitions

(a) The joint stock company

A joint stock company is a company whose capital is divided into shares of equal value that can be circulated in the manner set out in the law. A shareholder's liability is limited to the payment of the value of their subscribed shares. The company must have a trade name, derived from the object of its establishment.

(b) The limited liability company

A limited liability company is a company with no more than 50 partners. Each partner is only liable to the extent of the value of his shares. The company cannot be established, increase its capital or borrow using public subscription; nor may it issue negotiable shares or bonds. The transfer of the partners' shares are subject to the partners' recovery according to the conditions set out in the company's contract, as well as the conditions prescribed by this law. The company must have a trade name: this can include the names of the partner(s).

(c) Partnership limited by shares

This is a company whose capital is made up of a share(s) owned by a joint partner(s) with shares of equal value to which one or more shareholders have subscribed and which can be circulated in the manner set out in the law. The joint partner(s) have unlimited liabilities, whereas the shareholding partner is responsible only to the extent of their subscribed shares. The company's trade name can consist of one or more of the joint partners' names.

4.2 General rules applying to the three types of company

Partnerships limited by shares and limited liability companies cannot engage in insurance, banking or savings or accept deposits or invest money on behalf of third parties.

All contracts, invoices, trade names and titles, advertisements, papers and other printed material issued by the company should show the company's title and type (this should be shown before or after the title, in clear legible letters), the address of the company's head office and its issued capital as per its latest valuation.

4.3 Incorporation

The company founder signs the agreement or the licence application for the incorporation of the company or provides a share in kind on incorporation.

Under the provisions of Law 159/1981, there must be at least three founding partners in joint stock companies; in all other companies there cannot be fewer than two. If there are not enough partners, the company will be deemed to be dissolved unless it achieves the requisite number of partners within six months. The existing partners are responsible for the company's liabilities during this period.

The contract to be signed by the founders cannot include any conditions that exempt some or all of them from responsibility resulting from the incorporation of the company or any other conditions that apply to the company after it is established, unless these are included in the deeds of association or the articles of association. The founders are jointly responsible for any commitments they undertake in this capacity.

In transactions with, or on account of, the company under incorporation, the founders must act with due care. They are jointly responsible for any damage that may affect the company or a third party

Any contracts and actions undertaken by the founders in the name of the company will apply after it is established, as long as they are necessary for the incorporation of the company; if this is not the case, they will have no effect.

If the company's incorporation does not take place within six months of the public notification of its establishment, each subscriber can apply to a magistrate of summary jurisdiction to appoint someone to refund and distribute any money paid to the subscribers.

4.4 Incorporation procedures

The heads of agreement and the articles or deeds of association of the company must comply with the model issued by the competent authority and any signatures must be authentic. The documents must include the information specified in the executive regulations; these also specify the declarations and certificates that should be attached to the company's contract and the authentication status of the signatures by the competent administrative entity.

The founders or their delegated representatives shall notify the appropriate Public Administrative Authority of the following documents regarding the company's foundation and they should be attached to the notification:

- the heads of agreement and the company's articles of association, for a joint stock company or a partnership limited by shares, or the deed of association for limited liability companies;
- a certificate from one of the authorised banks confirming the subscription for all stocks or shares of the company, and that the value of the stocks or cash shares has been paid and placed at the company's disposal until it acquires its legal personality. The competent administrative entity shall issue a certificate to the person submitting the notification confirming that the written documents are attached to the notification and have duly been fulfilled; and

- the monies paid into the account of the company under incorporation should be deposited in one of the licensed banks by a decree of the competent minister. The company may not withdraw any money until its articles of association or deed of association have been recorded in the commercial register.

4.5   Provisions governing the incorporation of different types of company

(a)   Shares in kind

If shares in kind (material or moral) form part of the capital of a joint stock company or a partnership limited by shares or when the capital is increased, the founders or the board of directors should ask the competent administrative entity to verify whether the shares have been properly valued. A committee should be set up at the relevant administrative entity to undertake this verification process.

(b)   The constituent assembly

The founders or the company's agents will meet within one month of the expiry of the deadline for subscription or participation or the submission of a report on the valuation of the shares in kind, whichever comes first. All the partners shall have the right to attend this meeting, whatever the amount of their stock or shares.

For the meeting to be valid, partners holding at least half of the issued capital should attend.

The constituent assembly can examine the following matters:
- the valuation of the shares in kind in the manner provided for by law;
- the founder's report on the company's incorporation process and any expenditure incurred;
- the articles of association of the company – the assembly can only amend these with the approval of the founders and partners who hold at least two-thirds of the capital;
- endorsement of the selection of the members of the first board of directors and the auditor.

(c)   Limited liability companies

A limited liability company is established when all the cash shares provided for in the company's deed of association are divided among the partners and their value is paid in full. If a partner provided a share in kind, its type and value, the price that the rest of the partners accept for it, the partner's name and the amount of that partner's share in the capital in return for what he/she provides, must be set out in the deed of association.

5.   Joint stock companies

5.1   Capital and profits

The company's capital is divided into nominal shares of equal value. The articles of association set out the nominal value per share in Egyptian pounds, or their equivalent in foreign currencies. The shares are indivisible.

The company has an issued capital. The articles of association set out an amount of authorised capital, which cannot be more than ten times the issued capital. The minimum limit for the issued capital is set out in the articles of association.

The articles of association also specify the nominal value per share, and it must not be less than E£1 or more than E£1,000 or their equivalent in foreign currencies.

No incorporation shares or profit shares may be established except in return for a waiver of a concession granted by the government or a moral right.

Before a company can float its shares, it must obtain the approval of the Capital Market Authority. The subscriptions can be received through:

- an authorised bank;
- a company established for that purpose; or
- a company authorised to deal in securities.

All subscribers must pay at least one-quarter of the nominal value of the cash shares in cash, or by any other legally acceptable means of payment, in addition to the share premium and expenses.

5.2   Financial year

The company's financial year will be set out in the articles of association. Financial statements must be drawn up according to recognised accounting standards.

5.3   Share transactions

Incorporation shares and stocks that are given in consideration for shares in kind may not be negotiated, nor may the stocks to which the company's founders subscribed before publishing the balance sheet, the profit and loss account, and the documents attached thereto for two complete financial years that are not less than 12 months from the company's incorporation date.

The stocks and bonds of joint stock companies issued through public subscription must be presented to all the stock exchanges in Egypt no later than one year from the subscription closing date. These will be entered on their price schedules according to the terms and conditions set out in the stock exchange regulations.

If the company obtains a part of its stock, it must dispose of it to a third party within one year. Otherwise, it has to reduce its capital by the equivalent nominal value of the stock.

5.4   Bonds

The company can issue nominal bonds; these can be negotiable. They can only be issued by a resolution of the general assembly (see section 5.5 below) and after the issued capital has been paid in full, provided that their value is not greater than the net assets of the company as determined by the auditor according to the latest balance sheet approved by the general assembly.

The conditions of the issue of bonds may include their conversion to shares after a time limit specified by the company in the subscription prospectus. The conversion will be subject to the approval of the bondholder.

A bondholders' group will be established. The competent administrative entity should be notified of the establishment of the said group, its representative's name and copies of its decisions.

5.5 Management

Both the general assembly and the board of directors, together with the employees or any agents designated by either of these two bodies, shall have the right to take legal action on behalf of the company, taking account of its deed of association and its bylaws.

The board of directors has the power to manage the company and to do whatever is necessary to achieve its objectives, excluding actions falling within the jurisdiction of the general assembly that are exempted from directorial control by a special provision in law or the articles of association of the company. The general assembly can carry out any management functions if the board of directors is incapable of adjudicating on it because the required quorum has not been achieved. The general assembly also has the right to endorse any action taken by the board of directors or to issue recommendations about acts that fall within the board's jurisdiction.

Any decision or action taken by the general assembly, the board of directors or its committees or by any one of its members during the normal performance of management functions is binding on the company. A good-faith party may plead this in relation to the company even if the action exceeded the authority of its issuer or legally prescribed procedures were not observed. In all events, the company cannot avoid responsibility for carrying out any works or areas of business by arguing that they are not authorised by its articles of association.

(a) General assembly

Every shareholder shall be entitled to attend the general assembly of shareholders either personally or by proxy. A shareholder who is not a member of the board of directors may not deputise for a board member to attend the general assembly on his/her behalf. For a proxy to be valid, it must be evidenced by a written power of attorney and the proxy must be a shareholder.

The board of directors must be represented in the general assembly by the same number of members that must be available for its meetings to be valid. Non-attendance at meetings is not acceptable without a valid excuse.

The shareholders' general assembly will be held at the invitation of the chairman of the board of directors at a time and place designated by the articles of association. The general assembly should be held at least once during the six months following the end of the company's financial year. Even so, the board of directors may decide to call the general assembly to convene whenever necessary: this can be requested by the auditor or a number of shareholders representing at least 5% of the company's capital, if they can explain the reasons for this request. Stocks may not be withdrawn until the general assembly is over. Furthermore, the auditor or administrator may convene the general assembly if the board of directors does not do so; this can be done within a month of the date on which the meeting should have been called.

Subject to the provisions of the law and the company's articles of association, the ordinary general assembly's functions shall be to:

- elect or dismiss the members of the board of directors:
- monitor the work of the board of directors and consider releasing directors if necessary;
- approve the balance sheet as well as the profit and loss account;
- approve the board of directors' report on the company's business;
- approve the distribution of profits;
- carry out whatever the board of directors, the competent administrative entity or shareholders representing 5% of the capital decide to put to the general assembly; and
- undertake whatever else is vested in the ordinary general assembly by the law and the company's articles of association.

The board of directors should publish the balance sheet, the profit and loss account and an adequate summary of its reports as well as the full text of the auditor's report before the general assembly meets. The executive regulations determine the methods and dates of publication.

The ordinary general meeting will be valid only if it is attended by shareholders representing at least 25% of the capital (unless the articles of association stipulate a higher percentage, provided that it is not higher than half the capital). If the minimum limit is not available at the first meeting, the general assembly should be held within 30 days. The general assembly's resolutions shall be deemed adopted if passed by an absolute majority of the shares represented in the meeting.

The extraordinary general assembly can amend the company's articles of association subject to the following:

- Shareholders' liability cannot be increased – any resolution issued by the general assembly that would affect a shareholder's basic rights that are drawn from their capacity as a partner will be null and void; and
- Objects that are complementary to, associated with, or close to the original objects of the company may be added. In the meantime, the original object may be altered only for reasons acceptable to the committee provided for in the law "for reasons acceptable to the competent administrative entity".

The extraordinary general assembly may also consider prolonging or shortening the company's duration, terminating it prematurely or changing the percentage of loss that will result in its compulsory dissolution or merger.

(b)   *Board of directors*

The company is managed by a board of directors. The board should be composed of at least three members, who are selected by the general assembly for a three-year term as set out in the company's articles of association. By way of exception, the first board of directors shall be appointed by the founders for a term not exceeding five years.

A board meeting is not valid unless at least three members attend. Subject to the provisions of the preceding sentence, the board members may attend the meetings as proxies on behalf of each other provided that each proxy is in writing and has been endorsed by the chairman. The general assembly may, at any time, dismiss the board of directors or any of its members even if this was not included on the agenda.

The board of directors may apportion work among all its members according to the nature of the company's business. It may also:

- authorise one of its members or a committee of its members to carry out a specific job, to supervise an area of the company's activity or to exercise some of the powers or functions assigned to the board;
- delegate one or more of its members to undertake the actual management duties, with the board determining the terms of reference of the managing director. The managing director must be available on a full-time basis.

The minutes of board meetings should be recorded in a special register to be signed by the chairman and the secretary after every meeting. The terms and conditions that apply to the general meetings books are relevant here.

The board of directors may appoint a general manager from among its members. That manager may be invited to attend the board meetings but does not have a vote. The general manager shall perform their duties under the supervision of the managing director or the board chairman if undertaking the actual management functions. Further, the general manager is answerable to the managing director or the board chairman.

The board of directors shall appoint a chairman from among its members. It may also appoint a deputy chairman to replace the chairman in his/her absence. The board may assign the duties of the managing director to the chairman, who represents the company before the judiciary. The bylaws and the articles of association will determine the other functions of the chairman, members and employees.

Under the Egyptian Penal Code, any crimes committed will be penalised. Under the Civil Code, rules applying to contractual or delictual liability may be valid.

(c)   *Auditors*

A joint stock company must appoint an auditor who fulfils the requirements under law. The auditor is appointed and the auditor's fees decided by the general assembly. If there is more than one auditor, they shall be jointly liable. By way of exception, the company's founders appoint the first auditor.

6.   **Partnerships limited by shares**

Excluding those provisions relating to joint stock companies under the law (public subscription, to the composition of the board of directors and to some of the powers of the general assembly, the board of directors and the managing director according to Law 159/1981), all its provisions will apply to partnerships limited by shares under the rules set out in this chapter.

The management of a partnership limited by shares will be entrusted to joint partner(s) and the deeds of association will state the names and powers of those to be entrusted with management. Their status will, in terms of responsibility, be the same as that of the founders and the members of the board of directors in joint stock companies.

Every partnership limited by shares must have a controlling board made up of at least three shareholders. The board may ask the directors to provide them with accounts. It may examine the company's books and documents and take an inventory of the cash in hand, securities, and documents evidencing the company's rights and the goods found within it.

The shareholders' general assembly may neither transact nor approve any acts pertaining to the company's relationship with third parties, nor amend the company's deed of association without the directors' approval. The general assembly will act on behalf of the shareholders vis-à-vis the directors.

The company shall be terminated with the death of the partner entrusted with the management, unless otherwise provided. If there is no provision in the company's deed of association regarding what is to be done in this case, the controlling board may appoint an interim director to handle any urgent matters until the general assembly can be held. The interim director shall call a meeting of the general assembly within 15 days of his/her appointment, according to the procedures provided for in the deed of association. The interim director is only responsible for implementing his/her mandate.

7. Limited liability companies

7.1 The financial structure

The capital of a limited liability company may not be less than the limit specified by its articles or bylaws. Any profits or liquidation surplus must be divided among the shareholders in proportion to their shares, unless the company's deed of association provides otherwise.

The capital of a limited liability company may not be less than E£200 or its equivalent in foreign currencies. The capital is divided into equal shares of value not less than E£100; and if the capital is less than the said limit due to circumstances outside the company's control, the partners can increase the capital to that limit within one year of the date that it dropped below this limit. The company can be changed to another form that does not stipulate any minimum capital. Where the company does not proceed appropriately, any person of interest shall have the right to demand, by way of a court ruling, that the company be dissolved.

The shares may be sold by virtue of an official deed, or a deed with authentic signatures, unless the deed of association of the company provides otherwise. In this case, the rest of the partners shall have the right to recover the shares on the same terms.

Anyone who intends to sell his/her share should notify all the partners in the company, via the directors, of the offer he/she has received. If no offers are received within one month, the partner shall be free to dispose of his/her share. Each partner's share shall be transferred to his/her heirs and the status of the legatee shall be the same as that of an heir.

7.2   The company's management

The company shall be managed by a director appointed from among the partners, either for a definite or indefinite period. The directors are appointed by the deed of association of the company from the partners or others for an indefinite period. They shall be deemed to be appointed for the whole duration of the company, unless the deed of association provides otherwise. In all cases, the director(s) may be dismissed with the approval of the majority of partners so long as they possess three-quarters of the company's capital.

The directors have full authority to representing the company, unless its deed of association provides otherwise. Every decision issued by the company to restrict the directors' powers or to replace them must be recorded in the commercial register. This is only effective with regard to third parties five days after the decision has been recorded.

In terms of responsibility, the status of the directors is the same as that of the board of directors of a joint stock company. If the management is entrusted to one person, he/she should notify the partner's group about any conflict of interest in any transaction, for the purpose of authorising the transaction or for taking any action that the group deems fit.

If there are more than 10 partners, a board should be created. This should comprise at least three partners. The controlling board shall be determined as set out in the deed of association of the company, and its members are re-elected after the term set out in the deed of association. The controlling board can:

- ask the directors to submit reports;
- examine the company's books and documents and take an inventory of the cash in hand, the securities and the documents evidencing the company's rights and the goods found within it;
- monitor the balance sheet, the annual report and the draft of the distribution of profits; and
- submit a report about that to the partner's group at least 15 days before its meeting.

The members of the controlling board are not accountable for the work of the directors unless they knew about any mistakes that had been made and did not mention anything in their report.

The partners' decisions shall be issued in a general meeting by the majority of votes, unless the law or the deed of association provides otherwise. Every share has a vote even if the deed of association provides otherwise. The absent partners may vote in writing or deputise others to attend the general meeting on their behalf by virtue of a special proxy, unless the deed of association of the company provides otherwise. There shall be followed, in calling the general assembly to convene as well as in the deliberations, the rules applicable to joint stock companies.

The company's deed of association may not be amended, nor may its capital be increased or decreased, without the approval of the partners possessing three-quarters of the capital, unless the deed of association provides otherwise.

The provisions relating to the auditor, the inventory and the balance sheet in joint stock companies is the same as for limited liability companies. The balance sheet specifically shows the company's debts owed by the partners and the partners' debts owed by the company. The balance sheet should be deposited with the Commercial Registry within 15 days. Any interested party can ask to review it.

7.3 Dissolution of the company

If half of the company's capital is lost, the directors should submit a proposal for dissolving the company to the general assembly. This resolution needs the same majority as that required to amend the company's deed of association.

If the loss reaches 25% of the capital, the dissolution can be requested by the partners possessing 25% of the capital. If the capital falls to less the limit stated in the articles or bylaws, any interested party can ask for the company to be dissolved.

8. Merger and transformation

8.1 Merger

Any joint stock companies, partnerships limited by shares, companies in commendam, limited liability companies and general partnerships, whether Egyptian or foreign, that carry on their business in Egypt may be authorised, by a decree of the competent minister, to merge to form a new company. This will have the same status as that of the merged companies when applying the provisions of this law.

8.2 Transformation

The legal form of a partnership limited by shares or a limited liability company may be changed by a resolution adopted at an extraordinary general meeting or by a shareholders' group that holds more than three-quarters of the capital. The change will take place according to the procedures and conditions for the incorporation of the company.

9. Liquidation

Every company shall, after dissolution thereof, be in a state of liquidation. The liquidation shall be effected according to the provisions of the relevant Egyptian law, unless the articles of association or the deed of association of the company provide otherwise. The company shall maintain its legal personality during the liquidation period.

The phrase 'under liquidation' must be added to the company's name during the liquidation period. The company's entities will still exist, but their powers are restricted to work that does not fall under the liquidators' jurisdiction.

The general assembly will appoint the liquidators and will determine their fees. The liquidator will:

- discharge the debts owed by the company;
- sell the company's movable and immovable property at public auction or in any other way, unless his/her appointment deed specifies the way the sale is to be effected; and

- represent the company before the judiciary and agree to reconciliation and arbitration.

The liquidator is accountable to the company if he/she mismanages its business during the liquidation period. The liquidator shall also be accountable for any damage that affects the shareholders, the partners or third parties because of his/her mistakes.

10. **Official governmental dues for establishing a joint stock company and partnership in commendam limited by shares according to Law 159/1981**

Type of dues or tax	Value of due	Name of the party in favour of whom the dues are paid
Capital	1/1000 from the capital (with a maximum of E£1,000 and a minimum of E£100).	General Authority for Investment
Services	1/1000 from the capital (with a maximum of E£10,000 and a minimum of E£1,000).	
Publication	E£200 for 10 copies in the Arabic language. E£400 for 10 copies in the Arabic and the English language.	
In-kind share valuation	2/1000 from the total value of the assets or the share value as determined by the application demand (with a maximum of E£7,500 and a minimum of E£5,000).	
Certificate of the capital market	E£100.	
Registry fee	E£56.	Commercial Registry

continued

Type of dues or tax	Value of due	Name of the party in favour of whom the dues are paid
Capital dues less than E£500,000 Capital dues more than E£500,000	E£125. E£250.	Commerce Syndicate
Probate Duty (only for a company that has an issued capital not less than E£5000)	5/1000 with a maximum of E£5,000 and a minimum of E£100, + E£20 Attorney's stamp.	Bar Association
Probate duty	0.25/100 from the issued capital (with maximum of E£1,000).	Public Notarisation Authority
Practising licence Certificate of practice and the chapter membership dues plus stamp duty	2/1000 as annual subscription from the paid capital (with a maximum of E£2,000 and a minimum of E£24). E£29.	Chamber of Commerce
Dues of issuance of an establishment certificate	0.5/1000 (with a maximum of E£10,000 and a minimum of E£125).	Capital Market Authority
Tax card issuance	Stamp fees.	Taxation authority

11. **Official governmental dues for establishing a limited liability company according to Law 159/1981**

All fees are paid in at the Bank of Alexandria located at the General Investment Authority.

Type of dues or tax	Value of due	Name of the party in favour of whom the dues are paid
Official	1/1000 from the capital (with a maximum of E£1,000 and a minimum of E£100).	General Authority for Investment
Services	1/1000 from the capital (with a maximum of E£10,000 and a minimum of E£1,000).	
Publication	E£150 for the 10 copies in Arabic language. E£300 for the 10 copies in Arabic and English language; amount is doubled if extras are requested.	
In-kind share valuation	2/1000 from the in-kind shares value (with a maximum of E£7,500 and a minimum of E£5,000).	
Registry fees	E£56.	Commercial Registry
Capital dues less than E£500,000	E£125.	Commerce Syndicate
Capital dues more than E£500,000	E£250.	
Probate duty	5/1000 with a maximum of E£5,000 and a minimum of E£100, + E£20 Attorney's stamp.	Bar Association
Probate duty	0.25/100 with maximum E£1,000.	Public Notarisation Authority

continued

Type of dues or tax	Value of due	Name of the party in favour of whom the dues are paid
Practising licence	2/1000 as annual subscription (with a maximum of E£2,000 and a minimum of E£24).	Chamber of Commerce
Certificate of practice and the chapter membership dues and stamp dues	E£29.	
Tax card issuance	Stamp fees.	Taxation authority

12. **Official governmental dues for establishing a joint stock company and a partnership in commendam limited by shares according to Law 8/1997**

Type of dues or tax	Value of due	Name of the party in favour of whom the dues are paid
Capital duty	1/1000 from the capital (with a maximum of E£1,000 and a minimum of E£100).	General Authority for Investment
Services	1/1000 from the capital (with a maximum of E£10,000 and a minimum of E£1,000).	
Publication	E£200 for the 10 copies in Arabic language. E£400 for the 10 copies in Arabic and English language.	
In-kind shares evaluation	2/1000 from the in-kind shares value (with a maximum of E£10,000 and a minimum of E£5,000).	
Certificate of the Capital Market	E£100.	

continued

Type of dues or tax	Value of due	Name of the party in favour of whom the dues are paid
Registry fees for personal enterprises; registry fees for corporation and commercial partnership including foreign partners	E£56.	Commercial Registry
Probate duty	5/1000 with a maximum of E£5,000 and a minimum of E£100, + E£20 Attorney's stamp.	Bar Association (only for partnerships and companies that have an issued capital of not less than E£5,000)
Probate duty	0.25/100 from the issued capital (with maximum E£500 and a minimum of E£10).	Public Notarisation Authority
Dues of issuance of an establishment certificate	0.5/1000 from the issued capital (with a maximum of E£10,000 and a minimum of E£125).	The Capital Market Authority
Tax card issuance	Stamp fees.	Taxation authority

13. Official governmental dues for establishing a limited liability company according to Law 8/1997

All fees are paid at the General Investment Authority building.

Type of dues or tax	Value of due	Name of the party in favour of whom the dues are paid
Capital	1/1000 from the capital (with a maximum of E£1,000 and a minimum of E£100).	General Authority for Investment
Services	1/1000 from the capital (with a maximum of E£10,000 and a minimum of E£1,000).	
Publication	E£200 for the 10 copies in Arabic language. E£400 for the 10 copies in Arabic and English language.	
In-kind share valuation	2/1000 from the in-kind share value (with a maximum of E£10,000 and a minimum of E£5,000).	
Registry fee	E£56.50.	Commercial Registry
Contract probate duty	5/1000 with a maximum of E£5,000 and a minimum of E£100, + E£20 Attorney's stamp.	Bar Association (only for partnerships and companies that has an issued capital of not less than E£5,000)
Probate duty	0.25/100 from the issued capital (with maximum E£500).	Public Notarisation Authority
Opening the tax file and the tax card issuance	Stamp fees.	Taxation authority

14. **Official governmental dues for establishing a partnership and a partnership in commendam limited by share according to Law 159/1981**

Type of dues or tax	Value of due	Name of the party in favour of whom the dues are paid
Fees for a month	2/1000 without maximum limit.	Court
Registry fees	E£94.50.	Commercial Registry
Publicity fees	According to publicity area.	Publication
Dues + Subscription	2/1000 from the capital (with a maximum of E£2,000 and a minimum of E£24). E£86.	Chamber of Commerce
Tax card issuance	Stamp fees.	Taxation authority

15. **Official governmental dues for establishing a partnership according to investment Law 8/1992**

Type of dues or tax	Value of due	Name of the party in favour of whom the dues are paid
Capital	1/1000 from the capital (with a maximum of E£1,000 and a minimum of E£100).	General Authority for Investment
Services	1/1000 from the capital (with a maximum of E£10,000 and a minimum of E£1,000).	
Publication	E£465 for the contract in Arabic language.	
In-kind share valuation	2/1000 from the in kind shares value (with a maximum of E£10,000 and a minimum of E£5,000).	

continued

Type of dues or tax	Value of due	Name of the party in favour of whom the dues are paid
Registry fee	E£94.50. E£106.50 per individual company for foreigners.	Commercial Registry
Capital dues less than E£500,000	E£125.	Commerce Syndicate
Capital dues more than E£500,000	E£250.	
Control probate duty	5/1000 with a maximum of E£5,000 and a minimum of E£100, + E£20 Attorney's stamp.	Bar Association
Probate duty	0.25/100 from the issued capital (with maximum E£1,000).	Public Notarisation Authority
Scheduled taxes	E£90.	
Practising licence	2/1000 as annual subscription (with a maximum of E£2,000 and a minimum of E£24).	Chamber of Commerce
Different dues	E£86.	
Tax card issuance	Stamp fees.	Taxation authority

France

Nicola Mariani
Aurélie Maspétiol
Louis Néret
Dewey & LeBoeuf

1. Types of company with limited liability and applicable legislation

The most frequently used corporate vehicles in France are the *Société Anonyme* (SA), the *Société par Actions Simplifiée* (SAS) and the *Société à Responsabilité Limitée* (SARL). In these companies, financial liability is limited to the amount of the owners' capital contributions.

This chapter sets out the most notable features of these three types of companies. However, the choice of a company's legal structure in France depends on the shareholder's global strategy.

For instance, the SA allows the shareholders to initiate public offerings. The share capital of an SA is divided into freely transferable and negotiable shares and the administrative structure allows for the monitored delegation of powers.

An SAS is well suited for holding companies wishing to maintain 100% control of one of their subsidiaries and to set up a 'tailor-made' investment structure. The choice of an SAS allows for greater freedom, notably:

- in drafting the bylaws;
- in the determination of the management structure and governance; and
- in the setting up of the conditions relating to the transfer of shares.

An SARL is generally best suited for small to mid-size companies as it is easy to set up. An SARL offers greater security as its organisation and operating framework are both strictly regulated under French law.

Apart from the mainstream business corporations listed above, a wide range of other forms of company exist under French law. Some of these alternative corporate structures may be better suited for specific investment needs. However, these are subject to additional rules that fall outside of the scope of this chapter.

When reference is made to 'a company', without further specification, it refers to an SA, an SAS, an SARL or all three, as the case may be.

It is also possible to incorporate as a Societas Europaea (SE). Subject to certain conditions, the incorporation of an SE is likely to facilitate the merger or formation of a holding company or joint subsidiary between companies incorporated in different European Union member states, while avoiding certain legal and practical constraints arising from the existence of different legal systems within the European Union. The SE benefits from a consistent set of regulations, system of management and disclosure obligations relating to financial details throughout Europe. The SE's registered office is set out in the bylaws, and its location determines the applicable local legislation in so far as it does not contravene EC legislation. If the registered office is located in France, the SE will be subject to the legal regime of a French SA.

1.1 Applicable legislation

French-based companies are governed by both European and French legislation. The main provisions are set out in the French Civil Code, the French Commercial Code and the French Monetary and Financial Code.[1]

On August 4 2008, France enacted the *Loi de modernisation de l'économie*, which has introduced new corporate law aimed at simplifying company formation, such as:

- exemptions to the obligation to designate a statutory auditor for an SAS;
- removal of the requirement of a minimum share capital for an SAS (ie a €1 share capital is permitted); and
- removal of the requirement for members of the board of directors or supervisory board of an SA to be shareholders (unless otherwise provided in the bylaws).

2. Incorporation procedure

2.1 Proceedings prior to incorporation

(a) Foreign investment notifications

In most instances, foreign investment in France is not subject to any controls and requires only an administrative declaration, unless the investment is in one of a number of sensitive areas for which a specific control is set out.

Foreign investment may come from a foreign national, a French national residing abroad or from a foreign legal entity with its registered office abroad; however, in some cases a distinction may be drawn between foreign investments made by EU members and non-EU members. There is no general definition of 'foreign investor' under French law, so a case-by-case approach will need to be implemented in practice.

(b) Foreign investment declaration

Subject to certain exceptions, foreign investors are required to notify the French Ministry of Economy if the level of investment is greater than €1.5 million. This notification must be made at the time of the conclusion of the investment. It should be noted that the French administration considers that the filing shall be made on the execution of the binding agreement contemplating the investment, or on the completion of the investment should no prior agreement have been entered into. Failure to do so may result in a foreign investor incurring a fine of €750.

---

1   Updated versions of this legislation are available at www.legifrance.gouv.fr. These texts need to be read in conjunction with the European Community Treaty (notably Articles 44-2g and 293) and the numerous applicable directives relating to corporate law within the European Union.

(c)   *Foreign investment authorisation*
Prior authorisation from the French Ministry of Economy is required if the investment is made in one of the following sensitive industry sectors:
- gambling;
- regulated activities relating to civil security;
- research, development or production of life-science products to combat the effects of acts of terrorism, including health risks;
- wiretapping and eavesdropping equipment;
- services provided within the scope of evaluation and certification of security IT systems and devices;
- production of goods or provision of computer services offered to operators of certain strategic infrastructures (eg health, national defence);
- dual technologies;
- cryptology devices and services;
- business conducted by companies holding classified defence secrets;
- research, production and trade of weapons, munitions, powder and explosive substances for military use or war equipment; and
- defence-related contracts.

Once the French Ministry of Economy has received the application for authorisation, it will review the proposed investment and respond within a two-month period. The authorisation is deemed to have been granted if the French Ministry of Economy fails to respond. However, if the request for authorisation does not contain all requisite information and documentation, the two-month period is suspended until the missing information has been received.

Any agreement, undertaking or contractual clause purporting to carry out a foreign investment in one of the above-mentioned sensitive industry areas is null and void if due authorisation has not been rendered by the French Ministry of Economy. If so ordered, the foreign investor may be required to restore the original situation at its own cost. Failure to comply with the authorisation regime might also trigger a civil fine of up to double the value of the investment, as well as the imposition of criminal sanctions such as the seizure of the investment and imprisonment for up to five years.

(d)   *Statistical declaration*
If the investment exceeds a certain threshold (currently set at €15 million), a statistical declaration will have to be filed. As a consequence, the investment will have to be declared to the Banque de France within a 20-day period following its completion. In certain instances, an additional declaration needs to be made to the French Public Treasury.

(e)   *For foreign managers and shareholders*
Setting up a company in France does not require any specific formalities for EU citizens, or those of Iceland, Lichtenstein, Norway or the Swiss Confederation. There are additional formalities for other foreign nationals.

If a non-EU citizen wishes to carry out a business activity while residing in France, that citizen will need to obtain a temporary residence permit bearing the specification 'business activity'. If the future manager resides outside France, a request for a long-stay visa and a presentation of the contemplated business activity should be filed with the French consular authorities in that manager's country of residence. If the future manager is already residing in France with a residence permit that does not authorise business activity, they will need to apply for a change of status before the local district authorities (*Préfecture*) in their place of residence.

If a non-EU citizen wishes to set up a company in France but does not intend to reside in the country, that person must declare the company to the local district authorities (*Préfecture*) where the business will be based. The documents to be submitted include proof of civil status, a copy of criminal record or equivalent record in the country of origin, a copy of the bylaws of the company and the document appointing the company director.

2.2 Incorporation of the company

(a) Bylaws

Bylaws evidence the willingness of the shareholders to set up the company, and therefore must be put in writing. Bylaws must include the following information:

- the form of the company;
- the corporate purpose;
- the company name;
- the registered office;
- the share capital; and
- the term of the company.

The drafting of the other provisions may vary depending on the form of the company. Bylaws may be drafted in a simplified form for an SA or an SARL, since the contractual provisions are supplemented by extensive legal provisions, whereas bylaws of an SAS must detail numerous key elements such as the management structure, the decision-making process, or the restrictions on the transfer of shares. Professional guidance should be sought when drafting guidelines.

The legal representative of the company will generally be designated in the original bylaws of the company or through a separate decision of the shareholders.

(b) Execution of public instrument

In general, there is no need to have the bylaws executed by way of public instrument. However, there are certain instances when the bylaws must be executed by public instrument (eg when a building is transferred to a company in the process of formation). In addition, it is recommended that bylaws be executed by a public instrument in certain other cases – when, for example, the company is set up between heirs and/or spouses.

(c)   *Company registration number*

The company registration number (also referred to as the 'RCS' number) shall be indicated on all official documents issued by the company, and also, if applicable, on its corporate website.

The RCS number is made available upon the delivery of the 'Kbis' statement, (see section 2.2(e) below).

(d)   *Payment of taxes upon incorporation*

Upon incorporation of the company, a current (2009) fee of €83.96 will be payable to the Centre de formalités des entreprises.

Generally, the incorporation of a company is exempt from transfer taxes.

(e)   ***Registration with the competent Centre de formalités des entreprises and issuance of the Kbis certificate***

All incorporation documents must be filed with the competent Centre de formalités des entreprises (a 'one-stop shop' for corporate formalities). This communicates all relevant information to the tax authorities. The incorporation documents include the bylaws, the minutes evidencing the appointment of the executive managers, and, if applicable, the appraiser's report (Commissaire aux apports) on the contributions made in kind.

The clerk attached to the Centre de formalités des entreprises will verify the validity of the request for incorporation. A week or so after the incorporation documents have been filed, the clerk will publish a notice of incorporation in a legal journal and issue the company's Kbis certificate. The Kbis certificate issued by the clerk's office evidences the incorporation of the company.

Commitments entered into by the company before formal incorporation:

The company is formed as of the date of the signature of the bylaws, although it only enjoys legal personality and owns its assets as from the date of issuance of its Kbis certificate. All agreements entered into on behalf of the company under incorporation shall bind the company if the company commits to abide by the said agreements. The agreements not taken up by the company only bind the signatories of the said agreements.

(f)   *Corporate books*

The minutes recording the decisions of the shareholders and other corporate bodies must be kept in separate registers of minutes.

3. Number of shareholders

3.1 Number of partners/shareholders

	Société à Responsabilité Limitée (SARL)	Société Anonyme (SA) with a board of directors	Société par Actions Simplifiée (SAS)
Number of partners/ shareholders	1 to 100 natural and/or legal persons	At least seven natural and/or legal persons	At least one natural or legal person
Sanctions	Automatically dissolved if not regularised after one year	May be dissolved if not regularised after one year	N/A

3.2 Unipersonality

As mentioned above, the SAS and SARL may be formed by a single shareholder. Those types of company are regulated *mutatis mutandis* by legislation applicable to SASs and SARLs respectively.

4. Corporate name – limitations

The corporate name of a company can be freely chosen by the founding shareholders; however, it must not be contrary to public order or be immoral. In addition, the corporate name must not infringe third parties' intellectual property rights. To avoid this, it is highly recommended that an independent search of the availability of the corporate name be carried out with the *Institut National de la Propriété Industrielle* (INPI) database.

5. Registered office

Under French law, the registered office of the company must be the location from which the central management effectively operates. Its location will notably determine which courts will have jurisdiction over disputes involving the company as well as the place where most corporate formalities will have to take place.

Under certain conditions, the company may benefit from a collective domicile provided by a domiciliary agent, or use the personal address of a legal representative of the company as its registered office.

6. Object

The corporate purpose of a company must specify the activities that will be pursued by the company. The corporate purpose must be lawful, specifically defined in the bylaws and possible to achieve.

The corporate purpose limits the scope of action of the managers and may be used to protect the minority shareholders' interests. Any manager who does not act within the scope of the corporate purpose of the company may be removed. In addition, that manager could personally be held responsible if an act was committed that damaged the company.

Nonetheless, because of its limited liability, the company, is bound by the acts of its managers towards third parties, even if these acts do not come under the scope of the corporate purpose.

Finally, the corporate purpose will determine the collective bargaining agreement applicable to employees of the company. If the corporate purpose is not properly defined, the employees may seek a court order to obtain the implementation of the collective bargaining agreement corresponding to their effective activity.

7. Capital stock

The shares represent the contribution of each shareholder to the capital of the company. Contributions may generally be made in cash, in kind or via 'sweat equity' (ie a partner offers the company their time, work and professional knowledge). As opposed to contributions made in cash and/or in kind, sweat equity contributions are not taken into account when incorporating a company.

When setting up the company, a dedicated bank account will need to be opened to receive any cash contributions. The contributions will be held in a frozen account until the Kbis certificate is delivered.

Since 1983, title to shares has been dematerialised in France. Thus, no certificate will be given to the shareholders to evidence their ownership rights. Nonetheless, companies or intermediaries authorised by the stock market regulator (*Autorité des Marchés Financiers*) acting on their behalf keep track of shareholding structures.

Shares are, as a general rule, freely transferable. However, this freedom may be hindered by applicable legal provisions, by the bylaws of the company or by a shareholders' agreement.

Specific rules applying to each form of company are detailed in the table overleaf.

	Société à Responsabilité Limitée (SARL)	Société Anonyme (SA) with a board of directors	Société par Actions Simplifiée (SAS)
Minimum capital	No minimum requirement. €1 capital permitted. Must be sufficient capital to finance long-term needs. No public offerings allowed.	€37.000 Public offerings allowed if share capital greater than €225,000.	No minimum requirement. €1 capital permitted. Must be sufficient capital to finance long-term needs. No public offerings allowed.
Contribu-tions	Sweat equity allowed under certain conditions.	No sweat equity allowed.	Sweat equity allowed under certain conditions.
Partial payments	At least 20% of the nominal value of shares subscribed in cash must be paid up and the balance must be paid up within five years of registration. Shares subscribed in kind must be fully paid at the time of issue.	At least 50% of the nominal value of shares subscribed in cash must be paid up on incorporation and the balance must be paid up within five years of registration. Shares subscribed in kind must be fully paid at the time of issue.	At least 50% of the nominal value of shares subscribed in cash must be paid up upon incorporation and the balance must be paid up within five years of registration. Shares subscribed in kind must be fully paid at the time of issue.

continued overleaf

	Société à Responsabilité Limitée (SARL)	*Société Anonyme* (SA) with a board of directors	*Société par Actions Simplifiée* (SAS)
Represen-tation of shares	The shareholding structure is detailed in the bylaws, which must be regularly updated and registered with the *Registre du Commerce et des Sociétés* along with the relevant transactional documentation (as the case may be).	Stock registers kept by the company as evidence of the shareholding structure. For listed companies, an intermediary authorised by the *Autorité des Marchés Financiers* holds the ledgers.	Stock registers kept by the company as evidence of the shareholding structure.
Restriction on the transfer of shares	Shares are freely transferable between shareholders, subject to any restriction in the bylaws. Shares may be transferred to third parties following approval of shareholders representing at least 50% of the capital.	In principle, shares are freely transferable. Unless the company is listed, the bylaws may contain transfer restrictions.	In principle, shares are freely transferable. Bylaws may contain transfer restrictions.
Formalities on the transfer of shares	Approval of shareholders in the event of transfer to a third party. Deed of conveyance.	Unless the company is listed, share transfer form and entry on the stock register.	Share transfer form and entry on the stock register.

continued overleaf

	Société à Responsabilité Limitée (SARL)	Société Anonyme (SA) with a board of directors	Société par Actions Simplifiée (SAS)
Transfer taxes (payable when filing a copy of the deed of sale or the CERFA form)	3% of the price at which the shares are sold. If the company's assets are mainly composed of French real-property assets, the transfer tax amounts to 5%.	3% of the price at which the shares are sold (capped at €5,000). If the company is (i) not listed and (ii) its assets are mainly composed of French real-property assets, the transfer tax amounts to 5%.	3% of the price at which the shares are sold (capped at €5,000). If the company's assets are mainly composed of French real-property assets, the transfer tax amounts to 5%.

8. Equity

8.1 Balance between capital and own resources

(a) Equity funds amounting to less than one-half of share capital

Should the net equity (*capitaux propres*) be reduced to less than one-half of the share capital of the company due to losses, an extraordinary shareholders' general meeting should be convened within four months to decide whether the company should continue. The situation will be regularised within such period, failing which an action can be brought before the French Commercial Court by any interested person seeking the winding-up of the company.

(b) Thin capitalisation

From a corporate standpoint, for loans granted by a third party, financial expenses (interest) are in principle deductible from the taxable profits of the company as long as the loan is entered into in the best interests of the company, is commensurate with its financial capacity and the interest rate charged is an arm's-length rate.

There are specific tax rules that govern the deductibility of interest incurred in respect of loans granted by shareholders and, for tax years beginning on or after January 1 2007, by related entities.

Interest paid to a shareholder who is not considered a related party will be deductible for tax purposes up to the maximum rate defined in the French Tax Code. The rate is based on the average of annual floating rates applied by banks to enterprises for loans exceeding two years. It is reviewed every quarter. For the third quarter of 2008, this rate stood at 6.93%.

Interest paid to a legal entity that is a related party (as defined in the French Tax Code) will not be fully deductible if the following three thresholds are simultaneously crossed:

- a related debt-to-equity ratio of 1.5/1;
- interest paid to related parties exceeds 25% of adjusted current profits for the year; and
- interest paid to related parties exceeds income received from related parties (if the company uses the funds to finance other affiliated companies).

Interest is deductible up to the amount corresponding to the highest of the above ratio/thresholds, with the possibility of carrying forward the non-deductible amount within certain limits.

8.2 Securities

SAs or SASs may issue various types of securities. An SARL is only able to issue non-listed shares and, subject to certain conditions, ordinary bonds. Issuers may opt for various types of securities, such as:

- shares (including ordinary shares and preferred shares);
- securities giving deferred access to capital; and/or
- other bond instruments (eg ordinary bonds or complex securities such as bonds redeemable in shares or bonds with warrants redeemable in shares).

It is for the shareholders, gathered in an extraordinary general meeting, to decide whether to issue securities, unless the power to do this is delegated to the board of directors. Bonds that do not grant access to the capital may be issued upon a simple decision of the board of directors.

9. Administration of the company

9.1 General meeting of shareholders

There are a number of quorum, voting and challenge/annulment procedures applicable for a company, as set out next.

(a)   *Quorum and majority vote*

	Société à Responsabilité Limitée (SARL)	*Société Anonyme* (SA) with a board of directors	*Société par Actions Simplifiée* (SAS)
Quorum for meetings	For Extraordinary General Meeting (EGM), 25% of voting rights on first notice and 20% on second notice, unless bylaws provide for a higher quorum. For Ordinary General Meeting (OGM), no quorum is required.	For an EGM, 25% of voting rights on first notice and 20% on second notice. For an OGM, 20% on first notice and no quorum on second notice.	Determined by the bylaws.
Majority vote for adoption of resolutions	For EGM, 66% of voting rights + 1 vote notably required to ratify amendments to the bylaws. For OGM, 50% of the outstanding shares entitled to vote (ie absolute majority) on first notice and only the majority of shares represented at the meeting (ie simple majority) on second notice, notably required to approve the annual financial statements and to appoint or revoke managers.	For EGM, 66% of voting rights + 1 vote notably required to amend the bylaws. For OGM, 50% of voting rights + 1 vote notably required to approve the annual financial statements, to appoint or revoke members of the board of directors and to approve related parties' agreements.	Determined by the bylaws.
	Unanimous vote notably required to increase shareholders' contributions and in certain instances to change the corporate form or to transfer the registered office of the company outside France.		

(b)   ***Challenging resolutions***

Certain individuals may be entitled to request the annulment of a resolution. To do this, the individual will have to comply with the following:

- *Basis for action:* the nullity of a resolution may result only from an express provision of the French law or from the acts governing the nullity of contracts;
- *Legal capacity:* the right to challenge a resolution is available to all those who have a legitimate interest in the success or dismissal of a claim (notably shareholders, directors, managers, creditors, auditors); and
- *Statute of limitation:* the challenge must be brought before the relevant statute of limitation expires (ie three years in most cases save for resolutions pertaining to merger and share capital increases where the it drops to, respectively, six months and three months).

If the annulment of a resolution is the most commonly applied sanction, the courts may, in some instances, have discretion over it.

9.2   Administrative body

(a)   ***Different systems of governance***

(i)   SA

There are two possible systems of governance for an SA: (i) a board of directors (*Conseil d'Administration*) with a chairman of the board (*Président du Conseil d'Administration*) and a CEO (*Directeur-Général*) (it being understood that the CEO may combine the function with that of chairman (*Président-Directeur Général*)); or (ii) an executive board (*Directoire*) with a supervisory board (*Conseil de Surveillance*). In practice, the difference between the two forms of administration mostly lies in the strength with which each body exercises its powers.

The choice of a CEO with a board of directors will be favoured by investors who are looking for unhindered day-to-day management. The board of directors, composed of a minimum of three to a maximum of 18 members appointed by the shareholders, controls the management of the company and sets out the strategy. The CEO, appointed by the board of directors, is vested with the broadest powers to represent the company in all circumstances within the scope of the corporate purpose.

The choice of an executive board with a supervisory board will be favoured by investors who want to accentuate the distinction between the management and control functions. The executive board, composed of a minimum of two to a maximum of five members appointed by the supervisory board, is in charge of the management of the company and represents the company in its dealings with third parties. The supervisory board is composed of a minimum of three to a maximum of 18 members.

(ii)   *SAS*

The structure of the management of an SAS needs to be carefully defined in the bylaws. The only prerequisite is the appointment of a president to represent the company in its dealings with third parties. The powers of the president *vis-à-vis* the shareholders may be allocated relatively freely in the bylaws; to the extent that certain decisions may not be left to the discretion of the president – for instance, a change in the share capital, a merger, a split-off or a dissolution, which must be approved by the shareholders.

(iii)   *SARL*

One or several managers (*Gérant*) of an SARL will have to be appointed by the shareholders. There is no other executive body in an SARL. The managers are vested with the powers to represent the company in its dealings with third parties. The scope of these powers may be circumscribed in the bylaws.

(b)   **Term of office, resignation and removal of directors**

	Société à Responsabilité Limitée (SARL)	*Société Anonyme* (SA) with a board of directors	*Société par Actions Simplifiée* (SAS)
Terms of office	Freely determined in the bylaws. If no term is set, managers are appointed for the term of the company.	Determined in the bylaws but may not exceed three years for directors at the time of incorporation of a non-listed entity, and otherwise six years.	Freely determined in the bylaws.
Resignation	Conditions are to be determined in the bylaws.	At any time upon decision of the director, who does not have to justify its decision.	At any time upon decision of the president, unless otherwise determined in the bylaws.

continued overleaf

	Société à Responsabilité Limitée (SARL)	Société Anonyme (SA) with a board of directors	Société par Actions Simplifiée (SAS)
Removal of directors	At any time, upon decision of the shareholders representing 50% of the voting rights + 1 vote. In the event of removal without just cause, the manager may be entitled to damages. In the event of gross misconduct, at the request of any shareholder and upon decision of the court.	At any time upon decision of shareholders representing 50% of the voting rights + 1 vote. The decision does not need to be justified. If the circumstances of the removal of the director are considered to be abusive, he may be entitled to damages.	Freely determined in the bylaws. If the circumstances of the removal of the director are considered to be abusive, he may be entitled to damages.

(c) Directors' duties and liabilities

(i) Civil liability

Directors are liable for any breach of legislation applicable, any breach of bylaws, and any misconduct in their management. Directors may be liable towards third parties if their misconduct is severable from their functions.

(ii) Criminal liability

Directors may be held liable as a result of any misconduct, such as presentation of misleading financial statements or use of assets contrary to the company's best interests. Directors may incur up to five years' imprisonment and a fine, which may reach €375,000.

The company, as a legal person, may be held criminally liable for any misconduct carried out by its administration on its behalf. The amount of the fine incurred may reach €1,875,000. Other sanctions may apply, including the compulsory winding-up of the company.

(iii) Insolvency

In the event of insolvency of the company, the directors may be held liable for the debts of the company if the debts result from mismanagement (as established by a judicial decision).

In addition, when a company goes into liquidation, a director may be liable for the debts of the company if he engaged in one of the following:

- misappropriation of corporate assets;
- management of the company in furtherance of own personal interest; or
- presentation of misleading accounts.

(d) Employees' representative bodies

The staff representation system will vary depending on the size of the company.

In companies of more than ten employees, employees' representatives are elected by the employees to present individual and collective claims and to ensure compliance with labour laws under all circumstances.

A works committee (*Comité d'Entreprise*) must be set up if the company has more than 50 employees. This committee is elected for a period of four years by the employees to represent their interests when decisions are made about economic changes such as work organisation, and about social and cultural issues. If the company has fewer than 200 employees, it may be decided, after consultation with the employees' representatives, to opt for a single employee representation delegation that combines the employees' representatives and the works committee in the same body.

A *Comité d'Hygiène, Securité et Conditions de Travail* (CHSCT) will also be set up if the company has more than 50 employees. The CHSCT's role is to involve staff in training and other initiatives to prevent occupational risks and improve working conditions.

(e) Trade unions

Each year, the employer must conduct negotiations with trade union representatives regarding effective compensation, effective duration and organisation of working hours, and to deal with questions related to gender equality. The obligation to negotiate does not extend to an obligation to actually reach an agreement with union representatives.

Moreover, in companies of at least 50 employees, each representative union may appoint a union delegate (*délégué syndical*). Union delegates have, in principle, the monopoly over negotiation of collective bargaining agreements with the employer. They are granted a certain number of hours out of their effective working time in order to carry out their task. They benefit from protection against dismissal.

(f) Statutory auditors

The auditors who must issue various financial reports to the shareholders (see section 11 below) are appointed by the shareholders for a renewable term of six years. The chart overleaf details the appointment conditions of auditors.

	Société à Responsabilité Limitée (SARL)	*Société Anonyme* (SA) with a board of directors	*Société par Actions Simplifiée* (SAS)
Number of mandatory auditors	At least one statutory auditor and one replacement auditor if the company reaches two of the following threshold conditions: (i) a balance sheet reaching €1.55 million; (ii) a pre-tax turnover of €3.1 million; and (iii) 50 employees on average. Two statutory auditors when the company is required to publish consolidated accounts.	At least one statutory auditor and at least one replacement auditor. Two statutory auditors when the company is required to publish consolidated accounts.	At least one statutory auditor and one replacement auditor if the company reaches two of the threshold conditions: (i) a balance sheet reaching €1 million; (ii) a pre-tax turnover of €2 million; and (iii) 20 employees on average.[2] At least one statutory auditor must be appointed if the company is controlled by another company or controls another company under the meaning of Article L. 233-16 of the French Commercial Code. Two statutory auditors when the company is required to publish consolidated accounts.
Appointment	Appointed by the shareholders representing 50% of the voting rights + 1 vote.	Appointed by the shareholders' general meeting upon proposal of the board of directors.	Appointed by the shareholders' general meeting.

---

2 Thresholds are subject to confirmation since the implementing regulation has not yet been enacted upon the time of writing of this chapter (early 2009).

10. Fiscal year and duration and start of activities

The financial year of the company is for a 12-month period, subject to certain exceptions. It generally starts in January and ends in December but there are no specific rules and it may be decided otherwise depending on the seasonality of the business.

11. Financial statements

11.1 Company tax

If the company, whether incorporated in the form of a branch, a subsidiary or a permanent establishment, is making profits in France, it is liable to pay French taxes on its earnings in France. The standard applicable rate is currently (2009) 33.33% of the taxable business income, which is calculated by deducting eligible expenses (eg depreciation and amortisation, provisions, wages, energy consumption, and advertising) from revenue (ie all proceeds from the sale of goods and the provision of services and other proceeds).

An additional surtax of 3.3% is applied to the portion of corporate tax that exceeds €763,000, leading in this case to a marginal corporate tax rate of 34.43%.

11.2 Annual accounts

(a) *Documents*

Accounting obligations for French companies include:

- booking, in a chronological order, all movements having an impact on the patrimony of the company;
- controlling the existence and the value of assets and liabilities of the company using an inventory to be carried out at least every 12 months; and
- drawing up the financial statements (ie a balance sheet, profit and loss account and exhibits) at the end of every financial year according to the accounting and inventory books.

(b) *Audit report*

Subject to the appointment of a statutory auditor (either on a compulsory or voluntary basis), the statutory auditors of the company must produce a report in relation to the annual accounts, stating whether the accounts present an accurate picture of the company's financial situation or whether certain reservations need to be made. The auditor must also report the existence of certain related parties' agreements.

(c) *Approval and distribution of profits*

Before distributing dividends, 5% of the company's net income will have to be allocated to the retained earnings account, until the retained earnings account amounts to 10% of the capital of the company.

Dividends paid by a company (subject to corporate tax) to individuals who reside in France will be taxable at a maximum effective rate of approximately 33%.

Three methods are usually used by foreign residents to repatriate profits:

- transfer or distribution of net profit from branches or subsidiaries;
- interest on loans and advances granted by a foreign parent company; or
- royalties or management fees.

(d)   *Documents to be registered*
Within six months of the financial year end, the financial statements must be approved by the shareholders during the annual shareholders' meeting. The company's financial statements must then be filed together with the balance sheet, the profit and loss accounts with exhibits, the management report and the decision allocating the net income, and the statutory auditors' report (as the case may be).

12.   Company reorganisation

12.2   Transformation
A change of the company's legal form will result in its transformation, which will necessitate an amendment of the bylaws. However, such transformation will not lead to the setting-up of a new legal entity.

At least eight calendar days prior to the shareholders' meeting deciding on the transformation, a report will have to be drafted to assess the value of the assets of the company. Such a report will be drafted by the statutory auditor(s) of the company. If the company does not have a statutory auditor, a special auditor will have to be appointed to that effect by a decision of the French courts.

12.2   Merger
To successfully complete a merger, specific steps must be carried out. The companies involved must:
- make a merger plan, with the assistance of a lawyer;
- appoint special auditors to assess the value of the merging entities;
- file the merger plan with the *Registre du Commerce et des Sociétés*;
- publish a notice of the merger plan in a legal notices journal, in each local district where the registered offices of the participating companies are based;
- obtain approval of the plan from an extraordinary general meeting of each set of shareholders; and
- file with the *Registre du Commerce et des Sociétés* a declaration outlining all actions carried out and certifying that the operation has been completed in accordance with the applicable regulations.

If a French company is to merge with another EU entity, it should be noted that the parties may benefit from the European cross-border merger legal framework, which facilitates the process by overcoming obstacles caused by different national laws.

12.3   Split-off
A split-off of assets of a company into two or more, new or existing companies is subject to the same regulations as mergers.

13. Eventual separation of shareholders

As a general rule, French law is protective of shareholders' voting rights. Subject to a limited number of exceptions, shareholders may not be excluded from the company or be forced to transfer their shares against their will.

Under certain circumstances and pursuant to the bylaws, shareholders may be forced to purchase the shares of another shareholder, provided that the terms and conditions of purchase are determined in advance. Such terms and conditions must be included in the bylaws at the time of formation of the company or added to the bylaws through a unanimous decision of the shareholders.

More generally, the bylaws of the company or a shareholders' agreement may govern the transfer of shares and provide for exit conditions.

14. Dissolution and liquidation

The company may be dissolved in two ways other than through the expiry of its term and the fulfilment of its corporate purpose: (i) by decision of the shareholders; or (ii) by decision of a competent court.

14.1 A decision by the shareholders

The premature dissolution of the company may be decided by the shareholders at any time, subject to the approval of an extraordinary general meeting of shareholders (ie under the same majority-vote requirement as for the amendment of the bylaws of the company). The shareholders will have to appoint a voluntary receiver, set the place of liquidation and perform various other formalities.

However, if it can be shown that the purpose of the decision to dissolve the company is to harm the rights of the minority shareholders, or is motivated by fraud, the dissolution may be annulled and may trigger the majority shareholders' liability towards third parties.

14.2 A decision of a competent court

Subject to certain conditions, any shareholder may request the dissolution of the company before the courts. Such a request will have to be grounded on a 'just cause', which may be a breach by a shareholder of its duties, or some disagreement among shareholders. The dissolution of the company will only be ordered by the court if it can be ascertained that the management of the company and the conduct of its business are paralysed.

14.3 Liquidation

The dissolution of a company is always followed by its liquidation (ie the recovery of assets, the payment of debts and the distribution of any remaining net assets, except in the case of universal transfer of assets (which is similar to a merger)).

Liquidation will take place within a three-year period after the dissolution of the company and is decided on at a second general meeting, during which the shareholders must approve the final liquidation accounts, discharge the voluntary receiver of its mandate and decide on the distribution of any balance remaining.

15. Branches

As an alternative to setting up a subsidiary or a preliminary step to entering into the French market, it may be of interest for a foreign company to establish a branch in France.

The main difference between a branch and a subsidiary lies in the fact that, unlike a subsidiary, a branch of a foreign company is not considered to be a separate legal entity. As a consequence, the parent company is directly liable for any action undertaken by the branch, without any limitation to its liability.

A branch will nonetheless be regarded as a permanent establishment for tax purposes, and it will be liable to pay corporate income tax, VAT and any other applicable business tax.

The setting-up of a branch office requires no specific formalities other than that:

- the head of the branch office must hold or apply for the appropriate business permit (as mentioned above);
- the branch office must be registered with the *Registre du Commerce et des Sociétés*; and
- the branch manager must possess a power of attorney enabling him/her to ensure that the branch complies with French law.

Germany

Andreas Lachmann

Rotthege Wassermann & Partner GbR

1. Types of company with limited liability and applicable legislation

In Germany the Law for the Modernisation of the Private Limited Companies Act and to Combat its Abuse (MoMiG) entered into force on November 1 2008. It aims to reform the law on limited companies. Prior to its introduction, investors were advised to incorporate either as a limited liability company (*Gesellschaft mit beschränkter Haftung*) or as a public stock company (*Aktiengesellschaft*) to prevent personal liability and to install a corporate veil. Now, the legislator offers an alternative: an 'entrepreneurial company' (*Unternehmergesellschaft*). The share capital must at least be €1. This type of company must use the abbreviation 'UG' or the full German expression. The intention of the legislation is to create a German alternative to the British private limited company (suffix 'Limited' or 'Ltd').

Limited liability companies are governed by the Law on Limited Liability Companies, while public stock companies are governed by the Corporation Act. The ongoing legal reforms have been integrated into these two laws.

The Commercial Code also contains material provisions governing these types of company. A public stock company and a limited liability company are subject to stricter commercial requirements in dealings with third parties than other forms of company. The Commercial Code also sets out the fundamental principles on bookkeeping and accounting.

The bankruptcy regime is set out in the Insolvency Code, which determines the applicable proceedings where natural persons and companies, or their creditors, have filed for bankruptcy.

The transformation of companies is regulated by the Conversion of Companies Code.

2. Incorporation of a limited liability company

2.1 Entrepreneurial company

An entrepreneurial company requires a minimum share capital of €1. The capital must be paid up. Non-cash contributions are forbidden. The director of the company must declare that the contribution has been paid.

One-quarter of the annual net profit must be retained as a reserve within the company. This reserve cannot be distributed to the shareholder. It may be used as a capital increase or to cover losses in a particular year. If the capital is increased to €25,000, the entrepreneurial company can act freely without such restrictions. The company may then use the legal designation 'GmbH' (ie a limited company). Even though the provisions for the entrepreneurial company contain some peculiarities, the law on limited companies applies if there are no special circumstances.

Because of the costs of setting up a company, equipping an entrepreneurial company with only €1 is not sufficient if the company has to bear the costs of setting up. In this case the company would be insolvent from the start. The company should have a minimum capital of at least €300, or the shareholder should pay to set up the company. This also corresponds with the sample foundation protocols of the chamber of notaries.

2.2 Start-up or shelf company

Incorporation of a limited liability company requires registration in the companies register. There is no central companies register in Germany. Rather, registration occurs at the local registry court where the company has its principal place of business. Under Section 7 of the Law on Limited Liability Companies, the company must apply for registration to the court of the place where it has its registered office.

The length of the registration process depends on the respective registry court. However, the MoMiG implemented some changes, such as issuing sample statutes to help the setting-up procedure. Nonetheless, the reform does not provide for any fundamental changes with regard to the company formation procedure, except that administrative authorisation (eg for craft works) must not be obtained before the registration of the company and such authorisation may be applied for at a later stage before starting the business.

Even before it has been entered in the companies register, the company acquires the legal status of a pre-limited liability company once it has obtained notarial certification. There is a legal identity between the pre-limited liability company and the future limited liability company. However, at this stage the company may only do business as a pre-limited liability company, so its operations are very limited in practice.

An alternative is to use a shelf company. These are companies that have already been registered in the companies register and that manage their own assets exclusively. A shelf company is sold by the promoter – usually for a price between €2,000 and €3,000 – to a buyer who must then rename it and register the name change. In a decision of July 7 2003 the Federal Supreme Court ruled that the use of a shelf company constitutes a start-up and is subject to the respective legal provisions on capital contributions. Under Section 8(2) of the Law on Limited Liability Companies, the registry courts now require a guarantee from the new managing director that the required share capital payments have been made and are available to the managing directors.

As the renaming is treated as a start-up, there is little real advantage in using shelf companies.

The usual fees to set up a limited liability company with a capital of €25,000 are as follows:
- notarial fees – €380;
- court fees – €340; and
- chamber of commerce fees – €128.

However, these costs may vary depending on the method of incorporation and other circumstances.

Further, it is normal for foreign investors to entrust a German lawyer with the incorporation proceedings, which will normally incur additional costs of between €1,500 and €3,000. However, as most German lawyers charge for such work on an hourly basis, these figures may vary considerably.

There is no stamp duty in Germany.

2.3   Registration requirements

(a)   *Company name*

It is recommended that appropriate inquiries are made at the competent Chamber of Commerce to determine that there will be no objections to the company name. The name should not create any confusion and should not contain general terms that are not sufficiently specific. The Chamber of Commerce will often respond the next day or at least within a few days, but its approval does not guarantee that the name does not infringe the rights of third parties.

(b)   *Registered share capital, initial capital contributions*

The registered share capital of the GmbH must be at least €25,000. The prerequisite that each shareholder's initial contribution must be at least €100 was abandoned with the MoMiG. The same applies to the previous requirement that each initial contribution must be divisible by 50. The legislation now permits a more flexible handling. The only requirement is that the total contributions must equal the registered share capital.

If the capital has to be paid as cash, then it is not legitimate to re-disburse those payments to the shareholder (eg by the acquisition of assets from the shareholder) before the company is registered. However, the legislation is not as strict as before with regard to such back payments if they take place after the registration of the company and provided that it is possible to verify that the value of the assets was as least equivalent to the price agreed upon. These measures, however, require detailed advice from a German lawyer as such transactions are also to be reviewed beforehand to prevent criminal sanctions. This also applies for loans the German subsidiary provides to its parent company or companies. Even though the reform of the German law facilitates cash pooling, there are some restrictions (ie the subsidiary must be entitled to ask for the redemption at any time and that the recoverability must be ascertained). Foreign investors should be very careful because, under the new German law system, there is a fine line between allowed capital allocations and transactions that might be viewed by the state prosecutor as illegal.

The application for registration cannot be filed until at least one-quarter of each capital contribution has been paid. Moreover, at least half of the registered share capital must be paid up at the time of incorporation.

Before the MoMiG entered into force, the sole shareholder of a limited liability company with a single shareholder had to provide security for the unpaid portion (Section 7(2) clause 3 of the Law on Limited Liability Companies). To avoid this requirement, the registered share capital of such companies was usually fully paid up at the time of incorporation. The legislator has now abandoned this special treatment for the single-shareholder company.

In-kind contributions must be paid in full prior to incorporation. The shareholders must state the key facts establishing the reasonableness of the in-kind contribution in a special report. The MoMiG facilitates this way of setting up a company as the registration court can only refuse registration because of the missing equivalency where this is "not insignificant". Nonetheless, the procedure for setting up a company by in-kind contributions is normally not recommended for foreign investors. They are usually interested in getting the company established as quickly as possible.

(c)   *Shareholder agreement*

The MoMiG provides a basic template for a shareholder agreement. The use of the template serves to accelerate the registration of the company as the companies register may then rely on the lawfulness of its content. However, the template does not contain some of the basic provisions that are normally recommended by German lawyers, such as the exclusion of shareholders by way of forfeiture (eg in case of insolvency or death) and the right to terminate membership in the company, or the restrictions to the transfer of the shares.

The shareholder agreement of a limited liability company must be notarised. The shareholder agreement is appended to a notarised copy of the minutes of the foundation meeting, in which the voluntary mutual consent of the promoters is expressed. The shareholder agreement governs the basic foundation of the company and is binding on future shareholders.

If there are foreign shareholders, a dual-language version of the agreement can be created, with the German provisions on one side and the foreign-language provisions on the other. However, the predominance of the German version should be explicitly acknowledged.

The shareholder agreement must include:

- the name and registered office of the company;
- the corporate purpose;
- the amount of the registered share capital; and
- the initial contributions to be paid by each shareholder.

Where in-kind contributions are made, the item contributed and the amount of the initial contribution to which the in-kind contribution relates must be specified in the shareholder agreement.

Foreign promoters have often had problems specifying the principal place of business. In many cases premises have not yet been rented at the time of incorporation, as leases are often conditional on registration in the companies register. It is advisable to establish a temporary principal place of business (eg the offices of the solicitor assisting in the incorporation) for registration purposes. With the implementation of the MoMiG it is also possible to have the real seat of the company outside Germany if a business address exists within the country.

(d)   Timing of initial contributions

The initial contributions must be made after notarisation of the shareholder agreement and before registration in the companies register. In reality, this requirement is impossible to meet because the agreement is usually notarised and registration certified upon confirmation of payment at a single notary meeting. However, for technical reasons, payment cannot be made within the timescale of the notary meeting.

There is a common procedure available that avoids the need to have two notary meetings. The director declares before the notary that the initial contribution has already been paid – even though this is not true at the time – and trusts that the notary will not submit the statement to the registry court until payment has actually been made. However, this procedure is risky, given that it involves making a false statement before a public official.

German banks require individuals to be authorised to sign in person at the bank, so it can be difficult for non-Germans to open an account. However, it can usually be done. The legitimisation documents will then be sent internally to the German bank office. The banks will usually not allow transfers of the assets on the account if they exceed a certain amount (eg €2,000) until the company has been registered on the companies register. Furthermore, clients must undergo a second procedure to open the account after the company has been set up, which gives unlimited power to dispose of the assets. This procedure is quite time-intensive and is a serious burden on investors from abroad.

(e)   Application for registration

The following documents must accompany an application for registration:

- the shareholder agreement;
- proof of the identity of the directors, unless appointed in the shareholder agreement;
- a list of shareholders signed by the applicants;
- documentation relating to in-kind contributions; and
- if the corporate purpose requires government approval, the certificate of approval.

Care should be taken when formulating the corporate purpose of the company that (in so far as the activities do not require approval) the corporate purpose admits no doubt in this regard. This is particularly relevant where a foreign company is establishing a German subsidiary and wants it to adopt a corporate purpose that is formulated extremely broadly.

The application for registration must be filed personally by the managing director of the company under incorporation, as only the managing director has the power to declare the full payment of the capital; the managing director is also obliged to provide a specimen of his personal signature under Section 8(5) of the Law on Limited Liability Companies. Furthermore, the director must declare that he has not been convicted of insolvency by a court. Due to the MoMiG, the catalogue of declarations to be certified has been extended. This must to be taken into account to avoid a complaint from the companies register.

The declaration to the companies' register must be made after the company has been warned by a German notary about the consequences of making a false declaration. However, most non-German directors living abroad comply with this formality by way of a written instruction sent to them by a German notary. This must be countersigned by a director.

There is some disagreement among the German registry courts as to the evidence required to prove that a foreign company's acts during the incorporation process are legally effective. Some courts accept an uncertified extract from the register in which the foreign company is entered, in the original language. In order to avoid any objections, however, it is advisable to supplement this with a notarised power of representation from a notary of the foreign company.

The application to register the company must now be submitted electronically by a German notary to the companies register.

3.   Hiring of employees by a limited liability company

Employees are protected from termination by the Protection against Dismissal Act.

Since January 1 2004 this law has applied to companies that employ 10 or fewer full-time employees on a regular basis, provided they were hired after this date (Section 23(1) of the Protection Against Dismissal Act).

Part-time employees are counted *pro rata* as follows:

- employees working no more than 20 hours per week count as 0.5;
- those working no more than 30 hours count as 0.75; and
- those working more than 30 hours count as one.

Trainees do not count for such purposes.

The act covers only those employees whose employment in the same plant or company has lasted longer than six continuous months. As long as an employee is covered, dismissal is legally ineffective if it is socially unjustified – that is, if it is not based on grounds related to the person or conduct of the employee, or on urgent business needs that are adverse to the continued employment of the employee. As the German courts set a very high standard for grounds for dismissal, only very serious breaches of duty will justify dismissal and a warning must usually have been given beforehand.

The Protection against Dismissal Act does not apply to directors or senior management. In determining whether the act applies, whether the person to be dismissed is himself entitled to take personal decisions will prove decisive.

4.   Regulations governing limited liability companies

4.1   Directors

(a)   Appointment

A limited liability company must have one or more directors. The first directors are normally appointed in the company statutes. The decision to appoint directors at a later stage is normally taken by the shareholders' meeting. A director must declare his consent to his appointment.

Directors are appointed by decision of the shareholders and their appointment must be entered in the companies register (Section 39 of the Commercial Code). Often, a person to be appointed as director also acts on behalf of a shareholder. Under German law, such a contract whereby the same person represents both himself and a third party is invalid, except where the third party consents to the double representation or has been granted relief from this restriction on double representation (Section 181 of the Civil Code).

For example, where company A is the sole shareholder of company B and the president of company A intends to appoint himself as a director of company B, he will normally need the prior consent of the shareholders of company A.

Such consent must usually be obtained, and all documents necessary to verify this submitted, prior to registration. For foreign investors, this prerequisite often causes problems.

For example, French company A is the sole shareholder of German company B and the president of company A intends to appoint himself as the new director of company B. The registry court, if unfamiliar with French law, might ask the president of company A to verify that such double representation is permitted under French law without the shareholders' consent. Under French law (and in certain other jurisdictions), double representation is permitted without such consent. However, it may be necessary to submit to the registry court a legal opinion or a confirmation by a notary in this respect.

Similar problems often arise with regard to other legal acts of interrelated companies. It may therefore be helpful to grant the directors relief from the restrictions of Section 181 of the Civil Code on a general basis and have this entered in the companies register.

The appointment of a foreign national as director sometimes poses problems if he is not an EU citizen. Depending on which country he is from, a foreign national director who wishes to work in Germany may need to obtain a work permit and a visa to fulfil his duties. This should be clarified beforehand with the companies register.

(b) Employment contracts

A distinction must be drawn between the appointment of a director and any employment contract between the director and the company. A director need not be an employee of the company. Further, within a group of companies, a director may be employed by the parent company or another group member; in such cases, however, it is advisable to get the agreement checked by a tax adviser and/or lawyer.

The employment contract need not be in writing, although this is recommended. The duration of the employment contract can be either fixed or indefinite. If the duration is fixed, the director is entitled to receive his normal remuneration until the end of this contractual period if he is dismissed from office during this term. Where the duration is indefinite, a director who is dismissed is entitled to his contractual compensation until the end of the notice period. If the notice period is not specified in the employment contract, it will be determined by analogy to the legal notice periods of employees. While shorter notice periods may be specified, there are some limitations to such contractual agreements based on case law.

Where a director is to be restricted from competing with the company following dismissal, the non-competition agreement must fulfil the following legal prerequisites:

- There must be a legitimate reason for the agreement;
- The agreement must not be unfair in respect of the restrictions it imposes on the director;
- The agreement must not exceed two years in duration, except in exceptional circumstances;
- The agreement may encompass activities performed by subsidiary companies only if the director had direct access to their information; and
- Adequate compensation must be paid.

It is advisable to have a non-competition clause checked by a German lawyer in advance.

(c)   Management powers

A limited liability company is managed by the directors, who are entitled, in principle, to take all decisions within the ordinary course of business. However, this capacity is subject to any restrictions imposed on the directors by the company statutes. It is normal to include a catalogue of restrictions that limit the directors' right to manage the company. For example, the statutes might require that the shareholders give prior consent to a contract that would lead the limited liability company to incur obligations exceeding a predetermined amount of money.

Even if no such restrictions exist, the Federal Court has held that all measures that are fundamental to the structure of the limited liability company require the prior consent of the shareholders.

(d)   Powers of representation

A limited liability company is represented by the director or, where there is more than one director, by the directors jointly. In the latter case the shareholders can also empower the directors to represent the company individually. The company statutes can also provide for a single representation, which is very common.

(e)   Liability to third parties

A director is normally not liable for obligations incurred on behalf of the limited liability company towards third parties. However, there are some exceptions to this rule.

A director who acts in a way that persuades a third party to trust in his personal competence may be personally liable towards that third party. However, not all declarations of a director – not even those relating to the company's financial situation – will result in personal liability under normal circumstances. For example, the Federal Court has found that a director who ordered large amounts of stock for a limited liability company two months before applying for bankruptcy was not personally liable, even though the company was in crisis at the time. The legal situation would have been different had the director wrongly informed his business partner of the company's financial situation.

Personal liability may also be triggered by a delayed petition for bankruptcy. Section 64 of the Law on Limited Liability Companies requires a director to file for bankruptcy if the company is either over-indebted or illiquid. However, the Federal Court has ruled that an amount that is less than 10% of the total debts due will normally not be considered as illiquidity.

After the commencement of bankruptcy proceedings, creditors can sue a director only for debts incurred after the time the director was obliged to file for bankruptcy. Obligations incurred before this time are to be enforced by the insolvency administrator (Section 92 of the Insolvency Code).

(f)   *Liability to the company*
A director can also be liable with respect to the company if he does not act in accordance with his employment contract or the general duties to which he is subject according to German law. The main provision in this respect is Section 43(1) of the Law on Limited Liability Companies, which provides that directors must exercise the due care of a reasonable businessman. A director may further be liable if capital contributions are paid out to shareholders in breach of the capital maintenance provisions (eg where a loan is granted to a shareholder in times of financial crisis).

(g)   *Criminal liability*
'Criminal liability' as such does not exist in Germany. A director who commits a crime might be exposed to a claim of the victim under tort law. The victim may be a creditor, who can then sue the director directly, or the company, which has been disadvantaged by a criminal act by the director. Such claims must be pursued before the civil courts.

In theory, in certain circumstances it is also possible to seek civil compensation in criminal court proceedings. However, this possibility is of little practical relevance.

4.2   Directions by the shareholders
The managing directors must follow the directions of the shareholders, as long as these do not violate the law.

4.3   Capital maintenance
Conflicts between shareholder directions to managing directors and legal restrictions arise in particular in relation to capital maintenance provisions and duties to declare bankruptcy. German corporate law places great emphasis on capital maintenance.

The capital maintenance principle is enshrined in Section 30 of the Law on Limited Liability Companies, according to which company assets that are needed to maintain the registered share capital may not be paid out to shareholders. This kind of repayment occurs not only under the guise of an express repayment of capital contributions, but also in so-called 'hidden dividends'. These are allocations of any kind to shareholders from company assets that are not reported as dividends (eg excessive corporate rate assessments by a subsidiary, loans to a parent company at an excessively low interest rate, or the financing of the acquisition of another company from company assets).

However, those rules have been softened under MoMiG. The amended legal provisions now provide for exceptions with regard to the cash pooling, to facilitate financing within groups of companies. The rules on capital lock-up do not apply if the claim against the parent company is for full value or if a control agreement has been concluded between the respective companies.

Payments that violate the capital maintenance principle must be returned to the company pursuant to Section 31 of the Law on Limited Liability Companies. If the recipient took the payment in good faith, return of such payment may be demanded only to the extent necessary to satisfy the company's creditors.

The Law on Limited Liability Companies formerly also included restrictive provisions governing the reverse scenario, where the shareholders transfer resources to the company and subsequently demand them back. If a shareholder made a loan to the company at a time when shareholders, acting as prudent businessmen, would have transferred equity capital instead (ie a company crisis), they could enforce a claim for repayment of the loan in a bankruptcy action, but only as junior creditors (Section 32(a) of the Law on Limited Liability Companies). Under the new MoMiG regime, all repayment claims of shareholders arising from loans are considered those from junior creditors. The former provisions within the Law on Limited Liability Companies have been abolished and, instead, new provisions were implemented in the Insolvency Code – see in particular Sections 39, 135(1) and 135(2).

Formerly this principle applied to other legal acts of a shareholder or third party that were considered as the economic equivalent of making a loan, under Section 32(a)(3) of the Law on Limited Liability Companies. According to case law, the equity substitution rules applied in a number of situations that, on first impression, appeared to bear no resemblance to a loan. For example:

- Where a shareholder leases real property to the company, this is treated as equity substitution in a crisis and the shareholder must reimburse the company for rent it has paid. Further, the shareholder may not demand repossession of the property before the fixed term of the lease expires, even though he is receiving no rent payments;
- A parent company that delivers goods to its subsidiary but defers the purchase price during a crisis cannot demand payment in the future; and
- The provision of security by a shareholder in favour of the company is also treated as equity substitution during a crisis.

These principles were frequently overlooked, particularly by foreign investors. The MoMiG has not completely abandoned such principles. A shareholder who entrusts the company with assets (eg based on a lease) may not ask for the segregation, and thus the return of these assets, for a period of one year if the assets are relevant for the continuance of the business within the insolvency procedure. Even so, certain rules on compensation have recently been introduced.

4.4 Supervisory/advisory board

The normal legal structure of a limited liability company does not provide for a supervisory or advisory board.

Under the One-Third Participation Act, the employees of a limited liability company with more than 500 regular employees have a right of co-determination. The company must form a supervisory board; its composition, rights and duties are set out in the laws governing corporations.

Even if the One-Third Participation Act does not apply, a supervisory or advisory board may be established on a voluntary basis. In order to be recognised as an organ of the company, the company statutes must provide for the board's establishment. A supervisory or advisory board may be established to achieve one or more of the following goals:

- supervision of the directors;
- conclusion and termination of directors' employment contracts;
- advising of the directors;
- promotion of business activities; and
- arbitration/mediation with regard to conflicts within the company or group.

Where a public limited company is considered 'unguided' (eg the home addresses of the board members are unknown), each member of the supervisory board is obliged to file for insolvency, provided that the company is either over-indebted or illiquid.

4.5   Transfer of shares

Shares are disposable and inheritable. However, they may be transferred only pursuant to a notarised contract. Further, the assignment of shares may be tied to certain conditions in a shareholder agreement (eg the assignment of shares could be made conditional on the company's consent (Section 15(5) of the Law on Limited Liability Companies)). In family companies, it is also common to require the consent of all shareholders. The pledge of a share is subject to the same restrictions as its transfer.

With the MoMiG legislation, the possibility was introduced of acquiring shares of a private limited company in good faith. The correctness of the list of shareholders is the basis for such an acquisition, and the acquisition may still be valid even when the list does not reflect the true legal status. It is thus now more important than ever to check the standing of the shareholders, and the list has gained a new relevance. It must be kept up-to-date to avoid any fraud by former shareholders.

5.   Incorporation of a public stock company

A public stock company is incorporated through registration in the companies register.

Even before it has been entered in the companies register, the company acquires the legal status of a pre-public stock company once the shareholder agreement has been notarised. There is legal identity between the pre-public stock company and the future public stock company.

5.1 Registration requirements

(a) Company name

The company name may be the name of a natural person or thing, or a fanciful name. If it is a person's name, that person need not be a shareholder. If the company name is the name of a product or a fanciful name, and contains a reference to a certain branch, care should be taken to ensure that the name is sufficiently distinctive. This can be done by adding unique elements that lend the name individuality.

(b) Minimum share capital, initial contributions

The registered share capital must be at least €50,000.

Assuming that no in-kind contributions have been agreed to, the application for registration may not be filed until the amount called for every share has been duly paid and is at the disposal of the board of directors – unless such funds have already been used to pay the incorporation taxes and costs.

The amount that must be paid before the application for registration is filed must equal at least one-quarter of the lowest issue price of the shares subscribed (Section 36(a)(1) of the Corporation Act). In contrast, in-kind contributions must be fully paid (Section 36(a)(2) of the Corporation Act).

(c) Form and minimum price of shares

Shares can be issued either as par-value shares or non-par-value shares (Section 9 of the Corporation Act).

Par-value shares must have a value of at least €1. Non-par-value shares do not have a specific nominal value; instead, they represent a *pro rata* amount of the share capital, which must not be less than €1 per share. Thus, in the case of par-value shares, the shareholder's share of the registered capital is determined according to the ratio between the nominal value and the registered capital; in the case of non-par-value shares it is determined according to the number of shares.

A further distinction is made between registered shares and bearer shares. Shares must be registered if they are issued prior to full payment of the issue price (in other words, when electing not to pay the full amount as allowed by Section 36(a)(1) of the Corporation Act).

(d) Articles of association

The articles of association must be notarised.

The law distinguishes between the subscription declaration and the articles of association.

The subscription declaration must indicate:
- the promoter;
- the par value of par-value shares, the number of non-par-value shares, the issue price and, if more than one class exists, the class of shares subscribed by each promoter; and
- the amount of registered paid-up capital.

The articles of association must indicate:

- the name and registered office of the company;
- the corporate purpose;
- for industrial and commercial enterprises, the types of products and goods to be manufactured and traded;
- the amount of registered capital;
- the breakdown of the original share capital into par-value and non-par-value shares, the value and number of par-value shares and, if more than one class exists, the share classes and number of shares in each class;
- whether the shares are registered or bearer; and
- the number of members of the board of directors or the rules by which this number is to be defined.

The articles must also contain provisions on the form in which notices of the company are to be made.

The articles may deviate from the requirements of the Corporation Act only where expressly permitted. Supplemental provisions may be added to the articles unless this statute contains an exclusive rule. Given this restriction, it is unadvisable to adopt the articles of foreign companies word for word. Rather, in order to avoid impediments to registration, a German model meeting the usual standards should be used as the basis of the articles, which should then be modified to the requirements of foreign clients within the limits of the law.

(e)   *Incorporation report, audit*
The law requires the preparation of an incorporation report, regardless of whether the initial contributions are made in cash or in kind. Where in-kind contributions are made, the key facts establishing the reasonableness of such contributions or subscriptions must also be reported.

Section 32(3) of the Corporation Act requires the reporting of additional information when shares have been subscribed on behalf of a member of the board of directors or the supervisory board (ie incorporations using a 'straw partner').

(f)   *First supervisory board, statutory auditor*
The promoters must appoint the first supervisory board of the company and the statutory auditor for the first full or partial financial year, in which case notarisation is required.

5.2   Application for registration
A public stock company must be registered by all promoters and members of the board of directors and the supervisory board (Section 36 of the Corporation Act).

A notarised application must be submitted stating that the shares have been paid up; the price at which the shares were issued and the amount paid on the shares must be stated (Section 37 of the Corporation Act). Proof must also be given that this amount is at the disposal of the board of directors. If the amount was paid by way of a credit on an account, this must be confirmed by the respective banking institution.

The application must also indicate the powers of representation of the members of the board of directors, through an abstract statement as to whether there is collective representation, individual representation or pseudo-collective representation (through an authorised signatory).

The application for registration must be accompanied by:

- the articles of association, and documentation certifying notarisation of the articles and the subscription of shares by the promoters;
- other documentation relating to special benefits granted to shareholders or in-kind contributions;
- documentation on the appointment of the board of directors and the supervisory board;
- the incorporation report and the audit reports of the members of the board of directors, the supervisory board and the incorporation auditor, along with supporting documentation; and
- the certificate of approval, where the corporate purpose or any other provision of the articles requires government approval.

The members of the board of directors must sign the application themselves; representation by others is not allowed.

6.   Regulations governing a public stock company

6.1   Management and representation

Unless otherwise provided in the articles of association or unless the directors decide otherwise, management decisions must be made by all directors collectively. Similarly, in general the company may be represented only by the board of directors collectively. Any contrary rule of representation must be set out in the articles of association.

6.2   Supervisory board/co-determination

In principle, the supervisory board of a public stock company consists of three members, although the articles may specify a higher number. In any event, the number of members must be divisible by three. The number of members is further limited as follows:

- companies with a registered share capital of up to €1.5 million can have up to nine directors;
- companies with a registered share capital of more than €1.5 million can have up to 15 directors; and
- companies with a registered share capital of more than €10 million can have up to 21 directors.

As from July 1 2004, the One-Third Participation Act abolished the provisions of the Works Council Constitution Act of 1952. The 2004 statute deals with the election of employee representatives to the supervisory board of companies that employ between 500 and 2,000 workers. The right to representation on the supervisory board also exists where a public company with fewer than 500 regular employees was registered prior to August 10 1994 and is not a family company (Section 1(1) of the One-Third Participation Act). Companies that employ more than 2,000 people are subject to the Workers' Co-determination Act.

Under the One-Third Participation Act, one-third of the seats on a supervisory board must be occupied by employee representatives. If employees elect one or two members to the supervisory board, those members must be employees of the company. If more than two employee representatives serve on the board, at least two must be employees (Section 4(2) of the One-Third Participation Act).

6.3 General meeting

A general meeting is called as required by law or the articles of association, or whenever the well-being of the company requires it (Section 121 of the Corporation Act). It is called by the board of directors.

Under Section 122 of the Corporation Act, a general meeting must also be called if shareholders who collectively hold 5% of the registered share capital submit a written request for a meeting, indicating its purpose and the reasons for the request.

Each resolution of the general meeting is recorded in a notarised record of proceedings. For non-listed companies, the minutes signed by the chairman of the supervisory board are sufficient, provided no resolutions are adopted that require a three-quarters majority by law (Section 130 of the Corporation Act).

Under Section 131 of the Corporation Act, the board of directors must inform all shareholders in the general meeting of the company's affairs to the extent necessary for them to properly evaluate the items on the agenda. The duty to inform extends to legal and business relationships with affiliated companies.

Resolutions of the general meeting generally require a simple majority unless otherwise provided by law or the company's articles (Section 133 of the Corporation Act). Abstentions do not count for the purposes of determining a majority.

Resolutions may be challenged for violation of the law or the articles (Section 243(1) of the Corporation Act). A challenge may also be raised where a shareholder attempts to gain special advantages for himself or a third party to the detriment of the company or other shareholders by exercising his voting rights, and the resolution effectively serves such purpose. Under Section 246 of the Corporation Act, the notice of objection must be filed within one month of adoption of the resolution. If the objection is accepted and the resolution is invalidated, this decision applies to all shareholders, including those not party to the dispute.

6.4 Enterprise agreements

Enterprise agreements are agreements through which the directors are subordinated to another company (domination agreements) or are obliged to transfer all profits to another company (profit-and-loss transfer agreements) (Section 291 of the Corporation Act). An agreement in which one company undertakes to manage the company for the benefit of another is also considered a profi-and-loss transfer agreement.

Under Section 292 of the Corporation Act, enterprise agreements also include agreements through which a public stock company:

- undertakes to pool its profits or the profits of individual operations in whole or in part with the profits of other enterprises or individual operations of other enterprises for the purpose of apportioning a collective profit (profit pool);
- undertakes to transfer part of its profits or the profits of individual operations in whole or in part to another company (profit portion transfer agreement); or
- leases or otherwise surrenders the operation of its business to another company (lease agreement, company surrender agreement).

Such agreements can have significant economic consequences in light of Section 302(1) of the Corporation Act, which provides that the counterparty to a domination or profit transfer agreement must meet any annual deficit that arises during the term of the agreement in so far as this is not covered by amounts drawn from other profit reserves allocated during the term of the agreement. This does not apply to the other enterprise agreements under Section 292.

In cases governed by Section 292(1)(3) (ie an arrangement under which a dependent company leases or otherwise surrenders only the operation of its business to the dominant company), the dominant company must meet any annual deficit that arises during the term of the agreement to the extent that adequate consideration is not received for the agreed counter-performance.

Creditors are additionally protected by a requirement that, where a domination or profit transfer agreement is terminated, the other party must provide security to a creditor whose claim arises before termination is entered in the companies register, provided the creditor gives notice within six months once notice of the entry is given. Many German corporations, in response to the bad overall economic climate, are taking the opportunity to terminate enterprise agreements with unprofitable subsidiaries. Foreign creditors often fail to inform themselves of such changes, which can be discovered only by examining the companies register, and they therefore do not take advantage of their ability to obtain security.

All enterprise agreements (including those that do not create an obligation to compensate losses) become effective only when ratified by the general meeting, which requires the affirmative vote of at least three-quarters of the registered share capital represented at the meeting (Section 293(1) of the Corporation Act).

Under Section 293(2) of the Corporation Act, the approval of the general meeting of the counterparty to the enterprise agreement is also required if that company is a public company. This rule does not apply to foreign controlling companies, since German law does not aim to protect foreign companies. In the reverse case, involving a foreign subsidiary, the rule does not apply if the relevant foreign law does not contain a provision equivalent to Sections 302(f) and 304(f) of the Corporation Act.

The following formalities are also required to enter into an enterprise agreement:
- written form (Section 293(3));
- report of the board of directors on the enterprise agreement (Section 293(a));
- audit of the agreement (Section 293(b));

- audit report (Section 293(e));
- shareholders' opportunity to examine (Section 293(f));
- explanation of the agreement in the general meeting (Section 293(g)); and
- entry of the agreement in the companies register (Section 294).

6.5 Transfer of registered shares

Registered shares are entered in the company's share register by indicating the name, date of birth and address of the shareholder, along with the quantity of shares and, for par-value shares, the price (Section 67 of the Corporation Act). Where one share is converted into another, deletion and re-entry are made in the share register upon notification and proof. Since registered shares are instruments made out to order, they may be transferred by endorsement (Section 68 of the Corporation Act). Transfer by endorsement is just one of the acceptable alternatives; registered shares may also be transferred by assigning the certified rights, although it remains unsettled whether the share certificates must also be surrendered. In practice, the transfer is usually effected by means of an agreement on the transfer of ownership and assignment of the claim for possession as against the custodian bank.

Under Section 68 of the Corporation Act, the transfer of shares may be restricted in the articles of association; in particular, transfer may be made conditional on the approval of the company. The articles may also provide that the supervisory board or general meeting is to decide on approval. The articles may also set forth grounds justifying the withholding of approval.

6.6 Transfer of bearer shares

Where bearer shares are transferred as paper documents, ownership is transferred by agreement and surrender (Sections 929 and following of the Civil Code). Alternatively, a shareholding in a public stock company may be assigned to the transferee under Sections 398 and 413 of the Civil Code. Ownership of the shares then reverts automatically to the assignee under Section 952(2) of the Civil Code.

If, as is customary, the shares are held in a collective giro account at the central depository of securities (ie Deutsche Börse Clearing AG), then, instead of ownership of the share certificate, the shareholder takes co-ownership and co-possession of the deposit account (Section 6 of the Deposits Act). In such case the transfer is effected by transferring the share of ownership of the deposit account in accordance with Sections 929 and following of the Civil Code. The granting of co-possession is effected by entering the transfer in the depository's custody ledger (Sections 14 and 24(2) of the Deposits Act).

Bearer shares may also be kept in a special depository, with the name of the depositor identifiable externally (ie, either a credit institution or a central depository of securities (Sections 2 and 5 of the Deposit Act)). In such case the depositor remains the owner of the deposited shares and transfer is again carried out in accordance with Sections 929 and following of the Civil Code. Transfer of ownership is replaced by assignment of the claim of possession against the custodian under Section 931 of the Civil Code.

If a bank receives an order to acquire shares for a customer in the form of a buying commission, the principal (ie the customer) acquires the shares from the commission agent (ie, the bank) through transfer of the itemised list to the former (Section 18(3) of the Deposit Act). If a bank is given a buying or selling commission for the transfer of shares in a collective deposit account, the bank sells or acquires co-ownership of the deposit account according to the rules set forth above. The purchasing principal acquires co-ownership pursuant to either Sections 929 and 930 of the Civil Code or Section 24(2) of the Deposit Act, as desired. In either case the transfer of ownership to the principal is completed simply by means of an entry in the custodial ledger of the agent.

7. Taxes

A comprehensive reform of business tax law, which affects both corporations and partnerships, took effect on January 1 2008. From January 1 2009 the legislation introduced a flat-rate tax (*Abgeltungssteuer*): the various forms of capital gains in Germany will be taxed at a uniform rate for the first time. The capital gains compensation tax will establish a standardised tax rate of 25% plus a solidarity surcharge of 5.5%. In total there is now a 26.375% tax burden on all capital gains (interest, dividends, investment, certificates) and proceeds from the sale of private capital assets (securities, investment shares, participations in corporations, and others, with the exception of real estate).

The tax is retained directly at the source of the income by the debtor or by the bank and the amounts are paid directly to the fiscal authorities. The rate is fixed and does not depend on individual taxable income. Normally no additional income tax will be charged.

7.1 Types of tax

All companies must pay trade tax and value added tax (VAT). Corporations must also pay corporate income tax.

(a) Trade tax

Trade tax is a local tax (ie it is assessed by the local government and not by the Federal Finance Office). The amount of the tax depends on the respective municipality, which can determine this tax independently. The relevant figure is called the collection rate (*Hebesatz*). The tax is assessed on 'trade earnings', which are calculated by deducting certain amounts from business profits. Usually, the tax rate is higher in large cities than in smaller communities. Therefore, trade tax can be an important consideration in an investment decision.

The reform of the business tax law regime has also had an impact on trade tax. The basis of trade earnings has been extended but the basic rate for the assessment of trade tax has been considerably reduced.

(b) VAT

Currently (2009), the VAT rate is 19%.

Companies can deduct the VAT they pay, for instance when purchasing capital goods, from VAT collected (the so-called 'input tax deduction').

Companies must apply for a VAT identification number, which is assigned by the Federal Finance Office on request. A VAT identification number can be allocated only if a tax identification number has already been obtained (see section 7.2 below).

(c)   *Corporate income tax*

The legal basis of corporate income tax is the Corporate Income Tax Act. The corporate income tax rate in 2008 was 15% (formerly 25%). The total tax burden including a 5.5% solidarity surcharge is thus now 15.825%.

Foreign nationals are subject to tax on their German income. The German company withholds the corporate income tax (plus solidarity contribution), while the depositary bank withholds capital gains tax. A foreign national will receive a tax credit in the amount of the capital gains tax (plus solidarity contribution) payable.

The capital income tax rate for a foreign national may be reduced by applicable double-taxation treaties. The difference between the tax withheld and the tax due under the treaty will be paid by the Federal Finance Office.

7.2   Tax number

The tax authorities require that a questionnaire is filled out with regard to the relevant circumstances for the taxation of a company. This also implies that the prepayments are assessed on this basis by the tax authorities.

A tax number is obtained automatically from the local finance office when setting up a company in Germany. The tax number should not be confused with the VAT identification number. The VAT identification number must be applied for at the Central Authority for Taxes (*Bundeszentralamt für Steuern, BZSt*).

8.   Annual financial statements

The requirements regarding annual financial statements and auditing duties depend on the size of the corporation. According to Section 267 of the Commercial Code, small corporations are those that do not meet at least two of the following thresholds:

- a balance sheet total of €4.015 million after any deficit on the assets side is deducted (Section 268(3) of the Commercial Code);
- sales revenues of €8.03 million in the 12 months preceding the closing date; and
- an annual average of 50 employees.

Medium-sized corporations are those that exceed at least two of the above thresholds but do not meet at least two of the following thresholds:

- a balance sheet total of €16.06 million after any deficit on the assets side is deducted (Section 268(3) of the Commercial Code);
- sales revenues of €32.12 million in the 12 months preceding the closing date; and
- an annual average of 250 employees.

Large corporations are those that exceed at least two of the immediately preceding thresholds. A corporation is always considered large if the securities it issues are traded on an organised market within the meaning of the Securities Trading Act, or if the company has applied for admission to an organised market.

As small corporations are exempt from a number of accounting regulations, their balance sheets reveal less information about the company (Section 274(a) of the Commercial Code). In addition, small and medium-sized corporations can combine certain items as provided in Section 276 of the Commercial Code.

The most significant simplification for small corporations is that they are exempt from the audit duty (Section 316 of the Commercial Code).

The legal representatives of corporations must present the annual financial statements to the shareholders immediately after they are drafted. The statements must be filed with the Electronic Federal Bulletin (*elektronischer Bundesanzeiger*). A number of additional documents must also be filed. As many companies have neglected to do this, the government has increased the legal penalties for violating this provision. Furthermore, a penalty for not complying with this obligation shall be imposed. This no longer requires the application of a third party.

As the Electronic Federal Bulletin is publicly accessible, it often makes sense for creditors to examine the company's file there. If the company has not submitted its annual financial statements as required, the creditor can request the registry court to compel the company to do so.

9. Declaration of foreign investment

No such declaration is required in Germany.

10. Company reorganisation

The Conversion of Companies Code governs the restructuring of companies. Its scope of application is limited to German national companies and partnerships.

10.1 Merger

Through a merger, the assets of two companies are unified into a single company. There are different ways to achieve this goal, as follows:
- transfer of assets by way of universal succession;
- interchange of the shares of the transferor company with those of the transferee company; or
- termination of the transferor company without formal liquidation proceedings.

10.2 Split-up

Split-up is a type of merger through which only part of the assets are transferred. It may be effected in one of three ways:
- The assets of the transferor company are absorbed by several other companies (Section 123(1) of the Conversion of Companies Code), leading to termination of the transferor company without formal liquidation proceedings;
- Part of the assets remain with the transferor company, with other assets

transferred to one or more companies (Section 123(2) of the code); or
- Part of the assets are transferred to another company whose shares are held by the transferor company (Section 123(3) of the code).

The relevant assets may be transferred either to an existing legal entity or to a new legal entity.

10.3 Conversion

Through conversion, the corporate form of the company changes (eg, a limited liability company becomes a public stock company). Conversion does not lead to an asset transfer, as the company remains the same legal entity.

10.4 Asset transfer

The Conversion of Companies Code provisions on asset transfer become relevant only if state-owned entities or insurance companies are involved in the transaction. For foreign investors, this is thus of minor importance.

10.5 Legal prerequisites

A multitude of prerequisites under the Conversion of Companies Code must be fulfilled in order to reorganise. For example:
- The underlying contracts must be notarised;
- All participants must hold shareholders' meetings; and
- The transaction must be entered in the companies register.

10.6 Protection of creditors

The code includes numerous provisions aimed at protecting creditors from possible financial disadvantage.

(a) Merger

The creditors of participating companies have a right to demand collateral if they can verify that their claims would otherwise be endangered (Section 22 of the code). The demand must be made in writing and must be issued within six months of registration of the merger in the companies register. Foreign investors are not always aware that they must actively pursue their rights and that it is worth regularly obtaining extracts from the companies register. The collateral must be provided by the transferee company.

(b) Split-off

According to Section 125 of the code, the merger provisions also apply (with some exceptions) to split-up. The obligation to provide a creditor with collateral applies to split-ups involving both new and existing legal entities (Section 133 of the code). However, in the latter case only the company that incurred the respective obligation is obliged to provide the creditor with collateral.

Further, all companies involved in a split-up are jointly and severally liable for debts incurred by the transferor company. However, the liability of those companies that are not the debtors according to the split-up contract is limited to claims that fall due within five years of the split-up and are pursued by way of a lawsuit within that period.

(c)   *Conversion*

Creditors of a legal entity that participates in a conversion pursuant to Sections 22 and 204 of the code may request collateral.

The conversion of partnerships into companies is often used as a means to limit the personal liability of the partners. Section 224 of the code forestalls this possibility. It provides that the general partner of a partnership that converts into a company remains liable for a period of five years following the conversion for claims that fall due in that period and are pursued by way of a lawsuit. Limited partners remain liable indefinitely after the conversion.

11.   Liquidation

Voluntary liquidation of a company requires a decision of the shareholders, which must be approved by three-quarters of the voting rights unless otherwise provided for in the statutes. The statutes of a limited liability company can specify a lower majority (Section 60(1) clause 2 of the Law on Limited Liability Companies).

Upon a decision to liquidate, the appointment of the directors ends and they are replaced by one or more liquidators (who might in fact in practice be the former directors). The liquidator is responsible for winding up the company. Section 73 of the Law on Limited Liability Companies provides that, during the liquidation proceedings, no capital may be paid out to the shareholders before all claims have been satisfied and a 12-month period has subsequently elapsed.

12.   Bankruptcy proceedings

The Insolvency Code provides for the involuntary winding-up of a company. The assets are distributed to the creditors based either on an insolvency plan or on regular proceedings.

An insolvency plan allows the creditors to decide for themselves to a large extent on the way their claims are to be satisfied, although some rules on minority protection must be respected. Winding-up on the basis of an insolvency plan still remains the exception, although this option is becoming increasingly popular.

The regular proceedings are based on the principle of equal satisfaction of all creditors. However, some creditors can claim preferential satisfaction – for example, the commencement of insolvency proceedings does not prevent creditors that have delivered products under a retention-of-title clause from enforcing their rights.

Creditors should ensure that any collateral provided by the debtor will entitle them to preferential satisfaction in case of the commencement of insolvency proceedings. However, collateral that has been granted to a creditor may be challenged by the insolvency administrator if, at the time of grant, the creditor knew of the debtor's indebtedness or of circumstances that should have made it aware of such indebtedness. Depending on the motivation and the creditor's knowledge, the challenge period may be up to 10 years (Section 133 of the Insolvency Code).

Guatemala

Rodrigo Rosenberg Marzano
Eduardo Rosenberg Paiz
Rosenberg Marzano, Marroquin Pemueller & Asociados

1. Types of company with limited liability and applicable legislation

There are two main types of company with limited liability: joint stock corporations (*Sociedades Anónimas*) and limited liability companies (*Sociedades de Responsabilidad Limitada*).

As defined under Guatemalan law, a joint stock corporation is a type of company whose capital stock is divided into, and represented by, shares. The liability of each shareholder is limited to the payment of subscribed shares.

Limited liability companies are composed of various partners whose liability is limited to payment of their capital contributions. The capital is divided into partner contributions, which cannot be represented by bonds or titles of any kind, or by nominative shares.

In both types of company, the company itself is liable for obligations entered into by its legal representatives, to the extent of its capital stock. The partners themselves are responsible only for the contributions they offer at the time of incorporation, in the case of limited liability companies, or for payment of the shares they have purchased, in the case of joint stock corporations. Once they have fulfilled these obligations, they are freed from any further liability.

The joint stock corporation is very thoroughly regulated by the Code of Commerce (Legislative Decree 2-70), which governs almost every aspect of the company. The regime governing the limited liability company is more relaxed, leaving room for the founders to determine the structure of the company. This notwithstanding, the founding partners of a joint stock corporation also have significant freedom to shape their company, given that many provisions of the Code of Commerce are intended to apply in the absence of specific regulation in the bylaws.

The Guatemalan joint stock corporation allows for a certain degree of anonymity of the shareholders, and for the easy admittance of new shareholders and the transfer of shares; the reverse is true of the limited liability company. In addition, while a limited liability company can have only up to 20 partners, a joint stock corporation can have as many different shareholders as it has shares. The legal formalities relating to the incorporation and operation of joint stock corporations have led to the use of the limited liability company for smaller operations, where partners are usually related to one another or comprise closed groups, while the joint stock corporation is more commonly used for larger operations with a larger number of partners or groups of people whose relationship is purely financial.

The regulatory framework is set out in the Code of Commerce.

2.   Incorporation procedure

2.1   Proceedings prior to incorporation

(a)   Name registration

Joint stock corporation: The founders of a joint stock corporation can choose any corporate name they wish, as long as it has not already been registered. If the founders choose to name the corporation with the full name of one partner or the surnames of two or more partners, reference must also be made to the main corporate purpose. In any event, the corporate name of a joint stock corporation must be followed by a comma and the words 'Sociedad Anónima' or its abbreviation 'SA'.

Limited liability companies: The founders of a limited liability company can choose a corporate name that either refers to the main corporate purpose or incorporates the full name of one partner or the surnames of two or more partners. In any event, the denomination chosen must be followed by the words 'y Compañía Limitada' or the abbreviation 'Cía Ltda'. If the partners fail to include this designation, they become fully liable for the company's obligations.

The Guatemalan Mercantile Registry will confirm that a company name is not already in use by issuing a certificate stating that, as at the date of issuance, the relevant company name is free to be adopted by a company in formation.

(b)   Capital contributions

Shareholders in joint stock corporations and partners in limited liability companies can make contributions to the company's capital in the form of either cash or other goods of economic value. In the case of in-kind contributions, the goods must be detailed in the incorporation charter or an inventory previously approved by the partners or shareholders, who must determine the value of the in-kind contribution in monetary terms.

In the case of a limited liability company, partners who make in-kind contributions may eventually become personally liable in the following circumstances:

- if the value of the in-kind contribution as recorded in the incorporation charter or inventory is higher than its true value, all partners are liable for the difference; and
- if a partner offers any type of credit as a contribution, he is responsible for the debtor's liquidity at the time the contribution is made.

With these exceptions, however, the partner is in no way liable for the company's obligations.

Cash contributions must be deposited with a local bank before incorporation in an account under the name of the company in formation. The deposit slip must be presented to the notary public for the contribution to be included in the charter of incorporation.

(c)   ***Declaration of foreign investment***
No declaration of foreign investment is necessary.

(d)   ***Tax identification number for foreign shareholders***
Foreign shareholders are not required to obtain a tax identification number, since any eventual dividends or revenues paid on their shareholdings are tax free. This exemption is based on the fact that the company itself must pay tax on its revenue, and it is from this net revenue that dividends are distributed.

2.2   Incorporation

(a)   *Bylaws*

(i)   *Essential clauses*
The charter of incorporation of a limited liability company or joint stock corporation must include the following information at a minimum:
- the type of company that is being incorporated;
- the main corporate purpose;
- the company name;
- the corporate domicile;
- the capital and the amount that each founding partner is contributing. In the case of in-kind contributions, the value of the contribution must also be specified;
- the governing bodies of the company, their administration and powers;
- the share of profits corresponding to each partner or class of shares;
- the term of the company;
- the grounds for dissolution of the company before the term has expired;
- how to liquidate the company and divide its capital in case of dissolution;
- the period each year when the governing bodies must present their reports, inventory and financial statements; and
- whether disputes between the partners or shareholders must be resolved through arbitration and, where this is the case, how the arbitrator is to be appointed.

(ii)   *Clauses not foreseen by law*
The bylaws may also include any other clauses that the founders deem fit, as long as these do not contravene the Code of Commerce or any other law. The amendment of clauses that are governed by law is also possible, provided this does not violate specific legal norms. Guatemalan commercial law, in particular the Code of Commerce, has subsidiary application, which means that the founders of a company are free to structure their bylaws and govern their company as they wish, as long as they comply with the law.

(b)   ***Execution of public deed***
In Guatemala, the incorporation of a company, as well as the modification of the

bylaws and the admittance and separation of partners (in the case of limited liability companies), must be effected by way of public deed executed before a notary public. Guatemalan law provides that the incorporation document must be registered with the Guatemalan Mercantile Registry within one month of its execution.

The company is considered to be incorporated from the date on which the public instrument is executed. However, the company acquires legal personality and capacity only from the day it is registered in the Mercantile Registry.

(c)   ***Tax identification number***
Once the deed of incorporation has been provisionally registered with the Guatemalan Mercantile Registry, the company must be registered as a taxpayer and obtain a tax identification number. The registration process is simple, requiring only the presentation of a single, two-sheet form to the Superintendence of Tax Administration, accompanied by a copy of the charter of incorporation, certification from the Mercantile Registry that the company has been provisionally registered and the document of appointment of the company's legal representative.

(d)   ***Registration with the commercial registry***
The original charter of incorporation, together with receipt of payment of the mercantile registry tax and the official form requesting registration, must be presented to the Mercantile Registry within one month of execution of the charter of incorporation. The Mercantile Registry will review the incorporation document to ensure that it meets the legal requirements and will provisionally register the company. Once the provisional registration is granted, the company obtains legal personality. The Mercantile Registry will then issue an edict for publication in Guatemala's official newspaper, *El Diario de Centroamérica*. If no opposition to incorporation is presented in the eight days following publication, a copy of the publication must be presented to the Mercantile Registry to obtain definitive registration.

(e)   ***Legalisation of the official books***
Guatemalan companies are required to maintain the following official books:
- Joint stock corporations:
    - minute book for shareholders' meetings;
    - minute book for the administrative body; and
    - share register;
- Limited liability companies:
    - minute book for partners' meetings; and
    - minute book for the administrative body.

The official books must be authorised by the Mercantile Registry and the Superintendence of Tax Administration. Such authorisation is fairly simple to obtain, but a combined tax of Q0.65 (approximately $0.09) per authorised page must be paid to the corresponding authorities.

(f) *Declaration of start date and other tax declarations*

A new company is not required to present any document declaring the start date of corporate activities or make any other such declarations in order to commence operations. However, when registering as a taxpayer and applying for a tax identification number, the start date of activities must be stated.

(g) *Indirect taxes, incorporation fees and other levies*

Incorporation of a company in Guatemala is subject to the following indirect taxes:
- stamp duty on the charter of incorporation, in a fixed sum of Q250 (approximately $35);
- the mercantile registry tax, based on the amount of capital stock – the rate is currently (2009) 0.6% plus Q275; and
- stamp duty on the company's certificate of incorporation, in a fixed sum of Q200 (approximately $28).

3. Number of shareholders

As least two people are required to found any type of company, whether civil, mercantile or otherwise. One of the grounds for dissolution established in the Code of Commerce is where one person becomes the sole owner of all shares of one company (in a joint stock corporation) or the sole contributor to the capital of one company (in a limited liability company). Sole ownership of limited liability companies is not permitted under Guatemalan law.

4. Corporate name – limitations

The only limits to the company name, apart from those discussed in Section 2.1(a), is that it cannot contain terms that are contrary to law or that offend public decency and decorum. Also, since registration of a company in the Mercantile Registry grants the exclusive right to use the company name, any new company in formation must have a name that can be distinguished from all previously registered companies.

5. Corporate domicile

The domicile of a Guatemalan company must be stated in the incorporation charter. For such purposes, the domicile is the department in which the company has its main offices (the Guatemalan territory is divided into 22 administrative departments). This notwithstanding, the administrative body of the company may choose to establish branches and agencies in other areas of the Guatemalan territory and abroad.

The transfer of corporate domicile must be effected by way of public deed executed before a notary public, even if this transfer is within the Guatemalan territory, since it is usually this domicile that determines which court has jurisdiction over the company.

6. Corporate purpose

The corporate purpose must be stated in the charter of incorporation, and must define the main object as concisely and concretely as possible. The corporate purpose is included in the certificate of registration issued by the Mercantile Registry; it may be modified only by way of a public deed, which is subsequently registered with the Mercantile Registry so the relevant certificate may be amended accordingly.

7. Capital stock

7.1 Minimum capital requirement

There is no minimum capital requirement for limited liability companies.

Joint stock corporations have two types of capital: authorised capital and paid capital. The authorised capital is the maximum amount of shares representing capital that the company can issue without having to amend its bylaws. The paid capital is the amount of the contributions the shareholders have made. The authorised capital may be fully or partially paid up at the time of incorporation. At all times, however, a joint stock corporation must have at least Q5,000 (approximately $655) in paid-up capital.

This distinction between authorised and paid-up capital in joint stock corporations does not apply to limited liability companies, since the capital of a limited liability company must be paid-up in full at the time of incorporation.

7.2 Nature of contributions

See sections 2.1(a) and 7.1 herein.

Following the incorporation of a joint stock corporation, both cash and in-kind contributions may continue to be made, as long as these do not exceed the authorised capital.

7.3 Partial payments

New shares of a joint stock corporation, whether issued at the time of incorporation or as a result of a capital increase, can be partially paid up; the minimum payment is 25% of the nominal value of each share. The full value of the stock must be paid as required by the administrative body.

Partial payments are not possible for limited liability companies, since Guatemalan law requires that the capital be paid in full at the time of incorporation.

7.4 Representation of shares

The shares of joint stock corporations are issued in the form of certificates, which can represent one or more shares of company stock. Where the shares have been fully paid, these certificates may be either bearer or nominative; if the shares are only partially paid, the certificates must be made out in the shareholder's name. The certificates must contain certain information as required by law, including:

- the name of the company;
- its corporate domicile and duration;
- the particulars of the company's registration in the Mercantile Registry (eg registration number); and
- shareholder rights and obligations.

In limited liability companies, the partners' contributions are divided into *'aportaciones'* which cannot be represented by certificates of any kind.

7.5   Transfer of shares

(a)   *Restrictions*

The shares of joint stock corporation may almost always be freely transferred. The sole restriction on the transfer of shares that may be included in the bylaws is a provision making share transfers subject to the approval of the administrative body. However, this restriction applies only to nominative shares.

In a limited liability company, the transfer of one partner's share of the capital stock is severely restricted. A transfer of ownership or the admittance of a new partner to the company requires the unanimous consent of all partners. The sole exception to this restriction is if the bylaws allow a partner's heirs to succeed him in the event of his death.

(b)   *Formalities*

In the case of joint stock corporations, the formalities for the transfer of shares largely depend on whether the shares are nominative or bearer. There are no formalities for the transfer of bearer shares: as the bearer is considered to be the shareholder, physical delivery of the shares is sufficient to effect the transfer. To transfer nominative shares, the certificates must be endorsed and the shareholder register must be amended to reflect the change in shareholder. However, the bylaws may make the transfer conditional on the prior approval of the administrative body.

In limited liability companies, the transfer of one partner's share requires the unanimous consent of the other partners, as well as documentation of the transfer in a public deed that must subsequently be registered with the Mercantile Registry.

8.   Equity

8.1   Equity–capital ratio

The Code of Commerce stipulates that in order for a company to continue to operate, its equity must be at least 40% of the capital stock. Where the equity drops below the required minimum, this constitutes grounds for dissolution and liquidation of the company (see section 15 below).

8.2   Convertible bonds

Under Guatemalan law, debentures are contemplated as a means for a joint stock corporation to gain liquidity. The convertible bonds issued may be either nominative or bearer, and their value must be divisible by Q100. However, debentures are not commonly used in Guatemala since, even if the obligation contained in the convertible bonds is guaranteed by mortgage or collateral, the company is still liable with respect to the bonds to the full extent of its assets.

9. Administration of a joint stock corporation

The administration of a joint stock corporation is carried out by the general shareholders' meeting, the administrative body, management and internal auditors. These administrative bodies are the minimum required by law; the bylaws may be expanded to include additional bodies of control and organisation.

9.1 General shareholders' meeting

The general shareholders' meeting is the supreme organ within the corporation. As such, it has the power to:

- appoint and remove the members of the administrative body, and determine its competence; and
- decide on the distribution of profits, amendment of the bylaws, and other matters that involve the general corporate direction and will.

Shareholders' meetings can be either ordinary or extraordinary, depending on the importance of the matters to be dealt with during the meeting. Additional formalities and quorums are necessary for extraordinary meetings.

(a) Quorum requirements

(i) Attendance

For an ordinary shareholders' meeting, there is a quorum if shareholders holding half of the subscribed voting stock are present. For an extraordinary shareholders' meeting, there is a quorum if shareholders holding 60% of the subscribed voting stock are present.

A shareholder can attend shareholders' meetings either in person or by proxy. Proxy representation for a shareholders' meeting may be granted by means of a power of attorney or by written representation granted for each specific meeting.

However, in order to be considered as such for the shareholders' meetings, a shareholder must be listed in the shareholders' register, where the shares held are nominative, or must have presented his bearer shares at the main offices of the corporation at least five days before the meeting.

(ii) Voting

The quorum for the adoption of resolutions depends on the type of meeting being held. At an extraordinary shareholders' meeting, resolutions must be adopted by at least 50% of the subscribed voting stock. At ordinary shareholders' meetings, if the attendance quorum is met, simple majority vote of those present is sufficient for the adoption of resolutions.

(b) Challenging resolutions

Resolutions of the general shareholders' meeting may be contested before a Guatemalan court of law. Anyone who can demonstrate a legal interest in the resolution has the right to bring a challenge. However, it is common practice to include an arbitration clause in the bylaws, so as to avoid the protracted legal proceedings of the Guatemalan court system. The limitation period when challenging shareholder resolutions is restricted by law to six months from the date on which the meeting took place.

9.2 Administrative body

The administrative body of a joint stock corporation is its legal representative and is entrusted with the general direction of the company's affairs. Its competence is defined by the bylaws and by resolutions of the general shareholders' meeting that appointed the administrators. Hierarchically, the administrative body ranks below the general shareholders' meeting, which is responsible for the appointment of the administrators.

(a) *Different systems of administration*

The administration of a joint stock corporation may be entrusted to a single administrator or a group of administrators (board of directors). Where the former system is chosen, it is the sole administrator who is charged with the full responsibilities of the administrative body and who acts and deliberates independently on all corporate matters. A board of directors, on the other hand, must act jointly, convening meetings and adopting resolutions as a collegiate organ.

Within the board, a president is appointed as the legal representative of the corporation; he is its executive organ, responsible for executing the resolutions of the general shareholders' meeting. However, another board member may be entrusted with the execution of specific resolutions.

(b) *Term of office, resignation and removal of administrators*

By law, administrators may be appointed for a maximum term of three years, although they may be re-elected indefinitely for further three-year periods. The appointment of administrators must be registered with the Mercantile Registry.

Although not contemplated in local legislation, the bylaws usually allow for an administrator to resign before his term of office has expired. The administrator must present his written registration to the general shareholders' meeting, which in turn, and at the same meeting, will elect another representative to fill the vacancy.

The general shareholders' meeting may remove an administrator at any time and for any reason, and need not stipulate the grounds for removal. However, the resolution on removal of the administrator must name a new administrator to fill the vacancy.

(c) *Administrators' liability to third parties*

The administrative body's liability to persons other than shareholders and the corporation itself is limited to company creditors. The administrators are responsible to company creditors for any damages caused to them due to faulty administration. In any case, an administrator's liability towards a creditor is limited to those actions that will reconstitute the capital in order to guarantee the creditor's rights.

(d) *Non-competition*

The Code of Commerce stipulates that administrators cannot engage in any way in activities that are parallel or related to the corporate purpose of the company, unless otherwise stipulated in the bylaws and with the permission of the general shareholders' meeting.

Also, where an administrator has a special interest in a specific corporate operation or business relationship, he must inform his co-administrators or the general shareholders' meeting and abstain from involvement in the transaction. Failure to comply with this legal obligation makes the administrator liable for any damages caused to the corporation.

(e) Special duties of secrecy and loyalty

The Code of Commerce does not explicitly impose legal duties of loyalty or secrecy on the administrators. However, it is common local practice to have the administrators sign a non-disclosure and confidentiality agreement prior to taking office.

(f) Civil and criminal liability

Administrators are civilly liable towards the corporation and its shareholders for any damages caused to them due to faulty administration. The administrators are also specifically liable for the following:

- shareholders' contributions to the capital stock and the value assigned to them, in the case of in-kind contributions;
- the actual existence of profits distributed to shareholders;
- the proper and legal accounting of the company, and the veracity of the information contained in the company's financial statements; and
- the execution of resolutions adopted by the general shareholders' meeting.

If an administrator fails to perform his duties or causes any other damage to the corporation due to faulty administration, he may be held personally responsible for the breach by resolution of the general shareholders' meeting. The shareholder resolution causes the immediate removal of the administrator from office and, if convicted, the administrator must reimburse the corporation and shareholders for damages suffered.

The Penal Code holds administrators criminally liable only in case of tax evasion, tax fraud or similar crimes against the tax regime, where the administrator maliciously contributed to the execution of such crimes. If convicted, an administrator may be imprisoned for between one and six years.

(g) Management

The administrative body or the general shareholders' meeting can also appoint one or more managers entrusted with specific duties and with specific powers assigned at the time of appointment or by stipulation in the bylaws. Hierarchically, the managers rank below the administrative body, which directs and controls their activities. Managers must also present periodic reports of their actions to the administrative body, which in turn is liable for their actions. Managers have the same liability towards the corporation as administrators.

9.3   Others

(a)   *Internal controllers and auditors*

Guatemalan law provides that a joint stock corporation must be audited by the shareholders, one or more accountants and/or other professionals appointed for this purpose. Internal auditors are appointed and removed in the same way as administrators, and are responsible for:

- auditing and controlling the administrators' performance;
- verifying the company accounts;
- seeking reports from the administrative body on the progress of various corporate affairs; and
- convening general shareholders' meetings where they deem necessary.

The controllers and auditors are liable to the company for breach of their obligations.

10.   Administration of a limited liability company

The administration of a limited liability company is carried out by various organs that should include, at a minimum, the general partners' meeting and the administrative body. Since a limited liability company is conceived as a smaller type of company, most resolutions involving the general corporate direction must be taken by the general partners' meeting. The administrators are the legal representatives of the company and are entitled to act in the company's name. The Code of Commerce does not set out mandatory guidelines on the administration of a limited liability company, leaving room for the charter of incorporation to specify the preferred form of administration.

10.1   General partners' meeting

The general partners' meeting is entrusted with determining the general corporate direction. The bylaws should specify the majority necessary to adopt resolutions and the attendance quorum for meetings.

10.2   Administrative body, management and other organs

The administrative body has the power to execute acts and conclude contracts that relate to the corporate purpose. It is elected by the general partners' meeting, which will specify the administrators' powers and term of office. The appointment of the administrators must be registered with the Mercantile Registry.

Local legislation does not set out mandatory guidelines as to how the administration of a limited liability company should be carried out. The existence, organisation and competence of other administrative organs may optionally be included in the bylaws.

11.   Fiscal year, commencement of activities

The fiscal year in Guatemala coincides with the calendar year, beginning on January 1 and ending on December 31. The only exception to this legal rule is the year of incorporation, whereby the fiscal year begins at the moment of the company's registration with the Mercantile Registry and concludes on December 31 of the same year. Financial statements must be presented at the end of the fiscal year.

12. Financial statements

12.1 Company income tax

The tax base for individuals and corporations domiciled in Guatemala and engaged in trade or business activities is calculated on the basis of the accounting profits in the income statement prepared in compliance with Guatemalan generally accepted accounting principles (GAAP) (equivalent to International Accounting Standards), adjusted for non-deductible expenses, exempt income or foreign-sourced income, and some deductions or tax benefits.

According to Guatemalan law, the income tax rate is currently (2009) 31% calculated on taxable income, which is determined as follows:

Revenues (-) Costs (=) Gross income (-) Expenses (=) Net profit as per GAAP (+) Non-deductible expenses (-) Exempt and non-taxable income (-) Other deductions (=) Taxable income.

Guatemalan companies must submit their income tax returns within 90 business days of the end of the tax period.

12.2 Annual accounts

(a) Documents

Guatemalan law stipulates that all mercantile companies must present their general balance sheet and a statement of earnings and losses at least once a year. These documents must be signed by both the administrative body and the company accountant, and must comply with the particulars set out in Guatemalan law.

Once the documents have been approved by the general shareholders' meeting, they must be published in the official newspaper once the fiscal year has ended.

(b) Audit report

Local legislation contains no provisions on the preparation or presentation of an audit report.

(c) Approval and distribution of profits

Once the fiscal year has ended, the administrative body must prepare a proposal for the distribution of profits, based on the statement of earnings and losses and the general balance sheet. In joint stock corporations, it is the ordinary general shareholders' meeting that decides whether to approve the proposal and order the distribution of profits accordingly. In limited liability companies, the administrative body likewise prepares the proposal and presents it to the partners' meeting, which will decide whether to approve it.

In joint stock corporations, profits are distributed to each shareholder in proportion to shareholding. In limited liability companies, profits are distributed to each partner in proportion to capital contribution at the time of incorporation.

In Guatemala, it is the company itself that pays tax on income earned during each fiscal year, based on the amount stated in the statement of earnings and losses presented annually to the tax authorities. Therefore, the earnings distributed by a company are net earnings (after all tax deductions) and the dividends paid to shareholders are tax free, since the company has already paid tax on such earnings and to force the shareholders or partners to do so again would constitute unconstitutional double taxation.

(d)   *Deposit and publication*
The general balance sheet and the statement of earnings and losses must be published in the official newspaper. The general balance sheet must also be recorded in the company's book of general balance sheets, which is kept at the corporate domicile.

13.   Company reorganisation

13.1   Transformation
Any mercantile company may be transformed into another type of company recognised under the Code of Commerce. The general shareholders' meeting or general partners' meeting must agree to the transformation in a resolution that must subsequently be registered with the Mercantile Registry. The resolution must then be published – along with a copy of the last general balance sheet – in the official newspaper, as well as a local newspaper, on three occasions within a 15-day period. Two months after the last publication, the public deed of transformation may be executed. After execution, the document must be registered with the Mercantile Registry to complete the transformation. In a case of transformation, the company's legal personality is preserved.

13.2   Merger
A merger can be effected in one of two ways: either extinguishing two existing merging companies and creating a new company, or by merging one company into another surviving company. In either case, the new company or the surviving company acquires all rights and obligations of the merging companies. The procedure for merger is the same as that for transformation, except that each participant must publish the resolution to merge and its general balance sheet.

13.3   Split-off
The split-off of a mercantile company is not regulated under Guatemalan law. In order to effect a split-off, the company must first be dissolved and liquidated (see section 15 below).

14.   Eventual partner separation
The separation of a shareholder from a joint stock corporation is straightforward. If

a shareholder wishes to sell some or all of his shares, he may do so freely, with the only limitations being any restrictions in the bylaws on the transfer of shares.

A shareholder may be excluded from a joint stock corporation for various reasons stipulated in the Code of Commerce, including breach of the law or the bylaws, and the commission of fraudulent acts or acts against society. A shareholder may seek to separate from the joint stock corporation if:

- in the previous two fiscal periods the company had registered earnings but did not distribute profits representing at least 8% of the subscribed capital stock;
- the corporate purpose is changed;
- the company is to be the subject of transformation or merger; or
- the corporate domicile is transferred abroad.

In such cases the corporation must acquire the shareholder's shares using undistributed company profits and capital reserves. Should these funds be insufficient to pay for the shares in full, the company must reduce its capital stock until this amount is covered. Once the company has acquired the shares, they must be resold within six months; if they remain unsold at the end of this period, the company must reduce its capital stock by this amount.

In addition to those causes listed above for joint stock corporations, a partner of a limited liability company may also seek to separate from the company if:

- the bylaws are amended without his consent;
- the administration of the company is entrusted to someone outside the corporation without his consent;
- the company is to be the subject of a transformation or merger; or
- he voluntarily wishes to separate.

In such cases the company may reserve the right to retain the partner's share of his capital contributions and his portion of undistributed profits until pending corporate operations are concluded, after which his part will be liquidated and he will receive payment.

15. Dissolution and liquidation

A company may be dissolved on any of the following grounds:
- expiry of the term for which the company was incorporated;
- impossibility of achieving the corporate object;
- resolution of the shareholders or partners;
- a drop in equity to below 40% of the capital;
- the acquisition of all shares or contributions by a single person; or
- any other grounds stipulated in the bylaws.

Except where the company is to be dissolved due to the expiry of the term, dissolution requires a resolution of the shareholders or partners adopted at a meeting convened by the administrators within one month of becoming aware of the grounds for dissolution. Once the resolution has been adopted, the Mercantile

Registry must publish the declaration of dissolution in the official newspaper, as well as a local newspaper, on three occasions during a 15-day period. Once the resolution to dissolve has been adopted, the administrative body cannot enter into new corporate transactions and the company enters into liquidation.

Liquidation must be concluded within a year, during which time liquidators will be appointed to conclude all corporate business, pay off creditors and distribute the capital and undistributed profits. The liquidators are appointed by the partners or shareholders, and are empowered to take all actions necessary for the proper dissolution of the company.

16. Branches

In Guatemala, a branch office does not have limited liability with respect to its parent company. The Code of Commerce requires any foreign company wishing to operate in Guatemala to undertake to respond to all obligations in the country, not only with its local assets but also with all other assets it possesses abroad.

Hungary

Péter Komáromi
Sándor Szegedi Szent-Ivány Komáromi Eversheds

1. Types of company with limited liability and applicable legislation

The types of company with limited liability available in Hungary are as follows:

- the limited liability company (*Korlátolt felelősségű társaság*); and
- the company limited by shares (*Részvénytársaság*).

Moreover, in a limited partnership (*Betéti társaság*), the liability of at least one of the partners (the limited partner) is limited to the extent of his capital contribution.

The following main laws apply to both types of company:

- the Civil Code (Act IV/1959), which sets out the general legal framework;
- the Companies Act (IV/2006) – the operating statute that governs the formation, operation and dissolution of companies;
- the Act on Bankruptcy Proceedings, Liquidation Proceedings (XLIX/1991);
- the Act on the Investments of Foreigners in Hungary (XXIV/1988);
- the Act on Public Company Information, Company Registration and Winding-up Proceedings (V/2006);
- the Act on Corporate Tax and Dividend Tax (LXXXI/1996);
- the Act on the Capital Market (CXX/2001); and
- the Criminal Code (Act IV/1978).

2. Incorporation procedure

2.1 Proceedings prior to incorporation

(a) *Corporate name*

The law requires that all companies have a name that includes the corporate form and at least a lead word, which enables the company to be identified and distinguished from other companies. The lead word can be a combination of numbers and letters and can include the company's basic activities. The company name must be different from any other company in the same or similar line of business. Information on whether an identical name has been registered may be obtained from the register of companies and the Company Information System of the Ministry of Justice. This does not mean the name is automatically reserved; however, a company may now reserve its planned name before registration, according to new rules effective as of July 1 2006. If the company name can be registered, the Court of Registration reserves it for 60 days. During the term of registration, the initials 'ba' must be added to the company name; if the company is in liquidation, the initials 'fa' must be added, while the initials 'va' must be added if the company goes into voluntary dissolution.

(b) Declaration of foreign investment

Companies with foreign investment may be established in any form available under the Companies Act without special permission.

Additional rules applicable to foreign investments are set out in the Act on Foreign Investment in Hungary. Under this Act, investments and business establishments of foreigners in Hungary enjoy full protection and security.

The Companies Act requires both Hungarian and foreign participation to be registered in the register of companies, together with a note of the relevant country.

(c) Corporate powers

All companies, including wholly or partially foreign-owned companies, are entitled to engage in virtually any economic activity, unless it is prohibited or restricted by law.

(d) Tax identification number for foreign members/shareholders

Foreign members/shareholders do not need to obtain a Hungarian tax identification number unless they are resident for tax purposes in Hungary (ie if they reside in Hungary for at least 183 days per calendar year).

2.2 Incorporation

(a) Articles of association

The formative step in the creation of a company is the approval of the articles of association by the members/shareholders of the company. The articles of association must be executed in the form of a notarial instrument or an instrument countersigned by an attorney-at-law. Where the company has only one member, the operative document is called a deed of foundation.

(i) Essential clauses

The articles of association must include the following information:

- the company's name (which must include the word 'company') and address;
- the names and data (address/seat; mother's maiden name; company registration number) of the members/shareholders;
- the business activities to be conducted;
- the stated capital and the financial contribution of each member as well as how and when the subscribed capital was made available;
- the mode of representation and the method of signing for the company;
- the name and data (address/seat; mother's maiden name; registration number) of the managing directors, the supervisory board members and the auditor where applicable;
- the duration of the company if it is established for a limited period of time; and
- any other information required by the Companies Act.

Amendment of the articles of association requires the approval of 75% of the members unless otherwise prescribed by law. If the articles of association do not specify the duration of the company, this is considered to be indefinite.

(ii)   *Clauses not foreseen by law*
The members/shareholders may establish other clauses that are not foreseen by law, provided that these are not contrary to law.

(b)   **Pre-company**
Under the Companies Act, a company may pursue business activities as a 'pre-company' once the articles of association have been countersigned or notarised. A pre-company may not start to trade until registration has been completed, but it may otherwise operate as if it were fully registered, subject to the following restrictions:
- no changes may be made to the members of the pre-company, except in certain limited cases;
- the articles of association cannot be amended, except where the Court of Registration considers that it does not satisfy the statutory requirements;
- a lawsuit seeking the exclusion of a member may not be initiated;
- the pre-company may not engage in any activity that is subject to prior official authorisation;
- a resolution cannot be adopted with respect to termination without a legal successor or transformation into another company form, merger or de-merger; and
- the pre-company may not establish a business association, nor may it join one.

(c)   **Registration in the register of companies**
To legally exist, the company must be registered in the register of companies at the Court of Registration in the county where the company maintains its seat. As of July 1 2008 the incorporation documents can be submitted to the Court of Registration electronically to speed up the registration procedure. The request for registration must be filed within 30 days of signing the articles of association. Prior to filing the application, the pre-company must open a bank account with a Hungarian bank and the necessary capital contributions must be made available to the company.

(d)   **Corporate domicile**
The registered office of the company functions as the company's seat. The registered office also functions as the company's mailing address, where all business and official documents are received, filed, saved and archived. The indication of the seat must include the name of the town, the street and house number, as well as the postcode.

(e)   **Corporate purpose**
Information on the company's activities may be provided in the articles of association according to the nomenclature issued by the Central Statistical Office (called a TEAOR number/code). As from December 27 2008 the TEAOR numbers of the business activities are no longer registered on the company registry, and all numbers already registered

have been deleted under instruction from the Court of Registration. From now on, TEAOR codes will only be given to the Hungarian Tax Authority.

Among the activities to be carried out, the company's basic activity must be indicated first (if any other activities are also registered). The company's main decision-making body is entitled to change its corporate purpose. The change will be notified at the Court of Registration; the notification is free of charge and no publication fee needs to be paid.

(f) *Electronic registration proceedings*

The Court of Registration confirms the receipt of the applications submitted electronically by sending an electronic certificate to the applicant's legal representative. (Legal representation in the registration proceeding is obligatory.) The electronic certificate contains the company's name and seat, the company's registration number with the Court of Registration, the company's tax number and its statistical number. The Court of Registration obtains and records the company's tax and statistical numbers from the tax authority and the Central Statistical Office, electronically.

The following must be included with or attached to the application for registration:

- founding documents;
- specimen signature or sample signature of the person entitled to sign on behalf of the company;
- a statement of acceptance by the executive officers, by members of the supervisory board (if any), and by the auditor;
- the document authorising the executive officer to transfer his right of representation in respect of certain matters or groups of matters, if such exists;
- the document of authorisation of a foreign person's delivery agent in Hungary, if such authorisation is relevant;
- in the case of participation of a foreign company and if other Hungarian laws prescribe, the extract issued within three months from the register of companies of the foreign company and its attested translation in Hungarian;
- in the case of real property being contributed as a contribution in kind, the property title of such real estate issued within the last three months, as proof of the legal title of disposition over the property;
- power of attorney for the legal representative or verification of his right of representation;
- declaration in connection with value added tax for having a tax number issued;
- if any, the statement on the company name reservation, and the copy of the court resolution which ordered the reservation;
- foundation permit, if the foundation of the company is rendered subject to prior official authorisation by law;
- in the case of electronic signature, the certificate of electronic signature; and
- proof of payment of the duty and any publication fee.

Additional documents are required for the registration of companies for certain company forms specified in the Act on Public Company Information, Company Registration and Winding-up Proceedings (V/2006).

(g) **Simplified registration proceeding**
New rules came into effect as of September 1 2007 that introduced the so-called 'simplified registration proceeding'. This only applies if an unlimited partnership, a limited partnership, a limited liability company or a private company limited by shares is established by a standard contract form specified by law.

The legal representative must enclose a statement in the application for registration verifying that the legal representative has checked the company documents and they comply with the relevant legal regulations. In a simplified registration proceeding, the following documents must be submitted to the Court:
- founding documents prepared according to the standard contract form;
- a statement required of persons obliged to pay value added tax in connection with reporting the commencement of their taxable activity for issuing the tax number;
- power of attorney for the legal representative, or verification of his right of representation;
- proof of payment of the duty and the publication fee;
- in the case of a limited liability company the members' list, and if capital contributions are made jointly by several persons, the names of these persons and their representatives; and
- a foundation permit, if the foundation of the company is subject to prior official authorisation by law.

(h) **Company registration number**
The Court of Registration issues the company with a company registration number on receipt of the application for registration. This number is unique to the company.

(i) **Registration of participants**
The Companies Act requires that both Hungarian and foreign participants shall be registered in the register of companies together with an indication of the country of origin. (The list of such indications is included in Decree 21/2006 (V 18) IM of the Ministry of Justice.)

(j) **Date of articles of association**
The significance of the date of signing (and countersigning/notarising) of the articles of association lies in the fact that companies can commence partial operations as of this date.

(k) **Date of registration**
The date of registration is the date of the final court ruling on the registration of the company. As with all dates in the register of companies, it has a constitutive effect: the company has legal existence from the date of registration. As of January 1 2008 the

Court of Registration registers the companies (and the changes of the company's data) in the register of companies within 15 working days (not including any time granted for the correction of errors). The deadline for the registration is only one working hour as of July 1 2008 in the case of simplified registration proceeding (as specified above in section 2.2(g)). The registration is published in the *Company Gazette*.

(l)   Payment of indirect taxes

The Code on Duties (Act XCIII/1990) sets out levies and charges for administration and judicial services. The most relevant of these – that shall be paid in electronically – include the following:

- stamp duty for registration of a private company limited by shares or a limited liability company – HUF100,000;
- stamp duty for registration of a public company limited by shares or a European company limited by shares – HUF600,000;
- stamp duty for registration of partnerships – HUF100,000;
- publication fee for registration of companies – HUF5,000;
- publication fee for registration of changes in the companies' data – HUF3,000;
- stamp duty of only HUF15,000 and no publication fee if the company is established by a standard contract form in a simplified registration proceeding;
- stamp duty for registration of changes to the company's assets at a rate of 40% of the duty payable (which includes the duty payable for other changes reported at the same time).

3.   Auditing requirements

The auditing of accounts is obligatory at limited liability companies only if the company's annual net sales exceed HUF100 million (on the average of the two financial years preceding the financial year under review) or the average number of employees of the company (of the two financial years preceding the financial year under review) exceeds 50 people.

The auditor must be registered in the Register of Qualified Auditors maintained by the Ministry of Finance.

Companies limited by shares must always elect an auditor.

3.1   Minimum reporting obligations

Companies that satisfy the following criteria may prepare a simplified annual report where:

- the balance sheet total does not exceed HUF500 million;
- the annual net sales revenue does not exceed HUF1,000 million; and
- the average number of employees in the financial year under review does not exceed 50 people.

Entities that do not satisfy these criteria must prepare a full annual report. Separate guidelines apply to financial institutions and insurance companies.

3.2 Filing requirements

The company's management is responsible for issuing the annual report within 150 days of the end of the financial year (180 days in the case of a consolidated annual report). The annual report must include a balance sheet, an income statement and notes on the financial statements, which include the cash-flow statement. The preparation of a business report is also mandatory but this does not form part of the annual report.

All registered companies must file their annual financial statements and reports electronically to the Company Information Service. The company thereby fulfils its obligation of deposit and publication. Financial statements are available to the public.

4. Rules on conflicts of interest

Executive officers (ie managing directors of a limited liability company, and members of the board of directors of a company limited by shares) may not acquire any share – other than shares in public limited companies – in any business association where the main business activity is similar to that of the company, and may not accept an executive office in a business association or cooperative where the main business activity is similar to that of the company, unless permitted by the articles of association of the company or where the supreme body of the company has granted consent.

Anyone who has been sent to prison may not serve as an executive officer of a business association until he has been relieved of the legal consequences relating to his criminal record.

Anyone who has been barred from a certain profession cannot serve as an executive officer in a business association that pursues a related activity while the sentence remains in force.

For a period of two years after the cancellation of a business association from the register of companies based on winding-up proceedings, a person who served as an executive officer of a terminated business association cannot be an executive officer of another business association, during the calendar year prior to the cancellation.

5. Number of members/shareholders

Limited liability companies and companies limited by shares have one or more members/shareholders. Unless otherwise provided by law, a single-member business association may establish another single-member company and may be the sole member/shareholder of a business association. A single-member company cannot acquire its own shares.

If the sole member is a natural person, the deed of foundation of the single-member limited liability company may provide that the member is entitled to exercise management and representation.

All in-kind contributions (from the share capital) will be made available to the company before the application for registration. Only HUF100,000 (from the share capital) need be paid in before the application for registration is filed.

6. Antitrust rules

A member/shareholder has a qualifying control in the company if it has directly or indirectly 75% or more of the voting rights.

If the member/shareholder of a limited liability company or a private company limited by shares acquires a qualifying control in a company, it shall notify the Court of Registration within 15 days. Until the acquisition is reported, the member/shareholder may exercise its voting rights only to the extent that its participation is not subject to the disclosure obligation.

If there is any failure to comply with the obligation of notification in due time, the Court of Registration is entitled to impose the judicial oversight sanctions against the qualifying controller or its executive officer.

If the controlled company is going into liquidation, the qualifying controller bears unlimited liability if the court has declared that the qualifying controller is responsible because of its business decisions in the debtor company.

7. Fiscal year

Companies are assessed on a calendar-year or a business-year basis. The business year may differ from the calendar year only if the company is a fully consolidated subsidiary or a branch of a foreign parent company that uses a different tax year.

8. Taxation

A major review of corporate tax in Hungary took effect on January 1 2001 in parallel with the changes introduced by the new Accounting Act (C/2000). With effect from January 1 2004, another wave of changes was introduced into the Hungarian tax system. The major taxes imposed on corporations in Hungary are:

- corporate tax;
- solidarity tax;
- withholding tax;
- value added tax;
- excise and consumption tax;
- simplified business tax; and
- local taxes.

8.1 Full tax liability

The obligation to pay corporate tax applies to all types of businesses, with the exception of private enterpreneurs. The tax liability of resident taxpayers shall apply to both their income from Hungary and from abroad (full tax liability).

8.2 Restricted tax liability

The tax liability of non-resident entrepreneurs applies to any income from entrepreneurial activities performed in their Hungarian branches (restricted tax liability).

8.3 Corporate income tax system

The main characteristics of the corporate income tax system are as follows:

The tax base is calculated on the basis of the net profit before tax in the profit and loss statement, as modified by certain prescribed items (eg penalties, entertainment expenses, provision for bad debts).

The corporate tax rate is 10% on the part of taxable income not exceeding HUF50 million, and 16% on the part of taxable income over HUF50 million.

If the profit is left as retained earnings in the company or invested in another Hungarian-registered company, no additional tax is payable.

To the extent that profits are paid out to individuals (as members/shareholders) as dividends, the dividend is subject to a 25% (and, above a specific amount, 35%) rate of dividend tax. After Hungary's joining of the European Union, dividends payable to foreign members/shareholders – in line with Council Directive 90/435/EEC on the common system of taxation applicable to parent companies and their subsidiaries in different member states – are exempt from dividend tax if the foreign dividend-receiving party qualifies as a parent company of a Hungarian corporation for at least two years from the date of realising the dividend.

Hungarian-domiciled taxpayers, and foreign entrepreneurs who are subject to taxation on the activities of branch offices, must increase the corporate tax base by corporate tax actually paid (deducted) abroad and accounted for as expenditure pursuant to accounting regulations.

9. Company reorganisation

9.1 Dissolution

A company may be dissolved with the unanimous approval of all members. The receiver notifies the Court of Registration of the dissolution proceedings, announcing: the date of the resolution to dissolve; the time dissolution proceedings were opened; the name and address of the receiver; if the receiver is not a natural person, the registration number and the name and address of the natural person appointed; and the termination of the relationship of the former executive officer(s).

The Court of Registration decides the opening of the dissolution proceeding, and publishes it in the *Company Gazette*. The notice contains: the name of the company under dissolution, its registered office, tax and registration number; all information announced by the receiver (see above); and a notice to the creditors to notify their known claims to the receiver within 40 days following the date of publication of the notice.

Company assets may not be distributed until the company has been dissolved.

9.2 Transformation

A business association will terminate with succession in the case of conversion, merger and de-merger.

9.3 Conversion

Conversion occurs when a business association adopts a new form of business association subject to absolute succession.

9.4   Merger

Merger shall mean the operation whereby two or more business associations are wound up without going into liquidation and the companies combine as one legal entity.

According to the Companies Act, there are two kinds of merger:

- where the original company ceases to exist and all of its property is transferred to another existing company, which is regarded as the legal successor of that company in all respects (acquisition); or
- where two or more existing companies cease to exist and all of their property is transferred to a new company established through merger, which is regarded as the legal successor of the original companies in all respects.

9.5   De-merger

The de-merger of a business association occurs when the business association is split into two or more business associations with its members/shareholders and segments of the company's assets participating.

The Companies Act identifies two kinds of de-merger:

- where the original company ceases to exist and two or more separate and new independent companies come into existence with the assets of the original company, becoming the legal successors of the terminated original company (division); or
- where the original company remains in existence and continues to operate in its previous corporate form. One or more new companies are created by the members de-merging from the original company with certain of its assets. The new companies are the legal successors of the original company based on the proportion of their shared assets, unless the de-merger agreement states otherwise (separation).

10.   Liquidation

The dissolution of insolvent companies by way of liquidation is regulated in the Act on Bankruptcy Proceedings, Liquidation Proceedings (XLIX/1991).

Liquidation proceedings aim to satisfy creditor claims while at the same time dissolving an insolvent debtor. They may be initiated at the request of the debtor or a creditor, or in certain cases by order of the Court of Registration.

10.1   Insolvency

A debtor is insolvent if:

- undisputed and acknowledged contractual debts are not paid or are not disputed within 15 days of the due date, and the debtor fails to satisfy such debt upon receipt of the creditor's written payment notice;
- the debtor fails to settle his debt within the deadline specified in a final court decision;
- the enforcement procedure against the debtor was unsuccessful; or
- the debtor did not fulfil his payment obligation as stipulated in the composition agreement.

If the court finds that the debtor is insolvent, it orders the liquidation of the debtor. In its liquidation order, the court appoints a liquidator. All debts of the debtor fall due as of the initial date of liquidation. The liquidation order is published in the *Company Gazette* and, among other things, contains:

- the name of the court and the case number;
- the name, registered office, and tax number of the debtor and its subsidiaries;
- the date of filing the application for the liquidation proceeding;
- whether bankruptcy proceeding took place before the liquidation proceeding;
- the time of the opening of liquidation (the date of disclosure of the final decree of liquidation);
- the notice sent to the creditors to report their known claims to the liquidator within 40 days of publication of the decree of liquidation;
- the name and registered office of the liquidator and the name and mailing address of the receiver;
- the bank account number of the court;
- if the debtor is a single-member company, the name and address (registered office) of the founder (member/shareholder); and
- other material facts.

10.2 Registration of claims, creditors' committee

Claims against the debtor reported between 40 days and one year after publication of the liquidation order will nonetheless be registered and satisfied by the liquidator if there are sufficient funds remaining after all other claims have been satisfied.

The liquidator must convene all registered creditors within 90 days of publication of the liquidation order to establish a creditors' committee.

10.3 Composition agreement

Once 40 days have elapsed since the publication of the liquidation order, the creditors and the debtor may conclude a composition agreement at any time up to the submission date of the closing liquidation balance sheet. Where a composition agreement is reached, parties that did not come forward as creditors in the liquidation proceedings have no claim once the proceedings have closed.

10.4 Liquidator

Among other things, the liquidator:

- reviews the financial standing of the debtor and the claims against it;
- collects debts owing to it at the time of maturity;
- enforces its claims; and
- publicly disposes of its assets at the highest price that can be obtained on the market. Assets will be sold by tender or auction.

At the end of the liquidation proceeding, the liquidator prepares:

- the closing liquidation balance sheet;
- the statement of revenues and expenditures;

- the closing tax returns;
- the closing report; and
- a proposal for the distribution of assets.

This information must be submitted to the court and to the tax authorities. The liquidator also arranges for the retention of the debtor's documents.

10.5 Order of priority

Claims will be satisfied in the following order of priority:

- liquidation costs;
- claims secured by lien if the lien was created prior to the starting of the liquidation proceeding. The liquidator is entitled to deduct the marketing and saving costs, and the liquidation fee from the purchase price, but the remaining amount shall be paid to the secured creditor;
- in case of a lien on financial assets (a floating charge), in liquidation proceeding 50% of the purchase price of the sold financial assets subject to lien are paid to the secured creditor prior to the costs of liquidation, if the lien was created before the proceedings started.
- alimony, life annuity payments, compensation benefits and supplements to mining earnings payable by the company, as well as monetary contributions granted to members of agricultural cooperatives in place of household land or crops that the beneficiary is entitled to receive for his lifetime;
- with the exception of claims based on bonds, other claims of private individuals not originating from economic activities (in particular claims resulting from insufficient performance or compensation for damages, also including the amount of the guarantee obligations ordinarily expected in the given trade, as calculated by the liquidator), claims of small and micro companies as well as small-scale agricultural producers;
- social insurance debts and overdue private pension fund membership dues, taxes and public debts collectable as taxes, repayable government subsidies, and water and sewerage utility charges;
- other liabilities;
- irrespective of the time and grounds of occurrence, default interests and late charges, as well as surcharges and penalty and similar debts; and
- claims held by any executive officer or executive employee of the economic operator, or their close relative, or their domestic partner, or an economic operator under the debtor's majority control, and the claims resulting from the debtor's gratuitous commitment. Furthermore, claims held by any member/shareholder of the economic operator with majority control, that were filed before the insolvency.

11. Corporate crime

The Criminal Code regulates the following crimes, which may be committed either within or against the company:

- unlawful acquisition of economic advantage;

- violation of accounting regulations;
- criminal bankruptcy;
- unlawful preference of a creditor;
- marketing of substandard products;
- false attestation of quality;
- false marking of goods;
- deception of consumers;
- conclusion of agreements in restraint of competition in public procurement and concession procedures;
- concealment of assets to avoid liability;
- credit fraud;
- unauthorised foreign trade activities;
- illegal conduct by executive employees;
- impairment of registered capital;
- unauthorised financial activities;
- failure to supply economic data;
- insider trading;
- capital investment fraud;
- organisation of a pyramid scheme;
- breach of trade secrets;
- criminal conduct aimed at a breach of computer systems and data;
- compromise or defrauding the integrity of a computer protection system or device;
- profiteering;
- money laundering; and
- failure to comply with anti-money laundering reporting obligations.

12. Focus: limited liability company

12.1 Legal nature

A limited liability company is one of the two types of company with limited liability in Hungary. It is an independent legal entity characterised by the contribution of a fixed amount of capital by its owners, who are generally liable for its obligations only to the extent of their individual contributions, except as provided by law.

A limited liability company is one of the most popular vehicles for foreign investment in Hungary. It generally has relatively few owners (known as 'quotaholders' or 'members') who participate actively in its management and operation.

A limited liability company may be considered analogous to the closed corporation under US law. Ownership interests (referred to as 'quotas', since limited liability companies do not issue certificated shares) generally are not freely transferable without the consent of the other members. There are no restrictions on foreign ownership of a limited liability company.

12.2 Capitalisation

(a) Minimum capital requirement

The minimum required capital for a limited liability company is HUF500,000. The capital contributions of members may be of varying value, however, the value of each contribution may not be less than HUF100,000. Capital contributions must always be exactly divisible by ten thousand. Each member has one capital contribution; however, according to the provisions of common property, one capital contribution may have several owners.

Capital contributions may be made in cash or in kind. Half of the cash contribution must be provided before the submission of the request for registration of the company within one year from the registration of the company. In the case of a one-man company, the whole cash contribution to the capital is to be paid and all in-kind contributions must be provided prior to the submission of the request of the registration. In-kind contributions will be provided to the company at the time and in the manner specified in the articles of association. If the value of in-kind contributions at the time of foundation exceeds half of the initial capital, it must be fully provided to the company at the time of foundation. If the in-kind contribution was not provided fully to the company at the time of foundation, it must be provided within three years.

A limited liability company may not raise capital through public subscription.

(b) Nature of contributions

Capital contributions are to be expressed in Hungarian forints (HUF).

In-kind contributions may be any marketable object or intellectual work of pecuniary value, or any right representing pecinuary value. Only such objects, intellectual works, or rights that may be subject to execution may be taken into account as a contribution in kind and may be subsequently transferred by the company without the consent of a third party. Permission granted already on the provision of the contribution in kind qualifies as such.

Members determine the value of their own in-kind contributions, and these are approved by the other members. If the members determine the value of their in-kind contribution without the services of an auditor or other expert, they shall show what criteria were used to value the contributions. These statements are filed with the Court of Registration.

Members who have made in-kind contributions are liable to the company for a period of five years from the date of the contribution for any shortfall between the actual value of the assets (as at the date of the contribution) and their value as stated in the company's articles of association. Members who knowingly inflate the valuation of a contributed asset are jointly and severally liabile towards the company for any resulting damages.

If a member fails to make his capital contribution when due, the management will order him to make it within 30 days, specifying that failure to perform will result in the automatic termination of his/her membership. In such cases the member will be liable for damages caused to the company in accordance with the general rules of civil law.

(c)   *Increase or reduction of the registered capital*
The member's meeting is entitled to decide the increase of the registered capital of a limited liability company by a simple majority.

The registered capital may be increased by requesting cash or in-kind contributions, or it may be financed from the assets in excess of the registered capital.

The company's capital may not be increased unless all previously subscribed capital has been paid in full. If the registered capital is increased by capital contribution, the members shall have preferential rights within 15 days following the date of decision for the capital increase, unless the articles of association or the resolution of the members' meeting ordering the capital increase provides otherwise. If any member fails to exercise his preferential rights within the prescribed time limit, it may be exercised in his stead by the other members within an additional 15 days. If all members fail to exercise their preferential rights, the members' meeting shall designate other individuals on whom to confer the right to provide the capital contribution.

The minimum capital requirements do not apply to subsequent contributions. The increase in capital will be registered by the Court of Registration.

The capital may be reduced through a resolution adopted by a 75% majority at the members' meeting and, in certain cases, it is obliged to reduce the capital; however, the capital may not be reduced below HUF500,000. After notification of the Court of Registration, but before giving effect to any reduction in capital, the company is obliged:

- to publish two consecutive notices of the reduction in the *Company Gazette* at 30-day intervals; and
- to send specific notification to all known creditors requesting that they present their claims within 30 days of the last publication of the notice.

The notice must specify the content of the resolution on the capital's reduction.

The company must settle or provide security for the claims of all creditors that have timely objected to the capital reduction and presented their claims.

(d)   *Additional contributions*
The articles of association may provide that, with the approval of the members' meeting, the company may require the members to make additional contributions to cover any losses. The articles of association must also specify the maximum amount payable by members on this basis, as well as the method, frequency and timing of performing supplementary capital contributions. The amount of supplementary capital contributions is not part of any initial capital contributions.

(e)   *Transfer of quotas*
Quotas may be freely transferred to other members of the company. Members may grant each other pre-emption rights in the articles of association, or may restrict or render conditional the transfer of business quotas to third parties by other means. Quotas may only be transferred to third parties if they are fully paid and subject to a statutory pre-emption right in favour of:

- first, the other members;
- second, the company; and
- third, an alternative purchaser designated at a members' meeting.

The other members have 15 days from the date of notification of a proposed transfer to exercise their pre-emption rights.

(f) Treasury stock

A limited liability company can acquire its own quotas if the capital contributions have been fully paid.

No voting rights may be exercised by the company for any quotas acquired. The company must sell or transfer them to the members within one year in proportion to their capital contributions without compensation, or withdraw them in accordance with the rules relating to the reduction of registered capital.

12.3 Administration

(a) Members

(i) Members' meeting

The ultimate power in a limited liability company rests with the members. Except in limited liability companies with a single member, members' meetings must be held:

- at least annually;
- if it is deemed necessary in the view of the company's interest;
- if the company's equity capital has fallen to half of the registered capital due to losses;
- if the company is threatened by insolvency or has stopped making payments and its assets do not cover its debts; and
- if the articles of association prescribe that the members' meeting must be convened when requested by a certain percentage of members, or by any one member, for discussions over a draft decision;

Quotaholders must be given at least 15 days' notice of meetings, unless otherwise prescribed by the articles of association.

In addition to any other powers reserved under the articles of association, the power to resolve on the following issues is vested in the members' meeting:

- approval of the report prepared pursuant to the Accounting Act (2000/C);
- a decision to pay an advance dividend;
- order and repayment of additional payments;
- exercising the pre-emption right on behalf of the company;
- the appointment of the person who may exercise the pre-emption right;
- granting approval for the transfer of the quota to an outsider third party;
- a decision on the quota in the event an auction has failed;
- approval of the division of a quota and order for the redemption of same;
- initiating the exclusion of a member;

- the appointment, withdrawal and fixing of the managing directors' remuneration;
- the appointment, withdrawal and fixing of the supervisory board members' remuneration;
- the appointment, withdrawal and fixing of the auditor's remuneration;
- the approval of contracts to be concluded between the company and its members or managing director, or their close relatives or life partners;
- an assertion of claims against members, managing directors, supervisory board members and auditors;
- order of the examination of the company's report, management and activity by the auditor;
- a decision on the establishment of the recognised company group and on the content of the draft version of the dominance agreement; approval of the dominance agreement;
- resolving the liquidation of the company without legal successor or on its transformation;
- amendment of the articles of association;
- a decision to increase or reduce the registered capital;
- exclusion of pre-emption rights of the members;
- in connection with an increase of the initial capital, exclusion of the pre-emption rights of the members;
- the appointment of those persons who shall be entitled to exercise the pre-emption rights during the capital increase;
- the establishment of a deviation from the proportion of the quotas in the course of the capital increase or during the exercise of the pre-emption right;
- the establishment of a deviation from the proportion of the quotas in the course of the capital decrease; and
- all other matters referred to in the Companies Act or the articles of association.

There is a quorum if at least half of the initial capital or the majority of eligible votes is represented. The articles of association may specify a higher rate of participation but may not specify a quorum that is less than a simple majority.

Unless otherwise provided in the articles of association or by law, a simple majority is required to make decisions. Each quotaholder is entitled to one vote per HUF10,000 of capital held.

(ii) *Exclusion*

A member of a limited liability company with more than two members can be excluded from the company if 75% of the remaining members approve. This can take place if the continued membership of the person was preventing the company from achieving its objectives.

The excluded member has the right to appeal within 30 days of notification.

(iii) *Proxy*

Any member may be represented in the members' meeting by a person who has been duly authorised. Managing directors, directors, supervisory board members and the auditor cannot act as authorised representatives. Authority to act will be drawn up in a formal document.

(iv) *Decision making*

The articles of association may allow the members to participate in meetings by electronic means of communication, designed to handle dialogues between members and providing adequate facilities for unrestricted debate. In such a meeting, all those participating must be easily identified.

If permitted by the articles of association, members are entitled to make decisions without the need for a members' meeting. The draft of a proposed decision to be discussed without a members' meeting will be given to the members in writing, allowing at least eight days for a decision (unless a shorter period is prescribed in the articles of association). Members can vote in writing or in some other verifiable way.

(v) *Challenging resolutions*

Resolutions of the members' meeting may be contested before the court by any members, managing directors or supervisory board members of the company within 30 days of acknowledgement of the contested resolution.

(b) **Managing directors**

The company's affairs are managed by one or more managing directors. The position may be held by natural persons or corporate entities. In the latter instance, the personal requirements for a managing director apply to the representative of the corporate entity.

There is no legal requirement that managing directors be Hungarian citizens. Members may serve as managing directors.

The managing directors also represent the company with respect to third parties and in court proceedings. They may bind the company to agreements with third parties, notwithstanding any provisions in the articles of association that limit the power of directors to act on the company's behalf. Managing directors can delegate their responsibility to represent the company to certain employees.

Managing directors are responsible for maintaining the register of members and must notify the Court of Registration if there is any change in membership. They are also responsible for drawing up the annual accounts and the inventory of company assets for presentation at the annual members' meeting.

(i) *Term of office*

Managing directors are elected by majority vote of the members for a term of indefinite or definite period of time (in the latter case not exceeding five years).

(ii) *Acceptance*

The appointment of the managing directors takes effect from the moment their written acceptance is registered.

(iii)   *Reduction in number of managing directors*
If the number of managing directors falls, the remaining directors must convene a members' meeting and announce the changes to the Court of Registration within 30 days after the date of the resolution.

(iv)   *Initial managing directors*
The initial managing directors must be named in the articles of association.

(v)   *Non-competition*
Managing directors may not acquire any share – other than shares in public limited companies – in any business association where the main business activity is similar to that of the company, and may not accept an executive office in a business association or cooperative whose main business activity is similar to that of the company, unless the articles of association permits this possibility or where the supreme body of the company has granted consent.

(vi)   *Special duties*
The managing directors must act with the special care expected from persons in such positions in the course of their management activities. If they negligently or intentionally breach this responsibility, they are liable for damages incurred by the company, even if they are company employees.

(vii)   *Liability to third parties*
The company is directly liable for damage caused by the managing directors in relation to third parties. However, the company may bring indemnification claims against the managing directors in a case of termination of the company without a legal successor. Indemnification claims may be brought against the managing directors for one year following cancellation by members where the company is cancelled by the Court of Registration. The members may seek indemnification from the assets distributed on termination of the company in proportion to their quotas.

(viii)   *Removal*
Managing directors may be removed before their term of office has expired if 75% of the members approve.

(c)   **Supervisory board**
A limited liability company must have a supervisory board if:
- this is prescribed by law to protect public assets; or
- the number of full-time employees exceeds 200 people with regard to the exercise of the control rights of employees.

In all other cases the establishment of a supervisory board is optional.
The articles of association may provide for the creation of a supervisory board with between three and 15 members.
Neither members nor managing directors may serve on the supervisory board.

Members of the board must be natural persons. There are no requirements that the members of the supervisory board be Hungarian citizens.

(i) Employee participation

Where the annual average number of full-time employees exceeds 200, one-third of the supervisory board members must be elected by the company employees. The remaining members are appointed by the members of the company for a definite period of time (not exceeding five years). If in accordance with the articles of association the members have appointed the managing directors for an indefinite period of time, the members of the supervisory board may also be elected for an indefinite period of time.

(ii) Removal

Supervisory board members can be removed before their term of office has expired if 75% of the members approve.

The members' meeting is entitled to remove an employees' representative if this has been recommended by the works council, except where the works council failed to comply with the obligation to recall the representative subject to statutory grounds for disqualification, or failed to nominate a new representative within the time limit specified.

(iii) Duties and powers

The supervisory board is responsible for supervising the general business affairs of the company and its management. The board must review the annual financial report and all major reports and decisions submitted to the members' meeting for approval. The supervisory board has the power to request information from the management and employees and may inspect the company's books and records.

(iv) Quorum

There is a quorum if two-thirds or at least three members of the supervisory board are present. Decisions are made by majority vote of the board.

(v) Special powers

Pursuant to the Companies Act, the articles of association may authorise the supervisory board to:

- appoint and remove the managing directors;
- establish the managing directors' remuneration; and/or
- approve specific legal transactions.

The supervisory board must report measures it has taken in exercising these special powers at the next members' meeting. If the supervisory board has refused to approve a legal transaction in exercising these powers, the managing director is entitled to convene a members' meeting. The members' meeting can amend the resolution.

13.   Focus: company limited by shares (private and public)

13.1   Legal nature

Companies limited by shares are business associations with a share capital comprising shares of a predetermined number and nominal value, where the obligation of shareholders to the company extends to the provision of the nominal value or issue value of their shares. With certain exceptions set out in the Companies Act, shareholders are not liable for the company's obligations; their liability is limited.

A company limited by shares may be private (closed company) or public. A company limited by shares qualifies as public when its shares are publicly issued, in part or in full. The name of a company limited by shares must contain an indication as to whether it is closed or public; accordingly, the abbreviations 'zrt' or 'nyrt' respectively must be indicated in the company's name.

13.2   Shares

(a)   Classification

Shares are negotiable securities embodying membership rights. As of July 1 2006, there are only registered shares (ie, there are no bearer shares). The shares of a public company limited by shares may only be issued as dematerialised shares. Unless otherwise provided by law, shares are freely transferable. Any restrictions on the free transferability of the shares to third parties will be permitted only if expressly authorised by law.

Shares may further be divided into the following categories:
- ordinary shares (which must exceed 50% of the share capital at all times);
- preferential shares (preferred dividends; preferred liquidation quota on termination of the company limited by shares without legal successor; preference related to voting rights; preference for the appointment of executive officers or supervisory board members; and class of shares granting pre-emption rights for the shares of a closed company);
- employee shares (in case of an increase in share capital, such shares may be issued up to a maximum of 15% of the increased share capital);
- interest-bearing shares (which may be issued in the amount of 10% of the share capital); and
- redeemable shares (giving the company a purchase option or the shareholder a sale option; they may be issued in the amount of 10% of the share capital).

(b)   Convertible bonds

In addition to shares, a company limited by shares may issue registered convertible bonds, which can be converted into shares at the request of the holder, as well as bonds with subscription rights that grant pre-emptive rights for the purchase of shares to be issued later upon an increase in share capital. As with preferential shares, the aggregate value of convertible bonds cannot exceed 50% of the share capital.

(c) ***Share warrants, interim shares***

Before a company limited by shares is entered into the register of companies, share warrants are issued on contributions provided by the shareholders. Following registration, interim shares are issued for the contribution provided on shares subscribed or reserved by shareholders, until full payment is made for the share capital or the issue value of the shares.

(d) ***Transfer***

The deed of foundation of a private company limited by shares may restrict the negotiation of shares or may make such a transfer subject to the consent of the company. Such restrictions can be the stipulation of pre-emption rights or redemption rights attached to printed registered share certificates, as well as the right of option to purchase. However, such restrictive rights are valid for the company limited by shares or third parties only if they have been indicated on the share certificates by over-stamping.

Another restriction may be when the deed of foundation of a closed company restricts the categories or classes of shares to be acquired by certain persons by way of the transfer. The deed of foundation can stipulate that the transfer of registered shares is subject to the company's consent. This can be refused on substantial grounds, particularly if the shares are to be acquired by a competitor or the refusal is justified by some other reason set out in the deed.

13.3 Capitalisation

(a) ***Minimum capital requirement***

The share capital of a private company limited by shares may not be less than HUF5 million; in the case of a public company limited by shares, it may not be less than HUF20 million. A higher statutory minimum may be required by law in certain specific cases (eg banks must have a minimum share capital of HUF2 billion).

(b) ***Nature of contribution***

The shareholders may make their contributions in cash or in kind.

In the event that a contribution in kind is provided, the auditor's report must be attached to the deed of foundation, containing a description and valuation of the contribution, a statement as to whether the value of the contribution complies with the number and face value of the shares to be received in exchange, and a description of the valuation considerations applied by the auditor.

A company limited by shares may be registered only if, prior to the submission of the application for registration, the founders who have undertaken to provide contributions in cash have paid at least 25% of the face value or issue value of the shares to be received in the deed of foundation, and contributions in kind have been made fully available to the company except where the value is less than 25% of the share capital.

Shareholders that provide in-kind contributions will be liable to the company for a period of five years for any shortfall between the true value of the assets and their value as indicated in the shareholders' resolution at the time the contribution is made.

(c)   *Private company limited by shares*

In the course of private foundation, the founding shareholders undertake to receive all shares of the company. The deed of foundation provides for:

- the foundation of the company;
- the shareholders' obligation to receive the shares; and
- the organisation and operation of the company.

(d)   *Public company limited by shares*

Public foundation may occur by way of share subscription through a public offer in accordance with the Capital Markets Act (CXX/2001). The founders must prepare an information memorandum and draft deed of association, which must be published as part of the share issue prospectus. Share subscription must take place in accordance with the memorandum, by signing the subscription sheet and paying in 10% of the nominal value of subscribed shares. In a successful subscription, the statutory general meeting is held within 60 days of the closing date of the subscription. The meeting will resolve on the establishment of the company and accept its deed of association.

Before the statutory general meeting is convened, subscribers must supplement the amount paid by them upon subscription to 25% of the nominal value or issue value of the shares subscribed. In a public foundation, in-kind contributions may be provided only by founding shareholders and must be made available to the company before the statutory general meeting. (When establishing whether there is a quorum at the statutory general meeting, shareholders who have not provided their in-kind contributions in full will not be counted.)

Publicly founded companies limited by shares issue uncertified shares only.

(e)   *Operation*

The rules on the operation of private companies limited by shares are simpler (eg there is no need to disclose significant data in the annual report to shareholders or to publicly convene a general meeting).

A company limited by shares is a public company if its shares are issued publicly, whether fully or partially. A public share issue occurs if shares are issued through a public offering, or if privately issued shares are subsequently offered for sale through a public offer.

In the case of a public company limited by shares, significant data in the annual report must be disclosed and a general meeting may be convened after a public announcement giving at least 30 days' notice. The deed of foundation of a public company limited by shares may state that the public announcements of the company must be published on the company's official website.

13.4 Administration

(a) General meeting

The general meeting, which consists of all shareholders, is the supreme body of a company limited by shares. The deed of association specifies how frequently it must be convened; this must be at least once a year. If required, an extraordinary general meeting can be held at any time.

Unless otherwise provided for by the Companies Act, the general meeting must be convened by the board of directors according to the method stated in the deed of association. In the case of a private company, the meeting is convened by sending invitations to the shareholders at least 15 days in advance; in the case of a public company, it is convened by way of an announcement published according to the provisions of the deed of association at least 30 days in advance. The deed of association may allow invitations to be sent electronically to those shareholders who require it.

If an extraordinary general meeting is called in relation to a public takeover offer for the shares of a public limited company or at the request of the person having obtained a qualifying holding on the successful conclusion of a public takeover offer, the general meeting should be convened at least 15 days in advance.

Public limited companies must publish the key data of the report of the management and supervisory board at least 15 days before the general meeting, together with a summary of the proposals relating to the items on the agenda and the draft resolution in the provisions of the deed of association detailing the disclosure of official notices. The deed of association may allow the company to post any official notices on its website.

The shareholders at the general meeting will be listed on an attendance sheet. A record must be prepared; this is signed by the minute taker and the president of the general meeting.

The deed of association may allow the shareholders to participate electronically. The method used must allow dialogue between members and provide adequate facilities for unrestricted debate. It must also allow shareholders to exercise their rights as if they were there in person. Where the general meeting is held by conferencing, facilities that do not allow the identification of the persons participating in the general meeting may not be used, nor may the general meeting be held under such conditions. The meeting may not be held using facilities that could be discriminatory to any shareholder or any group of shareholders.

A general meeting may be held using conferencing and, unless the deed provides otherwise, shareholders are free to decide the way in which they wish to participate. Here, any shareholders who wish to attend the general meeting in person should notify the private limited company at least five days in advance. If they fail to do this, it will be assumed that they are participating by telephone.

The deed of association of a private company limited by shares may state that some issues can be resolved without holding a meeting. This is not possible in a public company limited by shares.

The ordinary general meeting must be convened in sufficient time to enable the company to comply with its tax obligations and its obligation to publish and deposit its annual reports by May 31 each year. Companies listed on the stock exchange must submit their approved financial reports by April 30.

(i)   Powers
The statutory general meeting may depart from the deed of association only with the unanimous approval of all the shareholders.

The general meeting may decide on matters that are not included on the agenda only if all shareholders are present and unanimously consent to such decision.

(ii)   Quorum
There is a quorum if shareholders representing more than half of the voting rights are present. However, the deed of association may grant an exemption from quorum requirements for issues requiring a simple majority, or may install different quorum requirements in certain cases.

(iii)   Decision making
As a rule, resolutions of the general meeting are approved by simple majority. The deed of association may require a higher percentage, even up to a requirement for a unanimous vote, for issues that are not regulated by the Companies Act.

Resolutions on the following issues must be approved by a majority of at least three-quarters of the voting rights:
- establishment and alteration of the deed of association;
- a change in corporate form;
- transformation or termination without a legal successor;
- variation of the rights attached to an individual series of shares, and transformation of categories or classes of shares; and
- any reduction in share capital.

The deed of association may require a higher percentage of the vote for resolutions involving these issues.

(iv)   Challenging resolutions
Resolutions of the general meeting can be contested before the court by any members or administrators of the company within 30 days of acknowledgement of the contested resolution.

(b)   Management board
The management board is the executive body that represents the company with respect to third parties, before the courts and other authorities.

The board is composed of between three and 11 directors; in a public company limited by shares the board has at least five, and a maximum of 11, members.

There is no legal requirement that any directors must be Hungarian citizens. Shareholders may serve on the board of directors.

Where the deed of association of a public company limited by shares so provides, it is controlled by the board of directors under the one-tier system instead of the management board and the supervisory board. In this case, the board of directors will discharge the duties of the management and supervisory board.

(i)   *Term of office*
The directors are elected by the shareholders at the general meeting for a definite period (a maximum of five years) or for an indefinite period of time. The directors then choose the chairman of the board from among themselves.

(ii)   *Acceptance*
The appointment of the board members takes effect from the moment their written acceptance is registered.

(iii)   *Director general*
The deed of association of a private company may provide that there is to be no board of directors, in which case the rights of the board are exercised by a director general.

(iv)   *Special duties*
The board of directors must prepare a report on the company's management, financial situation and business policy at least once a year for the general meeting and at least once every three months for the supervisory board. The board of directors must convene a general meeting within a period of eight days, providing simultaneous notice to the supervisory board, where it learns that:
- due to losses, the company's equity has fallen to two-thirds of the share capital;
- the equity of the private company limited by shares has fallen below HUF5 million, and the equity of the public company limited by shares has fallen below HUF20 million; or
- the company is on the brink of insolvency, or has stopped making payments and its assets do not cover its liabilities.

(v)   *Liability to third parties*
The company is directly liable for damage caused by the board of directors in relation to third parties. However, the company may bring indemnification claims against the directors if the company is terminated without a legal successor. Indemnification claims may be brought against the directors by shareholders where a company is cancelled by the Court of Registration, for up to one year following cancellation. The shareholders may seek indemnification from the assets distributed upon termination of the company in proportion to their shareholdings.

(vi)   *Removal*
Directors may be removed before their term of office has expired, with the approval of a simple majority of the shareholders.

(c) **Supervisory board**

The supervisory board is a controlling body similar to the board of directors of US companies. It comprises between three and 15 members. The supervisory board oversees the company's management. Its members participate in the general meeting; they may propose motions for inclusion on the agenda and may convene a general meeting. The rules on conflicts of interest with respect to the supervisory board members are identical to those for directors. With certain exceptions, the members of the supervisory board are elected by the shareholders for a term of five years. If the general meeting has appointed the managing board for an indefinite period of time, the members of the supervisory board may also be elected for an indefinite period of time.

(i) *Employee participation*

Where the annual average number of full-time employees exceeds 200, one-third of the supervisory board members must be elected by the employees of the company, unless there is an agreement to the contrary between the works council and the management of the company. The remaining members are appointed by the shareholders.

In the case of public limited companies controlled by the one-tier system, the procedures for exercising the right of employees – according to the deed of association – in supervising the company's management will be laid down in an agreement between the board of directors and the works council.

(ii) *Removal*

Supervisory board members may be removed by the general meeting at any time. The general meeting of the company may remove an employees' representative only if recommended by the works council, except where the works council failed to comply with the obligation to recall a representative subject to statutory grounds for disqualification, or to nominate a new representative within the time limit specified in the deed of association.

(iii) *Duties and powers*

The supervisory board is responsible for supervising the general business affairs of the company. The board must review the annual financial report and all major reports or decisions submitted to the shareholders' meeting for approval. The supervisory board has the power to require information from the management and employees, and it may inspect the company's books and records.

If, in the judgement of the supervisory board the activity of the management is contrary to the law, the deed of association or the resolutions of the general meeting, or otherwise infringes upon the interests of the company or its shareholders, the supervisory board shall call an extraordinary meeting of the general meeting and shall propose its agenda.

(iv) *Quorum*

There is a quorum if two-thirds or at least three members of the supervisory board are present. Decisions are made by majority vote of the board.

(v)   *Special powers*

Pursuant to the Companies Act, the deed of association of a private company limited by shares may authorise the supervisory board to:

- appoint and remove the directors;
- establish the directors' remuneration; and
- give prior consent to the passing of certain peremptory resolutions. In this case if the supervisory board refused to grant prior consent for a resolution, the management board of the company shall be entitled to convene the general meeting. In this case the supreme body shall have the right to overturn the supervisory board's decision.

(d)   *Audit committee*

In the case of public companies limited by shares, the general meeting sets up an audit committee composed of at least three members from among the independent members of the board (when there is a standard management system) or of the supervisory board.

(e)   *Cross-ownership restrictions*

Where a public limited company acquires control of 25% or more of the voting rights in another limited company or in a private limited-liability company, the business association is not entitled to acquire the shares of the public limited company and is required to alienate any shares obtained within 60 days. If the business association fails to comply with this obligation, the public limited company shall not be entitled to exercise any shareholders' rights attached to these shares.

14.   Branches

A branch is an organisational unit of a foreign enterprise, and it has no separate legal entity. However, the branch is authorised to pursue business activities independently. The branch cannot perform representative activities on behalf of the founding foreign company or other foreign non-resident entities.

The law regards a branch as a relatively independent part of the foreign parent and specifies that the foreign parent must continuously provide the assets needed for its operation and settle its debts. The foreign parent and the branch have joint and unlimited liability for debts incurred in the course of the activities of the branch. Execution may be levied over all of the foreign parent's assets located in Hungary for debts incurred in connection with activities pursued by the branch.

A branch comes into existence and may start to trade when it is registered by the Court of Registration.

The amount of capital available for the operation of a branch must be indicated in Hungarian forint, broken down into cash and in-kind contributions. A change in the registered capital of the branch must be reported to the Court of Registration, for registration and publication, at least once a year.

India

Aakash Choubey
Rabindra Jhunjhunwala
Khaitan & Co

1. Foreign investment regime

India has been a regulated economy since its independence in 1947. A new generation of economic growth was launched on July 24 1991 with the announcement of the New Industrial Policy Statement, which liberalised norms authorising foreign direct investment and technology collaborations in specific sectors, subject to certain limitations. Since then, foreign investment has been further liberalised, with the effect that in most sectors up to 100% foreign direct investment is permitted without any prior regulatory approval (the 'automatic route'). In other sectors, foreign direct investment is permitted up to certain specified limits – usually 26%, 49%, 51% or 74% of the total paid-in capital of an Indian company – and can be undertaken either under the automatic route or with the prior approval of the regulatory bodies of the Indian government, as may be required.

The Foreign Investment Promotion Board is the regulatory body that reviews all foreign investment proposals that do not fall under the automatic route. The Reserve Bank of India, which is also the central bank of India, administers and regulates exchange controls, and its approval may be required for certain cross-border transactions. Approval may also be required from the Securities and Exchange Board of India (SEBI), the statutory body regulating India's capital markets, for certain investments in listed public companies.

A foreign investor may enter India, subject to foreign investment policy, by forming a company or opening a branch, a project office or a liaison office, as appropriate to its requirements.

2. MCA 21

Along with liberalisation of the foreign investment policy, the Government of India has taken a benchmark initiative, known as MCA 21, with its vision of establishing a healthy business ecosystem by way of a comprehensive online portal to enable e-filing of corporate records.

Under MCA 21, the Ministry of Company Affairs (MCA) has made all the services provided by the Registrar of Companies (ROC) available online. The project provides e-services, including name search, registration of new companies, filing various returns and statutory documents under the Companies Act 1956 (Companies Act), which is the key legislation governing companies in India, and securing copies of available public documents registered with the MCA for business and industry.

3.   **Types of company with limited liability and applicable legislation**

The Companies Act provides for three types of company based on the liability of the members, as follows:

- company limited by shares;
- company limited by guarantee; and
- company with unlimited liability.

This chapter focuses on companies limited by shares, but the other two types of company listed above are briefly discussed in sections 9.4 and 9.5 below, respectively.

3.1   **Company limited by shares**

The chief characteristic of a company limited by shares is that the liability of a member is limited to any amount outstanding on the nominal value of his shares. A member is not liable to pay any balance due on his shares in the event of winding-up, except in pursuance of calls duly made in accordance with law and the articles of association while the company is a going concern. A company limited by shares can be either private or public.

(a)   *Private company*

A private company has the following characteristics:

- It must have a minimum paid-in capital of Rs100,000;
- There are restrictions on the transfer of shares, if any;
- It can have up to 50 members, excluding employees and previous employees who continue to be members after cessation of employment;
- It cannot invite the public to subscribe for any shares in, or debentures of, the company; and
- It cannot invite or accept contributions from persons other than the members, the directors or their relatives.

(b)   *Public company*

The Companies Act defines a 'public company' as a company that is not a private company and that has a minimum paid-in capital of Rs500,000, as well as any private company that is a subsidiary of a public company.

3.2   **Incorporation procedure for a private company**

To incorporate a private company, all relevant forms and applications must be submitted to the ROC in the state where the company is proposed to be incorporated. These forms and applications, along with the supporting documentation, may be signed and delivered by the authorised signatory of the applicant, who is authorised by way of either board resolution, where the applicant is a company, or power of attorney, where the applicant is an individual.

Incorporation is a three-step process, involving:

- selection and confirmation of the availability of the company name;
- stamping of the memorandum and articles of association; and
- registration of the company.

(a) *Selection and registration of name*

The applicant must submit a name availability application in e-Form 1 to the ROC in the prescribed form under the Companies (Central Government's) General Rules and Forms 1956, accompanied by the filing fee. The name application should mention six names, in order of preference. The names selected should indicate, as far as possible, the corporate purpose of the proposed company. When names are being chosen, applicable provisions of the Emblems and Names (Prevention of Improper Use) Act 1950, and the guidelines on the availability of names issued by the Indian government from time to time, should be followed. Names should be carefully chosen so that they do not infringe any trademark or violate other laws.

The ROC will process, verify and confirm the name within seven days of the date of filing the name application. If the requested names are unavailable or not approved, a fresh application selecting new names on e-Form 1A must be made. Once the ROC has approved the name of the proposed company, arrangements for drafting the memorandum and articles of association should be made.

The approved name remains valid for a period of 60 days from the date specified by the ROC by which all registration should be completed.

(b) *Memorandum and articles of association*

The memorandum of association sets out the powers of company to undertake certain specified objects and to do things incidental or conducive thereto. The articles of association are binding on the members of the company to the same extent as if the members have signed a contract with the company. In the past, the Indian courts have held that provisions of a shareholders' agreement that have not been incorporated into the articles of association are not binding on the company. In view of this, foreign investors should ensure that the provisions of any shareholders' agreement or pooling arrangement between shareholders are reflected in the articles of association.

One of the promoters should act as the signatory to the memorandum and articles of association, and the other promoters should issue a no-objection certificate in respect thereof. The following information should be included in the memorandum of association:

- the company name, with the suffix 'private limited';
- the state in which the company will have its registered office;
- the main corporate purpose to be pursued after incorporation, along with incidental and ancillary purposes;
- a statement that the liability of the members is limited by shares; and
- the amount of the share capital.

There must be at least two promoters. A company may be incorporated even if all promoters and proposed directors reside abroad, although the approval of the Foreign Investment Promotion Board or the Reserve Bank of India may be required.

The articles of association should further contain the restrictive clauses mentioned in section 3.1(a). The memorandum and articles of association should ideally be perused by a legal adviser, and must be approved by the ROC before printing.

The memorandum and articles of association must be stamped pursuant to the

Indian Stamp Act 1899 and at the applicable rate notified by the government of the Indian state in which the registered office of the company is situated.

(c) **Declaration**

A declaration for compliance with the provisions of the Companies Act must also be made in e-Form 1 by:

- an advocate of the Supreme Court of India or of a high court, an attorney or pleader entitled to appear before a high court, or a secretary or chartered account in full-time practice in India who is engaged in the incorporation of the company; or
- a person named in the articles of association as a director, manager or secretary.

(d) **Registration**

For the purposes of registration, the requisite documentation, along with certain other forms, must be filed with the ROC within 60 days of the date on which availability of the company name is confirmed, together with the specified registration and filing fees.

The fees for registration of the memorandum of association and filing of the articles of association and other forms, as per Schedule X to the Companies Act, must be paid in cash or by demand draft or treasury remitance slip. The minimum registration fee is Rs4,000 for registration of a company whose nominal share capital does not exceed Rs100,000; additional fees are levied according to the amount of the nominal capital. However, the registration fees cannot exceed Rs20 million.

After scrutinising the documents submitted, the ROC issues a certificate of incorporation to the company within three days of receipt of all the requisite documents in prescribed form.

3.3 Procedure for incorporation of a public company

The procedure for incorporation of a public company is almost identical to that of a private company, except for the following additional requirements:

- The company name should include the suffix 'limited';
- The authorised share capital should be at least Rs500,000 or such higher amount as may be prescribed as the minimum paid-up capital for a public company;
- There should be at least seven subscribers;
- A statement in lieu of a prospectus must be filed;
- An undertaking in the prescribed e-forms, duly stamped and signed by one of the directors or secretary, must be filed confirming that the application and allotment monies have been paid or will be paid in respect of the shares subscribed/to be subscribed by the directors; and
- A certificate of commencement of business must be obtained from the ROC.

3.4 Post-incorporation steps

The post-incorporation formalities to be undertaken by a company depend largely on the nature of the business of the undertaking and the sector in which it is engaged. The most important registrations that must be effected following incorporation are outlined in the remainder of this section.

(a) **Industrial licence**

Certain companies that intend to engage in specified manufacturing activities require an industrial licence. These industries are very limited (eg alcoholic beverages; cigars, tobacco cigarettes and manufactured tobacco substitutes; electronic aerospace and defence equipment; industrial explosives; and hazardous chemicals). Foreign investment cannot be made through the automatic route for companies that require an industrial licence.

(b) **Bank account**

A company may open one or more bank accounts with commercial banks in India.

(c) **Permanent account number**

A company requires a permanent account number from the Income Tax Department, which must be quoted in all documents pertaining to financial transactions notified from time to time by the Central Board of Direct Taxes, including the opening of bank accounts and the acquisition of immovable property.

(d) **Tax deduction and collection account number**

Any company that needs to deduct or collect tax also requires a tax deduction and collection account number from the Income Tax Department.

(e) **Service tax registration**

Where a company is a service provider and its services are taxable in India, it must register with the Service Tax Department.

(f) **Labour law registrations**

A company may be required to be registered as an employer under various labour laws such as the Employees State Insurance Act 1948, the Employees Provident Fund Scheme 1952 and other applicable legislation, depending on the nature of business of the company and company policies.

(g) **Software Technology Parks of India**

A company engaged in the export of software or other operations in the IT sector may register itself with the Software Technology Parks of India to avail itself of the 100% Export Oriented Unit Scheme for tax-related concessions. The company may also be required to obtain a customs bonding licence from the jurisdictional customs authority.

(h) **Other registrations**

Other registrations include:
- registration under the applicable Shops and Establishments Act;

- registration under the sales tax legislation, where applicable;
- application for an importer/exporter code, where applicable;
- professional tax registration, where required; and
- application for a trade licence.

4. Key distinctions between private and public companies

In addition to the difference in the minimum amount of paid-up capital, the key distinctions between a private company and a public company are outlined below. Foreign investors should consider these distinctions carefully so as to make an informed decision about which form of company is most suited to their needs.

4.1 Members

A private company should have between two and 50 members. A public company must have at least 50 members, but there is no such restriction on the maximum number of members.

4.2 Transfer of shares

The most noteworthy benefit available to a private company is the ability to restrict the transfer of shares by way of prescribing pre-emption rights, tag-along rights, drag-along rights and similar. The shares of a public company are freely transferable and any restrictions on the transfer of such shares are unenforceable.

4.3 Directors

A private company must have at least two directors, while a public company must have at least three directors. Each director should have a director identification number allotted by the Indian central government.

Further, directors of a public company must file their written consent to act as directors with the ROC and sign the memorandum of association for shares (relevant only at incorporation of the company), or enter into a contract for their qualification shares, if any.

Moreover, while directors of a private company may be appointed by a single resolution, each director of a public company must be appointed by a separate resolution. Directors of a private company are not required to retire by rotation, but in a public company at least two-thirds of the directors must retire by rotation at each annual general meeting.

Finally, the approval of the central government is not required for a private company either when appointing or when amending any provisions relating to the appointment or reappointment of a managing director or full-time director. In contrast, for a public company this requires either compliance with Schedule XIII of the Companies Act or the approval of the central government.

4.4 Commencement of business

A private company may commence business immediately after receiving the certificate of incorporation from the ROC. In contrast, a public company can commence business only when it receives a certificate to commence business from the ROC.

4.5 Managerial remuneration

In the case of a public company, the total managerial remuneration cannot exceed 11% of the net profits. Further, the remuneration payable to each managing/full-time director or manager cannot exceed 5% of the net profits. Restrictions also apply on the remuneration payable to ordinary directors. There are no such restrictions in the case of a private company.

4.6 Public deposits and further issue of capital

Subject to certain provisions under the Companies Act, a public company may accept deposits from the public. A private company cannot accept deposits from anyone other than the shareholders, directors and their relatives. Also, unlike a public company, a private company need not first offer its shares to existing shareholders in the case of any further issue of capital.

4.7 General meetings

Two members personally present constitute a quorum of a general meeting of a private company, whereas at least five members constitute a quorum in a public company.

Moreover, a private company is permitted to establish its own provisions relating to general meetings. Accordingly, a private company may call and hold its general meetings by giving less than the statutory 21 days' notice, or may establish its own regulations in the articles of association on the election of a chairman, proxies, voting, the content of the notice of a general meeting and so on. This flexibility is unavailable to public companies.

4.8 Inter-corporate investments

The restrictions with respect to investing in other companies apply only to public companies.

5. Share capital

The minimum paid-up capital share capital required for a private company is Rs100,000; for a public company it is Rs500,000. The Companies Act recognises two kinds of share capital: preference share capital and equity share capital.

In addition to equity and preference shares, companies in India are permitted to issue various other forms of securities, including debentures, bonds, derivatives and so on, depending on the needs of the issuing company.

5.1 Preference shares

Preference shares are shares that:

- with respect to dividends, carry a preferential right to be paid a fixed amount or an amount calculated at a fixed rate; and
- with respect to capital, in the event of winding-up or repayment of capital, carry a preferential right to be repaid the full amount of the capital paid in on such shares.

Unless these two features are present, the shares cannot be classified as preference shares.

Preference shares may carry certain additional rights, such as:

- a preferential right to be paid any arrears of dividends outstanding on such shares;
- a right to be paid a fixed-sum premium in accordance with the articles of association;
- a right to share surplus profits by way of additional dividends; and
- a right to share in surplus assets in the event of winding-up, after all kinds of capital have been repaid.

A company can issue preference shares of various kinds (eg redeemable preference shares, cumulative preference shares and participating preference shares).

5.2 Equity shares

Any shares that are not preference shares are regarded as equity shares. Equity shares can carry voting rights or differential rights as to dividends, voting or otherwise. Equity shares with differential rights can be created by a company that:

- has had distributable profits in the past three financial years;
- has not defaulted in filing its annual accounts and annual returns in the past three financial years; and
- has not failed to repay its deposits or interest thereon on the due date, or to redeem its debentures on the due date, or to pay dividends.

Private companies are not bound by these conditions and are free to issue share capital of such kinds as they deem fit.

5.3 Share certificates

Share certificates issued under the common seal of the company specifying the number of shares held by any member constitute prima facie evidence of title to such shares. The decision to issue a share certificate must be made by the board of directors or a committee consisting of at least three directors, where there are more than six directors in total, and at least two directors where there are six directors or fewer. Share certificates must be signed by two directors or their attorneys and the secretary or another person appointed by the board of directors for this purpose.

The particulars of every share certificate issued by the company should be maintained in a shareholder register kept by the company. Stamp duty on share certificates varies from state to state. Shares can also be issued in dematerialised form, thereby avoiding any need to pay stamp duty at the time of transfer of the shares.

5.4 Allotment of shares

Companies are permitted to allot shares for cash and in-kind consideration. However, in the latter instance there should be a duly stamped written contractual document (eg contract for sale or contract for services) reflecting the consideration in respect of which such allotment is made. Where no such written contract exists, a company must file with the ROC, within 30 days of the allotment of shares, the particulars of such oral contract along with the stamp duty that would have been payable had the contract been executed in writing.

6.   Management

The general meeting will appoint the board of directors to manage the affairs of the company. The general powers of management of the company are vested in the board of directors, although the members have ultimate control over the actions of the board. The meeting must be properly convened, notice of the meeting must be served in the prescribed manner on the persons entitled to receive such notice, and a quorum must be present. Meetings may be classified as follows:

- shareholders' meetings:
  - statutory meeting;
  - annual general meeting (AGM);
  - extraordinary general meeting; and
  - class meeting; and
- meetings of directors.

6.1   Statutory meeting

A public company must hold its first general meeting – known as the statutory meeting – between one and six months after it obtains a certificate of commencement of business. This meeting is held once only during the lifetime of the company. Private companies are not required to hold a statutory meeting. The board of directors must forward a 'statutory report' to each member of the company at least 21 days before holding the statutory meeting. The statutory report must be forwarded with a notice detailing, among other things, information on:

- the total shares allotted;
- cash received;
- an abstract of receipts and payments;
- the directors and auditors;
- contracts;
- underwriting contracts;
- arrears of calls; and
- commissions and brokerage.

The notice of the meeting must also specify that the meeting is a statutory meeting.

6.2   Annual general meeting

Each company is required to hold an AGM of shareholders every calendar year. The Companies Act mandates that there should not be an interval of more than 15 months between one AGM and the next. However, this period can be extended by a maximum period of three months for specific reasons set out in the Companies Act.

The AGM is an extremely important meeting for the shareholders, as they get an opportunity to discuss the affairs of the company and review its operations. Further, shareholders exercise control over the company's affairs through the AGM. The ordinary business to be discussed and approved at the AGM includes the following:

- company accounts and reports of the board of directors and auditors;
- declaration of dividends;

- appointment of directors to replace those who are retiring; and
- remuneration of the auditors.

As a statutory obligation, every AGM must be called during business hours on a day that is not a public holiday in India. This requirement does not apply to extraordinary general meetings. The Companies Act does not define 'business hours'; this is left to the working schedule of the company. The AGM must be held either at the company's registered office or at some place in the city, town or village in which the registered office is located. An AGM is called by giving at least 21 days' notice of the meeting, although a shorter notice period may apply if this is agreed to by all members entitled to vote at the AGM. This requirement does not apply to a private company, which has the flexibility to fix the time of a subsequent AGM by unanimous resolution of the members.

In the case of a public company, there is a quorum when five members are personally present at the general meeting; in the case of any other company, there is a quorum where two members are personally present. The articles of association may require a higher quorum, but cannot provide for a lower quorum than the statutory requirements.

6.3 Extraordinary general meeting

An extraordinary general meeting may be called to discuss administrative or financial issues that arise between two AGMs and that cannot be postponed until the next AGM due to their urgent nature. An extraordinary general meeting can be called either on the initiative of the board or at the request of a specified number of members. The board must proceed to call an extraordinary general meeting at the request of:

- members holding not less than 10% of the total paid-up share capital with the right to vote on the matter, in the case of a company with share capital; and
- members representing at least 10% of the total voting rights, in the case of a company with no share capital.

At least 21 days' notice of the extraordinary general meeting must generally be given. However, a shorter notice period may apply with the consent of:

- members holding at least 95% of the paid-up share capital with the right to vote at the meeting, in the case of a company with share capital; and
- members with at least 95% of the total voting rights, in the case of company with no share capital.

The quorum for an extraordinary general meeting is the same as that for an AGM. However, an extraordinary general meeting that is called at the request of the members will be dissolved if a quorum is not reached within 30 minutes of the prescribed time. In all other cases the meeting stands adjourned to the same day the following week, at the same time and place, or to such other date and time as the board may determine.

6.4 Class meeting

Class meetings are meetings of holders of a class of shares of a company. The provisions applicable to general meetings apply to class meetings, except in so far as the articles of association provide otherwise. The procedure applicable for general meetings also applies to class meetings, except with regard to the quorum.

Class meetings of different kinds of shareholder and creditor must be held under different circumstances. For example, class meetings of holders of different classes of shares must be held if the rights attaching to those shares are to be amended. Similarly, where a scheme of arrangement under a court order (eg amalgamation or de-merger) is proposed, meetings of the different classes of shareholder and creditor must be held. The quorum for a class meeting is two members holding, or representing by proxy, one-third of the issued shares of the class in question.

6.5 Board meetings

Meetings of the board of directors are usually termed 'board meetings'. Board meetings are conducted for the timely review of company policy, affairs and programmes. Board meetings involve fewer formalities than general meetings.

The board must meet at least once every three months and should hold at least four meetings a year at regular intervals; however, SEBI has increased the interval between meetings to four months for listed companies. Notice of each board meeting must be given to each director in India; where directors are abroad at the time, notice may be served at their usual address in India.

The quorum for a board meeting is one-third of the total number of board members or two directors, whichever is higher. If, at any time, the number of interested directors exceeds or is equal to two-thirds of the total number of directors, the number of remaining directors who are not interested directors will constitute a quorum (although again, this may not be less than two).

The Companies Act does not yet permit board meetings to be held via teleconferencing or videoconferencing.

There is no provision in law in India that restricts a company – whether public or private – from appointing non-residents and foreign nationals as directors.

6.6 Decisions by resolution

A 'resolution' is essentially a decision or determination taken at a meeting of shareholders or directors at which the relevant issue is deliberated. A resolution properly recorded in the minutes, which are signed by the chairman of the meeting of the board or shareholders, as the case may be, raises a presumption of accuracy of the minutes, until the contrary is proved.

6.7 Shareholders' resolutions

The Companies Act requires the shareholders to approve or authorise further action by the company by way of either ordinary resolution or special resolution. An ordinary resolution is a resolution of which due notice has been given and which is passed by simple majority of the votes cast by members and their proxies. For example, disposal of an undertaking of the company requires an ordinary resolution.

A special resolution is a resolution passed by at least three-quarters of the members who are entitled to vote and do so in person or by proxy at a general meeting, where due notice of the proposed special resolution has been given. For example, amendment of the articles of association requires a special resolution. Furthermore, while a defective ordinary resolution may be ratified, ratification of a special resolution or a resolution that requires special notice is not possible.

The Companies Act also requires that special notice be served on the company in certain cases (eg in the case of resolutions for the appointment of an auditor to replace a retiring auditor, removal of an auditor or removal of directors). This requirement is intended to encourage the company and its members to pay special attention to the matter.

6.8   Resolutions by postal ballot

Shareholders of public companies that are listed on recognised stock exchanges but scattered throughout India were afforded in 2000 the right to vote by postal ballot. In addition, voting may anyway be conducted by postal ballot, instead of at the general meeting, for certain businesses identified by the Indian central government.

Where a company decides to pass a resolution by postal ballot, it must send notice to all shareholders along with a draft resolution explaining the reasons for the postal ballot and requesting the shareholders to send their assent or dissent in writing within 30 days of the date of posting. Where the resolution is approved by the requisite majority of shareholders by way of the postal ballot, it is deemed to have been passed at a general meeting convened for that purpose.

6.9   Board resolutions

A simple majority is sufficient to pass any board resolution. Decisions of the board may be taken in two ways: either at board meetings or by circulation.

A circulation resolution must be circulated in draft among all directors in India; for directors who are abroad from India at the time, it must be sent to their usual address in India. All matters to be decided by the board can be decided by way of circular resolution, except those that expressly require a decision at a board meeting.

6.10   External and internal audit

Each company in India, at its AGM, must appoint an external auditor to hold office until the conclusion of the next AGM. Where eligible for reappointment, an auditor may be reappointed at the next AGM for a further one-year period.

The scope and objectives of the internal audit vary widely and apply to companies that have a paid-up capital of more than Rs2.5 million or an average turnover of more than Rs20 million for a period of three consecutive financial years (excluding banking, insurance and charitable companies).

While the external auditor is appointed to report independently on financial information relating to the company, the purpose of the internal audit system is determined by the management. Guidelines have been specified for general evaluation of the internal audit function by the statutory external auditor.

6.11 Power of attorney

The board of directors has the power – with the approval of the members, where required – to issue powers of attorney in favour of third parties for acts that are permitted to be delegated under the articles of association. The continuance of such powers depends on the terms and conditions under which the power of attorney is granted.

6.12 Directors' liability

The duties of directors, and possible liability for breach thereof, are not well defined under the Companies Act, but judicial decisions over the years have clarified the roles of directors. Directors are liable to punishment for any offence they commit, whether civil or criminal (eg failure to honour cheques or inclusion of mis-statements in the prospectus), while functioning on behalf of a company. They are also exposed to the risk of litigation from third parties and shareholders, and are open to claims against them from employees, creditors, governments and other interested parties due to losses suffered as a result of their negligent or fraudulent acts. However, the test for liability is whether, at the time the offence was committed, the director was in charge of and responsible to the company for the conduct of the business. The burden of proving such obligation rests with the prosecution, and not with the relevant director.

The court nevertheless has exceptional and discretionary powers to relieve a director from liability where it finds that the director has acted honestly and reasonably, and that, having regard to all the circumstances of the case, he ought fairly to be excused.

In addition to liability for illegal acts, directors will be personally liable as regards contracts and other transactions if they contract in their own names without disclosing that they are acting on behalf of the company.

However, the company can indemnify a director against any liability he incurs in defending any proceedings, whether civil or criminal, in which judgment is given in his favour, he is acquitted or relief is granted to him by the court. Further, both the company and directors are allowed to take out insurance cover for directors' liability arising out of wrongful acts.

6.13 Oppression and mismanagement

There are no provisions under the Companies Act that entitle the members of a company to challenge resolutions passed in general meetings that are contrary to law or public order, except where the meeting was improperly convened and without prejudice to the rights available under general laws and principles of equity. However, the Companies Act provides safeguards for protection of the interests of members where:

- the company's affairs are being conducted in a manner that is prejudicial to the public interest;
- the company's affairs are being conducted in a manner that is oppressive to any member or members; or
- a material change has taken place in the management or control of the company and, as a result, it is likely that the company's affairs will be

conducted in a manner that is prejudicial to the public interest or the interests of the company.

In such cases any member can approach the National Company Law Tribunal for such an order as may be appropriate to bring an end to the offending conduct or prevent such matters complained of.

7. Accounts and other reporting requirements

All companies must maintain certain statutory registers at their registered office or another place approved by special resolution of the members. They must also comply with certain reporting requirements with the ROC, in addition to filing all necessary prescribed forms from time to time. The registers and documents filed with the ROC constitute prima facie evidence of the matters reported therein. As mentioned above, the Indian central government has enabled the electronic filing of all the prescribed forms and supporting documents with the ROC.

7.1 Annual returns

A company with share capital must prepare and file an annual return in the prescribed form with the ROC within 60 days of the date on which the AGM is held deliberating the issues, including:
- the address of its registered office;
- the register of members;
- the register of debenture holders;
- the issue of shares and debentures;
- indebtedness;
- past and present members and debenture holders; and
- past and present directors, managing directors, managers and secretaries.

A company without share capital must prepare and file an annual return in the prescribed form with the ROC within 60 days of the date on which the AGM is held deliberating the issues, including:
- the address of its registered office;
- the names of members and the dates on which they became members, and the names of persons who ceased to be members since the date of the AGM in the preceding year, and the dates on which they so ceased; and
- all details of directors, managers and secretary of the company as are prescribed under the Companies Act.

7.2 Accounts

Each company must maintain at its registered office proper books of accounts reflecting the true and correct state of its financial affairs and containing the following disclosures:
- all sums of money received and expended by the company, and the matter in respect of which such receipt and expenditure took place;
- all sales and purchases of goods by the company;

- all assets and liabilities of the company; and
- in the case of a company engaged in production, processing, manufacturing or mining activities, particulars relating to the utilisation of material labour or other items of costs as may be prescribed by the central government.

The board must present the balance sheet and the profit and loss account to the general meeting; these documents must comply with the prescribed accounting standards.

The directors must also present to the general meeting a directors' report indicating:

- the state of affairs of the company;
- the amounts, if any, that the company proposes to contribute to any reserves in the balance sheet;
- the amounts, if any, that it recommends to pay by way of dividend;
- material changes and commitments, if any, affecting the company's financial position; and
- details of energy conservation, technology absorption, foreign exchange earnings and outgoings in such a manner as may be prescribed.

7.3 Accounting principles

The Institute of Chartered Accountants of India, in consultation with the National Advisory Committee on Accounting Standards, issues the accounting standards and practices that must be followed by companies in India. All 28 accounting standards issued by the institute are mandatory and companies must disclose their policies on these standards in their financial statements.

7.4 Formation of National Company Law Tribunal

The Companies (Second Amendment) Act 2002 paved the way for the formation of the National Company Law Tribunal. The tribunal is in the process of being formed and will replace various judicial and quasi-judicial bodies under the Companies Act, including the Company Law Board, the Board for Industrial and Financial Reconstruction, the Appellate Authority for Industrial and Financial Reconstruction and the high courts. The powers and jurisdiction currently being exercised by these judicial and quasi-judicial bodies will be consolidated and entrusted to the tribunal. A multiplicity of actions before various bodies regarding revival, rehabilitation, merger, amalgamation or winding-up will be avoided, and the tribunal will have sole competence to hear and decide on these matters. Moreover, the winding-up process will be shortened considerably.

8. Winding-up and dissolution

Exiting operations from India by way of winding-up and dissolution of a company is a tedious and time-consuming exercise that takes several years. The Companies Act lays down the provisions and procedure for winding-up, which eventually leads to dissolution of the company. Winding-up may be effected either through an order of the National Company Law Tribunal or voluntarily by the members or creditors. As the tribunal is in the process of being formed, this power is presently (2009) exercised by the competent high court.

A company must obtain clearance from the pertinent government authorities before it can initiate winding-up proceedings. For example, a company wishing to close down a manufacturing unit without dissolving requires clearance from the Indian government under the Industrial Disputes Act 1947.

8.1 Winding-up by National Company Law Tribunal

The National Company Law Tribunal can wind up a company on any of the following grounds, among others:

- if the company has resolved by special resolution that it should be wound up by the tribunal;
- if the company has not commenced business operations within one year of incorporation, or if it suspends its business for a year;
- if the number of members drops below the statutory minimum;
- if the company is unable to pay its debts; or
- if the company has defaulted in filing its balance sheet or profit and loss account for five consecutive financial years.

The power of the tribunal is discretionary and will not be exercised where this would be contrary to public policy or to the company's interests. As soon as the tribunal passes a winding-up order, an official liquidator is appointed to realise the company's assets in order to satisfy its liabilities.

8.2 Voluntary winding-up

A company may proceed to commence voluntary winding-up by:

- passing an ordinary resolution where the period fixed for the duration of the company in the articles has expired or where an event that constitutes grounds for dissolution has occurred; or
- passing a special resolution in other cases.

In a case of voluntary winding-up by members' resolution, the general shareholders' meeting will appoint a liquidator and establish his remuneration. However, in a case of voluntary winding-up by creditors' resolution, the creditors have the right to appoint the liquidator. The powers of the official liquidator in a winding-up by the National Company Law Tribunal are identical to those of a liquidator in voluntary winding-up.

9. Other company forms

9.1 Listed public companies

Listed companies are companies whose securities are listed on a recognised stock exchange in India pursuant to a listing agreement with the stock exchange. SEBI, which regulates the Indian capital markets, supervises listed companies with respect to the issue and transfer of securities and payment of dividends. Listed companies must comply with the listing agreement and with various rules, regulations and guidelines prescribed by SEBI from time to time. Listed companies are obliged to follow stringent corporate governance rules, as their actions have wider public impact.

9.2 Charitable companies

Companies limited by liability or guarantee that are formed in order to promote commerce, art, religion, charity or any other useful object and that do not distribute dividends to their members but instead apply their profits to the promotion of their objectives, may apply to the central government for a licence to dispense with the requirement to use the suffix 'Private Limited' or 'Limited'. Membership in such companies is generally controlled by decision of the governing body or management committee, and their officers and members enjoy immunity from personal liability.

9.3 Holding and subsidiary companies

A company is regarded as a subsidiary of another company if:

- the other company controls the composition of its board of directors; or
- the other company holds more than half the nominal value of its equity share capital.

A foreign company that is a holding and/or subsidiary company of an Indian company under its domestic law shall be deemed to be a holding and/or subsidiary company of the Indian company under the Companies Act.

The major advantage of a wholly owned subsidiary relationship is that the restrictions on inter-corporate loans and investments do not apply in respect of:

- any loan extended by a holding company to its wholly owned subsidiary;
- any guarantee given or security provided by a holding company in respect of a loan made to its wholly owned subsidiary; or
- any acquisition by a holding company, by way of subscription, purchase or otherwise, of the securities of its wholly owned subsidiary.

However, the balance sheet of the holding company must contain balance sheets, profit and loss accounts, and directors' and auditors' reports for all its subsidiary companies.

9.4 Company limited by guarantee

The Companies Act also provides for the incorporation of a company limited by guarantee in India. A guarantee company is essentially a private company. The liability of its members to pay in their contributions can be enforced during the lifetime of the company, while outstanding contributions may be recovered in the event of winding-up.

A guarantee company need not have a share capital. However, its articles of association must state the number of members with which it is to be registered. Generally, a guarantee company obtains funds through donations and the like. It is a suitable choice for all kinds of educational, charitable, research, training and scientific development institutions. A guarantee company can also apply to the central government to dispense with use of the suffix 'Private Limited' or 'Limited', a privilege reserved to companies that do not distribute their profits among members.

9.5   Unlimited company

A company with unlimited liability resembles a partnership, as the liability of each member extends to the entire amount of the company's debts and liabilities. Although creditors cannot institute proceedings against individual members, in the event of a winding-up the official liquidator can call upon the members to discharge the debts and liabilities without limitation. An unlimited company is not required to have a share capital; if it has, it may increase or reduce the share capital without restrictions.

The procedure for incorporation of an unlimited company is the same as for incorporation of a private company, except that the articles of association must state the number of members and, if the company has a share capital, the amount of share capital with which the company is to be registered.

An unlimited company can subsequently register itself as a company with limited liability. However, this kind of company is rarely incorporated in India.

9.6   Foreign companies

A foreign company can open a branch office, a liaison office or a project office in India. The establishment of a branch office or liaison office requires the prior approval of the Reserve Bank of India (as an exception, permission to open a liaison office of a foreign insurance company is granted by the Insurance Regulatory and Development Authority). A branch office, liaison office or project office that is owned or controlled by a person resident outside India enables to person to enjoy the status of a 'person resident in India', as per the Foreign Exchange Management Act 1999. Once a branch office, liaison office or project office is established in India, the foreign parent company is required to comply with the requirements outlined below.

To register itself with the ROC in New Delhi and the local ROC, a foreign company must submit a prescribed application, along with other prescribed documents, within 30 days of the establishment of a 'place of business' in India, including:

- a certified copy of its charter or memorandum and articles, or another instrument constituting or defining the constitution of the foreign company;
- the address of the registered or principal office of the foreign company;
- the names and addresses of one or more persons resident in India who are authorised to accept, on behalf of the foreign company, service of process and any notices or other documents required to be served on the foreign company;
- the full address of the office of the foreign company in India that is to be deemed as its principal business place in India; and
- a list and details of the directors and the secretary/joint secretaries of the foreign company.

However, if the foreign company is incorporated outside India by royal charter or any special act of parliament of its home country, then a simple notice to the ROC in New Delhi and the local ROC informing them of the foreign company's establishment of a place of business in India will suffice.

The foreign company must submit an annual balance sheet and profit and loss account for the place of business in India as though it were a company incorporated in India within the meaning of the Companies Act. The foreign company is also obliged to maintain books of accounts with respect to monies received and expended, sales and purchases made, and liabilities arising in the course of or in relation to its business in India.

The foreign company must wind up in accordance with the Companies Act provisions applicable to unregistered companies – that is, companies that can be but are not registered under the act. A foreign company can be wound up if, among other things:

- it has ceased to carry on business;
- it is unable to pay its debts; or
- the tribunal is of the opinion that it is just and equitable that the company be wound up.

(a)   *Branch office*

A foreign company engaged in manufacturing and trade activities abroad may open a branch office for:

- export/import of goods;
- provision of professional or consultancy services;
- research work in which the parent foreign company is engaged;
- promotion of technical or financial collaborations between Indian companies and the parent or overseas group company;
- representation of the parent company in India and acting as buying/selling agent in India;
- provision of services in information technology and software development in India;
- provision of technical support for the products supplied by parent/group companies; and
- foreign airline/shipping services.

A branch office may remit outside India the profits of the branch, net of applicable Indian taxes, upon production of certain documents. Subject to certain conditions, it can also acquire immovable property that is necessary for or incidental to the activity carried on in India. A branch office, as a foreign company, is taxed on its income at the rates applicable to foreign companies. A branch office is required to make annual filings with the Reserve Bank of India by submitting an annual activity certificate from a chartered accountant.

(b)   *Liaison/representative office*

A foreign company may open a liaison office to act as a channel of communication between the principal place of business or head office located outside India and entities in India. However, a liaison office cannot itself undertake any commercial/trading/industrial activity, directly or indirectly, and must not involve itself in any inward remittances received from abroad through normal banking channels.

A liaison office cannot acquire or own immovable property in India. It is also prohibited from undertaking any activity that results in income. However, where a liaison office creates a permanent establishment in India or a business connection is established through the liaison office, income attributable to that permanent establishment or business connection becomes taxable in India. A liaison office is required to make annual filings with the Reserve Bank of India by submitting annual activity certificate from chartered accountant.

(c)   *Project office*
A foreign company executing a project in India can open up a project office in India to represent its interests, provided it has secured a contract to execute a project in India and:
- the project is funded directly by inward remittance from abroad;
- the project is funded by a bilateral or multilateral international financing agency;
- the project has been cleared by an appropriate authority; or
- the company or entity in India that awarded the contract has been granted term loans by a public financial institution or bank in India for the project.

Like a branch office, a project office is treated as an extension of the foreign corporation in India and is taxed at the rate applicable to foreign companies.

10.   Corporate reorganisation
Various forms of corporate reorganisation are available, such as merger, share buy-back, capital reduction, de-merger and slump sale.

10.1   Merger
Reorganisation of a company by way of a compromise between the shareholders, creditors and other members on their claims and entitlements in order to revive the company, or by way of an arrangement between the company and its members, requires the sanction of the high courts of the respective states in which the merging companies are registered. The power to approve such schemes of compromise or arrangement for mergers have been transferred from the high courts to the National Company Law Tribunal, but the tribunal is still in the process of being formed.

10.2   De-merger or spin-off
De-merger is a process whereby an identified business of one company is transferred to another company, usually undertaken to segregate core and non-core businesses. As consideration for the spin-off, the shareholders of the selling company receive shares of the company into which the business is spun off. De-merger also requires

the prior sanction of the competent high court; again, this power has been transferred to the tribunal, which is still in the process of being formed.

10.3 Slump sale

A slump sale is another reorganisation tool that involves the transfer of identified businesses from one company to another. However, unlike a de-merger, a slump sale is not regulated by the courts; such hiving-off may be achieved by way of members' resolutions and a business transfer agreement.

10.4 Share buyback

A company can buy back up to 25% of the total paid-up capital and free reserves in the financial year in which the buyback is made. A buyback can be effected only out of the company's free reserves, the securities premium account and the proceeds of an earlier share issue. It requires a special resolution of the members, although a board resolution is adequate if the buyback is less than 10% of the total paid-up capital and free reserves in the financial year in which buyback is made.

10.5 Capital reduction

A reduction in share capital is a process through which a company can pay off its shareholders by cancelling or reducing its capital or by cancelling share capital against accumulated losses. A company limited by shares or limited by guarantee can reduce its share capital pursuant to a special resolution of members and upon confirmation by the competent high court. This power has been shifted to the National Company Law Tribunal, which is still in the process of being formed.

11. Taxation

Companies are subject to both direct tax (ie corporate tax) and indirect tax (eg customs duty, excise duty, VAT). The Indian fiscal year commences on April 1 and ends on March 31. Companies are required to file tax returns for each tax year by October 31. Corporate tax liability should be assessed by companies and discharged by way of advance tax payment in four instalments on June 15, September 15, December 15 and March 15 for a tax assessment year. The balance taxes, if any, should be paid on or before the date of filing the return. Delayed returns or a shortfall in tax may result in penal interest.

For the assessment year 2008–09, domestic companies will be subject to taxation at a rate of 30.9% (inclusive of surcharge and educational cess) where income is up to Rs10 million, and 33.99% (inclusive of surcharge and educational cess) where income exceeds Rs10 million. Foreign companies will be subject to higher taxation at a rate of 41.2% (inclusive of surcharge and educational cess) where income is up to Rs10 million, and 42.23% (inclusive of surcharge and educational cess) where income exceeds Rs10 million.

Dividends are non-taxable in the hands of shareholders, although a company issuing dividends must pay a dividend distribution tax of 16.995% (inclusive of surcharge and educational cess).

12.   Companies Bill 2008

On August 29 2008, the Union Cabinet of the Government of India gave its approval for the introduction of the Companies Bill 2008 (2008 Bill) to replace the Companies Act. The 2008 Bill has been introduced with a view to comprehensively revise the existing Companies Act in view of the changing economic and commercial environment of India. Some of the salient features of the 2008 Bill include:

- the introduction of a new entity in the form of a one-person company,
- applying the successful e-governance initiative, MCA 21 of the Ministry of Corporate Affairs, to all the processes involved in meeting compliance obligations;
- duties and liabilities of the directors and for every company to have at least one director resident in India; and
- statutory recognition to audit, remuneration and stakeholders grievances committees of the board of director and, further, recognition of the chief executive officer, chief financial officer and company secretary as 'key managerial personnel'.

It is expected that the 2008 Bill will replace the Companies Act in the near future.

Israel

Alon Kaplan
Orna Ronkin-Noor
Alon Kaplan Law Firm

1.   Types of company with limited liability and applicable legislation

Four types of corporation are available in the field of private law:

- partnership;
- collective corporation;
- non-profit organisation; and
- private company.

This is in addition to:

- public corporations, which operate and are legally formed only in the field of public law; and
- mixed corporations, which are formed under public law but whose field of business refers to both private and public law.

This chapter focuses on the private company, which is legally recorded by the registrar of companies pursuant to the Companies Law or Companies Ordinance.

In Israel, commercial activities may be carried out either through an Israeli company – defined as a company that is incorporated in Israel or whose activities are carried out and controlled in Israel – or through a foreign company.

The incorporation of a company is a legal act involving:

- submission of the incorporation documents to the registrar of companies;
- registration of the company; and
- issuance of the certificate of incorporation.

The company has independent legal personality separate from that of its shareholders, and it bears rights and obligations from the date of incorporation until liquidation. Its separate legal personality protects the shareholders and their assets from company creditors. The shareholders are liable for the company's debts only to the extent of their obligations towards it. This principle allows for risks to be taken and increases the potential for profit. An exception to this rule enshrined in company law allows for the corporate veil to be lifted in order to prevent harmful use of the principle of separate legal personality. The exception also applies where operation of the company is performed with the aim of cheating or exploiting someone, or where for some reason it involves unreasonable risk, taking into consideration the company's ability to pay its debts.

In the past, the legal framework governing companies was set out in the

Companies Ordinance, originally enacted in 1929 and significantly amended and improved over the years. With the enactment of the new Companies Law on February 1 2000, a significant portion of the Companies Ordinance was repealed, although certain provisions relating to bonds, liens and liquidations still remain under the ordinance and have not been included in the Companies Law.

During the past few years there have been certain changes in Israeli legislation concerning certain types of company. We focus here on two major changes:

- the Israeli underlying company; and
- a company for the benefit of the public (CBP).

1.1 The Israeli underlying company

An underlying company is a separate legal entity holding a trust's assets for the trustee. Every entity that possesses assets that are not its own, but belong to the trustee, fulfils the definition of an underlying company.

This may be useful where a common-law trust that is not a legal entity may wish to open and operate a bank account or where a continental trust (such as a foundation) may wish to undertake commercial activities using the underlying company.

The Taxation of Trusts Law, which came into effect on January 1 2006, provides for the establishment of an underlying company of a trust within Israel or abroad for the legal separation of the trustee's personal assets and the trust's assets.

The underlying company should be regarded as a 'flow-through entity'. The Israeli tax authority will 'look through' the company and treat any assets and income derived from it as if they were held directly by the trustee.

Since the trustee of a foreign settlor trust is not subject to tax or reporting requirements, a trustee may utilise an underlying company to hold its assets. Neither the trustee nor the underlying company is subject to tax or reporting obligations on the income derived from sources outside Israel. Where the underlying company derives income from sources within Israel, this is considered as earned by a foreign resident.

The general rules applying to any other private company will also be applied to the incorporation of an underlying company (ie name registration; the articles of association; certificate of incorporation; authorised share capital; one shareholder; administration of the company, etc).

1.2 Company for the Benefit of the Public (CBP)

On June 21 2007 Amendment No 6 to the Companies Law came into effect. This amendment reinforced new arrangements in respect of companies for the benefit of the public (CBP) and annulled the previous arrangements that applied to these companies according to the Trust Law. Under the amendment, a CBP is defined as a company whose articles of association incorporate only public aims, as per the addendum to the Law. These include companies whose main focus is:

- education;
- professional training;
- environmental protection;
- health or life saving;

- protecting animals;
- concern for human rights;
- research or higher education;
- sport; and
- absorption and settlement.

No profits (ie dividends) are distributed to its shareholders.

In order to ensure that the activity of the CBP will meet the above conditions, a series of strict requirements and demands apply to the company, its shareholders and its office-bearers. These restrictions apply to:

- any change to the company's aims;
- the transfer of shares;
- transactions with interested parties;
- payment for services by office-bearers or by corporations controlled by them.

Breaches of these obligations and demands may result in financial sanctions being imposed on the violator. A supervisory mechanism has been created (audit committee, internal auditor); in addition, the authority of the Registrar of Trusts has been strengthened with regard to these activities.

The CBP must be registered in two parallel registries – the companies' registry and the companies section of the registrar of trusts. However, only one application to register this type of company is required at the registrar of companies, as opposed to the previous situation where filing a separate application with both registrars was required.

The registrar of trusts must confirm that all the conditions required under law have been met. If the said confirmation is given and there is no other legal obstacle to the registration, the company will be registered simultaneously at the companies' registry and at the companies section for CPBs at the registrar of trusts, and a certificate of incorporation will be issued accordingly. After registration the company must add 'company for the public benefit' or 'CPB' on each and every document or advert on its behalf.

2.   Incorporation procedure

2.1   Proceedings prior to incorporation

(a)   Name registration

The law allows for the company name to be freely chosen, subject to certain restrictions. A company name will not be registered if:

- it is identical to the name of a corporation already legally registered in Israel, or is so similar to the name of an existing corporation that there is a possibility of confusion; or
- it is identical to the registered trademark of another company with the same corporate purpose, or is so similar to a registered trademark that there is a possibility of confusion, unless the written consent of the trademark owner is presented to the registrar.

In addition, the law affords the registrar of companies the discretion to decide whether a company name involves some sort of fraud or attempt to mislead; if he finds this to be the case, he will not register the company by that name.

The law further empowers the registrar to decide at his discretion whether a company name may harm public order or morality, in which case he will not authorise its registration.

The limitations imposed by law are intended to prevent a company from engaging in unfair competition, misleading the public or harming public order through use of the company name. The registrar's decision may be appealed to the court.

(b)   *Investment in the company*

There are a number of ways in which to invest in a company. The shareholders are obliged to make an initial investment of the amount of the redeemed share capital representing the guarantee of each shareholder for the company's debts. Like any other creditor, a shareholder may choose to make a financial loan to the company or to transfer to the company assets in his possession, and is entitled to repayment of the loan as well as the linkage differentials (up to the index increase) on a tax-free basis.

Israeli law obliges shareholders to calculate theoretical interest up to the level of market interest if they withdraw money from the company and are not charged interest or are charged at a lower rate than market interest. For such purposes, market interest is set at the consumer price index plus 4%. Some also hold the view that value added tax must be added to the amount of theoretical income. Further to court precedent, the company can register income interest on its books instead of the shareholder and charge the amount of interest to the shareholder.

Despite these provisions, the view of the income tax authorities with regard to shareholder withdrawals made for lengthy periods and without a proper repayment procedure is notoriously strict. If the loan is not repaid within a certain period, the shareholder will be compelled to pay tax as though the amount withdrawn was received not as a loan but rather as a dividend or salary. The income tax authorities will not only tax the withdrawing shareholder, but will usually consider the withdrawal as a net amount received after tax and will, for the purpose of calculating income tax, gross up the amount to the sum that was apparently received prior to receipt of the net amount.

It is therefore recommended that repayments of shareholder withdrawals be recorded in a register of loan agreements between the company and the shareholders.

2.2   Incorporation

(a)   *Articles of association*

(i)   *Essential clauses*

When incorporating a company, the main document which should be presented to the registrar is the articles of association. The articles, as they are recorded together with incorporation of the company, are legally valid from the date of incorporation.

The articles are the central document governing the relationship between the shareholders themselves and between the company and the shareholders.

Pursuant to the Companies Law, a number of issues must be included in or regulated by the articles of association (in the past, these issues were partially regulated by the memorandum of association, which no longer exists under the Companies Law). Outside these requirements, the founders have a significant degree of freedom in drafting the articles.

The following information must be included by law:
- the name of the company;
- the corporate purpose;
- the registered share capital, including the number and type of shares; and
- information on the limitation of shareholders' liability.

(ii) *Clauses not foreseen by law*

Under the Companies Law, the central document organising the company's internal operations is the articles of association. The articles act as a sort of 'constitution' of the company, and must include at least four clauses that were previously included in the memorandum of association. The company is entitled to add additional provisions as it deems fit.

The company can add clauses on matters that are not covered in the Companies Law. Such clauses have significant implications, as the articles bind all future shareholders of the company and affect all third parties who are not party to the articles.

(iii) *Optional clauses*

Under the Companies Law, a company can include in the articles of association any matters relating to its operations or its shareholders, including:
- the rights and obligations of the shareholders;
- instructions on the management of the company; and
- any other subject that the shareholders deem necessary to be included in the articles.

(b) **Execution of certificate of incorporation**

If the registrar of companies finds that all legal requirements and conditions for registration have been fulfilled, he will:
- register the company;
- allocate to it a registration number; and
- issue a certificate of incorporation to the company.

The company comes into existence on the date stated in the certificate of incorporation. The certificate acts as conclusive proof that all legal requirements and conditions of registration have been fulfilled.

Should there be a deficiency in the articles, the issuance of the certificate of incorporation is insufficient to cure that deficiency or to avoid the need to correct it.

(c) **Indirect taxes, incorporation fees and other levies**

The costs of incorporating an Israeli company are currently (2009) as follows:

- attorneys' fees – approximately $1,000 plus value added tax (VAT);
- registrar of companies' fees – approximately $680; and
- disbursements (agent's fees) – $150.

A number of indirect taxes are payable in Israel: VAT, purchase tax, customs duty and stamp duty.

VAT at a rate of 16.5% is imposed on transactions in Israel and on the import of goods into Israel (but not on exports). VAT at a rate of 0% applies at the personal level (eg for hotel accommodation). Where services are provided exclusively to an overseas resident and those services are not connected to a property in Israel, VAT at the rate of 0% also applies.

Stamp duty has not been charged on documents signed from January 1 2006 onwards.

(d) **Declaration of start date and other declarations**

Before commencing operations, the activities set out next should be performed.

(i) *Opening a bank account*

A company representative must present the founding documents of the company, together with confirmation of its incorporation, to the bank. He must also present confirmation by an attorney or accountant of the signatory rights on behalf of the company.

(ii) *Registration as authorised dealer with VAT authorities*

The first registration takes place at the office of the VAT authorities. To open a file, the following must be submitted:

- the articles of association;
- the certificate of incorporation received from the registrar of companies at the time of incorporation;
- the company's stamp;
- the company's bank account number (generally evidenced by means of a (cancelled) cheque); and
- the company's address.

The authorised dealer number is identical to the company's number.

(iii) *Registration with the income tax authorities*

Following registration with the VAT authorities and before commencing activities, the company must inform the income tax authorities about the new business. The notice may be sent by registered post and must be signed by an authorised signatory. A foreign company that must appoint a representative for VAT purposes must also appoint a representative for income tax purposes. The representative must be an Israeli resident, and must be given power of attorney to obtain income and profits, report to the authorities and pay taxes from the company's assets. If the company fails to appoint a representative, the representative appointed for VAT purposes will also be considered the representative for income tax purposes.

The tax authorities will then issue a confirmation regarding the management of the accounting books and will also issue a demand for payment of advance tax at a specified percentage of the turnover. The percentage is based on the experience of the tax authorities in the region where the company intends to operate, and it may be increased or reduced depending on the expected taxable income. Tax must be deducted at source for certain payments, and accordingly at the same time confirmation will be issued regarding the amount that must be deducted at source from the company's income, or alternatively an exemption on the grounds of payment of advance tax. Generally, in the first few months of a company's existence no certificate of exemption from income tax at source is given for its activities, and tax must be deducted at source by anyone making a taxable payment.

(iv) *Opening files for income tax deductions and at the National Insurance Institute*
Where the company intends to employ employees, it must open a deductions file with the income tax authorities as well as at the National Insurance Institute. Once this has been done, the company will be sent payment books through which deductions from employee salaries are to be made.

Where the company employs foreign workers, a 10% levy is imposed, which must be paid at the time of reporting on the employment of foreign workers.

(e) **Management of accounting books**
The company may keep its books either in Hebrew or in Arabic. It is also possible to request permission to keep the books in English. Additional bookkeeping obligations apply for income tax purposes. The bookkeeping requirements depend on the type of activity to be carried out, the turnover and the number of employees.

(f) **Tax identification number**
A foreign company can register with the income tax authorities and enjoy various legal benefits that are reserved to foreign companies. It can also choose to submit income tax reports for activities involving lower than usual costs or profits. The tax authorities will issue the foreign company with a special identification number.

3. Corporate domicile
Previously, prior to significant taxation reforms, a company was considered to be resident in Israel for tax purposes if it conformed to one of two models. The first model required that the company be registered in Israel and that its main activities be in Israel. Under the second model, the company's administration and control of its activities must be performed in Israel. Taxation reforms modified the first model only.

Today, every company that is incorporated in Israel is automatically considered an Israeli resident, even if its main activities are outside of Israel. The second model remains in place, with the implication that a company that has been incorporated and registered overseas will nonetheless be considered as an Israeli resident if its activities are controlled and managed in Israel. For such purposes, the places where daily control and management of the company are carried out, important business decisions are made and the board of directors meets will all be considered.

The income tax authorities have issued a circular explaining what information will be examined in this regard. This includes:

- the incorporation documents;
- protocols from board meetings;
- particulars regarding shareholders and employees;
- bank accounts;
- communication agreements with service providers; and
- the place where the books are kept.

4.   Corporate purpose

The company has separate legal personality that is fit for every right, obligation and legal activity. Legal fitness is generally unlimited. For registration purposes, the company must specify its corporate purpose in the articles of association. In the past, a company did not have the power to authorise activities that fell outside the scope of its corporate purpose (ie the *ultra vires* doctrine). Today, however, an Israeli company has the general power to undertake all activities that correspond to its corporate form. The fact that a company deviates from its corporate purpose does not in itself invalidate the relevant activity, since the company has the general power to undertake all lawful activities. At the same time, however, an activity that does not fall within the framework of activities defined by the company will not be legally binding on the company if the directors deviated from their authority and third parties involved in the activity knew or should have known about the extraordinary act.

The corporate purpose may be stated in the articles of association in one of three ways:

- to undertake all legal activities;
- to undertake all legal activities excluding certain types specified in the articles of association; or
- to undertake certain types of activity as specified in the articles of association.

The corporate purpose cannot be illegal, immoral or contrary to public order.

5.   Capital stock

5.1   Authorised share capital

A company may be established by a single shareholder and no minimum capital is required. The authorised (registered) share capital is determined in the articles and is composed of shares that are actually issued to the shareholders (issued share capital) upon establishment. If the company wishes to increase its authorised capital, it must do so by way of a resolution of the general shareholders' meeting. The increase must be reported and registered with the registrar of companies.

A reduction in the authorised share capital is possible provided that the cancelled shares have not been issued and there is no undertaking of the company for their issue (eg by a way of an option).

A company can establish several different classes of shares with varying rights and duties attached. In such a case, if the company wishes to amend the articles in a way that infringes on the rights of a certain class of shares, the amendment may take place only with the approval of the general meeting of shareholders of that class of shares. Many companies include a provision in the articles stating specifically that the issuance of a new class of shares will not be considered in itself to infringe on the other classes.

5.2 Issued share capital

The issuance of the share capital is carried out by the board of directors and must be reported to the registrar of companies. The board can issue shares only up to the limit of the authorised share capital. The company can reduce its issued share capital (eg by purchasing its own shares) if the consideration paid by the company does not exceed its revenues according to a formula that is specified in the law.

The company can have par-value shares and non-par-value shares. The company cannot issue par-value shares for consideration that is less than the par value, unless it transfers a similar portion of its surplus funds into the share capital.

5.3 Transfer of shares

In order to change a shareholding in a company, a written shareholder resolution is required. The company must be provided with a share transfer deed signed by the transferor and the transferee (usually confirmed by a witness). Further, to register the transfer, any relevant provisions of the articles of association must be complied with. Usually, the articles provide that a share transfer will not be effective and will not be registered unless approved by the directors. Once a board of directors' resolution has been passed confirming the transfer, notice will be sent to the registrar of companies.

6. Equity

6.1 Equity–capital ratio

This ratio is not relevant in Israel.

6.2 Convertible bonds

The board of directors is entitled to issue bonds and other share certificates that may be exchanged or executed for shares, up to the limit of the authorised share capital.

For this purpose, share certificates can be exchanged or executed for shares (eg bonds for exchange and options) as though they were exchanged or executed at the time of issuance.

7. Administration

7.1 Administrative bodies

The administration of the company is conducted by the different bodies. The main bodies under Israeli law are the shareholders, the board of directors and the general manager (chief executive officer).

(a) *General shareholders' meeting*

The general meeting elects the directors and the accountant, and it is authorised to make changes to the articles and to the authorised share capital. It also approves actions of the other bodies that require special approval due to a conflict of interest.

The company cannot delegate the authority to exercise these powers to other company bodies, but it can include in the articles other issues that fall within the competence of the general meeting. If competence for such powers is granted to other administrative bodies under the Companies Law and the shareholders take these powers from them, then the shareholders assume the same responsibilities and potential liability as the original body would bear while exercising these powers.

See also section 7.2 below.

(b) *Board of directors*

According to company law, the board of directors:

- determines company policy;
- supervises the general manager's activities;
- establishes the operating plans of the company;
- determines the principles for financing these plans and the priority of these principles;
- checks the financial situation of the company;
- identifies credit lines for which the company will apply;
- determines the organisational structure;
- determines the policy for payment of employees;
- prepares and approves the annual reports; and
- appoints and removes the general manager.

The board of directors further has residual authority to exercise any power not granted to a specific body under the law or the articles. See also section 7.3 below.

(c) *General manager*

The general manager is responsible for the day-to-day administration and management of the company, under the supervision of the board of directors, and must report to the board on any unusual issue of significance to the company. The general manager has residual power to exercise operating authority in relation to any matter that is not regulated under the law or the articles. See also section 7.4 below.

7.2 The general meeting

The company must hold an annual general meeting at least once a year, no later than

15 months from the last meeting, unless otherwise specified in the articles. The board of directors may call an extraordinary meeting and must do so at the demand of:

- at least one director;
- a shareholder holding at least 10% of the issued share capital and 1% of the voting rights of the company; or
- a shareholder holding at least 10% of the voting rights.

If the directors do not comply with this request, the court or shareholders holding more than half of the share capital can convene the meeting.

A general meeting (and a board of directors' meeting) can be held in any way that allows the shareholders to hear each other. Between seven and 45 days' notice of the meeting must be given, unless the shareholders (or the board of directors) have waived this right or the articles provide otherwise. Instead of holding a meeting, the shareholders can sign a written resolution as long as the resolution is accepted and signed unanimously (the same applies to the board of directors).

The notice must specify the agenda and include a reasonable description of the issues to be dealt with and the resolutions to be accepted. Regulations issued by the minister of justice provide that a deviation from the wording in the notice is possible if this is negligible or benefits the company. A shareholder who participates in a general meeting cannot claim that a resolution is void due to a default in the notice regarding the place or date of the meeting (the same applies to directors).

The quorum necessary to hold a general meeting in companies with more than one shareholder is two shareholders who together hold at least 25% of the issued share capital.

(a) Challenging resolutions

Where a minority shareholder is prejudiced, or there is a real threat that he may be prejudiced, he has the right to approach the court, which may decide to remedy or prevent the prejudice by giving instructions to the shareholders of the company. In addition, a shareholder who prejudices another will be subject to the laws of breach of contract.

Where a shareholders' meeting has not been properly convened (ie, has not been convened in accordance with the provisions of the Companies Law or the articles of association), the district court may decide to cancel any resolution taken at the meeting.

7.3 Board of directors

The first directors of the company are appointed upon registration of the company. Subsequent elections and dismissals of directors are conducted by the general meeting, unless the articles provide otherwise. Commonly, the articles will provide that directors are to be appointed and dismissed by certain shareholders, by issuing notice to the company.

Meetings of the board of directors are convened at least once a year, and the chairman of the board is entitled to call a meeting at any time. The chairman must further call a board meeting:

- at the demand of two directors, or of one director where there are five or fewer directors in the company;
- in any case of illegalities or irregularities;
- if the company accountant informs the chairman of substantial default in the accounting controls; or
- if the general manager has advised that there is a need for the board to take action.

The notice that must be given of a board meeting is determined in the articles, and no matter can be discussed unless it is included on the agenda specified in the notice (subject to the articles of the company).

(a)   *Conflict of interest*

The Companies Law is very strict when it comes to a possible conflict of interest for a director. A director or any other office holder of the company (including the general manager or any executive manager) who has a personal interest in a transaction of the company (whether existing or proposed) must reveal his interest no later than the first board meeting at which the transaction is discussed. A transaction in which an office holder has such an interest requires the approval of the board of directors; if the office holder is a director, he can neither participate in nor vote at the relevant meeting. If the transaction concerns a director and may have a substantial effect on the company's profits, property or obligations, or it is outside the ordinary course of business or not under free-market terms, there is a need for an additional approval by the general meeting. This is the case, for example, in approving the terms of employment of a director.

(b)   *Liability under civil and criminal law*

As a company is a legal entity separate from its shareholders, the question arises as to its criminal and civil liability.

Where a company causes damage it is generally impossible to claim against the shareholders, although where a director (who may also be a shareholder) is liable for the damage an action may be brought against him for contributory negligence.

Under criminal law, it may be possible to hold the company liable – for example, where the law extends criminal liability to the company for actions carried out in the course of its business activities. Moreover, where a central person in the company performs or endorses an offence, it may be possible to relate the offence to the company. Here, too, a distinction must be made between the liability of the company and its shareholders, who generally will not be held liable.

7.4   The general manager

The company is entitled to appoint one or more general managers; if a general manager is not appointed, the company will be managed by the board of directors. The board determines the scope and frequency of the general manager's reports, and both the board and the chairman of the board are entitled to demand reports from the general manager.

8. Company tax

The Income Tax Ordinance imposes tax at a uniform rate on taxable income. As the tax is uniform, it is imposed from the first shekel of profit rather than in a progressive manner.

Until 2004, company tax in Israel was levied at a rate of 36%. According to the national financial plan, the tax is to be gradually reduced as follows:

- 31% in the 2006 tax year;
- 29% in 2007;
- 27% in 2008;
- 26% in 2009; and
- 25% in 2010, when this process is expected to end.

The Israeli tax year is identical to the calendar year, although it is possible to approach the tax authorities with a request that the tax year begin on a date other than January 1 where this is the accounting practice in the parent company, or for other valid reasons.

The rate of tax on a dividend paid by a company to shareholders is 20%; where the shareholder is considered an essential shareholder (ie, holds at least 10% of the rights), the tax rate is 25%.

A company must submit income tax reports by May 31 each year, although with the permission of the income tax authorities it may postpone submission to a later date.

8.1 Types of corporate taxpayer

In addition to the classic company, other companies are recognised in Israel for taxation purposes, including the following:

- In a family company, taxable income is attributed to the representative debtor – that is, the family member who holds the majority of the shares.
- A transparent company is similar to a family company, but its income is attributed to all shareholders in proportion to their shareholdings. In fact there is no such company: the relevant law was meant to come into effect from 2003, but it was never implemented because associated regulations were never enacted.
- A home company is a company that is engaged exclusively in the holding of buildings. Its income may be considered as income of the shareholders and is attributed in proportion to their shareholdings.
- A company that holds trust assets to keep them separate from the personal assets of the trustee is not taxed and need not report its income, which is considered as income of the trustee.

Generally, a company in Israel is entitled to a credit on taxes paid overseas, including a mechanism for indirect credits on the taxation of dividends that a subsidiary company paid overseas.

According to the Taxation of Trusts Law, which become effective on January 1 2006, a company whose sole purpose is to be an underlying company of a trust will not be required to pay tax in Israel as long as the settlor of the trust is a foreign resident. This rule will apply even if the directors of the underlying company are Israelis.

8.2 Reporting requirements

A private company must file an annual report with the registrar of companies within 14 days of the annual general meeting. The directors will issue a declaration confirming that they have both approved the relevant reports and presented those reports to the annual general meeting.

A private company need not hold an annual general meeting if this is provided for in the articles and there is no objection from shareholders or the board of directors. In such a case the company need only file an annual report where:

- if it prepares annual financial reports, it must file this annual report once a year within 14 days of sending the financial reports to the shareholders; and
- if it is not active and does not prepare annual financial reports, it must file a report once a year.

A private company must attach the balance sheet (audited by a certified public accountant) to its annual report where the articles do not:

- limit the right to transfer its shares;
- prevent an offer to the public of its shares or bonds; or
- limit the number of shareholders in the company to 50.

9. Company reorganisation

9.1 Transformation

A private company can be transformed into a public company by amendment of the articles of association. The steps prescribed under the Securities Law for a change in corporate form must be followed, and the registrar of companies must be notified within 14 days of the change.

An unlimited company can be converted into a limited company by amendment of the articles within the framework of an application for a compromise or arrangement between the company and its creditors or shareholders. The application further requires court approval.

A limited liability company can become an unlimited company by agreement of all the shareholders.

9.2 Merger

The company may cease to exist either through liquidation or through dissolution.

Merger is a process through which the merging company is dissolved. Unlike liquidation, dissolution of the company by way of merger involves not the distribution of assets to the creditors but, rather, the transfer of the company's assets and obligations to another company.

The Companies Law recognises two alternative types of merger:

- merger without court authorisation; and
- merger with court authorisation.

Merger involves the transfer of the merging company's assets and obligations to the absorbing company in such a way as causes the dissolution of the merging company without liquidation. As a result of the merger:

- all assets and obligations of the merging company – including future debts, both known and unknown – will be transferred and assigned to the absorbing company;
- the absorbing company will take the place of the merging company in any pending legal proceedings, including execution proceedings;
- the registrar of companies will transfer the book of liens of the merging company to the absorbing company;
- the merging company will be liquidated and erased from the Register of Companies; and
- the registrar will give the merging company a certificate certifying performance of the merger and will register the merger in the register entries for the absorbing company.

10. Dissolution and liquidation

Until recently, a company could be struck off the register of companies if it did not pay the annual maintenance fee. As a result, many companies that ceased to be active merely stopped paying the annual maintenance fee and disappeared.

Today, as a result of a recent change in the law, a company can cease existing only through liquidation.

There are three kind of liquidation:

- voluntary liquidation;
- voluntary liquidation under court supervision; and
- involuntary liquidation under court supervision.

The most common forms are voluntary liquidation and involuntary liquidation under court supervision.

10.1 Voluntary liquidation

Voluntary liquidation is where a company initiates liquidation for reasons other than insolvency. The liquidator appointed by the company will pay off all its debts and transfer any remaining assets to the shareholders. A resolution stating that the company is no longer in existence will then be issued. If the directors do not declare in an affidavit that the company is solvent, the liquidation will become a voluntary liquidation under court supervision.

10.2 Involuntary liquidation

Most liquidations that take place in Israel are involuntary; most are requested by creditors due to the company's insolvency. The official receiver supervises the liquidations on behalf of the state, and every application to court must include the official receiver as a respondent. The official receiver files the application for appointment of the liquidator according to a vote that takes place at a creditors' meeting. If no liquidator is appointed, the official receiver will serve as liquidator. At each major step of the proceedings, and especially when making payments out of company funds, the liquidator will apply to the court for instructions; the official receiver must be addressed as a respondent to any such application.

10.3 Burdensome assets and contracts

The liquidator can ask the court to release him from burdensome assets and contracts, including real-estate assets with burdensome terms, company shares that were not fully paid up, and assets that cannot easily be sold.

The rationale behind this principle is that since the company in liquidation cannot fulfil its obligations in full, it is preferable that it waive all kinds of assets and benefits that do not justify additional liabilities.

A distinction must be drawn between the authority to release the liquidator from a burdensome contract and contracting with a liquidator (eg a contract for the sale of company assets).

This authority relates only to past contracts, and a liquidator cannot be released from a contract that was signed after the liquidation. Such contracts must also have court approval before signing.

11. Branches

In Israel, a branch has no separate legal personality from its parent company.

Italy

Marco Consonni
Pasquale Gerardo Marasco
Francesco Spreafico
Dewey & LeBoeuf

1. Types of company with limited liability and applicable legislation

Under Italian law, companies may be classified into three categories based on the members' liability:

- companies whose members have personal and unlimited liability for company obligations (*Società in nome collettivo*) – with the possibility of conventional derogation for those members who are not directors (*Società semplice*);
- companies in which some members have limited liability and others have unlimited liability; and
- companies that are exclusively liable for their obligations (*Società per azioni* (SPA) and *Società a responsabilità limitata* (SRL)), where none of the members is held liable for company obligations.

This chapter focuses exclusively on companies with a comprehensive limitation of liability: the SPA and the SRL.

The regime governing such companies was substantially reformed by Legislative Decree 6 of January 17 2003 and Legislative Decree 37 of February 6 2004 (and implementing provisions), which amended the relevant sections of the Civil Code. The reforms entered into force on January 1 2004.

The SPA is a joint stock company with the following characteristics:

- the company has separate legal personality from its members and is solely liable for its obligations to the full extent of its assets; and
- participation in the company is represented by shares, which are the minimum units of corporate capital.

The second characteristic distinguishes the SPA from the SRL, where participation is not represented by shares. Rather, each member of the SRL holds a quota of the corporate capital, the value of which depends on the amount of corporate capital subscribed by the member on incorporation or at the time of an increase in corporate capital.

The structure of the SRL is more flexible and the management less costly than those of an SPA (eg a lower minimum capital requirement applies). As such, this form is often used by foreign investors and multinational companies that are interested in commencing activities in Italy. The quotas of an SRL cannot be traded on the stock exchange. If the founding members want this type of company, their sole option is the SPA. Further, the SRL can issue bonds in limited cases, but only to professional investors and only if this is expressly provided for in the bylaws.

The SPA is the prototype for limited liability companies. The provisions governing SPAs largely apply to any limited liability company. The following discussion is valid for both SPAs and SRLs, except where otherwise indicated.

The SPA and SRL are governed by the general provisions applicable to all forms of company and by dedicated sections of the Civil Code, as recently amended (Articles 2247 to 2250 and 2325 to 2510).

As far as the SPA is concerned, the specific provisions of the Civil Code apply to both companies that issue shares listed on the stock exchange and companies whose shares are widely distributed among the public. In the former case, Legislative Decree 58 of February 24 1998 also applies.

Other specific rules are set out for companies operating in specific fields (eg banks).

2. Incorporation procedure

2.1 Before the incorporation

(a) Conditions for incorporation

Prior to proceeding with incorporation of a company, and as a condition of incorporation itself, the founding members must ensure that the following conditions are met:

- the corporate capital has been fully subscribed by the founding members;
- all requirements concerning cash and in kind contributions have been met; and
- the relevant government authorisations required to perform the intended activities have been obtained.

Upon execution of the incorporation deed, the notary public has the duty to ascertain that the above conditions have been fulfilled.

(b) Capital contributions

In order to participate in the incorporation of a company, it is necessary to subscribe a part of the corporate capital and either make, or undertake to make, the corresponding contribution. Future members contribute to the formation of the start-up capital in this way.

Contributions may be made in cash or in kind.

Where a contribution is in cash, the member must deposit at least 25% of the value of the contribution before incorporation. If the company is incorporated by a sole shareholder, the entire contribution (100%) must be paid before incorporation. Cash contributions are evidenced by means of a certificate issued by the bank where the funds have been deposited. The certificate must be submitted to the notary public upon incorporation.

The funds will remain deposited with the bank until the incorporation procedure has been completed; they will be returned to the directors, upon request, once proof is provided that the company has been registered in the companies register.

Where an in-kind contribution is made, the contribution must be paid in full on the date of subscription. Upon incorporation, the member must submit a sworn estimate report drawn up by an expert appointed by the president of the tribunal at the place where the company's registered office is located (for SRLs, the expert need not to be appointed by the president of the tribunal, although he must be listed in the register of accounting auditors). The estimate report must contain:

- a description of the goods or credits that form the object of the contribution;
- the value assigned to each of them;
- the criteria used to determine this value; and
- a statement that the value assigned is not lower than the nominal value, increased by the eventual premium of the shares issued against the contribution.

The estimate report must be attached to the incorporation deed and deposited with the companies register.

Within 180 days of the incorporation of an SPA, the directors must verify the evaluation of in-kind contributions contained in the estimate report and review them where necessary. Until the evaluations have been verified, the shares corresponding to the in-kind contributions are non-transferable and must remain deposited with the company. Should the directors discover that the true value of the goods or credits is 20% lower than the value assigned to them upon incorporation, the company must reduce the corporate capital proportionately.

For a cash contribution to an SRL, the payment due upon incorporation may be replaced by execution of an insurance policy or bank guarantee.

A contribution to an SRL may also be made in the form of an insurance policy or a bank guarantee through which obligations undertaken by the quotaholder to perform work or services in favour of the company are guaranteed up to their entire value. This rule does not apply to SPAs, as the performance of work or provision of services cannot constitute a contribution to the capital of an SPA (see section 7.2).

(c)   *Tax codes*

If the shareholders and/or directors of the company are foreign subjects, they must obtain a tax code prior to incorporation by filing a request with the local office of the Ministry of Finance. The process (which is based mainly on submission of papers) usually takes some time and requires particular care when drafting, completing and submitting the relevant documents (in particular, the application form containing the request for a tax code and the election of domicile in Italy).

(d)   *Special powers of attorney*

As SPAs and SRLs are incorporated through execution of a public deed, the shareholders must appear before a notary public, either in person or represented by attorneys in fact.

Where the incorporator is a foreign company, the individual appearing before the notary public should always be authorised by a special power of attorney, even if that individual is the legal representative of the foreign company. The signature on the power of attorney must be authenticated by a notary public in the country of issue and the document must be legalised by an apostille pursuant to the Hague Convention.

2.2 Incorporation

Both types of company are incorporated by the execution of an incorporation deed, which is a contract (or a unilateral deed, when the company is incorporated by a sole founding member) containing essential clauses set out in law and provisions regarding the operation of the corporate bodies. Usually, the documentation is executed in the form of two public deeds:

- the incorporation deed itself, containing the agreement of the founding members as well as the essential details regarding its structure; and
- the bylaws, containing the legal and procedural provisions governing the company's operation.

Even if they are drafted as two separate documents, the incorporation deed and the bylaws form a single contract, and the essential clauses can be included in either document. Nevertheless, in the case of a conflict between the clauses contained in the incorporation deed and the provisions of the bylaws, the latter will prevail.

(a) Incorporation deed and bylaws

(i) Essential clauses

SPA: The incorporation deed and the bylaws of an SPA must contain the following essential clauses:

- the details of the shareholders:
  - first name, last name, date and place of birth, domicile and citizenship, for natural persons; and
  - the name, country of incorporation and registered office for legal persons;
- the number of shares assigned to each shareholder (usually indicated in the incorporation deed and not reproduced in the bylaws);
- the company name (which must include an indication of the corporate form);
- the municipality in which the registered office of the company is located and details of any branch offices;
- the corporate purpose, with a specification of the activities the company will perform;
- the total amount of the corporate capital subscribed and paid in;
- the number of shares issued, their nominal value, if any, their characteristics, the methods of issue and the rules for their circulation;
- the value assigned to any in-kind contributions (usually indicated in the incorporation deed and not reproduced in the bylaws);
- the rules for the distribution of profits;

- the benefits assigned to promoters or founding members, if any;
- the system adopted for the management of the company, the number of directors and their powers, including the power of legal representation of the company;
- the number of members of the board of statutory auditors;
- the appointment of the first directors and statutory auditors (or members of the supervisory board) and, where necessary, of the person in charge of auditing the accounts (usually indicated in the incorporation deed and not reproduced in the bylaws);
- an estimate of the total incorporation expenses charged to the company (usually indicated in the incorporation deed and not reproduced in the bylaws); and
- the duration of the company. If the company is incorporated for an indefinite period and its shares are not listed, shareholders can leave the company when at least a year has elapsed since incorporation by giving at least 180 days' notice.

SRL: The incorporation deed and the bylaws of an SRL must contain the following essential clauses:
- the details of the quotaholders:
  - first name, last name, date and place of birth, domicile and citizenship, for natural persons; and
  - the name, country of incorporation and registered office for legal persons (usually indicated in the incorporation deed and not reproduced in the bylaws);
- the company name (which must include an indication of the corporate form);
- the municipality in which the registered office is located and details of any branch offices;
- the corporate purpose, with a specification of the activities the company will perform;
- the total amount of the corporate capital subscribed and paid in, which must be not less than €10,000;
- the contribution of each quotaholder and the value assigned to in-kind contributions (usually indicated in the incorporation deed and not reproduced in the bylaws);
- the quota of participation of each quotaholder (usually indicated in the incorporation deed and not reproduced in the bylaws);
- the rules for the company's operation, particularly in relation to administration and representation;
- the persons in charge of administration and those responsible for auditing the accounts; and
- an estimate of the total incorporation costs (usually indicated in the incorporation deed and not reproduced in the bylaws).

(ii)   *Clauses not set out in the law*

Shareholders may agree to include other clauses in the incorporation deed and the bylaws not expressly set out in the law in relation to the structure and operation of the company. Once the incorporation deed and the bylaws have been registered in the companies register, such clauses become enforceable not only between the members of the company, but also towards third parties (particularly for provisions limiting the transfer of participations: where such provisions are infringed, the other members of the company can take action to invalidate the transfer).

Examples of such additional provisions include the following:

* non-proportional assignment of shares;
* special rights reserved to promoters or founding members;
* special classes of shares;
* ancillary performances required by shareholders;
* restrictions on the free transfer of shares (eg a pre-emption clause);
* financing provisions;
* directors' fees;
* provisions regarding the issue and circulation of bonds;
* closing date of the fiscal year; and
* arbitration procedures.

(iii) *Optional clauses governed by law*

In establishing the regime governing the SPA and SRL, the law often contains provisions containing minimum requirements, with the possibility for the shareholders to extend the limits of such provisions in the bylaws. However, the minimum provisions apply by default in the absence of a specific agreement between the shareholders.

Examples of such provisions include:

* the duration of the company. The shareholders are free to choose the duration of the company or to incorporate the company for an indefinite period (in which case the law recognises the shareholders' right to withdraw from the company). Where an expiry date has been agreed in the bylaws, but is far away, the company must be considered as incorporated for an indefinite period and the right to withdraw is implicitly recognised;
* the corporate capital. This may be freely decided by the shareholders, provided that the minimum capital requirement (€120,000 for the SPA and €10,000 for the SRL) is met;
* withdrawal from the company;
* attendance and voting quorums; and
* powers of the administrative body.

(b)   **Execution of public deed**

The notary public must verify fulfilment of the conditions for incorporation and the lawfulness of the incorporation.

The control exercised by the notary public is both formal and substantive, because it aims to ascertain the company's compliance with the law. The notary public may refuse to request registration of the company in the companies register if, for instance, the incorporation deed or the bylaws contain a provision that conflicts with public order or with mandatory provisions set out in the law.

The cost of the notary public's assistance varies; it usually includes notary fees and taxes and duties anticipated by the notary on behalf of the client. Notary fees vary from district to district and depend mainly on the value and complexity of the transaction. For these reasons, it is advisable to clarify the effective incorporation costs with the notary public on a case-by-case basis.

(c)   *Tax code*

Once the company has been incorporated, the legal representative will file a request with the competent authorities to allocate a tax code to the company. The company must have a tax code to be registered in the companies register.

The steps to be followed are the same as those outlined in section 2.1(c).

(d)   *Registration*

When the incorporation deed has been executed and provided that all conditions for incorporation have been satisfied, the notary public will request that the Office of the Companies Register registers the company by filing the incorporation deed together with the relevant attachments within 20 days. The Office of the Companies Register will verify only that the documentation received meets the formal requirements.

A registration tax is payable for registration purposes. For cash contributions the tax is fixed (€168 in 2008), while for in-kind contributions the tax is calculated as a percentage of the value of the contribution (determined on the basis of the nature of the contribution). Administrative fees are also payable when filing a request for registration in the companies register.

Upon registration in the companies register, the company acquires legal personality and comes into existence.

Members who act in the company's name prior to registration in the commercial register are personally liable, without limitation, for any obligations incurred. A sole shareholder is jointly liable together with the company, while in companies with more than one shareholder those shareholders who ratified the activity performed in the company's name before registration are also liable.

(e)   *Tax issues*

All Italian-resident companies are subject to value added tax (VAT) (general rate 20%) and withholding tax, the *Imposta Regionale sulle Attività Produttive* – a regional tax generally levied at 3.9% on the value of productivity deriving from the business activity) income tax and social security contributions.

The profits of SPAs and SRLs are subject to the *Imposta sui Redditi delle Società* – a tax on earnings due in proportion to the registered income in each tax period – at a current rate of 27.5%.

The tax period coincides with the company's fiscal year, and the taxable base is calculated by adding all net revenues obtained by the company during the fiscal year. Payments made by the company as tax payments on account and withholding taxes by way of advance must be deducted from the taxable base.

The company must pay, by way of an advance payment, an amount generally equal to 100% of the taxes due under the income statement of the previous year. Payment must be made in two instalments if the amount of the first instalment is higher than €103. The first instalment (40% of the entire advance payment) must be paid within the term specified for payment of the balance due for the previous period. The second instalment must be paid during the month of November. The balance must be paid within the sixteenth day of the sixth month following the end of the tax period.

(f) **Registration for VAT purposes**

Before commencing activities in Italy, the company must register for VAT by filing the relevant request with the income tax authority (the form is provided by the authority).

(g) **Corporate books**

The company must keep the following corporate books:
- a shareholders' book, with details of the shareholders and their shareholdings;
- a bond book containing information on bonds issued, where applicable;
- a shareholders' meeting and resolution book, containing the minutes of the shareholders' meetings;
- a board of directors' meeting and resolutions book, containing the resolutions of the board (alternatively, where applicable, a management board's meeting and resolution book);
- a board of statutory auditors' meeting and resolutions book (alternatively, where applicable, a supervisory board's meeting and resolution book or a book of the committee for supervision of the management);
- an executive committee's meeting and resolutions book;
- a book of the meetings of bondholders, where applicable; and
- a book of financial instruments, where applicable.

The books listed above must be progressively numbered and stamped on each page before use, either by the Office of the Companies Register or by a notary public.

The company must also keep the following accounting books:
- a general journal;
- a VAT register for purchase invoices;
- a VAT register for sales invoices;
- an inventory book; and
- an assets book.

3. Number of shareholders

SPAs and SRLs may be incorporated by contract or by unilateral deed. In the latter case, the sole shareholder/quotaholder can benefit from the full limitation of liability if the following requirements are satisfied:
- The sole shareholder/quotaholder must pay the full amount of his cash contribution either on incorporation or at the time of any increase in the

corporate capital. Shares/quotas corresponding to in-kind contributions must be paid in at the time of subscription. If a company is incorporated by contract but the number of members is subsequently reduced to one, the sole shareholder/quotaholder remaining must pay in any outstanding cash contributions within 90 days.

- The directors of a company with a sole member must deposit with the companies register a statement containing the details of the shareholder/quotaholder within 30 days of registration of the sole member in the shareholders'/quotaholders' book. If the number of members is subsequently increased, the directors must communicate this fact to the companies register.

If one of the above requirements is not fulfilled, the sole shareholder/quota holder will be liable without limitation should the company become insolvent.

The sole member is liable, together with the individuals who performed the relevant acts, for obligations undertaken in the name and on behalf of the company prior to registration in the companies register.

Further, in order to ensure transparency, the law provides that any agreements between the company and the sole member are effective towards company creditors only if they are:

- reproduced in the book of resolutions of the board of directors; or
- concluded in writing with a true date that is prior to execution.

4. Corporate name

The corporate name may be freely chosen and changed during the life of the company. A change in corporate name requires an amendment to the bylaws and must be resolved in a extraordinary meeting. However, as the provisions concerning business names also apply to corporate names, it is advisable to choose a name that differs from those already in use by other companies. Where a corporate name is identical or similar to the name of another company and might create confusion, due to the corporate purpose of the companies and the places where their activities are performed, the company that registers later must integrate or amend the name so as to make it distinguishable.

The corporate name must always include a reference to the corporate form (ie *'Società per Azioni'*/'SPA' or *'Società a Responsabilità Limitata'*/'SRL').

5. Corporate domicile

The corporate domicile (registered office) is the place where the company's administrative body and the managing offices are located. It also determines the local Office of the Companies Register where the company must register.

Upon incorporation, the founding members must specify in the incorporation deed and in the bylaws the municipality where the registered office is located, although the exact address is not required. This rule was introduced by the recent reforms to simplify transfer of the registered office within the same municipality. Under the new regime, the transfer within the same municipality no longer requires the amendment of the bylaws (an extraordinary meeting is not required). The transfer may be resolved by the administrative body even if the bylaws do not contain a specific clause authorising it to do so.

The sole requirement in such cases is communication of the exact address to the Office of the Companies Register, both upon incorporation and at the time of transfer of the registered office. This is usually done upon incorporation by the notary public; where the registered office is transferred, the duty falls on the administrative body.

Upon incorporation, the founding members may establish branch offices in places where the company has a permanent representative (even outside Italy). The bylaws can empower the administrative body to transfer the registered office within the Italian territory and to open/close branch offices.

6. Corporate purpose

The corporate purpose is the type of activity that the company intends to perform during its life. It is common to list in the bylaws either a wide range of activities or an activity considered primary together with a series of secondary/ancillary/ complementary/instrumental activities (eg financial activities).

The description must not be so generic and wide as to make the corporate purpose substantially undetermined (eg the description of the corporate purpose cannot be "any industrial and/or commercial activity"). Further, the corporate purpose must be lawful.

If the corporate purpose is undetermined, vague or unlawful, there are grounds for nullification of the company. However, nullification cannot be declared if such grounds are remedied by an amendment to the bylaws that is filed with the companies register.

7. Capital stock

7.1 Minimum capital requirements

Different minimum capital requirements apply for incorporation, depending on the nature of the company:

- An SPA must be incorporated with a minimum start-up capital of €120,000; and
- An SRL must be incorporated with a minimum start-up capital of €10,000.

Higher minimum capital requirements are required for banking and financial companies, insurance companies, savings management companies (*società di gestione del risparmio*) and financial brokerage companies (*società di intermediazione mobiliare*).

7.2 Nature of contributions

The capital contributions represent the contribution of each member to the initial company equity and give the company the necessary risk capital to perform its activities.

In the SPA the nature of capital contributions may be freely determined in the bylaws, with the exception that work and/or the provision of services cannot contribute to the capital.

As a general rule, contributions must be in cash unless the bylaws state otherwise. In such case at least 25% of the corporate capital must be paid at the time of incorporation by depositing the relevant sums in a bank (see section 2.1(b)).

With respect to in-kind contributions, the transfer to the company of an asset is governed by the civil code provisions on the sale of goods. When the asset is acquired by the company, the risk of its loss rests with the company; if the loss occurs, the shareholder will still have the right to remain in the company. In contrast, where the right to use an asset is transferred, the risk of its loss rests with the shareholder, who loses the right to remain in the company, even if the loss of the asset is not his fault. In the case of transfer of a credit, the shareholder remains liable for the insolvency of the debtor.

7.3 Partial payments

Once the company is incorporated, the directors can ask the shareholders at any time to complete their contributions by paying the outstanding sums to the company. Such sums must be indicated in the share certificates; if the shares are transferred, the seller, together with the purchaser, will be obliged to pay in the outstanding contributions. However, the seller's obligation is limited in time (three years as from the registration of the transfer in the shareholders' book) and the company cannot seek payment from the seller before having unsuccessfully asked the purchaser.

If a shareholder fails to pay the outstanding sums within 15 days from publication of a request for payment in the *Official Journal*, the directors of the company may commence execution proceedings to obtain payment.

As an alternative, the directors may offer the shares subscribed and unpaid to the other shareholders in proportion to their shareholdings for a consideration not lower than the sum still due. Non-assigned shares may be offered on the market by the directors on behalf of the defaulting shareholder and at his own risk, through a bank or an authorised intermediary. If the there are no buyers, the directors are entitled to exclude the defaulting shareholder from the company, retaining the sums collected from him, without prejudice to compensation for further damages. If the unsold shares cannot be put into circulation during the fiscal year in which the exclusion is declared, they must be cancelled and the corporate capital reduced accordingly.

7.4 Shares

Shares grant the holder the title of shareholder. The bylaws can exclude the possibility of issuing shares and order that shares not be distributed to shareholders. In such case the title of shareholder and the authority to exercise the relevant rights are proved by registration in the shareholders' book.

(a) *Shares with no nominal value*

The company can issue shares without mentioning their nominal value. Here the provisions referring to the value of the shares apply according to the ratio between the relevant shareholding and the total number of shares issued by the company.

The division of the capital into shares without nominal value simplifies operations such as increasing capital by inserting reserves. A capital increase does not require the issue of new shares and their assignment to the shareholders, nor an increase in the nominal value of existing shares.

(b) Representation of shares

The shareholder has the right to release the shares corresponding to the participation in the capital stock. Unless special laws provide otherwise, the bylaws can exclude the issue of shares or decide to use different methods of representation (Article 2346 of the Civil Code).

In effect, the bylaws can provide for dematerialised shares (so-called 'optional' dematerialisation), which allows the financial instruments to circulate without having to effect a material transfer of title.

(c) Classes of shares

An SPA can issue different kinds of financial instrument (participatory and non-participatory) and, due to its statutory autonomy, can diversify the property and administration rights attached thereto.

Article 2348, paragraph 1 of the Civil Code states that all shares have equal value and grant their holders equal rights (each share grants the holder the right to vote at the meeting and the right to participate proportionally in the profits and the equity to be liquidated).

Each share carries one voting right; shares granting plural votes are forbidden.

Pursuant to the bylaws, the company can create different classes of shares with different rights attached.

In defining the content of the different share classes, the autonomy granted to the company under the statutory provisions is extremely broad.

If the company is not listed, and in cases where a single shareholder holds a significant majority of the shares, the bylaws may provide that the right to vote is limited to a maximum extent or is otherwise restricted (Article 2351, paragraph 3 of the Civil Code).

The company can also issue similar financial instruments pursuant to contributions by shareholders or third parties, including contributions of work and services (Article 2346, paragraph 6 of the Civil Code). The bylaws can entitle the holders of such financial instruments to vote on particular issues and provide for the appointment of one of them, according to established procedures, as an independent member of the board of directors or supervisory group, or as an auditor (Article 2351, paragraph 5 of the Civil Code).

Finally, a company can issue shares with rights that are proportionate to the results of business activities in a specific sector.

(d) Transfer of shares

(i) Restrictions

The bylaws can impose restrictions on the transfer of registered shares or shares that have not been issued. The bylaws can also forbid the transfer of shares for a period of up to five years from incorporation (Article 2355*bis*, paragraph 1 of the Civil Code).

Any limitation on transfer must appear on the share (Article 2355*bis*, paragraph 4 of the Civil Code), under penalty of invalidity; this requirement aims to guarantee transfers to third parties and satisfies the need for certainty regarding shares in circulation.

Pursuant to Article 2355*bis*, paragraph 2 of the Civil Code, a clause can be inserted in the articles of association that makes the transfer of shares conditional upon the approval of company bodies or of the other shareholders, provided that the company or shareholders are subject to an obligation to buy the shares on offer, or the shareholder has a right to withdraw, if they do not approve the transfer. If not, the restriction will be considered void. The criteria set out in Article 2437*ter* of the Civil Code on shareholders' withdrawal should be used to determine the price of the shares on offer.

The bylaws can also impose limitations on the transfer of shares in case of death. However, the corresponding clause will be considered void if it does not oblige the company or other shareholders to purchase the relevant shares in such cases. For such purposes, the provisions of Article 2355*bis*, paragraph 2 of the Civil Code apply.

The bylaws of an SRL can further limit and exclude the circulation of shares. Further, the transfer of shares may be made conditional (without limitation) on the approval of a company body, a shareholder or a third party. In such cases the regulations provide that the shareholder and his heirs have the right to withdraw from the company.

(ii)   *Formalities*

The law regulates the prerequisites for the transfer of shares and the corresponding effects of the transfer.

For a share transfer to be effective as between the parties, bearer shares must be transferred by simple delivery of the securities (Article 2355, paragraph 2 of the Civil Code). In contrast, registered shares must be transferred by endorsement attested by a notary or another authorised person pursuant to special legislation (Article 2355, paragraph 3 of the Civil Code).

A share transfer is valid as against the company once the new shareholder is registered in the shareholders' book. The endorsee has the right to obtain registration of the transfer and is authorised to exercise the rights resulting from the shares.

In any event, the company must update the shareholders' book pursuant to the special laws.

The transfer by deed of shares of an SRL between living people must result from a private contract attested by a notary public. The notary public must deposit this contract for registration in the companies register within 30 days of execution. Where the same share is sold to two different buyers, the purchase that is first registered in the companies register prevails. The transfer becomes effective towards the company only once it is registered in the shareholders' register. The purchaser requests such registration by showing the share purchase agreement.

8. Equity

8.1 Equity–capital ratio

In SPAs and SRLs the company's equity cannot drop below two-thirds of the capital stock due to losses. If, during a fiscal year, losses are higher than one-third of the capital stock, a shareholders' meeting must be held immediately to adopt the necessary measures. If these losses are not reduced by at least one-third during the subsequent fiscal year, the capital must be reduced in proportion to the verified losses.

If, due to losses higher than one-third of the capital, the capital stock drops below the statutory minimum requirements, the shareholders' meeting may decide to reduce the capital with a simultaneous increase up to the minimum amount, or alternatively to transform the company.

8.2 Bonds

An SPA can fall back on external financing by issuing certain bonds. The issue of bonds is subject to various conditions: in particular, bonds cannot be issued for an amount exceeding the sum of twice the capital stock, the legal reserve and the available reserves as indicated in the latest approved financial statements.

9. Administration

According to the traditional model of administration, the management of an SPA or SRL is shared between the shareholders' meeting and the directors. The shareholders' meeting has a defined function and can decide only those subjects that fall within its competence by law. The shareholders' meeting is essentially responsible for the most important decisions in the company's life.

The directors manage the company. Their competence has a general character. The directors are the legal representatives of the company and execute decisions taken by the shareholders' meeting.

9.1 General shareholders' meeting

Depending on the issues to be discussed, the shareholders' meeting can be ordinary or extraordinary.

The ordinary meeting:
- approves the financial statements;
- appoints and removes the directors, the board of statutory auditors and, where applicable, the person responsible for auditing the accounts;
- determines the remuneration of directors and auditors, where this is not specified in the incorporation documents;
- decides about the directors' and auditors' liability;
- decides all other subjects that fall within its competence under the law; and
- approves standing orders.

The directors can ask the ordinary meeting for authorisation to execute certain acts of management (although they have sole liability for the executed acts).

An extraordinary meeting:

- decides on amendment to the bylaws;
- appoints, replaces and empowers the liquidators; or
- decides all other subjects that fall within its competence under the law.

The bylaws can allocate certain powers of the shareholders' meeting to the directors. In particular, the directors can:
- execute any merger between controlling and controlled companies (if the absorbing company holds at least 90% of the capital stock of the merging company);
- indicate which directors are the legal representatives of the company;
- constitute and eliminate any secondary office;
- move the registered office within the home territory;
- reduce the capital stock in case of a shareholder's withdrawal; and
- amend the bylaws pursuant to the law.

The powers allocated to the shareholders of an SRL are broader than those of an SPA; in particular, the bylaws can place additional matters to those specifically provided for by law before the shareholders' meeting. The shareholders' meeting of an SRL will also decide on matters presented by one or more directors, or by shareholders representing at least one-third of the capital stock.

The shareholders' meeting is usually called by the directors, as appropriate. The meeting must be called at least once a year to approve the financial statements. The directors must further call the meeting when requested to do so by shareholders representing 10% of the capital stock, or such lower percentage as is provided for in bylaws (and the request must indicate the issues to be discussed).

The meeting must be called through a notice indicating the agenda, the time and place of the meeting, and the issues to be discussed. This notice must be published in the *Official Journal*, or in a newspaper indicated in the bylaws, at least 15 days before the date scheduled for the meeting – or 30 days where the company is listed. For all other companies, the bylaws may provide that the meeting be called through a notice sent to the shareholders at least eight days before the meeting by any means that guarantees evidence of receipt by the addressee (eg registered letter with advice of receipt, fax, e-mail). The call notice can also cite the date of the second call (which cannot be the same as the date of the first call).

In the absence of a call, a meeting is nonetheless convened as usual if representatives of the entire capital stock are in attendance, together with a majority of the directors and the members of the board of statutory auditors.

The bylaws can provide for the meeting to be held using various communication technologies and can also provide for a postal ballot.

(a)   *Quorum requirements*
Shareholders with the right to vote can participate in the general meeting, either in person or through a representative. In the latter case, the proxy is always revocable, must be given in writing and must indicate the name of the representative. Companies or corporations must appoint one of their employees or assistants for such purposes.

For listed companies, a proxy can be granted only for individual meetings.

A proxy cannot be granted to members of the administrative body or board of statutory auditors, or to company employees (or other people specially indicated by law). The regulations provide that a single person can represent only a limited number of shareholders at a meeting.

The ordinary meeting is validly constituted if the shareholders in attendance represent at least half of the capital stock (excluding those shares without voting rights). Decisions are taken by simple majority of the capital in attendance. At second call the ordinary meeting is validly constituted regardless of the number of participants, and decisions are taken by simple majority of the capital in attendance.

At first call, an extraordinary meeting takes decisions by absolute majority of the capital stock. At second call the extraordinary meeting is validly constituted if more than one-third of the capital stock is in attendance, and decisions are taken by at least two-thirds of the capital in attendance. A specific quorum is required for certain resolutions.

The bylaws can provide for higher majorities, although this does not apply to the approval of the financial statements and the appointment and revocation of company officers.

For listed companies, the extraordinary meeting is validly constituted if shareholders representing at least half of the capital stock are present at first call and at least one-third of the capital stock is present at second call. In both cases, decisions are taken by two-thirds of the capital in attendance.

The majority required to adopt resolutions in SRLs is higher than that for SPAs.

(b) Class meetings

If the company has issued different classes of shares or financial instruments, and these grant administrative rights, then special class meetings must be held alongside the general meeting. Where a decision taken during the general meeting will affect the rights of particular classes of shares or financial instruments, it must be approved by meetings of those members belonging to the relevant classes. The regulations on extraordinary meetings apply to such special meetings.

(c) Challenging resolutions

A decision of the shareholders' meeting may be invalid due to either breach of the provisions for the convening of meetings or defects in the decision itself. Decisions may be void or voidable.

Invalid decisions may be challenged only by those parties who are empowered by law to do so – namely:

- shareholders who were absent from the meeting;
- dissenting or abstaining shareholders representing at least 5% of the capital (or one per thousand, for listed companies);
- directors;
- supervisors; and
- members of the board of statutory auditors.

If the company has issued savings shares, the decision can also be opposed by the common representative of this class.

In SRLs, invalid decisions may be challenged by each dissenting shareholder, regardless of the size of his shareholding.

9.2 Management bodies

(a) Systems of administration in SPAs

Under Italian law, three systems for the administration and control are available.

In the 'traditional' system:

- the management and powers to represent the company are attributed to a sole director or a board of directors; and
- the board of statutory auditors controls the management, and an external auditor or audit company controls the accounts.

In the 'dualistic' system:

- the management is attributed to a supervisory board (appointed by the shareholders' meeting), which also carries out the typical functions of the general meeting;
- the administration is attributed to a management board (appointed by the supervisory board), which carries out the typical functions of the directors; and
- the accounts are controlled by an external auditor or auditing company.

In the 'monistic' system:

- management is attributed to the board of directors appointed by the shareholders' meeting;
- control is exercised by the committees created within the board of directors. The members of the control committee must meet high standards of professionalism and independence; and
- the accounts are controlled by an external auditor or auditing company.

In an SRL, the appointment of a board of statutory auditors is compulsory only if:

- the company has a capital stock that is at least equal to the minimum capital requirement for SPAs; or
- the company compiles financial statements according to the ordinary form.

(b) Term of office, resignation and removal of directors

The number of directors is specified in the bylaws. The directors need not be shareholders and are appointed for no more than three fiscal years. Their appointment is renewable and expires once the last financial statements of their term of office have been approved. Their office will also be terminated in the event of:

- removal by the shareholders' meeting;
- waiver;
- lapse (due to the occurrence of grounds for ineligibility); or
- death.

Both the appointment of directors and the termination of their term of office must be registered in the companies register.

(c) Directors' liability towards third parties

Directors are liable for their activities towards the company, the shareholders, third parties and company creditors.

Directors are liable towards the company if they do not perform their duties as required by law and if they do not maintain the accuracy required by the nature of their office and by their particular powers. Directors are usually not responsible for mere negative results of the business (if their behaviour is not negligent).

Directors have joint liability. If prejudicial behaviour is the direct responsibility of one director only, the other members of the board of directors will also be considered liable unless they can prove that they could not have prevented such prejudicial behaviour.

The decision to bring a liability action is taken by the ordinary shareholders' meeting. This decision can also be taken at the time the financial statements are discussed, even if there is no express note to this effect on the agenda.

A liability action can also be promoted by minority shareholders representing 20% of the capital stock (5% for listed companies). The bylaws can provide for different percentages within the limits of the law. The action proposed by the minority shareholders must have the aim of restoring company assets, rather than compensating for possible damage suffered.

Directors are liable towards company creditors if they breach their obligations to preserve company assets. A liability action can be proposed by creditors only if the company assets are insufficient to satisfy their claims.

Directors are further liable towards shareholders or third parties who have directly suffered damage because of the directors' fraudulent or negligent acts.

(d) Non-competition

Company directors cannot:
- be shareholders with unlimited liability in competing companies;
- carry out competing activities either for their own account or on behalf of third parties; or
- serve as directors or general managers in competing companies.

However, the shareholders' meeting can authorise directors to carry out such activities. This authorisation may be previously inserted in the bylaws.

Breach of the non-competition obligations provides grounds for removal of the director for cause and for a claim for damages caused to the company.

(e) Special duties of secrecy and loyalty

Directors are liable for damages caused to the company as a result of any use by them – for their own advantage or that of third parties – of information or business opportunities that come to their attention in the performance of their duties.

(f) Criminal liability

Italian law identifies and sets out penalties for numerous crimes that may be committed either within or against the company, such as the following:

- omission of information on the economic or financial situation of the company or corporate group which must be disclosed by law;
- falsification of statements;
- false reports or communications by the audit companies;
- barred control;
- undue repayment of contributions;
- illegal distribution of profits and reserves;
- illegal operations involving stocks or shares, of the company or of a controlling company;
- operations to the detriment of creditors;
- failure to make declarations, communications and deposits;
- failure to convene the meeting in the cases and under the terms provided for by law;
- fictitious creation of capital;
- undue distribution of capital goods by the liquidators;
- illegal influence on the assembly;
- share manipulation; and
- obstruction of public authorities in the exercise of their functions.

Criminal liability is also extended to those who exercise, in a continuous and significant manner, the typical powers relating to the office or function to which the crime relates.

9.3 Others

(a) Power of attorney

The directors have a general power to represent the company. Limitations in the powers of the directors (even if published) are not effective against third parties who have acted in good faith.

The company can also appoint other attorneys. The proxy, together with an attested signature, must be deposited for registration in the companies register. The acts modifying or revoking this proxy are also subject to registration.

(b) Internal controllers and auditors

Italian law sets out specific regulations on the internal control of corporations, both at management level and at accounting level.

The board of statutory auditors can be composed of three to five members (whether shareholders or not), who must satisfy certain prerequisites of professionalism and independence.

The board of statutory auditors (in the alternative control systems, the supervisory board and control committee) must supervise:

- compliance with the law and the bylaws;

- observance of the principles of correct management; and
- in particular, the adequacy of the organisational, administrative and accounting structure that the company has adopted, including its operation in practice.

The board of statutory auditors has certain powers to act and stimulate the company's operations.

10. Financial statements

10.1 Annual accounts

SPAs must compile the financial statements for each fiscal year. The financial statements are documents showing a clear and accurate picture of the company's economic and financial situation, and listing the financial results for each fiscal year.

The financial statements are composed of:

- the balance sheet;
- the profit and loss account; and
- supplementary notes.

They are filled together with the management report prepared by the directors, as well as the reports prepared by the board of statutory auditors.

The fundamental function of these documents is to verify periodically the state of the company's assets and profitability. They are the only legal instrument through which the shareholders can obtain accounting information on the company's operations, and through which creditors can verify the company's financial situation.

When drawing up the documents comprising the financial statements, the directors must follow the order and format provided for by Italian law, as interpreted and integrated by the Italian generally accepted accounting principles (Italian GAAP) or by the International Financial Reporting Standards (IFRS), if applicable.

The supplementary notes describe the items on the balance sheet and profit and loss account, and provide additional information on the company's assets and economic and financial situation, as well as on other issues defined by law (eg employees, remuneration of directors and auditors, and shareholder financing).

The management report must include information such as:

- relationships with controlled, connected and controlling companies, and with other companies controlled by such companies;
- the predicted evolution of the management; and
- significant events that occurred after the end of the fiscal year.

The board of statutory auditors must also prepare a report on the results of the fiscal year, as well as the activities undertaken in performance of their duties, and present it to the general meeting. The board must then make remarks and proposals regarding the financial statements and the relevant approvals. A similar report must be prepared by the person responsible for controlling the company accounts.

10.2   Approval of accounts

In companies that have adopted the traditional and monistic systems of administration, all corporate bodies cooperate to produce the financial statements.

The accounts must be approved by the ordinary meeting within 120 days of the end of the fiscal year. The bylaws can provide for a longer period of up to 180 days where the company is obliged to compile consolidated statements or where this is required due to the structure and the corporate purpose of the company.

The directors must prepare the accounts and send them to the board of statutory auditors, together with the directors' report, at least 30 days before the date scheduled for the meeting at which they will be approved.

The accounts and accompanying documentation must be deposited at the registered office for a period of 15 days before the date scheduled for the meeting.

Once the accounts have been approved, the directors must deposit a copy, together with the report and the minutes approved by the meeting, with the Office of the Companies Register.

In companies using the dualistic system, the financial statements are prepared by the managing board and approved by the supervisory board. The bylaws can provide that the general meeting may approve the financial statements where the supervisory board has not approved them or where this is demanded by at least one-third of the members of the management board and the supervisory board.

Any actions that make the accounts voidable or void pursuant to Articles 2377 and 2379 of the Civil Code cannot be taken if the subsequent financial statements have been approved.

10.3   Approval and distribution of profits

The general meeting approving the financial statements also decides on the distribution of profits to shareholders (this rule also applies for companies that have adopted the dualistic system: the meeting is called by the supervisory board).

Before any distribution is made to the shareholders, the profits as stated in the accounts must first be used to cover any losses from previous fiscal years. The remaining profits must be then used to fill up the legal reserve (5% per year until the reserve has reached 20% of the capital stock) and in part for any reserve provided for by the articles of association. The remaining funds (together with profits that were not distributed in previous fiscal years) can be distributed among the shareholders.

The fact that the accounts are approved does not automatically mean that the shareholders are entitled to receive their portion of the profits; this right arises only once a specific decision has been taken by the general meeting.

SPAs and SRLs are subject to the ordinary Italian corporate income tax (IRES), currently (2009) levied at 27.5%. The taxable basis is the profit resulting from the annual accounts adjusted according to IRES tax rules. With reference to foreign income that is subject to tax in Italy, the taxpayer is awarded a credit for final taxes paid on income abroad.

In addition, the regional income tax of productive activities (IRAP) is generally levied at a rate of 3.9% on the net production value (which is approximately equal to the EBIT (earnings before interest and tax) of the company, decreased by labour costs and interest expenses) deriving from business activities carried on in Italy.

Dividends paid by an Italian-resident SPA or SRL to its foreign shareholders are subject to a definitive withholding tax (or to a definitive substitute tax, in the case of shares held in the centralised securities clearing system managed by Monte Titoli SpA) levied at a rate that varies from 0% to 27% according to the fiscal status of the shareholder (a company or an individual), its country of tax residence (an EU member state, a country with which Italy has established a procedure for the exchange of information regarding tax matters, a tax haven or other countries), the applicability of EU Directive No 90/435/EEC (the Parent-Subsidiary Directive) or the existence of a convention against double taxation entered into by Italy with the country of residence of the shareholder. Dividends received by foreign shareholders who carry out their business activity in Italy through a permanent establishment to which the shareholding is connected are included in the taxable basis of the permanent establishment for 5% of the amount.

10.4 Consolidated statements

Consolidated statements are accounts compiled by holding companies in addition to their own accounts. They show the assets and economic and financial situation of the whole company group. Groups of smaller companies are not obliged to compile consolidated statements (as long as none of the group members is listed). Consolidated statements must be compiled in accordance with Italian law, as interpreted and integrated by the Italian GAAP or pursuant to the IFRS, if applicable.

11. Company reorganisation

11.1 Transformation

Transformation involves a change in the organisational structure of the company. Transformation may be homogeneous (ie transformation from a partnership into a corporation or vice versa) or heterogeneous (ie transformation from a corporation into other structures, or vice versa).

Transformation can occur even if examination proceedings are pending, as long as this is not incompatible with the purposes and status of the proceedings.

11.2 Merger

The preliminary phase of a merger involves the preparation of:

- the merger plan, which must meet the minimum requirements of Article 2501*ter* of the Civil Code and be deposited with the companies register of the place where each participating company has its registered office;
- the financial statements, which must cover the period up to 120 days before the date on which the merger plan is deposited at the registered offices of the participating companies;
- reports of the administrative bodies commenting on and justifying the merger plan from a legal and economic point of view, with particular reference to the criteria for the exchange of shares; and
- a report drafted by one or more experts for each participating company on the criteria for the exchange of shares.

During the resolution phase, an extraordinary shareholders' meeting is held before a notary public to resolve on the merger plan. Each resolution must then be deposited with the companies register, together with the documentation previously deposited at the registered offices.

The opposition phase lasts for 60 days from the date on which the final company resolution on the merger is deposited with the companies register. During this period the merger plan cannot be practically executed and creditors can file an opposition to the merger. There is no duty to inform creditors directly of the proposed merger; notification takes place through publication of the resolutions and the documentations by depositing them with the companies register.

In the final execution phase, the merger deed is executed before the notary public. The merger becomes effective once the merger deed is registered in the companies register.

11.3 Split-off

A company can be split in two ways:

- by transferring, fully or partially, the property of the company to one or more existing companies; or
- by transferring the company to new companies.

The shareholders of the company that is being split are assigned the shares relevant to the part to be split off at the same time.

The rules for split-off are identical to those for merger.

The regulation sets out rules to protect the creditors of the companies participating in the split-off. In particular, creditors can object to the split-off, and the participating companies are jointly liable to the full extent of the equity that is transferred or left to them.

12. Eventual shareholder separation

Shareholders are expressly entitled by law to withdraw from the company if they did not participate (either because they dissented or abstained from voting or were absent from the meeting) in resolutions on the following issues:

- amendment of the corporate purpose;
- transformation;
- transfer of the registered office abroad;
- revocation of liquidation;
- deletion from the bylaws of one or more grounds for withdrawal;
- amendment of the criteria for determining the value of shares in case of withdrawal; or
- amendment of provisions in the bylaws relating to voting or participation rights.

Any provision that aims to exclude or hinder exercise of the right of withdrawal in the above cases is null and void.

Unless the bylaws provide otherwise, shareholders who did not participate in resolutions on the following matters may also withdraw from the company:

- extension of the duration of the company; and
- the imposition or elimination of restrictions on the transfer of shares.

The bylaws of non-listed companies may also provide for other cases of withdrawal.

The right of withdrawal is exercised by sending a letter to the company within 15 days of the date on which the relevant resolution is registered with the companies register. The letter must contain the details of the withdrawing shareholder and the shares in relation to which the right of withdrawal is being exercised.

13. Dissolution and liquidation

Limited liability companies are dissolved when one of the following occurs:

- expiry of the duration of the company (the duration may be extended before it expires by resolution of the extraordinary meeting);
- achievement of the corporate purpose or impossibility to achieve it (unless the general meeting resolves to amend the bylaws accordingly);
- impossibility for the company to function due to continuous inactivity of the general meeting (deadlock);
- reduction in the corporate capital to below the statutory minimum (€120,000 for SPAs and €10,000 for SRLs) due to losses – unless the general meeting resolves either on a reduction in corporate capital and a simultaneous increase to an amount at least equal to the statutory minimum, or on transformation of the company;
- a resolution to dissolve taken by the general meeting when:
  - a shareholder withdraws from the company;
  - the relevant shares cannot be reimbursed without reducing the corporate capital; and
  - the creditors oppose the reduction;
- anticipated dissolution of the company resolved by the general meeting;
- other grounds for dissolution set forth in the incorporation deed or in the bylaws;
- a court decision declaring the nullification of the company; and
- bankruptcy or administrative liquidation (in such cases liquidation follows the rules of the specific insolvency proceedings).

Where there are grounds for dissolution, the directors must ensure that the appropriate resolutions are taken immediately and must file them with the companies register accordingly. If the directors fail to file the information, the court will do so at the request of the shareholders.

After dissolution, the company enters into liquidation thus:

- Liquidators are appointed by the extraordinary meeting;
- Upon registration of the liquidators' appointment in the companies register, the directors' office is terminated and the directors must deliver to the liquidators the corporate books, a review of the accounts and a report on the

period following approval of the latest balance sheet;

- The liquidators' activities are aimed at the satisfaction of claims of company creditors; the liquidators are personally and jointly liable for damage caused to those creditors;
- Once they have completed liquidation of the assets, the liquidators will draft a final balance sheet of the liquidation and a distribution plan; the final balance sheet must be approved by all shareholders;
- Once the final balance sheet of the liquidation has been approved, the liquidators will request deletion of the company from the companies register and the corporate books will be deposited with the companies register; and
- Creditors who are not satisfied with the liquidation may take action directly against the shareholders or against the liquidators for outstanding claims.

14. Branches

The setting-up of an Italian branch office by a foreign corporation is governed by Articles 2507 to 2510 of the Civil Code. According to these provisions, if a branch office is established in breach of the procedure outlined below, all persons acting in the name of the foreign company are jointly and severally liable, without limitation, for obligations undertaken on behalf of the branch.

In order to set up an Italian branch office of a foreign company, the following documentation is required:

- a copy of the original incorporation deed and the bylaws of the company;
- minutes of the meetings of the board of directors concerning the opening of the Italian branch office; and
- a certificate of existence of the company issued by the competent civil court or other competent administrative office, or by a notary public, indicating the company's registration number at the local civil court/companies register. The certificate should also indicate that the board of directors has the power to create a branch.

These documents must be authenticated by a notary public, legalised with an apostille pursuant to the Hague Convention and translated into Italian; the translation must be certified in Italy. They must also be deposited with an Italian notary public, who will take care of their registration with the companies register.

One of the main reasons why a foreign company may prefer to establish a branch rather than a separate legal entity is that the head office may be able to offset immediately possible initial losses abroad against its income. However, this can also be easily achieved through a limited liability company.

The general rule on foreign companies with branches in Italy is that they are treated as foreign non-resident taxpayers under Italian tax law; as such, they are subject to Italian income tax only in respect of Italian-sourced income.

The branch office is not obliged to compile and file an annual balance sheet. However, it must file the balance sheet of the controlling company (the ultimate parent company) with the Office of the Companies Register.

Japan

Hirokazu Amemiya
Hiromasa Ogawa
Kojima Law Offices
Yusuke Oyama
Hirakawa Sogo Law Office
Lynn F Pickard
Kojima Law Offices

---

1. Types of companies with limited liability and applicable legislation

At present, four types of company are available under the Companies Act of Japan.

- joint stock company (*Kabushiki-Kaisha* (KK));
- partnership company (*Goumei-Kaisha*);
- limited partnership company (*Goushi-Kaisha*); and
- limited liability company (*Goudou-Kaisha* (GK)).

A new Companies Act was approved by the Japanese *Diet* (the national legislature) on June 29 2005 and took effect on May 1 2006. The Companies Act introduced a new category of company – *Mochibun-Kaisha*, consisting of *Gomei-Kaisha, Goushi-Kaisha* and a completely new type of company, *Goudou-Kaisha,* which is similar to the US limited liability company.

For foreign investors intending to incorporate a company in Japan, the KK or the GK are the most feasible. The GK has a simpler structure than the KK and the reliance among equity holders is higher. As opposed to the original expectations of the Companies Act, however, the GK does not have pass-through tax status. Therefore tax is levied on the GK in the same way as the KK. The KK is the most widely used form of company, especially for foreign investors: in 2007 there were approximately 1.23 million KKs out of total about 1.62 million companies. The incorporations of GKs are increasing (in 2006, 3,500 GKs were incorporated; this number had risen to 6,000 GKs by 2007) but are far fewer than the incorporations of KKs (in 2007, 95,000 KKs were incorporated). For the near future at least, the KK will be the most common corporate form. This chapter focuses on the KK under the Companies Act, making reference to the GK where it differs significantly from the KK.

2. Incorporation procedure

A company is incorporated through registration with the Legal Affairs Bureau with jurisdiction over its registered office. The founders must undertake certain incorporation activities, including filing an application with the Legal Affairs Bureau. The Companies Act imposes no restrictions on the eligibility or number of founders, which may be natural or legal persons. In principle, no prior government approval is required to incorporate a company in Japan, even in the case of a wholly owned subsidiary of a foreign company.

2.1 Proceedings prior to incorporation

(a) Name registration
No name registration is required prior to filing the application for incorporation.

(b) Capital contributions
Contributions to the capital of a KK may be made in cash or in kind. Most commonly, however, companies are incorporated with cash contributions, since in-kind contributions involve additional (and sometimes time-consuming and/or costly) procedures. There are no minimum capital requirements under the Companies Act.

(c) Declaration of foreign investment
Under the Foreign Exchange Act of Japan, foreign investors must submit a declaration to the Ministry of Finance through the Bank of Japan, stating the name, date, number of shares acquired and acquisition price, within 15 days of the acquisition. Prior government approval of the investment is not required, unless the company to be incorporated will operate in certain industries such as nuclear power or the manufacture of weapons.

(d) Tax number for foreign partners/directors
Foreign investors and directors need not obtain a tax number to incorporate a company in Japan.

2.2 Incorporation

(a) Bylaws
The bylaws of Japanese companies are set out in the articles of incorporation, a constitutional document of all companies. The original articles of incorporation are prepared by the founders. The articles of incorporation must be prepared in Japanese and must be filed with the Legal Affairs Bureau.

(i) Essential clauses
The articles of incorporation must include clauses on the following matters:
- the corporate purpose;
- the company name;
- the district in which the head office is located;
- the total capital to be issued at the time of incorporation;
- the names and addresses of the founders; and
- the total number of shares to be issued.

The Legal Affairs Bureau is strict about the description of the corporate purpose. It is generally advisable to use wording that is similar to other companies or consult with officials at the Legal Affairs Bureau before formal filing of the incorporation application.

The articles of incorporation of a *Goudou-Kaisha* (GK) must state the names of the equity holders, and both the form (cash or in-kind) and the amount of capital contribution.

(ii)   Clauses not foreseen by law

The founders can decide on issues concerning the management of a KK without stipulating them in the articles of incorporation, such as:

- the chairman of the shareholders' meeting;
- the number of directors and/or corporate auditors; and
- procedures for the registration of shareholders' names.

(iii) Optional clauses governed by law

Clauses on the following matters become binding on a KK (and its shareholders) when included in the articles of incorporation:

- in-kind contributions;
- the acquisition of agreed assets by the company after its incorporation;
- fees to be received by the founders;
- expenses incurred by the founders and to be refunded by the KK after incorporation; and
- restrictions on the transfer of shares.

As the first four items must be approved by a court-appointed inspector, founders generally try to avoid their inclusion.

(b)   Execution of public deed

The articles of incorporation must be notarised before they are filed with the Legal Affairs Bureau. Certain other documents are also required for the incorporation of a KK, such as a certificate of the founders' signatures.

(c)   Tax identification number

After incorporation, a KK must file certain reports with the Tax Office in order to obtain a tax identification number.

(d)   Indirect taxes, incorporation fees and other levies

In order to incorporate a KK, stamp duty must be paid when the incorporation application is filed. The amount depends on the amount of the paid-in capital. The minimum stamp duty levied for incorporation of a KK is ¥150,000; the minimum stamp duty for a GK is ¥60,000.

Other costs for the incorporation of a KK include:

- the fees of the notary public for notarisation of the articles of association (¥50,000); and
- stamp duty, with the revenue stamp to be affixed to the original articles of incorporation (¥40,000).

A GK does not need to have its articles of incorporation notarised at a notary office.

(e) *Registration with the Legal Affairs Bureau*
The company obtains corporate status upon registration with the Legal Affairs Bureau. The registration process normally takes about one to two weeks from the date of filing of the application. The KK must designate its registered office in the application.

Certain information (ie the names of directors and the addresses of representative directors) is registered with the Legal Affairs Bureau, and this information is open to the public. However, the names of company equity holders are not registered with the Legal Affairs Bureau; therefore, third parties have no means of identifying the equity holders of Japanese companies.

(f) *Legalisation of official books*
A KK must maintain certain books (ie minutes of shareholders' meetings and board meetings, and a list of shareholders) in addition to the accounting books. However, apart from notarisation of the articles of incorporation during the incorporation process, there is no particular process under which the official books of KKs are legalised.

(g) *Declaration of start date and other tax declarations*
After completion of the incorporation process, a KK must submit various declaration forms to the Tax Office and other government offices for tax and social insurance compliance.

A KK must submit to the tax office:
- a declaration of incorporation;
- a declaration of the opening of an office to pay salaries;
- a declaration of the estimated inventory assets; and
- a declaration of amortisation of depreciable assets.

Where applicable, a KK must also submit documentation to the Labour Standards Inspection Office, the Public Employment Security Office and the Social Insurance Office.

3. Number of partners
There is no minimum number of equity holders for either a KK or a GK under the Companies Act. One individual or legal entity can own the entire equity of a KK or GK.

4. Corporate name – limitations
The Companies Act imposes several restrictions on company names. Under the previous regime (before May 1 2005), a company name that was already registered by another company could not be registered again in the same city; however, the Companies Act includes no such restriction. Therefore, a company can be registered even if there is another company with the same name in the same city. (As companies are identified by name and address, however, two companies with the same name cannot be registered at the same address. In addition, under the Unfair Competition Prevention Law it is prohibited to use a company name that is identical

or similar to another company name such that it could cause confusion with another company's business.)

The company name must include the term '*Kabushiki-Kaisha*', '*Goudou-Kaisha*', '*Goumei-Kaisha*' or '*Goushi-Kaisha*' as appropriate, depending on the corporate form. Companies cannot use a name or character that is likely to cause confusion with another type of company.

The words 'bank', 'securities company' and 'insurance' may be included only in the names of banking, securities and insurance companies respectively, pursuant to the Bank Act, the Securities and Exchange Law and the Insurance Business Law. A bank must include the Japanese characters for 'bank' in its name.

Since November 1 2002 it has been possible to use Japanese characters, Roman script, Arabic numerals and some signs (eg '&') in company names, under the Mercantile Registration Rule. Greek characters, Cyrillic characters and certain other signs (eg '@') may not be used.

5. Domicile

A company must register in the local district of its head office as stated in the articles of incorporation and must register branch offices with the Legal Affairs Bureau in the jurisdiction where each branch is located. The head office determines jurisdiction and is the place for tax payment.

6. Corporate purpose

The company's corporate purpose must be stipulated in the articles of association and registered with the Legal Affairs Bureau. Activities exceeding the corporate purpose are *ultra vires* (ie beyond the scope of the company's authority).

7. Capital stock

At the time of incorporation, a KK can issue shares up to the value of its authorised capital as decided by the founders. After incorporation, shares can be issued up to the value as decided by the board of directors (or the director with authority to represent the company, if the KK does not have a board of directors). The price of the shares may be determined by the founders or the board of directors (or the representative director) at the time of issuance.

In addition to common shares, the articles of incorporation of a KK may provide for the issue of preference shares. The terms and conditions of preference (eg preferential dividends or preference in distribution of residual property) may vary, as determined by the board of directors (or the representative director) at the time of issuance of such preference shares.

The shares of a KK are all non-par-value shares. The concept of par-value shares was recently abolished and all outstanding par-value shares were deemed to have been converted into non-par-value shares.

7.1 Minimum capital requirement

The Companies Act imposes no minimum capital requirements on either KKs or *Goudou-Kaisha* companies.

7.2 Nature of contributions

Shares in KKs are issued in proportion to the capital contribution. Shareholders' liability is limited to the price of the subscribed shares. Shareholders have the right to dividends and the right to exercise control in proportion to their shareholding.

7.3 Partial payments

Partial payments for shares are not permitted. Subscribers for shares must pay the full price of the shares into the bank account designated by the issuing company before the application for incorporation is filed.

7.4 Representation of shares

Under the Companies Act, KKs need not issue share certificates unless the articles of incorporation so provide.

KKs must maintain a shareholder register containing the names and addresses of all shareholders and other information stipulated in the Companies Act. Shareholders can demand that the company enrols his/her name in that shareholder register.

Shareholders listed in the shareholder register are entitled to receive dividends and to vote at shareholders' meetings, among other things.

In the case of a *Goudou-Kaisha*, the names of shareholders must be listed in the articles of incorporation. A *Goudou-Kaisha* cannot issue share certificates.

7.5 Transfer of shares

(a) Restrictions

In principle, the shareholders of KKs may freely transfer their shares to third parties under the Companies Act. However, a KK may impose restrictions on the transfer of shares by including provisions to this effect in the articles of incorporation.

At present, the only legally permissible way to restrict the transfer of shares of a KK is to provide in the articles of incorporation that shares cannot be transferred without the approval of the board of directors (or shareholder's meeting for KKs that do not have a board of directors). The Companies Act provides that the authority to approve a share transfer rests with the shareholders' meeting (or the board of directors for KKs that have a board of directors), unless otherwise stipulated in the articles of incorporation. Therefore, the articles of incorporation may transfer this authority to another party, such as the representative director. Note that the restrictions on the transfer of shares must not only be provided in the articles of incorporation, but must also be registered with the Legal Affairs Bureau. Otherwise, the KK cannot deny the transfer of shares to a third party who is innocent of the restriction.

Where the transfer of shares is restricted under the articles of incorporation, the KK must purchase the shares to be transferred or nominate a third-party buyer if it refuses to approve the proposed transfer. This provision of the Companies Act safeguards the right of shareholders to exit their investments.

In contrast, equity interests in a *Goudou-Kaisha* cannot be transferred without the consent of all other equity holders, unless the articles of incorporation provide otherwise. Where this consent is refused, the only way to exit the investment is to withdraw from the company, with the amount of capital to be returned calculated on the basis of the economic state of the *Goudou-Kaisha* at the time of withdrawal.

(b) Formalities

The transfer of certificated shares is effected by physical delivery of the share certificates. Where the KK has not issued share certificates, an agreement between the transferor and transferee is sufficient to effect the transfer; however, the transferee cannot exercise shareholder rights until its name is entered in the shareholder register as the successor of the transferor. If the company negligently fails or unreasonably denies entering a name in the register, the shareholder whose name has not been entered in the shareholder register may nevertheless exercise shareholder rights.

8. Equity

8.1 Equity–capital ratio

In principle, the paid-up capital of a KK is calculated by multiplying the issue price of the shares by the number of shares issued. However, a KK may allocate up to half of the capital contributions to the capital reserve account.

A KK must deposit at least 10% of the amount to be distributed as dividends into the capital reserve account or earned surplus reserve account until such amount equals one-quarter of the paid-up capital. A KK can pay out dividends as long as the reserves exceed the sum of the paid-up capital, the capital reserve requirement and the retained earned surplus reserve.

There is no legal requirement to adjust the balance of the capital stock if the company accumulates losses.

8.2 Convertible bonds

A KK may issue convertible bonds in various ways (eg bonds with pre-emptive rights, reverse convertible bonds). Regarding bonds with pre-emptive rights, a KK may generally issue shares in two ways. The first is to exchange the bonds for new shares; the second is to issue shares upon payment of fresh funds. While the former results in an increase in capital stock but no increase in assets, the latter results in an increase in both capital stock and assets.

9. Administration

Under the Companies Act, the organisational structure can be designed quite freely. However, the following structure – as applied under the previous regime, ie before May 1 2005 when the Companies Act took effect – is still fairly standard, where there are two types of organisational structure for KKs.

The first structure comprises the shareholders' meeting, the board of directors, the representative director and the statutory auditor. (Where the KK has a share capital of ¥500 million or more, or a total of at least ¥20 billion stated in the liability section of its latest balance sheet, an accounting auditor – which must be a certified public accountant or accounting firm – is also required.) The second structure comprises one or more executive officers, a nominating committee, an audit committee and a compensation committee, in addition to the shareholders' meeting and the board of directors. A statutory auditor need not be appointed; as a result, this is known as a 'non-corporate auditor' system. The system was introduced in 2002 for large companies; by June 2005, more than 100 companies had adopted it.

In the case of a *Goudou-Kaisha*, the organisational structure can be designed with even greater flexibility. A *Goudou-Kaisha* is a company in which ownership and control are not separated. Each equity holder in the *Goudou-Kaisha* basically has the power to manage the company's affairs, unless otherwise stipulated in the articles of incorporation. A *Goudou-Kaisha* may arrange its organisational structure freely through its articles of incorporation.

9.1 General shareholders' meeting

The general shareholders' meeting decides on the basic policies of the KK. The role of the shareholders' meeting differs depending on whether or not the KK has a board of directors. If there is no board of directors, matters stipulated in the Companies Act and other matters concerning the organisation, operation or management of the KK can be decided by the shareholders' meeting. However, where the KK has a board of directors, matters stipulated in the Companies Act or the articles of incorporation must be decided by the board of directors.

A shareholders' meeting must be held at least once a year. If all shareholders of voting rights agree in writing or electronically with the resolutions on the agenda provided by directors or shareholders, companies may deem that the resolutions have been adopted and there is no need to hold a shareholders' meeting.

(a) Quorum requirements

(i) Attendance

In order to transact business at a shareholders' meeting, shareholders representing a majority of the voting rights must be in attendance, unless otherwise provided for in the Companies Act or the articles of incorporation of the KK.

Companies can eliminate this quorum requirement through a provision in the articles of incorporation, and they may stipulate in the articles of incorporation that the resolution can be adopted by the majority of voting rights of attendees. However, if directors are to be elected, the quorum can never be reduced below one-third of the voting rights.

For certain other material matters, such as the introduction of restrictions of the transfer of shares, a higher quorum is required under the Companies Act.

(ii) Voting

Ordinary resolutions: Unless the Companies Act or the articles of incorporation provide otherwise, ordinary resolutions of the shareholders' meeting are adopted by a majority of the voting rights represented at the meeting. A director can be removed by ordinary resolution.

Special resolutions: Special resolutions are adopted by shareholders holding two-thirds of the voting rights present at the meeting. Matters that require a special resolution include the amendment of the articles of incorporation, merger proposals and liquidation.

Exceptional resolutions: Exceptional resolutions are required for certain material matters under the Companies Act, such as the introduction of restrictions on the transfer of shares. The requirements for adoption of an exceptional resolution are stipulated in the Companies Act, depending on the matter at issue. For instance, a resolution on restricting the transfer of shares must be approved by one-half of all shareholders in number representing two-thirds of the outstanding shares.

(c) **Challenging resolutions**

Shareholders, directors or corporate auditors may request the court to cancel a resolution of the shareholders' meeting within three months from the resolution on the following grounds:

- the procedure by which the resolution was adopted contravened the Companies Act or the articles of incorporation, or was significantly unfair;
- the content of the resolution contravenes the articles of incorporation; or
- the resolution is significantly inappropriate because of the vote by a shareholder who had a conflict of interest

Moreover, anyone may at any time request the court to confirm the non-existence or invalidity of a shareholders' resolution on the grounds that the resolution is against the law.

9.2   Administrative body

(a) **Different systems of administration**

The Companies Act sets outs certain principles that must be observed when designing the administrative body of a KK, depending on the size of the KK and the transferability of shares. A KK with paid-in capital of at least ¥500 million or whose total liability is at least ¥20 billion is defined as a 'large company'. Where the transfer of all classes of shares (common and preference) is not restricted, the KK is defined as a 'public company'.

The principles established in the Companies Act are as follows:

- All KKs must have one director in addition to the shareholders' meeting;
- A KK that has a board of directors must have a statutory auditor (or a board of statutory auditors); alternatively, the KK must have three committees (nomination committee, audit committee and remuneration committee) plus officers (although this requirement does not apply to a KK which is a public company but is not a large company), as well as an accounting adviser.
- Public companies must have a board of directors;
- KKs cannot have both a statutory auditor and three committees plus officers;
- A KK that does not have a board of directors cannot have a statutory auditor or three committee plus officers;

- An accounting auditor cannot be appointed unless the KK has a statutory auditor or three committee plus officers;
- Three committees plus officers cannot be established without appointing an accounting auditor; and
- Large companies must have an accounting auditor.

The Companies Act has also introduced a new type of organisation – the *Kaikei-Sanyo* (accounting adviser). This is a certified public accountant (or accounting firm) or a tax accountant (or tax accounting firm) that assists the directors in preparing the financial statements of the KK. The term of office for the accounting adviser is the same as that of directors.

An accounting auditor (*Kaikei-Kansanin*) audits the financial statements of the KK. While there are no qualification requirements for statutory auditors (*Kansayaku*), an accounting auditor should be a certified public accountant (or accounting firm). The term of office for the accounting auditor is one year.

KKs are free to design their management organisation within the limits of the above principles. For a non-public company, the minimum requirement is one director. However, the recommended structure for a subsidiary of a foreign company would be the standard model (ie a board of directors and a statutory auditor). If a suitable candidate for the position of accounting adviser can be found, the accounting adviser may be considered instead of the statutory auditor. This is because, for administrative and management control purposes, a Japanese subsidiary must have a board of directors to avoid the risk of abuse of power or authority by a single director.

An important requirement for a foreign investor planning to incorporate a KK in Japan is to have a resident director (or a resident representative director where the KK has a board of directors), although Japanese nationality is not required.

(b)   *Term of office, resignation and removal of directors*

The term of office of directors is two years, although the articles of incorporation may specify a shorter term. Non-public companies may extend the term of office up to total period of 10 years by including provisions to this effect in the articles of incorporation. While there are no specific requirements for the number of directors, three or more directors are necessary in companies that have a board of directors.

Directors are eligible for re-election.

Directors are elected at a shareholders' meeting. They may resign, or be removed at any time by ordinary resolution of the shareholders' meeting. The KK is liable for a director's loss of compensation where he is removed without reasonable grounds during his term of office.

(c)   *Directors' liability to third parties*

Directors are liable for their actions in performing their duties. The Companies Act includes the following provisions on directors' liability:

- Where directors perform their duties in bad faith or with gross negligence, they shall be liable for damage caused to the KK or to third parties; and
- Where directors falsify the record of share application certificates or other

material matters, and cannot prove they were not negligent, they will be liable to third parties.

Derivative actions are available in Japan. Any shareholder who has held shares continuously for six months is entitled to bring an action. To do this, the shareholder must demand that the company file a lawsuit against directors (and maybe others) to pursue their responsibility. If the company does not file a lawsuit within 60 days after the shareholder's demand, the shareholder can bring an action to the court.

(d) *Non-competition*

When a director transacts business on behalf of himself or a third party, he must disclose the material facts and any potential conflicts of interest to the board of directors or shareholders' meeting, which will then decide whether to approve the transaction. Where a director fails to obtain prior approval of the transaction, the KK can demand the profits arising from the transaction.

(e) *Special duties of secrecy and loyalty*

The Companies Act includes several further provisions that aim to prevent directors from taking action that might damage the interests of the KK either for their own benefit or for that of third parties.

Directors have a duty of loyalty based on the relationship of trust with the KK. They have the duty to oversee the representative director's performance of his duties. While the Companies Act includes no specific provisions on the obligation of secrecy, directors and other officers of the KK owe a duty of secrecy under the Unfair Competition Prevention Law and other general principles of law.

(f) *Civil and criminal liability*

Directors who violate their duties are jointly and severally liable to the KK for the compensation of damages. Moreover, if the violation is malicious, directors and other officers may be found guilty of an aggravated breach of trust – an offence punishable by up to 10 years' imprisonment with forced labour or a fine of up to ¥10 million.

Technical non-compliance, such as failure to renew the term of office of a director, is punishable by administrative fines of up to ¥1 million.

9.3   Others

(a) *Attorneys*

The Companies Act is silent as regards the appointment of general counsel. A Japanese attorney-at-law may be appointed as a director of a KK upon notification to the bar association. There is attorney–client privilege in Japan. (It is necessary to meet the requirement under the Civil Procedure law of "a matter to be kept confidential". Not all communications between an attorney and a client are protected. In addition, not all documents retained by a client are protected.) If the attorney is serving in the company, this privilege may not extend to communications with the directors.

(b) **Controllers and internal auditors**

A KK that has a board of directors must appoint a statutory auditor or establish an internal audit committee (except in the case of the large non-public company that has an accounting advisor (*Kaikei-Sanyo*)) and may have an accounting auditor to audit financial statements. No particular qualifications are required to become a statutory auditor and a non-resident foreigner may be appointed as the statutory auditor. The accounting auditor must be a certified public accountant or an accounting firm.

While there are no specific requirements for the number of statutory auditors, three or more statutory auditors are needed and the majority of auditors must be external auditors, in the case of companies that have a board of auditors. The term of office for the statutory auditor is four years, and this term cannot be shortened. Non-public companies can extend this term to ten years.

Although the statutory auditor has a right to audit the acts or decisions of the representative director or the board of directors after their occurrence, he does not have a right to act operationally within the business.

10. Fiscal year, commencement of operations

The fiscal year of most Japanese companies commences on April 1 and ends on March 31 of the following year. A company is free to decide on its fiscal year, but this cannot exceed one calendar year.

11. Financial statements

11.1 Company tax

Corporate income tax: Corporate income tax is a national tax based on all net profits from worldwide income. A company must file its income tax return within two months of the end of its fiscal year. The current (2009) rate of tax is 22% to 30%, depending on the amount of capital.

Other taxes: A company must pay corporate enterprise tax, corporate inhabitant tax and other taxes. Corporate enterprise tax is levied by the local authority based on net profits at a rate of between 3.8% and 11.52% (the companies whose capital stock is more than ¥100 million, and the companies whose capital stock is more than ¥10 million and that have offices in more than three prefectures must pay additional corporate enterprise tax based on value added at a rate of 0.48% and based on capital stock at a rate of 0.2%).

Corporate inhabitant tax is levied by the local authority based mainly on the corporate income tax (where the rate is between 17.3% and 20.7% of the corporate tax amount, in addition to an amount somewhere between ¥70,000 and ¥3.8 million according to the amount of capital stock). These taxes are due within two months of the end of the fiscal year.

While corporate enterprise tax may be offset by profits, corporate inhabitant tax cannot be offset.

Blue return system: Subject to the approval of the Tax Office, the special 'Blue Return' system (*Aoiro-Shinkoku*) affords certain advantages, including carry-back to the previous year, (at present, only small businesses obtain this advantage for five fiscal years after their incorporation), or carry-forward (for seven years) of net losses, under condition that the company keeps its books in accordance with the orders of the Ministry of Finance. To avail themselves of this system, companies must submit an application to the Tax Office within three months of incorporation, or by the end of the fiscal year, whichever is the earlier.

11.2   Annual accounts

(a)   *Documents*

The directors are obliged to prepare financial statements (balance sheet, profit and loss account, and statements on any changes to the 'capital' section of the balance sheet). The directors may choose to record this information in electronic or hard-copy form.

(b)   *Audit report*

The results of the audit must be summarised in an audit report issued by the Justice Ministry under the Companies Act. Where appointed, the statutory auditors and accounting auditors will be required to state in the audit report whether the financial statements are accurate.

(c)   *Approval and distribution of profits*

Directors must submit the financial documents to the statutory auditor and accounting auditor (where appropriate). The documents must also be approved by the board of directors if one has been established.

The documents must then be approved by the annual shareholders' meeting and allocatable profits may be distributed to the shareholders.

KKs that satisfy certain criteria may distribute dividends more than twice per fiscal year; in-kind dividends are also permitted.

The rate of withholding tax on dividends is basically 20% for individuals (15% national income tax and 5% local inhabitant tax) and 15% for companies. Reduced rates apply to individuals and companies owning shares of Japanese publicly listed companies: these stand at 10% for individuals (7% income tax and 3% inhabitant tax) and 7% (income tax only) for companies.

In the case of dividends paid to foreign shareholders, the rate of withholding tax may be reduced or exempted by an applicable double-taxation treaty.

(d)   *Deposit and publication*

KKs must keep their financial statements, audit reports and certain other important documents at their head office for five years from a week before the annual shareholders' meeting (or two weeks before for the companies that have a board of directors), and they must preserve copies for three years at branch offices. During this period, creditors and shareholders may inspect and take copies of these documents.

KKs must publish their balance sheet and, in the case of large companies, their profit and loss account. KKs may choose to publish in the *Official Gazette*, in a daily newspaper or on their website. When KKs publish their balance sheet in the *Official Gazette* or a daily newspaper, only a summary of their balance sheet needs to be published. In the case of website publication, the website address must be registered with the Legal Affairs Bureau; and the KK must publish the entire text of its balance sheet on its website, maintaining such information for a period of five years from the relevant annual shareholders' meeting.

12. Company reorganisation

12.1 Transfer and acquisition of a business

The transfer of all or a major part of a business must be approved by special resolution of the shareholders' meeting of the transferor. The acquisition of another company must also be approved by special resolution of the shareholders' meeting of the acquirer (although the acquisition only of part of a business does not require a resolution). Dissenting shareholders in either company are entitled to demand that the KK evaluate and purchase their shares. The procedures also protect the interests of creditors, which may object to the transfer/acquisition.

There is no need to obtain shareholder approval where:

• the value of the transferred business is less than 20% of the company's total value; or
• the acquirer holds more than 90% of all shares in the seller.

12.2 Merger

Merger is permissible under the Companies Act. There are two types of merger: in the first, one company survives the merger; in the second, a new KK is incorporated as a result of the merger.

One or both of the companies shall dissolve without liquidation as a result of the merger. The surviving KK or new KK will assume all assets, debts, rights and liabilities of the merging companies.

A merger must be approved by special resolution of the shareholders' meetings of the participants. Dissenting shareholders are entitled to demand that the KK evaluate and purchase their shares. A so-called 'short-form merger' is available where certain conditions similar to those explained in section 12.1 above are satisfied. In such a case the approval of the shareholders' meetings is not required.

To protect the interests of creditors, disclosure through the *Official Gazette* and notification to known creditors are both required.

One important point in the case of merger (as well as in a corporate spin-off or stock-for-stock exchange) is that the surviving KK can pay cash or other assets (eg stock of a foreign parent company) instead of its own shares.

If there is a substantial defect in the merger proceedings, shareholders, directors, statutory auditors, officers, liquidators, bankruptcy administrators or creditors who did not approve of the merger may bring an action to invalidate the merger within six months from the date on which that merger took effect.

12.3 Corporate spin-off, stock-for-stock exchange and stock transfer

Corporate spin-offs are permissible under the Companies Act. There are two types of corporate spin-off: in the first the divided KK is incorporated into an existing KK, while in the second the divided KK is transferred to a new KK. A KK can use the spin-off system to rationalise its operations.

Stock-for-stock exchanges and stock transfers are also permissible. In both transactions a KK becomes a wholly owned subsidiary of another KK upon special resolution of the shareholders' meeting. In a stock-for-stock exchange the parent company is already incorporated, while in a stock transfer a new parent company is incorporated. Using these systems, a company can incorporate a holding company or turn a target company into a wholly owned subsidiary.

In principle, the procedures to be followed for a corporate spin-off, stock-for-stock exchange and stock transfer are similar to those for a merger. However, in general, procedures to protect the interests of creditors are not required.

The procedures for an action for invalidation are also similar to those for a merger.

13. Eventual partner separation

A shareholder of a KK can separate itself from the KK by transferring its shares to another shareholder or a third party. This is the basic mechanism for eventual partner separation.

However, the Companies Act entitles shareholders of a KK to demand that the KK purchase their shares in certain cases involving corporate reorganisation. The purchase price will be determined by the court if the shareholder and the KK fail to reach agreement.

In the case of a *Goudou-Kaisha*, eventual partner separation is achieved through withdrawal.

14. Dissolution and liquidation

Dissolution involves the termination of corporate status, while through liquidation the remaining assets are distributed to the shareholders following dissolution.

The causes for dissolution are as follows:
- expiry of the duration of the company or the occurrence of any other event provided in the articles of association;
- special resolution of the shareholders' meeting;
- merger;
- bankruptcy;
- a dissolution order issued by the court (where the company's existence is obviously against the public interest);
- a judgment for dissolution; or
- dormancy of the company.

In liquidation, directors lose their powers and the liquidators assume control of the company. Generally, the directors become the liquidators, although a shareholders' meeting may appoint other persons as the liquidators.

During the liquidation process, all debts will be satisfied and the remaining assets of the KK will be returned to the shareholders on a *pro rata* basis, unless otherwise stipulated in the articles of association.

15. Branches

If a foreign company establishes a branch in Japan, it is required to appoint a representative in Japan and to register his/her name and address. One representative must be a Japanese resident. The foreign company is liable for all of the branch's debts. To avoid the foreign company's direct liability, it is advisable to form a wholly owned subsidiary.

Luxembourg

Guy Harles
Saskia Konsbruck
Arendt & Medernach

1. **Types of limited liability company and applicable legislation**

The most common forms of limited liability companies incorporated in Luxembourg are private limited companies (*sociétés à responsabilité limitée,* Sàrl) and public limited companies (*sociétés anonymes*, SA). Both forms of company are governed by the Luxembourg Law on Commercial Companies of August 10 1915, as amended, the Civil Code and the Commercial Code.

1.1 **Private limited companies**

Private limited companies may be incorporated by one or up to 40 shareholders. The shareholders are liable up to the amount of their contribution. Their versatile character, low capitalisation requirements and simple operating rules make this a very popular form of company.

1.2 **Public limited companies**

Public limited companies may be incorporated by one or more shareholders (there being no maximum number). Shareholders are liable up to the amount of their contribution only. Public limited companies are able to raise capital by means of public subscription.

2. **Incorporation**

2.1 **Prior to incorporation**

(a) *Name registration*

Subject to availability and the limitations described under section 4 below, the corporate name of a private or public limited company may be freely chosen. The Trade and Companies' Register will, upon formal request and payment of a fee, issue a certificate of availability. The certificate will be valid from its date of issuance until registration of the corporate name with the Trade and Companies' Register. Given that the issue of a certificate of availability does not provide its beneficiary with a right to reserve the proposed corporate name, it will be important to minimise the time between the date of issuance and the date of incorporation of the company.

(b) *Contribution to the company equity*

Contributions to private and public limited companies are usually made in cash.

A bank account must be opened in the name of the company. For practical reasons, it is advisable to open the account with a bank having at least a branch in Luxembourg. The funds representing the initial share capital must be wired to and deposited on such account for the purpose of incorporation. A blocking certificate issued by the bank must be provided to the notary at incorporation. Immediately after incorporation, the notary issues a de-blocking certificate rendering the funds available.

Contributions may also be made in kind. To be valid, they must be economically valuable. While no audit report is required for contributions in kind to private limited companies, such a report is required for public limited companies. The founding shareholders are solely responsible for the valuation.

(c) *Declaration of foreign investment*

The Luxembourg constitution guarantees freedom of trade and industry, a principle that has been extended by the courts to foreign investors. However, for anti-money-laundering compliance reasons, the ultimate beneficial owner of a company must be identified and disclosed to the bank, the notary and the legal counsel involved in the setting-up of the company. All information so disclosed will be covered by applicable confidentiality laws.

2.2 Incorporation of the company

(a) *Bylaws*

(i) *Essential clauses*

The following is a non-exhaustive list of clauses typically contained in the articles of incorporation of public and private limited companies:
- corporate name;
- corporate purpose;
- registered office;
- amount of subscribed capital and, if applicable, authorised share capital;
- amount of issued shares and details on classes of shares, if applicable;
- specific rights attached to each class of shares;
- composition and functions of the management bodies;
- formalities and majority requirements of shareholder meetings;
- distribution of proceeds;
- supervision; and
- liquidation.

(ii) *Clauses not foreseen by the law*

Shareholders are free to provide for any additional clauses that may not be expressly foreseen by law, provided that such clauses are not prohibited.

(iii) *Enlargeable clauses ruled by law*

It is possible to deviate from the legal provisions as long as those legal provisions are only supplementary. No alteration may be made to imperative provisions (eg a clause that would deprive a shareholder from its rights to share in distributions of the company's income would be deemed void).

(b) *Execution of a public instrument*

Private and public limited companies must be incorporated by written instrument of a notary public. The deed of incorporation may be drafted in French, German or, if followed by a French or German translation, English. The notary must register the deed of incorporation within one month with the Luxembourg Registration Administration (*Administration de l'Enregistrement et des Domaines* – hereafter AED), file it with the Trade and Companies' Register (*Registre du Commerce et des Sociétés*) and arrange for publication in the official gazette, entitled *Mémorial*.

Under Luxembourg law, a company is deemed to be incorporated as soon as the constitutive document has been signed in front of the notary.

(c) *Tax identification number*

After their registration with the Luxembourg Trade and Companies' Register, private and public limited companies receive a tax identification number and are registered with the Luxembourg Tax Administration (*Administration des Contributions Directes*).

(d) *Payment of indirect taxes*

No indirect taxes are levied on contributions made to the share capital or premium of private and public limited companies. As an exception, contributions of Luxembourg-situated immovables, as well as contributions of movables that are not remunerated by shares, may remain subject to proportional duties.

(e) *Registration with the Mercantile Registry*

As noted above, the deed of incorporation of private and public limited companies must be registered with the Trade and Companies' Register. A file will be opened in the name of the company and the register will proceed with the publication in *Mémorial*.

A failure to register with the Trade and Companies' Register will render the deed of incorporation of a company without effect towards third parties. The company will furthermore be unable to bring legal actions and, potentially, incur liability.

Companies have an ongoing obligation to file any amendment to their articles of incorporation, delegations of powers and changes in the composition of their management bodies with the Trade and Companies' Register.

(f) *Official books*

All corporate documents, including, but not limited to, annual accounts, securities' registers, books of minutes of board and shareholders' meetings and contracts of the company, must be kept at the registered office and made available to shareholders and/or, where so provided for by law, third parties.

(g)   *Declaration of set up activity and other tax declarations*

Under Luxembourg law, any company undertaking commercial or industrial activities must obtain a special authorisation delivered by the competent government ministry (*Ministre des Classes Moyennes*) upon proof that the holder of the authorisation is of sufficient standing and professional qualification and upon payment of a fee of €24. Specific authorisations apply to insurance companies, banks and financial activities as well as to certain activities that could endanger public safety.

With regard to employment matters, a company must register with the Luxembourg social security within eight days from the commencement of its business activities. The registration can be carried out on a dedicated website. In addition, when recruiting a new employee, the company must provide a special declaration form (*declaration d'entrée*) to the Luxembourg social security administrative body (Centre Commun de la Sécurité Sociale) within eight days. Failure to provide such a declaration would expose the company to a fine.

All Luxembourg taxable persons or foreign taxable persons having a fixed establishment in Luxembourg must register for value-added tax purposes with the competent tax administration (AED) within 15 days of the beginning of their activities, unless they are formally excluded from this obligation.

3.   Number of partners, unipersonality

A private limited company can be incorporated with one shareholder only but the number of shareholders cannot exceed 40. Public limited companies may be incorporated with one shareholder and no maximum applies.

In both cases, shareholders may be natural persons or legal entities. There is no requirement as to the nationality of the shareholders.

4.   Corporate name – limitations

As noted above (see section 2.1(a) above), the corporate name of private and public companies may be freely chosen. It may be a pure creation or a description of the purpose of the company, provided that the name is not contrary to public policy. The name of a shareholder may appear in the corporate name of a private limited company, but not of a public limited company.

Should the chosen corporate name already be used by another company and a risk of confusion exist, then that company may bring legal action in order to protect its corporate name, as well as an action for unfair competition.

5.   Domicile

The articles of incorporation of a company must indicate its registered office. The registered office must correspond to the company's place of effective management (ie the place where the business of directing the company's activities effectively takes place).

Under Luxembourg law, the place of effective management of a company is an indicator of its nationality and the applicable law. Consequently, a company registered abroad, but having its head office in Luxembourg, will be deemed to be a Luxembourg company.

Companies may establish their office at their own premises or with a domiciliation agent based in Luxembourg.

6. Object

The corporate purpose of a company must be stated in its articles of incorporation. It must be lawful – ie it must exist, be realisable, not be contrary to public policy, and be sufficiently specific. An unlawful purpose may trigger a potential action for cancellation of the company. Companies are generally authorised, as a matter of their articles of incorporation, to perform any operation directly or indirectly related to their purpose.

7. Capital stock

7.1 Minimum amount

The minimum share capital of public limited companies is approximately €31,000 and €12,500 for private limited companies. The par value of each share may be freely determined. The share capital may be denominated in euros or a foreign currency.

7.2 Nature of contributions

As stated above, contributions to private and public companies can be made in cash or in kind.

7.3 Partial payments

Shares in the share capital of private limited companies must be fully paid-up at the time of subscription, whereas shares in a public limited company may each be paid-up to one-quarter only.

7.4 Share certificates, systems of representing shares

Shares in private companies must be issued in registered form and must be voting shares, while public companies may issue bearer or registered shares as well as non-voting shares. Shares in public companies must be in registered form until they are fully paid-up.

In the case of registered shares, certificates evidencing the entries in the shareholders' register can be delivered to the shareholders.

Conclusive ownership of: (i) bearer shares is established by the mere possession of the corresponding share certificate; and (ii) of registered shares is established by registration on the register of shareholders.

7.5 Preferential subscription right

In a public limited company, the law provides that the existing shareholders shall in general have pre-emption rights in respect of any new shares to be issued for a consideration in cash, *pro rata* to their existing shareholding at the time of issuance. Such pre-emption rights may be limited or disapplied in certain conditions provided by law.

There is no equivalent right by law in private limited companies but shareholders may provide for one in the articles of incorporation.

7.6 Restrictions to the transfer of shares

Shares of private and public limited companies are freely transferable among shareholders.

Transfers of shares in public limited companies to third parties can be freely made whereas the shares of private limited companies may only be transferred to third parties subject to the approval given by the shareholders (including the transferor) at a majority vote of shareholders representing at least three-quarters of the issued share capital.

In a public company any transfer of shares in registered form will be effective towards the company and third parties as from either the declaration of transfer entered in the register of shareholders or upon notification to or upon acceptance of the transfer by the company.

Any transfer of shares in a private limited company must be documented through a transfer agreement under private seal or in notarised form, and, unless the company is a party to the transfer document, it becomes effective towards the company only upon notification or acceptance of the transfer.

8. Equity

8.1 Balance between capital and own resources

Under Luxembourg law, in the event of a loss of half the share capital, the board of directors or the management board of public limited companies must convene a meeting of shareholders to discuss the possible dissolution of the company. This decision must be adopted in compliance with the rules on an extraordinary meeting of shareholders (see section 9.1 below). However, if the shareholders do not take such a decision, then the company is not dissolved. It must be noted that when the loss equals three-quarters of the share capital, dissolution may be approved by only one-quarter of the votes cast at the meeting.

These provisions do not apply to private limited companies.

The capitalisation of private and public companies must, from a Luxembourg tax perspective, comply with the arm's-length principle (ie financing provided by shareholders or affiliates must be based on market conditions between unrelated parties).

8.2 Convertible bonds

Because of their convertible nature, the issuance of convertible bonds (in private and public limited companies) requires a vote of the extraordinary general meeting of shareholders (unless otherwise provided by the articles of incorporation). Existing shareholders in public limited companies have pre-emption rights in respect of the bonds. There is no equivalent right for existing shareholders in a private limited company.

The issuance of convertible bonds in a public company is considered as a contribution in kind and therefore requires an auditor's report. An auditor's report is not required for private companies.

9. Administration of the company

9.1 General meeting of partners

(a) *Quorums of attendance to meetings and majority for adoption of resolutions*

(i) *Resolutions not amending the articles of incorporation*

In a public limited company, resolutions of ordinary general meetings of shareholders are generally passed with a simple majority of the votes validly cast, regardless of the portion of capital represented.

In a private limited company, collective decisions are validly taken in so far as they are adopted by shareholders owning more than half of the share capital on first call and, on second call, the resolutions will be validly passed with a majority of votes, regardless of the portion of capital represented.

(ii) *Resolutions amending the articles of incorporation*

In a public limited company, resolutions of extraordinary general meetings are passed, on first call, with a majority of at least two-thirds of the votes validly cast at a meeting where at least half of the share capital is present or represented. On second call, there is no presence quorum. Abstention and nil votes are not taken into account.

In a private limited company, such resolutions are passed by approval of a majority of shareholders, representing at least three-quarters of the issued share capital, or by a resolution of the sole shareholder, as the case may be.

(b) *Challenge of resolutions*

Resolutions amending the articles of incorporation may be cancelled by a court decision and on any of the following grounds:

- absence of an authentic deed;
- unlawful corporate purpose;
- absence of at least one validly committed founding shareholder; or
- if the modified articles of incorporation do not state the name and the purpose of the company, the contributions and the amount of the subscribed capital.

Any other resolutions may be challenged for breach of legal procedures (eg quorum of attendance, voting threshold for adoption of resolutions), provided that the challenging shareholder expressed his disagreement at the relevant general meeting during which the resolution was adopted. Resolutions may also be challenged if the consent of a shareholder has been obtained by fraud, misrepresentation or force. In each case, the irregularity must have had an impact on the vote results. Any cancellation of a resolution will have a retroactive effect.

9.2 Administrative body

(a) Different systems of administration

A private limited company may be managed by one or several managers, who do not need to be shareholders. The managers are appointed by the general meeting of shareholders.

Public limited companies can be managed based on a single-tier or a two-tier management system. According to the single-tier system, management of a company is performed by a board of directors, which must consist of at least three directors – except where the company has one single shareholder, in which case only one director is required. In a two-tier system, the company's management is undertaken by a management board and the supervision of such management board is entrusted to a supervisory board. The number of the members of the management board and of the supervisory board is determined by the articles of incorporation; however, if the capital of the company is equal to or greater than €500,000 or if the company has two or more shareholders, the management board must consist of at least two members and the supervisory board must consist of at least three members.

The board of directors/management board/managers have the broadest powers relating to the management of the company, except for those matters expressly reserved by law or the articles of incorporation to the shareholders.

(b) Term of office, resignation and removal of directors

Managers of a private limited company may be appointed for a limited or an unlimited duration. Unless otherwise provided in the articles of incorporation, the managers may be re-elected and may only be dismissed for cause by the shareholders.

In a public limited company, the term of the directors' office may not exceed six years. Directors may be re-elected unless otherwise provided in the articles of incorporation, and they are freely dismissible by the shareholders or the supervisory board, as applicable, at any time and without cause.

Managers and directors may resign at any time and without cause or authorisation.

(c) Directors' liability to third parties

Directors and managers in public and private limited companies are jointly and severally liable both towards the company and any third parties for damages resulting from the breach of the Luxembourg Law on Commercial Companies or the articles of incorporation of the company.

(d) Non-competition

Non-competition clauses are, in general, valid and binding under Luxembourg law provided that they do not violate the principle of freedom of trade and industry by effectively prohibiting the exercise of an activity.

(e) Special duties

Directors and managers must act at all times in the best interests of the company. They must act in good faith and competently towards the company and are subject to a general duty of care and confidentiality.

Directors and managers also have a duty to avoid conflicts of interest. Indeed, any director or manager having an interest in a transaction submitted for approval to the board, which conflicts with that of the company, is obliged to advise the board thereof and to make sure that a record of his statement is included in the minutes of the meeting. He may not take part in the deliberations. At the next following general meeting, before any other resolution is put to the vote, a special report must be made on any transactions of this kind. However, if there is only one board member, any transactions in which such member has a conflicting interest must be recorded, and if it is a member of the management board, the transactions must be authorised by the supervisory board.

(f) Civil and criminal liability: legislative framework and consequences

Directors and managers are civilly liable towards third parties on the grounds mentioned above (see section 9.2(c)).

The directors and managers in public and private limited company do not assume any personal obligation by reason of the commitments of the company. They are liable towards the company in accordance with general law for the execution of their mandate and for any misconduct in the management of the company's affairs. They are discharged from such liability in the case of a violation to which they were not a party provided no misconduct is attributable to them and they have reported such violation to the first general meeting after they had acquired knowledge thereof.

It is important to distinguish between an action brought by a shareholder in the name of the company and an action brought by a shareholder for the defence of its own interests. Indeed, a shareholder who has suffered personal damages may initiate legal proceedings against a director on civil liability grounds. If the company itself has suffered damages, then the general meeting of shareholders shall decide on the appropriateness of bringing an action against the directors/managers by a simply majority vote. An action of a single shareholder in the name of the company is not recognised under Luxembourg law.

The current legal situation in Luxembourg is that such liability is not recognised, although a bill of law that will introduce the criminal liability of companies is being prepared. Directors may, however, be liable for criminal offences such as fraud, fraudulent use of corporate property or breach of trust.

9.3 Others

(a) Attorneys

Private and public limited companies may delegate specific matters falling within their daily management as well as their representation to any person(s), shareholder(s) or not, acting alone or jointly, as agent(s) of the company. Special powers can be delegated to any person acting alone or jointly as agents of the company.

(b)   *Controllers and internal auditors*

The operations and annual accounts of private limited companies with more than 25 shareholders, as well as of every public limited company, must be supervised by one or more statutory auditors. They are appointed by the general meeting of shareholders and may be removed at any time, without notice and without cause. They are a corporate body of the company and may or may not be shareholders. Statutory auditors have an unlimited right of permanent supervision and control of all the operations of the company.

If a company exceeds, for two consecutive years, two of the three following criteria: (i) balance sheet total of €3.125 million; (ii) net turnover of €6.25 million; and (iii) an average number of 50 full-time staff employed during the financial year, the statutory auditors will be replaced by one or several independent auditors to be appointed by the general meeting of shareholders. The role of the independent auditors is to control the annual accounts, but they have no right of control or intervention in the management of the company.

10.   Fiscal year, duration and start of activities

The fiscal year generally corresponds with the calendar year. Private and public limited companies may, however, close their accounts on another date, provided that the accounting year does not exceed 12 months. Any amendment of the date of the fiscal year contained in the articles of incorporation constitutes an amendment of the articles of incorporation.

A company may be incorporated for a limited or unlimited duration and exists as from the signing of the notarial incorporation deed.

11.   Financial statements

11.1   Company tax

Taxable profits realised by private and public limited companies are subject to corporate income tax and municipal business tax at an effective maximum rate of 28.59% in 2009 in Luxembourg city (inclusive of the 4% surcharge for the employment fund). However, dividends, liquidation proceeds and capital gains may be partially or wholly tax exempt under certain conditions. Qualifying intellectual-property (IP) rights (eg patents, trademarks and copyrights on computer software) may also be exempt for up to 80%.

Moreover, private and public companies are subject to an annual net worth tax at the rate of 0.5% applied on their net assets as valued on January 1. Qualifying shareholdings and IP rights may, under certain circumstances, be exempt from net worth tax.

11.2   Annual accounts

(a)   *Documents*

Under Luxembourg GAAP, private and public companies must hold annual accounts consisting of:

- a balance sheet,
- a profit and loss account, and
- the notes to the accounts.

The directors/managers must submit all materials and their report on the operations of the company to the auditors at least one month before the annual meeting of shareholders, to allow them to prepare their report.

(b) *Audit report*

The results of the work of the auditors (statutory or independent) must be detailed in a report made available to shareholders at least 15 days before the annual meeting. The report must be in writing and detailed and end with a conclusion by which the auditor summarises the extent of his report on the annual accounts.

(c) *Approval and distribution of profits*

Shareholders of private and public limited companies must approve the annual accounts of the last financial year within six months after the close of the financial year. From a company's annual profits, 5% must be allocated to the legal reserve until the aggregate amount of such reserve amounts to 10% of the company's share capital. The general meeting of shareholders will determine how the remainder of the annual net profits will be used.

In a public limited company no interim dividends may be paid unless the articles of incorporation authorise the board of directors or the management board to do so. Payment of interim dividends may only be made:

- after interim accounts have been drawn up showing that sufficient funds are available;
- if the amount to be distributed does not exceed total profits made since the end of the last financial year for which the annual accounts have been approved, plus any profits carried forward and sums drawn from reserves available for this purpose, less losses carried forward and any sums to be placed to reserve pursuant to the requirements of the law or of the articles of incorporation;
- if the resolution of the board of directors or the management board, as applicable, to pay an interim dividend has not been passed more than two months after the date at which the interim accounts have been drawn up; and
- if the auditor(s) has/have stated in a report to the board of directors or the management board, as applicable, that the first three conditions have been satisfied. It is disputed, however, whether interim dividends may be paid during the first financial year.

The possibility for a private limited company to pay interim dividends is now commonly admitted, even in the absence of a specific legal provision to that effect. It is advisable for a careful board of managers to ensure that:

- interim accounts have been drawn up showing that sufficient funds are available;

- the amount to be distributed does not exceed total profits made since the end of the last financial year for which the annual accounts have been approved, plus any profits carried forward and sums drawn from reserves available for this purpose, less losses carried forward and any sums to be placed to reserve pursuant to the requirements of the law or of the articles of incorporation; and
- the auditors of the company, if any, have stated in their report to the board of managers that the first two conditions have been satisfied.

The general meeting of shareholders typically resolves upon the payment of interim dividends, unless the articles of incorporation expressly provide that the manager(s) are competent to do so.

(d)   *Deposit and publicity*
The balance sheet, income statement and annex must be filed with the Trade and Companies' Register within a month of their approval by the shareholders. A note of such filing will be published in the *Mémorial*. Failure to do so, with fraudulent intent, is a criminal offence.

12.   **Company reorganisation: transformation, merger and split-off**
Private and public limited companies may be converted into one another or into any other available corporate form, provided that such conversion is not prohibited by law. A conversion will not give rise to a liquidation or to the creation of a new legal entity.

In Luxembourg, businesses may combine via acquisitions, mergers or takeovers and they may also divide. Since 2007, such operations have been extended to all forms of companies and interest groups. A company may transfer branches of activity as well as all of its assets and liabilities in accordance with the legal provisions applicable to the division procedure. Simplified procedures apply to mergers by acquisition of an affiliated company by its parent company if the parent holds at least 90% of the subsidiary.

13.   **Eventual partner separation**
A shareholder may be excluded from a company in accordance with the articles of incorporation, provided that the procedure and the grounds for exclusion are sufficiently described. It is possible to apply for judicial exclusion of a shareholder but this should be the last resort for attempting to save a company.

It is worth mentioning partner separation in the context of a mandatory takeover bid. Indeed, if the offeror, further to a mandatory takeover bid, holds securities representing not less than 95% of the capital carrying voting rights and 95% of the voting rights of the target company, it may require the holders of the remaining securities to sell their securities to him at a fair price.

14.   **Dissolution and liquidation**
Dissolution may result from a resolution voted by an extraordinary general meeting

of shareholders (see section 9.1 above) or following the loss of half the share capital of a public limited company. Dissolution may also be ordered by a court under the conditions provided for by law.

Private and public limited companies are deemed to exist for the purpose of their liquidation. The extraordinary general meeting of shareholders will appoint a liquidator to realise the assets of the company and, to the extent possible, pay off the debts. Unless otherwise stated in the articles of incorporation, the liquidators are vested with a general managerial power. However, they must obtain an authorisation from the shareholders to perform some of their duties (eg to borrow money to pay the debts of the company, issue negotiable instruments, etc). Each year, the results of the liquidation must be submitted to the general meeting of shareholders.

When the liquidation is complete, the liquidators must make a report to the general meeting of shareholders which shall appoint an auditor in charge of verifying such report. Once all assets have been realised and, to the extent possible, debts have been paid off, the general meeting of shareholders will resolve upon the termination of the liquidation. This decision must be published in the *Mémorial*.

15. Branches

Under Luxembourg law, a branch of a foreign company does not constitute a legal entity separate from that of the company. In contrast, a subsidiary of a foreign company does have a separate legal personality and does therefore assume the liability applicable to the corporate form under which it exists (ie limited liability if it is a private or public limited company).

Malaysia

Dato' Johari Razak
Grace CG Yeoh
Shearn Delamore & Co

---

1. Types of limited liability company and applicable legislation

In Malaysia, limited liability companies may be incorporated under either the Companies Act 1965 (the CA) or the Offshore Companies Act 1990. Under the CA, limited liability companies are companies limited by shares, companies limited by guarantee and companies limited by both guarantee and shares. This chapter focuses on companies incorporated under the CA and limited by shares – the most common form of company used to conduct business in Malaysia.

2. Incorporation

2.1 Proceedings prior to incorporation

(a) Name registration
An application to the Companies Commission of Malaysia (CCM) must be made to determine the availability of a proposed name. A private company is required to have the words *'Sendirian Berhad'* or its abbreviation *'Sdn Bhd'* at the end of its name, whilst a public company must have the word *'Berhad'* or its abbreviation *'Bhd'* at the end of its name.

(b) Contributions to the company equity
Shareholders may subscribe for shares in the company's equity either by payment in cash or in the form of assets.

(c) Declaration of foreign investment
As a general rule, there is no requirement for investors to declare their investments in Malaysia. However, the Foreign Investment Committee's Guidelines on the Acquisition of Interests, Mergers and Takeovers by Local and Foreign Interests (FIC Guidelines) provide that prior approval of the Foreign Investment Committee (FIC) is required for certain acquisitions, details of which are contained in the FIC Guidelines. The FIC Guidelines are government policy guidelines and not statutory rules, but if they are not complied with there may be consequences. For example, FIC approval may be a precondition for obtaining other regulatory approvals.

In addition to the FIC Guidelines, there are other guidelines and legislation relating to equity participation in respect of specific industries.

(d) **Tax number for foreign partners/directors**

Where foreign partners/directors who are non-taxpaying residents in Malaysia carry on business in Malaysia and have sources of income that give rise to chargeable income, the non-taxed resident partners/directors should obtain from the Inland Revenue Board of Malaysia (IRB) tax reference numbers for the purposes of filing a Malaysian tax return for that year of assessment. The information/documents that should be furnished to the IRB include the following:

- names of the partners/directors;
- date of birth;
- correspondence addresses of the partners/directors;
- year of assessment in which the partners/directors first received income from the company;
- address of the company and the employer's number of the company; and
- a copy of the first page of the passport of the partners/directors.

2.2 Incorporation of the company

(a) **Bylaws – the memorandum and articles of association**

The bylaws of a company are contained in the memorandum and articles of association of a company.

(i) *Essential clauses*

The memorandum of association sets out the objects and powers of a company, whilst the articles of association are the internal regulations of the company.

For a company with limited liability, the memorandum of association must contain the following:

- a clause specifying the name of the company;
- the objects of the company;
- the amount of authorised and issued share capital and the nominal value of the shares;
- a statement that the liability of its members is limited;
- the full names, addresses and occupation of the subscribers; and
- a subscription clause stating that the subscribers are desirous of forming a company and respectively agree to take the number of shares in the capital of the company set out against their respective names.

In respect of the articles of association, there are no mandatory requirements as to the inclusion of specific provisions. The Fourth Schedule (Table A) of the CA provides standard articles known as Table A – Regulations for Management of a Company Limited by Shares (the Table A Regulations). If articles are not registered, or if articles are registered, then so far as the articles do not exclude or modify the regulations contained in Table A, the Table A Regulations will be the articles of the company so far as they apply in the same way and to the same extent as if they were contained in registered articles.

(ii)   *Clauses not foreseen by law*

Where Table A is not adopted, the following matters should, at the very least, be covered:

- share capital and variation of rights;
- transfer of shares;
- alteration of capital;
- general meetings;
- directors;
- dividends;
- winding-up; and
- notices.

(iii)   *Enlargeable clauses ruled by law*

The CA sets out provisions that apply to companies notwithstanding any provision in their memorandum and articles of association. A few examples are as follows:

- A public company may by ordinary resolution remove a director before the expiration of his period of office; but where any director so removed was appointed to represent the interests of any particular class of shareholders or debenture holders, the resolution to remove him shall not take effect until his successor has been appointed;
- Subject to certain exceptions, every member shall have a right to attend any general meeting of the company and to speak and vote on any resolution before the meeting; and
- Any provision, whether contained in the articles or in any contract with a company, for exempting any officer or auditor of the company from, or indemnifying him against, any liability that by law would otherwise attach to him in respect of any negligence, default, breach of duty or breach of trust of which he may be guilty in relation to the company, is void.

(b)   **Execution of public instrument**

For the purposes of incorporation, the memorandum and articles of association are required to be signed by each subscriber to the memorandum, in the presence of at least one witness (not being another subscriber) who shall attest the signature and add his address. As a matter of policy, the general practice of the CCM is that if the subscriber is a corporate body, the seal of the corporate body shall be affixed onto the memorandum and articles of association and signed by any two directors, or one director and the secretary, or such mode of execution by authorised signatories as is permitted under the constitution of the corporate body. This must be witnessed by a notary public, a solicitor, an attorney-at-law, an auditor or a chartered secretary.

(c)   **Tax number for the company**

Once a company commences its operation in Malaysia, a tax reference number should be obtained from the IRB. The company should provide the following information/documents in writing:

- address registered with the CCM;

- name and address of tax agents (if any);
- date of commencement of business;
- accounting period;
- address of place of business;
- certified true copy of memorandum and articles of association of the company;
- two certified true copies of Form 8 (Certificate of Incorporation of a Public Company) or Form 9 (Certificate of Incorporation of a Private Company); and
- two certified true copies of Form 24 (Return of Allotment of Shares).

The tax reference number is required when the company submits its tax return form or when making a tax payment, and it is quoted on all correspondence with the IRB.

(d)   *Payment of indirect taxes*

The Royal Customs and Excise Department Malaysia (Customs) has the care and management of indirect taxes.

(i)   *Customs duty*

Customs duties are levied upon certain goods imported into or exported from Malaysia and are to be paid by the importer or exporter, as the case may be. The relevant rates are set out in the Customs Duties Order 2007 whereas the valuation of the goods would be in accordance with the Customs (Rules of Valuation) Regulations 1999, giving effect to the WTO Valuation – WTO Guidelines.

(ii)   *Excise duty*

Excise duties are levied upon specified goods manufactured in or imported into Malaysia.

(iii)   *Sales tax*

Sales tax is charged and levied on taxable goods:
- manufactured in Malaysia and sold, used or disposed of by any person who is, or is required to be, licensed under the Sales Tax Act 1972; or
- imported into Malaysia by any person for home consumption.

(iv)   *Service tax*

Service tax is payable on any taxable service provided by any taxable person (ie a person carrying on the business of providing such taxable service). The current (2009) rate of service tax is 5%.

(v)   *Goods and services tax (GST)*

The implementation of GST in Malaysia was proposed in the 2005 Budget to replace sales tax and service tax. However, no date has been set for its implementation.

(e) **Registration with the Mercantile Registry**
Companies formed under the CA must be registered with the CCM.

(f) **Legalisation of official books**
A company is required by the CA to maintain the following books:
- the register of members;
- the register of directors, managers and secretaries;
- the register of option holders;
- the register of debenture holders;
- the register of charges;
- the register of substantial shareholders; and
- the register of directors' shareholdings, etc.

(g) **Declaration of set-up activity and other tax declarations**
A company is required to determine and submit an estimate of its tax payable in the prescribed form to the IRB not later than 30 days before the beginning of the basis period for that year of assessment. Where a company first commences operation in Malaysia, the estimate of its tax payable for that year of assessment must be submitted to the IRB within three months of the date of commencement of operations.

For each year of assessment a company is required to furnish the Director-General of the Inland Revenue (DGIR) with a return in the prescribed form within seven months from the date following the close of the accounting period that constitutes the basis period for the year of assessment. Under the self-assessment system, the tax return filed by the company is deemed as a notice of assessment.

A company is also required to notify the IRB about employees of the company who are likely to be chargeable to tax within one month from the date of commencement of employment. The company is required to make an annual return showing the names and addresses of its employees and the income paid to them.

3. **Number of partners: unipersonality**
A limited liability company in Malaysia has a separate legal personality and can transact business in its own name. A private company cannot have more than 50 members.

4. **Corporate name: limitations/restrictions**
The registrar of companies can reject an application where, amongst others, the proposed name is undesirable, a name is identical or closely resembles the name of a existing company or if a name has been reserved or is prohibited by law.

5. **Domicile**
Malaysian income tax is imposed on a territorial basis and is generally chargeable on the income of any person accruing in, or derived from, Malaysia or received in Malaysia from outside Malaysia. As such, domicile is not relevant in relation to the imposition of income tax in Malaysia.

6. Objects

A memorandum of association containing the objects of a company to be incorporated must be lodged with the CCM.

7. Capital stock

7.1 Minimum amount

The authorised capital of a company is the amount of share capital it is authorised to issue. The issued capital of a company represents the authorised capital that has been issued to shareholders of a company.

For the purpose of incorporation, all companies incorporated in Malaysia must issue a minimum of two shares and have at least two members.

7.2 Nature of contributions

Shares may be allotted for cash or in exchange for assets.

7.3 Partial payments

Shares may be issued partly paid or fully paid.

7.4 Share certificates and systems of representing shares

A certificate under the common or official seal of a company specifying any share held by any member of the company shall be prima facie evidence of the title of the member to the shares. Every share certificate shall be under the common seal of the company.

Every company shall keep a register of its members in accordance with the CA.

7.5 Restrictions to the transfer of shares

The CA stipulates that a private company can only be incorporated if its articles of association restrict the rights to transfer its shares. In the case of a public limited company, there is no requirement under the CA as to the restriction in the transfer of its shares. A company may be subject to conditions imposed by relevant authorities requiring their prior approval for transfers of shares.

7.6 Transfer of shares: formalities required

The relevant steps for the transfer of shares for companies other than companies listed on Bursa Malaysia, the Malaysian stock exchange, (listed companies) are as follows:

- the member disposing of shares executes the relevant transfer form(s);
- the transfer form must be submitted to the Malaysian Stamp Office for adjudication of the stamp duty payable on the transfer of the shares;
- upon issuance by the Stamp Office of a notice of assessment as to the proper stamp duty chargeable, stamp duty must be paid;
- the transferee must submit to the company secretary of the company the stamped instrument of transfer together with the share certificate(s) representing the shares;

- a directors' resolution must be passed authorising the registration of the transfer of shares; and
- a new share certificate(s) representing the shares is issued in the name of the transferee.

However, the transfer of shares in listed companies is carried out on a scripless basis. Records of shareholders are maintained in the record of depositors maintained by Bursa Malaysia Depository Sdn Bhd. Individual share certificates are not issued to shareholders of listed companies.

8. Equity

8.1 Balance between capital and own resources

There is no requirement that paid-up capital should be of any minimum amount. The CA does not specify that any balance is required between the paid-up capital of a company and the assets and liabilities of the company. However, if in the course of the winding-up of a company or in any proceedings against a company it appears that an officer of the company who was knowingly a party to the contracting of a debt had, at the time the debt was contracted, no reasonable or probable ground of expectation, after taking into consideration the other liablities, if any, of the company at the time, of the company being able to pay the debt, the officer may be liable for imprisonment for up to one year or a fine of RM5,000.

8.2 Convertible bonds

A company may issue convertible bonds subject to obtaining the relevant approvals. Convertible bonds do not form part of the share capital of a company unless and until the bonds are converted into shares.

9. Administration of the company

9.1 Meetings

(a) *General meeting of members*

The first annual general meeting of a company must be held within 18 months from the date of incorporation and thereafter once every calendar year at intervals of not more than 15 months from the last annual general meeting. All general meetings other than the annual general meeting are called extraordinary general meetings.

In addition, a public limited company with a share capital is also required to hold a statutory meeting (a general meeting of members) within a period of not less than one month and not more than three months after the date at which it is entitled to commence business.

(b) *Meeting of directors*

There is no statutory requirement as to when a company must hold the first directors' meeting. However, for practical reasons, a directors' meeting should be called soon after the company has been incorporated so that the administrative operations of the company may be regularised.

(c) **Quorums of attendance to meetings**

(i) *Board of directors' meeting*
The quorum for a board of directors meeting is stipulated in the articles of association of a company. Generally, companies fix the quorum at two directors.

(ii) *Shareholders' meeting*
The quorum for its shareholders' meetings is stipulated in the articles of association of a company. Generally, companies fix the quorum at two members.

(d) **Quorums for adoption of resolutions**
There is no statutory requirement for different quorums for the adoption of different type of resolutions and the articles normally provide for the same quorum requirement. Under the CA and under the articles, it is normally provided that the quorum for the general meeting would be the same regardless of the type of resolution to be passed. However, the majority for passing of a resolution differs according to the type of resolution.

An ordinary resolution requires a notice in writing of not less than 14 days or such longer period as is provided in the articles of association of a company. Generally, an ordinary resolution must be passed by a simple majority of the members present and voting.

A special resolution must be passed by a majority of not less than three-quarters of such members that are entitled to vote, of which not less than 21 days' notice specifying the intention to propose the resolution as a special resolution has been duly given.

A resolution requiring special notice requires a notice of the intention to move it to be given to the company not less than 28 days before the meeting at which it is moved, and the company shall give its members notice of any such resolution at the same time and in the same manner as it gives notice of the meeting. If that is not practicable, the company shall give them notice, in any manner allowed by the articles, not less than 14 days before the meeting. If, after the notice of the intention to move such a resolution has been given to the company, a meeting is called for a date 28 days or less after the notice has been given, the notice, although not given to the company within the time required, shall be deemed to have been properly given.

(e) **Challenge of resolutions**
A resolution passed by a general meeting can normally be challenged in law if it is passed by a meeting where notice has not been duly given or the necessary quorum is not present or there are some other irregularities in respect of the meeting. Further, a resolution can be challenged on the grounds that the affairs of the company are being conducted or the powers of the directors are being exercised in a manner oppressive to any member(s), or that some act of the company has been done or is

threatened, or if the resolution has been passed or is proposed that unfairly discriminates or is otherwise prejudicial to any the member(s).

9.2 Administrative body

Under Malaysian law, a company is made up of two distinct decision-making bodies: the board of directors and the shareholders.

(a) *Different systems of administration*

The CA and the articles of association of a company set out the different duties and powers conferred on the directors and shareholders. Table A provides that the business of the company shall be managed by the directors and may exercise all such powers of the company as are not, by the act or by articles, required to be exercised by the company in general meeting.

(b) *Term of office, resignation and removal of directors*

The CA requires a company to have a minimum of two directors and at least two directors must have his/her principal or only place of residence in Malaysia. Any resignation in contravention of this provision will be deemed invalid. The CA does not impose a limit as to the maximum number of directors, though the company's articles may do so.

A director of companies that are not listed companies may hold office for an indeterminate period unless he/she vacates that office under the articles of association or the CA. Typically, under the articles of association, the grounds for vacation of office include:

- bankruptcy;
- that the director is of unsound mind or has been absent for more than six months without permission of the other directors; or
- the director ceases to be a director by virtue of the CA.

In the case of listed companies, all directors are required to retire at least once in each three-year period.

Further, notwithstanding anything in the memorandum or articles of association of a company, no person aged 70 years or more may be appointed as a director of a public company or a subsidiary of a public company. The office will become vacant at the conclusion of the next annual general meeting after the director attains the age of 70. However, if a majority of not less than three-quarters of the members of the company vote to retain the director, either in person or by proxy, the director can be appointed or reappointed and can hold office until the next annual general meeting of the company, or can be authorised to continue in office as a director until the next annual general meeting of the company.

Resignation is normally carried out by way of written notice to the company.

Apart from the provisions contained in the articles of association of a company in respect of the removal of directors, the CA provides that a director of a public company may be removed by way of an ordinary resolution of the shareholders.

In private companies, any removal of a director will need to be carried out in the manner contained in the articles of association of a company.

When a director resigns or is removed, a company is required to file the prescribed forms with the CCM within one month of the resignation or removal. This is a procedural requirement and does not affect the validity of the resignation or removal.

(c)   ***Directors' liability to third parties***

Generally a director is not liable to a third party. This liability arises where:

- a director expressly contracts in the company's name or on its behalf but does not have authority from the company to enter into the contract as its agent;
- a director of a company expressly or impliedly contracts to make himself personally liable;
- in the course of a winding-up of a company or in any proceedings against a company, it appears that any business of the company has been carried on with intent to defraud creditors of the company, and then the court may, on the relevant applications being made, declare any director (or any other person) who was knowingly a party to the carrying on of the business in that manner to be personally liable for the debts or other liabilities of the company;
- a director has authorised, directed and procured the commission of a tort by the company, whereupon that director may, depending on the facts of the case, be held personally liable; or
- a director commits a tort in the course of his function as a director, whereupon the director may be liable, depending on the facts of the case.

(d)   ***Non-competition***

The directors are under a fiduciary duty to the company and this includes not putting themselves in the situation where there is any conflict of interest with the company. In particular, a director shall not, without the consent or ratification of a general meeting:

- use the property of the company;
- use any information acquired by virtue of his position as a director or officer of the company;
- use his position as such director or officer;
- use any opportunity of the company that he becomes aware of in the performance of his functions as the director or officer of the company; or
- engage in business that is in competition with the company;

in order to gain a direct or indirect benefit for himself or any other person, or cause detriment to the company.

(e)   ***Special duties of secrecy and loyalty***

A director of a company shall at all times exercise his powers for a proper purpose and in good faith in the best interests of the company and shall also exercise reasonable care, skill and diligence. A director will have a duty of secrecy and loyalty to the company to the extent required to comply with the aforesaid obligation.

Additionally, a director who has a contract of employment may have an express provision in his contract of appointment imposing a duty of confidentiality.

(f) *Civil and criminal liability: legislative framework and consequences*

The CA contains various provisions imposing obligations on a director. Some examples are as follows:

- Section 67 of the CA provides that a director may be personally liable for imprisonment of five years or a fine of up to RM100,000 if, except as is otherwise expressly provided by the CA, the company gives any financial assistance in connection with a purchase or subscription made by any person for any shares in the company (whether directly or indirectly and whether by means of a loan guarantee or the provision of security) or, where the company is a subsidiary, in its holding company or in any way purchases, deals in, or lends money on its own shares;

- Section 364 of the CA provides that a director who in any return, report, certificate, balance sheet or other document required by the CA makes or authorises the making of a false or misleading statement knowing it to be false or misleading in any material particular or intentionally omits or authorises the omission or accession of any matter or thing, thereby making the document misleading in a material respect, could be liable for imprisonment for 10 years or a fine of up to RM250,000;

- Various other statutes impose personal liability on directors. Some examples are as follows:

  - Section 214 of the Capital Markets and Services Act 2007 (CMSA) provides that a director could be personally liable to a fine of up to RM3 million or a term of imprisonment for up to 10 years or both, where false or misleading statements are submitted to the Securities Commission in connection with proposals (as outlined in the CMSA) to be undertaken by the company;

  - Section 46 of the Employees Provident Fund Act 1991 (EPF Act) provides that if a company fails to make contributions as required under the EPF Act, the directors of the company (and those who were directors when the contributions were liable to be paid) shall, together with the company, be jointly and severally liable for the contributions due;

  - Where a company contravenes any provision of the Occupational Safety and Health Act 1994 or regulations made thereunder, its directors may be charged jointly in the same proceedings with the company; and

  - Section 75A(1) of the Income Tax Act 1967 (ITA) imposes joint and several liability upon a 'director', as defined in Section 75A(2), where any tax is due and payable pursuant to the ITA by a company. The definition of director under Section 75A(2) only extends to those occupying the position of director (by whatever name called, and includes those concerned in the management of the company's business) who, either on their own or with one or more associates, directly or indirectly own or control more than 50% of the ordinary share capital of the company.

9.3 Others

(a) *Company secretary*

The CA requires a company to have at least one company secretary qualified under the provisions of the CA who has his principal or only place of residence in Malaysia.

(b) *Attorneys*

The company may appoint any attorney subject to any restriction in the articles.

(c) *Controllers and internal auditors*

A company is required to appoint an approved external auditor to audit its books. Although there is no statutory requirement to appoint tax agents, most companies would appoint qualified tax agents for proper tax management and to ensure compliance.

10. Fiscal year, duration and start of activities

The determination of the date in which the business of the company commences is important for purposes of tax and is a question of fact. The date of incorporation of the company should be distinguished from the date of commencement of the business of the company.

As tax is charged and assessed in respect of a year of assessment, the calendar year coinciding with a year of assessment shall constitute the basis year for that year of assessment. The ITA provides that the basis year for a year of assessment shall constitute the basis period for that year of assessment.

In instances where a company makes up its accounts of its operations for a period of 12 months ending on a day other than December 31 in the basis year, that period shall constitute the basis period for that year of assessment.

11. Financial statements

11.1 Company tax

(a) *Annual accounts*

(i) *Income tax*

The principal legislation governing the imposition of income tax in Malaysia is the ITA. The prevailing corporate tax rate is 26% for Year of Assessment 2008 and there will be a further reduction to 25% for subsequent years of assessment. The effective tax rates can be significantly reduced with tax holidays, incentives, exemptions and concessionary or reduced tax rates where applicable.

(ii) *Documents*

With the implementation of a self-assessment system, tax audits and tax investigations conducted by the IRB against companies are key enforcement tools to ensure that tax returns submitted are correct and in accordance with the law.

It is important for companies to maintain a proper record of all documents relevant to the business of the company. The ITA requires that companies carrying on business in Malaysia keep and retain records for a period of seven years from the end of the year to which any income from that business of the company relates. Records for this purpose shall include books of account of the company that record receipts and payments or income and expenditure, invoices, vouchers, receipts, and any other documents that the DGIR thinks necessary to verify the entries in any books of account.

All records that relate to any business in Malaysia must be kept and retained in Malaysia.

(b) *Audit report*

A company must appoint auditors for the purposes of carrying out audits (see section 9.3(c) above) and presenting an independent report on the financial position of the company. The auditor's report must be attached to or endorsed on the accounts or consolidated accounts.

Pursuant to the CA, the directors of a company must, not later than 18 months after the incorporation of a company and subsequently at least once in every calendar year at intervals of no more than 15 months, lay before the company at its annual general meeting a profit and loss account (or, in the case of the first account since incorporation of the company, made up to a date not more than six months before the date of the meeting).

(c) *Approval and distribution of profits*

A company may distribute its profits to shareholders by way of a dividend declaration in accordance with its articles of association. Dividends cannot be declared except out of profits available for distribution.

(d) *Deposit and publicity*

Generally, all companies are required to make the necessary filings, including annual returns and audited accounts, with the CCM as stipulated under the CA. However, private companies (where no beneficial interest in the shares is held directly or indirectly by any corporation and which has not more than 20 members none of whom is a corporation) are exempt from filing audited accounts.

12. Company reorganisation: transformation, merger and split-off

Companies may reorganise themselves by way of a merger or scheme of arrangement or they be taken over, and these organisations are governed by various provisions under the CA, the Malaysian Code of Takeovers and Mergers 1998 and the Securities Commission Act 1993.

13. Eventual partner separation

A member will cease to be a member of a company upon disposal of the shares in the company in accordance with its articles of association.

14. Dissolution and liquidation

A company may be dissolved under the CA by way of winding-up. There are two primary modes of winding-up:

- voluntary winding-up; and
- winding-up by the court.

14.1 Voluntary winding up

There are generally two types of voluntary winding-up: members' voluntary winding-up and creditors' voluntary winding-up. A company may be wound-up voluntarily:

- when the period, if any, fixed for the duration of the company contained in the memorandum or articles of association expires, and the memorandum or articles state that the company is to be dissolved. and the company in general meeting has passed a resolution requiring the company to be wound up voluntarily; or
- if the company so resolves by special resolution.

14.2 Winding-up by the court

A company may be wound up by the court on the grounds as provided in the CA. These include circumstances where the company is unable to pay its debts, or the company does not commence business within one year of its incorporation.

15. Branches

A branch office set up in Malaysia does not have a legal status of its own but is viewed as having the same legal entity as the incorporated entity under which it is established. Accordingly, liability of a branch is limited to the same extent as the foreign company under which it is established.

Mexico

Fernando Cuesta
Ramón Macías Garcia
Cuesta Campos y Asociados SC

---

1. **Types of company with limited liability and applicable legislation**
    Various kinds of corporate vehicle are regulated by the General Law on Commercial Entities. However, two types are most commonly used because the partners' exposure to liabilities is limited to the amount of their capital contributions.

    The first type is the *Sociedad Anónima* (SA), essentially equivalent to a 'C' corporation in the United States; its shares may be freely transferred unless otherwise stipulated in the company bylaws. The SA is the only type of entity authorised by law to issue bonds or debentures (privately or publicly traded).

    The second is the *Sociedad de Responsabilidad Limitada* (SRL), which shares some similarities with a limited liability company or limited liability partnership in the United States. In such companies the admission of new partners and the transfer of partnership interests are generally subject to restrictions and requirements; therefore, by law, partnership interests cannot be publicly traded on a stock exchange.

    Both the SA and the SRL require at least two partners (Mexican or foreign individuals or entities) and a sole administrator or administrative body with similar responsibilities. Both may adopt the form of variable capital to reduce or increase the capital stock by way of partner resolution.

    There is no significant administrative advantage to either form, although the SRL has a slight advantage because an examiner is not required.

    The type of vehicle to be used rather depends on the specific needs of the partners, including:
    - the structure of the corporate partners in a foreign country;
    - their tax situation under the applicable income tax laws; and
    - the intention to have either a closely held company or an entity that admits transfers of stock and new partners or that will be publicly traded.

    In the United States, for instance, an important issue to consider in deciding whether to use an SA or an SRL is whether to defer the attribution of Mexican-source income to the corporate partners in the United States by using an SA or an SRL that has not elected 'pass-through' status, or immediately to pass through all Mexican-source income and deductions to the corporate partners through an SRL that has elected to be treated as a pass-through entity pursuant to certain Internal Revenue Service regulations. In addition to the deferral of income, there could be other benefits associated with the election of pass-through status, such as the ability to use Mexican losses in the United States and the avoidance of potential double taxation.

2. Incorporation procedure

A legal business entity in Mexico must be created by means of a public deed (through either a notary public or public broker), which includes the bylaws that will govern the new company.

At incorporation, the partners usually hold a general ordinary meeting covering issues such as:

- the initial distribution of capital stock;
- the appointment of a sole administrator or a board of directors;
- in the case of an SA, the appointment of at least one examiner to monitor the company's administration on behalf of the shareholders;
- the appointment of a general manager, and other officers or agents; and
- the granting of general or special powers of attorney to company officers or employees in addition to those usually granted in the bylaws to administrators or board members.

Once incorporated, a Mexican entity must apply for a series of governmental permits, licences and registrations, depending on its corporate purpose, the commercial activities to be conducted and whether it will have direct employees. In any event, all entities must be registered in, among others:

- the Public Register of Commerce;
- the Federal Taxpayers' Register;
- the Mexican Business Information System; and
- if applicable, the Foreign Investment National Register, the Social Security Institute, the Mexican Housing Fund Institute and the Retirement Savings System.

2.1 Proceedings prior to incorporation

(a) *Name registration*

An application must be made to the Ministry of Foreign Affairs for authorisation to use a name for the company. Three alternative names must be submitted in order of preference to avoid repeat applications in the event that a name is rejected. This authorisation does not grant any intellectual property (IP) protection.

(b) *Capital contributions*

For SAs, the minimum capital is Ps50,000 (approximately $5,000), divided into nominal shares with equal par value represented by stock certificates. For SRLs, the minimum is Ps3,000 (approximately $300), represented by as many partnership interests as there are partners.

Notwithstanding the above, it is generally advisable that the value of the company's capital stock is consistent with the size of the entity's operation.

(c) *Declaration of foreign investment*

Mexico welcomes foreign direct investment, granting foreign investors 'national treatment' (ie, the same rights to which Mexican investors are entitled).

Over the past three federal administrations, Mexico has continually expanded the areas in which foreign investment is allowed. Current policies encourage foreign participation in the capital stock of Mexican business entities unless specifically restricted in either the Constitution or the Foreign Investment Law. Consequently, only a few restrictions remain for activities reserved to Mexican investors or the Mexican government.

Further, Mexico's Foreign Investment Law includes a classification known as 'neutral' investment. A neutral investment is an investment contributed to Mexican corporations through shares with limited corporate rights or without voting rights, as well as by means of trusts authorised under the Foreign Investment Law. This type of investment is not considered when determining the percentage of foreign participation in the corporate capital of Mexican companies. Investments made by international financial development institutions into the capital stock of corporations may also be considered neutral investments with the prior authorisation of the National Foreign Investment Commission.

Foreign investors are required only to register with the National Foreign Investment Registry, which is under the control of the Ministry of Economy, and comply with certain reporting requirements.

Companies with foreign capital must register with the National Foreign Investment Registry and submit the required economic and statistical information to the Foreign Investment Commission, which is also under the control and supervision of the Ministry of Economy. Foreign investors must additionally provide notice of any variation in corporate capital or certain changes to the corporate bylaws, changes of domicile or changes of legal representatives, in order to maintain the validity of their registration and remain in good legal standing before the registry.

The following economic areas are considered strategic by the Mexican Constitution and the Foreign Investment Law, and foreign investment is therefore restricted:

- activities reserved to the Mexican government, including petroleum and some basic petrochemicals, radioactive minerals, nuclear energy, electricity, telegraph and satellite communications services, and the postal system (but not courier services); and
- activities reserved for Mexican citizens and corporations. No foreign direct investment is allowed (except as neutral investment) in the areas of land transportation of passengers and freight, distribution of gasoline and liquefied petroleum gas, radio and television services (excluding cable and direct satellite television), credit unions, development banking institutions, and certain professional and technical services, among others.

In the case of other activities, foreign direct investment is restricted to specific percentages provided by law. For some enterprises, such as air transport, the maximum limit is 25%. Others – such as insurance services, most financial services (except for banking, financial brokerage and financial holding activities, where 100% foreign direct investment is allowed subject to certain requirements), certain telecommunication operations (satellite pathways and their frequencies, band of frequencies, and public telecommunication nets), administration of ports, most fishing activities, guns and their supplies, as well as newspapers – are subject to a maximum limit of 49% foreign ownership.

Further, an investor must have a special permit from the National Foreign Investment Commission to hold more than 49% of the stock in certain other enterprises, including schools, port services, cellular telephony, insurance brokerage, legal services, securities qualifiers, operation of railroads and trains, and drilling for gas and petroleum.

Other legal provisions, such as free trade agreements entered into by Mexico with other countries and some other special laws, set out specific regulations that must be analysed to determine whether the specific business activity that the foreign investor will perform is prohibited, regulated or allowed under Mexican law. These regulations must be scrutinised on a case-by-case basis.

(d) Tax number for foreign partners/directors

According to the Federal Tax Code, non-resident foreign partners must file a notice to the Ministry of Finance indicating their address, tax domicile and tax identification number abroad; otherwise, they will be bound by registration and reporting requirements in Mexico.

Foreign individuals are deemed to have a residence in Mexico for tax purposes when they establish a home in Mexico or, if they also have a home in another country, when they have their 'centre of main interests' in Mexico. Under the code, a centre of main interests is deemed to exist in any of the following cases:

- more than 50% of the total income of the individual during the year is derived from Mexican sources; or
- the individual has his main place of professional activities in Mexico.

2.2 Incorporation procedure

(a) Bylaws

(i) Essential clauses

The General Law on Commercial Entities provides that the public deed of incorporation must contain:

- the name, nationality and address of the partners;
- the corporate purpose;
- the name of the company;
- the term;
- the fixed minimum capital stock;
- contributions made by the partners;
- the corporate domicile;
- the administration mechanism and the authority of the administrators;
- the appointment of directors and officers;
- the mechanism to distribute profits and losses;
- the amount of the reserve fund; and
- dissolution and liquidation provisions.

Companies with foreign partners must include a clause within the bylaws establishing that the company is organised according to Mexican law, and that present or future foreign partners commit and formally agree before the Ministry of Foreign Affairs to consider themselves as Mexican nationals in respect of their participation in the company, as well as of the goods, rights, concessions and participations of which the company will be titleholder, and not to invoke the protection of their governments; otherwise, they will forfeit their participation to the Mexican government.

(ii)   *Clauses not foreseen by law*
Under the General Law on Commercial Entities, the company bylaws must include the information outlined in section 2.2(a) above, along with any other rules freely agreed by the partners in connection with the organisation and functioning of the company, such as management and operating issues, budgeting, internal auditing controls and so on.

(iii)   *Optional clauses governed by law*
Almost all of the legal requirements that the bylaws must contain may be freely agreed by the partners, provided that certain public policy provisions of the General Law on Commercial Entities are complied with. These include provisions on, among other things:

- the distribution of profits and losses among the partners;
- responsibilities of the partners and administrators;
- obligations in favour of third parties, such as the maintenance of the reserve fund and publication obligations;
- voting rights; and
- the value of shares.

(b)   Execution of public deed
In order to incorporate a company by executing the public deed of incorporation, corporate partners must demonstrate their existence and that the individuals acting on their behalf have sufficient authority.

In the case of corporate partners, the main documents required to incorporate a Mexican company are as follows:

- a certificate issued by the corresponding governmental authority evidencing the legal existence of the company that will own an interest in the Mexican entity;
- a certificate issued by the corresponding company's director or officer evidencing that the person who will sign all documents on behalf of the incorporating company (ie a proxy) has sufficient authority to bind the company. This may also be accomplished through a resolution of the board of directors of the company appointing a specific person to act on behalf of the company; and
- a proxy to act on behalf of each shareholder or partner authorising the individual(s) in Mexico to sign the incorporation deed. The proxies must be signed before a notary public by the person legally authorised in the certificate of incumbency or board resolution.

In order for documents issued abroad to be valid in Mexico, they must be legalised before a Mexican consulate or embassy; alternatively, in the case of countries that have signed the Hague Convention, ratification by a local notary public and attachment of the apostille will suffice.

(c)   **Tax identification number**

A legal entity doing business in Mexico must register as a taxpayer with the Federal Taxpayers' Registry of the Tax Administration Service (the Mexican equivalent to the US Internal Revenue Service). Every taxpayer (whether a corporation or individual) must register in order to obtain a taxpayer identification number, which is necessary for all tax records and payments, must be printed on all company invoices and is an essential requirement in receipts for deductible expenses.

(d)   **Payment of indirect taxes**

Companies must maintain records of their operations and of their compliance with tax obligations. The main taxes payable by companies are income tax, value added tax (VAT), Single Rate Minimum Corporate Tax (*Impuesto Empresarial de Tasa Única* – IETU) and social security, Mexican Housing Fund Institute and state payroll tax (see section 11.1).

Foreign investors organising a commercial entity may opt to have local legal counsel analyse and prepare the provisions to be included in the company bylaws, to ensure they fit the partners' business purpose. Fees charged by local counsel may vary, depending on the firm's level of specialisation, prestige and the complexity of the business purpose upon incorporating the Mexican entity.

As the incorporation of a Mexican entity requires the involvement of a notary public or public broker, foreign investors must pay for their services, calculated according to the applicable state schedule of officially authorised public notary fees and charges. In general, the fees charged by a notary public or public broker range from approximately $300 to $700.

The relevant governmental fees are as follows:

- Public Registry of Commerce – Mexican commercial entities are recorded in the Public Registry of Commerce with jurisdiction in the territory where the new entity's corporate domicile is located. In this regard, state revenue laws specify whether the company must pay a fixed or variable fee (variable fees are commonly calculated based on the amount of capital contributed to the new Mexican entity). For instance, the Mexico City local revenue provisions specify that governmental fees shall be calculated based on capital stock and powers of attorney granted, among other things, up to a cap of approximately $800. The Jalisco state revenue law levies a fixed fee of approximately $110.
- National Foreign Investment Registry – entities with foreign investors must pay a fee of approximately $130 upon filing the application.

The Federal Taxpayers' Registry does not require payment of governmental fees.

(e) ***Registration with the Mercantile Registry***
According to the General Law on Commercial Entities, for a commercial entity to have legal status independent of its partners, it must be registered at the Public Registry of Commerce. The performance of activities prior to registration will result in the personal liability of the partners, administrators and representatives, who will not be protected by the corporate veil and will have unlimited liability to third parties.

Notaries public and public brokers present the public deed of incorporation for registration as part of their incorporation services. The registration data provided to the Public Registry of Commerce is then requested by governmental agencies and third parties – including the Ministry of Finance in order to enter the company in the Federal Taxpayers' Registry, and banks in order to open accounts.

(f) ***Legalisation of official books***
Companies must keep the following books at their corporate domicile:
- a minute book for partner meetings;
- a minute book for board of directors' meetings;
- a partners' registry book; and
- variations of the capital registry book.

These books remain under the custody of the administrators or anyone they appoint for this purpose, who will have joint and several liability if the books are not kept up to date or if the information contained therein is inaccurate.

(g) ***Declaration of start date and other tax declarations***
See section 11.1 below.

3. Number of partners
There are no sole-ownership commercial entities in Mexico. The General Law on Commercial Entities requires at least two partners. The maximum number of partners in SAs is unlimited, while in SRLs it is limited to 50 partners.

4. Corporate name – limitations
The company name must be authorised by the Ministry of Foreign Affairs and must be followed by the type of entity or its abbreviation.

5. Domicile
The partners must specify a corporate domicile for the company, but they may establish branches or agencies in other areas of the country or abroad, and choose conventional domiciles for other matters that will not imply a change in the company's corporate domicile.

6. Corporate purpose
The corporate purpose is a descriptive list, set out in the bylaws, of activities that the company may conduct. The company may not perform activities that are not

contemplated in its corporate purpose. Normally, general standard corporate purposes are used for all business entities, which include the general day-to-day operations of any corporation (eg leases, loans, transfers) along with the particular purpose of the company.

7. Capital stock

The capital stock of a variable capital company may be increased through additional contributions made by the partners, contributions made by new partners or capitalisation of previous contributions, profits, premiums or reserves, as well as reduced through amortisation of partners' participations. Each increase or reduction must be approved by the partners, following certain formalities pursuant to law or the company bylaws.

Each increase or reduction in the fixed or variable capital must be recorded in the variations of capital registry book of the company.

In the case of a capital increase, the partners have a right of first refusal in proportion to their partnership interests or shares, as the case may be, to subscribe to the newly issued partnership interests or shares within the terms indicated by the General Law on Commercial Entities.

7.1 Minimum capital requirement

See aection 2.1(b) above.

7.2 Nature of contributions

Contributions may be made in cash or in kind. Except as otherwise agreed, contributions of property to a company shall be understood as an absolute transfer of title thereto, and risk of loss will be transferred to the company until actual delivery of the property.

In the case of an SA, the General Law on Commercial Entities provides that any shares paid for in whole or in part with an in-kind contribution must be kept on deposit by the corporation for two years. If, during this two-year period, it appears that the actual value of the property thus contributed drops by more than 25% from the date on which it was contributed, the partner will be obliged to pay the difference to the company.

7.3 Partial payments

The incorporation deed or the partner resolution approving an increase in capital must indicate the terms and conditions under which the unpaid capital must be paid in order to allow for partial payments. However, at the time of incorporation of an SA, the partners must pay in at least 20% of each share payable in cash and 100% of the shares payable in kind. At the time of incorporation of an SRL, at least 50% of the capital stock must be subscribed and paid for.

7.4 Representation of shares

The capital stock of an SA is represented by nominal stock certificates, which are considered to be negotiable instruments. The capital of an SRL is formed by partnership interests that may eventually be represented by certificates if the partners so agree.

7.5 Transfer of shares

(a) Restrictions
Generally, the shares of an SA may be freely circulated. However, the General Law on Commercial Entities provides that the company bylaws may include a provision stating that shares may be transferred only with the board of directors' authorisation, and that such authorisation may be denied if the board designates another purchaser of the shares for market value.

The partnership interests of an SRL may be assigned only in the specific cases and pursuant to the requirements set out in the law and the company bylaws.

(b) Formalities
The share certificates of an SA may generally be freely transferred by endorsement, while the transfer of partnership interests in an SRL must be approved in advance by a majority of the partners, in accordance with the law.

8. Equity

8.1 Convertible bonds
Only SAs can issue bonds, which, pursuant to the general law on negotiable instruments and credit operations, represent the individual shares of the holders thereof in an interest-bearing loan payable by the issuer on a specific date. The same law also regulates the possibility of an issue of convertible bonds, in which case the company must hold treasury stock in an amount sufficient for the conversion.

9. Administration

9.1 General partners' meeting
The supreme authority of the company is the partners' meeting. Meetings are chaired by the general administrator or the president of the board of administrators and, in their absence, by a person unanimously appointed by the partners.

The authority of the partners' meeting includes the following:
- approval and modification of the financial report and approval of the actions required or necessary;
- distribution of profits;
- appointment and dismissal of the sole administrator or members of the board of administrators, the examiner or board of examiners, or any other officer of the company;
- modification of the company bylaws;
- acceptance of new partners in the company;
- determination of increases and reductions in capital stock;
- determination of dissolution; and

- resolution of any other matters referred to in the General Law on Commercial Entities and in the bylaws.

Partners may attend the meeting either in person or through representatives; in the latter case, it is sufficient that the representation is granted in a simple power of attorney executed before two witnesses.

Meetings may be called by the sole administrator or board of administrators, or by the examiner or board of examiners, if any. Where they fail to do so, partners representing 33% of the partners' interests may call a meeting.

Unless otherwise established in the company bylaws, in the case of an SA, meetings will be called by notice published in the local *Official Gazette* or a major newspaper at least 15 days before the date on which the meeting will take place. In the case of an SRL, the meeting is called by notice sent personally to each partner at least eight days before the date on which the meeting will take place.

The notice calling a meeting must specify the agenda, place, time and date of the meeting.

A call is not necessary when all the capital stock of the company is represented at the meeting and at the time the resolutions are taken.

The bylaws may provide that resolutions adopted by unanimous vote of the partners, without holding a partners' meeting, will have the same force and legal effect as resolutions adopted at a partners' meeting, as long as they are confirmed in writing by all partners.

Resolutions passed at meetings must be included in the minutes and incorporated into the partners' meeting book; they must be signed at least by the president and secretary of the meeting. The minutes must include a list of attendance.

In SAs, a partners' meeting must be held at least once a year within the four months following the end of the previous fiscal year. In SRLs, unless otherwise stated in the bylaws, a partners' meeting must be held at least every six months.

(a) **Quorum requirements**

In an SA, there are two classes of shareholders' meeting, depending on the matters to be addressed or the actions to be taken: ordinary and extraordinary. To be legally convened at first call, an ordinary shareholders' meeting requires a quorum of shareholders representing 50% of the capital stock. Resolutions will be valid only if adopted by a majority of votes present.

To be legally convened at first call, an extraordinary shareholders' meeting requires a quorum of shareholders representing at least 75% of the capital stock. Resolutions will be valid if approved by shareholders representing at least half of the capital stock.

There are no quorum requirements for an ordinary shareholders' meeting at second or subsequent call; resolutions will be valid when adopted by a majority of those present.

To be legally convened at second or subsequent call, an extraordinary shareholders' meeting requires a quorum of shareholders representing at least 50% of the capital stock, and resolutions will likewise be valid when adopted by shareholders representing at least 50% of the capital stock.

In an SRL, there is no distinction between ordinary and extraordinary partners' meetings. Resolutions are adopted by majority vote representing at least half of the capital. If this requirement is not achieved at the first meeting, the partners will be called for a second meeting, at which resolutions will be adopted by majority vote regardless of the capital represented.

9.2 Administrative body

(a) Different systems of administration

Administration of the company is the responsibility of either a sole administrator or a board of administrators. Administrators may be a partner or an individual outside the company. Typically, board members have authority only jointly and not individually, although they may be granted individual authority in the bylaws.

The administrators have extensive powers to administer the business of the company, with the broadest authority to represent the company and manage and dispose of its property, and all general and special authority established by law. Their powers are granted without restriction.

The board usually comprises a chairman, a vice chairman and a secretary. Board members may guarantee their performance through a bond, and their compensation, if any, is determined by resolution of the partners' meeting. Resolutions of the board are usually adopted by majority vote; where there is an even number of administrators, the chairman has the casting vote.

Board meetings will be held when called by any of the members and will be legally convened when the majority of the board members are in attendance. The board of administrators may meet in the corporate domicile or another place within Mexico or abroad.

The partners may determine that resolutions adopted by unanimous vote of the board members, without holding a meeting of the board, will have full legal effect and the same validity as resolutions taken at a board meeting, provided they are confirmed in writing and signed by all members of the board.

The officers of Mexican entities are usually the general manager and other managers of the company. SAs and SRLs follow the same pattern in relation to administration, although terminology may vary.

(b) Term of office, resignation and removal of directors

The sole administrator or board members will remain in their positions until removed by resolution of the partners.

(c) Directors' liability to third parties

Generally speaking, the administrators will be liable to third parties:

- if they fail to perform the duties inherent to their position;
- in any case of violations of the law (in which case liability may be criminal or civil); or
- if they carry out acts on behalf of the company not contemplated in the corporate purpose or in violation of an express limitation of authority established in the bylaws.

9.3 Others

As a general rule, there is no implied authority in Mexico, meaning that an agent cannot bind the company unless he has been granted specific authority to do so. There are some exceptions to this rule, but to protect the company it is advisable that only formally appointed attorneys in fact execute transactions on behalf of the company.

The Federal Civil Code, the civil codes of each state and Mexican commercial laws identify four types of power of attorney:

- acts of ownership or control (eg power to sell or encumber assets, or to take on debt);
- power to issue bills of exchange, promissory notes, cheques and other credit instruments;
- acts of administration (day-to-day operations); and
- for lawsuits and collection purposes.

It is recommended that authority be granted to at least one Mexican-resident officer, to facilitate post-incorporation and ordinary operations of the company.

10. Fiscal year, commencement of operations

The official fiscal year of a Mexican company commences on January 1 and concludes on December 31 – except during the first fiscal year, which may be irregular if the company commences activities after January 1. However, for internal accounting purposes or for the consolidation of financial statements, a company may follow an alternative internal fiscal year.

Companies are customarily established for a period of 99 years; however, the partners are free to establish a different term.

11. Financial statements

11.1 Company tax

(a) Income tax

Under the Income Tax Law, tax is mainly levied on:

- income of legal entities (irrespective of the type of entity or corporate vehicle);
- income of individuals;
- Mexican-source income of non-residents (whether individuals or legal entities); and
- non-profit organisations.

'Taxable income' is defined in the Income Tax Law as gross income, which includes any kind of income unless specifically excluded, minus allowable deductions and unexpired net operating loss carry-forwards from previous years. Gross income includes any inflationary gain, and any inflationary loss is fully deductible.

Legal entities residing in Mexico are taxed on their worldwide income from all sources, including profits earned in cash or credit. Mexican-resident entities are those incorporated under Mexican law or those with a principal place of business or management located in Mexico. Non-resident entities are taxed on income earned from a Mexican source.

The tax rate for the 2008 fiscal year is 28%.

The tax year must generally coincide with the calendar year, always ending on December 31 each year and not exceeding 12 months. An annual tax return must be filed by the end of the third month following the end of the fiscal year. Companies are also required to file monthly tax returns.

Dividends received from a Mexican entity are not subject to income tax if the earnings were already subject to income tax at the corporate level and the entity distributing the profits pays them from its so-called 'net tax profit account' (an account of net after-tax income that can be distributed to shareholders without any further taxation pursuant to the income tax provisions).

(b) VAT

VAT at a current general rate of 15% (10% in the border region) is payable on the sale of goods, provision of services, rent and importation of goods and services (except temporary imports under the Maquila or PITEX programmes).

A 0% VAT rate applies to some transactions involving certain products, such as food and medicines, which in general terms means that no VAT is payable in such cases.

VAT collected by taxpayers from their suppliers must be remitted to the tax authorities, and may usually be credited against the VAT paid by the taxpayers (eg in their purchases or the importation of goods) thereby reducing the net liability owed to the tax authorities. Excess credits may be reimbursed.

Since the 2003 fiscal year, VAT has been computed for each calendar month, except where the tax is incurred through occasional activities. Monthly returns must be filed by day 17 of the following month.

(c) IETU

The Single Rate Minimum Corporate Tax (*Impuesto Empresarial de Tasa Única*) or IETU (by its Mexican nomenclature) is a new flat-rate tax similar to a tax that is in force in various European nations.

The IETU is applicable to all individuals or entities, including permanent establishments of foreign persons and entities executing the following activities:

- the transfer of goods;
- the rendering of independent services; and
- the grant of temporary use and enjoyment of goods.

IETU is designed as a minimum tax and replaces the Asset Tax.

Under the IETU Tax Law, the IETU would be levied at a flat 17.5% rate (with an introductory 17% rate for the 2009 fiscal year).

The IETU is aimed at taxing the perceived income (effectively received). The base of the IETU is determined on a cash-flow basis: perceived income (effectively received) minus authorised deductions (effectively paid). Deductions are tied to cash expenditures.

Against the IETU determined as mentioned herein, authorities may credit an amount equivalent to the income tax of the taxpayer and determined according to the Income Tax Law for the corresponding period. If the credited amount is inferior to the estimated IETU, such difference may be the estimated IETU to be paid by the taxpayer.

The payment of the IETU must be carried out within the same periods and at the same dates as the income tax.

(d)   Excise tax

An excise tax called the 'special production and services tax' applies to entities and individuals that sell and import certain goods or render certain services. The law establishes different rates for such products and services, which include: alcoholic beverages, alcohol and denatured alcohol; tobacco and cigarettes; gasoline and diesel; mineral water, hydrating or re-hydrating beverages; and certain services such as telecommunications.

(e)   Employment taxes

Salaries are subject to the following taxes:

- income tax – according to a percentage established by law, which is based on the level of income;
- social security tax – a two-part payroll tax paid partly by the employee and partly by the employer. This contribution includes access to benefits such as a retirement pension, insurance against occupational accidents and illnesses, and health services provided by the federal government;
- housing fund – a tax that is paid to the government-operated Mexican Housing Fund Institute, which provides workers with special benefits for obtaining loans to build, purchase or repair their homes; and
- state payroll tax – based on the amount received by the worker. It is a source of revenue for state governments.

(f)   Import duties and tariffs

The Mexican government charges duties on items that are imported into Mexico. To determine the applicable import tariffs, one must first look at the General Import Tariff Law. However, depending on the country of origin of the goods, preferential tariffs may apply under an applicable free-trade agreement, provided that the origin of the goods is evidenced with a proper certificate. In recent years, Mexico has negotiated and signed free trade agreements with a number of countries. Accordingly, numerous import–export duties have been reduced or even eliminated. Applicable import duties and taxes must therefore be determined on a case-by-case basis, taking into account the specific goods to be imported or exported and any applicable free-trade agreement.

In addition to the preferential tariffs established in the free trade agreements, a series of reduced tariffs is contained in the Decree Establishing the Sector Promotion

Programmes, through which companies incorporated in Mexico (both exporters and producers for the domestic market) may enjoy lower tariffs than those established in the General Import and Export Tariff Law (at rates of 0% or 5%) for certain imports.

11.2   Annual accounts

(a)   Documents

It is recommended – and may be necessary – to retain a firm of certified public accountants based in Mexico to compile the requisite records and file tax returns in accordance with the requirements of Mexican law.

(b)   Approval and distribution of profits

Profits are distributed as follows:

- Five per cent of the company's gross profits must be used to create or increase the legal reserve fund, until it has reached at least 20% of the capital stock;
- A certain amount may be distributed to company employees as part of a profit-sharing system;
- An amount determined by the partners' meeting will be used to pay the board of administrators; and
- The remaining profits will be distributed as determined by the partners' meeting, which may be called as needed to distribute profits or losses contained in the annual financial statements.

The partners must absorb any losses in proportion to their interests, but their liability is always limited to the amount of their contribution.

12.   Company reorganisation

The General Law on Commercial Entities includes a dedicated chapter (Chapter IX) that regulates the terms, conditions and formalities required to carry out transformations, mergers and split-offs of commercial entities.

13.   Dissolution and liquidation

A company will be dissolved upon the earlier of:

- a resolution of the partners' meeting to dissolve the company; or
- any of the reasons stated in Articles 229 and following of the General Law on Commercial Enterprises.

Once the company has been dissolved, it will be liquidated. The partners' meeting will appoint a liquidator, who will have the necessary authority to conclude the company's businesses and activities and to reimburse the balance to the partners, if any.

The Netherlands

Berth Brouwer
Jan-Willem Wiertsema
Boekel de Nerée NV

1. Types of limited liability company and applicable legislation

In the Netherlands there are two types of companies with limited liability: the private company with limited liability (*besloten vennootschap met beperkte aansprakelijkheid*, BV), and the public limited company (*naamloze vennootschap*, NV). Both types of company are separate corporate entities and limit the liability of their shareholders to the value of their shares. The BV and NV have a similar structure and similar corporate law is applicable to both legal forms, but there are also a number of differences. An NV is usually used for the somewhat bigger companies. All Dutch companies listed on stock exchanges need to have the form of an NV since the BV has a mandatory share-transfer restriction. A third type of limited liability company, *societas Europeae* (SE), was introduced a few years ago; basically it shares many characteristics with an NV, and because this legal form is rarely encountered it is not discussed here.

The Dutch Civil Code (*Burgerlijk Wetboek*) applies to companies in the Netherlands, and all non-tax issues discussed below are covered by the Dutch Civil Code. The Corporate Income Tax Act 1969 (*Wet op de vennootschapsbelasting* 1969) and the Turnover Tax Act 1968 (*Wet op de omzetbelasting* 1968) apply to all tax-related issues discussed below. Conveniently, most relationships that a company has with third parties (eg employees, clients, landlords, and creditors and debtors in general) are also covered by the Dutch Civil Code.

Industry-specific regulations, stemming from public law, are included in a number of separate laws and leave certain industries much more regulated than others.

2. Incorporation

2.1 Proceedings prior to incorporation

(a) Corporate name

The envisaged name of a company to be incorporated does not need to be registered prior to incorporation. However, if a company is to conduct business even before its incorporation, a company 'to be incorporated' (*in oprichting*, or *io*) can be registered under its envisaged statutory name with the Trade Register of the Chamber of Commerce. (See section 4 below.)

(b) **Capital contributions**

Contributions to a company's equity can be made either in kind or in cash (see section 7.2 below). If a contribution is made in cash, it is essential that the incorporator pays up the shares to be issued to him and not another person or legal entity. If the payment is made by a third party and the company petitions for bankruptcy, a receiver may argue that the incorporator did not pay up his shares and so he can be held liable for any deficit that exists on the day the company goes bankrupt.

A bank account with a Dutch bank needs to be opened to receive all cash contributions. After the fully issued share capital has been paid into such an account, which is always held in the name of the company to be incorporated, a so-called bank declaration needs to be provided by the bank to the civil-law notary who will execute the deed of incorporation. Usually this account will only be fully operational after the company has been incorporated.

(c) **Declaration of foreign investment**

This is not generally applicable. Investment in the banking industry is highly regulated and regulatory provisions include the approval of the Dutch Central Bank for certain inbound or outbound investments. Under the Act on Financial Supervision (*Wet financieel toezicht*), any investment that results in the acquisition of a minimum of 5% of the shares in a listed company must be reported to the Authority for Financial Markets (AFM).

(d) **Tax number for foreign partners/directors**

Foreign shareholders, partners or directors do not necessarily need to obtain a Dutch tax number in case an interest is held in a Dutch company. Under certain circumstances a director may become liable to pay Dutch income tax and will therefore need to apply for a Dutch tax number.

2.2 Incorporation of the company

(a) **Bylaws**

(i) *Essential clauses*

Clauses that are too important to leave out of the articles of association are those that stipulate a company's name, object, registered office, share capital, system of representation, and type of administrative body. Clauses that elaborate on voting rights pertaining to shares and the system for the allocation and distribution of profits are essential (see section 7.5 below).

(ii) *Clauses not foreseen by law*

Any special share structure needs to be facilitated by special provisions in the articles of association of a company. Examples of special structures are:
- the use of tracking stock;
- cumulative preference shares (*cumulatief preferente aandelen*);

- shares with limited voting rights (*degressief stemrecht*); and
- the use of depository receipts for shares (*certificaten van aandelen*).

Dutch corporate law only facilitates the adoption of shareholders' resolutions outside a meeting (*besluiten buiten vergadering*) or the payment of an interim dividend in cases where these options are explicitly mentioned in the articles of association. Most articles of association create these possibilities.

(iii) *Enlargeable clauses ruled by law*

Although the powers of the general meeting of shareholders, the board of managing directors and the supervisory board (if any) are indicated in Dutch corporate law, the articles of association can marginally expand and restrict these powers. The current legal framework is considered by many to be inflexible. New legislation, which most likely will become effective in 2009, provides for a so-called 'Flex BV'. The new legislation will open the possibility of creating shares without voting rights, or shares without the right to receive dividends. Simultaneously, new legislation has been drawn up (but is not in force yet) to introduce a one-tier board in the Netherlands.

(b) **Execution of public deed**

The bylaws, or articles of association, are included in the deed of incorporation of a company. This is to be executed in the form of a notarial deed by a civil-law notary. The full text of any deed of incorporation must be filed with the Trade Registry of the Chamber of Commerce within eight days after such deed has been executed. Any document in which the articles of association of a company is amended also needs to be executed in the form of a notarial deed.

(c) **Tax number for the company**

Upon incorporation of a company and its subsequent registration with the trade register of the Chamber of Commerce, new companies need to apply for a tax number by sending a form to that effect to the Dutch tax authorities. Once granted, the tax number of the company is almost the same as its VAT number (add B.01).

(d) **Payment of indirect taxes**

Companies will have to file a tax return (*belastingaangifte*) in order to pay indirect taxes, mainly VAT and customs duty. Except for a few assets such as cars, no customs duty or similar tax exists in relation to the import of goods from other EU member states. VAT is currently (2009) levied at two rates: 19% and 6%. The rate of 6% applies to food and non-alcoholic beverages, books, cultural services, agricultural products and medication. Certain services are VAT exempt (eg banking services and rental of real estate). VAT is to be paid on either a monthly, quarterly or annual basis and can usually be reclaimed (see section 2.2(g) below).

(e) **Registration with the Mercantile Registry**

Registration of each new company with the trade register (*handelsregister*) is mandatory and should be completed within eight days of a company being incorporated. Usually the civil-law notary who has executed the deed of incorporation will register the company.[1]

Details to be registered include:

- personal data of the managing directors (name, address, date of birth, place of birth);
- information about sole shareholders;
- number of employees;
- registered office;
- principal place of business; and
- telephone number, fax number, website and e-mail address.

(f)   *Corporate books*

No legalisation of documents is required in the Netherlands. either to commence business activities or to finalise the incorporation of a company. Upon incorporation. banks usually require an original extract of the trade register and an original signature of each officer of the company who is authorised to operate bank accounts on behalf of the company. Before the bank has this information, an account can be opened but it cannot be operated.

(g)   *Declaration of set-up activity and other tax declarations*

Generally most business activities, except activities in the banking industry, will not be exempt from VAT (*omzetbelasting*). Invoices sent by a company must include VAT. To reclaim VAT, a VAT number should be obtained from the Dutch tax authorities. Normally a VAT number will be provided within a few days after a request by (the tax advisor of) the company.

In certain types of business (eg banking, hospitality) a permit to carry out business activities is required. A user's permit (*gebruiksvergunning*) is required to start using office space that exceeds a certain net lettable floor area.

3.   Number of partners

Companies can be incorporated by any number of partners/shareholders. Other enterprises in the form of limited liability partnerships (*commanditaire vennootschappen*) and commercial partnerships (*vennootschappen onder firma*), which are not considered separate legal entities, need to be incorporated by a minimum of two partners. It is envisaged that new legislation will become effective in 2009. This means that the types of partnerships referred to above will be able to acquire the status of separate corporate entities (though without the limited liability that characterises a BV and an NV).

4.   Corporate name – limitations

The corporate name needs to begin or end with either BV or NV. Both the corporate name and a possible trade name used by a company next to its corporate name may not infringe rights of other parties who already use these names in the form of a trade name, a brand name or a corporate name. To avoid conflicts, it is advisable to

---

1   For more information about the Trade register please visit the following website: www.kvk.nl/English/

have the Chamber of Commerce conduct a name search prior to the incorporation of a company. Words that do not exist in the Dutch language can be used in a corporate name as long as the words are written in letters using the Roman alphabet. Few other restrictions exist in relation to corporate names.

5. Domicile

The articles of association of Dutch companies include the address of one registered office (*statutaire zetel*). However, this may be different from the company's principal place of business.The registered office muist be located in the Netherlands. The company can have several branch offices other than its principal place of business.

Unless the articles of association provide for another address, all general meetings of the shareholders are to be held at the company's registered office. Resolutions adopted in a shareholders' meeting not held at the registered office of the company where the articles of association do not specify another location are open for annulment unless all shareholders were present or represented at such meeting.

6. Object

Transactions that are conducted beyond the scope of the object of a company may be open to annulment. *Ultra vires* transactions can only be annulled by the company (ie not by a third party involved – where the other party was aware that the company was acting beyond the scope of its object). Special purpose companies tend to have a very 'narrow' object clause so that shareholders can ringfence their investment in such a company.

7. Capital stock

7.1 Minimum amount

The minimum amount of capital for a BV is currently set at €18,000; for an NV the minimum capital is €45,000.

7.2 Nature of contributions

Shares may either be paid up in cash or in kind. Where shares are paid in kind, a chartered accountant needs to provide a statement in which the value of the assets is assessed. This will be transferred to the company by way of contribution in kind. The assets can be either tangible or intangible, corporate law in the Netherlands does not restrict the nature of the assets that can be contributed. New legislation is being discussed in the Dutch parliament under which the mandatory assessment by chartered accounts is to be abolished.

7.3 Partial payments

Following an agreement to that effect between a company (existing or to be incorporated) and its (prospective) shareholder, 75% of the nominal value of shares can be paid after the shares have been issued. No restriction of the duration of the postponement exists. In each case the minimum capital needs to be paid up when the company is incorporated. This payment cannot be postponed.

7.4 Share certificates, systems of representing shares

Share certificates (*aandeelhoudersbewijzen*) are not widely used in the Netherlands. Where a shareholder of a company is represented at a shareholders' meeting by another legal entity or natural person, the shareholder must provide a proxy to this effect.

7.5 Restrictions to the transfer of shares

Many companies have a clause restricting the free transfer of shares; for each BV a clause must be included in the articles of association – hence the name: 'private company with limited liability'. Two types of clause exist: a clause including the approval procedure (*goedkeuringsregeling*); and a clause including a right of first refusal procedure (*aanbiedingsregeling*). For a transfer of shares to a third party in the former clause, an approval is required from either the management of the company or the general meeting of shareholders. In the latter clause, all co-shareholders need to refrain from making use of their right of first refusal for a shareholder to be able to transfer his shares to a third party. In the case of an NV, a clause regarding the restriction to transfer shares does not need to be included. However, in practice a clause restricting the transfer of shares is included in the articles of association.

7.6 Transfer of shares: formalities required

For the transfer of shares in non-listed companies, a notarial deed of transfer is required. When the notarial deed of transfer is executed, the management of the company must record the transfer in its shareholders' register – although registration of the transfer is not a constitutive requirement for the transfer. The NV offers the only exception to this system in the form of bearer shares. This kind of share is hardly used today. Bearer shares can be transferred by physically handing over the particular shares by the seller to the buyer.

8. Equity

8.1 Balance between capital/own resources

For most businesses the balance between the equity and debt in a company is bound to a certain maximum or minimum level. However, companies in the financial industry such as banks are highly regulated and need to comply with specific rules that cover the debt–equity ratio. The Basel II recommendations have been integrated into national regulatory provisions. Dutch tax law imposes a limit on the deductibility of interest by introducing rules on thin capitalisation. Interest may be non-deductible where companies are highly leveraged, in excess of a debt–equity ratio of 3:1, and where the debt that exceeds the said level amounts to €500,000 or more.

8.2 Convertible bonds

Convertible bonds can be viewed, from a corporate law perspective, as a conditional issuance of shares. A resolution to issue shares must be adopted by a general meeting of shareholders unless the general meeting has delegated such authority to the board of managing directors. Convertible bonds are used in both private and public companies, though their use is not widespread. When used in public companies, convertible bonds can form part of a private interest in public equity, or 'PIPE', deal.

9. Administration of the company

9.1 General meeting of partners

(a) Quorum requirements
Attendance by shareholders at shareholders' meetings is not regulated by Dutch corporate law in the same way as is the attendance by directors of meetings of the board of directors. However, the fact that a director rarely attends meetings may, in connection with other circumstances, lead to the conclusion that he/she is not fulfilling his/her obligations towards the company (see Article 2:9 of the Dutch Civil Code; see also section 9.2(c) below).

(b) Adoption of resolutions
Dutch corporate law does not provide for a quorum for meetings of shareholders in relation to the types of corporations that are used most frequently, namely a BV or an NV. Usually a quorum is required for certain resolutions such as dissolution, merger, split-off, or amendment of the articles of association. Articles 2:134 and 2:244 of the Dutch Civil Code create a restriction for the articles of association of an NV and a BV, stipulating that the articles of association cannot include a quorum of more than 50% of the votes where there is a resolution to appoint or remove a director.

(c) Challenge of resolutions
Generally, all resolutions of either the board of directors and the meeting of shareholders can be reconsidered as long as resolutions have not yet been executed or as long as no binding contracts have been entered into with third parties. Where resolutions have been adopted contrary to the articles of association of a company, such resolutions can be nullified.

9.2 Administrative body

(a) Different systems of administration
Companies may opt to have a management board only or a management board and a separate supervisory board. New legislation will create the possibility for companies to opt for a one-tier board that will include both executive and non-executive members.

Currently, it is expected that the legislation will become effective during 2009. Where a company exceeds a certain size, a special set of corporate regulations – ironically referred to as 'the wonder of The Hague' – will apply. The critical size is currently roughly a shareholders' equity of more than €13 million and 100 employees or more based in the Netherlands. Any Dutch company exceeding this size for three consecutive years has a full statutory two-tier status and will have to introduce a supervisory board into its corporate structure. Managing directors are appointed and removed by the supervisory board in companies with a full statutory two-tier status (*structuurvennootschappen*). The power to appoint members of the supervisory board is shared between the supervisory board itself, the general meeting of shareholders and the works council of the company.

(b) *Term of office, resignation and removal of directors*

No mandatory minimum or maximum term of office exists under Dutch law, although companies are not barred from including limitations to this effect in their articles of association. The relationship between a managing director and a company has a hybrid character; usually both employment law and corporate law apply. A voluntary resignation of managing directors will usually only be restricted by a notice period, a typical aspect of employment law. The general meeting of shareholders can adopt a resolution to remove a director. This may be effective immediately although employment law may prevent the immediate termination of the underlying employment contract. In companies with a full statutory two-tier status (*structuurvennootschappen*), only the supervisory board may adopt a resolution to remove a director.

(c) *Directors' liability to third parties*

The basic rule of corporate law in the Netherlands is that creditors of a company cannot demand performance of a contract from parties other than the company itself. In practice, a number of exceptions exist, for instance in the case of mismanagement. In a landmark case concerning a company called Ceteco NV that was listed on the EuroNEXT stock exchange, the district court of Utrecht pierced the corporate veil and found the managing directors of the company and the members of its supervisory board, next to a majority shareholder, jointly and severally liable for the deficit at the date of bankruptcy of the company. According to this judgment, even the fact that managing directors do not adapt corporate procedures and the number and quality of staff to match corporate growth might lead to liability. The judgment is open for appeal. According to case law from the Dutch Supreme Court, personal liability occurs when managing directors knew or should have known that a company was unable to meet its obligations.

(d) *Non-competition*

Neither corporate law nor employment law provides for a special form of post-contractual reasonableness and fairness between the former parties to a contract. Therefore, the use of non-compete clauses is widespread in the Netherlands and the clauses are generally upheld by Dutch courts of justice. Non-compete clauses and the inseparable penalty clauses may not be upheld in certain cases (eg where the penalty is not in proportion to the potential damage to a company or the clause is effective for a long period (ie more than one year)).

(e) *Duty of secrecy and loyalty*

The duration of clauses in employment contracts that obligate an employee/

managing director to not disclose confidential information do not need to be restricted (see section 9.2(d) above).

(f) Civil and criminal liability: legislative framework and consequences

Both a company and its managing director(s) can commit criminal offences. A criminal offence committed by a company can also impose criminal liability on the director who ordered the act on behalf of the company. A director who is aware of an offence and who has the authority to act but who refrains from doing so can also be criminally liable. Next to the managing directors, other natural persons who exercise control over the day-to-day management of the company may also become liable (see section 9.2(c) above).

9.3 Others

(a) Attorneys

Even micro-cap companies usually have in-house lawyers. In-house lawyers have been admitted to the bar since January 1997, though this is currently still an exception. Court proceedings are generally handled by external lawyers.

(b) Controllers and internal auditors

The accounts departments of most larger companies in the Netherlands are headed by controllers who help the managing directors of a company to prepare financial statements. Except for small and group companies, financial statements must be audited by an external auditor.

10. Fiscal year, duration and start of activities

The fiscal year of a company may differ from the calendar year. In some types of businesses a fiscal year that coincides with the calendar year may even be an exception. However, most Dutch companies have a fiscal year that coincides with the calendar year. Activities of a company can be started directly after the registration of the company with the trade register of a Chamber of Commerce, as activities before this date render the managing directors of the company jointly and severally liable for any obligations created before registration.

11. Financial statements

11.1 Company tax

Corporate profits below €40,000 are currently (2009) taxed at a rate of 20%, corporate profits between €40,000 and €200,000 are taxed at a rate of 23% and corporate profits above this are taxed at a rate of 25.5%. The Netherlands is known for its many favourable tax treaties, and the ease with which the taxation of certain profits have been capped has resulted in bilateral negotiations with the tax authorities known as 'tax rulings'. Please consult a tax advisor before creating or amending a corporate structure to avoid any tax leakage.

11.2 Annual accounts

Each company needs to draw up annual accounts within five months after its fiscal year has ended. This deadline can only be postponed once, for six months. Companies listed on the EuroNEXT stock exchange must draw up their annual accounts in line with the International Financial Reporting Standards.

(a) Documents

Annual accounts (*jaarrekening*) consist of a balance sheet (*balans*) and explanatory notes (*toelichting*). Next to the annual accounts an annual report (*jaarrekening*) must be drawn up, within which comments are included regarding the state of affairs on the balance sheet date and any expected developments in the period beyond this date.

(b) Audit report

The audit report (*accountantsverklaring*) is to be issued by a chartered accountant (*registeraccountant*) or by a specially qualified accounting consultant (*Accountant-Administratieconsulent*). Small and group companies do not need to audit their annual accounts provided that – in relation to group companies – the financial position and the financial results of the company are included in a consolidated balance sheet of the main corporate entity within the group and that entity has filed a so-called declaration pursuant to Article 2:403 of the Dutch Civil Code. The declaration causes the main legal entity to become liable for all the group companies in respect of which such a declaration has been made.

(c) Approval and distribution of profits/withholding tax

Once the management of a company has drawn up annual accounts, a general meeting of shareholders is required to approve and adopt the annual accounts. The general meeting of shareholders also needs to adopt a resolution to either distribute profits to the shareholders or to allocate profits to the company's reserve fund. Profits can only be distributed where the company's shareholders' equity exceeds the share capital and the statutory reserves. Profits may also be distributed in kind. Interim dividends can only be distributed where this is permitted in the articles of association.

A withholding tax of 15% is imposed on dividends. In general, the tax withheld may be credited against the corporate income tax liability of the recipient. In general, the participation exemption is applicable if a Dutch company owns at least 5% of the nominal paid-up capital of the subsidiary. No Dutch withholding tax needs to be withheld if the participation exemption applies to the recipient. If the recipient is a company domiciled within the European Union and subject to corporate income tax, no dividend withholding tax is due if the recipient owns at least 5% of the capital. In certain situations the withholding tax could be decreased or nullified if a tax treaty is applicable – in general this applies if the recipient is a company that owns at least 25% of the capital in the Dutch company. There is no withholding tax on interest or royalties in the Netherlands.

(d)   *Deposit and publicity*
Within eight days of the annual accounts having been approved and adopted by the general meeting of shareholders, the annual accounts, the annual report and the audit report need to be made publicly available by filing them with the trade register of the Chamber of Commerce. Again, group companies do not need to file such documents as long as the conditions referred to above are met. Small companies need only publish a simplified balance sheet.

12.   Company reorganisation: transformation, merger and split-off
An NV can be easily converted to a BV and likewise a BV may be converted into an NV or an SE. These types of company can also be converted into a foundation, an association, or a cooperative society. These latter legal forms can also be converted (back) to a BV or an NV. Any conversion requires the prior approval of a district court since any of the conversions might entail a change of control and a change of ownership which are delicate topics.

Based on EU law, Dutch corporate law provides for the possibility of a merger or split-off of companies. Recently, legislation has been implemented to facilitate international mergers. In the case of a merger, all assets and liabilities will be transferred under universal title to the acquiring company. When a certain part or business of a company is split off to form a new corporate entity, both the new corporate entity and the existing company are liable for all liabilities existing on the date on which the split-off is effected.

13.   Eventual partner separation
Most joint-venture entities have articles of association that reflect the joint-venture character of the entity and, secondly, all shareholders of such entities will usually create a separate shareholders' agreement. It is highly advisable to draw up a shareholders' agreement since shares in a non-listed corporate entity are usually quite illiquid; and, in the case of a separation in combination with a conflict between the partners/shareholders the price of the shares that are to be transferred is one of the classic matters that cause a dispute.

Partner separation in cases of conflict that occur without a contractual basis will usually lead to court proceedings. This can take up to two years to resolve, perhaps even longer. A judgment may typically order a shareholder to transfer his shares to another shareholder. An extrajudicial solution is to apply a split-off; this solution works best for holding companies.

14.   Dissolution and liquidation
The general meeting of shareholders can adopt a resolution to dissolve the company. Dutch corporate law does not require such a resolution to be adopted with a special majority, although many articles of association require a qualified majority of the votes cast at a meeting of shareholders that has been convened for the purpose. The Dutch Chamber of Commerce has the power to dissolve inactive companies.

The liquidation of a company will be executed by one or more liquidators appointed by the general meeting of shareholders. The liquidators have the responsibility of using the sales proceeds of all the assets of the company to pay all debts and, more broadly, to meet all of the company's liabilites. A custodian must also be appointed by the general meeting of shareholders. The custodian needs to keep the books, records and other data carriers of the company for seven years after the company has ceased to exist.

The dissolution and liquidation of a company must be published in a nationally distributed newspaper. The company will cease to exist after all assets known to the liquidators have been distributed.

15. Branches

A company may have several branches other than its principal place of business. Activities carried out in the branch offices of a company will not lead to a different liability position of the company; usually the same general conditions apply to all of its business activities and its liability is capped by the level of the shareholders' equity in the company. Certain creditors may nevertheless demand a superior position by requesting a bank guarantee, a right of pledge, or a right of mortgage in relation to continuing performance contracts.

Nigeria

L Fubara Anga
ÆLEX

---

1. Types of company with limited liability and applicable legislation

Nigerian companies may be broadly classified into private and public companies. Any company, whether private or public, may be limited by shares or limited by guarantee.

Private and public companies limited by shares are companies in which the liability of shareholders is limited to the amount outstanding, if any, on the shares they hold. Once a member has fully paid up his shares, he no longer has any liability in the event of the company being wound up. The liability of the members of private and public companies limited by guarantee is limited to the amount that they have undertaken to contribute in the event of the company being wound up.

A company limited by shares must have a share capital, whereas a company limited by guarantee is not required to have a share capital.

Private and public companies limited by shares are established for commercial purposes and for the distribution of profits to their members. In contrast, private and public companies limited by guarantee are established for the promotion of commerce, art, science, religion, sports, culture, education, research, charity or other similar purposes. The income of companies limited by guarantee is to be applied solely towards the promotion of their purpose, and no part of it may be paid or transferred directly or indirectly to the members.

Furthermore, in the event of the winding-up of a company limited by guarantee, any property or assets remaining after the company's debts have been discharged must not be distributed among the members, but must instead be transferred to another company limited by guarantee with a similar purpose. This is in contrast to a company limited by shares, whose property upon winding-up will be applied in satisfaction of its liabilities and then, subject to such application and any contrary provisions in the articles of association, will be distributed among the members according to their rights and interests in the company.

There is also a form of business organisation known as a limited partnership. This is not a company in the strict sense of the word. It is an organisation consisting of not more than 20 persons, one or more of whom are general partners liable for all debts and obligations of the organisation, and one or more of whom are limited partners, whose liability is limited to the extent of their contributions. The limited partnership must be registered in the Register of Limited Partnerships.

The Companies and Allied Matters Act (Chapter C20) Laws of the Federation of Nigeria 2004 (CAMA) is the primary statute regulating the establishment and administration of all company affairs and activities. The following regulations are issued pursuant thereto:

- the Companies Proceedings Rules 1992; and
- the Companies Winding up Rules 2001.

Other relevant statutes and regulations include:
- the Investment and Securities Act No 13 2007;
- the Nigeria Investment Promotion Commission Act (Chapter N117) Laws of the Federation of Nigeria 2004;
- the Companies Income Tax Act (Chapter C21) Laws of the Federation of Nigeria 2004;
- the Insurance Act (Chapter I17) Laws of the Federation of Nigeria 2004 and its subsidiary legislation; and
- the Immigration Act (Chapter I1) Laws of the Federation of Nigeria 2004 and its subsidiary legislation.

2. Incorporation procedure

2.1 Proceedings prior to incorporation

(a) Corporate name
The first step is to conduct a name availability search and reserve the proposed name of the company at the Corporate Affairs Commission by filing the prescribed form and paying the prescribed fee. If the name is available and acceptable, the commission will issue a statement of availability. The name will be reserved for such a period as the commission deems fit, up to a maximum of 60 days. During this period, no other company will be registered under the reserved name or any other name that, in the opinion of the commission, bears too close a resemblance to the reserved name.

(b) Indirect taxes, incorporation fees and other levies
The official fees that must be paid in the course of incorporation are as follows:
- the Corporate Affairs Commission registration fee, at approximately 1% of the nominal capital; and
- stamp duty at the Stamp Duties Office, at approximately 0.75% of the nominal capital.

Professional fees for incorporation vary and depend on the rates of the solicitor undertaking the incorporation procedures. The fees are negotiable. The notarisation fees of a notary public or commissioner of oaths are usually nominal.

(c) Registration with the companies registry
The companies registry in Nigeria is the Corporate Affairs Commission.

To incorporate a company in Nigeria, the following documents must be submitted to the commission, together with evidence of payment of stamp duty and the registration fee:

- the memorandum and articles of association;
- notice of the address of the registered office of the company, and the head office if different from the registered office (a postal box or private mailbag address is not acceptable);
- a statement in the prescribed form containing the list and particulars, together with the consent, of the persons who are to be the first directors of the company;
- a statement of the authorised share capital signed by at least one director;
- any other document required by the commission to satisfy the requirements of any law relating to the formation of a company; and
- a statutory declaration in the prescribed form by a legal practitioner that the requirements of CAMA for the registration of a company have been complied with.

Upon receipt of these documents, the commission will register the memorandum and articles unless, in its opinion:

- they do not comply with the provisions of CAMA;
- the business that the company is to carry on, or the purpose for which it is formed, is illegal;
- a subscriber to the memorandum is incompetent or disqualified under CAMA;
- there is non-compliance with a requirement of any other law regarding registration and incorporation of a company; or
- the proposed name conflicts with, or is likely to conflict with, an existing trademark or business name registered in Nigeria.

Anyone aggrieved by a decision of the Corporate Affairs Commission may give notice to the commission requiring it to apply to the court for directions, which the commission must do within 21 days of receipt of such notice.

Upon registration of the memorandum and the articles of association, the commission will certify under its seal that:

- the company is incorporated;
- in the case of a limited company, the liability of the members is limited;
- in the case of an unlimited company, the liability of the members is unlimited; and
- the company is private or public, as the case may be.

(d) Bylaws

Subject to CAMA, the memorandum and articles of association, when registered, have the effect of a contract under seal between the company and its members and officers, and between the members and officers themselves, whereby they agree to observe and perform the provisions contained therein.

(i) Essential clauses

The memorandum of association must include the following information:

- the name of the company;

- that the registered office of the company shall be situated in Nigeria;
- the nature of the business that the company is authorised to carry out;
- any restrictions on the powers of the company;
- whether the company is private or public;
- the share capital of the company (not being less than N10,000 in the case of a private company and N500,000 in the case of a public company); and
- the number of shares that each subscriber to the memorandum will take (the cumulative value of which shall not be less than 25% of the authorised share capital) – each subscriber must write his name opposite the number of shares he takes.

The articles of association must be signed by the subscribers to the memorandum of association. The articles contain the regulations for the management of the company. Its clauses regulate such matters as:

- classes of shares;
- restrictions on the transfer of shares and pre-emptive rights of existing shareholders (in the case of a private company);
- commissions and brokerage;
- increases and reductions in capital;
- meetings;
- voting;
- use of company seals; and
- notices.

The articles of association must be stamped as a deed.

(ii)   *Clauses not foreseen by law*
Where CAMA makes no express provision for certain circumstances, the shareholders are free to include the relevant regulations in the articles of association.

(iii)   *Optional clauses governed by law*
CAMA prescribes default clauses in several instances and permits the shareholders to modify these clauses in the articles. For example, CAMA states that unless the articles provide otherwise, the quorum for directors' meetings shall be two where there are not more than six directors and one-third of the directors where there are more than six. CAMA similarly provides that unless otherwise provided in the articles, the quorum for the general meeting shall be one-third of the members or 25 members (whichever is less), present in person or by proxy.

(iv)   *Standard format for memorandum and articles*
The Corporate Affairs Commission has recently introduced a standard format for memorandum and articles of association with effect from 2009.
The features of the new format are as follows:

- The objects of the company stated in the memorandum of association should not exceed five;

- The relevant provisions of the articles of association stated in Table A of Schedule 1 of CAMA are incorporated into the articles of association of the company by ticking the relevant box on the first page of the new format subject to additions, omissions and alterations; and
- Any additions, alterations and omissions to the provisions of the articles of association stated in Table A of Schedule 1 of CAMA should not exceed one page.

(e)   Execution of public deed

A company must have a common seal, the use of which is regulated by the articles of association.

Anyone who has dealings with a company is entitled to assume that a document has been duly sealed by the company if it bears what purports to be the company seal attested to by two persons purporting to be a director and the secretary of the company.

Any contract that, if executed between individuals, would be legally required to be in writing under seal, or that could be varied or discharged only in writing under seal, must be made, varied or discharged, as the case may be, in writing under the company seal.

However, a document or proceeding requiring authentication by a company may be signed by a director, secretary or other authorised officer, and need not be under its common seal unless otherwise required by law or the terms of the agreement.

Prior to incorporation, a legal practitioner must attest on oath before a notary public or commissioner of oaths that all requirements of the law in respect of incorporation have been complied with. No further intervention or participation is required by a notary public or a commissioner of oaths. The costs of notarisation are usually nominal.

(f)   Legalisation of official books

CAMA requires companies to keep the following registers:
- register of members;
- index of members, where the number of members exceeds 50;
- register of substantial shareholders (ie holders of at least 10% of the share capital), where the company is a public company;
- register of charges;
- register of debenture holders;
- register of directors' interests; and
- register of directors and secretaries.

However, there are no requirements as to formal legalisation of the registers. The registers constitute prima facie evidence of the content contained therein and may not be amended except by order of the court.

(g)   Declaration of foreign investment

A company with foreign participation must register with the Nigerian Investment

Promotion Commission. Upon registration, the company obtains a business permit. The company may also obtain expatriate quotas through the commission, which allows it to employ foreign nationals.

Companies with foreign investment can freely transfer profits and dividends, repay foreign loans and repatriate capital. In order to remit these funds at the official foreign exchange rate, the foreign investor should have obtained from a bank a certificate of capital importation that confirms the initial importation of foreign capital.

(h)   *Tax number for foreign partners/directors*

Non-resident shareholders and directors are liable to pay tax on Nigeria-sourced income. However, tax identification numbers are not issued, as the tax is deducted at source by the company. Expatriates employed in Nigeria are also liable to pay tax on Nigeria-sourced income.

(i)   *Tax identification number*

Upon incorporation, the Corporate Affairs Commission allocates an incorporation number to the company. Thereafter, the company must register with the tax authority (the Federal Inland Revenue Service). As part of the registration process, a unique 14-digit tax identification number is issued.

3.   Company membership

Members of a company include subscribers to the memorandum of association and persons who have agreed in writing to become members of the company. The prima facie proof of membership of a company is entry of the member's name in the register of members. In Nigeria, anyone who has the capacity to enter into a contract may become a member of a company, excluding persons declared to be of unsound mind, corporate bodies in liquidation and undischarged bankrupts. While a person under the age of 18 years may become a member of a company, he will not be counted for the purpose of determining the legal minimum number of members.

Under Nigerian law, foreign nationals can own up to 100% of the authorised share capital of a company, as long as the business the company intends to carry on is not on the 'negative' list (ie production of arms and ammunition, production of uniforms for military and paramilitary services, and the production of and dealing in drugs and narcotics). Businesses included in the negative list are prohibited to both Nigerian and foreign investors.

The carrying on of any business for profit or gain by a group of more than 20 persons – whether as a company, association or partnership (excluding any cooperative society registered under the provisions of any law in force in Nigeria, or any partnership of legal practitioners or accountants) is prohibited unless the group is registered as a company under CAMA or pursuant to any other law in force in Nigeria.

Further, no company – whether public (limited by shares or by guarantee) or private (limited by shares or by guarantee) – may have fewer than two members. The total number of members in a private company may not exceed 50. There are no restrictions on the maximum number of members that a public company may have.

4. Corporate name – limitations

The name of a private company limited by shares must end with the word 'Limited' or 'Ltd'. The name of a public company limited by shares must end with the words 'Public Limited Company' or 'PLC'. The name of a company limited by guarantee must end with the words '(Limited by Guarantee)' in parentheses or '(Ltd/Gte)'.

No company may be registered under a name that:

- is identical to that under which an existing company is already registered;
- so closely resembles that of an existing company as to be calculated to deceive, except where the existing company is in the course of being dissolved and signifies its consent;
- contains the words 'chamber of commerce', unless it is a company limited by guarantee;
- is capable of being misleading as to the nature or extent of the company's activities, or is undesirable, offensive or otherwise contrary to public policy; or
- would violate an existing trademark or business name registered in Nigeria, unless the consent of the owner of the trademark or business name has been obtained.

Except with the consent of the Corporate Affairs Commission, no company is to be registered under a name that:

- includes the word 'federal', 'national', 'regional', 'state', 'government' or any other word suggesting or calculated to suggest that the company enjoys the patronage of the federal government or a Nigerian state, or any governmental ministry or department;
- contains the words 'municipal' or 'chartered', or suggests or is calculated to suggest a connection with any municipality or other local authority;
- contains the word 'cooperative' or 'building society'; or
- contains the word 'group' or 'holding'.

A company that breaches these provisions will be directed to change its name.

5. Corporate domicile

The registered office of all Nigerian companies must be situated in Nigeria.

6. Corporate purpose

The corporate purpose of a company must be stated in the memorandum of association. A company limited by shares may carry on any lawful business for the purpose of making a profit. For a company limited by guarantee, the corporate purpose must involve the promotion of commerce, science, art, religion, sports, culture, education, research, charity or other similar purposes, and profits derived must be applied solely towards the promotion of this purpose.

A company is prohibited from carrying on any business not authorised by the memorandum or exceeding its powers under the memorandum or CAMA. This notwithstanding, no act of a company, and no conveyance or transfer of property to or by a company, shall be invalid merely because such act, conveyance or transfer was not done or made in furtherance of any of the authorised business of the company, or because the company otherwise exceeded its purpose or powers. A company will not escape liability to third parties for an act merely because such act was not done in furtherance of the business objects specified in the company's memorandum of association.

7. Capital stock

7.1 Minimum capital requirement

For private and public companies without foreign shareholders, the law prescribes the minimum authorised share capital as N10,000 and N500,000 respectively. For companies with foreign shareholders, the minimum authorised share capital is N10,000,000 (Exchange rate as at January 2009: N147 to US$1).

7.2 Nature of contributions

Shares may be paid for either in cash or in kind, or through a mix of cash and in-kind contributions.

Where an in-kind contribution is made, the company must appoint an independent valuer to determine the true value of the consideration and furnish the company with a report accordingly. Within three days of receiving this report, the company must send a copy to the proposed purchaser and indicate whether it will accept the consideration.

7.3 Partial payments

It is possible for shares to be allotted but not paid for immediately. A company may, from time to time, make calls upon members in respect of any monies unpaid on their shares. However, no call may exceed one-quarter of the nominal value of the shares; nor may a call be made within one month of a previous call.

7.4 Representation of shares

Share certificates must be issued within two months of subscription or within three months of the date on which a share transfer is lodged with the company. A share certificate should bear the company's common seal and identify the shares to which it relates and the amount paid on them.

7.5 Transfer of shares

(a) Restrictions

All private companies must restrict the transfer of shares through provisions in the articles of association.

The first schedule of CAMA provides templates for the memorandum and articles of association. They contain clauses to the effect that, in a private company:
- the directors may, in their absolute discretion and without giving any reason, refuse to register any share transfer, irrespective of whether the shares are fully paid; and

- the company will not allocate any new or unissued shares unless these are offered in the first instance to all shareholders or to all shareholders in the class or classes being issued, in proportion to their existing holdings.

(b) Formalities

The transfer of shares is effected by an instrument of transfer and, except as expressly provided in the articles, shall be without restrictions. The instrument of transfer must be executed by or on behalf of the transferor and transferee; the transferor is still considered the shareholder up until the name of the transferee is entered in the register of members.

On the application of the transferor of any share or interest in a company, the company will enter the name of the transferee in its register of members. The company may not register the share transfer unless a proper instrument of transfer is delivered to the company.

8. Equity

8.1 Equity–capital ratio

There are no statutory stipulations as to what proportion of a company's capital must be constituted by equity. The law requires merely that at any point in time at least 25% of the authorised share capital must have been issued. Where the share capital is increased, this obligation must be met within six months of the increase. It is not mandatory that issued shares be paid for in full at allotment.

8.2 Convertible bonds

A company may issue debentures, debenture stock and other securities in respect of money borrowed for the purpose of its business or corporate purpose. Within 60 days of allocation of the debentures, the company must deliver to the debenture holder either the debenture or a certificate of the debenture stock bearing the company's common seal.

A company may also offer debentures to the public for subscription or purchase. Before doing so, the company must execute a debenture trust deed in respect of the debentures and procure the execution of the deed by the trustee for the debenture holders appointed by the deed.

Each debenture trust deed must state, among other things, in the case of convertible debentures, the dates and terms on which the debentures may be converted into shares, and the amounts that may be credited as paid in on those shares in rights of the debentures held by them.

9. Administration

The corporate governing bodies are the general meeting and the board of directors. The directors are responsible for the day-to-day running of the company. The general meeting makes resolutions to enable the directors to carry out functions for which resolutions of the general meeting are a precondition. The general meeting is the ultimate decision-making body of the company.

9.1   General meeting

There are three types of general meeting through which members may take decisions.

(a)   *Statutory general meetings*

These must be held by each public company within six months of the date of incorporation. At least 21 days prior to the date of the meeting, the directors must forward to every member a copy of the company's statutory report, stating:

- the total number of shares allotted, distinguishing them as fully or partly paid in otherwise than in cash and, in the case of shares partly paid up, the extent to which they are so paid in, and in either case the consideration for which they have been allotted;
- the total amount of cash received by the company in respect of all shares allotted, distinguished as above;
- the names, addresses and descriptions of the directors, auditors, managers (if any), and secretary of the company;
- the particulars of any pre-incorporation contract, together with details of any modification or proposed modification thereof;
- any underwriting contract that has not been carried out and the reasons why;
- the arrears (if any) due on calls from each director; and
- the particulars of any commission or brokerage paid or payable in connection with the issue or sale of shares or debentures to any director or manager.

The report must contain an abstract of company receipts and payments made up until at least seven days before the report, showing under separate headings:

- receipts from shares and debentures and other sources;
- payments made from such receipts and the particulars of the remaining balance; and
- an account or estimate of the company's preliminary expenses.

Failure to comply will render the company and any officer in default guilty of an offence and liable to a fine.

The statutory meeting must be held in Nigeria.

(b)   *Annual general meetings*

These must be held annually in Nigeria; in any event, no more than 15 months may elapse between one annual general meeting and the next. This timeframe may be extended, upon application to the Corporate Affairs Commission, by a period not exceeding three months.

The business that may be transacted at the annual general meeting may be classified as ordinary business and special business. Ordinary business comprises the following:

- declaration of dividends;
- presentation of financial statements and the reports of the directors and auditors;

- election of directors to replace those retiring;
- appointment of the auditors and determination of their remuneration; and
- appointment of the members of the audit committee.

(c)   ***Extraordinary general meetings***

These include all general meetings of the company other than the statutory meeting and the annual general meeting. They may be held outside Nigeria. All business transacted at an extraordinary general meeting shall be presumed to be special business. Full and proper notice of at least 21 days must be given of an extraordinary general meeting and the proposed special business to be conducted at the meeting.

(d)   ***Quorum requirements***

(i)   *Attendance*

Unless the articles of association provide otherwise, the quorum for a company meeting is either one-third of all of members of the company or 25 members present in person or by proxy (whichever is less).

Where the number of members is not evenly divisible by three, the number closest to one-third will suffice as a quorum; where there are six members or fewer, the quorum is two members.

Unless otherwise stated in the articles, if a quorum is lost during the course of a meeting due to the withdrawal of members for what the chairman considers to be insufficient reasons, the meeting may continue with the numbers present and any decisions taken will be binding on all members.

On the other hand, if members withdraw during the meeting for sufficient reasons, the meeting will be adjourned to reconvene at the same time and place one week later; if there is still no quorum at the adjourned meeting, those members present will constitute a quorum and their decisions will be binding on all members.

In both instances, if only one member is left after withdrawal, that member may seek the direction of the court.

(ii)   *Voting*

Proposals put before a general meeting are adopted by either ordinary resolution or special resolution.

An ordinary resolution is passed by simple majority of votes cast by members attending a general meeting either in person or by proxy. A special resolution is passed by a majority of at least 75% at a general meeting where at least 21 days' notice specifying the intention to pass a special resolution was given.

(iii)   *Challenging resolutions*

Resolutions passed during a general meeting that contravene the law or the memorandum and articles of association may be challenged by any member or director and, in some instances, by creditors or debenture holders or liquidators (where the company is being wound up).

9.2 Administrative body

(a) Different systems of administration

Unless the articles of association provide otherwise, the business of the company is to be managed by the board of directors. The board may exercise its powers through committees or may appoint a managing director from within the board and delegate all or some of its powers to the managing director.

(b) Term of office, resignation and removal of directors

Unless the articles of association provide otherwise, all directors must retire from office at the first annual general meeting. At each subsequent annual general meeting, one-third of the directors must retire; where the number of directors is not divisible by three, then the closest number to one-third shall retire. The directors to retire every year are those who have been longest in office; where persons became directors on the same day, those to retire are determined by lot.

A director may be appointed for life.

A director may resign from office by giving written notice to the company.

Notwithstanding any provisions to the contrary in the articles of association, or any agreement between the company and the director, a director may be removed from office by ordinary resolution. Special notice is required before this resolution can be passed, and the company must forward a copy of the notice to the director to be removed. The director is entitled to defend himself before the resolution for removal is passed. A person appointed to fill the vacancy created by the removal of a director will be deemed to have become a director, for the purposes of determining when he must retire, on the day on which the person he replaces was last appointed as a director.

(c) Directors' liability to third parties

The company acts through its members in general meeting or through the board of directors. Thus, any act of the members in general meeting, or of the board of directors or managing director while carrying on the usual business of the company, shall be treated as an act of the company itself, and the company shall be liable for such act.

However, where a company receives money by way of loan for a specific purpose, or receives money or other property by way of an advance payment for the execution of a contract or project and, with the intent to defraud, fails to apply the money or property for the specified purpose, each director or officer who is in default shall be personally liable to the payer for refund of the money or property.

Where a company carries on business without having at least two members for a period of six months, each director or officer will thereafter be jointly and severally liable together with the company for company debts contracted during this period.

(d) Non-competition

CAMA contains no provisions on non-competition. However, it provides that the fact that a person holds more than one directorship does not derogate from his fiduciary duties to each company, including a duty not to use property, opportunities or information obtained in the course of the management of one company for the benefit of another, or for his own advantage or that of a third party.

(e) *Special duties of secrecy and loyalty*

In addition to the duty not to misuse company information, a director stands in a fiduciary relationship towards the company and must observe the utmost good faith towards the company in any transaction concluded with it or on its behalf. He must at all times act in what he believes to be in the best interests of the company so as to preserve its assets, further its business and promote the purposes for which it was formed, in such a manner as a diligent, careful and ordinarily skilful director would act in the circumstances. A director is prohibited from making secret profits or other secret benefit.

(f) *Civil and criminal liability*

A director is prohibited from making any secret benefit in respect of any transaction involving the company. Where he does so, he commits a breach of duty and the company is entitled to recover the benefit and then sue him for damages sustained, without any deduction in respect of what the director has returned.

Persons who are knowingly involved in carrying out business in a reckless manner or with the intent to defraud creditors or for any fraudulent purpose will be personally responsible for all or any debts of the company or other liabilities, such as the court may direct. They are also guilty of an offence and liable upon conviction to a fine or imprisonment.

9.3 Others

Every company must have a secretary. The company secretary may have an assistant. The directors must ensure that the company secretary has the requisite knowledge and experience to discharge the functions of his office. The secretary of a public company must be:

- a member of the Institute of Chartered Secretaries and Administrators;
- a legal practitioner;
- a member of the Institute of Chartered Accountants of Nigeria or such other bodies of accountants as are established from time to time by legislation;
- a person who has held the office of secretary of a public company for at least three of the five years preceding his appointment in a public company; or
- a body corporate or firm consisting of members who are each qualified under any of the above points.

There is no mandatory requirement that a company have a lawyer.

10. Fiscal year

The directors will determine the commencement and closing dates of the fiscal year. This is usually done at their first meeting following incorporation, during which the directors will determine the date each year up to which the company's financial statements will be prepared. Notice of this date must be given to the Corporate Affairs Commission within 14 days of its determination.

11. Financial statements

11.1 Company tax

A tax of 30% is currently (2009) chargeable on the profits of any taxable company accruing in, derived from, brought into or received in Nigeria. Where the true profits of the company cannot be readily ascertained, the tax authority may deem a proportion of the company's turnover to be its taxable profit. In practice, 20% of a company's turnover is usually deemed to be its taxable profit.

All taxable companies are required to file returns on their income with the Federal Inland Revenue Service within six months of the end of each accounting period. They must also calculate tax payable and pay such tax when forwarding their returns.

11.2 Annual accounts

(a) Documents

The directors must prepare financial statements for each fiscal year. The financial statements must include:

- a statement of the accounting policies;
- the balance sheet as at the last day of the fiscal year;
- a profit and loss account or, in the case of a non-profit company, an income and expenditure account for the year;
- notes on the accounts;
- the auditors' report;
- the directors' report;
- a statement of the source and application of funds;
- a value-added statement for the year;
- a five-year financial summary; and
- in the case of a holding company, the group financial statements.

CAMA further provides that at least once a year, all companies must make and deliver to the Corporate Affairs Commission an annual return in the form and containing the information required under CAMA.

The annual return of a company with shares, other than a small company, must include the following information with respect to the registered office:

- the registers of members and debenture holders;
- shares and debentures;
- indebtedness; and
- past and present members, and directors and secretary.

(b) Audit report

At the annual general meeting, each company must appoint an auditor or auditors to audit the financial statements and to hold office until the conclusion of the next annual general meeting.

The auditors will prepare a report on the accounts they examine, and on each balance sheet and profit and loss account, and on all group financial statements. Copies of this report must be presented to the company in general meeting during the auditors' tenure. The auditors' report must be countersigned by a legal practitioner and must expressly state the following:

- whether the auditors have obtained all information and explanations that, to the best of their knowledge and belief, were necessary for the purpose of the audit;
- whether, in their opinion, proper books of account have been kept by the company, so far as appears from their examination of the books, and proper returns adequate for the purposes of the audit have been received from the branches they have not visited;
- whether the balance sheet and profit and loss account accord with the books of accounts and returns;
- whether, in their opinion, and to the best of their information and according to the explanations given to them, the financial statements provide the information required under CAMA and give a fair view of the state of the company's affairs; and
- in the case of a holding company submitting group financial statements, whether, in their opinion, the group financial statements have been properly prepared in accordance with the provisions of CAMA so as to give a true and fair view of the state of affairs and profit or loss of the company and its subsidiaries.

(c)   ***Approval and distribution of profits***
A company may declare dividends in respect of any year or other period only on the recommendation of the directors. The company may, from time to time, pay the members such interim dividends as appear to the directors to be justified by the profits. The general meeting has the power to reduce the dividend amount recommended by the directors, but it cannot increase the recommended amount.

The company may pay dividends out of the following profits, subject to its being able to pay its debts as they fall due:

- profits arising from the use of company property that is a wasting asset;
- revenue reserves; and
- profits realised on a fixed asset sold or, where more than one asset is sold, the net profit realised on the assets sold.

A company must not pay or declare dividends if there are reasonable grounds to believe that, as a result of the payment, it would become unable to pay its liabilities as they fall due.

The company must deduct a withholding tax of 10% on dividends paid and remit the amount thus withheld to the appropriate tax authority. The tax remitted will be held by the tax authority as a credit for the recipient and may be offset against income tax due from that recipient. For non-resident shareholders and directors, however, the withholding tax is a final tax.

(d)   *Annual returns*

All registered companies must complete their annual returns within 42 days of the annual general meeting and forward them to the Corporate Affairs Commission. In the case of a company with share capital, the annual returns should include:

- the company name;
- the address of the registered office;
- the location of the registers of members and debenture holders;
- a summary of share capital and debentures;
- particulars of the company's indebtedness;
- a list of past and present members; and
- the particulars of the directors and secretary.

Annual returns must be accompanied by the following documents:

- a written copy, certified by a director and the company secretary to be a true copy, of every balance sheet and profit and loss account presented to the general meeting in the year to which the return relates; and
- a copy, certified as above, of the auditors' report on, and the directors' report accompanying, each balance sheet.

12.   Company reorganisation

12.1   Transformation

A private company may be transformed into a public company, and a company limited by shares may be transformed into an unlimited company, by submitting an application to the Corporate Affairs Commission in the prescribed form. The reverse is also possible in both cases. However, certain restrictions apply:

- a public company and a company that has previously been transformed from an unlimited company into a limited company cannot be transformed into an unlimited company;
- a company that has been previously transformed from a limited company into an unlimited company cannot be transformed back into a limited company; and
- an unlimited company cannot be registered as a public company or a company limited by guarantee.

In order for a company limited by shares to be transformed into an unlimited company, the company must pass a special resolution authorising the transformation and making the necessary amendments to the memorandum and articles of association. Where there is a transformation from a private company into a public company, the company must comply with the minimum share capital requirement for a public company and must issue at least 25% of its new authorised share capital.

12.2   Merger

Mergers and acquisitions are governed by the Investment and Securities Act. There are three classes of mergers: small, intermediate and large. All intermediate and large mergers are subject to the prior review and approval of the Securities and Exchange Commission (SEC). The SEC may also direct parties to a small merger to seek its approval for any merger that it considers may substantially prevent or lessen competition or is not in the public interest.

13. Eventual shareholder separation

In Nigeria, the separation of a shareholder may occur in the event of:

- forfeiture of shares;
- sale of his entire shareholding;
- winding-up; or
- merger or acquisition.

Where a shareholder fails to pay any call or instalment of a call on his shares, the company's directors may issue a notice in writing to such shareholder demanding payment of the outstanding sums within a period not less than 14 days from the date of service of such notice. Where the shareholder fails to make payment as directed in the notice, his shares shall be liable to forfeiture.

Where a shareholder divests himself of his entire shareholding, he ceases to be a member of the company.

The winding-up process is explained in section 14 below.

In the case of merger or acquisition, a shareholder may dissent from the arrangement. Where such dissent is signified, the shares of that member may be purchased at fair market value by the acquiring or newly formed company.

14. Dissolution and liquidation

The winding-up of a company may be voluntary or involuntary.

A company may be wound up by the court in the following circumstances:

- if the company has resolved by special resolution that the company be wound up by the court;
- in a case of default in delivering the statutory report to the Corporate Affairs Commission or in holding the statutory meeting;
- if the number of members is reduced to fewer than two;
- if the company is unable to pay its debts; or
- if the court is of the opinion that it is just and equitable that the company be wound up.

The petition for winding-up may be presented to the court by:

- the company;
- a creditor;
- the official receiver;
- a contributory;
- a trustee in bankruptcy to or a personal representative of a creditor or contributory;
- the Corporate Affairs Commission; or
- a receiver, if authorised by the instrument under which he was appointed.

A company may be voluntarily wound up:

- when the period (if any) fixed for its duration under the articles expires, or an event occurs that the articles provide will cause the company to dissolved, and the general meeting passes a resolution requiring the company to be wound up voluntarily;
- if the company resolves by special resolution that the company should be wound up voluntarily; or
- by its creditors.

The body with the power to appoint a liquidator depends on the method of winding-up. Upon the appointment of a liquidator, the powers of the directors cease.

15. Branches

CAMA does not provide for separate legal personality of company branches. There is joint liability between a branch and its headquarters, and any purported claims against a branch should be directed to the head office.

Norway

Marte Solberg
Øystein A Sverre
Brækhus Dege Advokatfirma ANS

1. Types of company with limited liability and applicable legislation

Norwegian corporate law is based on two acts: the Act on Private Limited Companies and the Act on Public Limited Companies. Both acts were passed by Parliament on June 13 1997 and took effect on January 1 1999. The two acts are largely similar in structure and content, and they are divided into the same chapters. Where this chapter makes reference to a statutory provision, that provision applies to both corporate forms unless otherwise indicated.

Upon incorporation, founders of a business entity select the corporate form through which they wish to carry out their business activities. Small companies are normally organised as private limited companies, while large companies often choose to establish themselves as public limited companies. Companies wishing to conduct business as a public limited company must expressly state this in the articles of association. Where a private limited company is formed, Chapter 15 of the Act on Private Limited Companies regulates how conversion to a public limited company may be effected.

The main differences between private limited companies and public limited companies are as follows:

- Only public limited companies may invite subscriptions from the general public in order to obtain new share capital. A private limited company must issue shares to a limited and identified group of investors.
- The minimum share capital of a private limited company is NOK100,000 while for public limited companies it is NOK1 million. The total registered share capital must be paid in before the company can be registered in the company register.
- As a general rule, the shares in a public limited company are freely negotiable. The articles of association may stipulate that the consent of the board of directors is required for all share transfers, and that the shareholders have a right of first refusal when ownership to shares is transferred.
- The acquisition of shares in a private limited company requires the consent of the board of directors, although the articles of association can stipulate that such consent is not necessary. Unless the bylaws provide otherwise, the shareholders in a private limited company have a right of first refusal when ownership to shares is transferred.
- The shares and shareholders of a public limited company must be registered in the Norwegian register of securities. This is optional for a private limited company.

- Up to half of the share capital of a public limited company may take the form of non-voting shares or shares with limited voting powers. A private limited company can freely limit the voting rights of its shares.
- The formation rules and procedures for private limited companies and public limited companies are largely identical. However, the documentation requirements regarding in-kind capital contributions are greater for public liability companies, both at formation and when increasing equity.
- In certain cases, a shareholder in a private limited company can demand that the company redeem his shares. A public limited company can, subject to approval from the Ministry of Justice, redeem small shareholdings (less than NOK500).
- In a private limited company with fewer than 20 shareholders, the board can convene a general meeting without the shareholders being present. However, if a shareholder objects to this procedure, a general meeting must be held. In a public limited company, a general shareholders' meeting must be held in order to adopt valid resolutions.
- There are different requirements regarding the constitution of the board of directors and for the management.
- In general, more stringent requirements regarding equity, accounting and financial reporting apply to public limited companies than to private limited companies.

2. Incorporation procedure

The only legal way in which to incorporate a private limited company or a public limited company is by 'simultaneous formation'. Simultaneous formation means that the drafting of the memorandum of association and the subscription of shares take place at the same time. All of the share capital must be paid in before the company can be registered in the company register. Registration papers must be submitted to the Company Registry within three months of incorporation. If the company pays its own incorporation costs, these costs must be paid in by the subscribers as a premium in addition to the share capital.

The share capital and other equity can be paid either in cash or in kind, both at formation and upon subsequent capital increases. The valuation procedures applicable to in-kind contributions are quite rigorous.

2.1 Proceedings prior to incorporation

(a) Corporate name

It is not possible to register a company name prior to registration of the company itself. In some instances, the name may be registered as a trademark. Interested parties can make an inquiry to the Company Registry to find out whether a name is legal or already in use. If the name is already in use, the company cannot be registered under the same name.

(b) **Capital contributions**
Contributions to the company equity cannot be made before the formation meeting. Normally, the equity is committed at the formation meeting and paid in during the first couple of weeks after the meeting.

(c) **Declaration of foreign investment**
There is no requirement to declare foreign investment at the time of formation.

(d) **Tax number for foreign directors**
Foreign individuals who are directors or employees of a Norwegian company must register for tax purposes in Norway. The Central Census Office will duly issue a so-called 'D-number' – an 11-digit number that incorporates the individual's date of birth.

2.2 Incorporation

(a) **Bylaws**

(i) *Essential clauses*
The bylaws must specify:
- the company's name;
- the municipality in which the company will have its office;
- a description of the company's corporate purpose and the business activities it will carry out;
- the amount of the share capital, the number of shares and the par value of one share;
- the exact number, or the minimum and maximum number, of directors on the board;
- whether the company will have more than one managing director;
- the matters that must be decided by the general meeting; and
- whether the company's shares will be entered in the Register of Securities.

(ii) *Clauses not foreseen by law*
The founders and shareholders of a company are at liberty to add to the articles of association more or less anything they wish. The most usual clause that is not required by law is one specifying when and how the shareholders' right of first refusal shall apply if ownership to shares is transferred.

(b) **Execution of public deed**
Once the formation meeting has been conducted and the equity has been paid in, the registration papers should be sent to the Company Registry in Brønnøysund. Upon registration, the Company Registry issues a company certificate or letter of good standing containing the key information registered and the company's organisation number.

(c)   **Tax identification number**

The National Register for Entities (which is separate from, although located in the same place as, the Company Registry) issues a nine-digit organisation number, which is used for identification for both tax and value added tax (VAT) purposes.

(d)   **Indirect taxes, incorporation fees and other levies**

To register a company with the Company Registry in Norway costs NOK6,000. In addition, there are legal fees and auditors' fees totalling from NOK10,000 upwards, depending on the complexity of the company to be incorporated and registered.

Whether a company must register for VAT purposes depends on the nature of the business conducted. Until 2001 the liability to pay VAT was mainly limited to the supply of goods. In July 2001 the government passed new regulations that also included the supply of services in the VAT regime.

The standard rate of VAT is currently (2009) 25%. However, the rate varies depending on the kind of service provided, down to 7% for airline tickets.

A VAT account must be filed every two months by the tenth day of the month after the month following the end of the two-month period (eg the January–February VAT account is due on April 10). In the VAT account, incoming (paid) VAT is deducted from outgoing (charged) VAT, and the balance is received or must be paid quickly after the account has been filed.

3.   Number of shareholders

There are no requirements regarding the minimum or maximum number of shareholders. A company can be the sole shareholder of another company, which is then a subsidiary of the first company.

4.   Corporate name – limitations

The name of a company cannot contain terms contrary to law or be offensive to the public. The name must be distinctive (ie not already in use by someone else).

The name of a private limited company must contain the designation *'Aksjeselskap'* or 'AS'.

The name of a public limited company must contain the designation *'Almenaksjeselskap'* or 'ASA'.

5.   Corporate domicile

The bylaws must specify the municipality in which the company's registered office will be located. This is normally where the company will be considered to have its domicile. A company can change its domicile by moving its offices to a new location. The bylaws should be changed accordingly.

6.   Corporate purpose

The corporate purpose must be stated in the bylaws. If the purpose changes or new business activities are initiated after incorporation, the bylaws must be changed accordingly.

7.   Capital stock

7.1   Minimum capital requirement

For a private limited company, the minimum share capital is NOK100,000. For a public limited company, the minimum share capital is NOK1 million.

7.2   Nature of contributions

Contributions are normally made by cash payment. However, in-kind contributions are also allowed; in such cases the company's auditor must confirm the value of the contribution.

7.3   Partial payments

The committed share capital must be paid in its entirety before the company can be registered.

7.4   Representation of shares

Norway abolished share certificates with the Companies Acts of 1999.

Private limited companies are now obliged to keep an updated log of all issued stock. The log must show the name, address and date of birth of each shareholder, as well as the number of shares and percentage of shares held. The log must be available at all times at the company's premises. It is the board of directors' responsibility to ensure that the log is kept up to date at all times.

Public limited companies are obliged to subscribe to the register of securities, which contains the same information as the logs of private limited companies.

7.5   Transfer of shares

(a)   Restrictions

Unless the bylaws provide otherwise, the board of a private limited company must approve all transfers of shares. In contrast, the shares of a public limited company are freely transferable, unless the bylaws provide otherwise.

When the share capital is increased in a public or private limited company, the existing shareholders have a right of first refusal to subscribe to the new shares.

The bylaws can contain a clause granting a right of first refusal to existing shareholders in cases of a transfer of ownership to one or more of the company shares.

(b)   Formalities

A shareholder who wishes to sell all or some of his shares in a private limited company must report the transfer to the board of directors, unless relieved of this duty by the bylaws. The board of directors may oppose the transfer if it finds that the transfer would be detrimental to the development of the company. Otherwise, the board must approve the transfer and enter the new owner of the shares in the shareholder log.

The shares of a public limited company are normally freely transferable. A copy of the contract note must be sent to the Registry of Securities for registration.

The bylaws of both types of company can include a clause granting a right of first refusal to existing shareholders in cases of a transfer of shares. Where such a clause is included, the transferor must notify the board of directors that he has received an offer on some or all of his shares. The board must then inform the other shareholders about the offer without undue delay. If a shareholder matches the offer, the transferor must transfer the shares in play to him; where more than one shareholder matches the offer, the shares in play are split between the offering shareholders in proportion to their previous holdings. The bylaws will specify deadlines for each step and can also deviate from this procedure.

8. Equity

8.1 Equity–capital ratio

The board of directors has a general duty to act if the equity drops below what must be considered a sound level, taking risks and the size of the company's business activity into account.

In this regard, an equity level below 50% of the share capital is always considered unacceptable, prompting the board to take action.

If the board finds the equity levels indefensible, the board must call a general meeting, inform the general meeting of the economic situation and suggest remedies. If the board of directors does not find grounds for proposing measures, or if such measures cannot be implemented, the board of directors must move that the company be dissolved.

8.2 Convertible bonds

The general meeting can decide, by a two-thirds majority, to enter into agreements on convertible loans. The conditions of the convertible loan must be decided by the general meeting. For a private limited company, only existing shareholders or specifically named persons and entities can be invited to participate in a convertible loan. A public limited company can invite the public or an undefined pool of investors to participate.

9. Administration

9.1 General shareholders' meeting

(a) Quorum requirements

(i) Attendance

If the general meeting has been legally called, there is no lower limit on the number of attendees to achieve a quorum.

(ii) Voting

The quorums for the adoption of resolutions are stated by law or the company's bylaws.

Normal resolutions, such as those on the election of board members or the acceptance of the annual accounts, are decided by simple majority of the shareholders, both in number and in value, present at the general meeting.

Changes to the bylaws must be approved by two-thirds of the shareholders, both in number and in value, present at the general meeting.

Resolutions that alter the rights of some shareholders (ie change the internal relationship between shares) must be approved unanimously by all shareholders of the company.

(b)   Challenging resolutions

A shareholder can challenge resolutions of the general shareholders' meeting before the Norwegian courts on the grounds that the resolution was made on an illegal basis – for example, because:

- the summons for the general meeting at which the resolution was adapted was illegal; or
- certain votes that were accepted should not, for legal reasons, have been accepted.

Mere disagreement with the content of a resolution does not constitute grounds to challenge it in the courts.

9.2   Administrative body

(a)   Different systems of administration

A public limited company must have at least three directors on the board. A private limited company can have a board consisting of one director with a registered alternate director. If the share capital of a private limited company is more than NOK3 million, the board must consist of at least three directors.

The board of directors is responsible for the day-to-day administration of the company. The board hires the managing director. It also adopts budgets, is responsible for the financial planning of the company and adopts business plans.

In wholly owned subsidiaries the importance of the board is diminished, as decisions are often made by other bodies such as the board of directors of the parent company. The subsidiary must still have a separate board of directors, which will take care of the minimum responsibilities imposed by law on the board of directors. The board of directors can issue proxies where this is permitted by the bylaws.

(b)   Rules on gender representation on company boards – public limited companies

In December 2003 the Norwegian Parliament passed an amendment to the Public Limited Companies Act, stating that public limited companies must have a gender balance in the companies' boards. The legislation was adopted by a large majority of the Parliament; only one party voted against.

By doing so, Norway was the first country in the world to demand gender balance within the boards of public limited companies.

The requirement of the gender representation law is that both sexes shall be represented on company boards as follows:

- If the board has two or three members, both genders must be represented;
- If the board has four or five members, each gender shall be represented by at least two representatives;
- If the board has six to eight members, each gender shall be represented by at least three representatives; and
- If the board has nine members, each gender shall be represented by at least four representatives, and if the board has more than nine members, each gender must make up at least 40 per cent of the representatives.

These rules also apply to the election of alternates.

For employee representatives there are special requirements. Where two or more board members are elected from among the employees, both genders must be represented; this also applies to alternates. However, this rule will not be applicable in companies where one of the genders represents less than 20% of the total number of employees on the date of the election.

If the board's composition does not meet the statutory requirements, the central company register will refuse to register the board.

A company that does not have a board that fulfils the statutory requirements may, according to the Public Limited Companies Act, be dissolved by order of the court.

(c)   *Term of office, resignation and removal of directors*

Directors of the board are elected by the general shareholders' meeting for two-year periods. If a new director is not elected as a replacement at the end of this term, the director continues in this post indefinitely. He can resign from the board mid-term simply by issuing a letter to the Company Registry or by writing to the general meeting stating that he will resign after the next general meeting.

The bylaws can deviate from these rules. In some companies, the chairman of the board is appointed by the shareholders' meeting, while in others the board constitutes itself after it has been elected.

At least half the members of the board and the managing director must be resident in Norway or nationals and residents of an EEA (European Economic Area) member state.

(d)   *Directors' liability to third parties*

A director may be held liable for losses suffered by third parties due to the director's gross negligence or wilful misconduct. However, such cases are rare. The most common circumstance in which liability is triggered is where the board delays calling in the receivers, thus running the company at the creditors' expense for too long.

(e)   *Non-competition*

Non-competition clauses for directors and employees must be incorporated into their individual contracts with the company. The law does not impose non-competition requirements.

(f) **Special duties of secrecy and loyalty**
Board members and employees are bound by general – albeit unwritten – rules of secrecy and loyalty to the company for which they work. Because these rules are unwritten, they are normally included in employment contracts and in a written declaration of non-competition and secrecy signed by each director of the board, where this is deemed necessary.

(g) **Civil and criminal liability**
Chapter 19 of both the Act on Private Limited Companies and the Act on Public Limited Companies establishes the basis for criminal charges against board members or others who, through their position in a company, wilfully or negligently breach any provision of the acts.

Historically, criminal charges have rarely been brought against elected officials of a company due to misconduct in the execution of their duties. Where individuals have actually been imprisoned for such offences, fraudulent behaviour aimed at personal gain has been part of the charge. Such behaviour is regulated in the Penal Code in addition to the company's legislation.

9.3 Others

(a) **Auditors**
All limited companies must keep accounts, which must be audited by an external, registered or state-authorised auditor.

(b) **Controllers and internal auditors**
It is up to the board of directors, in cooperation with the management, to decide whether a controller or internal auditor is required; there is no legal requirement for such positions to be filled. The appointment of controllers and internal auditors becomes common only as and when the business reaches a certain magnitude.

10. Fiscal year, commencement of operations
The normal fiscal year in Norway is the calendar year. Upon application, an alternative fiscal year may be allowed where there is good reason to do so (eg the parent company of a Norwegian subsidiary has a different fiscal year).

A company can commence operations upon formation; it does not have to wait for completion of the registration. In the period before registration, the founders are liable for all liabilities incurred by the company. During this period, the term 'under formation' or words to this effect should be added to the company name.

11. Financial statements

11.1 Company tax
Companies must submit their annual tax return by March 31 (on paper) or May 31 (electronically) each year (this deadline can be extended upon application). The tax return is based on the financial accounts, with some deviations based on the tax law.

One-third of the expected corporate tax for the fiscal year must be paid by February 15 the following year, with the second third due by April 15. The remainder is paid once the assessment is issued in early autumn. The current (2009) corporate tax rate in Norway is 28%.

11.2   Annual accounts

(a)   *Documents*
The annual accounts of Norwegian companies comprise a profit and loss account, a balance sheet and a multitude of various specific accounting forms required by law, depending on the type of business. The accounts are presented to the ordinary general shareholders' meeting together with the board of directors' annual report. The ordinary general shareholders' meeting must be held before June 30 in the year following the relevant fiscal year.

The tax reporting is based on these documents; any deviations between the annual accounts and tax accounts are made through so-called 'year-end dispositions'.

(b)   *Audit report*
The auditor reports to the ordinary general shareholders' meeting. The auditor's report is usually presented at the meeting, and the meeting will enclose it together with the annual report of the board of directors.

(c)   *Approval and distribution of profits*
In the annual report, the board of directors proposes how the profits should be distributed, including how much should be paid out in dividends to the shareholders. The general meeting will vote on whether to approve these proposals.

If the proposals are approved, the dividends will usually be distributed within a couple of weeks of the general meeting, even though it is not specified by law when such distribution should take place.

Shareholders resident in Norway currently pay a tax of 28% on dividends received from a Norwegian company. Shareholders resident in another EEA member state are exempt from withholding tax. Other foreign resident shareholders are subject to withholding tax on dividends at a rate that, depending on the relevant tax treaty, varies from 0% to 25%.

(d)   *Deposit and publication*
The annual report, together with the annual accounts, must be submitted to the Registry of Accounts by August 1 of the year following the relevant fiscal year. The accounts submitted to the registry are public, in the sense that anyone can ask to see them or have a copy sent to them.

12.   **Company reorganisation**
All forms of transformation are possible. The Act on Private Limited Companies includes a chapter on conversion to a public limited company. Basically, this involves:

- an increase in share capital (if necessary);
- amendment of the bylaws to state that the company is a public one; and
- enrolment of the company and its shareholders in the register of securities, if not already included therein.

Mergers and de-mergers are relatively simple and can be effected tax free where strict requirements are satisfied in respect of equity and how the balance of the merging companies is valued. Loss carry-forwards can be lost if the merger/de-merger is tax motivated. If the reorganisation is motivated by business considerations, then losses may be maintained and carried forward after the merger/de-merger.

13. Dissolution and liquidation

The general shareholders' meeting can decide to liquidate the company. At the same time, the general shareholders' meeting will elect a liquidation board. The decision and the liquidation board are registered with the Company Registry, which will advertise the liquidation twice in both local and national newspapers. After this advertisement, there is a period of two months during which all creditors should present their claims to the liquidation board.

Once this period has expired, the liquidation board pays the creditors and sets up a liquidation balance. It then reports the company as ready for dissolution to the company register. The company is then dissolved and deleted from the register.

14. Branches

In Norway, a branch of a company is not considered to have its own equity. When registering a branch of a foreign entity in Norway, it is the foreign entity itself that is registered. Thus, the branch has the same liability and the same equity as the head office.

If the branch is sued for any reason, then the head office is sued, risking its equity.

Panama

Yadira Moreno
Aguilar Castillo Love

Panamanian laws provide for several different types of commercial companies: collective companies (*sociedades colectivas*); simple or by-shares limited partnerships (*sociedades en comandita simples o por acciones*); limited liability corporations (*sociedades anónimas*); and limited liability companies (*sociedades de responsabilidad limitada*). The most common are limited liability corporations and limited liability companies.

Limited liability companies are intended for businesses with a limited number of partners and capital. The procedures and rules to set up this type of company, making changes to them and administering them, are more formal than those for corporations. However, limited liability corporations have more flexible rules for organisation, amendment, and administration, are more flexible and have no limitations regarding the number of partners or the amount of capital they have.

1. Types of limited liability company and applicable legislation

Limited liability companies are mainly governed by Law 24 of February 1 1966. In the absence of specific provision within this law, provisions of the Commercial Code apply.

Limited liability corporations are mainly governed by Law 32 of February 26 1927. In the absence of specific provisions within this law, provisions of the Commercial Code apply.

2. Incorporation of limited liability companies and limited liability corporations

2.1. Prior to incorporation proceedings

(a) Name registration

Article 38-A of the Panamanian Commercial Code allows the name of a company or corporation to be reserved for 30 days. This must be done by means of an application before the Public Registry Office. The documents for registering the company or corporation must be filed within the 30 days. If the company or corporation documents are not filed within 30 days, the reservation will expire.

This is not a mandatory procedure but an option given to any party wishing to reserve a particular name to prevent it being used by another company while the registration documents are gathered.

(b)   ***Contributions to company equity***
For limited liability companies, the law requires that, at the moment the company is constituted, all of the company capital must be subscribed and at least 50% of the in-cash capital must have been paid.

For limited liability companies, there is no mandatory rule requiring that any part of the capital be subscribed or paid.

(c)   ***Declaration of foreign investment***
There is no legal requirement to declare whether the investment is foreign or not.

(d)   ***Tax number for foreign partners/directors***
There is no need for foreign partners directors to obtain a tax number prior to registering a limited liability company.

2.2.   Incorporation of the company

(a)   ***Bylaws***
Both types of company described here must sign an incorporation agreement. This must be contained in a public deed and recorded at the Public Registry Office. For limited liability corporations, this document is called the articles of incorporation. The bylaws are internal rules of the corporation and are not required to be recorded at the Public Registry Office; this registration is optional. Limited liability companies must have more specific provisions in their organisation document. In this section, unless otherwise indicated, we will refer to the incorporation document (articles of incorporation) and not specifically to the bylaws.

(i)   *Essential clauses*
The following clauses are required for both limited liability companies and corporations:

- **Name of the company or corporation:** In both cases, the name of the company must be accompanied by a suffix indicating the type of company (SdeRL) or corporation (Corp, SA, Inc, etc).
- **Object of the corporation:** For limited liability companies, objects must be specific and the company is not allowed to enter into activities other than those listed, except if the bylaws are amended. In the case of corporations, the objects are of a general nature and the corporation is allowed to enter into any business, even if it is not listed, as long as the business is legal (although some exceptions apply for some regulated activities, such as banks and insurance companies).
- **Capital:** For limited liability corporations, the amount of authorised capital must be established, as well as the number and nominal value, and any classes if these are different. It can also establish that the shares will have no nominal value (in this case, some additional information would be required). There is no need to establish what the contributions of the shareholders are, only the amount of shares that signatories to the articles of incorporation

have agreed to take. For limited liability companies, the amount of capital must be expressed in Panamanian balboas (PAB) as well as the contribution made by each partner, and the way that this is divided between them.

- **Domicile:** Limited liability companies must include the detailed and complete domicile, as well as the address of any establishment it operates or purports to operate. Corporations can establish their domicile in a more general manner (could be only the country).
- **Duration:** Limited liability corporations can establish a perpetual duration. They must establish not only the duration, but also how the duration is to be counted, as well as how it can be extended, if the partners decide they wish to do so. (In this case, no perpetual duration can be established).

The following clauses are required for limited liability companies:
- the complete names, nationality, marital status, occupation, domicile and the personal identification number of each person who signs the document (the partners – personally or by proxy – and the administrators if they are not partners);
- the cash, goods or rights contributed by each partner (describing the nature of these), the value attributed to in-kind contributions (and the justification of said attributed value), and when and how the cash contributions that have not been satisfied will be paid;
- the person or persons that will administer and represent the company (who may or may not be partners in the firm), and their term of appointment. If no term of appointment is established, it is considered to be for an indefinite term; and
- how the general assembly of partners will deliberate and adopt agreements, as well as how said assembly is to be constituted and the dates when it must meet. If there are five partners or less, there is no need for a general assembly, but the agreement must indicate how will the partners be consulted and how will they express their opinions in writing.

The following clauses are required for limited liability corporations:
- the names and addresses of the subscribers (who can be expressed in a general manner) – and there is no need to establish other particulars about these individuals. The subscribers are not necessarily those who will become the partners of the corporation. They must establish how many shares of the company they agree to acquire when the company decides to issue shares, but they could transfer their subscription rights to a third party. There is no mandatory timeframe in which shares have to be issued;
- the name and domicile of the resident agent in Panama, which must be a Panamanian lawyer or law firm; and
- the names and addresses of the directors, of whom there must be a minimum of three.

(ii)   *Clauses not foreseen by law*

The requirements listed in (i) above referred to the minimum requirements for organising a company. The parties can agree on any other provisions as long as they are not against the law. Bylaws can be recorded at the Public Registry Office, although this is not mandatory. The consequence of this registration would be that the provisions of the said bylaws could be opposed to third parties, since they become publicly available; otherwise, they would only be mandatory for the company or corporation partners.

Although not established by law, limited liability corporations must include the names of the officers of the corporation (president, treasurer, secretary and others) in their articles of incorporation. These need not to be partners or directors of the corporation; and one person can hold more than one office.

(iii)   *Enlargeable clauses ruled by law*

Unless prohibited by law, provisions can be enlarged or established in a manner that is different from the one provided by the applicable law. These include (among others) the faculties reserved to the different governing bodies of the company or corporation. Limited liability corporations have more flexibility in this regard, in terms of formalities as well as with regard to the terms of the matters that can be enlarged or amended.

(b)   **Execution of public instrument**

Both limited liability companies and corporations must be executed by means of a public deed, notarised by a Panamanian notary public, prior to being recorded at the Public Registry Office.

For limited liability companies, the chart of incorporation must be signed by all the partners and administrators (if these are not partners). For limited liability corporations, any two people can sign the said document.

The organisational document can be executed in a foreign country, and in a foreign language. The document must be legalised by a Panamanian consul or by means of an apostille seal, and translated into the Spanish language by an authorised Panamanian public translator, and then submitted before a Panamanian notary to proceed with its registration. The company legally exists from the date the articles of incorporation are recorded at the Public Registry Office.

(c)   **Tax number for the company**

The tax number for the company is formed from those numbers registered at the Public Registry Office (microfiche and document registration numbers). The full tax number is obtained by registering with the Ministry of Economics and Finance. This registration is granted automatically by filling in a form at the ministry's offices, or submitting it online. The tax number is the identification number of the company.

(d)   **Payment of indirect taxes**

To constitute a company or corporation, an annual fee (the *Tasa Única*) must be paid. This fee must be paid before the company is registered, and afterwards on an annual basis. It currently (2009) amounts to US$250 for the first year, and US$300 for subsequent years. It is subject to surcharges and a fine in cases of late payment.

(e) **Registration with the Mercantile Registry**

All companies and corporations must obtain a licence from the Ministry of Commerce and Industry before they can commence operations. Due to a recent law (Law 5 of 2007) this can be filed online for most companies. There are some exceptions, such as those activities that need prior authorisation (ie those that require expenditure on alcoholic beverages, pharmaceutical companies, expenditure on weapons, etc, as well as regulated activities (insurance companies, banks, trusts, and others).

(f) **Legalisation of official books**

The minimum mandatory books for companies are a journal, a general ledger, a minute book, and a shareholders' and shares book. The law allows for these books and registrations to be kept in an electronic format, so long as they clearly show the operations of the company and can be printed.

(g) **Declaration of set-up activity and other tax declarations**

With limited exceptions, besides registering the company with the tax authorities and filing the notice of operation at the Ministry of Commerce and Industries no other filing is required to commence operations.

3.   Number of partners – unipersonality

Both limited liability companies and limited liability corporations can be formed by one person. In the case of limited liability companies, this must be established in the name of the company, which must include the name of the owner, followed by the words 'Empresa de Responsabilidad Limitada', or the suffix 'EdeRL' or 'Ltda'. If the limited liability company does not establish this wording, the company owners will be severally responsible for the company's obligations and liabilities.

4.   Corporate name – limitations

Corporate names must not be identical or similar to that of a previously established company. It should not be misleading (eg include the word 'insurance' or 'bank', unless it is authorised to enter into that type of business). Corporate names must also contain the suffix pertaining to the type of company. There are no limitations in terms of language of the corporate name.

5.   Domicile

Companies and corporations are free to determine their domicile, which for legal purposes could be established in a country other than Panama. However, if the company does business that produces what Panamanian fiscal law determines to be "of a Panamanian source", they must establish a domicile for tax purposes.

For the purposes of the articles or charts of incorporation of the limited liability companies, detailed domicile and addresses of the company establishments must be included. This is not required for limited liability corporations; however, the address of the company must be given to the Ministry of Commerce and Industry when the company files its operation notice.

6.   Object

In general terms, all companies and corporations are free to establish their objectives, as long as they are of a legal nature.

In the case of limited liability corporations, unless specific approval is required for regulated businesses, corporations can engage in any legal activity even if it is not listed at the corporation's articles of incorporation.

Limited liability companies can only engage in those activities that are expressly listed in their chart of incorporation.

7.   Capital stock

7.1   Minimum amount

Limited liability companies must have a minimum amount of capital of PAB2,000 and a maximum of PAB500,000. Capital can only be divided in so-called quotas of PAB100 or amounts divisible by 100.

Limited liability corporations do not have minimum or maximum amounts of capital. For payment of registration fees only, the minimum amount is PAB10,000 of authorised capital – ie the corporation could have an authorised capital of less than PAB10,000, but registration fees will be calculated on a minimum of said sum. Shares can be issued in any amounts. Non-par-value shares can also be issued, but there must be an indication regarding how many shares of this type will there be, plus some additional provisions regarding how the total capital is formed when there are non-par-value shares.

7.2   Nature of contributions

Contributions can be made in cash or in kind (goods, work, services, and rights).

For limited liability corporations, determination of the value of in-kind contributions is done by the board of directors. These are presumed to be correct, except in the case of fraud.

For limited liability companies, the value of in-kind contributions is established at the charter of incorporation (when the contribution is made at that moment) or at the moment when said contribution is documented.

7.3   Partial payments

Partial payments are allowed in limited liability corporations, as long as the shares to be acquired are to be issued in the form of a nominal (not bearer) stock certificate. In such cases, the amount due must be noted on the stock certificate, as well as in the company share registry. The shareholder wis required to respond for the company's obligations up to the amount he owes for the acquisition of his/her shares.

Limited liability companies can also issue quota certificates for partially paid quotas. In such cases, there should be a note indicating the amount paid, and the due date for payment of the remaining amount.

7.4 Share certificates – systems of representing shares

For limited liability companies, the law establishes that the partners have a right to receive a certificate signed by the administrator of the company detailing ownership of the relevant shares. The certificate must contain the name of the company, the capital, the registration data of the Public Registry Office, the partners' name, the amount of the participation (including amounts paid and owed, in this case indicating when the contribution has to be completed) and the date and place of issuance. However, since quotas are established by public deed and are recorded at the Public Registry Office, participation can also be shown on the relevant public deed.

In the case of limited liability corporations, acquisition of the shares that constitute the capital of the company must be documented by means of a stock certificate. This document has to contain the following information:

- proof of registration at the Public Registry Office;
- authorised capital of the company;
- amount of shares corresponding to the owner;
- type of action (if there is more than one type);
- indication regarding amounts owed (if any); and
- the name of the owner (if not in bearer form).

As mentioned above, no bearer stock certificates can be issued unless the price of the share has been fully paid.

7.5 Restrictions to the transfer of shares

Unless otherwise established in the charter of incorporation, participation in a limited liability company can be freely transferred, in whole or in part, as long as the amount transferred is in an amount divisible by PAB100. To proceed with the transfer, the relevant partner has to communicate, in writing, to the administrator, his/her intention to transfer the shares, indicating the name of the acquirer, if any, the number of shares to be transferred and the price. The administrators will notify this information in writing to the other partners within 15 days, and they are allowed to opt to buy these quotas within 30 days following this notice. If several partners are interested, they will be divided in proportion to the number of shares they hold or, if this is not possible, by drawing lots.

Unless otherwise established by the articles of incorporation of the company, there is no limit to the transfer of the shares of a company.

7.6 Transfer of shares: formalities required

The transfer of quotas of limited liability companies has to be done by means of a public deed, after complying with the procedure established in section 7.5 above and must be recorded at the Public Registry Office within the 30 days of the transfer.

The transfer of shares of limited liability corporations can be done by transferring the stock certificate (in the case of bearer-form certificates) or by means of the endorsement of a stock certificate in a nominative form. In the latter case, the transfer will not be valid before the corporation until the new owner presents the endorsed document and the transfer is recorded in the shareholders' registry. The company can refuse the transfer if part of the price of the shares is still due, until this amount is paid in full.

8. Equity

8.1 Balance between capital and own resources

There are no specific provisions in either law (corporations or limited liability companies) requiring a particular balance between capital and own resources of these entities. What is applicable are the general accounting laws and principles and/or those established by regulatory agencies for specific business (banking, for example).

8.2 Convertible bonds

Bonds and other negotiable instruments are the subject of other specific laws and regulations. Generally speaking, instruments that are to be publicly traded need to comply with the pertaining Law for Negotiable Instruments, and the Securities laws, and are subject to supervision from the National Securities Commission.

For limited liability corporations, as long as there is compliance with the previously mentioned laws, partners can agree on the terms and conditions for issuing convertible bonds, preferred stock and other instruments. Limited liability companies are not prohibited from doing so, but if there were to be bonds convertible into shares, there could be some limitations based on the regulation on transfer of their social quotas (acceptance of the new partner by the others).

9. Administration of the company

9.1 General meeting of partners

(a) Quorums of attendance at meetings

Limited liability companies require, for a meeting to be duly convened, the presence of the majority of the paid-up capital, unless the incorporation document establishes a qualified majority.

For limited liability corporations, although the laws do not expressly establish a specific majority required for a meeting, in practice a simple majority of the issued and outstanding shares is sufficient.

The articles of incorporation (for both limited liability companies and corporations) can include specific provisions in this regard.

(b) Quorums for adoption of resolutions

For the adoption of resolutions in the case of limited liability corporations, the general rule, unless otherwise established in the articles of incorporation, is that a simple majority of the shareholders present at a given meeting suffices for the resolutions thereby adopted to be valid.

In the case of limited liability companies, agreements have to be adopted by a majority of the authorised capital, unless the articles of incorporation require a higher percentage of votes.

(c)   *Challenge of resolutions*

Any partner of a limited liability company can challenge the agreements adopted in violation of the articles of incorporations and the pertaining laws. The competent courts to decide these matters are those presided over by circuit judges. The same right is granted to partners at limited liability corporations.

9.2   Administrative body

(a)   *Different systems of administration*

Administration of limited liability companies is exerted by one or more administrators, appointed by the partners of the company, depending on what the articles of incorporation establish.

Limited liability corporations, on the other hand, are administered by a board of directors, also appointed by the shareholders. There must be a minimum of three directors. In order for an individual to be able to administer a corporation, the board of directors must grant him/her a general power of attorney, indicating the faculties granted.

Neither administrators nor the board of directors can dispose of the company's assets or enter into agreements different from those of the ordinary course of business of the entity, unless they obtain authorisation from the partners/ shareholders.

(b)   *Term of office, resignation and removal of directors*

There are no pre-established term for the administrators/directors to be in office. This is left to the decision of the partners/shareholders. The shareholders can, however, remove the administrator(s) and/or director(s) at any time. Administrators/directors are also free to resign from their office.

(c)   *Directors' liability to third parties*

Generally speaking, directors of a limited liability corporation are only severally responsible to third parties for the corporation's obligation when they knowingly approve or give their consent to acts that reduce the corporation's goods to less than the amount of its liabilities or if capital stock is reduced or if a false declaration or report regarding a substantial matter is given.

The administrators of a limited liability company are responsible for damages caused by negligence, gross negligence or violation of legal provisions, clauses of the articles of incorporation or agreements adopted by the company and, in general, for very bad performance of the obligations assigned to them.

(d)   *Non-competition*

There is no specific provision prohibiting directors and partners or administrators of a limited liability corporation or company to engage in other business related to the business of the corporation that they represent. However, it is very common that the articles of incorporation include this provision, and partners anyway usually decide to replace the directors/administrators that they deem are not responding to the best interests of the corporation.

There is, however, a prohibition for partners of limited liability companies to engage in business that is similar or that in any way creates difficulties for the normal development of the company's operation (unless the partners agree otherwise).

(e) *Special duties of secrecy and loyalty*

There are no specific provisions in this regard for limited liability companies or corporations.

(f) *Civil and criminal liability: legislative framework and consequences*

For civil liability, what was indicated in section 9.2(c) above applies.

In criminal matters, Article 241 of the Panamanian Criminal Code establishes criminal sanctions on those directors, managers or administrators of banking, financial or financial intermediation legal entities who directly or indirectly approve one or more credits or other financing transactions beyond or against legal regulations, hence making it possible to cause the forceful dissolution, insolvency or permanent lack of liquidity of their institution.

Other financial crimes for which directors and administrators can be penalised are not providing information or providing false information to the authorities, in order to hide insolvency or lack-of-liquidity situations. In addition, there are criminal sanctions for directors who retain employees' social security payments.

9.3 Others

(a) *Attorneys*

Both limited liability companies and corporations are required to have a resident agent, who has to be a Panamanian lawyer or a law firm. Resident agents are not legal representatives or administrators of these entities.

(b) *Controllers and internal auditors*

There are no legal requirements for controllers and/or internal auditors for companies or corporations in general, but such requirements are stipulated for specifically regulated entities (such as banks).

10. Fiscal year, duration and start of activities

Ordinary fiscal years in Panama (for corporations, companies, and all types of persons or entities) go from January 1 to December 31. However, all such entities are allowed to change their fiscal period, with the pertaining information/approval of the fiscal authorities.

11. Financial statements

11.1 Company tax

Companies and corporations are required to pay an annual corporate tax in order to remain valid. This tax amounts to US$250 for the first year, and US$300 for all subsequent years, provided that the tax is paid on time – there are fines and penalties for late payment.

Income tax for juridical persons (of all types) is currently (2009) 30%. Panama has a territorial tax system; therefore income that is not considered of a Panamanian source is not taxable.

11.2 Annual accounts

(a) Documents
Persons in general (not only corporations) that engage in commercial activities are required to have, as a minimum, three types of books: a diary, a general ledger, and an inventory book. These books are permitted to be in an electronic form.

(b) Audit report
Audit reports are not required for all companies but only for those regulated ones.

Administrators of limited liability companies are required to present an annual report to the shareholders, but not necessarily an audit report.

(c) Approval and distribution of profits
Limited liability companies' and corporations' laws do not indicate restrictions on distributions of profits. They only stipulate that partners will participate in profits and losses in proportion to their participation in the company.

(d) Deposit and publicity
Limited liability companies have to record at the Public Registry Office the names of the partners and administrators.

Limited liability corporations are not required to publicly disclose information on the partners. Only information regarding directors and officers is required to be recorded at the Public Registry Office.

12. Company reorganisation: transformation, merger and split-off
Limited liability companies, as well as limited liability corporations, can be merged into other entities (whether domestic or foreign), as well as transformed into other types of entity, provided the pertaining procedures and approval by the partners are complied with. Unless these entities engage in certain government-regulated activities, there is no need to ask for prior approval by any governmental entity.

Regarding split-off, this is not contemplated by these laws. Generally, this is handled through the opening or formation of a new legal entity, and a transfer of assets and business by means of several types of transactions (capital contribution, transfer by sale or donation, etc).

13. Eventual partner separation
For limited liability corporations, a partner who wishes to separate from the corporation would have to sell or otherwise transfer his/her shares in the corporation to another party (and right of first refusal or similar would have to be established in the articles of incorporation.

Limited liability companies can establish procedures for voluntary separation of a partner or partners when they have not agreed to an extension of the company's term of existence, a modification of the company's objective, an increase or reduction of capital, a transformation of the company into another type of entity, or the merger of the company. In any of these cases, they would have to communicate their decision to the other partners within 30 days following the date when such a resolution had been approved, and they are entitled to receive payment of a just price for their participation.

There is also the possibility of voluntarily retiring from the company by giving the other partners three months' prior notice, and during the 60 days following said notice the remaining partners may acquire the retiring partner's interest in the company. Detailed procedures would be subject to the provision of the articles of incorporation.

Partners of limited liability companies could also be excluded from the company by the other partners in five specific situations:

- when partners engage in competitive activities;
- when they do not pay their quotas on time;
- when they are declared bankrupt;
- when they somehow impede the company's activities or operations; or
- when they engage in serious misconduct against the company.

14. Dissolution and liquidation

Limited liability companies can be dissolved for the following causes:

- in the cases provided for in the articles of incorporation;
- by agreement of the partners;
- because the objective has been fulfilled or by a manifest impossibility to continue the operations;
- because the duration of the company has elapsed without being extended by the partners;
- in the case of a merger with another legal entity, with the company not remaining as the surviving one;
- by justified cause declared by a judicial judgment;
- in a case where the assets of the company have been reduced to less than half the capital established in the articles of incorporation, unless the partners make additional contributions within 30 days from the date this situation has taken place; and
- in a case where the partners are reduced to fewer than two, unless a new partner is found within the subsequent 60 days.

For limited liability corporations, the law only provides for dissolution by agreement of the partners or by termination of the corporation's duration.

The entities will remain in existence only for the purposes of collecting and paying debts and for distributing the proceeds among the partners/shareholders (and this period is permitted to be no more than three years for corporations).

15. Branches

In order to establish a branch in Panama, foreign companies and corporations are required to determine the capital that is going to be assigned to the Panamanian branch. Generally speaking, the local branch is responsible for the local operations, and the head office is liable for the capital that it has committed to the Panamanian operations and other activities or transactions in which the head office has participated. For Panamanian tax purposes, only Panamanian activities are subject to income tax and other local laws in Panama.

Paraguay

Esteban Burt
Peroni Sosa Tellechea Burt & Narvaja

1. Types of company with limited liability and applicable legislation

Two types of company with limited liability are available in Paraguay:

- corporations (*Sociedades Anónimas*); and
- limited liability companies (*Sociedades de Responsabilidad Limitada*).

2. Incorporation procedure

2.1 Execution of public deed

(a) Corporations

The founding shareholders must enter into a corporate contract, which must be executed as a public deed. A notary public must officially record the corporate contract, which must then be registered at the Commercial Registry.

The legal fee of the notary public is 0.75% of the corporate capital, plus publication expenses.

(b) Limited liability companies

The partners must enter into a contract, which must be executed as a public deed. A notary public must officially record the contract for registration with the Commercial Registry.

2.2 Tax number for foreign partners/directors

All natural and legal persons who are taxpayers must be registered for tax purposes and have a corresponding tax identification number.

2.3 Bylaws

(a) Corporations

(i) Essential clauses

The bylaws of a corporation must include the following information, at a minimum:

- the full name, nationality, profession, civil status and domicile of each shareholder, and its respective shareholding;
- the full name of the corporation and its corporate domicile;
- the nature of the business;

- the specific duration of the corporation;
- the amount of subscribed and paid-up capital;
- the nominal value of the shares and an indication of whether they are nominal or bearer;
- the value of any in-kind contributions;
- the basis on which profits will be distributed;
- special privileges and rights, if any, conferred on founders or holders of preferred shares;
- dispositions regarding management and supervision, the number of administrators and their powers and duties;
- the powers of the shareholders' meetings, provisions regulating the shareholders' right to vote, and the procedure for adoption of decisions at shareholders' meetings; and
- the grounds for liquidation of the corporation.

(ii) *Clauses not foreseen by law*

Apart from the above minimum clauses, which must be included in the bylaws, the shareholders of a corporation are free to establish additional clauses as long as these do not conflict with Paraguayan legislation.

(b) **Limited liability companies**

There are nor specific legal requirements for the bylaws of limited liability companies under Paraguayan law.

2.4 Tax identification number

The Undersecretariat of Taxes, within the Secretariat of Finance, is responsible for the administration and application of the Tax Code. All corporations and limited liability companies must be registered with the undersecretariat, which will issue a tax number for each contributor.

2.5 Registration with the Mercantile Registry

All corporations and limited liability companies must register their bylaws, executed in the form of a public deed, with the Registry of Legal Persons and Associations and the Commercial Registry. Once the registries have approved and registered the bylaws, the company acquires separate legal personality from its members.

2.6 Legalisation of official books

(a) **Corporations**

Corporations are required to maintain the following official books:
- general shareholders' meetings
- board of directors' meetings;
- share register;
- register of obligations;
- register of shareholder assistance;

- inventory; and
- diary.

All books must be legalised by the Commercial Registry and kept at the corporate domicile.

(b) *Limited liability companies*

Limited liability companies are required to maintain the following official books:
- general shareholders' meeting book;
- minute book;
- share register;
- register of obligations;
- register of shareholder assistance;
- inventory; and
- diary.

All books must be legalised by the Commercial Registry.

3. Number of shareholders

3.1 Corporations

The Civil Code provides that a corporation must have at least two shareholders.

3.2 Limited liability companies

Limited liability companies may have between two and 25 partners.

4. Corporate name – limitations

4.1 Corporations

The corporate name of a corporation must include the words '*Sociedad Anónima*' or the abbreviation 'SA', and it cannot contain any term that is contrary to law. The corporate name must be stated in the bylaws.

4.2 Limited liability companies

The corporate name of a limited liability company must include the words '*Sociedad de Responsabilidad Limitada*' or the abbreviation 'SRL', and it cannot contain any term that is contrary to law. The corporate name must be stated in the bylaws. The name of one or more partners may be used as the corporate name.

5. Corporate domicile

The legal domicile of a corporation or limited liability company must be specified in the bylaws. Normally, the legal domicile is the place where administration of the business takes place.

6. Corporate purpose

6.1 Corporations

The corporate purpose of a corporation must be stated in the bylaws. It must be lawful and possible to achieve. All activities carried on by the corporation must aim towards the achievement of its proposed objectives.

6.2 Limited liability companies

Limited liability companies must be commercial enterprises, even where they undertake civil activities. They cannot operate as a bank, insurance or savings/loan company. The corporate purpose is set out in the bylaws.

7. Capital stock

7.1 Minimum capital requirement

(a) *Corporations*

Paraguayan legislation imposes no minimum capital requirements on corporations. However, the corporate capital must be sufficient to carry out the activities and achieve the corporate purpose of the corporation. The initial capital stock must be stated in the bylaws and cannot be modified unless they are amended.

(b) *Limited liability companies*

Paraguayan legislation imposes no minimum capital requirements on limited liability companies. However, the corporate capital must be sufficient to carry out the activities and achieve the corporate purpose of the company. The initial capital stock must be stated in the bylaws and cannot be modified unless they are amended.

Export and import companies must meet certain requirements set by the Paraguayan Central Bank.

7.2 Nature of contributions

Partner and shareholder contributions may be made in cash or in kind.

7.3 Partial payments

(a) *Corporations*

The capital stock is generally paid in at the time of incorporation. The founder shareholders undertake to subscribe to a certain number of shares, which they can pay for either immediately or within 30 days.

(b) *Limited liability companies*

In general, the capital stock is fully paid up at the time of incorporation. Partial payments are allowed, but at the time of incorporation at least 50% of the capital must be paid in cash and deposited with the Banco Nacional de Fomento. The difference must be paid within two years of incorporation.

7.4   Representation of shares

(a)   *Corporations*

The share certificates must:

- be numbered;
- be signed by one or more directors; and
- contain the name of the company, the date and place of registration, the amount of subscribed capital, and the value and type of share.

In order to issue bearer share certificates, the shares must be paid in full; until then, shareholders will be given provisional certificates and remain liable for their payment. The bylaws may establish different classes of shares, with different rights, which may be nominative or bearer.

(b)   *Limited liability companies*

The shares of limited liability companies are represented by nominal non-endorsable quotas of G1,000 or multiples thereof.

7.5   Transfer of shares

(a)   *Corporations*

There are no restrictions on the transfer of bearer shares, and transfer is effected by simple delivery of the shares.

To effect a transfer of nominal shares, the purchaser's information (eg name, profession, address) must be entered in the company's share register and the shares must be signed and dated by the endorser.

(b)   *Limited liability companies*

Where a limited liability company has five or more partners, the transfer of quotas requires the prior approval of partners representing three-quarters of the capital. Where there are fewer than five partners, the transfer must be approved by unanimous vote.

Partners wishing to transfer their quotas must advise the other partners accordingly, who must respond within 15 days. If no opposition is made during this 15-day period, the partners' consent is presumed. In any case of opposition, a partner wishing to transfer his quotas may request authorisation from a judge.

A transfer of quotas must be realised by a notary public and has effect from the date of registration at the Commercial Registry.

8.   Administration

8.1   Administrative body

(a)   *Corporations*

The administration of a corporation is carried out by one or more directors, as stated in the bylaws. The directors are appointed in the bylaws or elected by the ordinary shareholders' meeting. Directors can be shareholders or not. They may be re-elected, but their appointment is revocable by the shareholders' meeting. Directors are usually appointed for one fiscal year, although a different term may be specified in the bylaws.

The administrators are not responsible for the corporation's obligations, except in a case of non-performance of their duties, mismanagement or personal violation of the law or bylaws. In such cases the administrators are jointly and severally liable towards the corporation and third parties. Directors who opposed, voted against, or were not present at the time the illegal decisions were taken are not liable.

The Criminal Code further sets out various types of corporate crime and the applicable penalties. The legal representative of a corporation is liable for its illicit acts or omissions, and will suffer the consequences established in the Criminal Code.

(b) Limited liability corporations

The administration and representation of a limited liability company is performed by one or more managers, who may or may not be partners. The managers have the same rights and obligations as the directors of corporations. They are appointed at the time of incorporation, and there are no limits on how long they can remain in office.

Managers cannot act on their own initiative in respect of any business transaction that is not included in the bylaws. Managers are jointly and severally liable to the company and the partners in case of bad management or violation of the bylaws.

(c) Non-competition

The Civil Code establishes that a company may not have as a director anyone who also acts for a direct competitor.

(d) Special duties of secrecy and loyalty

There are no special regulations on secrecy and loyalty. Nevertheless, special clauses covering this matter may be included in the contract between employer and employee.

8.2 Shareholders' meeting

(a) Corporations

Shareholders' meetings may be ordinary or extraordinary, and must take place at the corporate domicile.

An ordinary shareholders' meeting must be called at least once a year by the directors or trustees, and it must consider and decide on the following:

- the annual directors' report, statements of accounts, balance sheet, distribution of dividends and trustees' reports;
- the election, removal and responsibilities of directors and trustees; and
- the issuance of shares.

An extraordinary shareholders' meeting may be convened by the directors at any time, or by the corporate trustee when necessary or convenient, or at the request of shareholders representing 5% of the capital. It must consider and decide on the following:

- modification of the bylaws;
- increases or reductions in capital;
- redemption, reimbursement or amortisation of shares;
- merger, transformation or dissolution;
- issuance of debentures; and
- issuance of participation bonds.

8.3 Others

(a) Attorneys

The bylaws of a corporation or limited liability company may allow the administrators to grant power of attorney to a third party, who may be a natural or legal person. Depending on the object of the power of attorney, it must be granted through a notary public, who in some cases must also register the power of attorney.

(b) Controllers and internal auditors

Paraguayan law does not require corporations or limited liability companies to have internal auditors or controllers. Companies may choose to have their accounts audited by external independent auditors.

9. Fiscal year

Normally, all Paraguayan companies follow a fiscal year that begins on January 1 and ends on December 31. Depending on the nature of business (eg agricultural) the company may issue a request to the Undersecretariat of Taxes to work to a different fiscal year.

10. Financial statements

The tax regime is set out in the Tax Code Law (125/91, as amended by Law 2421/04). The Undersecretariat of Taxes is responsible for the application of the Tax Code Law.

10.1 Company tax

The general tax rate is currently (2009) 10%. In the case of distribution of net profits to shareholders or partners, an additional tax at a rate of 5% is applied.

The withholding tax on dividends is 15% when paid to non-resident shareholders (ie corporate income tax at a rate of 10%, plus an additional 5% when profits are distributed rather than reinvested).

10.2 Annual accounts

(a) Documents

(i) Corporations

The directors of a corporation must prepare the financial statements and present them to the trustees on a quarterly basis. Each year, the directors must also prepare a complete inventory and a detailed statement showing the financial condition of the company. All of these documents must be approved by the ordinary shareholders' meeting.

(ii)   Limited liability companies

As for corporations, the financial statements of limited liability companies comprise the balance sheet, in which the profit and loss account is reflected. All documents relating to the annual accounts must be considered and approved at the ordinary shareholders' meeting.

(b)   Audit reports

Corporations and limited liability companies may choose to appoint independent external auditors to review the annual accounts, following which the auditors will issue a report on the relevant fiscal year.

(c)   Approval and distribution of profits

A balance sheet must be prepared each year according to the methods established by law and the bylaws, and must be approved by the ordinary shareholders' meeting. Five per cent of the net profits must be set aside each year, with the goal of creating a reserve fund of not less than 20% of the subscribed capital.

Corporations may pay dividends to shareholders out of net profits only.

(d)   Deposit and publication

Copies of the balance sheet must be made available at the corporate domicile at least 15 days before the shareholders' meeting. The company diary and trustees' report must also be made available at least 15 days before the meeting. There is no requirement to publish the annual accounts.

10.   Company reorganisation

Paraguayan law allows for the transformation of any company into another type of company, without prejudice to the rights and obligations of the previous company.

The merger of companies is also allowed. Through merger, two or more companies are dissolved and their respective assets and liabilities are assumed by the new company.

(a)   Corporations

The transformation of a corporation requires the prior approval of an extraordinary shareholders' meeting.

(b)   Limited liability companies

All partners of a limited liability company have the right to participate in the decisions of the company. If the bylaws do not establish how the partners are to reach decisions, the rules applicable to corporations will apply.

The partners' unanimous consent is required for a change in corporate purpose, transformation, merger or other amendment of the bylaws.

11. Eventual partner separation

The separation of a partner from a limited liability company does not affect the company's existence. A partner may be excluded from the company in any case of violation of the law or bylaws.

12. Dissolution and liquidation

12.1 Corporations

A corporation may be dissolved:

- where the duration established in the bylaws has expired;
- where the corporation has achieved its corporate purpose, or it has become evident that achievement of the corporate purpose is impossible;
- where the shareholders unanimously agree to dissolution;
- for corporations with two shareholders, in the case of the death of one shareholder; and
- for causes established in the bylaws.

Judicial dissolution may also take place; a judicial resolution has effect from the date on which the grounds for dissolution arose.

Liquidation is the final step once dissolution has taken place. During liquidation, the company's liabilities and debts are settled; any assets remaining will be distributed to the shareholders in proportion to their contributions.

12.2 Limited liability companies

A limited liability company may be dissolved:

- where the duration established in the bylaws has expired;
- where the company has achieved its corporate purpose, or it has become evident that achievement of the corporate purpose is impossible;
- where the members unanimously agree to dissolution; and
- for causes established in the bylaws.

Limited liability companies do not dissolve in the event of a partner's death, interdiction, bankruptcy or the dismissal of a manager, unless otherwise stipulated.

13. Branches

Branches have legal autonomy, and can acquire rights and contract obligations for the parent company.

Foreign companies that conduct regular business in Paraguay must establish a branch office in the country. Like Paraguayan companies, these are subject to the Civil Code provisions on publication of corporate documents and registration with the Commercial Registry and the Registry of Legal Entities and Associations. Foreign companies are considered to be domiciled where their principal place of business is located, but branch offices established in Paraguay are considered domiciled in Paraguay for the purpose of transactions and business carried out within Paraguay. They must therefore comply with all formalities and obligations established under

Paraguayan law for similar entities.

Representatives of foreign companies are authorised to engage in all actions, transactions and activities in which the parent company can engage in its own country. Any limitation to this capacity is null and void. Representatives are subject to the same Civil Code provisions as administrators in general.

Once the branch office has been registered and the accounting forms have been filed with the tax authorities and other public offices, the branch can commence operation and carry out business transactions. Government authorisation is not required. The branch office must comply with the taxation and disclosure requirements of local companies. Publication and registration of balance sheets, reports and statements are controlled by the Ministry of Finance, although, since branches do not hold annual shareholders' meetings, such control is more relaxed.

Poland

Michał Barłowski
Wardyński & Partners

1. Introduction

Traditionally, limited liability companies, irrespective of their form, played an important role in Polish law and practice both before and after World War II. There are two legal forms for capital companies that have a legal personality and where the liability of all shareholders is limited:

- *spółka z ograniczoną odpowiedzialnością* (sp z oo, which is similar to a UK private limited company (Ltd) and which is denoted 'LCC' here); and
- *spółka akcyjna* (SA), which is a joint stock company similar to a UK public limited company (plc) and which is denoted 'PLC' here.

Only one form of limited liability company exists – the LLC. However, a shareholder's obligations and liabilities towards a PLC are even more limited. This chapter deals with the regime that applies to both.

A PLC can either be publicly owned,where its shares (stock) can be acquired on a stock exchange where its shares are listed, or as a private company where its shares are not listed and are not admitted to public trading. Here, shares are held privately and the share certificate cannot be de-materialised (ie it must always be issued by the PLC).

Although the legal form, organisational functioning, formation, and liquidation of both an LLC and a PLC appear to be similar, there are some major differences between them. Usually LLCs have a smaller number of owners and, apart from contributing capital, the shareholders usually know each other and there is an element of trust between them. In a PLC these features can be totally absent.

The legal requirements and regulations for the formation of a PLC are also more stringent. For example, in a PLC there must be a supervisory board; this does not apply to an LLC. Whenever shares are paid for in a PLC by an in-kind contribution, the market value must be confirmed by an accountant who has been nominated by the appropriate registry court. Shares in a PLC are securities and can be admitted to public trading and listed on a stock exchange, whereas those in an LLC are not – no share certificates are issued. A PLC can issue both bearer and registered shares; an LLC does not issue shares *per se* and the rights of shareholders are always registered in their names. Shares in an LLC must always be fully paid in advance (the concept of declared and paid-up share capital is unknown); there are exceptions to this rule in a PLC. A minority shareholder who possesses up to 5% of shares in a PLC can be excluded by a squeeze-out; this is not possible in an LLC.

2. Applicable legislation

The Commercial Companies Code of 2001 (as amended) (the CCC) deals with corporate regulations. It replaced the Companies Code of 1934. Other regulations that apply to the two forms of company are found in the:

- Civil Code 1964;
- Corporate Income Tax Act 1992;
- Unfair Competition Act 1993;
- Accountancy Law Act 1994;
- National Court Register Act 1997;
- Tax Ordinance Act 1997;
- Commercial Companies Code 2000;
- Tax on Civil Law Transactions Act 2000;
- Foreign Exchange Law Act 2002; and
- Freedom of Business Act 2004.

3. Incorporation

3.1 Proceedings prior to incorporation

(a) *Registration of corporate name*

A corporate name is required by law. It must be on the company's deed of association, which is registered in the National Court Register (NCR). The corporate name must be different from those of companies already registered in the same legal form.

There are no additional, special registries for corporate names.

If a corporate name is a company trademark, the name can also be registered as a trademark with the Patent Office (*Urząd Patentowy*).

(b) *Payment of the initial capital of a company*

LLC shareholders must pay the initial capital in full, before a company is registered in the NCR. If shares are issued at a premium, these must also be paid for in full before registration.

All company management board members (ie the executive board of directors) must jointly declare and represent that all shareholders have paid the initial capital in full. Under the CCC, it is an offence for board members to make false declarations. The declarations are registered and thereby incorporated. The management board members are personally liable for any false statements.

For PLCs, non-cash contributions must be fully paid in kind within a year of registration, whereas shares issued for cash need at least one-quarter of the nominal value to be paid before registration. If shares are issued only for in-kind contributions, or for in-kind and cash contributions, at least one-quarter of the initial capital must be contributed before registration.

Company founders must submit a report on in-kind contributions. This should contain:

- a detailed description of the contribution, the number and type of shares or other rights to participate in any profit, or in any distribution of company assets;

- the names of contributors; and
- the method of valuation.

If the in-kind contribution is an enterprise (ie an ongoing business), financial statements for the last two financial years must be attached to the report.

The report is to be audited by one or more NCR-registered auditors; the CCC exempts some reports from audit (ie reports concerning non-monetary contributions that have already been audited (without reservations) by auditors and securities or other financial instruments whose average (median) listed price can be established for the previous six months)). The details of when these exemptions apply are covered by the CCC.

Payment is made into the company's account either directly, or through an investment company. The account must be held by a bank within the European Union, or the European Economic Area.

(c) *Declaration of foreign investment*

Under the Foreign Exchange Law Act 2002 (or, if a foreign national or a foreign company owns more than 10% of share capital, under the Accountancy Law Act 1994) a company that has a registered office in Poland and is a branch of a foreign company must file an annual report detailing the foreign investment to the National Bank of Poland.

This does not apply to banks, branches of foreign banks, or branches of credit institutions.

(d) *Tax identification number for foreign shareholders and members of management boards*

Foreign nationals who are management board members or shareholders – including foreign corporations – who will have to pay tax after the incorporation of a company must obtain a tax identification number (NIP), which is issued by the Tax Office.

3.2 Incorporation of a company

(a) *Deed of association*

(i) *Essential clauses*

During the process of incorporation, a deed of association of a company (articles of association for an LLC or statute for a PLC) must be formally accepted in the form of a notarial deed by shareholders.

A company deed of association must indicate, at least:
- a corporate name and registered office;
- the object of the business;
- the duration of the company, if a time is set;
- the initial capital (in a PLC the amount paid for initial capital prior to registration);
- whether a shareholder can own more than one share (applicable to an LLC);

- the number and nominal value of any shares issued (applicable to an LLC);
- the object of in-kind contributions (if any), identifying the in-kind contributor, number and the nominal value of any shares issued for the contribution (applicable to an LLC);
- any special shareholder benefits or duties (applicable to an LLC);
- the number and nominal value of any shares, and whether these are ordinary or preference shares (and, for PLCs, whether issued shares are to be registered or bearer shares);
- classes of shares and any rights thereunder, if different classes are to be issued (applicable to a PLC);
- full personal or corporate names of the founders (applicable to a PLC);
- the number of management and supervisory board members (the latter being an option in an LLC), or the lowest numbers possible and the entity authorised to determine the composition of the management or supervisory board (applicable to a PLC); and
- specification of where announcements will be published if the company is not to use the *Monitor Sądowy i Gospodarczy* (*Court and Business Gazette*) (applicable to a PLC).

In addition, if these are to be legally effective provisions, then a deed of association for a PLC must include:
- the number and type of rights to profit, or assets and related rights;
- all duties of shareholders, in addition to paying for shares;
- the terms and manner of share redemption;
- any restrictions on share transfer;
- the personal rights of the shareholders (if any); and
- an estimate of the costs of incorporation.

(ii)   *Optional clauses*
LLC: There are a number of provisions that although not compulsory when registering a company, are often found in the deeds of association. They may:
- specify shares that have special rights;
- set down a definition of a shareholder's obligation to act unpaid for the company;
- allow additional payments of capital, in proportion to a shareholding;
- allow the transfer of a part of share, if a shareholder is limited to one share;
- specify conditions for the transfer of all, or a part, of a share on consent of the company, or other requirement;
- limit, or exclude, the rights of heirs to join the company in place of a deceased family member and to determine the terms of paying off such heirs;
- limit or exclude the division of shares among heirs, where the deceased shareholder had more than one share;
- allow division of shares among a shareholder's heirs after death, if the shareholder is entitled to hold only one share;
- limit, or exclude, the right of a shareholder's spouse to join the company if

the share, or shares, is joint marital property;
- provide that a pledgee or usufructuary of shares can vote;
- authorise shareholders to determine a dividend day;
- authorise a management board to pay an advance dividend;
- grant preference to dividends not paid in preceding years and define the maximum number of years for which this dividend can be paid from successive annual profits;
- allow the voluntary or compulsory redemption of shares, and define the reasons and procedure;
- allow redemption of shares without a shareholders' resolution when certain events occur;
- restrict the right to recall management board members to important reasons;
- limit the liability of management board members;
- provide that the president of a management board has a casting vote and allow the president to direct the work of the board;
- appoint a supervisory board, and exclude or limit shareholder supervision of the company;
- extend the authority of a supervisory board, specifically by providing that a management board must obtain the consent of the supervisory board when acting under the company deed, and by giving the supervisory board the right to suspend any board member for important reasons;
- define matters that require the resolution of shareholders, other than the matters in the CCC;
- allow persons other than the supervisory board to convene a shareholders' meeting when the management board fails to do so;
- set the maximum increase permitted for initial capital and allow a certain period of time for the management board to do so; and
- define when a company can be dissolved.

PLC: A deed of association can:
- set the minimum or maximum initial share capital;
- define the ownership of shares;
- set the time and amount of payment for shares;
- provide that registered shares that are jointly-owned marital property can only be owned by one spouse;
- require that the company must consent to alienation of shares, or otherwise restrict the freedom to alienate registered shares;
- allow a pledgee or usufructuary of a share to vote, or make such voting conditional upon consent of company management;
- allow shareholders to define the day a dividend is paid;
- authorise the management board to pay an advance dividend;
- define special rights that are to attach to shares;
- give personal rights to a shareholder, specifically the right to appoint and recall management board and supervisory board members, or the right to obtain benefits from the company;

- regulate how destroyed or lost shares, provisional certificates or other documents are cancelled;
- define the voluntary and compulsory redemption of shares, and when there can be redemption without a shareholders' resolution;
- provide for the partial reappointment of a management board, or a common term of office;
- restrict the recall of management board members to important reasons;
- extend the authority of the supervisory board, specifically by providing that the management board must obtain the consent of the supervisory board prior to acting under the company deed;
- provide that supervisory board members can vote in writing, or by other means of direct communication over distance through another supervisory board member;
- provide that supervisory board members can be paid;
- define the matters that require a resolution of shareholders, other than the matters in the CCC; or
- define the creation of reserve capital for exceptional losses, or for expenditure.

Neither list is comprehensive.

(iii)   *Statutory provisions that can be altered by a deed of association*
There are certain provisions that apply by force of law even if they are not specifically dealt with by the deed of association. A number of the provisions are based on the equal (proportional) treatment of shareholders and their rights and obligations.
    LLC: In an LLC they include:

- shareholder equality – a company deed can provide otherwise;
- shareholder rights to audited profit, as is resolved by shareholders – a company deed can provide for a different manner of profit distribution;
- that profit is to be proportionate to a shareholding of a shareholder in the registered capital – although a company deed can provide a different manner of distribution of profit;
- that management board and supervisory board members are to be appointed and recalled by a resolution of shareholders – although a company deed can provide otherwise;
- rules for the statutory length of the term of offices of management board and supervisory board members,
- rules for company representation by a management board that has more than one member;
- the rule that each supervisory board member can supervise independently of any other member;
- that shareholder meetings are to be convened in the registered office of the company;
- that shareholder meetings are to be valid regardless of the number of shares represented at a meeting;

- that shares of equal nominal value have one vote per share, whereas shares of different nominal values have one vote for each PLN10 of nominal value (unless the articles of association of the company state otherwise);
- that shareholders can participate in shareholder meetings and vote through a proxy;
- that shareholder resolutions are to be passed by an absolute majority of votes;
- requirements to amend the company deed, to dissolve the company, or to transfer the whole or an organisational part of the enterprise (ongoing business) of the company;
- the priority for existing shareholders to subscribe for shares in an increase of the existing share capital, in proportion to the shares held;
- that management board members can be liquidators of the company and can be recalled by shareholders;
- the terms for distribution of assets to shareholders.

PLC: In a PLC these include:
- that a shareholder can demand that bearer shares are converted into registered shares or vice versa – although a company deed can limit that right;
- that the management board members are to be appointed, and recalled, by the supervisory board;
- that if the management board has more than one person, they all have the duty and right to jointly manage the company;
- that rules of company representation apply to a management board that has more than one member;
- that the supervisory board is to determine the remuneration of management board members employed under contracts of employment, or any other type of contract;
- that consent to management board members who may be conducting an activity categorised as being competitive to the activity of the company in which they are board members is to be given by the body authorised to appoint the management board;
- that the supervisory board is to be appointed and recalled by the shareholders;
- the rules for a quorum of a supervisory board; and
- that resolutions of the supervisory board are to be passed by an absolute majority of votes.

(b)   ***Signing a deed of association***
The deed is to be in the form of a notarial deed and is to be signed before a notary public, who will charge a fee. The shareholders, or founders, must appear, or be represented, at the signing.

(c)   ***Tax number***
The company must apply for a tax number. The application must accompany an

application to be registered in the NCR. The application form can be downloaded from the website of the Polish Ministry of Finance.[1]

An application is to be accompanied by a notarially or legally certified:

- extract from the NCR;
- company deed;
- proof of right to occupy the registered office of the company;
- REGON given by the Central Statistical Office of Poland (see section 3.2(g) below); and
- bank statement.

The application must be filed before the first act of business of the company that is taxable, or together with the first declaration on corporate income tax.

(d) Payment of indirect taxes

The incorporation of a company is taxed under the civil law transactions tax if the company is managed in Poland. However, there are statutory exemptions.

The tax is currently (2009) 0.5% of the contributions to the share capital or amount of initial capital. The tax is paid to the notary public that assists with incorporation.

(e) Registration in the register of entrepreneurs

The management board must register a 'company in organisation' in the NCR that has jurisdiction over the location of the registered office of the company.

The application to register must include:

- corporate name, and registered office (or service address for a PLC);
- object of company activity;
- amount of initial capital (the number and nominal value of shares in a PLC);
- amount of target capital, if provided in the company deed (applicable to a PLC);
- number of preference shares and the preferences (applicable to a PLC);
- proportion of initial capital paid prior to registration (applicable to a PLC);
- whether a shareholder can have more than one share (applicable to a PLC);
- surnames, forenames, and addresses of management board members and rules of company representation;
- surnames and forenames of supervisory board members, if such a board exists in the company;
- if shareholders have contributed in kind, a notation to that effect;
- if the duration of the company is to be limited;
- the name of the specific gazette in which company announcements are to be made; and
- if the company deed gives to shareholders any personal rights, right to participate in profit, or assets, other than the rights attaching to shares, a notice to that effect (applicable to a PLC).

---

1   www.mf.gov.pl

The application form and information is available on the website of the Polish Ministry of Justice.[2]

The following documents, or certified copies, must accompany the application:

- the company deed;
- the notarial deed and issuance of shares (applicable to a PLC);
- a list of shareholders, signed by all members of the management board (applicable to an LLC);
- a declaration signed by all management board members that the shareholders have made full contributions to the initial capital (applicable to an LLC);
- a declaration signed by all management board members that contributions to share capital are lawful (applicable to a PLC);
- a bank or investment firm certificate for payment for shares into the account of a company in organisation, should the company's statutes provide that some in-kind contributions are to be made after company registration – in which case a representation signed by all members of the management board is required that this has been done properly and on time;
- proof of the appointment of company management bodies, listing the members, if the bodies and members are appointed otherwise than under the company deed (the second part of this sentence only applies to an LLC); and
- specimen signature(s) of the management board member(s) issued and certified by a notary or court officer.

An application to register in the NCR must be made within six months from the date of the signing of a company deed. Otherwise:

- the company deed expires (an LLC);
- the management board must forthwith notify the persons that have a legal interest in receiving the notification and return the cash and in-kind contributions, or either of the two, that have been made (a PLC).

In practice the time taken to register a company is around one month, but this varies between registry courts and no guarantee can be given as to the time required for court (NCR) registration.

(f)   *Official records*

Each LLC or PLC must keep company records, which must include:

- a share register;
- a minute book; and
- books of accounts.

LLC: In an LLC the management board keeps a share register. Any shareholder can inspect it. Any changes must be filed with the NCR.

A minute book covers shareholders meetings. The minutes must state: whether

---

the meeting was properly convened; whether it was capable of passing valid resolutions; the resolutions that were passed; the votes cast for each resolution; and any objections. A list of attendees, signed by them, is to be attached to the minutes. If a resolution is in writing, it is to be recorded in the minute book. If the minutes are drawn by a notary, an excerpt is to appear. Shareholders can inspect the minute book and request copies of any resolutions, which must be certified by the management board.

PLC: In a PLC the management board must keep a register of registered shares and provisional share certificates if these were issued. A purchaser, pledge, or usufructuary of registered shares can request the board to record that shares have been transferred or have been encumbered, as the case may be. A shareholder can inspect and request a copy of the register and must pay any costs.

The share register can be kept in electronic form. A PLC can commission a bank or brokerage house to do this.

A minute book must have a copy of minutes, including evidence of shareholder meetings having been convened and powers of attorney issued by shareholders. The minutes are recorded by a notary and state that a meeting was properly convened; was capable of passing valid resolutions; specify the resolutions passed; the number of votes cast; and any objections. A list of attendees, signed by them, is to be attached to the minutes.

Shareholders can inspect the minutes book and have copies of resolutions certified by the management board.

Books of accounts are to be kept in the registered office of a company. If the books are kept outside the registered office, the tax office must be notified. In general, books of accounts must be kept within Poland.

The books, source documents, and interim financial statements must be stored for five fiscal years. Annual financial statements must be stored indefinitely.

(g) *Incorporation and post-incorporation applications*

Apart from filing an application for registration in the NCR, which, after registration by the court, terminates the process of establishing a company (a company becomes a legal person and is no longer 'in organisation'), other registrations must be obtained before the company can start to operate. These applications must be made to:

- the Polish Central Statistical Office (Główny Urząd Statystyczny) for a so-called REGON number;
- the Tax Office for a tax number and registration for VAT; and
- the Social Insurance Institution (Zakład Ubezpieczeń Społecznych).

4. Number of shareholders

A company can have any number of shareholders, but an LLC cannot be incorporated by a single shareholder. However, there is nothing to prevent this happening after incorporation.

Special provisions apply to a sole shareholder company. A sole shareholder cannot represent a company in organisation, except with regard to the application to the NCR to register the company (applicable to an LLC). Rights vested in shareholder meetings are exercised by the sole shareholder. There are special rules for acts performed by a sole shareholder (the same rules also apply to situations where there are two shareholders, but one is the company itself that has acquired – as an exception to the general prohibition – its own shares.)

In the above situations, any legal declarations, representations of a shareholder (eg where a shareholder and the company enter into a contract) or similar acts must be made in writing to be legally effective. Should such acts exceed the scope of ordinary company business, a certificate containing the signatures of the shareholder representatives is required.

5. Corporate name – limitations

A company must have a name, which is registered in the NCR.

In general, the name should include the company's object, registered office and any other expressions. A company name must also specify the form of incorporation of the company, which may be abbreviated. The name can contain a surname or pseudonym if it indicates a connection to the company, but an individual would have to consent in writing to the use of their name. An abbreviated corporate name can be used. A company's name must differ from any competitors; it must not be misleading.

A branch office is identified by the word '*oddział*' (branch), and details of the branch's registered office.

Any change of name must be registered with the NCR. If the form of a company changes, the name can be retained but the new form must be incorporated.

A name cannot be sold, but a company can authorise another to use it, unless that would be misleading.

If another company feels that the right to their name has been breached, it can demand that the use ceases and that any adverse effects be removed. It can also claim damages, or a return of unjust enrichment from the party at fault.

6. Registered office

A registered office is required, and is to be specified in the company deed.

The office must be in Poland, and a transfer abroad will result in dissolution of the company (except for the situation where this is done under the cross-border merger provisions of the CCC). As a rule, the office is at the same location where the management board is based. A change of office location must be registered in the NCR within seven days.

A company can have only one registered office.

A management board could be held to be liable to a company for not having a registered office.

A company that has a registered office abroad can have branches, or agencies, inside or outside Poland.

7. Object of activity

A company can be incorporated for any lawful purpose, but Polish legislation can restrict certain activities to a specific type of company.

The object of activity must be defined in the company deed, meaning that if an object is to change, the deed will have to be changed.

Objects of company activity must be registered with the NCR on incorporation. Any major change of object requires a shareholders' resolution passed by the three-quarters of the votes in an LLC, or two-thirds in a PLC.

The business activity of an LLC or a PLC is defined in compliance with the Polish Activity Classification 2007 (*Polska Klasyfikacja Działalności* 2007 or PKD 2007), which is available on the website of the Central Statistical Office of Poland.[3]

8. Share capital

8.1 Minimum amounts
The minimum amount of a registered share capital for an LLC is PLN50,000 and the nominal value of one share cannot be less than PLN50; the minimum for a PLC is PLN500,000 and the nominal value of one share cannot be less than PLN0.01.

8.2 Nature of contributions
Shareholders can pay for shares in cash, or in kind. Any movable or immovable property, as well as any transferable rights, including receivables, can be contributed. An in-kind contribution must always have value, but services or the delivery of work cannot be used as an in-kind contribution. They should always be contributed at market value so as to fully pay for the shares that are issued in exchange for the contribution to the company.

8.3 Partial payments
Shares in an LLC must be paid for in full before a company can be registered, so shares cannot be taken for a value less than nominal value. Shares can have a premium on the nominal value, and the premium is transferred to the supplementary capital of the company.

Shares in a PLC that are paid for by in-kind contributions must be fully paid no later than one year after the registration of the company. At least one-quarter of the nominal value of shares paid for by monetary contributions must be paid for before the company is registered. If shares are issued in return for in-kind contributions, or contributions both in kind and in cash, at least one-quarter of the amount of the initial capital must be paid before the registration of the company.

The time and amount of payments for shares is set out in the company's deed or in a resolution of shareholders, but shareholders can authorise the management board to decide the timing of payments.

8.4 Share certificates
In an LLC the share capital must be divided into shares that are of equal value (unless there is just one share). As a rule, one share means one vote, but a company deed can give other preferences. In general there are no more than three votes per share.

---

3   www.stat.gov.pl

In a PLC a management board issues share certificates in the form of a document. This must contain the:

- corporate name, and registered office of the company – the issuer;
- the relevant NCR and company reference number;
- date of registration and date of issue of the share;
- nominal value, series and number, type of share and any special rights attached to the share;
- amount already contributed, if the share is an ordinary registered share;
- restrictions on the alienation of a share; and
- provisions of a company deed on duties of the shareholder to the company encompassed in the share.

A PLC share certificate must bear the seal of the company and the signature of the management board. The signature can be mechanically reproduced. A company statute can have additional requirements on the content and form of a share certificate. Multiple-share certificates can be issued.

Registered shares can be issued before being paid for in full. Bearer shares must be paid for in full before they are issued, but a registered provisional certificate can be issued if only partial payment has been made.

A PLC whose shares have been admitted to public trading and are listed on a stock exchange can have a dematerialised form and, instead of a share certificate, shareholders can receive a registered certificate of deposit from the entity holding the company's securities account.

In a PLC, the initial share capital is divided into shares of equal nominal value Each shareholder can have more than one share. As a rule, one share equals one vote, but a company deed can provide otherwise. Generally there are no more than two votes per share.

8.5 Restrictions on the transfer of shares

In an LLC the articles of association can limit or exempt the transfer of shares, or make the transfer conditional upon the company's consent. If a deed of association is silent on who should provide consent, this is given by the management board in writing; the registry court can consent to the transfer if the board refuses to do so.

The deed of association can also limit or exclude the rights of heirs to join the company in place of a deceased shareholder, and also the right of a shareholder's spouse to join the company when shares are joint marital property.

Shares in a PLC can be transferred, but the statute can make this conditional on the company's consent, or impose other limitations. The management board decides in writing whether or not to consent if this is not stated. If a company refuses consent to a transfer, it must provide an alternative buyer within a specific time.

A contract can limit the transferability of shares, or parts of them, for a period of up to five years. A contract can restrict the alienation of the whole, or part, of a share for up to five years.

Rights of pre-emption, or of giving other priority rights to acquire a whole or part of a share, are permitted, but not for more than 10 years.

8.6 Transfer of shares

The transfer of a share in an LLC is to be in writing and to have signatures certified by a notary. The company is to be notified by the parties participating in the transfer, and proof of transfer must be provided. The transfer will apply from the moment of notification.

A transfer of registered shares, or a provisional certificate in a PLC, must be in writing. This can be done on the share certificate or the provisional certificate, or on a separate document (agreement).

The Competition and Consumer Protection Act 2007 applies to some transfers. The President of the Office of Competition and Consumer Protection must be notified when the permitted levels of market concentration are exceeded.

9. Equity

9.1 Balance between capital and own resources

If a balance sheet prepared by the management board of an LLC shows a loss in excess of the total of the supplementary and reserve capital and half of the initial capital (one-third for a PLC), a meeting of the shareholders must be convened to adopt a resolution on the continued existence of the company.

In a PLC a supplementary reserve capital must be created to be applied to losses, into which no less than 8% of the annual profit is to be transferred until the reserve reaches more than one-third of the registered share capital.

9.2 Convertible bonds

A PLC can issue convertible bonds if a company statute provides for this. Shareholders can pass a resolution by a majority of three-quarters of votes cast. The resolution is to be registered with the NCR.

10. Administration of the company

10.1 Shareholder meetings

(a) Quorums at meetings

As a rule, a quorum is not required for shareholder meetings in either type of company. A company deed can provide otherwise.

(b) Quorums for passing resolutions

An absolute majority of votes is required, unless otherwise provided in the CCC or the company deed.

A resolution to dissolve a company can be passed by an absolute majority of votes when a loss in excess of the total of supplementary and reserve capital and half of the initial capital for an LLC, or one-third of the initial capital for a PLC, is shown on the company's balance sheet. A company deed can provide different thresholds.

In an LLC, a two-thirds majority is required to pass a resolution to amend the articles of association, to dissolve the company, or to transfer the whole or an organisational part of an enterprise (ongoing business).

A three-quarters majority is required to pass a resolution to make major changes in the object of the company business activity defined by the articles.

Any shareholders' resolutions that change the deed of association and impose any new obligations on any shareholders, or that decrease or increase any shareholder rights or obligations already granted or imposed by the deed of association, require the consent of the shareholder who is affected by such a change.

A three-quarters majority is required to pass a resolution in a PLC for: issue of convertible bonds or bonds giving a pre-emptive right to shares; amendment of the company deed; redemption of shares; any decrease in the registered share capital; a transfer of the whole or organisational part of an enterprise (ongoing business) ; or dissolution of the company.

A two-thirds majority is required to finance an acquisition of own shares, but if more than half of the initial registered capital is represented at a shareholders meeting, only an absolute majority of votes is required.

A 95% majority is required to be able to compulsorily acquire the shares of minority shareholders (a 'squeeze out' procedure).

A company deed may have more rigorous requirements for passing these kinds of resolutions, for either type of company.

(c) *Challenges to resolutions*

In either type of company, a resolution that is contrary to the company deed or good practice, and that threatens the company's interests or is intended to harm a shareholder, can be invalidated. An action for invalidation must be brought within one month of the resolution, but no later than six months (three months for a public PLC) from when the resolution was passed.

An illegal resolution can be declared invalid by bringing an action against the company. The action would have to be brought within six months (30 days for a public PLC) of the resolution, but no later than three years (two years in a PLC, or one year in a public PLC) from the resolution being passed.

The following persons and/or company bodies have the right to bring an action:

- members of the management or supervisory board;
- a shareholder that voted against the resolution whose objection was recorded in the minutes of the shareholders' meeting (holders of non-voting shares in a PLC are excluded);
- a shareholder wrongfully excluded from a shareholders' meeting;
- a shareholder absent from a shareholders' meeting only because the meeting was improperly convened, or the resolution was not on the agenda; and
- a shareholder who was bypassed during voting, or who did not agree to vote in writing, or who voted against the resolution and when informed of the resolution objected within two weeks (applicable to an LLC).

In an action to invalidate a resolution, the company is represented by the management board, unless shareholders have appointed a lawyer. If the management board, in either type of company, cannot act for the company, and shareholders do not appoint a lawyer, the court will appoint a guardian.

A judgment that is final in law and that invalidates a resolution binds the company, shareholders and members of managing bodies. Where the validity of an act depends on a resolution of shareholders, invalidation will not apply to third parties that have acted in good faith.

10.2 Management board

(a) System of administration

A management board is compulsory in both types of companies. Appointments can be made from among shareholders or other individuals (either Polish or foreign national(s)). A board must have one or more members.

In an LLC, a board that has more than one member can and must manage and represent the company in all court and out-of-court acts. For a PLC, all members of the board must jointly manage the affairs of the company, and this cannot be limited in application to third parties.

Each LLC board member can, without a prior resolution of the board, manage matters within the ordinary course of business of the company, but a resolution is required where at least one member objects, or where the ordinary course of business is exceeded.

If the board in either type of company has more than one member, the company deed defines the company representation. If it does not, two members of the board must act jointly, or one member must act jointly with a proxy.

Documents can be served on one board member, or a proxy.

When the company and a board member are entering into a contract, or if there is a dispute involving a board member, the company must be represented by the supervisory board, or by a lawyer appointed by shareholders. If a sole shareholder is the sole member of the management board, any legal act between the shareholder and the company must be shown in a notarial deed.

A board can pass a resolution when board members have been notified of a meeting. Board resolutions are passed by an absolute majority of votes, but all members must consent to the appointment of a proxy. A proxy can be revoked by a single member.

In PLCs, resolutions are recorded in the minutes. These are signed by the board members in attendance.

(b) Terms of office, resignation, and recall of management board members

The shareholders of an LLC, or the supervisory board of a PLC, can recall members of a management board at any point. Management board members can be recalled, or suspended, by shareholders.

The statutory term of office for board members of an LLC expires when shareholders meet to approve financial statements for the first full financial year in which the member served on the board. This also applies to a PLC if no term of office had been set out in the statute (but this cannot be longer than five years).

If management board members in either type of company are appointed for a common term of office, the term of office of a member appointed before the lapse of the common term of office expires at the same time. The term of office expires on death, resignation, or removal from the board. A member can be removed at any time by shareholders, or supervisory board of a PLC.

The company deed can restrict the right of recall.

(c) **Management board member liability to third parties**

In either type of company, management board members are jointly and severally liable to creditors of the company for three years for any intentional or negligent declarations, including submitting false details to the NCR when the company is registered, or where the share capital has been increased.

The board members are jointly and severally liable for company obligations when enforcement against the company is ineffective. A member is not liable when the member proves that:

- a petition for bankruptcy was filed on time;
- debt arrangement proceedings were instituted on time;
- failure to file a petition for bankruptcy, or institute debt arrangement was not the fault of a management board member; or
- a creditor suffered no loss, even though there was failure to file for bankruptcy or arrange the payment of debt.

Board members in a LLC are also jointly and severally liable for tax arrears if the company cannot pay and the board member cannot prove that:

- a petition for bankruptcy was filed, or action to prevent bankruptcy were taken on time;
- the board member was not at fault in failing to file for bankruptcy, or trying to prevent bankruptcy; or
- the board member has not identified assets that could satisfy the tax arrears.

The liability for tax arrears applies to present and former members of the board.

(d) **Non-competition**

Management board members cannot by law operate businesses that compete against the company.

Members in either type of company must not compete in business, or be a partner or a shareholder of such a business. They cannot be on the management board or own shares in such companies. This applies when a member has more than a 10% interest in a competitor or has the power to appoint a least one member to a management board.

(e) **Special duties of confidentiality and avoidance of a conflict of interest**

Under the Unfair Competition Act 1993, management board members must maintain confidentiality for three years after they cease to be a board member, subject to receiving compensation. When there is a conflict of interest, the member must not act and must note the conflict of interest in the minutes of the company's board meeting.

(f)   ***Civil and criminal liability***

In an LLC, members of the management board are liable for any losses due to illegal acts or omissions unless they are not at fault. Board members can be held jointly and severally liable for the loss.

In a PLC, management board members are liable for any losses caused by negligence, or illegal acts, unless they are not at fault. Management board members may also be held liable for losses during the incorporation process, or for losses caused by false information in publications, or records, to do with the issue of company shares, bonds, right to a dividend, or distribution of assets. The liability is joint and several.

In either type of company it is an offence to:

- act to the detriment of the company;
- fail to file for bankruptcy when there is good reason to do so;
- announce false information, or present such information to company bodies, Polish state authorities, or auditors;
- allow the company to acquire its own shares, or pledge them, unless the CCC permits this;
- issue registered documents, bearer documents, or documents to order, for shares or for rights to profits in the company;
- enable unlawful voting at shareholders' meetings, or unlawful exercise of minority rights or (in a PLC) issue a false certificates authorising the exercise of voting rights; or
- release rights to a share that has not been paid for, before the company is registered, or before an increase of initial capital is registered.

It is also an offence if a management board does not:

- file a list of shareholders in the NCR;
- keep a share register;
- convene a shareholders' meeting when required to do so;
- provide explanations to an auditor when required to do so;
- apply to the NCR for the appointment of auditors; and
- manage the company for more than three months without a proper supervisory board.

10.3   Other specific provisions

(a)   ***Shareholder representation by proxy***

A proxy can represent shareholders at shareholders' meetings and vote, unless otherwise provided in the CCC or company deed. Powers of attorney that are not in writing are invalid; a document of a power of attorney must be attached to the minute book.

A management board member or company employee cannot act as an attorney-in-fact at a shareholders' meeting.

A proxy appointed by shareholders can represent a company in a dispute over invalidating a shareholders' resolution.

(b)   *Company representation by a commercial proxy*

A commercial proxy (*procura*) can act in or out of court in all matters involving company business. The deed of association defines the representation of a company. The consent of all management board members is required to appoint a commercial proxy, but any member can revoke a proxy.

A commercial proxy must be registered in the NCR. It must be granted in writing to be valid, and can be given to more than one person. A commercial proxy's authority can be limited to the right to represent a branch.

(c)   ***Supervisory board and shareholder personal rights of supervision***

Any shareholder in an LLC can supervise the company.

The shareholder, either alone or together with an appointee, can inspect records of the company, prepare a balance sheet for that purpose, or call on the management board to provide explanations, at any time.

An LLC's deed of association can provide for the establishment of a supervisory board. A supervisory board is usually optional, but it is obligatory when a company has a registered share capital of more than PLN500,000 and has more than 25 shareholders. An LLC's articles of association can limit shareholder supervision when a supervisory board is appointed. A supervisory board supervises day-to-day company management, but it cannot bind (instruct) a management board in how to manage a company. Any supervisory board member can supervise the company alone unless a company deed provides otherwise.

A supervisory board is to have no less than three members appointed for a one-year term of office by shareholders, unless otherwise provided in a deed of an LLC. They can be recalled at any time by shareholders. The rules governing terms of office for a supervisory board member are the same as for the management board.

Resolutions of the board can be passed when at least half of the members are present and all members have been invited to the meeting. A company deed can set more rigorous requirements for a quorum.

A PLC must have a supervisory board and its powers are more extensive than the supervisory board of an LLC. A supervisory board can suspend any members of a management board and delegate other board members to temporarily (for a period not exceeding three months) assume the responsibilities of any board members who have been recalled, resigned, or are unable to carry out their role.

In addition, a company deed can extend the authority of a supervisory board, specifically by providing that the management board is to obtain the consent of the supervisory board prior to acting as provided in the company deed. If, however, the supervisory board refuses to consent, the management board can request shareholders to authorise the acts.

A supervisory board must have a minimum of three members (five, in a listed PLC), who are appointed, and recalled, by shareholders. A company statute can provide for a different manner of appointing, and recalling, members. The term of office of a supervisory board member cannot be longer than five years.

A shareholder holding more than one-fifth of the initial capital of a company can require that a supervisory board be elected by another shareholders' meeting by voting in separate groups, even if a company statute provides a different way to appoint a supervisory board. In that situation, each group can delegate one supervisory board member to supervise and act independently of others.

A supervisory board is to pass resolutions by an absolute majority, unless the PLC's statute provides otherwise. Furthermore, a supervisory board is to act collectively, but it can delegate duties to specific members.

11. Fiscal year, duration and start of activities

In general, a fiscal year in Poland is the calendar year, but there are statutory exceptions.

A company has a first fiscal year that lasts from the start of business until the last day of the fiscal year that is chosen, but it cannot be longer than 12 months. If, however, that company commences business in the second half of a calendar year and chooses a calendar year to be the fiscal year, the first fiscal year lasts from the first day of business until the end of the next calendar year. The statute of a PLC can define a fiscal year to be other than a calendar year. If so, the company must inform the Tax Office and the fiscal year will be successive 12 monthly periods.

11.1 Financial statements

(a) Taxation

Corporate income tax is payable on company income less deductible expenses and allowances. Specifically, this is likely to cover normal trading expenditure, capital allowances, and donations to charities. The basic corporate income tax rate is currently (2009) 19%. No separate capital gains tax is added to corporate income tax.

Dividends to be paid to foreign shareholders usually attract a withholding tax currently of 19% (unless a double-taxation treaty provides otherwise). Poland has concluded double taxation agreements with more than 80 countries.

However, special tax rules apply when a company pays dividends to shareholders in the European Union, the European Economic Area or Switzerland, and the dividends can be exempt from withholding tax. The shareholders can benefit from the special tax regime based on the Parent–Subsidiary Directive 2003/123/EC dated December 22 2003, but only if statutory preconditions are met.

Value added tax (VAT) applies to the sale and supply of goods and services by Polish companies, and on the import and export of goods and services into and out of Poland. The VAT rates are currently 22%, 7%, 3%, 0%, and there are exemptions. The general VAT rate is 22%.

Social security is currently payable at the rate of 34.12% of premium base, and 21.16% of premium base is covered by an employer (including 2.45% of premium base to the Labour Fund and 0.10% of premium base to the Fund of Guaranteed Employee Benefits).

Real estate tax is currently payable up to a maximum of PLN17.31 per square metre of useable area of real estate, other than agricultural land, in which a business operates. Land tax is payable up to a maximum of PLN0.62 per square metre of land in which a business operates. The local authority sets the rate per square metre of real estate and land tax.

11.2   Annual accounts

(a)   Documents

A company must prepare a balance sheet, a profit and loss account, notes to financial statements, a cash flow statement, and a management board report. All books of accounts and financial statements must be denominated in Polish zlotys. Foreign source documents in accounting records need to be translated into Polish.

Annual accounts must be true and fair, and they must comply with the requirements in the CCC and other relevant regulations. Annual accounts must be signed by management board members, and the person in charge of accounting – usually an accountant.

Annual accounts are sent to the tax office, the NCR, and shareholders of the company. Company shareholders must receive them no later than 15 days before an annual ordinary shareholders' meeting.

All source documents, books of accounts, and interim financial statements must, as a rule, be stored for five complete fiscal years. Annual financial statements must be stored permanently. Books of accounts are to be maintained in the registered office of a company or, if they are not, the tax office must be notified. In general, they must be maintained within Poland.

Companies that operate as small businesses and can satisfy at least two of following three criteria can prepare and file annual accounts in a simplified form:

- total assets do not exceed €2 million in value;
- turnover does not exceed €4 million; or
- the total number of employees does not exceed 50.

(b)   Audit reports

An auditor must provide a written declaration as to whether annual accounts comply with the relevant accountancy principles and whether they are a true and fair indication of a company's financial position.

An auditor's report is required for a PLC. Such a report is required for an LLC if it satisfies at least two of following three criteria:

- the average number of full-time employees is more than 50;
- total assets at the end of a fiscal year are a minimum of €2.5 million in value;
- net income sales, or financial transactions, for a fiscal year are a minimum of €5 million.

The obligations of an auditor are defined in the Accountancy Law Act 1994. Among other characteristics, the auditor must be impartial and independent.

An auditor is appointed by shareholders, unless otherwise provided in a company deed.

A company must make an audit report available to shareholders within 15 days of an ordinary shareholders' meeting.

(c)   Approval and distribution of profits

In general, shareholders can resolve to distribute profit, which is to be paid as a dividend in proportion to possessed shares in the registered capital. A company deed can provide a different manner of distribution of profit.

A company deed can authorise a management board to pay shareholders an advance dividend, but the advance can only be paid when approved annual financial statements for a previous financial year show a profit. A company deed can provide for preferences related to shares in terms of the payment of a dividend.

A shareholder that received a dividend that is contrary to law, or to a company deed, must return it and is liable to the company for it jointly and severally with those members of the management board that authorised it.

(d)   Publication of accounts

Annual financial statements, audit reports (if prepared) and resolutions of shareholders to accept annual financial statements and to distribute, or allocate, profit must be filed with the NCR within 15 days of the ordinary shareholders' meeting that deals with those matters.

All companies must publish certain information in the *Official Journal of the Republic of Poland* (*Monitor Polski B*). This information includes: balance sheets, and profit and loss accounts; a statement of the source and application of funds; statements of cash flows; an audit report; and a copy of the resolution of shareholders to accept the annual financial statements, and any resolution to distribute, or allocate, profit. Publication must be within 15 days of an ordinary shareholders' meeting that has dealt with those matters.

12.   Company reorganisation: transformation, merger and split-off

(a)   Transformation

Either type of company can change the legal form of its operation and be transformed into another type of company or partnership. A company is transformed from the time when the change is registered with the NCR.

The transformed company acquires all rights and obligations of the company or partnership, unless otherwise provided by law. As a rule, the transformed company retains the permits, concessions, and allowances that applied before the transformation. Shareholders that participate in the change remain as shareholders after the change, as from the day of the change.

A transformed company must use its previous name in parentheses beside the current corporate name, accompanied by the word '*dawniej*' (formerly) for at least one year.

(b)   Merger

Either type of company can merge with another company or partnership. Companies can merge with the foreign companies in accordance with the newly implemented principles of the EU Directive 2005/56/EC dated October 26 2005 on cross-border mergers of LLCs.

A company in liquidation, or one in the process of dividing assets, or one in bankruptcy cannot take part in a merger.

A merger can be executed through:

- acquisition, that is by way of transferring all assets of a company or a partnership (the target) to another company (the acquirer) in exchange for shares from the acquirer to the shareholders, or partners, of the target; or
- forming a separate company, by way of a transfer of all assets in exchange for shares in the separate company.

On the day of a merger, the acquirer, or separate company, acquires all rights and duties of a target. As a rule, the acquirer, or separate company, acquires any permits, concessions, or allowances, granted to a target. Furthermore, on the day of a merger, the shareholders, or partners, of a target become the shareholders, or partners, of the acquirer, or separate company, as the case may be.

The acquirer, or separate company, needs to apply to register the change in the legal status of the held real-estate properties in a land and mortgage register. Similar registration-update obligations apply in relation to other registries where merged company assets have been registered.

The assets of a merged company or partnership are to be managed separately by an acquirer, or separate company, until all creditors of the pre-merged companies that gave notice of debt within six months of the announcement of the merger are paid or given security of payment.

(c)   *Split-off*

A company can be divided into two or more companies. A division of a PLC is not permitted unless the initial capital has been paid in full. In addition, a company in liquidation that has started a division of assets, and a company in bankruptcy, cannot be divided.

A split-off is possible through:

- acquisition by way of transfer of all assets of the company being divided to another company in exchange for shares in an acquiring company, which are issued to the shareholders of the company under division;
- formation of separate companies, to which all assets of a company under division are transferred in exchange for shares in that separate company;
- acquisition and formation of a separate company by a transfer of all company assets under division to an existing company and a separate company or companies; or
- separation by way of transfer of part of the company assets under division to an existing company or a separate company.

On the day of split-off, the acquiring or newly formed companies acquire the rights and duties of a company under division specified in the split-off plan. In general, an acquirer, or separate company, that came into existence as a result of split-off acquires any permits, concessions, or allowances that have been held prior the division or separation.

The acquirer, or separate company, must apply to be registered in a land and mortgage register, or other registers, to update the legal status of rights that are disclosed in those registers.

13. 'Squeeze-out' procedure

In an LLC, a court can, at the request of other shareholders that hold more than half of the registered share capital of a company, exclude a shareholder from the company. The company deed can decrease that threshold. The shares of an excluded shareholder must be acquired by existing shareholders, or by third parties. A court must set the price for the shares at their market value.

Majority shareholders in a PLC can resolve to compulsorily acquire shares only if the minority shareholders hold less than 5% of the registered share capital. The resolution must be passed by no more than five shareholders whose cumulative holding is no less than 95% of the registered share capital and who hold no less than 5% of initial capital. The quorum for passing the resolution is 95% of votes cast. A company statute can set more rigorous requirements.

The minority shareholders whose shares are to be compulsorily acquired must deposit their share certificates at the company within one month of the publication of the resolution for acquisition. The management board can annul the share certificates and issue replacement share certificates, which are transferred to purchasers of these shares, if this deposition does not happen. Compulsory acquisition does not apply to public PLCs.

A shareholder, or shareholders, representing not more than 5% of the registered share capital can demand that the agenda of the next shareholders' meeting contains a resolution on compulsory acquisition of their shares. These can be purchased by not more than five shareholders representing jointly not less than 95% of initial capital, where each of the purchasing shareholders holds not less than 5% of initial capital.

The provisions on compulsory purchase of shares do not apply to public companies, companies in liquidation, or companies in bankruptcy unless a resolution of compulsory purchase was passed at least three months before the declaration of liquidation or bankruptcy.

14. Dissolution and liquidation

(a) Dissolution

A company can be dissolved for the following reasons:
- reasons listed in a company deed;
- a resolution of shareholders to dissolve the company, or transfer the registered office abroad (confirmed in a minute prepared by a notary, for an LLC);
- a declaration of bankruptcy; or
- other causes provided by law.

In addition, the Registry Court can decide to dissolve a company when:
- the deed of association has not been validly executed by shareholders;
- the object of company activity specified in the company deed is illegal;
- the company deed does not contain any provisions on a corporate name, object of activity, initial capital or contributions thereto; or

- those that concluded the company deed lacked the capacity in law to be able to do so.

A company cannot be dissolved by the Registry Court for any of the reasons mentioned above if five years have passed from the time when it was registered. The registry court is to decide whether to dissolve a company after an examination *ex officio*, or on application of a person having a legal interest in the dissolution. A court decision to dissolve a company does not affect the validity of company acts.

In addition to the instances mentioned above, the Registry Court can also decide to dissolve an LCC at the request of:
- a shareholder, or a member of the company's management body, if it has become impossible to meet company objectives for important business reasons; or
- a state authority if a company's unlawful activities threaten the public interest.

A company is dissolved at the point when it is deleted from the NCR.

(b) *Liquidation*

Liquidation commences on the date when the Registry Court decision to dissolve the company becomes final in law, or when the shareholders pass a resolution to dissolve the company. Liquidation means the company name must be supplemented by the additional designation *'w likwidacji'* (in liquidation).

During liquidation a company retains legal personality. However, profits cannot be paid to shareholders, nor can company assets be divided before all obligations have been paid in full.

Liquidators are the members of the management board of the company, unless otherwise provided in a company deed or by a resolution of shareholders. When the Registry Court decides to liquidate a company, it can also appoint liquidators. Liquidators can be recalled by a resolution of shareholders (applicable only to an LLC). However, if the Registry Court appoints liquidators, only the registry court can recall them.

The liquidators must notify the Registry Court of the opening and completion of liquidation. They announce (twice for a PLC) the dissolution of the company and the start of the liquidation procedure, and they give notice that creditors have three months (six months for a PLC) from the date of announcement to file a claim.

The liquidators must complete outstanding company business; collect debts; fulfil obligations; and sell company assets. They manage and represent the company to the extent that they have the authority to do so.

The opening of liquidation causes proxies to expire. Moreover, a proxy cannot be given during liquidation.

Books of accounts and documents of a dissolved company must be placed in the custody of the person indicated in the company deed or in a resolution of shareholders. In the absence thereof, the NCR will appoint a custodian. Shareholders and persons having a legal interest can inspect the company's books.

If a company is bankrupt, it is dissolved on completion of the bankruptcy, by deletion from the NCR. In liquidation, the official officer in bankruptcy applies for the deletion of a company from the NCR. A company will not, however, be dissolved if the bankruptcy ends in a scheme of arrangement or is discontinued for other reasons.

A liquidator, or an official receiver in bankruptcy, is to notify the Tax Office of the dissolution of a company, and supply a liquidation report.

In a PLC, the liquidator or official receiver in bankruptcy needs to notify other bodies and institutions of the termination of existence of a company, including:

- the Central Statistical Office of Poland (Główny Urząd Statystyczny);
- the social insurance institution (Zakład Ubezpieczeń Społecznych); and
- the relevant banks.

15.   Branches

Either type of company that has a registered office in Poland, or abroad, can establish a branch in Poland.

Under Polish law, a branch is not a separate entity from its parent company and the parent company is liable for the obligations of its branch. A branch must be registered in the NCR and the provisions on liquidation of companies apply to the liquidation of branches.

Romania

Alina Deiac
Marius Nita
Pachiu & Associates

---

1. **Types of limited liability company and applicable legislation**

The most frequent types of limited liability companies incorporated in Romania are limited liability corporations (*societate cu raspundere limitata* – SRL, denoted in this chapter as LLCs) and joint-stock companies (*societate pe actiuni* – SA). As a general rule, the legal form of the company may be freely chosen by its founders. However, certain activities, such as banking and insurance, may only performed by joint stock companies.

LLCs and joint stock companies are governed by the following legislation:

- Law 31/1990 on companies, republished with the *Official Gazette* No 1066/17.11.2004, as further amended (company law);
- Law 26/1990 on the Mercantile Registry, republished with the *Official Gazette* No 49/04.02.1998, as further amended;
- Law 359/2004 on the simplification of the registration process with the Mercantile Registry of individuals, family associations and legal entities, as well as the functioning authorisation for legal entities, published in the *Official Gazette* No 839/13.09.2004, as further amended; and
- Law 571/2003 regarding the Fiscal Code, published with the *Official Gazette* No 927/23.11.2003, as further amended.

2. **Incorporation**

2.1 **Proceedings prior to incorporation**

(a) *Corporate name*

Each company incorporated in Romania must have a corporate name. The corporate name is obtained by submitting a standard application with the competent Mercantile Registry, providing for three alternative names in order of preference. If one of the preferred names is available, the Mercantile Registry will issue proof of availability the same day. This is valid for a period of three months as of the date of issue and can be extended for an additional three-month period.

(b) *Contributions to company equity*

The contributions to the company's equity can be performed in kind, in cash or by contributing account receivables. In-cash contributions are mandatory when establishing any form of company.

Cash contributions, regardless of the currency in which they are disbursed, must always be stated in RON (the Romanian new leu) in the bylaws. In-kind contributions are allowed for any form of company.

(c)   *Declaration of foreign investment*

Foreign investments are encouraged in Romania. However, when incorporating a company, the partners must submit a statement detailing the amount of foreign investment to the competent Mercantile Registry for statistical purposes.

(d)   *Tax number for foreign partners/directors*

Upon registration as partners or directors of a Romanian company, foreign citizens must present a certified affidavit demonstrating compliance with Romanian legislation and declaring that they are not resident in Romania and do not have fiscal debts there. A tax number does not have to be obtained prior to the incorporation of a company. Directors must also present a notarised signature specimen.

2.2   Incorporation

(a)   *Bylaws*

(i)   *Essential clauses*

As provided by company law, the bylaws must contain the following information:
- identification data of the partners, which must include:
  - for individuals: first and second name; personal numerical code (or equivalent under applicable law); place and date of birth,; domicile and citizenship;
  - for legal entities: name; domicile; nationality; number of registration with the mercantile registry; or sole registration number, in compliance with their national law;
- form, name and registered domicile;
- the company's object of activity, stating the main field of activity and the main activity;
- the capital stock, mentioning the contribution of each partner in cash or in kind; the value of the contribution and the method of evaluation; the number and value of shares;
- directors' identification data, the powers granted to them and whether they exercise such powers jointly or severally;
- the identification data of appointed censors or internal auditors;
- each partner's share for profit and loss;
- secondary headquarters – subsidiaries; agencies; representative offices or such other entities without legal personality – if established simultaneously with the company or the terms for their subsequent establishment;
- duration of the company; and
- the method of dissolution or liquidation of the company.

In addition to this, for a joint stock company the bylaws must also provide for:

- the number and nominal value of the shares, specifying whether they are nominative or bearer shares;
- whether there are one or several classes of shares; the number, nominal value and rights associated with each class of shares;
- any restriction with regard to the transfer of shares;
- provisions relating to the management, administration, control of management and operation of the company, the number of the directors and method to determine such number;
- powers of representation granted to directors and, as applicable, to the managers, and whether they are to exercise them jointly or severally;
- any special advantages granted upon formation or authorisation of the company to any person participating in the formation of the company or in transactions resulting in the authorisation of the company, as well as identification data of the beneficiaries of such advantages; and
- the total (or estimated) value of all incorporation expenses.

(ll)   *Clauses not foreseen by law and enlargeable clauses ruled by law*

Besides the clauses required by company law, the partners in a LLC or in a joint stock company can include provisions in the bylaws that focus on particular situations, such as pre-emption rights given to a partner in a case of the assignment of shares, tag-along or drag along rights, or provisions that may refer to deadlock situations.

Moreover, in several situations, the legal framework set out by company law can be adjusted. One situation refers to the necessary quorum/majority for adopting a resolution within the general meeting of the partners, or within the supervisory board or the board of directors, as applicable. The quorum/majority requirements can be adjusted upwards or downwards by the partners within certain limits.

(b)   **Execution of public deed**

The bylaws of a company must be concluded in writing and executed by all partners or by attorneys of such (based on a power of attorney granted by the partners), and as a general rule they are concluded under private signature or are certified by a lawyer.

However, these documents must be concluded in authentic form if there is an in-kind contribution to the capital stock consisting of land, or when a joint stock company is incorporated by public subscription.

(c)   **Tax identification number**

Upon the incorporation of the company with the competent Mercantile Registry, a certificate of registration will be issued, which provides the company's unique registration code issued by the Ministry of Public Finances.

If the company pays VAT, it must submit an application to the competent fiscal authority for a VAT payment certificate, containing the fiscal attribute 'RO'.

(d) Indirect taxes

If the activities of the company are taxable for VAT and the forecasted turnover exceeds €35,000, the company must be registered for VAT with the proper fiscal authority. If the company anticipates that its turnover will be less than €35,000, it can decide whether or not to pay VAT. If the company's activities are exempt from VAT, it can register as a non-payer.

The standard VAT rate is currently (2009) 19%, and the reduced VAT rate is 9%.

(e) Registration with the Mercantile Registry

Within 15 days of signing the bylaws, the partners or their representatives must apply for the company's registration with the Mercantile Registry in the jurisdiction where the company has its domicile. In this respect, the bylaws of the company, together with a standard registration application form and various other documents, must be submitted. Registration takes about five working days after the submission of the file. The company acquires legal personality as of the registration date. Registration is performed by a judge working in the Mercantile Registry.

(f) Legalisation of official books

Both LLCs and joint stock companies must keep: (i) a shareholders' registry stating the name, the address or domicile of the shareholders; and (ii) a record of financial statements. Law 252/2003 regarding a unique register of controls requires each company to keep such a register issued by the competent fiscal authority, in which all controls and sanctions performed by authorities on the activities carried out by the company must be mentioned.

As regards the accounting books, Law 82/1991 on accounting procedures provides that companies must also keep: (i) a journal; (ii) an inventory; and (iii) a main register. An employees' evidence register, issued by the competent territorial labour inspectorate, must also be kept by each company.

Joint stock companies must also keep a register of:

- the meetings and issues discussed by the general meetings of partners;
- the meetings and issues discussed by the board of directors, respectively the directorate and the supervisory board;
- the meetings and facts found by the censors or, as the case may be, by the internal auditors within their term of office; and
- bonds, stating the total number both of issued bonds, if any, and of redeemed bonds.

(g) Declaration of set-up activity and other declarations

When submitting the file of incorporation to the Mercantile Registry, the appointed director of the company must complete a statement regarding the activities to be performed by the company. This serves as authorisation for the activities to be performed by the company as regards labour protection, environmental protection, sanitary and sanitary-veterinary legislation.

Furthermore, a declaration regarding the fiscal status of the company must be submitted to the Mercantile Registry stating whether the company is registered for

VAT and regarding any tax to be paid by the company (profit tax or tax on revenues).

3. Number of partners: unipersonality

A joint stock company must have at least two partners. Company law prohibits the establishment of a joint stock company by a sole partner.

The number of partners for LLCs can range from one to 50. Although unipersonal LLCs are not regarded by law as a distinct type of company, the legislation contains special provisions for this category. The main relevant special provisions are:

- an individual or a legal entity may hold the position of sole partner in only one Romanian LLC;
- an LLC having a sole partner cannot act in its turn as a sole partner of another LLC; and
- the agreements between the LLC and its sole partner must be concluded in writing under the sanction of absolute nullity.

4. Corporate name: limitations

The name of the company is represented by one or several words or letters, and as a general rule it must contain at least one Romanian word. Registration of a company's name containing words such as 'national', 'Romania', 'Romanian', 'institute' and/or their derivates, or those that would suggest that the company is a public institution or is of local or national public interest, requires the prior written approval of the General Secretary of the Romanian government.

Moreover, registration of a company name containing words such as 'academic-scientific', 'academy', 'university', 'school' and/or their derivates is not permitted.

5. Corporate domicile

A company must establish its domicile in premises that are appropriate for its activity. It is not allowed to register the domicile of a company in a fictitious location. Moreover, the domicile of a company must always be registered with the Mercantile Registry.

6. Corporate purpose

All the activities registered in the bylaws of a company as an object of activity for the company must be codified according to Order 337/2007 on National Classification of Economic Activities (NCEA) issued by the National Statistics Institute (each activity to be performed by a company has an NCEA code, which must be reflected in the bylaws). The object of each activity is expressed by NCEA groups of three figures for the field of activity and by NCEA classes of four figures for the main and secondary object of activity.

7. Capital requirements

7.1 Minimum capital requirements

The minimum threshold of the capital stock of joint stock companies is RON90,000 (€25,000). The value of one share may not be less than RON0.10.

As regards LLCs, the capital stock may not be less than RON200 (€60) and is divided into shares of equal value of at least RON10 each.

7.2 Nature of contributions

The capital stock may be subscribed to and paid in by the partners by in-kind, cash and/or receivables contributions.

Cash contributions are attested by an account excerpt issued by the bank where the equity amounts were deposited. The excerpt is presented to the competent Mercantile Registry on incorporation of the company.

In-kind contributions can be made in all forms of companies and shall be paid in by transfer of the applicable rights and actual delivery of the goods to the company. Moreover, such contributions must be economically assessable. In an LLC having a sole partner, the value of in-kind contributions will be established by an expert.

Contributions to work or services are not allowed, regardless of the type of company. As regards contributions in receivables, these are allowed in joint stock companies other than those established by public subscription; but they are not allowed at all for LLCs.

The increase of the capital stock can also be performed by issuing new shares by incorporating reserves, except legal reserves, as well as profits or issue premiums, or by converting liquid debts payable by the company into shares.

7.3 Partial payments

In the case of LLCs, the contributions to the capital stock must be paid in full.

For joint stock companies, each partner must pay at least 30% of the subscribed capital stock on incorporation, while the remaining 70% must be paid: (i) within a maximum 12 months of the company registration date for in-cash contributions; and (ii) within two years of the registration date for in-kind contributions. Furthermore, a partner whose contribution consists of receivables is not released from the obligations attached to the contribution until the company has received that contribution.

7.4 Representation of shares

In joint stock companies, the shares may be represented by nominative or bearer shares. Shares may be ordinary (giving the holder the right to vote and to receive dividends proportionate to the percentage of the capital stock owned) or preferential (without voting rights, but with priority for dividends). The nominative shares may be issued in material or dematerialised form; the latter being registered in the shareholders' registry. If the company has not issued material shares, it shall issue, *ex officio* or at the partner's request, a partner's certificate comprising the relevant data regarding the shares.

In case of LLCs, the shares may not be represented by negotiable titles.

Any paid share gives the right to one vote in the general meeting of partners, unless otherwise provided in the company's bylaws. One share may be owned by several people; in such a case, the joint owners must appoint a representative.

(a)   *Restrictions*

The shares of a LLC may be freely transferred among partners. As regards the transfer of the shares outside the company, the preliminary approval of the partners representing at least three-quarters of the capital stock is required.

In case of joint stock companies, if not otherwise provided in the bylaws the partners can transfer their shares without any restrictions. Should the shares be listed on a publicly traded market, the transfer must comply with the rules provided by the relevant market. Moreover, as a general rule a company may not subscribe to its own shares – although some temporary exceptions are provided by company law.

(b)   *Formalities*

In LLCs, the transfer of shares must be registered in the shareholders' register held by the company and with the Mercantile Registry. The transfer of shares becomes effective between the parties and the fiscal authorities at the execution date of the shares' sale–purchase agreement or at a subsequent date provided therein. However, as regards third parties the transfer of shares becomes effective only on the registration date of the transfer of shares with the competent Mercantile Registry.

The shares of joint stock companies may be directly transferred to third parties, as follows:

- bearer shares – by material delivery;
- nominative shares issued in a material form – by a statement made in the shareholders' register of the company and on the share, signed by the assignor and assignee or by their authorised representatives;
- nominative shares issued in a dematerialised form:
  - by a statement made in the shareholders' register of the company, signed by the assignor and assignee or by their authorised representatives;
  - by capital market procedures where the shares are traded on a stock exchange.

The shares may be subject to security interests. Any pledge on the shares of a company must be registered in the shareholders' register and with the electronic archive for security in movable property, so as to be opposable towards third parties.

8.   Equity

8.1   Equity–capital ratio

If the value of the net assets of a company falls to less than half of the value of the capital stock, the partners of the company may decide to dissolve the company or to decrease the value of the capital stock in a ratio that would render the value of the net assets to more than half the value of the decreased capital stock.

No intervention is required provided that the net assets are replenished to exceed half of the capital stock within the fiscal year following the one where the losses where recorded. If the share capital is found to have decreased, it must be replenished or reduced prior to any profit allocation or distribution.

If the ratio between the long-term debt and the total value of the capital stock of a company is less than or equal to three, the interest paid by the company is fully deductible. If it is higher than three, the interest paid by the company is not deductible during that fiscal year but will be carried over to the following years, until it is fully deducted. However, this rule does not apply to the interest paid by the company to banks and/or other credit or financial institutions for any loans obtained.

8.2 Convertible bonds

Only joint stock companies may issue bonds. The bonds convertible into shares shall have a nominal value equal to the value of the shares. Moreover, the public-offer prospectus should provide for the ways in which the bonds may be converted.

9. Administration

9.1 General partner's meeting

(a) Quorum requirements

In the case of joint stock companies, company law provides for two types of partner's meeting: (i) ordinary general meetings; and (ii) extraordinary general meetings. There are also some situations when special meetings of the partners who own shares with a dividend-related priority may take place.

The ordinary general meeting shall be held at least once a year, within five months after the end of the financial year. In order for the ordinary general meeting to be validly assembled, at first call, the presence of at least one-quarter of the total number of voting rights is required. If this quorum is not obtained, at second call the partners may resolve regardless of the number of partners present at the meeting.

Extraordinary general meetings are held whenever it is necessary to make a decision regarding amendment of the bylaws of the company. On first call, the attendance of partners representing at least one-quarter of the number of voting rights is required for valid decisions to be passed (one-fifth, at second call).

In both types of general meetings, the partners adopt resolutions with a straightforward majority of the expressed votes unless the bylaws stipulate a higher majority. However, resolutions regarding the amendment of the company's main activity, a capital stock increase or decrease, a change in legal form, and the split-off or dissolution of the company require a majority of at least two-thirds of the voting rights held by the attending partners.

For LLCs, the decisions are taken by the partner's general meeting. As a general rule, at first call a unanimous vote of all partners is required to any amendment of the bylaws. At second call, the decision can be taken regardless of the number of partners attending the assembly or their capital stock percentage.

To adopt resolutions, a double majority is required before valid resolutions can be passed: (i) a majority of the number of shares; and (ii) a majority of the number of partners. For example, where a LLC has three partners and a total capital stock of 30 shares, where the first partner holds 20 shares and the second and third partners hold five shares each, the first partner, although it holds a majority, cannot solely adopt resolutions: the consent of at least one other partner is required in order to meet the double majority. However, this rule only applies if the bylaws of the company do not provide otherwise. Resolutions regarding amendments to the bylaws require all partners to vote, except if otherwise provided by the bylaws.

(b) Challenge of resolutions

In the case of joint stock companies, any resolutions of the partners' general meetings that run counter the law or the bylaws of the company may be challenged in court, within 15 days after the publication in the *Official Gazette* of Romania, by any partner who did not attend the meeting or who voted against and requested that this be recorded in the minutes of the meeting. Moreover, the right to challenge the resolutions is not subject to any time limitation, and can be filed by any interested party, when the challenge is grounded in absolute nullity.

Under the same conditions, the partners of LLCs have the right to challenge the resolution of the general meeting provided that the 15-day period commences as of the date the partner acquires knowledge of the resolution of the general meeting.

Directors may not challenge the resolutions of the partners' general meeting approving their revocation.

9.2 Administrative body

(a) Different systems of administration

Joint stock companies may be managed in two different ways: either by a unitary system, or by a dualist system that incorporates two bodies, namely the directorate; and the supervisory board.

If a joint stock company has opted for the unitary system, the company is managed by one or several directors (and the number is always odd). If several directors are appointed, they form a board of directors.

If a joint stock company opts for the dualist system, the supervisory board includes three to 11 members elected by the general meeting of partners, and the directorate consists of an odd number of members that are appointed by the supervisory board. The members of the directorate cannot act as members of the supervisory board. The directorate represents the management body of the company, whose activity is overseen by the supervisory board.

LLCs are managed by one or several directors. Where several directors are appointed, they form a board.

(b) Term of office, resignation and removal of directors

In a joint stock company that has opted for the unitary system, the removal of a director from office is decided by the general meeting of partners. Under the dualist system, the decision to remove the members of the supervisory board is also taken by the general meeting of partners, while the members of the directorate are removed by a decision of the supervisory board.

A director's term of office cannot exceed four years, except for the first directors' term (which cannot exceed two years).

In LLCs, the directors' removal from their office is decided by the general meeting of partners or, as the case may be, by the sole partner. The legislation does not provide for limitations as regards the term of office.

For both types of company, directors may be removed without a specific cause although they may be entitled to compensation. Moreover, the company cannot be compelled to reinstate a director. The directors may resign, usually by giving a notice period, according to the management agreement concluded with the company.

(c)   *Director's liability to third parties*

While acting within the limits of their mandate, in principle the directors may not be held responsible toward third parties. Considering the duties performed by the directors in the course of their mandate, the responsibility of the company shall be entailed because the directors, in performing their mandate, represent the company. Company law limits the liability of the directors only to the case of a company's bankruptcy. Moreover, Law 85/2006 on insolvency procedures provides for certain conditions under which the directors of a company may be compelled to bear a part of the company's debts.

(d)   *Non-competition*

The directors of an LLC are not allowed to hold the position of director in a competitor company or companies having the same object of activity as the company, or exercising the same trade or other competitive trade, on their own or on another person's account, without the approval of the general meeting of partners, and subject to revocation and liability for damages.

Directors of both LLCs and joint stock companies may nevertheless undertake non-competition obligations based on a management agreement concluded with their company.

(e)   *Special duties of secrecy and loyalty*

The directors of either a joint stock company or an LLC must act in good faith and in accordance with the obligations of non-disclosure and confidentiality. Under company law the directors of the company cannot disclose any confidential information and trade secrets to which they had access in their capacity as directors. This duty continues after the termination of their mandate. Furthermore, the directors shall loyally exercise their mandate, considering the company's interest at all times. These duties can also be stipulated within the management agreement to be concluded with the company.

(f)   *Civil and criminal liability: legislative framework and consequences*

Under company law, a director of a company may be held criminally liable for fraudulent management, embezzlement, forgery, use of forgery, as well as other criminal offences, and can be punished by a term of imprisonment ranging from one month to 12 years, depending on the seriousness of the crime.

Moreover, the directors shall have a civil responsibility towards the company for any damage incurred due to their actions. The directors are also liable for the violation of obligations incumbent on them based on the management agreement.

The general meeting of partners has the authority to bring an action for liability against directors where they fail to carry out their duties and the company suffered as a result. Where the general meeting of partners decides to start an action for liability against the directors, the mandate granted to such directors shall end as of the date when the decision was taken.

The directors of a joint stock company must take out an insurance policy for professional liability.

9.3   Others

(a)   Attorneys

Companies may appoint persons, other than the directors, to act in their name and on their behalf for specific situations or matters, to represent the company before official authorities or towards third parties, or to have signatory rights in representing the company severally or jointly with the directors. This appointment must be made using a power of attorney, which must be registered with the Mercantile Registry to become opposable toward third parties.

(b)   Controllers and internal auditors

The activity of joint stock companies must be audited by at least three censors and one deputy censor. There must be an odd number of censors in all cases. Censors are elected by the general meeting of partners for a term of three years and can be re-elected.

Joint stock companies opting for a dualistic administration system shall be subject to financial audit.

The censors must:

- supervise the management of the company;
- verify the accounting books of the company;
- ensure the conformity of the financial statements of the company and of the accounting registers; and
- ensure the correctness of the valuation of the assets and property of the company.

With regard to LLCs, the appointment of censors is mandatory only if the company has more than 15 partners. Here, the censors' attributes are similar to those of the censors of joint stock companies. If no censors are appointed, any partner that is not a director of the company may exercise the right of control.

10.   Fiscal year

The financial year starts on January 1 and ends on December 31 each year. The company's first financial year start on the date of registration and ends on December 31.

11. Financial statements

11.1 Company tax

Companies pay a profit tax at a current (2009) rate of 16%. As an alternative, companies may be incorporated as micro-enterprises and can choose between a 3% tax on revenues and the 16% profit tax.

A micro-enterprise is a legal person that must cumulatively observe the following conditions:

- Its scope of activity comprises manufacturing of material goods, provision of services or/and trade (where it obtains more than 50% of its income from activities other than management and consultancy);
- It has between one and nine employees;
- The revenues obtained by the company (the estimated revenues) in one financial year do not exceed the equivalent in RON of €100,000; and
- The capital stock of the company is entirely private (ie the company must not have partners from the Romanian state, public authorities or public institutions).

Newly established companies may be incorporated as micro-enterprises upon registration with the Mercantile Registry when they comply with the conditions specified above.

The provisions regarding micro-enterprises do not apply to companies with 250 employees or more. Banks, insurance and reinsurance companies, securities brokers and gambling businesses do not qualify for the micro-enterprise taxation regime.

11.2 Annual accounts

(a) *Documents*

The directors of a company must draft an annual financial report, an annual report of the board of directors (unitary system) or of the directorate and of the supervisory board (dualist system), as well as a proposal with regard to the distribution of dividends.

The annual financial reports include: the balance sheet; the profit and loss account; and the accounting policies and other explanatory notes. In companies that apply accounting regulations in line with the Directives of the European Union and International Accounting Standards, the annual financial reports include: balance sheet; profit and loss account; statement of changes in equity; cash-flow statement; accounting policies and explanatory notes.

(b) *Audit report*

Under Order 1752/2005 of the Ministry of Public Finances, the companies that fulfil certain criteria – namely (i) the total value of the assets is of at least €3.65 million; (ii) the net turnover is of at least €7.3 million; and (iii) the average number of employees is of at least 50 – have the obligation to conclude an annual audit report. Public-interest institutions, such as credit or insurance companies and joint stock companies opting for the dualist system, are also subject to a financial audit.

Apart from such companies, for which the conclusion of an audit report is mandatory, any company may choose to have its financial situation audited.

(c)   *Approval and distribution of profits*

The general meeting of partners has a duty to approve the financial statements and distribute the net profit.

The profit is paid to the partners as dividends. Dividends are distributed to the partners according to the amount of the paid-up capital stock that they hold, unless otherwise provided for in the bylaws. The dividends are paid within the term agreed by the general meetings of partners or, as applicable, under special laws – but no later than six months as of the date of approval of the annual financial statements for the relevant financial year.

At least 5% of the company profits will be set aside each year for the reserve fund until this reaches a minimum equivalent of one-fifth of the capital stock. If the reserve fund is reduced, it must be replenished.

In joint stock companies, the general meeting of partners are not permitted to approve the balance sheet and the profit and loss account unless they are accompanied by the censors' report.

(d)   *Deposit and publicity*

Within 15 days of the general meeting of partners approving the financial statements (and within 150 days of the end of the financial year), the directors of the company will submit the financial statements to the relevant Mercantile Registry, accompanied by the directors' report and auditor's report as well as the minutes of the resolution of the general meeting of partners.

For companies with an annual turnover exceeding RON10 million (approx €2.7 million), an announcement regarding the submission of the documents is published with the *Official Gazette* of Romania. For companies whose annual turnover does not exceed RON10 million, the announcement will be published on the Mercantile Registry's website.[1]

The data included in the annual financial statement will be transmitted in electronic format by the competent Mercantile Registry to the Ministry of Public Finances.

If the company has not submitted its financial statements within six months after the expiry of the legal deadlines, the competent court may declare the dissolution of the company at the request of any interested party.

12.   Company reorganisation

Companies may take another legal form based upon the resolution of the general meeting of partners.

12.1   Merger and Split-off

Companies may merge either by absorption of one company by one or more other

---

1   http://semnal.onrc.ro/cgi-bin/bilant.cgi

companies, or by merger of two or several companies, which cease to exist on the formation of a new company.

A company split-off may be performed either by transferring the net assets of one company, which ceases to exist, to several existing or newly formed companies or by transferring a part of the company's net assets to one or more existing or newly formed companies. If the merger or split-off means that the company ceases to exist, it will be dissolved without a liquidation process and a universal transmission of the assets to the benefiting company (or companies) will occur.

Each company participating in the merger or split-off process must approve the process under the terms and conditions set out for the amendment of the company's bylaws. The merger and split-off decisions and any plans prepared to consider such a transaction will be registered with the Mercantile Registry and published in the *Official Gazette* of Romania.

12.2 Eventual partner separation

Separation is performed when a partner decides to sell their shares to another partner or to a person who will become partner in their place. The separation of partners can be also performed by withdrawal and exclusion. Company law provides that exclusion of partners can be performed only for partners in LLCs when:

- a partner fails to make the contribution that it was supposed to make; or
- a director–partner commits fraud, causing damages to the company, or uses a registered signature or capital for their own or another's benefit.

A partner in a LLC can withdraw from the company in one of the following situations:

- in the cases stipulated in the bylaws;
- with the agreement of all the other partners; or
- for good reasons on the basis of a court decision.

As regards joint stock companies, a partner may withdraw from the company if it voted against a resolution of the general meeting of partners and may request the company to purchase that partner's shares, but only if the relevant resolution had as its object one of the following:

- change of the main object of activity;
- change of company' domicile abroad;
- change of the legal form of the company; or
- merger or split-off of the company.

The right to withdraw may be exercised within 30 days of publication of the resolution of the general meeting of partners in the *Official Gazette* of Romania, for the situations provided in the first three bullet points immediately above (resolutions referring to the change of the main object of activity, the change of the company' domicile abroad and any change of the legal form of the company); and as of the date of adoption of the resolution by the general meeting of partners in relation to the fourth bullet point (resolutions approving a merger or split-off of the company).

12.3   Dissolution and liquidation

Under company law, a company shall be dissolved in the following situations:

- where the duration of the company has expired;
- where it has become impossible to achieve the company's objectives or, conversely, where they have been achieved;
- where the company is declared null and void;
- by a decision of the general meeting of partners;
- where there is severe conflict between partners, if this is preventing the company from operating;
- bankruptcy;
- where one-half of the registered capital has been lost;
- where the registered share capital has dropped under the legal limit; or
- where the number of partners has dropped under the legal limit.

At the request of any interested party, as well as at the request of the National Mercantile Registry, the court may declare the company's dissolution where the company:

- no longer has statutory bodies or they can no longer meet;
- has not submitted, within six months of the expiry of the legal deadlines, the annual financial reports or other documents that, according to the law, are to be submitted to the Mercantile Registry;
- has ceased its activity, or does not have headquarters, or its partners are missing, or their domicile/residence is unknown; or
- has failed to replenish its registered capital according to the conditions prescribed by the law.

The court's decision to dissolve the company will be registered with the Mercantile Registry and published in the *Official Gazette* of Romania. When the court decision becomes final, the company goes into liquidation. During the process, the company maintains its legal status only for the purpose of its liquidation.

13.   Branches

According to Law 105/1992 regarding private international law relations, the organic status of a branch established by a company in Romania is governed by the national law of that company (*lex societatis*).

According to this legal provision, a foreign company may establish a branch in Romania as long as such a right is acknowledged by its *lex societatis* and the company observes the law that applies to the registration and publicity formalities (ie Romanian law).

The branch does not become a distinct legal entity, as it remains a part of the structure of the foreign company. The branch is considered to have the same legal personality as the foreign company and the assets and liabilites of the branch belong to the foreign company, while the branch's activities cannot be more extensive than the activities of its parent company.

Russia

Dmitry Lyakhov
Jonathan Russin
Russin & Vecchi LLP

1. Types of company with limited liability and applicable legislation

The most commonly used forms of companies with limited liability in Russia are the joint stock company and the limited liability company. Russian law also provides for companies with additional liability, but this form is rarely encountered in practice.

Limited liability companies do not issue share certificates; instead, the share percentages are stated in the foundation documents. Where numerous shareholders are anticipated, the joint stock company is the preferred form, since large numbers of shareholders can be more easily accommodated through the use of share certificates. Joint stock companies can be either open or closed. In open joint stock companies, shares may be bought and sold without limitation, while in closed joint stock companies, shares may be freely bought and sold only among existing shareholders or a predetermined group of persons who enjoy a right of first refusal when shares are sold by a shareholder.

The fundamentals of the legal regulation of limited liability companies and joint stock companies can be found in the Civil Code of the Russian Federation (Part One) No 51–FZ, dated November 30 1994 (as amended). These basic rules are fleshed out in regard to limited liability companies in the Federal Law on Limited Liability Companies No 14–FZ, dated February 8 1998 (as amended), and in regard to joint stock companies in the Federal Law on Joint Stock Companies No 208–FZ, dated December 26 1995 (as amended). There are also some specialised laws and enactments detailing certain related issues, such as the Federal Law on State Registration of Legal Entities and Individual Entrepreneurs, the Federal Law on Foreign Investments in the Russian Federation and the Federal Law on Insolvency (Bankruptcy). In addition to laws passed by the legislative chambers, Russian legal materials include governmental enactments, presidential orders and other obligatory documents of various state bodies (eg the Central Bank, the Federal Service on Financial Markets and the Federal Anti-monopoly Service) as well as court practice which, while not an official source of law, guides the interpretation of all legal materials.

2. Incorporation procedure

The procedures for incorporating limited liability companies and joint stock companies are similar; the chief difference is the requirement for joint stock companies to register the issuance of share certificates, which does not apply to limited liability companies. The state body responsible for registering legal persons such as limited liability companies and joint stock companies is the Russian

Federation Tax Service, with incorporation taking place at the local Tax Service office of the place where the company is located. The State Register of Legal Entities is a public record and all information contained therein is open for examination by third parties, except for passport data of physical persons and information on the bank accounts of a legal entity or an individual entrepreneur. Information is provided upon written request and payment of a state fee of Rb200 (approximately $8).

A company's registered office is generally the place where the main executive body is located.

The first step in registering a company is the adoption of a joint resolution by the founders, which is executed in the form of minutes of the founding meeting (or a decision of the sole founder, where the company has only one founder). The founders also draft a charter (bylaws) and execute a foundation agreement (if there are several founders). In the case of a limited liability company, the foundation agreement is considered as a founding document and should be submitted to the Tax Service at the moment of registration of the company. But in the case of a joint stock company,[1] the foundation agreement is not a founding document; it is simply considered to be an internal document of the company, which should be kept in the company's files.

The founders are free to choose any company name they desire, but use of the words 'Russia', 'Russian Federation' and derivative phrases is restricted. This requirement is established by a newly adopted Part IV of Russian Civil Code and came into legal force in 2008. According to this new requirement, the use of the word 'Russia' and derivatives may be allowed only under individual permission of the Government and if more than 75% of equity of the company is owned by the Russian Federation.

According to current legislation, no declaration of foreign investment is required where the company is established by foreign founders. However, in some cases involving 'strategic' industries, preliminary approvals will be required. Also, where the company has a foreign founder, no foreign tax number or special tax registration is required under the general registration procedures.

For the purposes of registration of a company with limited liability, the following documents must be submitted to the Tax Service:

- the application for registration. The applicant must be either the founder (if the founder is an individual) or the founder's general director (if the founder is a legal entity). The applicant's signature should be witnessed by a Russian notary public (or at a Russian consulate abroad). The application should contain a list of the main activities that the company plans to perform;
- the minutes of the meeting of the founders (or decision of the sole founder) expressing a decision on registration of the company;
- the company's foundation documents;
- where the founder is a legal entity, its certificate of incorporation or similar document (eg extract from the trade register);[2] and

---

1   It should be noted, however, that new amendments to the legislation on limited liability companies will come into force on July 1 2009. According to these amendments, the foundation agreement will no longer be a foundation document of a limited liability company, but will simply serve as an internal document of the company.

- a receipt confirming payment of the applicable state registration fee, which is currently set at Rb2,000 (approximately $80).

2.1 Charter

The sole foundation document of a joint stock company is its charter. The foundation documents of limited liability companies with two or more founders are the foundation agreement and the charter;[3] limited liability companies with a single founder require only a charter. The charter is a private document of the company and there is no need to certify it with a notary public.

The charter of a limited liability company must include the following information, at a minimum:

- the object and purposes of incorporation;
- the full and short trade name of the company;
- information on the company's location;
- the structure and competence of the governing bodies;
- a list of issues falling within the exclusive jurisdiction of the general meeting of shareholders;
- a list of issues that must be adopted unanimously or by a qualified majority of the shareholders;
- information on the procedures for the adoption of resolutions by the executive bodies;
- the amount of the charter capital;
- the amount and nominal value of each share;
- the rights and obligations of the shareholders;
- the terms and conditions for withdrawing from the company, and the consequences of withdrawal;
- the terms and conditions for the transfer of shares;
- rules on the storage of company documents and information, and the provision of such information to company shareholders;
- the procedure for conducting the general meeting of shareholders that will adopt the annual reports;
- the powers of the general director;
- procedures governing the general director's activities and decision-making powers; and
- the number of members of the audit committee and their powers.

The foundation agreement of a limited liability company should contain:

- the founders' obligation to incorporate the company;
- the terms of joint cooperation regarding incorporation;
- the amount of charter capital;

---

2   Where the founder is a foreign legal entity, this document should be duly apostilled or legalised to be valid in Russia. The choice among the two mentioned procedures depends on whether the country of the company's origin is a party to the Hague Convention of 1961 on Waiver of Requirement for Legalisation of Foreign Official Documents.
3   See footnote 1.

- the amount and composition of each founder's contribution;
- the nature of the founders' contributions;
- the terms of the founders' contribution;
- the founders' liability for failure to make agreed contributions;
- the structure of the governing bodies;
- the conditions of the founders' participation in company activities;
- the terms and conditions for the distribution of profits and losses;
- the corporate governance procedures; and
- the terms and conditions governing withdrawal from the company.

In addition to these required provisions, the Law on Limited Liability Companies contains optional provisions that may be established in the charter. The founders may agree to include other provisions in the charter that do not contradict the provisions of the law or other current legislation.

The bylaws of a joint stock company must include the following information, at a minimum:

- the full and short trade name;
- information on the company's location;
- the type of joint stock company (closed or open);
- the quantity, nominal value and type (ordinary or preferred) of distributed shares;
- the rights of holders of each type of shares;
- the amount of charter capital;
- the structure and competence of the governing bodies, and procedures for the adoption of resolutions;
- procedures for convening and conducting the general shareholders' meeting, along with a list of issues that should be adopted unanimously or by two-thirds qualified majority vote;
- information on branch and representative offices;
- information on the rights of the Russian Federation or municipality to participate in the management of the company; and
- other clauses provided by law.

2.2   Registration requirements

The company's tax number is issued by the registration body (ie the local Tax Service office) during registration, together with the company number (ie the unified state registration number).

The Tax Service should complete registration of the company within five days of receipt of the required documents, along with proof of payment of the applicable state fee. The Tax Service was designated as the registration authority in order to act as a 'one-stop shop'; as a result, upon registration with the Tax Service, a company is also registered with all applicable state pension, social and medical insurance funds. After this, the company should register itself with the state statistics committee.

Upon registration, no further declaration of commencement of activities or other tax declaration is required. Moreover, no legalisation of the official books is required.

3. **Number of shareholders**

Limited liability companies may have between one and 50 shareholders, whether natural or legal persons. However, a limited liability company may not have as its sole shareholder another legal entity that itself has only one shareholder. Like limited liability companies, closed joint stock companies may have between one and 50 shareholders. Open joint stock companies may have an unlimited number of shareholders.

4. **Corporate name – limitations**

Companies may adopt any name the founders want. The company may not include the words 'Russia', 'Russian Federation' and derivative phrases in its corporate name, unless the Russian Federation owns more than 75% of the equity in the company. In this case the company must also receive special approval from the Russian government.

The full official name of a company consists of an indication of its corporate form – OJSC (OAO in Russian), CJSC (ZAO) or LLC (OOO), followed by the company's name.

5. **Corporate domicile**

A company's domicile is the place where its general director (chief executive officer) is located, which should be indicated in the charter and in the application for registration. If the company changes its officially registered domicile, it must register the change with the Tax Service. In practice, many Russian companies use nominal addresses for registration with state bodies and then rent their main office in a different area, which is permitted.

6. **Corporate object**

Although there is no legal requirement to include the company's goals, purposes and types of activities in the charter, this information is commonly included. Since such information could be construed as limiting the company's activities to those listed, the phrase "and any other types of activities which are not prohibited by law" is often included at the end of any such list. Some types of activity may be performed only if the company has obtained a licence issued by an authorised state body (each body specialises in issuing licences in its field), or a special permission for performing some type of activity (eg permission for construction, permission for using radio frequencies, etc).

7. **Capital stock**

The minimum charter capital for both limited liability companies and closed joint stock companies is Rb10,000 (approximately $400), while for open joint stock companies it is Rb100,000.

7.1 **Nature of contributions**

Cash, assets, rights and other property or property rights with monetary value may be contributed to the charter capital of a limited liability company. In the case of in-kind contributions, the general meeting of shareholders must determine the value of the property; where the in-kind contribution is valued at more than Rb20,000 (approximately $800), an independent appraisal is required.

Shares in a newly incorporated joint stock company must be fully distributed among the initial shareholders before registration.

7.2 Partial payments

Partial contributions of the initial capital are allowed for both limited liability companies and joint stock companies. For limited liability companies, at least 50% of the charter capital must be contributed prior to registration, with the remainder being contributed within one year of state registration unless a shorter term is required under the foundation agreement. For joint stock companies, at least 50% of the charter capital must be paid in within three months of registration and the remainder within one year of state registration. Shares that are not fully paid cannot be voted on at the general shareholders' meeting.

7.3 Representation of shares

Limited liability companies do not issue share certificates or other similar documents. Joint stock companies issue shares, which are always registered. Shares may be only non-certificated (ie exist only as entries in a special shareholder register).

The shares of a joint stock company may be ordinary or preferred, but preferred shares may not comprise more than 25% of the company's charter capital. Ordinary stock may be of only one type, but various types of preferred share may be issued, with varying rights including defined dividends and liquidation preferences, as set out in the charter. Preferred shares carry no voting rights as long as defined dividends are timely paid.

7.4 Transfer of shares

(a) Restrictions

Shares in joint stock companies and limited liability companies may be sold only to the extent that they are fully paid.

Shareholders in joint stock companies may transfer their shares without limitation, except that closed joint stock company shareholders enjoy a right of first refusal in the case of a sale of shares by another shareholder.

Similarly, limited liability company shareholders may transfer their shares without limitation, unless such limitations are set out in the charter, including a prohibition against sales to third parties.[4] In addition, limited liability company shareholders enjoy a right of first refusal in the case of a sale of shares by another shareholder.

A shareholder of a closed joint stock company or limited liability company who is selling his shares may not vary the substantive terms (especially including price) in the event of a failure of the other shareholders to exercise their right of first refusal.

---

4   New amendments to the legislation on limited liability companies will come into force on July 1 2009. The described rule will change to the opposite. Shareholders of a limited liability company will not be allowed to sell their shares to a third party unless this is directly set out in the company's charter.

Rights of first refusal for both limited liability companies and closed joint stock companies arise only in connection with sales. In other words, the transfer of shares by will, intestate succession or successorship in interest by operation of law does not trigger rights of first refusal, although the charter may provide otherwise.

Limited liability company shareholders may encumber their stock or shares with liens (unless the charter provides otherwise), subject to the approval of the general meeting.

(b) *Formalities*

The transfer of shares in a limited liability company requires the corresponding amendment of the charter. The transfer itself should be executed in a written document.[5] The transfer of shares in a joint stock company is effected by making a corresponding entry in the shareholder register.

8. Equity

8.1 Equity–capital ratio

Joint stock companies are required to maintain a reserve fund, which is established by contributing at least 5% of the net profits to the fund until it reaches the level specified in the charter.

If, by the end of the second year following incorporation or thereafter, the net assets of a joint stock company are less than its charter capital, the company must undergo a reduction in charter capital to the amount of net assets (but not less than the minimum capital requirement established by law).

Limited liability companies may form reserve funds at their own discretion, as set out in the charter.

8.2 Convertible bonds

Limited liability companies may, with the approval of the general meeting, issue bonds to an amount not exceeding the charter capital. Joint stock companies may, with the approval of the board of directors (unless otherwise provided in the charter), issue bonds that are convertible into shares.

9. Administration

9.1 General shareholders' meeting

A detailed procedure for making decisions is required for the general shareholders' meeting. Each shareholder in a limited liability company and shareholders of a joint stock company having at least 2% of shares has the right to propose matters for inclusion on the agenda for the meeting and to vote on all matters. This can sometimes be a limitation. For example, a provision in a charter entitling one

---

5   A new rule will come into legal force on July 1 2009 that will oblige the shareholder of a limited liability company to notarise a share purchase agreement when selling his share. The obligation to provide the documents to the Russian Federation Tax Service registering a change of shareholder will now be imposed on the notary, not on the shareholder himself.

shareholder to nominate the general director will be void and unenforceable as unlawfully limiting the rights of other shareholders. The other bodies of the company are usually determined by the general shareholders' meeting.

For limited liability companies, most decisions are adopted by the general shareholders' meeting by a simple majority of votes of all shareholders of the limited liability company (not of attendees). However, the charter may require qualified votes for some decisions. According to the Law on Limited Liability Companies, resolutions on changes to the foundation agreement and on liquidation or reorganisation must be adopted unanimously. Resolutions to change the charter or charter capital must be adopted by at least a two-thirds majority. The charter cannot reduce these qualified votes. The quorum for attendance at the meeting is not specified in the Law on Limited Liability Companies, but it should be at least a majority of shareholders in order to meet the 'simple majority' rule.

The following issues fall within the sole competence of the general shareholders' meeting:

- determination of the company's main areas of operations, and decisions on the company's participation in associations and other unions of commercial entities;
- approval of amendments and additions to the charter, and increases in the charter capital;
- approval of amendments to the foundation agreement;
- formation of the executive bodies of the company and termination of their powers, approval of the transfer of powers vested in the executive body to a commercial entity or to an individual entrepreneur (manager), approval of the manager and the terms and conditions of his powers;
- election of the members of the audit committee and the members of the board of directors, and their dismissal prior to the expiry of their terms of office;
- approval of annual reports and annual accounting balance sheets;
- approval of distribution of net profits;
- approval of documents governing company operations (internal regulations);
- approval of bonds and other securities issuance;
- instruction to conduct an audit, approval of the auditor and determination of the amount of remuneration;
- approval of reorganisation or liquidation of the company;
- appointment of the members of the liquidation committee, and adoption of liquidation balances; and
- resolution of other matters specified in the charter and the Law on Limited Liability Companies.

The general shareholders' meeting should be convened at least once a year between two and four months after the end of the fiscal year. The annual meeting approves the financial results for the year. It is possible to hold meetings by survey, provided that all shareholders record their votes in writing. The use of an authorised representative at the meeting acting pursuant to a proper power of attorney is permitted.

In joint stock companies, the shareholders' meeting should be held at least once a year between two and six months after the end of the fiscal year. The following matters should be resolved at the meeting:

- election of the members of the board of directors and the audit committee (or comptroller);
- nomination of company auditor;
- approval of the financial results of the year;
- distribution of dividends; and
- other matters that should be resolved by the ordinary annual shareholders' meeting according to the charter.

The following matters fall within the exclusive competence of the shareholders of joint stock companies:

- amendments and additions to the charter;
- reorganisation;
- liquidation, appointment of the members of the liquidation committee and adoption of liquidation balances;
- determination of the number of members of the board of directors, and their election and dismissal prior to the expiry of their terms of office;
- determination of the quantity, nominal value and types of shares and the rights attaching to such shares;
- any increase or reduction in charter capital;
- the formation of executive bodies and their termination prior to expiry of their term of office (if this does not fall within the competence of the board of directors according to the charter);
- election of audit committee members;
- approval of the company auditor;
- distribution of dividends;
- approval of the annual report and accounting balance sheets;
- approval of the procedure for holding shareholders' meetings;
- approval of the members of the electoral commission;
- approval of stock splits and consolidations;
- approval of transactions with interested parties;
- approval of major transactions;
- share repurchases by the company;
- participation in financial and industry groups, associations and other unions of commercial organisations;
- approval of documents governing company operations (internal regulations); and
- other matters regulated by the Law on Joint Stock Companies.

(a) *Challenging resolutions*
A decision adopted by limited liability company shareholders that violates legal requirements or the charter, or that otherwise infringes the rights and interests of a shareholder, may be nullified through court action at the request of a shareholder who did not participate in the meeting or voted against such decision. This request

must be filed within two months of the date on which the shareholder knew or should have known of such decision.

The same provisions apply to decisions of joint stock company shareholders, although the term during which decisions may be challenged is six months.

9.2 Administrative body

(a) Different systems of administration

Management functions are performed either by a sole executive body (general director) or by two executive bodies – a general director and an executive committee. The company may also have a board of directors where the charter so provides; joint stock companies with more than 50 voting stockholders are obliged to have a board of directors. The board of directors carries out the general management of the company, and its functions and competence should be defined in the charter. Where a board of directors is not established, its functions are generally performed by the shareholders.

Foreign citizens may occupy administrative positions in the company without limitation, but they must hold a work permit or other document that entitles them to work in Russia. The company must also obtain separate permission to employ foreigners.

(b) Term of office, resignation and removal of directors

Members of the board of directors of joint stock companies are elected each year at the ordinary shareholders' meeting. For limited liability companies, the procedure for the composition and election of the board of directors is established by the charter. For both limited liability companies and joint stock companies, the general director is elected by the shareholders. The power to appoint the general director may be granted to the board of directors where the charter so provides.

(c) Directors' liability to third parties

Members of the board of directors, the general director and members of the executive committee are liable to the company for any damage that results from illegal decisions. Members who did not vote or who voted against such decisions are not liable.

(d) Non-competition

In both limited liability companies and joint stock companies, members of the executive committee may not make up more than one-quarter of the board of directors. The general director may not serve as chairman of the board of directors.

(e) Limitations on executives and interested-party transactions

Interested-party transactions require the approval of the general shareholders' meeting or the board of directors. These are defined as transactions of the company in which its general director, members of the executive committee, members of the board of directors, and shareholders holding, together with affiliated persons, more than 20% of the shares in the company are 'interested'. Being 'interested' in a transaction means (in terms of Russian legislation) being personally (or through a number of close relatives) a party to such transaction, or a shareholder of a party to such transaction, owning more than 20% of shares of such party, or having a position in one of the executive bodies of a party to a transaction.

(f)   *Special duties of secrecy and loyalty*
The general director and members of the board of directors and the executive committee are obliged to act for the benefit of the company, and to perform their obligations to advance the interests of the company.

(g)   *Civil and criminal liability*
The company is not subject to criminal liability; it has only civil liability to the extent of its assets. The general director is liable for offences and crimes committed by the company in administrative and criminal matters, such as non-payment of taxes, fictitious bankruptcy or similar illegal acts. Also, criminal liability may be imposed in certain cases on the chief accountant of the company.

9.3   Others

(a)   *Internal controllers and auditors*
Joint stock companies are obliged to have an audit committee and internal auditor. In limited liability companies, the appointment of an audit committee is optional where there are fewer than 15 shareholders. Members of the audit committee may not occupy any other position in the company.

In joint stock companies, the audit committee should review the reports on the company's financial activity at the end of each fiscal year, and at any time at the request of shareholders holding more than 10% of the voting rights. In limited liability companies with more than 15 shareholders, the annual reports and balance sheets may not be approved by the shareholders until they have first been reviewed and approved by the audit committee.

10.   Fiscal year, commencement of activities
The official fiscal year starts on January 1 and ends on December 31. However, companies have the right to choose any dates for their financial year.

11.   Financial statements

11.1   Company tax
Company profit is subject to tax, which is generally payable on a quarterly basis. The profit subject to taxation is calculated as income less expenses. The general tax rate is currently (2009) 24%; however, certain categories of profit are taxed at specific rates. Under certain circumstances, the company may apply one of the special tax regimes instead of the tax on profit, as follows:
- Unified tax on imputed income is a levy on some forms of business activity where tax control is difficult. Such activities are subject to taxation based on imputed income, which is defined as their estimated gross income.

- The simplified taxation system may be used by organisations that satisfy certain eligibility requirements. The tax rate here is 6% of their gross income or 15% of gross income minus expenses.
- Unified agricultural tax is levied on agricultural manufacturers whose average portion of income from the sale of agricultural products for the first nine months in a year constitutes at least 70% of the whole income. The tax rate is currently 6% of the value of income minus expenses.

11.2   Annual accounts

(a)   Documents

The main documents reflecting the company's yearly financial results are as follows:
- balance sheet;
- profit and loss statement;
- value added tax declaration;
- declaration of tax on profits; and
- declaration to the pension fund and to unified social tax allocations.

Where the simplified system of taxation is availed of, only the profit and loss report and the declaration to the pension fund need be filed.

(b)   Audit report

An audit report by an independent auditor is required in the following cases:
- for open joint stock companies;
- for certain types of financial organisation, such as lending institutions, insurance companies and similar organisations;
- where the profit for the year exceeds Rb50 million (approximately $2 million) or the value of assets according to the balance sheet exceeds Rb20 million (approximately $800,000); and
- in certain other cases that do not relate to companies with limited liability.

(c)   Approval and distribution of profits

For joint stock companies, the decision on the distribution of dividends is taken at a shareholders' meeting. The dividends may be paid yearly or at three, six or nine-monthly intervals.

For limited liability companies, the decision on the distribution of profits is taken by the shareholders. The profits are distributed in proportion to the capital contributions. An alternative basis for distribution may be specified in the charter with the unanimous approval of all shareholders.

The tax on dividends is currently set at the following rates:
- 0% for Russian companies that hold 50% or more in the company that distributes the dividends if the contribution of the shareholder in the charter capital of such company was more than Rb500 million;
- 9% for Russian companies and individuals who are Russian tax residents;
- 15% for foreign companies; and

- 30% for non-resident individuals.

Applicable double-taxation treaties may establish lower rates.

(d)   *Deposit and publication*
Limited liability companies must publish their annual financial statements and balance sheets in the case of equity securities (bonds and other) issuance. Open joint stock companies must disclose their annual financial statements and balance sheets in a printed publication, issue prospectuses (where required by law) in a printed publication or online, and publish certain information in advance of their annual shareholders' meeting in a printed publication.

12.   Company reorganisation

Joint stock companies and limited liability companies may be reorganised through merger, accession, division, split-off or transformation. The property of new companies created through reorganisation may be formed only from property owned by the companies that participated in such reorganisation. The company is considered to be reorganised as of the time of state registration of the newly created company or, in the case of accession, from the date of registration of the cessation of activity of one of the companies.

The company must publish an announcement and notify all creditors in writing no later than 30 days after the decision to reorganise. Creditors then have 30 days in which to demand acceleration of the performance of obligations and compensation of losses. The company must draft an act of transfer or a separation balance sheet reflecting the transfer of property and obligations during the reorganisation.

12.1   Merger

In the case of a merger, the shareholders of each participating company must approve:
- the merger agreement between the companies;
- the charter of the merged company; and
- the act of transfer.

The merger agreement should determine the procedure for voting at the common shareholders' meeting of the merging companies. The common shareholders' meeting should elect the executive bodies of the new company.

12.2   Accession

In case of accession, a company transfers all its property, rights and obligations to another company and then terminates. The participating companies must sign an accession agreement that specifies the procedure and conditions for accession, and the procedure for share conversion. The general shareholders' meeting of each company must approve the accession agreement (which should contain provisions on the procedure for voting at the common shareholders' meeting). Shareholders of the acquired company should adopt an act of transfer. The common shareholders' meeting should adopt amendments to the charter.

12.3 Division

As a result of division, a company transfers all its rights, obligations and property to new companies and terminates. The general shareholders' meeting approves:

- the division;
- the procedure and conditions for such division;
- the new companies to be created;
- the procedure for share conversion; and
- the separation balance sheet.

The general shareholders' meeting of each newly created company should adopt its charter and elect its executive bodies.

12.4 Split-off

As a result of split-off, a company transfers some of its rights, obligations and property to new companies but does not terminate. The procedure is the same as for division.

12.5 Transformation

A joint stock company may be transformed into a limited liability company, a production cooperative or a non-commercial partnership. A limited liability company may be transformed into a joint stock company, a company with additional liability or a production cooperative.[6]

13. Eventual partner separation

A shareholder in a limited liability company may withdraw from the company at any time without the consent of the other shareholders. In such a case his share reverts to the company. The company must pay the actual cost of the share to the withdrawing shareholder within six months of the end of the fiscal year during which the shareholder announced his withdrawal. The value of the share is determined on the basis of data in the annual accounting balance sheets.

Shareholders of joint stock companies may dispose of shares at their own discretion, including by selling them to third parties.

14. Dissolution and liquidation

A company may be liquidated voluntarily or by court decision. In a case of voluntary liquidation, decided at a shareholders' meeting, the company terminates without transfer of its property, rights and obligations to other persons. The shareholders must immediately notify the registration body in order to include information that the company is under liquidation in the state register of legal entities.

The shareholders' meeting appoints a liquidation commission, which acquires all management rights. The liquidation commission will publish an announcement of the liquidation and identify and notify all company creditors and debtors. Creditors have two months from the announcement in which to make their claims. The

---

6   According to the new amendments to legislation that come into force on July 1 2009, it will also be possible to transform a limited liability company into a partnership.

liquidation commission will prepare an intermediate balance sheet to be approved by the shareholders. If the company does not have sufficient funds to satisfy all creditor claims, the liquidation commission will sell company assets. Payments to creditors are made in the following order of preference:

- payments for damage caused by the company to the health and lives of persons;
- payments of salary and other similar payments;
- payments to state budget and non-budget funds; and
- all other payments.

Payments to creditors of each rank are made only once the creditors of the preceding rank have been paid in full.

Once all company debts are paid, the liquidation commission will prepare a liquidation balance sheet to be adopted by the shareholders.

Once all creditors have been paid, the rest of the property is distributed among the shareholders. In a joint stock company, the remaining property must be distributed among the shareholders in the following order:

- payments for shares that must be redeemed;
- payments of accrued but unpaid dividends and the liquidation value of preferred shares; and
- payments to all other shareholders.

Payments to shareholders of each rank are made only once all shareholders of the preceding rank have been paid in full.

The liquidation ends and the company is terminated once the state body enters the appropriate record in the state register of legal entities.

A company may be deemed insolvent when it is unable to satisfy creditors' claims totalling at least Rb100,000 within three months of their falling due. The company, together with creditors, may take a decision on insolvency and liquidate voluntarily. The right to petition a court to declare a company insolvent may be exercised by the debtor itself, by creditors or by authorised governmental bodies.

15.   Branches

Companies may have branch and representative offices in Russia. Representative offices may only represent the company and may not perform any commercial activities, while branch offices may perform such activities. Both branch and representative offices act in the name of the parent company, which is liable for their activities. The company charter must contain information on all branch and representative offices.

The authors would like to thank Elena Iourkina for her kind assistance as co-author of the chapter on Russia for the first edition of this publication.

Singapore

Sophie Lim
Ng Shen Li
Allen & Gledhill LLP

1. Introduction

This chapter gives a brief overview on the formation and administration of limited liability companies in Singapore – in particular, private companies limited by shares.

1.1 Limited liability companies: a dichotomy

There are two types of limited liability company in Singapore: companies limited by shares and companies limited by guarantee.

In the context of a company limited by shares, a shareholder's liability would be limited to the amount he has invested in the shares of such a company. In contrast, a shareholder's liability in respect of a company limited by guarantee is limited to the amount he has agreed to guarantee.

As companies limited by guarantee are usually set up for a specific purpose,[1] the more common form of limited liability company in Singapore comprises companies limited by shares. Accordingly, this chapter will not discuss private companies limited by guarantee.

Companies limited by shares are typically classified as private companies and public companies. Whilst there are many similarities in the way they are administered, public companies are comparatively more regulated under the Companies Act, Chapter 50 of Singapore (the Companies Act). Private companies are more commonly incorporated in Singapore than public companies[2] unless there are specific reasons[3] for utilising a public company structure.

1.2 Applicable legislation and regulatory authorities

The main legislation governing limited liability companies in Singapore is the Companies Act and its subsidiary legislation.

The regulatory authority that is primarily responsible for regulating such companies in Singapore is the Accounting and Corporate Regulatory Authority (the ACRA).

---

1   Companies limited by guarantee are usually incorporated for non-profit purposes and are generally engaged in charitable or educational activities.

2   The type of limited liability company that is set up ultimately depends on the commercial factors underlying the particular incorporation. For example, where there is an intention to list the shares of the company on a stock exchange, the company is typically structured as a public company limited by shares.

3   For example, a public limited company structure must be used where there are more than 50 shareholders (excluding any employee of the company or its subsidiary or any person who, while previously in the employment of the company or its subsidiary was, and thereafter has continued to be, a member of the company).

2.   Incorporation procedure

2.1   Proceedings prior to incorporation

(a)   The 'Bizfile' electronic filing system
All incorporation applications must be made electronically using the ACRA's electronic 'Bizfile' filing system.

(b)   Corporate name
The proposed name of the company must first be approved by and reserved with the ACRA. All applications for new company names must be submitted electronically using Bizfile. The application is usually processed within a day unless the application is referred to a referral authority. If so, the processing time may take up to 14 days from the application date.

If the application is approved, the name will be reserved for a period of 60 days from the application date. This may be extended once (before the expiry of the initial reservation date) for a further period of 60 days from the application date for the extension via Bizfile. If the company is not incorporated within this extended reservation period, a fresh application must be submitted.

(c)   Share capital
The share capital of a company can be increased by the shareholders by way of cash or in consideration other than cash. Notwithstanding the nature of the increase in share capital, a specific value in the form of the issue price must be ascribed to each share. The share capital of a company can be denominated in any currency.

(d)   Foreign investments
As a general rule, there is no prohibition against a company being wholly owned by a foreign individual or corporation.

However, for certain regulated industries, there is industry-specific legislation that imposes restrictions in respect of foreign ownership of shares in the company.

2.2   Incorporation
Once the name of the company has been successfully reserved, certain information and the incorporation documents have to be lodged with the ACRA via Bizfile.

The main incorporation document to be lodged is the memorandum and articles of association of the company.

Upon successful incorporation, the ACRA will transmit an electronic notification to the applicant by e-mail, stating that the company has been incorporated and providing the date of incorporation as well as the company registration number.

2.3   Memorandum and articles of association

(a)   Contents
The memorandum of association incorporates the name of the company, the nature

of the liability of the shareholder(s) (ie that their liability is limited), and the full name(s), address(es) and occupation(s) of the subscriber(s).

The objects of the company need no longer be stated in the memorandum. Under the Companies Act, a company is conferred full capacity, rights, powers and privileges to carry on or undertake any business or activity, do any act or enter into any transaction unless its capacity, rights, powers and privileges are expressly limited otherwise in the company's memorandum and articles.

The articles of association incorporate the internal regulations of the company. This could be drawn up as a full-length document or, alternatively, the prescribed form of articles incorporated in Table A in the Fourth Schedule to the Companies Act could be adopted with any relevant modifications.

Matters that are usually set out in the articles of association are as follows:

- variation of the rights of shareholders;
- alterations to the share capital of the company;
- restrictions and procedures on the transfer of shares and the rights of directors to decline to register a transfer;
- administration and regulation of shareholders' and directors' meetings;
- appointment and resignation of directors;
- powers and duties of directors; and
- distribution of assets of the company upon its winding-up.

(b) *Execution*

The Companies Act requires a copy of the memorandum of a company to be signed by the subscribers, stating the number of shares that each subscriber has agreed to take. Once lodged with the ACRA, the memorandum and articles of association become a publicly available document.

2.4 Costs of incorporation

The fee for incorporation of a private limited company with a share capital is S$300 irrespective of the size or currency of the issued capital. There is no separate fee for issuing the notice of incorporation; this is issued by the ACRA via e-mail. The application for the reservation of a company name is S$15 and any extension of this application is S$10.[4]

3. Shareholders

A company must have at least one director and one shareholder. Unless the proposed business activity of the company falls within a regulated industry, there are generally no residency requirements applicable to the shareholders of a company under the Companies Act. Where the company has only one shareholder, the sole director and shareholder can be the same person. The sole director must be resident in Singapore and he must not act or be appointed as the secretary of the company.

---

4   Costs are current as at January 6 2009.

4. Company name

The Companies Act regulates the names that may be used for a Singapore company. As a general rule, the Registrar of Companies (the registrar) is empowered under the Companies Act not to register a name of a company that is:

- undesirable;
- identical to that of any other company, limited liability partnership or corporation, or to a business name that is already registered with the ACRA; or
- a name of a kind that the government minister for finance has directed should not be accepted for registration.

The Registrar may force a change of name if it is established that the name of the company is so similar to that of another Singapore-registered entity that it would cause confusion.

5. Share capital

5.1 Capitalisation of issued share capital

(a) *Minimum share capital*

Whilst there is no express minimum capital requirement prescribed in the Companies Act, in practice at least one share in the capital of the company must be issued at incorporation.

(b) *Shareholder approval*

The Companies Act prohibits the directors of a company from allotting and issuing additional new shares in a company without prior approval from the shareholders in a general meeting.

5.2 Nature of increase in issued share capital

As highlighted in section 2.1 above, the new shares in the capital of a company may be issued for cash or non-cash consideration. Where additional shares are allotted by the company after incorporation, notification must be lodged with the ACRA via Bizfile within 14 days.

5.3 Partially paid-up shares

Shares need not be paid-up in full at the point of allotment; they can be allotted and issued to a shareholder as partially paid-up shares. This results in a 'debt' between the shareholder and the company for the unpaid portion of the shares. The shareholder must repay the company when the latter makes a 'call' for the debt to be paid. Calls by a company are typically regulated by the articles of association.

5.4 Share certificate: evidence of title

A share certificate specifying the number of shares held by a shareholder of a company is prima facie evidence of title. Each share certificate should be issued under the common seal or, if applicable, the share seal of the company and should state the requisite information prescribed under the Companies Act such as the class of shares, the amount paid on the shares and the extent to which the shares are paid up.

5.5   Restrictions on transfer of shares

The Companies Act states that a private company limited by shares must have in its memorandum and articles of association:

- restrictions on the rights to transfer its shares; and
- a requirement that such company shall not at any time have more than 50 shareholders.

Restrictions on the transfer of shares should be set out in the articles of association. There is no requirement under the Companies Act for a public company to impose restrictions on the transfer of its shares.

The restrictions that are most commonly reflected are set out next.

(a)   *Rights of pre-emption to existing shareholders*

The articles of association may confer upon the existing shareholders of a company certain rights of pre-emption over any prospective transfers of shares.

In the absence of language to the contrary in the articles of association, rights of pre-emption may generally be waived by the existing shareholders.

(b)   *Discretion of directors to refuse to register a transfer*

The directors of a company may also be conferred with the discretionary power of refusing to register any transfer of shares in the statutory registers of the company. Where the directors refuse to do this, the Companies Act provides that a notice of refusal must be issued by the company to both the transferor and the transferee of the shares, within one month after the date the transfer was lodged.

(c)   *Formalities of transfer of shares*

The formalities in respect of the transfer of shares are governed by the articles of association. The Companies Act provides that a transfer of shares should be effected by a "proper instrument of transfer".

Typically, the procedure for a transfer of shares in a private company limited by shares is as follows:

- The instrument of transfer is executed by the transferor and the transferee (the articles of association may require a witness to these signatures);
- The instrument of transfer is duly stamped[5] with the appropriate stamp duty;
- The share certificate, a duly executed instrument of transfer and a certificate of stamp duty are lodged with the company;
- Where the directors are satisfied that the transfer may be registered, the transfer is registered on the statutory registers of the company; and

---

5   It is an offence to register any instrument chargeable with duty if it has not been stamped.

- Within one month of the transfer, a new share certificate must be issued to the transferee.

6. Administration of a company

6.1 Statutory registers

The Companies Act requires a company to maintain the statutory registers described next.

(a) Register of members

A register of members must contain information including (but not limited to):
- names and addresses of the shareholders;
- the date at which the name of each person is entered into the register as a shareholder;
- in the case of a company having a share capital:
  - a statement of the shares held by each member, distinguishing each share by its number, if any, or by the number, if any, of the certificate evidencing the shareholder's holding;
  - the amount paid or agreed to be considered as paid on the shares of each shareholder; and
  - the date of every allotment of shares to shareholders and the number of shares comprised in each allotment.

(b) Register of directors, secretaries, managers and auditors

A register of directors, secretaries, managers and auditors must, with respect to each officer, contain information including (but not limited to):
- full name;
- residential address;
- nationality; and
- means of identification – ID card number (if card issued) or particulars of the passport or such other similar evidence of identification as is available (otherwise) (Section 173(9) of the Companies Act).

This register is kept at the registered office of the company and may be inspected by shareholders of the company, or any third party upon payment of a nominal fee.

(c) Register of directors' shareholdings

A register of directors' shareholdings must, in relation to each director, contain information including (but not limited to):
- the particulars of shares, debentures or participatory interests of the company or its related corporations that are held or in which the shareholder has an interest;
- debentures of or participatory interests made available by the company or a related corporation which are held or in which the shareholder has an interest;
- any rights and options in respect of the acquisition or disposal of shares in

the company or its related corporations; and

- the contracts to which the shareholder is a party or under which he is entitled to a benefit, being contracts under which a person has a right to call for or to make delivery of shares in the company or its related corporations.

This register is kept at the registered office of the company and may be inspected by shareholders of the company, or any third party upon payment of a nominal fee.

(d) Register of charges

A register of charges must record information on any charges created by a company over its assets. This is kept at the registered office of the company and may be inspected by shareholders, any creditor of the company, or any third party upon payment of a nominal fee.

(e) Register of debenture holders

A register of debenture holders must, in respect of each debenture holder, contain information such as the name and address of such holder and the amount of debentures held.

This need not be kept at the registered office of the company, but if it is held at a location within Singapore other than the registered office, the requisite notifications have to be lodged with the ACRA via Bizfile. A copy may be inspected by every registered debenture holder and by any shareholder on request and on payment of a nominal fee.

6.2 General meetings of the shareholders

(a) Types of general meeting

These are governed by the Companies Act and the articles of association of the company. There are three types of general meetings:

- **Statutory meeting:** to be held only by newly incorporated public companies limited by shares only once in the company's existence, not less than one month and not more than three months after the date that the company is entitled to commence business;
- **Annual general meeting:** to be held by a company at least once every calendar year,[6] and in any case not more than 15 months after the last preceding annual general meeting; and
- **Extraordinary general meeting:** any general meeting of a company other than its annual general meeting or (if applicable) its statutory meeting. There is no minimum requirement or restriction on the maximum number of extraordinary general meetings that must or can be held by a company.

---

6   Except in the first year of incorporation of the company – when such company is required to hold its annual general meeting within 18 months of its incorporation.

(b) **Types of resolution**

Under Singapore law, there are two types of resolution:

- **Ordinary resolutions:** resolutions passed by a simple majority of shareholders present and voting. All resolutions may be passed by an ordinary resolution unless otherwise specified under the Companies Act; and
- **Special resolutions:** resolutions passed by a three-quarters majority of shareholders present and voting. The following are non-exhaustive examples of matters that the Companies Act requires approval by way of a special resolution:
  - alteration by the company of its articles of association;
  - alteration of the memorandum of association (other than alterations to entrenching provisions (if any));
  - change of name of the company; and
  - any winding-up of the company.

(c) **Notices**

Notices of general meetings must be issued to the registered shareholders and the auditors of the company. Notices may also be issued to any other persons as may be identified in the articles of association.

The Companies Act requires notice of the intention to propose a special resolution to be given 14 days before the relevant general meeting for private companies, whilst a longer notice period of 21 days is prescribed for public companies.

(d) **Quorum**

The quorum requirement of general meetings is determined by the articles of association of the company. It is typical for the presence of at least two shareholders to constitute a quorum, unless the company has only one shareholder.

6.3 Administrative body

(a) **Roles of the board of directors and the shareholders**

The Companies Act prescribes the distribution of powers between directors and shareholders of a company and stipulates that the business of a company shall be managed by or under the direction of the directors and, further, that the directors may exercise all the powers of a company, except any such power that the Companies Act or the memorandum and articles of the company requires the company to exercise in a general meeting.

(b) **Appointment, removal and resignation of directors**

Generally, the appointment, removal (for public companies, certain procedural requirements for the removal of directors under the Companies Act must be complied with) and resignation of directors are regulated by the articles of association of a company.

In terms of residency requirements, every company must have at least one director who is ordinarily resident in Singapore. Whilst there is no statutory definition on the expression 'ordinarily resident', this is generally understood to mean a Singapore citizen or permanent resident, or a holder of a valid work pass issued by the Ministry of Manpower who usually resides within Singapore. A director of a company is not allowed to resign or vacate his office (notwithstanding the provisions in the company's memorandum and articles or any agreement with his company) unless there is remaining in the company at least one director who is ordinarily resident in Singapore. Any such resignation or vacation in contravention of the aforesaid requirement is deemed invalid.

The Companies Act does not prescribe a minimum or maximum length of time for which a director may be appointed, except that the office of a director of a public company (or a subsidiary thereof) shall become vacant at the conclusion of the annual general meeting commencing after he attains the age of 70.[7] If required, the articles of association of a company can stipulate such time limitations.

Subject to the conditions specified in the Companies Act, a Singapore court may, under certain circumstances, make an order disqualifying a person from being a director or being concerned with or taking part in the management of any company for a period of time specified by the court, if that person:

- was a director of a company that has at any time gone into liquidation (whether while he was a director or within three years of his ceasing to be a director) and was insolvent at that time and the conduct of the individual makes him unfit to be a director or in any way be engaged in the management of a company;
- was a director of a company that had been ordered to be wound up by the court on the grounds that it was being used for purposes against national security or interest; or
- was convicted in Singapore of any offence in connection with the formation or management of a corporation.

(c)   *Fiduciary and statutory duties of directors*

The common law, the Companies Act and certain statutes[8] prescribe strict rules in relation to duties imposed upon any person who becomes a director of a company. A director is under a statutory duty to act honestly and use reasonable diligence in the discharge of the duties of his office at all times. At common law, a director is regarded as a fiduciary of a company and accordingly he is bound to observe all fiduciary duties imposed by the common law. As a general rule, a director owes this duty to the company, not to the individual shareholders. Some non-exhaustive examples of a director's fiduciary duties are set out below:

- Directors must act in what they consider to be the best interests of the company and not for any collateral purpose;
- Directors must not allow themselves to get into a position where there is a conflict between what they ought to do for the company and what they might

---

7   There is a prescribed procedure under the Companies Act for the reappointment of a director of a public company (or a subsidiary thereof) after he attains the age of 70.
8   For example, the Banking Act, Chapter 19 of Singapore and the Insurance Act, Chapter 142 of Singapore impose additional duties on directors of companies that are regulated by these statutes.

do for themselves. Notwithstanding anything in the articles of association of the company, if a director is aware of any conflict of interest he must, as soon as he becomes aware of the relevant facts, declare it at a board of directors meeting. This must be recorded by the secretary in the minutes.

(d) Liabilities of directors
In addition to being criminally liable under the Companies Act or any other relevant statute, a director who commits a breach of his fiduciary duties or wilfully commits certain breaches of the Companies Act may also be liable to the company or to third parties for losses so incurred.

7. Audited accounts

7.1 Retention of records
Except for a company that is a dormant or an exempt private company, all other companies are required to file their audited accounts with the ACRA,[9] resulting in their audited accounts becoming a document of public record. In addition, a company is required to keep such accounting records as are necessary to explain the transactions and financial position of the company and enable true and fair profit and loss accounts and balance sheets (together with the requisite documents) to be prepared.

Such records are to be retained for a period of not less than five years from the end of the financial year in which the relevant transactions are completed.

7.2 Approval
The directors of a private company or a public company (which is not listed on a securities exchange in Singapore) have an obligation to lay before the company's annual general meeting a profit and loss account for the period since the preceding account made up to a date not more than six months[10] before the date of the meeting. A balance sheet as at the date to which the profit and loss account is made up should also be laid before the company at the annual general meeting. Unless certain exemptions apply, both the profit and loss account and the balance sheet of the company should be audited in accordance with the Singapore Financial Reporting Standards.

7.3 Annual returns
Within one month of its annual general meeting, a company is required to file an annual return with the ACRA via Bizfile.[11] The annual return must contain information prescribed under the Companies Act, including (but not limited to:

- particulars of the amount of indebtedness of the company;

---

9   An exempt private company is exempted from filing its accounts with the ACRA.
10 In respect of public companies listed or quoted on a securities exchange in Singapore, the profit and loss account and the balance sheet should be made up to a date not less than four months before the date of the annual general meeting of such public listed company.
11 Where a company maintains a branch register outside Singapore, such company is required to file its annual return within two months after its annual general meeting.

- a summary of the share capital and the shares of the company; and
- particulars of the officers of the company.

8. Declaration of dividends

The Companies Act provides that dividends of a company may only be declared out of profits. The act is silent on the manner in which dividends may be declared – this is usually a matter stipulated in the articles of association. Typically, the articles of association provide that final dividends are declared by the company at an annual general meeting, upon the recommendation of the directors; directors are usually empowered to declare interim dividends.

With effect from January 1 2008, all companies that are tax-resident in Singapore have moved to the 'one-tier' corporate tax system. Under this system, the tax collected from corporate profits is final and the Singapore-resident company can pay tax-exempt (one-tier) dividends that are exempt from Singapore income tax in the hands of its shareholders, regardless of their tax residence status.

9. Corporate taxation

For the year of assessment 2009, a company is taxed at a flat rate of 18%. There may be scope for certain companies to be given a tax exemption or rebate under prescribed circumstances.

From 2010, the corporate tax rate will be reduced to 17%.

Slovak Republic

Julian Juhasz
Squire, Sanders & Dempsey LLP

1. Types of company with limited liability and applicable legislation

The companies with limited liability available in the Slovak Republic are:

- the joint stock company (*akciová spoločnosť*); and
- the limited liability company (*spoločnosťs ručením obmedzeným*).

The joint stock company and limited liability company are the most commonly used corporate forms in the Slovak Republic.

They are governed by the following laws:

- the Commercial Code (Act 513/1991, as amended and supplemented);
- the Commercial Register Act (530/2003 Coll.);
- the Trade Licensing Act (455/1991);
- the Court Fees Act (71/1992 Coll., as amended and supplemented);
- the Securities and Investment Services Act (566/2001 Coll.);
- Decree 25/2004 Coll. (as amended and supplemented), providing sample forms for the filing of applications for registration in the Commercial Register and a list of deeds to be attached to such applications;
- the Social Insurance Act (461/2003 Coll.);
- the Health Insurance Act (581/2004 Coll.);
- the Tax Administration Act (511/1992);
- the Value Added Tax Act (222/2004 Coll.); and
- the Penal Code (Act 300/2005 Coll., as amended and supplemented).

2. Joint stock company

In general, joint stock companies are used as vehicles for large commercial transactions involving high volumes of capital and a large number of parties. A joint stock company is a company whose registered capital is composed of a certain number of shares of a certain nominal value as set out in the founding agreement (or founding deed, in the case of a sole founder.

2.1 Incorporation procedure

(a) Establishment

A joint stock company organised under the Commercial Code may be established by one shareholder, provided it is a legal entity; if the joint stock company is founded by individuals, at least two shareholders are required. The maximum number of shareholders is unlimited. The business name of the company must include the designation *'akciová spoločnosť'* or the abbreviation 'akc spol' or 'as'.

(i)   *Founding agreement*

To establish a joint stock company, the founders must enter into a founding agreement (or founding deed in the case of a single founder). The founding agreement must be executed in the Slovak Republic in the Slovak language.

The founding agreement must contain the following information:

- the business name of the company, its seat or registered office (ie the principal place of business) and its corporate purpose;
- the suggested amount of the registered capital;
- the number of shares, the nominal value of such shares, and the form and type of shares;
- where different types of shares are issued, the different rights attached thereto;
- any restrictions on the transfer of bearer shares;
- the issue rate of the shares;
- the number of shares subscribed by the individual founders;
- details of any in-kind contributions;
- the name of the deposit trustee (which may be either the founder or a bank based in the Slovak Republic);
- the amount of the statutory reserve fund (if created at the time of establishment) and the manner in which it is to be replenished; and
- estimated costs of the company related to its incorporation and establishment.

(ii)   *Establishment through public offering*

The establishment of a joint stock company through a public offering is a gradual method of establishing the company. Once the founders have entered into a founding agreement, an offer for the subscription of shares is published. The founding agreement must be prepared in the form of a notarial deed or a legal act. As neither the founding agreement nor the draft articles of association forms part of the call for the subscription of shares, the terms of the offer must be consistent with the founding agreement and cannot be changed during the subscription period. In order for each subscription to be effective, a subscriber must subscribe for the shares and pay at least 10% of the subscription price in cash by the end of a specified period. If, by the end of this period, the total amount of subscribed shares fails to reach the proposed amount of the registered capital, and the outstanding amount is not subscribed by the founders within one month, the subscription is ineffective.

The founders must convene a constitutive general meeting within 60 days of the effective subscription of the whole amount of the proposed registered capital. The constitutive general meeting will decide on the establishment of a joint stock company, the articles of association will be approved and the corporate bodies elected. Any decision of the constituent general meeting must be approved by subscribers to shares having aggregate nominal value equal to not less than 50% of the nominal value of all the shares. At least 30% of the nominal value of all subscribed shares payable in cash must be paid in by no later than the beginning of the constitutive general meeting. The balance of the subscription price must be paid by the subscribers within one year of establishment of the company.

If the joint stock company is established by a public offering for the subscription of shares, the founding agreement must also specify the following:

- the place and time of the share subscription;
- the procedure in case of subscription of shares in excess of the proposed registered capital – in particular, a specification as to whether the founders will allow the subscription of additional shares following the full subscription of the proposed registered capital. If this is allowed, the agreement should also specify whether:
  - the subscription of additional shares will cause an increase in the proposed registered capital;
  - the number of shares subscribed by the individual subscribers will be reduced in proportion to their subscriptions, while maintaining the proposed registered capital; or
  - there will be a partial increase in the proposed registered capital.

The founding agreement may also specify some other procedure to be followed in such cases:

- the place and term for the payment of fractions of the subscribed shares and the percentage thereof; and
- the procedure for convening the constitutive general meeting.

All benefits that may be granted to persons involved in the establishment of the joint stock company, and in obtaining its permits and authorisations, must be agreed in the founding agreement.

If the founder is a legal entity, the founding deed must be executed by the director(s) of the founder with the authority to sign on behalf of the founder. The power of the director(s) to act on behalf of the founder must be evidenced by an extract from the Commercial Register or by similar supporting documentation. The founding deed may also be executed by an attorney in fact.

(iii) *Establishment without public offering*

Where a joint stock company is established without a public offering, the founders subscribe the entire proposed registered capital and at the same time exercise the powers of the constitutive general meeting. The company is established by a founding agreement that contains the wording of the approved articles of association and a determination of the first members of the corporate bodies, elected pursuant to the articles of association by the general meeting. For the validity of the agreement of founders on the establishment of a company without a public call, the law formally requires that the founding agreement be prepared in the form of a notarial deed. At least 30% of the registered capital must be paid in cash (and in-kind contributions must be paid in full prior to the company's registration in the Commercial Register).

(iv) *Memorandum of association*

The articles of association of a joint stock company have the function of the memorandum of association. The founding agreement is binding only on the founders of the company, but not on other subscribers or shareholders; such subscribers or shareholders are bound solely by the articles of association. In the case of subscription based on a public offering, draft articles of association must be made available for inspection by subscribers at each subscription venue. The general meeting may decide what majority is necessary to adopt the articles of association; otherwise, approval by subscribers holding a majority of the subscribed shares is sufficient.

Amendment of the articles of association following incorporation falls within the powers of the general meeting and must be approved by two-thirds of the shareholders in attendance, unless the articles of association specify a higher majority. If necessary, the articles of association also provide for:

- the issuance of various classes of shares;
- the designation thereof;
- the number of such shares and the rights attached thereto; and
- rules for the issuance of bonds and the rights attached to such bonds.

(b) **Proceedings prior to incorporation**

To perform most activities included in the corporate purpose clause of the founding agreement, a joint stock company must be granted a trade licence. Whether the company needs to obtain a trade licence and/or a concession deed (trade permit certificate) depends on the nature of the activities to be carried out.

A trade licence is issued by the local branch of the Trade Licence Office. As there are several types of licence (some requiring proof of certain professional qualifications, experience, skills or equipment, as well as prior approval of other regulatory authorities), it is essential to formulate carefully the corporate purpose clause in the founding agreement.

The application form must be accompanied by the following documents:

- a notarised copy of the founding agreement or founding deed;
- a notarised power of attorney, issued by the founders, for the authorised representatives empowered to file the application and liaise with the Trade Licence Office;
- if required, a notarised copy of evidence of the applicant's qualifications. If the applicant is a foreigner, he must provide evidence of his qualifications as above (which must be comparable to such qualifications in the Slovak Republic), translated into Slovak and notarised;
- an acceptance deed signed by the responsible person accepting this position; and
- stamp duty of €3 for the issuance of a trade licence for free (unqualified) trade, €16.50 for the issuance of a trade licence for vocational and professional trade and €33 for the issuance of a concession deed.

The most recent amendment of the Trade Licensing Act, effective from October 1 2007, introduced, in the interest of improvement of the business environment, several more significant changes. Pursuant to this most recent amendment of the act, a trade licence may contain only one notifiable trade, and a concession deed may contain only one object of business. Valid trade licences with several objects of business issued prior to October 2007 shall remain in force.

In relation to the limitation of the number of objects of business (one trade licence – one object of business), administrative fees for issuance have been decreased.

Further, the following was cancelled through the amendment: a duty to prove a licence to operate a business premises and a duty to submit copies of the criminal records that will be obtained by the Trade Licence Office itself via an electronic form. A natural person and a legal entity shall specify, together with a notification of the trade, data necessary for requesting for a copy of the criminal records. If the copy of the criminal records contains a record on the sentence for an intentional crime, the Trade Licence Office shall request the entrepreneur to submit the valid and effective judgment on the sentence.

A natural person and a legal entity may also specify, together with a notification of the trade, data required under special laws:

- fulfilment of tax registration with respect to income tax and notification duty; and
- registration to the system of compulsory health insurance.

A natural person who is registered in the system of compulsory health insurance shall specify, together with a notification of the trade, the trade name of the insurer with which he/she is registered and may notify any change of the insurance payer. The Trade Licence Office shall distribute such data to the relevant authorities and shall record that data in a non-public part of the trade register.

If the Trade Licence Office discovers that the notification and the particular entrepreneur meet the conditions established by law, it shall issue a trade licence not later than five business days from the day it is delivered the notification of the trade and copies of the criminal records.

The Trade Licensing Act applies to all trades and businesses except those specifically excluded from its scope of application (eg activities reserved for operation by the state, banking and insurance, forestry, farming, fishing, telecommunications, and radio and television broadcasting). It usually takes one to three weeks to obtain the licence.

(c)   *Incorporation*

Within 90 days of execution of the founding agreement, the board of directors must apply for registration of the joint stock company in the commercial register, submitting the following documents:

- a completed application form with notarised signatures of all directors or their attorneys in fact;
- a notarised copy of the founding agreement or founding deed;
- the articles of association;
- a decision of the supervisory board on the appointment of the board of directors, if the board of directors is appointed by the supervisory board under the articles of association;

- a deed proving entitlement to pursue the relevant business activity (eg a trade licence for each object of business);
- a written representation of the contribution administrator;
- a valuation report proving that the value of the in-kind contribution corresponds to the subscription price of the shares paid up by such contribution, where an in-kind contribution has been made;
- notarised specimen signatures and acceptance deeds of all members of the board of directors;
- acceptance deeds of members of the supervisory board;
- where a founder is a foreign person, a certificate of registration of the foreign person in the relevant commercial register;
- powers of attorney for submission of the applications for registration in the commercial register, if any; and
- a document confirming payment of the court fee amounting to €830.

If a joint stock company is being established based on a call for the subscription of shares, in addition to the specified deeds the following shall be enclosed with the application for registration:

- the call for the subscription of shares, together with the document proving its publication;
- the deed of subscribers, or copies of written manifestations of the will of the subscribers; and
- a notarial deed from the session of the constituent general meeting.

All of the documents listed in the two bullet lists above must be officially translated into the Slovak language, as the translation must be attached to all foreign-language documents submitted to the Slovak registration authorities.

If the court finds that all the requirements have been fulfilled, the joint stock company will be registered within five days of submission of the completed application, together with the supporting documentation, to the district court, unless a later date is requested in the application. The joint stock company obtains legal personality for the purpose of Slovak law on the day of registration in the commercial register.

(d) Post-incorporation proceedings

Once the registration certificate has been issued, the company must register with the respective tax authority for the assessment of value added tax (if its turnover in the previous 12 months reaches the registration threshold of €35,000).

The joint stock company must also register for pension, sickness, disability, unemployment, injury and guarantee insurance with the Slovak Social Insurance Company within eight days of its first employment contract becoming effective, and with one of the health insurance companies for payment of its employees' health insurance.

2.2　Shareholders

(a)　*Rights and obligations*

A subscriber becomes a shareholder of the joint stock company upon registration of the company in the commercial register. Shareholders are entitled to:

- participate in the general meeting;
- vote at the general meeting;
- be elected to company bodies; and
- exercise proprietary rights – that is:
  - the right to a profit share (a dividend);
  - the right to *pro rata* distribution of the assets remaining upon liquidation;
  - a pre-emptive right to subscribe to shares in the event of an increase in registered capital; and
  - the right to information – the right to request information and explanations from the board of directors at the general meeting involving the affairs of the company and of persons controlled by the company, relating to items on the agenda of the general meeting; and the right to inspect deeds included in the collection of deeds at the company's seat, and to request copies thereof.

(b)　*Minority shareholders' rights*

Shareholders holding at least 5% of the shares are entitled to request the convening of an extraordinary general meeting to discuss proposed issues. In such a case the board of directors must convene a general meeting within 40 days of delivery of the written request. The board of directors is not entitled to modify the agenda of the general meeting proposed by the minority shareholders without their prior consent. If the board of directors fails to convene the general meeting within the prescribed period, the minority shareholders may request a court to authorise them to convene the meeting. Any costs incurred by the minority shareholders in this regard must be borne by the company. The members of the board of directors are jointly and severally liable to the company for the compensation of such costs.

In addition, minority shareholders holding at least 5% of the shares may request that certain issues be included on the agenda of the general meeting and that the general meeting deal with such issues. Minority shareholders may at any time request the supervisory board to investigate the performance of the duties of the board of directors. At the request of the minority shareholders, the supervisory board will pursue any claims of the company for damages against the board members. The board of directors, if approached by the minority shareholders, must take action against any shareholders who fail to pay the issue price of the subscribed shares duly and on time.

(c)　*Expulsion of a shareholder*

If a shareholder fails to pay in the subscription price of shares, or any fraction thereof, within the specified timeframe, he will become obliged to pay default interest in an amount of 20% annually, unless the articles of association provide otherwise. The joint stock company may expel a shareholder from the company if he fails to pay in the issue price of the shares, or any fraction thereof, within the term for payment despite having been notified by the board of directors. The board of directors will decide on whether expulsion is appropriate. The decision will then be served on the shareholder and filed in the collection of deeds. The shares of the expelled shareholder will pass over to the company on the date of receipt of the decision to expel the shareholder from the company.

2.3 Registered capital

(a) Minimum capital requirement

The Commercial Code sets the minimum amount of registered capital at €25,000. A joint stock company is liable for breach of its obligations to the full extent of its assets. Shareholders bear no liability for the obligations of the company.

(b) Shares

Shares are securities to which are attached shareholders' rights, as defined by the Commercial Code and the articles of association. Each share must include the following:

- the business name and registered office of the company;
- the nominal value of the share;
- an indication as to whether the share is 'registered' or 'bearer'. If it is a registered share, it must also include the business name, registered office and identification number of the shareholder if it is a legal entity, or the name, residence and birth certificate number of the shareholder if he is an individual. If the shareholder is a non-resident legal entity, an identification number will be indicated only if assigned. If the shareholder is a non-resident individual, his date of birth will be indicated if no birth certificate number has been assigned;
- the registered capital and the number of all shares of the company outstanding at the time of issue;
- the date of issue; and
- if several classes of shares are outstanding, the class thereof. Ordinary shares (ie shares to which no special rights are attached) need not specify any class.

The shares may be issued in certificated or book-entry form. In addition to the general requirements outlined above, certificated shares must also indicate:

- a serial number;
- the signature(s) of the director(s) authorised to act on behalf of the company at the time of issue; and
- a specification of the rights attached thereto, at least by reference to the provisions of the articles of association.

Registered shares may be issued in certificated or book-entry form, while bearer shares may be issued only in book-entry form (ie they must be registered with the Slovak Central Depository of Securities or one of its licensed members). If the company has issued registered shares, it must arrange for the maintenance of a shareholder list with the Central Depository of Securities.

The company may issue preference shares to which a preferential right to dividends is attached. However, the aggregate sum of the nominal value of preference shares may not exceed one-half of the total amount of the registered capital.

(i)   *Transfer of shares*
The transfer of book-entry shares is effected through the Slovak Central Depository of Securities or its licensed members that administer the accounts of the owners of securities. Certificated shares may be transferred by endorsement and delivery to the transferee. The transfer of registered shares only becomes effective with respect to the company when the new shareholder is registered in the shareholder list. The articles of association may restrict, but not exclude, the transfer of certificated shares. If the articles of association make the transfer of certificated shares subject to the approval of the company, they must also specify the grounds on which the company may refuse to give its approval and the timeframe within which the company must inform the requesting shareholder of its decision. If the grounds for disapproval of a transfer, as specified in the articles of association, do not apply, the company must approve the transfer. The company is liable for any damage that the shareholder may suffer as a result of a breach of these duties.

(ii)   *Subscription of own shares*
In limited cases, and under conditions stipulated by the Commercial Code, the company may subscribe its own shares – for example:

- only a maximum of 10% of the registered capital may be subscribed by the company;
- the equity must not drop below the aggregate of the registered capital and the reserve fund; and
- the issue rate of the shares to be acquired must be fully paid up.

A company holding its own shares cannot exercise the voting rights attached thereto.

(c)   **Convertible bonds and priority bonds**
Pursuant to a decision of the general meeting, a joint stock company may issue convertible bonds with a right of exchange against company shares (convertible bonds) or bonds with a right to preferential subscription of company shares (priority bonds). This decision may be taken only if the general meeting simultaneously decides on a conditional increase in the registered capital. Both the right to exchange convertible bonds against company shares and the right to preferential subscription of company shares may be transferred as separate rights.

(d)   **Interim certificates**
An interim certificate is a registered security and is transferable (by endorsement and

delivery in the case of a physical interim certificate, and by registration of the transfer in the records of book-entry securities in the case of a book-entry interim certificate). The interim certificate enables a shareholder to exercise rights if he has not yet paid in the nominal value of his shares. If a shareholder transfers its interim certificate to another party prior to the paying-up of the nominal value of shares, the shareholder will be liable for paying up the remaining fraction of the nominal value of the subscribed shares. The company will provide shares in exchange for the interim certificate once the shareholder has fully paid in the issue price of the shares subscribed.

(e)   *Increase in registered capital*

An increase in the registered capital through the subscription of new shares may be carried out only if the issue price of all previously issued shares (other than employee shares) has been paid in full. This restriction does not apply to an increase in the registered capital through in-kind contributions and in the case of the issuance of employee shares. The decision to increase the registered capital must be approved by two-thirds of the votes at the general meeting. If several classes of shares are outstanding, a two-thirds majority of votes is required with respect to each class of shares.

(f)   *Reduction in registered capital*

Unless a special act provides otherwise, any reduction in the registered capital is to be decided, further to a proposal of the board of directors, by a two-thirds majority of votes at the general meeting. If several classes of shares are outstanding, a two-thirds majority of votes is required with respect to each class of shares.

(g)   *Reserve fund*

Pursuant to Section 67(2) of the Commercial Code, a joint stock company must create a reserve fund to be used to cover losses of the company. The reserve fund must be created at the time of establishment of the company, in an amount of at least 10% of the registered capital. The reserve fund must be subsequently replenished on an annual basis by at least 10% of the net profits until the funds allocated in the reserve fund reach 20% of the registered capital. The reserve fund may be created by subscription of shares at an issue price that is higher than the nominal value of the shares (ie share premium).

2.4   Administration

(a)   *General meeting*

The general meeting is the supreme body of a joint stock company and consists of all attending shareholders. A general meeting is held at least once a year and is convened by the board of directors, with a few exceptions provided for by the Commercial Code. There is no quorum requirement for a general meeting. A general meeting adopts resolutions by simple majority vote, unless the articles of association or the Commercial Code requires some other majority. The Commercial Code stipulates a two-thirds majority of the shareholders present for:

- an increase or reduction in the registered capital;
- winding-up;
- the issuance of convertible or priority bonds;
- amendment of the articles of association; and
- a change in legal form.

The articles of association may specify a higher majority for the adoption of resolutions at a general meeting.

(i)   *Competence*
The powers of the general meeting include the following:
- to approve changes to the articles of association, unless the law specifies otherwise;
- to decide on an increase or reduction in the registered capital and the issuance of convertible or priority bonds;
- to elect and remove members of the board of directors, unless the articles of association vest this power in the supervisory board;
- to elect and remove members of the supervisory board or other bodies established by the articles of association, except for members of the supervisory board elected by company employees;
- to approve the annual individual financial statements and extraordinary individual financial statements, distribute profits, cover losses and decide on the remuneration of the members of the statutory bodies of the company;
- to decide on the conversion of registered shares into book-entry shares and vice versa;
- to decide on the dissolution of the company or any change in its legal form;
- to decide on the termination of trading in the company's shares on a stock exchange;
- to set out the principles of remuneration of the members of the corporate bodies, unless such power is vested in a supervisory board;
- to decide on the approval of a contract on the transfer of an enterprise or of part of an enterprise; and
- to decide on other matters entrusted to the authority of the general meeting by law or the bylaws.

(ii)   *General meeting of sole-shareholder company*
If a joint stock company has a sole shareholder, the powers of the general meeting are exercised by this shareholder. Any resolutions of a sole shareholder exercising the powers of the general meeting must be in writing. A written resolution must be delivered to the board of directors and supervisory board of the company. In cases where the Commercial Code stipulates a two-thirds majority of votes as specified above, the resolutions must be executed in the form of notarial deed and must be delivered to the board of directors and to the supervisory board.

(b) **Board of directors**

The board of directors is the statutory body of the joint stock company that manages its operations and acts on its behalf. Unless the articles of association provide otherwise, any member of the board is authorised to act on behalf of the company. The authority of the board of directors to act on behalf of the company may be restricted by the articles of association, or by resolutions of the general meeting or the supervisory board. However, such restrictions have no effect with respect to third parties.

Members of the board of directors are elected by the general meeting for a term specified in the articles of association, up to a maximum period of five years. A sole-member board of directors is permitted. Members of the board of directors who are not nationals of an Organisation for Economic Cooperation and Development (OECD) or an EU member state require a residence permit in order to obtain registration in the commercial register.

Unless the articles of association provide additional restrictions, members of the board of directors are not allowed:

- to conclude business deals that are associated with the business of the joint stock company in their own name and for their own account;
- to mediate the company's transactions for other parties;
- to participate in the business of any partnership as a member with unlimited liability; or
- to discharge the office of a statutory body or be a member of a statutory or similar body of another legal entity with a similar corporate purpose, unless the primary company has an interest in the other company's business.

Board members who are in breach of their duties are jointly and severally liable to indemnify the company for any damage caused. However, the board members are not liable for any damage caused to the company by implementing a resolution of the general meeting, unless the resolution is contrary to the law or the articles of association. The board members will not be released from their liability if their conduct has been approved by the supervisory board. The liability of the board members cannot be excluded or restricted by any agreements with the company, nor by the articles of association.

The company may waive its claims to indemnity against the board members or make a settlement therewith, but:

- not earlier than three years after the claims arose;
- only if the waiver is approved by the general meeting; and
- only if no objection against such a resolution is raised by any shareholder with a stake of at least 5% in the company.

Indemnity claims against board members may be made by a creditor of the company in its own name and for its own account if the creditor is unable to satisfy its debt from the company's assets. The claims of creditors towards the board members do not lapse even if the company waives its claims to indemnity or enters into a settlement agreement with the board members. In the event of the company's bankruptcy, creditors' claims may be enforced against the board members by the bankruptcy trustee.

The other standards for criminal and civil liability are identical for members of the board of directors and those of a supervisory board; the differences in their application arise from the differences in the types of decision and supervisory activities for which they are each responsible. Members have no other criminal or civil liability, either to the company or to third parties, arising solely out of their role as members in a company. Pursuant to Section 19 of the Penal Code, a member of the board of directors or a supervisory board member may also be liable as an individual if he breaches Slovak law.

(c) *Supervisory board*

(i) *Competence*
The supervisory board supervises the exercise of powers by the board of directors and the company's business activities. Members of the supervisory board are entitled to inspect any documents and reports concerning the company's activities. The supervisory board also monitors whether the books are properly kept and reflect the actual state of affairs. The supervisory board reviews the annual financial statements as well as the proposal for the distribution of profits, and submits its comments to the general meeting. Members of the supervisory board shall attend general meetings of the company and are obliged to report the findings of their monitoring and inspections to the general meeting.

(ii) *Members*
The supervisory board consists of at least three members. Two-thirds of the supervisory board members are elected by the general meeting and one-third by the company's employees, provided that there are more than 50 full-time employees at the time of election. The members are elected for a period stipulated by the articles of association, up to a maximum of five years. Members of the board of directors may not serve as members of the supervisory board, as procurist, or as any other person authorised to act on behalf of the company. The scope of liability and the prohibition on competition applicable to the members of the board of directors also apply to the members of the supervisory board.

2.5 Financial statements
The annual and extraordinary financial statements of joint stock companies must be audited by an auditor according to the Accountancy Act. Both the annual and extraordinary financial statements must be approved by the general meeting. A copy of the annual and extraordinary financial statements is included in the collection of deeds in the Commercial Register and is publicly accessible. The members of the board of directors are obliged to include a copy of the annual and extraordinary financial statements in the collection of deeds.

2.6 Distribution of profits

Each shareholder is entitled to a share in the profits allocated for distribution by the general meeting based on the company's performance. Unless the articles of association provide otherwise, the entitlement to dividends is based on the ratio between the nominal value of shares held by the shareholder and the nominal value of shares held by all other shareholders. The right to dividends may be transferred as a separate right as of the date on which the general meeting adopts the decision to distribute profits.

3. Limited liability company

The Commercial Code defines a 'limited liability company' as a company with registered capital consisting of cash or in-kind contributions paid by its members. A limited liability company may be established by a single natural person, subject to certain restrictions; the maximum number of members is limited to 50.

3.1 Incorporation procedure

(a) Establishment

Slovak law distinguishes two phases in the process of setting up a limited liability company: establishment and incorporation/registration. Establishment is made by the execution of a memorandum of association or, in the case of a sole founder, a founding deed. After the company has been established, a filing is made in the commercial register maintained at the respective district court. The company is incorporated and fully recognised as a corporate entity capable of entering into relationships with third parties on the date of registration in the commercial register. Persons acting on behalf of the company prior to incorporation are jointly and severally liable for their actions. Obligations incurred prior to incorporation will become binding on the company only if the general meeting approves such actions within three months of the incorporation date. In general, the company will not assume liabilities that are not directly connected to incorporation (eg lease of office premises, opening of a bank account), unless the company assumes such other liabilities under the condition of subsequent approval by the general meeting.

(i) Memorandum of association or founding deed

The founding deed is used instead of the memorandum of association where the company is established by a sole founder. The memorandum must be executed in the Slovak Republic in the Slovak language. The memorandum can provide for the adoption of articles of association that regulate the company's internal organisation and elaborate on the general matters included in the memorandum; however, the adoption of articles of association is not mandatory.

The memorandum must contain the following information:
- the business name of the company and its seat or registered office (ie the principal place of business);
- the name and registered address of the founder;
- the corporate purpose (ie a list of the activities in which the company will engage);

- the amount of the initial registered capital (which must be at least €5,000) and the form of payment (either cash or in-kind contributions);
- the names, addresses and dates of birth (or birth numbers, if applicable) of the first executives of the company, and the manner in which they will represent the company;
- the names, addresses and dates of birth (or birth numbers, if applicable) of the first members of the supervisory board (if one is created);
- the name of the deposit trustee (which can be either the founder or a bank based in the Slovak Republic);
- the amount of the statutory reserve fund (if created at the time of establishment) and the manner in which it is to be replenished;
- any benefits that may be granted to persons involved in the establishment of the company, and in obtaining its permits and authorisations;
- an estimate of the costs of establishment and incorporation; and
- further details where required by law.

If the founder is a legal entity, the founding deed must be executed by the director(s) of the founder with the authority to sign on its behalf. The authority of the director(s) to act on behalf of the founder must be evidenced by an extract from the commercial register or by similar supporting documentation. The founding deed may also be executed by an attorney in fact.

(ii) *Notarial fees*
The memorandum of association or founding deed must be certified by a notary, along with the specimen signatures of all executives. The final amount of the notarial fees depends on several factors, in particular the number of company founders – each signature must be certified on each copy of the memorandum (three copies are required for the commercial register and Trade Licence Office, while one additional copy is usually made for the company and each founder). The fee for certification of each signature is currently (2009) approximately €2 plus 19% VAT.

(b) **Proceedings prior to incorporation**
The process of registration with the Trade Licence Office is identical to that for joint stock companies (see section 2.1(b) above).

(c) **Incorporation**
Within 90 days of execution of the memorandum of association, the executives must apply for registration of the company in the relevant commercial register, submitting the following documents:
- a completed application form with notarised signatures of all executives or their attorneys in fact;
- the founder's corporate documentation (eg extract from the commercial register);
- a notarised copy of the memorandum of association;
- an extract from the bank account evidencing the deposit of the initial

registered capital or a corresponding declaration of the deposit trustee;
- a trade licence or other permit, where applicable;
- notarised specimen signatures and acceptance deeds of all executives;
- powers of attorney for submission of the application for registration in the commercial register, where applicable;
- if the founder is a Slovak legal entity, an affidavit stating that the founder is not owned by the sole member/shareholder;
- if the founder is an individual, an affidavit stating that the founder is not the sole member in more than three companies; and
- stamp duty (currently of €331.50).

(d) *Post-incorporation proceedings*

The same post-incorporation registrations and periods apply to a limited liability company as for a joint stock company (see section 2.1(d)).

3.2 Members

(a) *Number of members*

A limited liability company may have a minimum of one member, subject to certain restrictions, and a maximum of 50 members. The company is liable for breach of its obligations to the full extent of its assets. The liability of each member for the company's obligations is limited to any amount outstanding on its pledged contribution registered in the commercial register.

(b) *Rights and obligations*

A member is obliged to pay up his pledged contribution within the terms and by the date prescribed by the Commercial Code or, as appropriate, set out in the memorandum of association. However, such a payment must be made within five years of incorporation or of the date on which the member joined the company, or of the date of subscription of a new contribution. No member may be released from this obligation. The executive directors must notify without undue delay the body esponsible for the commercial register of the payment in full of each member's contribution.

(c) *Ownership interest*

The ownership interest represents the rights and duties of a member and the corresponding participation in the limited liability company. It is determined by the ratio between the member's pledged contribution to the company and the company's registered capital, unless the memorandum of association provides otherwise.

(d) *Termination of partnership*

(i) *Termination by the court*

A member may not directly withdraw from a limited liability company. He may, however, propose that the court terminate his participation in the limited liability company if he cannot be reasonably required to remain in the company any longer.

(ii)   *Expulsion of a member*
A limited liability company may request the court to expel a member who is in serious breach of his duties even though he has been reminded of his duties and has been given a written warning of the possibility of expulsion. A member whose contributions in the company amount to not less than 50% of the registered capital must approve such a request.

(iii)   *Settlement*
A member whose partnership in a limited liability company is terminated by the court or who has been expelled is entitled to a settlement share. The same right inures to the benefit of the heir or legal successor of such a member, unless the ownership interest has been transferred thereto.

3.3   Registered capital

(a)   *Minimum capital requirement*
A limited liability company must have a minimum registered capital of €5,000. If the company has more than one founder-member, the contribution of each member must be at least €750. The amounts of individual contributions may vary; however, it must be expressed by a positive integer number. The aggregate amount of all individual contributions must correspond to the registered capital.

(b)   *Nature of contributions*
If a member undertakes to make an in-kind contribution, the memorandum of association must specify the nature of such contribution and its value in monetary terms (which is offset against the pledged contribution of the member). In-kind contributions must be paid in before filing the application for registration in the commercial register, as must all cash contributions where there is a sole founder. If there are several founders, the contribution of each member must be at least €750 and at least 30% of the contribution must be paid in before registration in the commercial register. The aggregate value of the paid-up contributions in cash, together with the value of contributions in kind that have been handed over to the company, shall be no less than 50% of the statutory minimum amount of the registered capital.

(c)   *Increases and reductions in registered capital*
The registered capital of a limited liability company may be increased by new cash contributions only once all existing cash contributions have been fully paid in. This restriction does not apply if the registered capital is to be increased by in-kind contributions. Unless the memorandum of association or a decision of the general meeting to increase the registered capital provides otherwise, the current members have a pre-emptive right to subscribe new contributions *pro rata* to their ownership interests. This right must be exercised by the date specified in the memorandum of association or, if no date is specified, within one month of the date of the decision of the general meeting to increase the registered capital. If the new contribution is

subscribed by someone other than a current member, this must be effected by means of a written statement through which the new member agrees to adhere to the memorandum. His signature must be officially authenticated.

Any resolution on a reduction in the registered capital must be passed by the general meeting. The amount of the registered capital and the amount of each member's contribution may never be reduced below the statutory limits. The executives shall be obliged to publish the reduction of the registered capital (together with its extent) for the first time within 15 days of the date of such a resolution and for the second time within 30 days from the date of the first notice. The notice shall be addressed to the company's creditors, asking them to file proofs of their claims within 90 days from the date of the most recent notice.

(d)   Reserve fund

Pursuant to Section 67(2) of the Commercial Code, a limited liability company must create a reserve fund to be used to cover losses of the company. The reserve fund may be created either at the time of establishment or as soon as the company generates profits. In the latter case, the first contribution to the reserve fund must amount to at least 5% of the company's net profits and cannot exceed 10% of the registered capital. The reserve fund must subsequently be replenished on an annual basis by amounts of at least 5% of the net profits until the funds allocated in the reserve fund reach at least 10% of the registered capital.

3.4   Administration

(a)   General meeting

The general meeting is the supreme body of the company. General meetings must be held at least once a year and are convened by the executives. The number of votes of each shareholder shall be determined as a proportion between the value of its contribution and the registered capital of the company, unless the memorandum of association provides otherwise. There is a quorum if at least a simple majority of members, together holding at least half of all votes, are present, unless the memorandum provides otherwise. The general meeting adopts resolutions by simple majority of votes, unless the memorandum or the Commercial Code requires a higher majority. The Commercial Code requires a majority of two-thirds of the members present for the adoption of resolutions on the following matters:

- approval of actions taken by the founders prior to incorporation;
- approval and amendment of the articles of association;
- amendment of the memorandum of association;
- deciding on increases and reductions in registered capital and deciding on in-kind contributions; and
- dissolution of the company or any change in its legal form, if the memorandum of association so permits.

In addition to the above issues, the general meeting also has the power to decide on matters that include:

- the annual individual, extraordinary individual or consolidated financial statements, distribution of profits and settlement of losses;
- appointment, removal and remuneration of executives;
- appointment, removal and remuneration of members of the supervisory board (where applicable);
- expulsion of a member in accordance with Sections 113 and 121 of the Commercial Code;
- approval of a contract on the sale of an enterprise or part thereof; and
- other matters entrusted to the authority of the general meeting by law or by the memorandum or articles of association.

The general meeting may reserve the right to decide other matters that would otherwise fall under the authority of other company bodies.

If a limited liability company has a sole member, the powers of the general meeting are exercised by that member. Any resolutions of a sole member exercising the powers of the general meeting must be in writing.

(b) *Executives*

(i) *Term of office, resignation and removal of directors*

One or several executives may constitute the statutory body of a limited liability company. Only a natural person can be an executive. If there are multiple executives, each is entitled to act individually on behalf of the company, unless the memorandum or articles of association stipulate otherwise.

The consent of the majority of the executives is required for any decision concerning the company's business management, provided it falls within their authority. The executives must:

- make arrangements to keep the records and accounting books prescribed by law, maintain a list of company members and inform the members on company matters; and
- submit an ordinary individual financial statement, an extraordinary individual financial statement, a proposal for the distribution of profits or settlement of losses and an annual report, as required by law.

Executives are appointed by the general meeting for a term specified in the memorandum of association. The powers of executives to act on behalf of the company may be limited by the memorandum or by decision of the general meeting. However, no limitations of executives' powers are effective with respect to third parties.

Executives must discharge their office with due care and in the interests of the company and all of its members. In particular, they:

- must collect and take into account any available information in making business decisions;
- must not disclose any confidential information; and
- must not favour their own interests, the interests of certain members only, or of third parties, over the interests of the company while discharging their duties.

(ii)   *Liability*

Executives who are in breach of their duties are jointly and severally liable to indemnify the company for any damage caused. However, executives are not liable for any damage caused to the company by implementing a resolution of the general meeting. This does not apply if the resolution is contrary to the law or the memorandum or articles of association. If there is a supervisory board, the executives will not be released from their liability if their conduct has been approved by the supervisory board. The executives' liability cannot be excluded or restricted by any agreements with the company, nor by the memorandum of association.

The company may waive its claims to indemnity against the executives or make a settlement therewith, but:

- not earlier than three years after the claims arise;
- only if a waiver is approved by the general meeting; and
- only if no objection against such a resolution is raised by any member with at least a 10% interest in the company.

Indemnity claims against the executives may be made by a creditor of the company in its own name and for its own account if it cannot satisfy its debt out of the company's assets. The claims of creditors against the executives do not lapse even if the company waives its claims to indemnity or enters into a settlement agreement with the executives. In a case of bankruptcy, creditors' claims may be enforced against the executives by the bankruptcy trustee.

The other standards for criminal and civil liability are identical for executives and supervisory board members; the differences in their application arise from the differences in the types of decision and supervisory activities for which they are each responsible.

The members have no other criminal or civil liability either to the company or to third parties arising solely out of their role as members in a company. For criminal liability of the executives and the supervisory board members, see section 2.4(b).

(iii)   *Non-competition*

Unless the memorandum of association provides additional restrictions, the executives are not allowed:

- to conclude business deals in their own name and for their own account that are associated with the business of the company;
- to mediate the company's transactions for other parties;
- to participate in the business of any partnership as a member with unlimited liability; or
- to discharge the office of a statutory body or be a member of a statutory or similar body of another legal entity with a similar scope of business, unless the primary company has an interest in the other company's business.

(iv)   *Residence permit for foreign executives*

Executives who are not members of an OECD or EU member state require a residence permit in order to register with the commercial register.

(c) *Supervisory board*

A supervisory board may be established if permitted by the memorandum of association. The supervisory board is entitled to:

- supervise the executives' activities;
- inspect business and accounting books;
- review the annual financial statements; and
- submit reports to the general meeting.

The members of the supervisory board (there must be at least three) are elected by the general meeting. Executives may not serve as members of the supervisory board. The scope of liability and the ban on competition applicable to executives and described in section 3.4(b) above also apply to members of the supervisory board. The supervisory board shall convene a general meeting at all times if the interests of the company so require. Members of the supervisory board shall not have any voting right at the general meeting.

3.5 Financial statements

The annual and extraordinary financial statements of a limited liability company need not be audited unless certain conditions are met. A copy of the financial statements must be included in the collection of deeds in the commercial register and is publicly accessible.

3.6 Distribution of profits

Each member is entitled to share in the profits (dividends) in proportion to his paid-up contribution, unless the memorandum of association provides otherwise. The company shall not pay any interest on contributions made to the company and advances on dividends. The members must refund to the company any profits paid to them in conflict with these provisions. Each member shall have such a duty, regardless of whether it acted or did not act in good faith in the payment of the dividend. Executive directors who approve such payments will have joint and several liability for the refund.

4. Corporate name

The corporate name of a joint stock company or limited liability company is the name under which the company performs its business activities and is registered in the commercial register. The corporate name may not be interchangeable with the corporate name of another entrepreneur, and may not create a false impression of the entrepreneur or its scope of business. A different corporate form cannot be considered to be sufficient to distinguish the corporate name of a legal entity.

5. Corporate domicile

The corporate domicile of a joint stock company or limited liability company is the address that is registered in the commercial register.

6.   **Corporate purpose**

The corporate purpose must be listed in the founding agreement or founding deed
of a joint stock company or a limited liability company. To perform most activities
listed in the corporate purpose clause, the company must be granted a trade licence
as outlined in Section 2.1(b).

7.   **Company taxation**

The corporate income tax rate in the Slovak Republic is currently (2009) 19%. Within
three months of the end of the preceding fiscal year (generally the calendar year), all
persons liable to pay income tax must file a tax return for the preceding fiscal year
and pay any tax accordingly.

Taxpayers whose tax due in the preceding fiscal year exceeded a certain threshold
(currently €16,596.96) must pay monthly advances on the tax due in the current
fiscal year, amounting to one-twelfth of the tax due in the preceding fiscal year. The
taxpayer must then pay the difference between the aggregate advances paid and the
tax due for the current fiscal year within three months of the end of the fiscal year.

Taxpayers whose tax in the preceding fiscal year was between a lower set
threshold (currently €1,659.70) and the threshold mentioned in the previous
paragraph must pay quarterly advances on the tax due in the current fiscal year,
amounting to one-quarter of the tax due for the preceding fiscal year. The taxpayer
must then pay the difference between the aggregate advances paid and the tax due
for the fiscal year within three months of the end of the fiscal year.

If the difference is negative, any overpayment will be refunded to the taxpayer.

8.   **Company reorganisation**

A joint stock company may transform into a limited liability company and vice
versa. Both types of company can also reorganise into another form of partnership,
company or cooperative. The company does not cease to exist as a legal entity
because of a change in corporate form.

For limited liability companies and joint stock companies, the decision on a
change in corporate form must be approved by two-thirds of the members or
shareholders (respectively) present at the general meeting, unless the memorandum
or articles of association provide otherwise.

A branch cannot be directly transformed into a limited liability company or joint
stock company, but it is possible to create a new company and then sell the branch
to the new company as a part of an enterprise. As a branch has no legal personality,
all its obligations and liabilities remain with the previous controlling company
(except for employment relations, which may be transferred to the new company,
depending on the circumstances).

9.   **Dissolution and liquidation**

The termination of a company involves two phases: winding-up, and then deletion
from the commercial register. Deletion from the commercial register is preceded by
winding-up either with or without liquidation.

In the event of voluntary winding up of a company, it may be simultaneously decided that the company is to be taken over, merged or split. This decision affects no restrictions specified by law. In the case of merger, takeover or split-off, the company to be deleted from the commercial register must have the same corporate form as the company that takes over the assets and liabilities of the deleted company, unless the Commercial Code provides otherwise. A takeover between a limited liability company and a joint stock company is the exception to this rule: the limited liability company will be deleted and its assets and liabilities will be taken over by the joint stock company.

In a case of liquidation, all the company's assets and liabilities are transferred to a legal successor. Liquidation is not required if:

- the company owns no property;
- a bankruptcy petition is dismissed due to lack of funds;
- the bankruptcy proceedings are abandoned because the debtor's assets are insufficient to cover the expenses and fees of the bankruptcy trustee; or
- there is no property left after the termination of bankruptcy proceedings.

A company will cease to exist on the date it is deleted from the commercial register.

South Africa

Sizwe Msimang
Claire van Zuylen
Bowman Gilfillan

---

1. Applicable legislation

The principal legislation governing companies in South Africa is:

- the Companies Act 61 of 1973 (the Companies Act), as amended;
- a new Companies Act, which will repeal and replace the Companies Act with effect from 2010 (the new Companies Act); and
- the Close Corporations Act 69 of 1984.

The following legislation and rulings apply only to public companies that are listed:

- the Securities Services Act 36 of 2004 (if listed on the Stock Exchange)
- the Securities Regulation Panel Code (the SRP Code); and
- Johannesburg Stock Exchange Equity Rules of August 1 2005 (the JSE Rules);

When the new Companies Act comes into force in South Africa in early 2010, it will bring about significant changes to corporate law and the incorporation of companies. Where the new Companies Act will introduce significant changes to the existing corporate law, we note here the new developments where appropriate. The most significant change is that the current Registrar of Companies will be substituted by the Companies and Intellectual Property Commission.

2. Types of limited liability company

There are currently two forms of limited liability company in South Africa: a private company and a public company. There is also a simpler form of corporate entity known as a close corporation, which is subject to simpler secretarial duties and where only natural persons can be members. Close corporations are due to be phased out under the new Companies Act. Thus for the purposes of this chapter, these are not considered.

2.1 Private company

In a private company:

- the number of shareholders can be between one and 50;
- the transfer of shares is restricted by the articles of association;
- shares or debentures cannot be offered to the public;
- only one director is needed; and
- financial statements do not have to be lodged with the Registrar of Companies (the registrar).

2.2 Public company

A public company:

- must have at least seven shareholders (there is no limit to the number of shareholders, but there must not be fewer than seven);
- may offer its shares to the public;
- has freely transferable shares;
- can list its shares on a stock exchange;
- is obliged to lodge its financial statements with the Registrar of Companies; and
- must have at least two directors.

Under the New Companies Act, companies will be classified into two types: a 'for profit' company and a 'not for profit' company. The for-profit company is defined in Section 1 of the new Companies Act as a company incorporated for the purpose of financial gain for its shareholders. The definition includes: a state-owned company; a private company; a personal liability company if it meets the criteria of a private company; or a public company. A not-for-profit company is defined as a company incorporated for a public benefit or other prescribed object, the income and property of which are not distributable to its incorporators, members, directors, officers or persons related to any of them except for limited purposes.

3. Incorporation procedure

3.1 Proceedings prior to incorporation

(a) Corporate name

The name of a new company must first be reserved with the registrar before the name can be registered. The rationale behind this is so that the shareholders can first establish from the registrar (by means of the reservation) that the name is not undesirable. A company name will be considered undesirable if it is similar to the name of a company already registered by the registrar or if, in the registrar's opinion, it will be misleading to the public, who may believe that two companies are related while in fact they are not. In such circumstances the proposed name will not be reserved or registered unless the existing company consents to the use of the name. Consent from existing group companies can simply take the form of a letter.

The name is reserved for two months, after which the reservation expires – although it can be extended for a further two months. Once the name is reserved, an application for registration is made and the name is registered.

In addition to the legal name being registered, a 'shortened' name of the company and a defensive name can be registered. Ordinarily, a company on the verge of deregistration or dissolution can register its name as a defensive name to stop the name being used at a later stage by third parties. However, a name can only be registered as a defensive name if the registrar is satisfied that the person wanting to register it as a defensive name has a "direct and material interest" in the name in question.

A company name may contain any letters, numbers or punctuation marks or symbols such as +, &, #, % or =.

In the case of a for-profit company, the name may be the registration number of the company together with the expression '(South Africa)'. The name reservation period will be six months and any extension period is two months.

(b) *Capital contributions*

Generally, shareholders have no obligation to contribute to the equity of the company save for a nominal amount (such as ZAR1.00) payable for the issue of shares.

Once the company is established and the shares issued, the shareholders may decide to fund the company either by means of equity or debt funding.

Equity funding is generally understood to be the act of raising money for company activities by selling common or preference shares (stock) to individual investors or where individual investors, in return for money paid, receive ownership interests in the company. This is commonly known as share capital.

Debt funding is also generally understood to mean the raising of money for working capital or capital expenditure through the lending of money to the company by individuals or institutions. In return for lending the money, the individuals and/or the institutions become creditors of the company and receive a promise that the principal and, if applicable, interest on the debt will be repaid (ie the promise represents a shareholder or bank loan).

The generally accepted method of funding a new company is by way of the new company issuing shares. It is more common in South Africa to keep the authorised share capital of the company at a minimum (eg 100 shares). The shareholders can subscribe and take up all or part of the shares. Further financing would then be provided to the company by means of shareholders' loans.

(c) *Declaration of foreign investment*

A company incorporated in South Africa will be subject to exchange control legislation if it has a foreign shareholder (or where a foreign company has majority holding) or if it receives financial assistance from a foreign creditor. South Africa's exchange control legislation is aimed at preventing the export of capital (which includes anything of monetary value in addition to cash) from South Africa to other jurisdictions. Ordinarily, before a company can export capital, it will need to apply to the Reserve Bank of South Africa for approval for the remission of capital.

Thus, where any non-resident elects to invest in South Africa, the Exchange Control Department of the South African Reserve Bank (SARB) must authorise the investment upfront through its authorised dealers. Authorised dealers are banks appointed by the Minister of Finance and they are able to buy and sell foreign exchange and, in certain instances, approve transactions. In other instances, a potential investor would liaise with an authorised dealer, who would then approach the Exchange Control Department to authorise a specific transaction. However, persons other than authorised dealers cannot approach the Exchange Control Department directly.

When establishing a local subsidiary, exchange control permission becomes important in two areas: where the shares in a local company are held by a non-resident; and capitalisation of the local entity by a foreign shareholder.

(d)   *Shareholding*

When a foreign company acquires a shareholding in a South African company, the share certificate evidencing the shareholding must be submitted to an authorised dealer, together with details of the transaction (eg the full name and country of residence of the owner of the securities, together with a signed declaration by the holder that, to the best of his knowledge, the owner is resident in the country stated, the name of the company issuing the securities, the total number of securities and the name and residential address of the person in possession of the securities). The authorised dealer will then place a 'non-resident' endorsement on the share certificate. The effect of this endorsement is twofold: to ensure that, if the shares are later sold, the foreign shareholder can remit the sale proceeds back abroad or credit the proceeds to a non-resident account. In addition, once a share certificate has been endorsed as 'non-resident', all dividend income resulting from the shareholding is freely transferable to a non-resident bank account.

(e)   *Loans and funding*

Regulations 3(e) and (f) of the Exchange Control Regulations provide:

> *Subject to any exemption which may be granted by the Treasury or a person authorised by the Treasury, no person shall, without permission granted by the Treasury or a person authorised by the Treasury and in accordance with such conditions as the Treasury or such authorised person may [impose] –*
>
> *(e) grant any financial assistance to any person in the Republic, where as security for such financial assistance, the person granting the financial assistance in turn relies on any security, guarantee, undertaking or financial assistance, directly or indirectly furnished by –*
>
> *(i) any person resident outside the Republic; or*
> *(ii) an affected person;*
>
> *(f) grant any financial assistance to any person in the Republic, where such person –*
> *(i) is not resident in the Republic; or*
> *(ii) is an affected person.*

An 'affected person' is effectively a local entity that is controlled by foreign shareholders and is formally defined as meaning:

> *a body corporate, foundation, trust or partnership operating in the Republic, or an estate, in respect of which –*
>
> *(i) 75 per cent or more of the capital, assets or earnings thereof may be utilised for payment to, or to the benefit in any manner of, any person who is not resident in the Republic; or*
>
> *(ii) 75 per cent or more of the voting securities, voting power, power of control, capital, assets or earnings thereof, are directly or indirectly vested in, or controlled by or on behalf of, any person who is not resident in the Republic.*

'Financial assistance' is widely defined, but excludes the granting of credit by a seller for any commercial transaction that directly involves passing ownership of the goods sold by seller to the purchaser and the granting of credit solely for payment for services rendered.

Accordingly, if a non-resident shareholder wishes to grant financial assistance (give a loan) to its South African subsidiary, permission must be obtained. Approval is also required for the creation of loan accounts by the South African company in favour of a non-resident. If permission is granted for a non-resident shareholder to provide financial assistance to a South African subsidiary, any repayments would also require approval.

With regard to local borrowings, non-residents may borrow up to 100% of the rand value of funds introduced into, and invested in, South Africa. However, if a non-resident wishes to borrow locally to finance a foreign direct investment into South Africa, the borrowing would be considered by SARB up to 300% of the rand value of the funds introduced from abroad and invested in South Africa.

A foreign-shareholder-controlled local entity would be able to borrow locally up to 300% of its foreign shareholder's total investment (which means the paid-up equity capital, preference shares, undistributed earned profits, shareholders loans and, in some instances, shareholders' trade credit). If a portion of the shares in the local company are held locally, this increases the amount that the local company could borrow locally, based on the following formula:

$$\left[\frac{\% \text{ South African interest}}{\% \text{ non-resident interest}} + 3 \right] \times 100\%$$

Accordingly, the greater the local shareholding, the more the South African company is entitled to borrow locally.

Thus exchange control restrictions must be carefully considered when making a decision on funding and capitalising a South African subsidiary.

(f) *Tax number for foreign partners/directors*

Ordinarily, a shareholder or a director of a company need not provide a tax number when establishing a company in South Africa.

However, once the company is registered and then seeks to register for income tax, value added tax (VAT) or employees' tax, its shareholder(s) and directors must provide their tax numbers. If the shareholder(s) and directors are not South African residents, they need not provide their tax number unless they are registered as taxpayers in South Africa.

3.2 Incorporation

(a) *Bylaws*

The incorporation of a company includes, principally, the registration of its memorandum and articles of association. The memorandum of association is the founding document (constitution) of the company, while the articles of association serve as the 'code of conduct' of the company, regulating the manner in which the company is to function. The memorandum of association basically sets out, among others, the:

- name and registration number of the company;
- company's main and ancillary objects;
- authorised and issued share capital;
- financial year end (in most cases a company will choose a financial year end to coincide with the end of the tax year (ie February 28));

The articles of association mainly provide for, among others, the:

- powers, duties, number, proceedings and meetings of the directors;
- relationship of the company with its directors;
- rights of the shareholders (eg minority protection);
- shares, share certificates and share register;
- transfer and conversion of shares;
- general meetings of shareholders; and
- declaration of dividends.

(b) *Shareholders' agreement*

The shareholders may endeavour to strike a balance between themselves or safeguard their interests, particularly if they are minorities, by making provision for protections that are neither in the Companies Act nor in the articles of association. To do this the shareholders may enter into a shareholders' agreement. This is does not replace the articles of association. The shareholders' agreement can override the articles of association, but only between the shareholders and not against third parties.

Usually, a shareholders' agreement is used to provide greater minority shareholder support or to regulate pre-emptive rights clauses, quorum requirements both for directors and shareholders, majorities required for special resolutions, 'come along' and 'tag along' provisions, forced sale provisions, dispute resolution provisions, etc.

(c) *Execution of public deed*

Save for the registration of the memorandum and articles of association and other documents of incorporation (eg CM22 (registering the physical and postal address of the company); CM29 (register of directors); and CM31 (appointment of auditor)), a public instrument does not need to be executed for a company to be registered.

(d) *Tax number of the company*

In South Africa a trading company will register as a taxpayer for income tax, VAT and employees' tax. On registration, a company is allocated a tax number on registration for a particular tax with the South African Revenue Service (SARS). The company's tax number serves as its identification number and it cannot be changed.

(e) *Indirect taxes, incorporation fees and other levies*

Save for the prescribed registration fees payable to the registrar, no indirect taxes are payable upon registration of a company. However, stamp duty and/or securities transfer tax must be paid upon transfer of issued shares or beneficial ownership in issued shares from one shareholder to another.

(f) ***Registration with the Mercantile Registry***
The particulars of the company, together with those of its directors, are registered with the registrar. The registrar issues a certificate of incorporation together with a certificate to commence business. The certificate of incorporation is evidence that the company has been incorporated and the certificate to commence business grants permission to trade as a company. Where a company trades or enters into transaction prior to this certificate being issued, its directors and shareholders will be personally liable for any debts incurred by the company and be guilty of an offence.

The directors of the company can assume office before their appointment is registered by the registrar. However, their appointment must be registered within 28 days or an offence is committed. By contrast, the auditor of the company cannot start doing work for the company until the appointment has been registered.

(g) ***Corporate books***
There is no requirement that the books and records of a private company be legalised by the registrar. Public companies must file their financial statements with the registrar. Under the Companies Act the following books and records must be maintained at their registered addresses:
- minute books;
- an asset register;
- financial records;
- register of members (shareholders);
- all documents of incorporation; and
- share certificates and share transfer forms.

(h) ***Declaration of start date and other tax declarations***
As mentioned above, no company can commence business unless the registrar has issued a certificate to commence business. This is normally issued on the date of incorporation. The certificate to commence business is basically the company's licence to trade.

All companies are required to file tax returns with SARS at their financial year ends. A tax return is a declaration of income and expenditure of the company for that particular financial year to enable SARS to determine whether the company has overpaid or underpaid tax. VAT returns must also be filed.

4. Number of partners (shareholders)
As mentioned above, a private company can have between one and 50 shareholders, and a public company must have a minimum of seven shareholders.

5. Corporate name
This is discussed in section 3.1(a) above.

6.   Domicile

Under South African law (and also as recognised in most other jurisdictions), a company's domicile is its country of incorporation and its shares are located in the country of domicile, not where the shareholder is domiciled.

7.   Corporate purpose

The company may only have one principal object and can have more than one ancillary objects. The object of the company must not be illegal.

8.   Capital stock

8.1   Share types and share capital

In South Africa there are two types of shares: par-value shares and non-par-value shares. The former are the shares of a fixed amount (nominal value) and the latter are fixed in number. The share capital of a company may consist of both the par-value and non-par-value shares and each type can be converted into the other type.

Limited liability companies have an authorised share capital (authorised by the memorandum of association of a company) and the issued share capital (a portion of the authorised share capital determined by the number of shares issued). If a company has already issued all of its authorised share capital and then finds that it needs to issue more, the shareholders must first, by means of a special resolution, alter the company's memorandum of association to provide for an increased authorised share capital. If a company, without an authorising resolution from its shareholders, purports to issue capital in excess of the capital authorised by the memorandum of association, the issue is void.

Under Schedule 5 of the new Companies Act, a share will not have a nominal or par value. The shares of a pre-existing company issued at a nominal value under the current Companies Act and held by a shareholder continue to have the nominal value that was assigned to them when they were issued.

8.2   Nominal amount (par value)

The par value of a share is an arbitrary figure arrived at by the directors of a company. It does not have to be the market price of a share and does not fluctuate in accordance with market conditions. The nominal amount of a share could be ZAR2, ZAR1 or even ZAR0.50. The proceeds of any issue of par-value shares must be credited to the share capital account or share premium account, if any.

8.3   Stated capital account

The amount of issued non-par-value shares is represented by a stated capital account in respect of a particular class of shares. If non-par-value shares are issued for a consideration other than cash, a sum equal to the value of the consideration, as determined by the directors, must be transferred to the stated capital account. This may be applied to settle the preliminary expenses of the company or the expenses of, or the commission paid to, the creation or issue of such non-par-value shares.

8.4 Nature of shareholders' contributions

Save for the nominal amount for par-value shares and the amount payable for the issue of non-par-value shares, the shareholders of a company have no general duty to contribute to the working capital of the company. However, the shareholders' agreement may impose a duty to contribute towards the company's share capital on the shareholders.

Ordinarily, the shareholders would advance money to the company in a form of a loan account, which is quite often subordinated at the request of the auditors to maintain the cash flow of the company. Subordination of loan accounts simply means that the shareholders waive the right to payment until all other creditors of the company have been paid.

Shareholders' loans can be interest bearing or not, depending on what is agreed.

Where the shareholder is a foreign entity, the company must obtain exchange control permission before the loan is advanced and must also obtain exchange control permission when the loan is repaid. Exchange control approval will not be granted if the interest charged on the loan is deemed excessive.

8.5 Partial payments

The Companies Act prohibits the allotment or issue of shares unless they have been paid for in full and the company has received payment. The exception is where the shares are to be issued and allotted to the public (this only applies to public companies). If the shareholders agree that new subscribers to the shares of the company pay the subscription fee in instalments, the shares will be issued and allotted piecemeal upon receipt of an instalment until the full subscription fee has been paid.

8.6 Share certificates

The share certificate is a declaration in which the company affirms that the person to whom it issued the shares is the registered shareholder and entitled to the shares mentioned therein, and that the amount appearing on the certificate as consideration for the shares has been paid. The share certificate is prima facie evidence of the title of the shareholder to the shares concerned. However, it is recognised in South African law that the registered shareholder may only be a nominee and that true beneficial ownership in and to the shares could vest in another party.

The Johannesburg Stock Exchange (JSE) Rules require a public company listed on the Johannesburg Stock Exchange to keep a register of nominee shareholdings.

8.7 Restrictions to the transfer of shares

As mentioned above, private companies are restricted from offering their shares to the public, while public companies have no such restrictions. Typically, clauses in a shareholders' agreement or in the articles of association prohibit a shareholder from selling shares on the open market without first offering them to the other shareholders. The JSE Rules require an offer of shares to be made by means of prescribed circulars to all other shareholders; however, the directors of listed public companies can remove some of the shares from the offer to comply with the requirements of any regulatory body of any territory recognised as having import on the offer.

8.8 Transfer of shares

Under normal circumstances, the transfer of shares is initiated by a share sale agreement between a shareholder and the prospective purchaser – and the agreement need not be in writing. South African law classes shares as incorporeal movables. Following the conclusion of a share sale agreement, the seller signs a cession of shares (and loan account if any) for the benefit of the purchaser for the transfer of the shares. A share transfer form is also executed by the seller for registration of the transfer of shares from him to the purchaser.

9. Equity

9.1 Balance between capital/own resources

The principle in English Law of maintenance of capital for the benefit of the persons who have dealings with the company has been embodied into South African law. The capital of the company is separate and must at all times be separated from the profits of the company. The capital of a limited company is not a debt owed by it to the shareholders: in the event of capital loss, the company is under no legal obligation either to make it good or on that ground alone wind up its affairs. The rule is, accordingly, not that the company must maintain the capital it raises but, rather, that it must actually raise capital that it purports to raise and, when not in liquidation, it must not return that capital to its shareholders otherwise than in terms of a reduction of capital authorised by the Companies Act. The capital is reduced, for example, when a shareholder surrenders his shares to the company and the company retains those shares as unissued shares available for reissue or when a company buys back its shares from a shareholder and the shares are cancelled.

9.2 Convertible bonds

A convertible bond is a financial instrument that may be issued only if the value of the consideration received equals the fair value of the instrument issued. A convertible bond is convertible into ordinary shares that are proportional to the value of such convertible bond. Upon conversion, the fair value of the convertible bond tendered in exchange for the proportionate shares will reflect both the fair value of the option and the fair value of the bond.

10. Administration of companies

10.1 General meetings of shareholders

(a) Quorum requirements

Unless the articles of association provide for a greater number to constitute a quorum, the quorum of a general meeting of a public company is constituted by three shareholders entitled to vote and that of a general meeting of a private company is constituted by two shareholders (unless there is only one). In the case of a wholly owned subsidiary of another company, the representative of a holding company constitutes a quorum. The shareholders may fix the quorum of the meetings in a shareholders' agreement, but the number suggested must not be less than that provided for in the Companies Act.

(b) *Quorum for the adoption of resolutions*
A general meeting at which a special resolution will be passed requires a two-thirds majority, while a meeting at which an ordinary resolution will be passed requires a simple majority (eg 51% of the shareholders' votes).

(c) *Challenge of resolutions*
A resolution passed at a meeting where the necessary quorum was not present is void. Similarly, a special resolution passed at a meeting for which a notice was not given or a notice of less than 21 clear days' notice was given is void. However, the shareholders may consent to the waiver of notice of meeting or period of notice of meeting. Any resolution contravening the Companies Act, common law, any other statute or the articles or memorandum of association of the company is also void.

10.2 Administrative body

(a) *Different systems of administration*
The administrative function of the company is vested in the directors. No other person has a duty or a right to administer the company unless so authorised by the directors by resolution or power of attorney.

(b) *Term of office, resignation and removal of directors*
The appointment of the directors and their term of office is determined by the shareholders. However, a director may resign his office at any time by tendering a written resignation to the company to that effect. The date of its resignation is the date of the letter, not the date of its registration by the registrar.

A director may also be removed from office by other directors by means of a resolution. A shareholder may remove a director appointed by him if in the opinion of that shareholder the director no longer represents his interests in the company. A director may also be removed from office if his estate is sequestrated, he has been removed from another position of trust for dishonesty, he has been convicted of fraud, theft, forgery, perjury, uttering a forged document or corruption.

(c) *Directors' liability to third parties*
The general rule is that the directors are not personally liable for the debts of the company. However, there are, exceptions to this:
- The memorandum of association of a private company may provide for unlimited liability of the directors and erstwhile directors of the company in that they are jointly and severally liable, together with the company, for the debts of the company incurred during their tenure of office.

- As indicated above, if a company having share capital commences business or exercises any borrowing power before the registrar has issued a certificate entitling it to commence business, the directors and shareholders are jointly and severally liable for all debts arising from the business so conducted. In this regard, liability ensues to all directors and shareholders despite the fact that the some of them may not played an active role in such transactions.
- If any director of a company signs or authorises to be signed on behalf of the company any bill of exchange, promissory note, endorsement, cheque or order for money or goods in which the company's name is not mentioned in eligible characters, he is personally liable to the holder of the bill of exchange, promissory note, cheque or order for money or goods for the amount of it unless duly paid by the company.
- Failure to appoint an auditor within three months of the resignation of the company's auditor renders any person who was a director during that period or who became a director after that period and had knowledge of the vacancy, but who failed to take reasonable steps to ensure that it would be filled, jointly and severally liable together with the company for any company debt incurred when the vacancy existed.
- When it appears that the business of the company was conducted recklessly or with the intention to defraud creditors of the company or creditors of any other person, or any fraudulent purpose, any person who was knowingly a party to such conduct may be declared personally liable for all or any of the debts of the company.

(d) **Non-competition**

Directors of a company stand in a fiduciary relationship with the company, which comes with fiduciary duty towards the company. No fiduciary duty is owed by the directors to individual shareholders of a company nor do shareholders owe a fiduciary duty towards the company in which they hold shares. A director commits a breach of a fiduciary duty if, among others, he:

- acts for the benefit of any other person to the detriment of the company for which he is a director;
- fails to prevent conflict arising between his own interests and those of the company he serves; or
- takes away a business opportunity available to the company.

Where it appears that a director has breached his fiduciary duty, the company can claim back any benefit resulting from the breach. Moreover, the company may apply to set aside any transactions and request that the court declare that any benefit belongs to the company.

(e) **Confidentiality**

A director is under a fiduciary duty not to disclose confidential information entrusted to him by virtue of his office or to use it for his own purposes. This may be extended to cover a particular period of time after the termination of the director's employment with the company. Confidential information includes, but is not limited to, information of direct commercial value, (eg trade secrets or customer lists). The director's fiduciary duty reinforces and extends the company's rights in regard to the confidential proceedings of its board. A director must respect the confidential nature of the board's affairs. Confidentiality is not determined by merely looking at the form of the item but the substance. The directors are obliged to keep secret any matter that is discussed; any correspondence that might detrimentally affect the vote of directors in a particular matter are also confidential.

(f) Civil and criminal liability

The directors may be held criminally liable if they, among others:

- fail to keep the register of members;
- provide false information in the prospectus;
- are directors of a public company and fail to issue half-yearly interim reports;
- fail to issue annual financial statement within six months after the end of the financial year;
- provide interim reports or provisional financial statements not signed by two directors if there are more than one;
- fail to lodge copies of the interim report and provisional financial statement with the registrar;
- conduct the business of the company before the registrar issues a certificate to commence business;
- publish the name of a person who has not been validly appointed as a director;
- fail to hold a specified number of the qualification shares within two months and continue to hold office of directorship thereafter;
- fail to maintain the register of directors and officers;
- are not qualified to act as a director, but they purport to be one;
- fail to disclose their interests in contracts that are being entered into by the company;
- fail to record the interests declared by each director;
- do not keep the minutes of their meetings; and
- falsify books and records;

For civil liability, please refer to what is said above about the certificate to commence business and personal liability to third parties (see section 10.2(c) above).

10.3 Others

(a) Attorneys

Attorneys play a vital role in the formation of a company; however, they usually have no role to play in the administration of the company.

(b) Controllers and internal auditors

South African companies do not have controllers. The company may have internal auditors but its financial statements must be audited by an independent auditor who is capable of expressing an unbiased opinion on the financial affairs of the company. While listed companies must have a company secretary, the position is optional in the case of a private company.

11.   Financial year end

The company must set out the date of its financial year end in its application for the certificate to commence business. The date of incorporation (which is usually also the date of commencement of business) is the first date of the company's financial year-end. This runs until the date immediately preceding the anniversary of the date of commencement of business or the date to be determined as the end of the financial year in the calendar year. The financial year-end is a 12-month cycle. A company may change its financial year end to align with that of its group companies at any time.

12.   Financial statements

12.1   Company tax

Companies have the following tax liabilities:

*   income tax: levied on the annual gross income of the company;
*   value added tax: levied on sales and purchases by the company; and
*   employees' tax: includes pay as you earn (paid by the employees but the employer must register for it), unemployment insurance fund contributions (minimal contribution by the employer towards the employees' unemployment insurance fund) and skills development levy (minimal contribution by the employer towards the skills development fund run by the government).

12.2   Annual accounts

(a)   Documents

One of the functions of annual accounts is to enable the shareholders to determine whether the company's affairs are being competently managed. Falsifying the annual accounts can lead to the directors of the company being held personally liable for the debts of the company.

(b)   Audit report

The audit report is one of the ways in which the financial statements can be validated. After the auditor has examined the financial statements, he must satisfy himself:

*   that proper accounting records have been kept by the company and that proper returns adequate for the purposes of audit nave been received;
*   that the minute books and attendance register with regard to the meetings of the company have been kept;
*   that the register of interests in contracts has been kept and that the records

tally with the minutes of directors' meetings;

- as to the existing securities of the company;
- of the sufficiency of the information gathered to enable him to carry out the audit;
- that the financial statements of the company are not in conflict with its accounting records and returns;
- that the financial statements comply with the requirements of the Companies Act;
- that the financial statements accurately represent the financial affairs of the company; and
- that the company is in operation.

The auditor may then issue his report to the shareholders, stating that he has examined the financial statements and that in his opinion they accurately represent the financial position of the company and the results of its operations as required by the Companies Act.

(c)   ***Approval and distribution of profits***
Dividends can only be paid out of profits and must first accrue before they are declared. The shareholders generally have no right to dividends and the company does not have a duty to declare them. The dividends are declared at the discretion of the directors. The directors, with guidance from the Companies Act and the articles of association, declare dividends by means of a resolution passed at the annual general meeting of directors. Once a dividend has been declared, a shareholder can claim payment from the company (ie he becomes a creditor of the company). The articles of association may authorise the directors to declare interim dividends as and when they deem this is justified by the profits of the company. However, there is no provision for the declaration of an interim dividend that is then followed by payment. The directors may rescind their own resolution to pay an interim dividend, so a shareholder has no right to an interim dividend prior to payment.

(d)   ***Deposit and publicity***
Not applicable.

13.   Company reorganisation: merger and split-off

13.1   Merger
Mergers are regulated by the Competition Act 89 of 1998. When one or more companies directly or indirectly acquire or establish direct or indirect control over the whole or part of the business of another company, a merger has taken place. A 'merger' is very widely defined and may be achieved by the purchase or lease of the shares, an interest or assets of the other company or through amalgamation or other combination with the other company. For the purposes of the merger as defined, a person controls the company if he, among others:

- beneficially owns more than half of the issued share capital of that company;

- is entitled to vote a majority of votes that may be cast at a general meeting of the company;
- is able to appoint or veto the appointment of the majority of the directors;
- is a holding company and the company in question is a subsidiary thereof; or
- has the ability to materially influence the policy of the company in a manner comparable to a person who can exercise control as referred to above.

Mergers must be brought to the attention of registered trade unions representing a substantial number of employees in the workplace or to the employees concerned or their representatives in the absence of registered trade unions.

Mergers are classed as small, intermediate or large. There are two categories of notifiable mergers: intermediate mergers and large mergers. Small mergers are those that fall below the thresholds and are not notifiable. If the authorities are of the opinion that the merger may substantially prevent or lessen competition or cannot be justified on public interest grounds, they are entitled to call upon the parties to notify the merger. This procedure must be initiated within six months after the merger has been implemented.

Intermediate mergers are those that meet the following 2009 thresholds:

- the combined annual turnover in, into or from the Republic of South Africa for the acquiring firms and the target firms are valued at R560 million or more; or
- the combined assets in the Republic of the acquiring firms and the target firms are valued at R560 million or more; or
- the annual turnover in, into or from the Republic of the acquiring firms plus the assets in the Republic of the target firms are valued at R560 million or more; or
- the annual turnover in, into or from the Republic of the target firms plus the assets in the Republic of the acquiring firms are valued at R560 million or more; and
- in addition (and, logically, the first step in the assessment), the annual turnover in, into or from the Republic or the asset value of the target firm must be R80 million or more.

A large merger is one where one of the first four calculations given above results in a figure that is equal to or exceeds R6.6 billion and the turnover or asset value of the target firm equals or exceeds R190 million.

No merger can be implemented unless approved in advance by the Competition Commission or Competition Tribunal, if necessary.

13.2   Split-off

Where group companies purport to split off, the process is called 'unbundling'. The unbundling transaction is a transaction where equity shares of a resident company (the unbundled company) are held by another company (the unbundling company). This distributes all equity shares (the unbundled shares) to its shareholders in accordance with their effective interests in the shares of the unbundling company.

There is tax relief for group transactions and unbundlings.

14. Eventual partner separation

Where the shareholders no longer need to keep the company, they may sell their shareholding to third parties or back to the company itself. Alternatively, they can pay all the debts of the company and distribute the residual capital among themselves and thereafter deregister the remaining shell of the company. Furthermore, the shareholders may liquidate the company by means of a special resolution regardless of whether the company has debts or not.

15. Liquidation and dissolution

Under South African law, there are three ways in which a company can be wound up:

- a de-registration of the corporate shell of a dormant company with no assets or liabilities;
- a voluntary winding-up by way of a special resolution (75% majority) at the instance of the shareholders, either in terms of:
  - a member's winding-up (where the company can pay its debts); or
  - a creditors' winding-up (where the company cannot pay its debts); and
- a compulsory winding-up by means of an application to court.

After the company has been placed into liquidation by means of a shareholders resolution or a court application, the liquidator is appointed and the winding up process begins. The process can take from six months to two years.

16. Branches

External companies (ie companies incorporated in countries other than South Africa) can register their branches in South Africa. If an external company registers in South Africa, the company remains a separate legal personality incorporated in its country of origin and the registration in South Africa only creates branch of that external company. Once registered, it is for all purposes deemed to be a South African company and enjoys legal personality separate from that of its parent company. The company pays tax in South Africa and if its external parent company were to be liquidated, it would not be liquidated on that basis. Its directors cannot be held personally liable for the debts of the company unless the factors mentioned above are present.

Spain

Maria Luisa de Alarcón Elorrieta
Nuria Clemente Farré
JAUSAS

1. **Types of company with limited liability and applicable legislation**
    The companies with limited liability that are most commonly used in Spain are:
    - joint stock companies (*Sociedades Anónimas*); and
    - limited liability corporations (*Sociedades de Responsabilidad Limitada*).

    Their operating systems, corporate structures, governing bodies and formal, accounting and fiscal obligations are very similar, but each has certain peculiarities outlined below and examined in more detail in the course of this chapter.

    Limited liability corporations have a more personal character and are intended for so-called 'closed' corporations (eg a small number of partners, or family groups) irrespective of size. For this reason, the formalities for the convening of meetings, in-kind contributions and so on are simpler and less costly than those for joint stock companies. On the other hand, in some cases liability can be extended to the partners in respect of what they receive.

    In a limited liability corporation, the partners' will prevails as stated in the bylaws; many specific regulations are possible (eg different voting rights depending on the class of shares; special provisions on separation and exclusion; specific regulation of the distribution of dividends and the transfer of shares). In principle, shares are not freely transferable; strict clauses may be established to regulate this matter further. It is also possible to give the shareholders' meeting direct control over the administrative body – even to the extent that it can interfere in management tasks.

    The joint stock company is a more 'open' type of company. It aims to protect minority interests. To this end, there are stricter publication requirements for the convening of shareholders' meetings. The participation of experts is also necessary for in-kind contributions, and the participation of auditors is required for capital increases that reduce reserves or the capitalisation of credit. Partial payment of the capital stock is permitted (25% minimum). Shares – which may be nominative or bearer – may be freely transferred; while it is possible to establish clauses restricting this right, they cannot be as strict as those of limited liability corporations. The administrator's duties are regulated in greater detail as a guarantee to minority shareholders, who also have the right to ask questions at shareholders' meetings. To facilitate minority shareholder participation, the time limit for the convening of shareholders' meetings is longer than for limited liability corporations. There is a clear separation between the functions of the shareholders' meeting and the functions of the management bodies.

Only joint stock companies can obtain loans from the public through the issue of bonds and list their shares for trading on the stock exchange.

Joint stock companies are governed by:

- Royal Legislative Decree 1564/1989 of December 22 1989, the Revised Text of the Joint Stock Companies Law (as amended).

Limited liability corporations are governed by:

- Law 2/1995 of March 23 1995 on Limited Liability Corporations.

Both types of company are governed by:

- the Commercial Code;
- Royal Decree 1784/1996 of July 19 1996 Approving the Mercantile Registry Regulation;
- Royal Decree 171/2007 of February 9 2007 regarding the publicity of the familiar protocols;
- Law 2/2007 of March 15 2007, on professional companies; and
- Royal Decree-Law 10/2008 of December 12 2008, on financial measures taken to improve the liquidity of small and medium enterprises.

2. Incorporation procedure

2.1 Proceedings prior to incorporation

(a) Corporate name

In order to establish a company, a corporate name is required. This is obtained by submitting an application from one of the founding shareholders to the Central Mercantile Registry. The registry has a website and interested parties can consult this to see if their corporate name is available. Within three days of receipt of the application, the registry will either:

- issue the certificate of registration; or
- reject the name if it does not conform to law or has already been registered to a third party.

The certificate of registration remains valid for six months.

(b) Capital contributions

The shareholders can make cash or in-kind contributions to the company's capital, but all contributions must consist of assets or rights with economic value. The future performance of work or the provision of a service cannot be the subject of a contribution, although in certain cases the bylaws may require the provision of services ancillary to the specific cash or in-kind contribution.

Cash contributions – whether in national currency or foreign currency (but stated in euros) – are evidenced by a certificate issued by the bank or credit institution with which the funds have been deposited. This is valid for two months. The certificate will be delivered to the notary upon incorporation of the company.

In the case of in-kind contributions, a detailed description of the assets will be made and an economic value attributed to them. In joint stock companies, this evaluation must be carried out by an independent expert appointed by the mercantile registrar of the place where the company is to be domiciled – except in the case of securities quoted on a secondary stock market, in which case the expert evaluation can be replaced by a certificate of the relevant stock exchange. In limited liability corporations, an expert evaluation is not expressly required by law, but it may nonetheless be advisable to avoid any liability on the part of the contributor.

In no event can the performance of work or the provision of a service by a shareholder be considered a contribution. This notwithstanding, the bylaws may require the provision of ancillary services alongside the capital contribution, stating the specific content of such services and whether these are gratuitous or subject to remuneration, but without becoming part of the capital stock. The amount of eventual remuneration cannot exceed the value of the service provided.

In limited liability corporations, the shareholders are jointly and severally liable to the company and third parties for in-kind contributions and for the value assigned to them in the charter of incorporation. The statute of limitations for such liability is five years from the date on which the contribution was made. Shareholders whose in-kind contributions were subject to expert valuation are excluded from joint and several liability.

(c) **Declaration of foreign investment**
Foreign investments – and their liquidation – are liberalised in Spain, without prejudice to specific systems governing particular sectors and with the exception of investments from territories or countries regarded as tax havens, which require prior authorisation.

This notwithstanding, for administrative and statistical purposes all foreign investments (and their liquidation) must be declared to the General Directorate of Commerce and Investments, a division of the Ministry of Industry, Commerce and Tourism.

(d) **Tax number for foreign partners/directors**
If the shareholders and/or administrators of the company are foreign, they must obtain a Spanish tax identification number prior to incorporation.

In the case of individuals, this procedure is handled by the civil government and is relatively simple, although it can take some time. A tax identification number may also be obtained through the corresponding Spanish consulate in the country of residence of the foreign shareholder. In the case of foreign corporations, the tax identification number must be obtained from the Spanish tax authorities.

2.2 Incorporation

(a) **Bylaws**

(i) *Essential clauses*
The company's operating system is set out in the bylaws, which must include the

following information, at a minimum:

- the name of the company;
- the corporate purpose, with an indication of the activity or activities to be carried out;
- for joint stock companies, the duration, which may be indefinite (there is no obligation to state this for limited liability corporations);
- the corporate domicile, specifying for joint stock companies the body with competence to resolve on the establishment, closure or transfer of branches;
- for joint stock companies, the date of commencement of operations (there is no obligation to state this for limited liability corporations);
- the capital stock;
- the bylaws, which for joint stock companies must state:
  - the portion still outstanding and the procedure and time limits for assessments (payment of up to 75% of the capital stock may be deferred);
  - the number of shares into which the capital stock is divided;
  - their nominal value, class and series; and
  - the amount of paid-up capital, and whether it is represented by nominative or bearer shares or by means of book entry;

  and for limited liability corporations must state the number of shares into which the capital stock is divided and their nominal value (and it should be noted that the capital must be fully paid upon incorporation);
- the structure of the administrative body and representation, as well as the number of administrators, their terms of office (in joint stock companies, the maximum term is six years and must be the same for all directors; in limited liability corporations, the directors may be appointed indefinitely), and the remuneration system, as the case may be;
- whether the company has opted for stricter quorum requirements in respect of attendance at shareholders' meetings and/or the adoption of resolutions;
- the procedure for deliberation and adoption of resolutions by the board of directors if established as administration body;
- the financial year-end;
- for joint stock companies, any restrictions on the free transfer of shares that may be desirable; for limited liability corporations, any modifications to the legal regime restricting the transfer of shares;
- if the company has opted for the provision of ancillary services:
  - their specific content;
  - whether the services are gratuitous or for remuneration;
  - the shares to which the obligation attaches; and
  - eventual penalties in case of infringement;
- for joint stock companies, any special rights that may be reserved to founding or promoting shareholders;
- for limited liability corporations, the voting rights and systems for profit sharing and/or distribution of dividends that attach to the shares, if these are other than *pro rata*;
- for limited liability corporations, causes for the separation of a shareholder or

shareholders other than those established by law, and the procedures and time limits for exercise or suppression of this right; for joint stock companies, express provisions on all causes for separation;

- for limited liability corporations, the procedure for granting third-party representation at meetings. Failure to establish express provisions in the bylaws will trigger the application of provisions set forth in the applicable law, which make the granting of representation more complicated; and

- an arbitration clause, if desired. If no arbitration clause is expressly included in the bylaws, any dispute among the shareholders will be settled by the Court of Justice in accordance with the applicable law.

(ii)   *Clauses not foreseen by law*

The bylaws are the internal rules governing the company. Although the law states specific minimum clauses that must be included in the bylaws, the shareholders can also establish other clauses as long as these are not contrary to law.

It is important to include any such optional clauses because, if they are specified in the bylaws and registered with the Mercantile Registry, they are enforceable not only among the shareholders but also in respect of third parties.

(iii)   *Optional clauses governed by law*

In some cases the regime set out by law can be amended by the corporate bylaws. In general terms, the system for limited liability companies is more flexible in this respect and greater weight is granted to the will of the partners as stated in the bylaws.

(iv)   *Agreements between shareholders (family protocols)*

Family protocols were conceived for companies where the shareholders/partners were part of one family, but they can also apply to any kind of shareholders or partners. In some cases a special regime of behaviour, governance or transfer of shares, etc, may be established between the shareholders/partners that is more complicated than those set out in the bylaws. These sorts of agreements are compulsory between the parties. Now, under Royal Decree 171/2007 they can have access to the mercantile register and in this way be effective for third parties to varying degrees.

The registrar registers the content of the agreement reached between shareholders/partners, reviews its content and assesses that it is in accordance with law. The agreement has full effect between shareholders/partners and third parties.

The registrar proceeds to the deposit of the agreement entered into between the shareholders/partners, without reviewing the legality of the contents, just the formalities of its execution. For the agreement to be enforceable between the shareholders/partners, its fulfilment is established as an ancillary obligation attached to the shares.

The registrar is informed that the agreement exists, but the content is not published.

(b)   ***Execution of public deed***

Joint stock companies and limited liability corporations are incorporated by means of a public deed executed before a notary public. In order for the company to benefit from limited liability, the public deed must be registered with the Mercantile Registry at the corporate domicile within two months of the date of incorporation.

Unless the bylaws expressly provide otherwise, the company will be considered to have been incorporated from the date on which the charter of incorporation is executed before the notary public.

The company acquires legal personality when the charter of incorporation is registered with the Mercantile Registry. If registration is still pending one year after the date of incorporation, the shareholders may ask for it to be dissolved 'in the course of formation' and demand a refund of any contributions made.

The charter of incorporation is executed by all founding shareholders, present or represented. It contains, together with the bylaws, all covenants and provisions deemed appropriate, provided that these are not contrary to law or to the principles governing the company.

Upon incorporation, the following must be submitted for incorporation into the public deed:

- a certificate of the corporate name issued by the Central Mercantile Registry (names department);
- a bank certificate evidencing payment of the capital stock and, in the event of in-kind contributions for joint stock companies, the report issued by the independent expert appointed by the mercantile registrar; and
- a declaration of foreign investment, if applicable.

The notary fees for incorporation of a company with the minimum statutory capital are approximately €400 for limited liability corporations and €550 for joint stock companies.

(c) *Tax identification number*

In order for the company to be registered with the Mercantile Registry and conduct activities in Spain, a tax identification number must be obtained from the state tax agency. This number is granted with immediate effect when the corresponding form, together with the original charter of incorporation, is presented. The declaration form must be signed by the administrator, who must be in possession of a Spanish tax identification number if he is a foreign person.

The tax identification number is also required to proceed with payment of the corresponding indirect taxes (see section 2.2(d) above).

(d) *Payment of indirect taxes*

The incorporation of joint stock companies and limited liability corporations is subject to a tax on the transfer of assets and documented juridical acts. The applicable rate is currently (2009) 1% of the capital stock (but where the capital is not fully paid up, the outstanding portion is not deducted for this purpose). The tax must be paid in the month following the date of the incorporation deed, by submitting the corresponding form (Form 600) prior to registration of the charter of incorporation with the Mercantile Registry.

(e) **Registration with the Mercantile Registry**

The original charter of incorporation – together with a receipt evidencing payment of the indirect tax and a copy of the document evidencing presentation of the application for a tax identification number – must be submitted to the Mercantile Registry in the province where the corporate domicile is located. Some fees must also be paid to cover expenses relating to publication of the registration in the *Official Gazette* of the Mercantile Registry. If approved by the registry, the company will be regarded as registered and will acquire legal personality from that date.

The registration fees for incorporation of a limited liability company with minimum share capital are normally estimated at €320, and for a joint stock company at €440. Additionally, a fee of €53.50 must currently be paid for publication in the *Official Gazette*.

(f) **Legalisation of official books**

Companies must keep the following books:
- journal;
- inventory and annual accounts book;
- minute book;
- registered share book for joint stock companies or shareholders' record book for limited liability corporations; and
- sole shareholder contracts record book, for sole-ownership companies.

The books must be legalised by the Mercantile Registry in the province where the company is registered. (The books cannot be legalised until the company has been duly registered with the registry.)

The books must be kept, together with all other company documents, for a period of six years from the date of the last entry, even in a case of liquidation.

(g) **Declaration of start date and other tax declarations**

In order to start up activities, a number of other steps must be taken.

(i) *Licences*

A municipal opening licence is necessary before opening the premises at which the company's activities are to be carried out. The application must be submitted to the city council of the district where the company is domiciled.

(ii) *Registries*

If industrial activities are to be conducted at the company's premises, the premises must be registered with the Industrial Registry and the relevant start-up authorisation obtained.

(iii) *Fiscal matters*

The tax on economic activities (*Impuesto sobre Actividades Económicas*) is a local tax assessed on business activities. It is compulsory for all companies – although joint stock companies and limited liability corporations are exempt from the tax for their first two years of business activity, and subsequently if their net turnover is less than €1 million. Registration for the tax is still obligatory, however.

A census declaration is also required in order to communicate for fiscal purposes the commencement, modification or cessation of activities. This may be submitted on the same form as the application for a tax identification number.

If the company owns any real estate, it must pay real estate tax (an annual municipal tax assessed on real estate).

(iv) *Employment matters*

The company must:
- register with the social security general system;
- enrol with social security;
- take out a workers' compensation insurance policy to cover occupational accidents and illnesses; and
- register its employees with social security.

These tasks are performed by submitting the corresponding form to the General Treasury of Social Security. The company cannot register employees with social security unless it has obtained an entrepreneur's contribution code.

(v) *Labour and social security matters*

The company must:
- communicate the opening of the work centre;
- obtain and legalise the visitors' book;
- obtain and legalise the employee register book; and
- obtain a working-day calendar.

3. Number of partners

Sole ownership exists where:
- the joint stock company or limited liability corporation is incorporated by a single shareholder (whether a natural or legal person); or
- all shares of a company incorporated by two or more shareholders become the property of a single shareholder.

The status of sole ownership must be registered with the Mercantile Registry by way of a public deed stating the identity of the sole shareholder; any change to this status must also be registered.

Reference to sole ownership must also be made in all company documentation and on all notices to be published in accordance with the law or bylaws.

All agreements entered into between the sole shareholder and the company must be executed in writing and transcribed in a contracts register. Such contracts must also be itemised in the annual report.

If the status of sole ownership arises after incorporation and is not recorded in the Mercantile Registry within six months, the sole shareholder will have unlimited personal and several liability for company debts incurred while registration was pending. This liability lapses from the date on which the sole ownership is registered.

4.   Corporate name

Where the name of a joint stock company or limited liability corporation refers to the company's purpose and this purpose subsequently changes, the amendment of the corporate purpose cannot be registered without simultaneous amendment of the corporate name.

As a general rule, the corporate name cannot contain terms that:
* are contrary to law, public order or good customs; or
* might create confusion as to the nature of the company.

5.   Corporate domicile

The bylaws will specify the corporate domicile, which must:
* be located in Spain; and
* coincide with the actual centre of administration or management or the principal place of business.

While the administrative body can resolve on a transfer of domicile within the same municipal district (unless the bylaws provide otherwise), a shareholder resolution is required for a transfer to another municipal district.

Foreign companies may transfer their corporate domicile to or from Spain (from or to both EU and non-EU countries), subject to the Mercantile Registry Regulations on this matter.

6.   Corporate purpose

The corporate purpose must be stated in the bylaws, giving a clear, precise and concise description of the activities to be carried out.

7.   Capital stock

7.1   Minimum capital requirement

The company's capital is stated in the bylaws and is calculated by multiplying the number of issued shares by the nominal value of the shares. This figure cannot be amended unless the bylaws are also amended.

For joint stock companies, the minimum capital stock is currently €60,101.21. This must be subscribed in full and a minimum initial payment of 25% of each share must be made prior to incorporation. The remainder will be paid in accordance with the bylaws, or alternatively as resolved by the administrators.

For limited liability corporations, the minimum capital stock is currently €3,005.06. The capital stock must be subscribed in full and fully paid in upon incorporation.

7.2   Nature of contributions

Please see section 2.1(b) above.

7.3 Partial payments

In the case of joint stock companies, new shares – whether issued at the time of incorporation or as a result of a capital increase – may be partially paid in; the minimum payment is 25% of the nominal value of each share.

However, ancillary services and stock premiums do not constitute part of the capital stock and must be fully paid in upon subscription of the shares.

If payment is not made within the established timeframe, the shareholder is considered in default and the company can seek payment together with legal interest and damages; the shareholder is penalised by the suspension of his rights attaching to the shares (eg voting rights, rights of first refusal, entitlement to dividends).

7.4 Representation of shares

The shares of joint stock companies represent aliquot parts of the capital stock and confer on their holders the status of shareholder, together with all inherent rights and obligations. The shares must be nominative where:

- the capital stock is only partially paid;
- a clause in the bylaws restricts the free transfer of shares;
- the shares involve ancillary services; or
- this is required by specific rules in the relevant commercial sector.

In all other cases, the shares may be nominative or bearer.

The shares of limited liability corporations are indivisible and cumulative. They do not have the nature of securities, cannot be represented by certificates or account entries, and are known as *participaciones* (quotas). The partners are vested with title to the quotas, which confer similar rights and obligations to those conferred by shares.

7.5 Transfer of shares

(a) Restrictions

In principle, the shares of joint stock corporations are freely transferable. Consequently, clauses that aim to prevent the free transfer of shares are prohibited. However, specific restrictions may be established in the bylaws or by law in certain exceptional cases, as set out next.

(i) Legal restrictions

These include the following:

- a general prohibition on all share transfers until the charter of incorporation or capital increase deed, as the case may be, has been duly registered with the Mercantile Registry;
- restrictions stemming from foreign investment regulations applicable to specific activities;
- restrictions affecting the company's or parent's own shares; and
- restrictions on the transfer of shares involving ancillary services, which require the authorisation of the company unless otherwise stated in the bylaws.

A share transfer effected in breach of legal restrictions is invalid.

(ii)   *Restrictions imposed by shareholder agreement*
These are agreed between the shareholders for shares held by the parties to the agreement. They are not included in the bylaws and their legal validity is *inter partes*.

A share transfer effected in breach of such restrictions constitutes a breach of contract but will remain valid if the purchasing party ignores the agreements.

Royal Decree 171/2007 of February 9 2007 means that these kinds of agreement appear in the mercantile register so that they are in the public domain (see section 2.2(a)(iv)).

(iii)   *Restrictions stated in the bylaws*
In joint stock companies, these are expressly permitted by law, subject to certain limitations (eg they cannot prevent the transfer of shares and can affect only nominative shares). If the restrictions are breached, the transfer can be annulled, but it is also possible to remedy the breach.

In limited liability corporations, the situation is just the opposite – clauses allowing for the free transfer of shares between living parties are prohibited, and as such are null and void (except as among partners, spouses, ascendants or descendants, or companies in the same corporate group). Clauses prohibiting the free transfer of shares *inter vivos* are valid if the bylaws entitle the partner to separate from the company at any time. Clauses forbidding the free transfer of shares *inter vivos* or exercise of the separation right for a term not exceeding five years from the incorporation of the company or the capital increase, as the case may be, are also permissible.

(b)   **Formalities**
With regards to joint stock companies, a distinction must be made amongst bearer shares, nominative shares and intangible certificates or book entries. In general, all shares may be transferred by means of a public deed executed before a notary public, but, depending on the type of shares involved, other possibilities are available as regulated by the Commercial Code, stock exchange regulations and the like. Nominative shares may be transferred by way of endorsement, but the transfer must be recorded in the nominative share register in order to be valid against the company.

The transfer of shares in a limited liability corporation must be executed in a public document and entered in the partners' record.

Share transfers that breach the law or the bylaws are invalid.

8.   Equity

8.1   Equity–capital ratio

For joint stock companies, the equity cannot be less than two-thirds of the capital stock. If this ratio is breached for an entire fiscal period, a capital stock reduction becomes compulsory. For both joint stock companies and limited liability corporations where the equity is less than one-half of the capital stock, the administrators must convene a general shareholders' meeting to discuss the possible dissolution of the company and how otherwise to restore the balance between its assets and liabilities. If the administrators fail to convene this meeting as required, they will incur joint and several liability together with the company in respect of debts sustained.

In some contexts (eg when certain losses are not computed as such) the legal rules differ from the accounting rules. When calculating the company's equity, some specific legal rules apply (see Royal Decree Law 10/2008 on financial measures taken to improve the liquidity of small and medium enterprises).

8.2 Convertible bonds

Only joint stock companies may use convertible bonds as a means to obtain external financing.

9. Administration

The governing bodies are the general shareholders' meeting, which resolves on corporate decisions, and the administrative body, which is responsible for the management and representation of the company.

9.1 General shareholders' meeting

The shareholders' meeting has the power to:

- amend the bylaws;
- appoint and dismiss the administrators; and
- approve the accounts.

In limited liability corporations, the general shareholders' meeting can also give instructions to the administrative body and make the adoption of resolutions on certain management issues subject to its prior authorisation, unless the bylaws provide otherwise.

In joint stock companies, the most significant meetings are as follows:

- *Formally convened meeting* – this is convened by means of a notice published in the *Official Gazette* of the Mercantile Registry and a newspaper of the province in which the company's corporate domicile is located, one month prior to the date on which the meeting is to be held, with an indication of the agenda. Shareholders owning 5% or more of the capital stock may request the administrative body to convene the meeting and/or include issues on the agenda. The notification of the meeting can establish a first-call date and a second-call date, at least 24 hours apart. In limited liability corporations, the bylaws may specify other call procedures, provided that receipt of notification of the meeting is ensured (eg by registered mail), no second call is provided and the term for calling the meeting is 15 days prior to the meeting.
- *Universal meeting* – this is considered to be convened and validly constituted when the attending parties unanimously resolve to hold the meeting and the meeting is attended by all those representing the capital stock.

(a)   Quorum requirements

(i)   Attendance

Shareholders may attend general shareholders' meetings either in person or by proxy.

In joint stock companies, the proxy need not necessarily be a shareholder, but the power of representation must be granted in writing and specifically for each meeting.

In limited liability corporations, the shareholders can be represented by:

- another shareholder, or his or her spouse, ascendant or descendant;
- a person holding general powers of attorney to administer the assets of the shareholder in the national territory; or
- any other person as set forth in the bylaws.

The bylaws can therefore change the system of representation. Representation is revocable in general terms, except in certain cases established in Royal Decree 171/2007.

For joint stock companies, as a rule, the general shareholders' meeting is validly constituted when formally convened at first call if the shareholders present or represented hold at least 25% of the subscribed voting stock. If the meeting cannot be constituted at first call because a quorum is not present, then at second call the meeting is validly constituted regardless of the percentage of capital stock represented in the attendance.

The bylaws cannot reduce, either directly or indirectly, the legal quorum required for constitution of the meeting at first call, although they can establish a higher quorum than that required by law (as long as unanimity is not effectively required).

If the meeting is to decide on certain matters (ie, the issue of debentures, capital increases or reductions, transformation, merger or split-off and any amendment of the bylaws), a special attendance quorum is required as follows:

- at first call, at least 50% of the subscribed voting stock; and
- at second call, at least 25% of the voting stock; if the meeting is attended by less than 50% of the voting stock, resolutions require the approval of at least two-thirds of the capital stock in attendance.

The bylaws can increase the above quorums, as long as unanimity is not required and a lower quorum at second call is maintained.

The general shareholders' meeting of a limited liability corporation is validly constituted if it is attended – either in person or by proxy – by shareholders representing a percentage of votes sufficient to adopt resolutions, in accordance with the law and the bylaws. In this case there is no difference between the attendance quorum and the voting quorum.

(ii)   Voting

In joint stock companies, decisions of the shareholders' meeting are adopted by simple majority of votes and are expressed in resolutions.

In limited liability corporations:

- regular corporate resolutions (eg, approval of the accounts) are passed by a simple majority of the votes validly issued, provided that these represent at least one-third of the votes;

- resolutions for capital increases and reductions, and other amendments to the bylaws for which no higher majority is required, must be approved by at least one-half of the votes corresponding to the shares into which the capital stock is divided; and

- resolutions on transformation, merger or split-off, elimination of the right of first refusal and the exclusion of partners must be approved by at least two-thirds of the votes corresponding to the shares into which the capital stock is divided.

The bylaws can require a higher majority for the adoption of certain resolutions, with the following exceptions:

- Liability actions against the administrators must always be adopted by simple majority; and

- The quorum required for the separation of partners in limited liability corporations cannot exceed two-thirds of the voting stock.

(b) Challenging resolutions

Resolutions of the general shareholders' meeting that are contrary to law, and in particular to public order, may be contested. Resolutions that contravene the bylaws, or that damage the interests of the company for the benefit of shareholders or third parties, may be annulled.

Any shareholder, administrator or third party with a legitimate interest can contest invalid resolutions. Annullable resolutions may be contested by:

- shareholders who did not attend the meeting at which the resolution was passed; and

- dissenting shareholders whose opposition to the resolution was recorded in the minutes of the meeting.

9.2 Administrative body

The administrators have the power to manage and represent the company. They are appointed and dismissed by the general shareholders' meeting.

(a) Different systems of administration

In joint stock companies, the administrative system adopted must be expressly stated in the bylaws. By contrast, the bylaws of limited liability corporations can provide for different systems, with the shareholders' meeting ultimately choosing the system to be adopted.

The available administrative systems are as follows:

- sole administrator;

- various joint and several administrators;

- joint administrators (in joint stock companies the maximum is two, while in limited liability corporations there can be more, acting jointly at least in pairs); and

- board of directors (composed of at least three directors who act together as a corporate body, but without prejudice to the power to delegate competence to one or more of the members for a resolution adopted by at least two-thirds of the board).

(b)   *Term of office, resignation and removal of directors*

The administrators' appointment takes effect from the moment they accept their post. The term of office is established in the bylaws. In joint stock companies this term is the same for all administrators and cannot exceed six years (although re-election is possible). In limited liability corporations the term is indefinite, unless the bylaws provide otherwise.

The appointment and cessation of administrators must be registered with the Mercantile Registry to be effective with respect to third parties.

(c)   *Directors' liability to third parties*

With regard to administrators' liability, the Law on Limited Liability Corporations refers to the Joint Stock Companies Law.

This law provides that an administrator will be civilly liable both to shareholders and to company creditors for damage caused to the company by an illicit act or omission that is contrary to law or to the bylaws, or by failure to perform the duties inherent in the office. This liability arises where there is a causal link between the damage to the company and the illicit act or omission on the part of the administrator.

Liability may be organic, in which case it does not extend to individuals who are not members of the administrative bodies or in other positions of power; and personal, in which case all members of the administrative body who performed the act or adopted the resolution in question will be held jointly liable, unless they can prove that they did not participate in, were unaware of or expressly opposed the act or resolution. The fact that the damaging act or resolution was adopted, authorised or ratified by the general shareholders' meeting does not discharge the administrators from liability.

A liability action against the administrators may be brought in two ways, as follows:

- To bring a corporate action, the damage must have been caused directly to the company. The action can be filed by the company either through the general shareholders' meeting by simple majority or through minority shareholders representing at least 5% of the capital stock. Alternatively, a corporate action may be filed by the creditors if the company's assets amount to less than the value of their claims.
- An individual action may be filed either by shareholders or by third parties whose interests have been damaged by the administrators' acts.

The company can file a liability action against the administrators by way of a resolution of the general shareholders' meeting, which may be adopted even if the matter does not appear on the agenda (as is the case with the dismissal of an administrator).

Approval of the annual accounts by the general shareholders' meeting has no effect on a liability action.

The administrators have a duty to convene a general shareholders' meeting to discuss the dissolution of the company in certain specific circumstances – for example, where:

- the company is unable to fulfil its corporate purpose;
- the corporate bodies are paralysed;
- its assets have fallen to below half of the capital stock;
- the capital stock has dropped below the statutory minimum; or
- there are other circumstances specified in the bylaws.

If the administrators fail to convene this meeting to dissolve the company or to remove the contrary circumstances, or subsequently fail to apply for judicial dissolution or bankruptcy, within two months of such a trigger event occurring, they will have joint and several liability for the company's obligations.

(d) Non-competition

The Law on Limited Liability Corporations provides that administrators cannot engage in activities that are identical, similar or complementary to those undertaken by the company, except with the express approval of the general shareholders' meeting. Any shareholder can address the court of the place where the company has its domicile in order to request the dismissal of an administrator who infringes this prohibition.

The Joint Stock Companies Law does not expressly prohibit competition. However, in accordance with the principles of transparency and loyalty, it imposes an information obligation where an administrator intends to carry out, either directly or through related parties, investments or activities that are similar to those carried out by the company. The authorisation of the general shareholders' meeting is required for such activities.

(e) Special duties of secrecy and loyalty

Articles 127 and following of the Joint Stock Companies Law set out strict provisions on the administrators' duties of diligence, fidelity, loyalty and secrecy. If the office of administrator is held by a legal person, the duty of secrecy rests with its legal representative.

In contrast, the Limited Liability Corporations Law states merely that administrators must discharge their office with diligence and observe the duty of secrecy.

(f) Criminal liability

The Criminal Code lists a number of crimes that might be committed within the company or against the company, as follows:

- inclusion of falsehoods in company information;
- imposition of abusive and damaging resolutions;
- imposition or advantage from damaging resolutions adopted by fictitious majorities;

- obstruction or denial of rights;
- fraudulent or unfair administration; and
- obstruction of the administration supervisory activities.

In principle, only the aggrieved party or its legal representative may prosecute in such cases. Moreover, the crime must have caused damage to a third party and there must have been intent on the part of the perpetrator; mere negligence is therefore excluded.

Criminal actions may be brought against directors and de facto directors. Claims based on abusive agreements may additionally be filed against those shareholders who influenced the directors' resolutions. Third parties may also be joined as defendants with directors and shareholders for claims filed on the grounds of abusive resolutions passed for their own benefit.

9.3. Others

(a) *Representatives*
In principle, the power to represent the company rests with the administrative body. However, a joint stock company or limited liability corporation can grant power of attorney to a natural or legal person. The power of attorney is extinguished by revocation or waiver, and it is effected by the initiation of bankruptcy proceedings against or liquidation of the company.

In order to have effect with respect to third parties, the power of attorney must be registered with the Mercantile Registry.

(b) *Internal controllers and auditors*
Spanish law includes no provisions on internal controllers or auditors.

The company may voluntarily appoint an external auditor to review its accounts. In some cases specified by law a mandatory audit is required (see section 11.2(b) below).

10. Fiscal year, commencement of activities
The bylaws specify the date of the fiscal year-end. The fiscal year cannot exceed one calendar year.

While the company may have a definite duration, it is more common to establish a company for an indefinite period. In any event, the duration of the company must be specified in the bylaws.

The bylaws must indicate the date on which the company is to commence activities. This cannot be prior to the execution of the charter of incorporation, except where a limited liability corporation is transformed into a joint stock company or vice versa, in which case the start date is the date on which the company, in its former legal form, commenced operations.

11.   Financial statements

11.1   Company tax

Both joint stock companies and limited liability corporations must submit their tax returns, prepared on the basis of the annual accounts as approved by the general shareholders' meeting, within six months plus 25 days of the end of the fiscal year.

In general, the current (2009) tax rate in Spain stands at 30%. For some small companies (ie, companies with a net turnover of less than €8 million in the preceding fiscal year), the first tranche of profit (currently up to €120,202.41) is taxed at a rate of 25%. (These figures are updated each year.) A number of deductions may also be made that reduce the tax payable.

11.2   Annual accounts

(a)   Documents

The annual accounts of joint stock companies and limited liability corporations comprise the balance sheet, profit and loss account and annual report.

The balance sheet must generally be submitted in the standard form required by law. However, an abbreviated balance sheet may be submitted by companies that satisfied at least two of the following conditions in the two preceding years:

- the total assets did not exceed € 2.85 million;
- the net annual turnover was less than € 5.7 million; and
- the average number of employees was less than 50.

Similarly, the profit and loss account must generally be submitted in the standard form required by law. However, an abbreviated form (grouping several items together under the single heading of 'Operating income') may be submitted by companies that satisfied at least two of the following conditions in the two preceding years:

- the total assets did not exceed € 11.4 million;
- the net annual turnover was less than € 22.8 million; and
- the average number of employees was less than 250.

Companies may also submit an abbreviated balance sheet or profit and loss account for the first fiscal period following incorporation, transformation or merger if, at the close of the fiscal period, they satisfy at least two of the conditions above that apply to either the balance sheet or the profit and loss account.

The annual report complements, explains and comments on the balance sheet and the profit and loss account.

The profit and loss accounts of joint stock companies must be accompanied by a management report, which explains how business is progressing and outlines important events that occurred between the end of the fiscal period to the date on which the accounts were drawn up. No management report is required where an abbreviated balance sheet is submitted.

(b) *Audit report*
For both joint stock companies and limited liability corporations, the annual accounts and management report will be revised by an independent auditor, who will issue an opinion accordingly. Companies that submit an abbreviated balance sheet are released from this obligation.

The auditor may be appointed by the general shareholders' meeting during the fiscal period covered by the audit, by the Mercantile Registry or by the court of the place where the company has its corporate domicile.

(c) *Approval of accounts and distribution of profits*
The administrative body must prepare the accounts and the management report within three months of the end of the fiscal period. Once the documents have been examined by the auditor, they must be submitted to the general shareholders' meeting for approval within six months of the end of the fiscal period.

The general shareholders' meeting will then decide on the approval of the accounts and the distribution of profits. Dividends may be distributed only if the company's net worth is not less than the capital stock and after the allocations required by law or the bylaws have been made. In any event, 10% of the profits must be assigned to the legal reserve until this reaches 20% of the capital stock. In the absence of specific provisions in the bylaws, the remaining profits may be freely distributed by the general shareholders' meeting. Dividends will be distributed to shareholders on a *pro rata* basis.

A withholding tax currently of 18% will be levied on dividends paid to resident shareholders who are natural persons. Such a withholding tax does not apply to active Spanish legal entities.

Dividends distributed to non-resident shareholders will be subject to the tax on non-residents, which varies depending on:

- whether the beneficiary is an EU parent company or affiliated company (in general, these are not subject to withholding tax); and
- the existence of a double-taxation treaty (the provisions contained therein will prevail).

(d) *Deposit and publication*
The annual accounts must be filed with the Mercantile Registry at the place of the company's corporate domicile within one month of their approval. Copies of such information may be freely obtained.

12. Company reorganisation

12.1 Transformation
Where a company is transformed into another type of company, it retains its legal personality and shareholding composition. The law outlines in detail the alternative types of company into which joint stock companies and limited liability corporations may be transformed.

12.2 Merger

Where two or more companies merge into a new or existing joint stock company, they cease to exist and their assets and liabilities are transferred to the new company, which acquires by universal succession all assets and liabilities of the companies absorbed in the merger. The merger procedure is regulated by detailed provisions in the Joint Stock Companies Law (which also apply to limited liability corporations). The simplest mergers are those in which there is a direct or indirect control relationship between the merging companies.

12.3 Split-off

A split-off can take place in one of the following ways:
- The assets and liabilities of a joint stock company are divided into two or more parts, which are transferred to an existing or newly created corporation, while the original joint stock company ceases to exist; or
- Certain assets and liabilities of a joint stock company are separated out and transferred to one or more existing or newly created corporations, while the joint stock company continues to exist.

The split-off can be resolved only if all shares of the companies involved are fully paid up. The beneficiaries of the split-off can choose a different corporate form from that of the original company.

The split-off procedure is similar to the merger procedure and is regulated in detail by the Joint Stock Company Law and the Law on Limited Liability Corporations.

13. Eventual separation of shareholders

For joint stock companies where a resolution is passed on a change in corporate purpose, transformation or the transfer abroad of the corporate domicile, shareholders who have no voting rights or who voted against the particular resolution have a right to withdraw from the company. It is recommended that a provision to this effect be included in the bylaws in case of failure to provide ancillary services as obliged.

For limited liability corporations, dissenting shareholders have a right to withdraw where a resolution is passed on the following matters:
- a change in corporate purpose;
- transfer abroad of the corporate domicile;
- amendment of the procedures on the transfer of shares;
- transformation;
- creation, amendment or early termination of the obligation to provide ancillary services;
- extension or reactivation of the corporation; and
- other matters stated in the bylaws.

The procedure for separation is set out in the applicable legislation and in regulations that may be included in the bylaws.

For limited liability corporations, a shareholder may also be excluded from the company for failure to provide ancillary services, infringement of the non-competition clause, or other causes established in the bylaws with the agreement of all shareholders.

14. Dissolution and liquidation

There are various reasons to dissolve a company; the most common are as follows:
- resolution of the general shareholders' meeting;
- expiry of the duration established in the bylaws;
- termination or impossibility of achieving the corporate purpose;
- reduction of corporate assets to less than one-half of the capital stock;
- reduction of the capital stock to less than the minimum legal limit;
- full merger or split-off;
- bankruptcy stemming from a judicial resolution; and
- other reasons specified in the bylaws.

Dissolution generally requires a resolution of the general shareholders' meeting, which must be convened within two months of:
- the date on which the cause for dissolution occurred, if the meeting is called at the administrators' initiative; or
- the date on which a shareholder requested that the meeting be convened, where there are legal grounds for dissolution.

The general shareholders' meeting need not be convened where the company is to be dissolved because the term specified in the bylaws has expired.

Upon a resolution to dissolve a limited liability corporation, the administrators automatically become the liquidators, unless other liquidators are appointed pursuant to the bylaws or a resolution of the general shareholders' meeting.

The liquidators of a joint stock company are appointed by the general shareholders' meeting. Shareholders who represent 20% of the capital stock may request the court to appoint a controller to supervise the liquidation process.

During the liquidation process, the liquidator realises company assets and uses the proceeds to satisfy its liabilities. Real estate must be sold through notarial or judicial auction, unless the transaction has been authorised by the general shareholders' meeting.

15. Branches

Company branches are regulated by the Mercantile Registry Regulations. A 'branch' is defined as a secondary establishment that serves as a permanent representative of the parent company in Spain and has a certain degree of management autonomy, through which activities of the parent company are carried out in whole or in part.

As branches do not have separate legal personality, creditors may address the parent company directly. Where a claim is made against a branch, the parent will be liable.

Foreign companies with branches in Spain must file company accounts at the Mercantile Registry of Spain in accordance with the applicable regulations.

16. Professional companies

Law 2/2007 of March 15 2007 on Professional Companies introduced a new regulation for companies incorporated and run by professionals with a university degree and registered with the relevant professional association (eg lawyers listed with their bar association) as to the manner in which they discharge their activities. They may be incorporated as any type of legal company, but must follow the Law on Professional Companies for:

- corporate purpose;
- duration;
- corporate name;
- capital stock and increase of capital;
- dissolution;
- transfer of shares;
- separation and exclusion of professional partners;
- rules for valuation of contributions;
- ancillary services;
- distribution of profits and losses;
- composition of administration body; and
- arbitrage.

Sweden

Peder Hammarskiöld
Sandra Hein
Hammarskiöld & Co

1. Types of limited liability company and applicable legislation

In Sweden '*aktiebolag*' (AB) is the term used to describe companies limited by shares. These can be either private or public. Only public limited liability companies are allowed to raise capital by public offerings.

The main legislation governing the limited liability companies, private as well as public, is the Swedish Companies Act of 2005 (*Aktiebolagslagen* (2005: 551), often referred to as 'ABL' but hereinafter 'the Companies Act'). For limited liability companies in the banking and insurance sectors, the general corporate regulation in the Companies Act is also supplemented and modified by sector-specific laws.

Accounting and taxation issues are not governed by the Companies Act. The most important legislative acts in these fields are the Annual Accounting Act (*Årsredovisningslagen* (1995: 1554)), the Bookkeeping Act (*Bokföringslagen* (1999: 1078)) and the various tax laws.

Since December 2004, Sweden has also had its own corporate governance code, (*Svensk kod för bolagsstyrning*). A revised code came into force on July 1 2008. There is no legal obligation for companies to comply with the code but, as of July 1 2008, the listing rules for OMX Nordic Exchange Stockholm and NGM Equity require that all Swedish companies listed on these markets comply with the code.

2. Incorporation

2.1 Proceedings prior to incorporation

The quickest and easiest way to set up a limited liability company in Sweden is to buy a ready-made 'shelf company' and amend its bylaws and appoint new directors and auditors.

Setting up a company from scratch is more time-consuming and involves the following steps:

- One or more founders drafts a memorandum of association containing, among the bylaws, information about the directors of the board and auditors (as well as deputy directors and deputy auditors) and information about the price and other conditions for shares to be issued and subscribed for;
- The founders subscribe for all the shares in the company;
- Full payment for the shares is effected;
- The founders finalise, date and sign the memorandum of association; and
- The board applies for registration of the company by the Swedish Companies Office (the 'companies office').

The founders must be Swedish legal persons or natural or legal persons domiciled in the European Economic Area (EEA).

(a) Corporate name

The company name is registered when the Companies Office registers the new company in the companies register. To avoid a delay in the registration process, it is often wise to check whether the intended name is available and, if possible, provide an alternative.

(b) Capital contributions

Contributions to the company's equity can be made in cash or in kind (*apportegendom*).

Payments in cash are to be effected as payments to a bank account opened by the company for this purpose. A bank certificate confirming the payment is required to register the company in the companies register.

In-kind contributions have to be property that is, or may be assumed to be, of value for the operations of the company. An undertaking to perform work or provide services is not accepted as in-kind contributions. If capital contributions are made in kind, the value of these contributions must not be set higher than the actual value to the company. The fulfilment of these requirements is to be confirmed in a statement by an auditor, which also confirms that all the property has been conveyed to the company.

(c) Declaration of foreign investment

There is no requirement to declare foreign investments in Swedish companies, unless the company is active in a sector where material changes of ownership (regardless of nationality) are to be approved by the Swedish Financial Supervisory Authority, such as banks, insurance companies and others.

(d) Tax identification number

Foreign directors who receive compensation for their work will in principle be liable for income tax in Sweden and will be provided with a tax number from the Swedish tax agency. The directors' liability for tax in Sweden may be reduced or exempted under a double-taxation treaty.

2.2 Incorporation

(a) Bylaws

(i) Essential clauses

A company's regime and operating system is set out in the articles of association, which must contain, at a minimum, the following information:
- the name of the company;
- the location in Sweden of the registered office of the company;
- the objects of the company;
- the share capital;
- the number of shares or, where a minimum share capital and a maximum

share capital are stated in the articles of association, a corresponding minimum and maximum number of shares;

- the number, or the minimum and maximum number, of members of the board of directors;
- the number, or the minimum and maximum number, of deputy directors, where these are appointed;
- the number, or the minimum and maximum number, of auditors;
- the procedure for convening general meetings; and
- the period of time to be covered by the company's financial year.

(ii) Clauses not foreseen by law

As long as they are not contrary to law, other clauses than those stated above may be included in the bylaws. Nevertheless, bylaws of Swedish companies tend to be quite standardised. Issues that fall outside the required minimum content of the bylaws are usually governed by shareholders' agreements. The primary consequence of including additional information in the bylaws is that the information is considered to be in the public domain.

(iii) Enlargeable clauses ruled by law

The Companies Act provides for some optional clauses that may or may not be included in the bylaws. The most important of these are the share transfer restriction clauses described in section 7.5 below.

(b) Execution of public deed

When the new company is registered, the Companies Office issues a certificate of registration that contains a summary of the information registered about the company. Additional and updated certificates can be obtained at any time in Swedish or in English. There is a small cost for this.

(c) Tax identification number

A limited liability company must register with the Swedish Tax Agency, which will issue a certificate of registration and a tax account. In addition, the company should apply for a certificate to show that the company is liable for the so-called 'F-tax' (taxation as a business) and a VAT registration number. The company must also register as an employer if it is to have employees or otherwise make payments that are subject to income tax.

(d) Payment of indirect taxes

The registration of the newly incorporated company by the Companies Office is subject to an administrative fee (presently SEK2,200). Similar fees will be charged for any subsequent change to the registered information, such as a change of director or changes to the bylaws.

(e)   **Registration with the Mercantile Registry**
The Swedish companies register is administrated by the Companies Office. When a limited liability company is incorporated, it has to be registered in the companies register in order to gain status as a legal person and be able to hold rights and obligations, act as a party in legal proceedings, etc.

If, before the company has been registered, representatives of the company act on its behalf so that liability arises, those individuals who have participated in the act or decision in question are jointly and severally liable. In some circumstances, the liability may be assumed by the company following registration.

Many other subsequent decisions that are of importance for the governance of the company or its registered equity (eg a change of directors, new issues of shares, warrants or convertible instruments) must also be notified to the Companies Office for registration.

(f)   **Corporate books**
There is no procedure for the legalisation of company books in Sweden. The company is obliged to keep a share register, minutes of board meetings and general meetings as well as accounting books, but none of these documents is officially legalised.

(g)   **Declaration of set-up activity and other tax declarations**
New companies must register with the Companies Office and the Tax Agency. Further, certain kinds of business activities, involving financial services, alcohol, weapons, public transport, environmental risks etc, may require official licences or permits.

3.   Number of partners – unipersonality
Swedish limited liability companies may be founded and held by one or more founders/shareholders. Nevertheless, the board of a private limited liability company must have a minimum of two people: one director and one deputy director (see section 9.2 below). A minimum of three directors is required for public companies.

4.   Corporate name – limitations
The company name must include the word '*aktiebolag*' or the abbreviation 'AB'. The name of a public limited liability company must also include the term '*publikt*' or '(publ)'.

The name of the company must distinguish the company's business from those of others and cannot be merely a description of the business or of the company's products and services. In addition, the name must not be confusingly similar to someone else's family name, artistic name, protected trade name, trademark or other distinctive mark, or a protected literary or artistic work. It must also not include the name or abbreviation of a public authority or an international organisation, be offensive to decency and public order, or otherwise be misleading to the public.

5.   Domicile
A Swedish company is considered to be domiciled where it has its registered office.

The registered office may be located anywhere in Sweden and does not need to be the actual place of business. The location of the registered seat is usually the place where the company may be sued in court.

6. Corporate purpose

The purpose of the company must be stated in its bylaws. It may consist of any lawful business and does not have to be commercial. If the company's operations have another purpose than generating profits for distribution to the shareholders, this must be clearly set out in the bylaws. The statement defines what kinds of activities the company may engage in. Acting outside this might incur liability for damages for the board or the managing director in relation to the company, the shareholders or a third party. Nevertheless, legal acts that are performed on the company's behalf, in violation of the company's purpose, are generally enforceable against the company.

Another important implication is that it is within the bounds of the company's purpose that the company's name is protected.

7. Capital stock

7.1 Minimum amount

Private companies must have a share capital of at least SEK100,000. In public companies the share capital must amount to a minimum of SEK500,000.

7.2 Nature of contributions

In connection with a new issue of shares, contributions to the share capital can be made in cash or in kind (see section 2.1(b)). In-kind payments may include payment set-off against a debt.

The share capital may also be increased through a bonus issue of shares where capital is transferred from the statutory reserve, the revaluation reserve, unrestricted equity or by writing up the value of a fixed asset.

7.3 Partial payments

An increase in the share capital becomes effective through registration by the Companies Office of the resolution to issue new shares. Registration requires that the subscribed and allotted shares have been fully paid up and that these shares represent the minimum amount by which the share capital is to be increased according to the issue resolution.

If the issue resolution provides a minimum and maximum amount by which the share capital is to be increased, it is possible to register the issue in parts in the sense that shares issued as a consequence of the same issue resolution are registered gradually as they are paid for. The first registration can then be effected as soon as payment has been made for shares representing the minimum amount by which the share capital is to be increased.

7.4 Share certificates – systems of representing shares

The Companies Act distinguishes between companies whose shares may be represented by physical share certificates and companies whose shares are registered in a Central Securities Depository (CSD) register pursuant to the Financial Instruments Act (SFS 1998:1479) (CSD companies). Only public companies may be CSD companies. Companies that are not CSD companies must issue share certificates if the holder of the shares in question so requires, but not otherwise.

Share certificates are promissory notes and may be subject to acquisitions made in good faith. For that reason it is very important that share certificates are not lost. Lost share certificates can only be cancelled by a court decision – something that takes more than a year to obtain.

Companies whose shares may be represented by physical share certificates are obliged to keep a separate register with information about the shares issued and the shareholders. The share register is managed by the board, and mismanagement of the register is considered a criminal offence.

Shares may be issued in different classes. Each share represents an equal portion of the share capital, but share classes may differ in voting rights or rights to the company's assets or profits. If the share classes differ in voting rights, no share may carry voting rights that exceed the voting rights of any other share by more than 10 times.

Existing shareholders hold pre-emption rights to new issues of shares, warrants and convertible instruments.

7.5 Restrictions to the transfer of shares

Unless otherwise stipulated in the bylaws or agreed between the shareholders, shares may be freely transferred. Nevertheless, a change of ownership of companies that are supervised by the Swedish Financial Supervisory Authority (*Finansinspektionen*) (eg insurance companies, banks and stock markets) needs the approval of that authority.

In the bylaws, only three specific kinds of restrictions can be registered:

- a so-called 'consent clause' (*samtyckesförbehåll*) (Chapter 4 Section 8 of the Companies Act);
- a right-of-first-refusal clause (*förköpsförbehåll*) (Chapter 4 Section 18 of the Companies Act); and
- a post-sale purchase clause (*hembudsförbehåll*) (Chapter 4 Section 27 of the Companies Act).

CSD companies that are not listed on a stock exchange may have a post-sale purchase clause in their bylaws, but they do not have any of the other transfer restrictions.

A consent clause in the bylaws means in brief that the transfer of a share to a new owner requires prior consent from the company (acting through the board). Where the company refuses to grant consent, it must state its reasons for refusal. If the transferor so requires, the company must also designate another transferee who is prepared to acquire the shares.

A right-of-first-refusal clause in the bylaws means, in brief, that existing shareholders, or another party set out in the clause, has the right to purchase shares before they may be transferred to a new owner.

A post-sale purchase clause in the bylaws means, in brief, that an existing shareholder or another person identified in the post-sale purchase clause is entitled to purchase shares that have already been transferred to a new owner.

Other kinds of restrictions or obligations to share transfers (eg tag-along and drag-along clauses) may follow from shareholder agreements.

7.6 Transfer of shares – formalities required

As between the parties, shares are transferred through an agreement between the existing and the new holder. There are no formal requirements that the agreement must comply with to be valid; even oral agreements are accepted. For CSD companies, perfection of the share transfer (in relation to third parties) requires that the new owner is registered in the CSD register; non-CSD companies must ensure that the new owner comes into possession of the share certificates for the transferred shares. The new owner should also notify the board of the acquisition so that he can be registered in the company's share register.

8. Equity

8.1 Balance between capital and own resources

Swedish company law does not require any particular balance between external funding and own resources. The capital protection rules still mainly rely on the concept of a minimum share capital. Nevertheless, the rules regarding distribution of profits and other beneficial value transfers from the company to shareholders (or others) require the observance of a 'rule of caution' (see section 11.2(c) below).

8.2 Convertible bonds

Besides shares, a limited liability company may also issue convertible bonds (*konvertibler*) or warrants (*optioner*).

Convertible bonds grant the holder or a particular person (or order) a right or obligation to exchange for shares in the company the claim he or she has against the company according to the bond. Convertible bonds may be paid in cash, in kind or by set-off against a debt, depending on the conditions set out in the resolution for issuing the convertible bonds.

Warrants grant the holder the right to subscribe for new shares in the company in exchange for payment in cash. Warrants can be – but do not have to be – issued against payment. The price for the new shares must, however, never be lower than the quotient value of the previously existing shares.

The rules for the issue of convertible bonds and warrants are very similar to the rules for share issues. A resolution by the general meeting is required in all cases and the shareholders' pre-emptive rights to new shares apply equally to the issue of convertible bonds or warrants.

9. Administration of the company

9.1 General meeting of partners

The general meeting of the shareholders holds the ultimate decision-making powers in the company. According to the Companies Act, some kinds of decisions may only be resolved by the general meeting. This applies, for example, to the appointment of the board of directors and auditors, changing the articles of association, distribution of profits and new issues of shares, warrants or convertible instruments. The bylaws may reserve additional questions for decision by the general meeting than those issues that follow from law.

In addition, the general meeting may also provide instructions to the board or even overturn a prior decision by the board.

As a minimum, one annual general meeting must be held each year. Extra general meetings are to be convened where necessary, or when demanded by the auditors or the holders of at least one-tenth of the shares.

(a) Quorums for attendance

As a main rule, no quorum is required for a general meeting, as long as the rules for convening it have been observed. Nevertheless, there are a few types of resolution that require the support of a certain amount of the total numbers of shares or votes in the company to be valid, thereby creating an indirect quorum requirement.

(b) Quorums for adoption of resolutions

The main rule is that a resolution is adopted by a single majority of the votes cast. In matters that do not concern an election, the chairman has the casting vote. Certain matters (eg altering the bylaws) require a higher majority. The quorum rules set out in the Companies Act may to some extent be modified by provisions in the bylaws.

(c) Challenge of resolutions

A shareholder, the board, a single board member or the managing director may challenge resolutions by the general meeting in court. This type of proceeding may be brought by a person whom the board of directors has refused to enter as a shareholder in the share register.

Action for the annulment or amendment of a resolution by the general meeting must, as a main rule, be brought within three months of the date of the resolution. The three-month time limit does not apply to certain cases of fundamentally erroneous decisions (eg when the meeting has not been properly convened).

9.2 Administrative body

The board of directors is in charge of the company's business and its organisation. It is responsible for ensuring that the company's organisation in respect of accounting, management of funds and its general financial position includes satisfactory controls. The board is also required to assess the company's financial situation regularly.

The board of directors may appoint a managing director to be in charge of the company's day-to-day management in accordance with the guidelines and instructions provided by the board. In public limited liability companies the appointment of a managing director is mandatory. The managing director can be a member of the board but must not be its chairman.

The concept of 'day-to-day business' basically means measures that, in consideration of the scope and nature of the company's business, are of normal current character and not of great significance. The board can also entrust the managing director with specific tasks that fall outside the scope of day-to-day business.

The managing director is also responsible for taking any necessary measures to ensure that the company's accounts are maintained in accordance with applicable laws and regulations and that the management of funds is conducted in a sound manner. Further, the managing director is a channel for information between the board of directors and the operational business of the company. The managing director should keep the board informed about the operations of the company.

(a) Different systems of administration

The Companies Act is rather strict when it comes to the organisation of a company. The fundamental division of functions and powers between the general meeting, the board and the managing director (if any) may not be altered.

In addition to the corporate organs provided for by the Companies Act, the Swedish Corporate Governance Code also requires companies that apply the code to have a nomination committee, an audit committee and a remuneration committee.

(b) Term of office, resignation and removal of directors

Board members are as a main rule appointed by the general meeting of shareholders. The bylaws may prescribe that one or more directors is appointed in another way (eg by a particular shareholder or a municipal body). The board itself, or board members, may never appoint other board members. In a public company, more than half of the members of the board must be appointed by the general meeting. No less than half of the board members must be resident within the European Economic Area.

In addition to the principles outlined above, Swedish labour law provides the employees with certain rights to board representation; these rights are exercised by the unions.

The term of office of the board members is to be stated in the bylaws. Generally, board members are appointed at each annual meeting, for a term of one year. Board members can choose to resign from their appointment at any time during their term of office. Shareholders representing more than half of the shares can also change the composition of the board at an extra general meeting.

A change of directors must be notified to the Companies Office. It is important to note that the change is not effective until the Companies Office has received this notification.

(c) Directors' liability to third parties

Directors of the board, as well as the managing director, may be held liable for damages that they wilfully or negligently cause third parties or shareholders in the fulfilment of their duties if the damage is caused by a violation of the Companies Act, the applicable annual reports legislation, or the bylaws.

(d) **Non-competition**

Swedish company law does not foresee any direct prohibition for directors of the board to engage in competing activities, in person or via another company. The directors must, however, be able to act in the best interests of the company, something that follows from the duty of loyalty further outlined below. It is a matter for the shareholders to decide who they consider will be most fit for the job as director of the board. Consequently, the Swedish Corporate Governance Code provides that the appointment or re-election of a board member should always be preceded by the disclosure of any other assignment of material importance held by the person to be elected.

Furthermore, a member of the board of directors may not participate in a board decision where he or she has a conflict of interest.

(e) **Special duties of secrecy and loyalty**

The board of directors has a general duty of care towards the company and is obliged to act in the best interests of the company. As part of that duty, board members have a duty of secrecy where publicity could be detrimental to the company.

(f) **Civil and criminal liability: legislative framework and consequences**

The board of directors and the managing director will be held liable for criminal offences conducted in the company's operations. Criminal liability requires a wilful or negligent act or omission on behalf of the board member in question, depending on how the criminal offence is worded. Failing to take action despite actual or assumed knowledge of unlawful activities might also be a cause for liability. If a specific task has been clearly delegated from the board or managing director to someone else who is competent for the task, criminal liability might, under some conditions, follow the delegation of the task.

The liability of the managing director and the directors of the board for any damage caused to third parties or shareholders has been described in section 9.2(c) above. The directors of the board and the managing director may also be held liable for damages to the company if they wilfully or negligently have caused damage to the company in the performance of their duties. In addition to the liability rules in the Companies Act, company officials may also under general tort law be liable to provide compensation for any damage caused by criminal offences that they have committed.

9.3   Others

(a) **Attorneys**

In Sweden, there is no licence required to be able to practise law. The professional title *'advokat'* may only be used by members of the Swedish Bar Association. No distinction is made between attorneys who plead in court and those who do not.

(b) **Controllers and internal auditors**

Pursuant to the Companies Act, it is the board that is ultimately responsible for ensuring that the company has good internal controls. As a help to fulfil this duty, larger enterprises tend to employ internal auditors, but that is not required under law. The code favours the employment of internal auditors by stating that "for companies that do not have a separate internal audit function, the board of directors is to evaluate the need for such a function annually and to justify its decision in its report on internal controls." (Section 10.6 of the Corporate Governance Code.)

10.   Fiscal year, duration and start of activities
The financial year is 12 months and the company is able to choose to end it by the December 31, April 30, June 30, or August 31. During the company's first year of business, or if the fiscal year is changed, the financial year may be shortened or prolonged to a maximum of 18 months. All companies within one company group must apply the same fiscal year.

11.   Financial statements

11.1   Company tax
As of January 1 2009, the company tax for limited liability companies has been lowered to 26.3% of the company's taxable income. In addition, companies are liable to pay social security fees for employees, VAT and real-estate taxes.

11.2   Annual accounts

(a)   Documents
Annual reports, consisting of a report of the board of directors, a profit and loss account and a balance sheet for the company and, if applicable, a consolidated profit and loss account and consolidated balance sheet, are to be prepared, signed by the board and adopted by the annual general meeting of the shareholders.

Accounting records, vouchers and all other accounting material must be kept in Sweden and be stored for at least ten years.

(b)   Audit report
Audit reports are to be submitted annually and presented at the annual general meeting together with the annual report.

(c)   Approval and distribution of profits
When the annual accounts are adopted by the annual general meeting, the meeting must also decide how the company's profits or losses during the year are to be allocated. Profits may only be distributed to an amount that leaves the company's restricted equity fully covered. In addition, a so-called 'rule of caution' must be observed, meaning that the dividend has to be justifiable when taking into account the demands with respect to the size of the shareholders' equity that are imposed by the nature, scope and risks associated with the company's operations and the company's need to strengthen its balance sheet, liquidity and general financial position.

The general meeting's decision to distribute profits to the shareholders is to be based on a proposal from the board. To its proposal, the board must issue a reasoned statement in which it confirms that the proposed dividend is justifiable under the rule of caution described above.

If the annual general meeting does not resolve to distribute all of the company's profits that, according to the annual accounts that were adopted at that meeting, were available for distribution, additional profit distributions may be resolved by subsequent general meetings held until the next annual general meeting. In this case, the resolution to pay a dividend must be notified to the Companies Office.

The tax rate on dividends is currently 30%, but for companies the lower company tax of 26.3% (until recently 28%) applies. Dividends paid between Swedish companies may often be exempt from tax according to an exemption for dividends on "business related shares" (*näringsbetingade andelar*). This exemption applies correspondingly where the shareholder recipient is a company resident in the European Economic Area. Dividends paid to foreign shareholders are in principle subject to a 30% withholding tax, but an exemption or lower tax rate may often apply under a double-taxation treaty. A tax number is not required for the taxation of dividends.

(d) Deposit and publicity

An annual report is to be submitted to the Companies Office for registration, within one month from the date when the annual accounts were adopted by the annual general meeting. The annual general meeting is to be held within six months from the expiry of the company's fiscal year.

Some companies (eg insurance companies) are also under an obligation to file interim reports.

12. Company reorganisation: transformation, merger and split-off

The most common form of merger between Swedish limited liability companies is when a parent company absorbs a subsidiary. It is also possible to do it the other way round and have the subsidiary absorb its parent company. Less frequently used is the option of a merger by 'consolidation', where two or more transferor companies are merged into a new transferee company, incorporated as a consequence of the merger. In all cases, a merger means that the assets and liabilities of the transferor company(ies) are transferred to the transferee company, in exchange for consideration to the shareholders in the transferor company(ies), and the transferor company(ies) is/are dissolved without liquidation. More than half of the consideration to be paid to the shareholders in the transferor company(ies) must consist of shares in the transferee company. The rest of the consideration may be paid in such shares or in cash.

A merger has to be approved by the general meeting(s) in the transferor compan(ies). This generally requires a majority of two-thirds of the shares voted for and represented at the meeting. If there are shares of different classes, a two-thirds majority must be reached within each class of shares. If required by holders of at least 5% of the shares in the transferee company, the merger must also be approved by the general meeting of that company. Stricter quorum rules apply when any of the transferor companies is a public company and the transferee company is a private company.

The companies' creditors are to be notified of a proposed merger. Should any of the creditors oppose the merger, the matter will be referred to a general court. The court will then allow the merger if the opposing creditor receives full payment or the company offers satisfactory security.

A merger normally takes about four to six months to conclude.

Since February 15 2008, it is also possible for Swedish limited liability companies to merge with corresponding companies incorporated according to the laws of an EEA member state and also having their corporate seat in an EEA state. A Swedish limited liability company may also merge with other EEA companies to form a European company.

As regards the possibilities to split off a part of a company's operations, this can be done either on a pure contractual basis, where assets and liabilities are transferred from one company to another in accordance with an asset-transfer agreement, or according to the de-merger rules in Chapter 24 of the Companies Act.

A split-off pursuant to the rules in the Companies Act means that a company is divided in a way where the company's assets and liabilities in whole or in part are taken over by one or more companies in exchange for consideration to the shareholders of the transferor company. If all of the transferor company's assets and liabilities are transferred, the transferor company will be dissolved without liquidation. If the split-off only includes parts of the transferor company's assets and liabilities, the transferor company will not be dissolved, but instead will continue its remaining operations. The de-merger procedures are very similar to the merger procedures.

13. Eventual partner separation

Unless the shareholders have an agreement to that effect, Swedish law provides very few possibilities for shareholders of a limited liability company to acquire the shares of other shareholders against their will, or the other way round, for single shareholders to demand that other shareholders acquire their shares. The most commonly applied rules are the buy-out rules in Chapter 22 of the Companies Act. Pursuant to these rules, a shareholder must hold more than one-tenth of the shares in a limited liability company to enjoy a right to buy out minority shares. Correspondingly, if one shareholder holds more than one-tenth of the shares, the minority shareholders may also compel the majority shareholder to purchase their shares.

There are also buy-out rules in the Companies Act that are aimed at situations where there is risk of continued fraud on the minority, but these rules are not known to have been applied in practice.

14. Dissolution and liquidation

A limited liability company can cease to exist as a consequence of a merger, de-merger, bankruptcy or liquidation.

Voluntary liquidation is the result of a resolution by the general meeting that the company shall go into liquidation. The resolution has to be supported by shareholders holding more than one-half of the votes cast, unless otherwise provided for in the bylaws.

Further, the Companies Act prescribes specific procedures for how the board and shareholders are to act in a situation of suspected capital deficiency. This may in the end result in a duty to place the company into liquidation. Failure to comply with these procedures might result in personal liability for company debts.

The Companies Office also has certain powers to place companies into liquidation, for example when the company fails to appoint board members or file annual reports.

15.   Branches

Foreign companies may also establish business in Sweden in the form of a branch office, administered by a managing director who is resident in the European Economic Area. A branch office is not considered to be a legal person on its own, so its liabilities are borne in full by the parent company. However, the branch is not obliged to have any share capital.

Switzerland

Martin Eckert
MME Partners

1. Types of company with limited liability and applicable legislation

Two types of company are at the forefront of business activity in Switzerland:

- the corporation (*Aktiengesellschaft* (AG)); and
- the limited liability company (*Gesellschaft mit beschränkter Haftung* (GmbH)).

These types of companies offer the following advantages:

- liability and risk that are limited to capital;
- simplified procedure for transfer of participation rights/shares;
- regulated representation rights; and
- comparability with foreign legal entities such as the German GmbH, the US joint stock company, the English limited liability company and the French *Société Anonyme*.

It is also possible to have a Swiss branch of a foreign corporation entered in the commercial register, or to set up a private company that is not a legal entity in its own right.

Articles 620 to 763 of the Code of Obligations form the general legal basis for the corporation.[1] The corporation is a legal entity in its own right, with its own company name, whose predetermined capital is divided into parts (shares) and whose liability is limited to its assets. In general the corporation has three governing bodies: the general shareholders' meeting, the board of directors and the auditors. Under certain circumstances the general shareholders' meeting can waive the annual audit. The shareholders exercise their rights in the general shareholders' meeting. Actual management of the corporation is the exclusive responsibility of the board of directors. The executive officers are appointed by the board.

Articles 772 to 827 of the Code of Obligations form the general legal basis for the limited liability company. Like the corporation, the limited liability company is a legal entity in its own right. In contrast to the corporation, however, a limited liability company's foundation capital must be at least CHF20,000. However, each share transfer must be approved by the partners' meeting and entered in the share register. It is possible to hold several shares. Contrary to the corporation as mentioned above, the members as well as the shares they hold are registered with the commercial register.

---

[1] The provisions of the Corporation Law are available online at www.admin.ch/ch/d/sr/220/index3.html

The corporation is the predominant company form in Switzerland for exclusively capital-related companies. The sole duty of a shareholder of a corporation is to pay in his share of the capital. In contrast, typical elements of a limited liability company are that the partners are known to the public, while the shareholders of a corporation are anonymous. Also, in a limited liability company there are duties connected with the person of a partner, such as the duty of confidentiality and loyalty. The articles of association of a limited liability company may set forth further duties, such as the obligation to pay in additional capital, and a non-competition clause. Like the corporation, the limited liability company may have up to three governing bodies: the general partners' meeting, the management and the auditors. The latter can be waived under certain preconditions.

A glance at the statistics shows that the corporation is by far the more popular type of company. There are various reasons for this. It is often said that the corporation's higher capital base makes it more creditworthy, and that the limited liability company is unsuitable for larger enterprises because of restrictions on the transfer of shares or the non-competition clauses that could be foreseen in the articles of association. Nevertheless, the limited liability company offers several advantages compared with the corporation, as follows:

- lower capital requirements;
- the flexibility to shape the articles of association to suit the partners' needs and therefore give the company a more capital-related character (exclusion of non-competition; no additional duties for the partners, etc) or to create a typical limited liability company that has a more personal character (non-competition clause; additional duties for the partners, etc); and
- the possibility of incorporating further duties for its partners into the articles of association.

As it is a legal entity in its own right, a limited liability company may also be subsequently converted into a corporation.

As the limited liability company is very similar to the corporation, this chapter is based on the applicable regulations governing corporations. For limited liability companies, reference can be made to these regulations unless otherwise indicated.

2.   Incorporation

2.1   Proceedings prior to incorporation

(a)   Name registration
The company name is registered together with the general registration of the company with the Commercial Register.

(b)   Capital contributions
The share capital of the company must amount to at least CHF100,000. At least 20% of the par value of each share must be paid in upon incorporation. In any event, the contribution made must be at least CHF50,000.

In a limited liability company, each member must pay or cover his whole contribution at the time of incorporation.

(c) Declaration of foreign investment
There are no restrictions on foreign investment and no declaration of foreign investment is required.

However, the Federal Act on Acquisition of Real Estate by Persons Resident Abroad restricts the acquisition of real estate by foreigners, foreign-based companies or Swiss-based companies controlled by foreigners. As a rule, such persons require authorisation from the competent cantonal authority. However, the Federal Office of Justice has decided that this act should be abolished in the future.

A company based in Switzerland that is controlled by non-Swiss nationals is not affected by this legislation if the non-Swiss nationals are resident in Switzerland.

(d) Tax number for foreign shareholders
No tax identification number is required for foreign shareholders.

2.2 Incorporation

(a) Bylaws

(i) Essential clauses
The articles of association must include provisions on:
- the company name and the legal seat of the company;
- the corporate purpose;
- the amount of the share capital and the contributions made;
- the number, par value and type of shares;
- the calling of a general shareholders' meeting and the voting rights of the shareholders;
- the administrative bodies and the audit; and
- the form in which the company will publish notices.

(ii) Clauses not foreseen by law
In addition to the clauses required by law, the articles of association include further provisions. However, such provisions should be included only if they are significant for the company.

(iii) Clauses valid only when included in the articles of association
In order to be valid, the following provisions must be included in the articles of association:
- amendment of the articles of association in deviation from legal provisions;
- allocation of profits;
- allocation of interest during construction periods;
- limitation of the duration of the company;
- liquidated damages in a case of delayed contribution;

- authorised or conditional increase in capital;
- possibility to convert registered shares into bearer shares and vice versa;
- restrictions on the transfer of registered shares;
- preferential rights of individual classes of shares, as well as participation certificates, profit-sharing certificates and founders' shares;
- restrictions on voting rights and the rights of shareholders to appoint a proxy;
- cases not provided for by law in which a shareholder resolution requires a qualified majority;
- authorisation to transfer the management to individual members of the board of directors or to third parties;
- organisation and functions of the auditors, where these exceed the legal provisions;
- contributions in kind, acquisition of assets of shareholders or a person closely affiliated to them and special benefits in favour of the founders;
- representation rights in the board of directors of classes and groups of shareholders; and
- special provisions for the protection of minorities or individual groups of shareholders.

If a shareholder makes an in-kind contribution, the articles of association should also indicate the asset and its value, the name of the contributor and the shares issued to him. After 10 years, provisions in the articles of association concerning in-kind contributions or acquisitions of assets may be repealed by shareholder resolution.

(b)   *Execution of public deed*
A corporation can be set up quickly and easily. The foundation document must be publicly notarised by an authorised notary (a lawyer or public servant who is licensed to act as a notary public). The following essential documents/information must be submitted to the notary:
- the articles of association;
- a declaration of the auditors' acceptance of their mandate (in cases where the founders appoint an auditor);
- confirmation from a recognised deposit agent (ie a Swiss bank) that the share capital or foundation capital has been paid in on a blocked account and is at the free disposal of the company;
- personal details of the members of the board of directors, with their specimen signatures notarised by a notary public; and
- a domicile acceptance statement, if the company does not have its own offices.

(c)   *VAT identification number*
If the company is liable for value added tax (VAT), it can request a VAT number prior to registration. The responsible authority is the VAT Main Division of the Federal Tax Administration[2]

---

2   Details are available at: www.estv.admin.ch/d/dienstleistungen/mwst.htm.

(d)   Indirect taxes, incorporation fees and other levies

The following incorporation costs are likely to arise when forming a new corporation or limited liability company with a share capital of CHF100,000.

Notary fees (eg Canton of Zug)	2% of the share capital (minimum CHF500).
Registration fees (commercial register)	Approximately CHF800.
Advisory fees (depending on requirements)	Approximately CHF4,000 to CHF7,000.
Federal stamp duty (1%)	The first CHF 1,000,000 of capital is exempt. Other costs (general expenses) will vary, depending on the company's needs.

(e)   Registration with the Commercial Register

To become a legal entity, the company must be registered with the Commercial Register. The application for registration must contain the document of incorporation, together with the other documents mentioned above. The Commercial Register will check whether the application is complete and conforms with the legislation.

During the registration procedure, the share capital that has been lodged with the deposit agent remains blocked. The procedure ends when the corporation is formally registered in the commercial register. However, the paid-in capital will continue to be blocked until the bank receives an extract from the commercial register proving that the company has been duly registered. Once the application is submitted to the commercial register, it takes five to eight business days for the registration and for receipt of an excerpt from the commercial register. Capital deposit accounts are provided by all Swiss banks.

(f)   Legalisation of official books

Legalisation of the official books is not required. Swiss companies do not have to publish figures (as long as they are not listed on a stock exchange).

(g)   Other declarations – social security

If the company has employees, it must register them with the social security institutions listed in the table overleaf. Premium contributions are, on average, the percentages overleaf of the underlying salary.

Old age and surviving dependants insurance	4.20%
Invalidity insurance	0.70%
Defence duty compensation	0.15%
Unemployment insurance	1%
Family allowance	1.60%
Accident insurance (average rate)	2%
Staff welfare fund (average rate)	6%
Total	**15.65%**

Each employee additionally pays some premiums.

3.   Number of founders

A corporation must have at least one founder (whether a natural or a legal person). The founder(s) can simply hold the shares in trust. If they are private individuals, it is irrelevant whether they are Swiss or foreign nationals. However, the incorporation can become more complicated if one or more founders are foreign companies; in such cases and for practical reasons, it is therefore advisable to authorise private individuals to set up the company and then transfer the shares to the foreign companies after incorporation.

4.   Corporate name – limitations

In principle, corporations and limited liability companies are free to choose their company names within the limits of the general principles of naming companies. The company names of corporations as well as those of limited liability must be clearly distinguishable from any company name already registered in Switzerland. The corporate name must be true and not be misleading or against any public interests. The name can be a fantasy name or it can be derived from the business activity of the company. The suffixes 'Ltd' (AG) for corporations or LLC (GmbH) for limited liability companies must be added to all company names.

Mere descriptive names are not suitable to individualise a legal entity, because they are not distinctive. Combinations of descriptive names or descriptions with fantasy character or with fancy elements are allowed.

It is advisable to check the intended name with the relevant Cantonal Commercial Registry before establishing the company. The names of every company already registered can be called up on the website of the Federal Commercial Registry.[3]

In most cases, it is advisable to protect not only the registration of the company name but also any relevant brands/trademarks and the domain name. The Federal Institute for Intellectual Property is responsible for the protection of brands and trademarks.[4]

5.   Corporate domicile

The corporate domicile can be anywhere within Switzerland. If the statutory

---

3   See www.zefix.admin.ch. More detailed information on companies that are already registered in the commercial register can be accessed online at www.teledata.ch (subject to charges) or at the particular cantonal commercial registries (without being charged).
4   See www.ipi.ch.

domicile differs from the place where the company is actually managed, this may be significant with regard to taxation: as a rule, tax liability arises at the place where the company is actually managed and not at the domicile listed in the registration documents. Cantons and communities/municipalities (*Gemeinden*) decide on their tax level. It is possible to negotiate special tax arrangements.

6. Corporate purpose

A corporation and a limited liability company may pursue any legal commercial and non-commercial purpose.

7. Capital stock

7.1 Minimum capital requirement

A corporation must have a share capital of at least CHF100,000. The share capital can be divided into bearer and/or registered shares. The par value of those shares must be at least CHF0.01. When establishing the corporation, at least 20% of the par value of each share must be paid in and the total paid-up share capital must amount to at least CHF50,000.

A limited liability company must have a foundation capital of CHF20,000. The par value of the shares must be at least CHF100. In the case of a financial restructuring, the par value can be decreased to a minimum of CHF1. When establishing a limited liability company, the respective contribution of the issue price of each share must be paid in full.

7.2 Nature of contributions

The easiest way to set up a corporation is through cash contributions. These must be deposited with an institution subject to the Federal Law of November 8 1934 on Banks and Saving Banks and placed at the exclusive disposal of the company. The bank will release the sums contributed only upon registration of the company in the commercial register.

Special provisions must be considered where in-kind contributions are made. An in-kind contribution is valid only if:

- it is made based on a written or publicly notarised contract for in-kind contributions;
- the company, upon registration with the Commercial Register, may immediately dispose of the asset; and
- a special auditors' confirmation is presented.

The in-kind contribution must be realisable. The articles of association must indicate the asset and its value, the name of the contributor and the shares issued to him.

The company can also acquire assets from shareholders or third parties, or it can intend to make such acquisitions of assets. The articles of association must indicate the asset, the name of the alienator and the consideration to be given by the company.

If, upon incorporation, particular benefits are stipulated in favour of the founders or other persons, the articles of association must list the names of the beneficiaries and precisely indicate the benefits with regard to content and value.

The assets acquired and consideration given by the company, as well as the content and value of any special benefits, must be registered with the Commercial Register.

Provisions in the articles of association concerning in-kind contributions or acquisitions of assets may be repealed by shareholder resolution after 10 years.

7.3   Partial payments

Upon incorporation, a contribution of at least 20% of the par value of each share must be made. In any case, the contribution must be at least CHF50,000.

Upon incorporation of a limited liability company, the full amount of the par value of each share must be paid in.

7.4   Representation of shares

There are three types of shares: bearer shares, registered shares and participation certificates.

Bearer shares are made out to the bearer – in other words, the person who possesses the share certificate is recognised as the shareholder. Bearer shares are issued only after payment of the full par value. Shares issued prior to full payment are null and void.

Registered shares are entered in the share register of the company under the name of the specific shareholder to whom the shares belong.

Part of the share capital may be issued in the form of so-called 'participation certificates'. Essentially, these are shares without voting rights.

7.5   Transfer of shares

(a)   Restrictions

There are no mandatory restrictions on the transfer of bearer shares. However, the law and the articles of association may impose restrictions on the transfer of registered shares.

Registered shares that are not fully paid up may be transferred only with the consent of the company, unless they are acquired through succession, division of an estate, matrimonial property law or debt enforcement. The company may refuse its consent to the transfer only if the acquirer's solvency is questionable and security is not provided.

The articles of association may provide that registered shares may be transferred only with the consent of the company. This restriction also applies to the creation of a life estate (usufruct). If the company goes into liquidation, these restrictions are deemed null and void. The company may refuse its consent if:

- it gives a valid reason that is mentioned in the articles of association; or
- it offers to take over the shares for its own account or for the account of other shareholders or third parties at the real value at the time of the request.

Valid reasons are deemed to be provisions regarding the composition of the shareholders' circle that justify refusal in view of the company's purpose or its economic independence. Further, the company may refuse the transfer if the acquirer does not expressly declare that he is acquiring the shares in his own name and for his own account. If the shares are acquired by succession, division of an estate, matrimonial property law or debt enforcement, the company may refuse its consent only if it offers to take over the shares at their real value.

The acquirer may request that the judge at the company's domicile determine the real value of the shares. The company bears the cost. If the acquirer does not reject the takeover offer within one month of learning the real value, it is deemed to be accepted.

The articles of association may not impose further restrictions on the transfer of registered shares.

(b) *Formalities*

Bearer shares are transferred simply by being physically handed over to the new owner. The transfer of registered shares requires the handing over of the duly endorsed share certificate.

8. Equity

8.1 Reserves

In addition to the share capital, the company is required to create reserves. Five per cent of the annual profit must be allocated to the general reserve until this has reached 20% of the paid-up share capital (the obligatory general reserve). The creation of extra reserves may be provided for in the articles of association.

8.2 Increase in share capital

There are three ways to increase the share capital:
- ordinary increase of share capital;
- authorised increase of share capital; and
- conditional increase of share capital.

All three ways require a shareholder resolution since amendment of the articles of association is required.

(a) *Ordinary capital increase*

The general shareholders' meeting resolves on the capital increase and empowers the board of directors to increase the capital within three months.

(b) *Authorised capital increase*

By amending the articles of association, the general shareholders' meeting may authorise the board of directors to issue new shares at its discretion within a period of up to two years.

(c) *Conditional capital increase*

The general shareholders' meeting may indirectly increase the capital subject to conditions by issuing (or authorising the board of directors to issue) rights to acquire new shares, such as options or conversion rights. Such rights may be issued to employees of the corporation or may be issued in connection with capital markets transactions such as the issuance of convertible bonds, bonds with stock options or similar instruments.

8.3 Equity–capital ratio

Swiss legislation does not oblige companies to maintain a balance between share capital and own resources. However, if the latest annual balance sheet shows that half of the share capital and the legal reserves are no longer covered, the board of directors must call a general shareholders' meeting and propose financial reorganisation.

In a case of substantiated concerns of over-indebtedness, an interim balance sheet must be prepared and submitted to the auditors for examination. If the interim balance sheet shows that the company's assets are insufficient to cover its liabilities, the board of directors must notify the judge accordingly.

9. Administration

The corporation has three governing bodies: the general shareholders' meeting, the board of directors and the auditors.

9.1 General shareholders' meeting

The general shareholders' meeting is the supreme governing body of the corporation and is empowered to:

- set out and amend the articles of association;
- approve the annual accounts;
- decide on the distribution of profits; and
- discharge the directors from liability.

The general shareholders' meeting elects the board of directors and the auditors.

The general shareholders' meeting must be convened at least once a year (within six months of the close of the business year). Extraordinary general meetings can be called at any time by:

- the board of directors;
- shareholders representing at least 10% of the share capital; or
- the auditors.

(a) Quorum requirements

(i) Attendance

There are no quorum requirements for a general shareholders' meeting to be legally convened. However, the articles of association may establish such quorums.

(ii) Voting

The general shareholders' meeting passes resolutions and carries out elections by absolute majority of the votes allocated to the shares represented, to the extent that the law or the articles of association do not provide otherwise.

A shareholder resolution passed by at least two-thirds of the votes represented and by absolute majority of the par value of shares represented is required for the following:

- a change in the corporate purpose;
- the issuance of shares with privileged voting rights;
- the introduction of restrictions on the transfer of registered shares;
- an increase in capital, whether authorised or conditional;
- an increase in capital out of equity against in-kind contributions or for the purpose of acquiring assets and the granting of special benefits;
- any limitation or withdrawal of pre-emptive rights;
- a change in the registered seat of the company; and
- the dissolution of the company.

(b) *Challenging resolutions*

The board of directors and any shareholder can take legal action against the company to challenge shareholder resolutions that violate the law or the articles of association. In particular, resolutions may be challenged that:

- withdraw or limit shareholders' rights, thereby violating the law or the articles of association;
- withdraw or limit shareholders' rights without proper reason;
- discriminate against or disadvantage shareholders in a manner not justified by the corporate purpose; or
- withdraw the profit orientation of the company without the consent of all shareholders.

The right to challenge lapses if a suit is not filed within two months of the general shareholders' meeting.

Furthermore, shareholder resolutions are null and void if they:

- withdraw or limit the shareholders' right to participate in the general shareholders' meeting, the minimum voting right, the right to sue or other rights granted by mandatory provisions of law;
- limit the shareholders' rights to control beyond the extent provided by law; or
- disregard the fundamental structures of the company or violate the provisions for protection of the capital.

9.2   Board of directors

The board of directors is the management body of the corporation. It has the following non-transferable and inalienable duties:

- ultimate management of the company and issuance of the necessary directives;
- establishment of the organisation;
- structuring of the accounting system and the financial controls, as well as financial planning in so far as this is necessary to manage the company;
- appointment and removal of persons entrusted with management and representation;

- ultimate supervision of persons entrusted with management, in particular in view of compliance with the law, the articles of association, regulations and directives;
- preparation of the business report and the general shareholders' meeting, and implementation of its resolutions; and
- notification to a judge in a case of over-indebtedness.

The board may, by means of internal organisational regulations, nominate individual members (delegates) or third parties (managers, authorised clerks) to carry out those functions of management that may be delegated.

The board of directors consists of one or more members. There is no requirement for a board member to be a shareholder. At least one member of the board must have signatory power to represent the company. Furthermore, the corporation must be represented by at least one natural person residing in Switzerland; this person can be a member of the board or a managing director.

When appointing members of the board of directors, it may be necessary to obtain work permits for non-Swiss people.

The board of directors must prepare an annual report that, in particular, includes information on the progress of the business, the company's economic and financial situation and any increases in capital that have taken place.

The annual general shareholders' meeting must be held at least once a year. This is called by the board of directors.

(a) Different systems of administration

The board of directors manages the business of the company. However, this does not mean that the board of directors must carry out all business itself. The articles of association can authorise the board of directors to delegate the management, fully or partially, to individual members or third parties by way of organisational regulation. Such regulation organises the management, determines the position to be held, defines the duties and regulates, in particular, reporting requirements.

The board of directors can assign only the preparation and implementation of its resolutions or the supervision of business transactions to committees or individual members. Therefore, it must provide for adequate reporting to its members.

(b) Term of office, resignation and removal of directors

Directors are elected by the general shareholders' meeting. The members of the board are elected for three years unless otherwise provided for by the articles of association.

Members of the board have the right to terminate their mandate at any time. The general shareholders' meeting is entitled to remove members of the board.

(c) Directors' liability to third parties

If, upon the founding of a company or upon the issue of shares, bonds or other securities, statements are made or disseminated that are incorrect, misleading or in breach of the legal requirements on issue prospectuses or similar instruments, anyone who intentionally or negligently contributed thereto is liable to the acquirers of the securities for any damage caused.

Founders, members of the board of directors and all persons who participated in the foundation become liable to the company, as well as to shareholders and creditors of the company, for any damage caused:

- if they indicate intentionally or negligently in an incorrect or misleading manner, conceal or disguise in-kind contributions, the acquisition of assets or the granting of special benefits to the shareholders or to other persons in the articles of association, a founders' report or a report on a capital increase, or if the approval of such measures violates the law in any other manner;
- if they intentionally or negligently cause the company to be entered in the commercial register on the basis of a confirmation or deed containing incorrect statements; or
- if they knowingly contribute to the acceptance of subscriptions from insolvent persons.

The members of the board of directors and all persons engaged in the management or liquidation of the company are liable, not only to the company but also to shareholders and to company obligees, for any damage caused by the intentional or negligent violation of their duties.

(d) Non-competition

Members of the board of directors are not bound by a duty of non-competition. However, they are obliged by law to carry out their duties with due care and must duly safeguard the interests of the company.

(e) Special duties of secrecy and loyalty

The members of the board of directors and third parties engaged in the management of the company must carry out their duties with due care and duly safeguard the interests of the company. They should give equal treatment to shareholders in equal circumstances.

(f) Corporate crime

If a crime is committed within the company and the perpetrator cannot be verified due to deficient organisation of the company, the company itself can be held responsible. In cases of money laundering, cooperation with criminal organisations, the financing of terrorism or the bribing of Swiss or foreign officials, the company may be prosecuted independently of the perpetrator if it failed to take all necessary and reasonable organisational precautions to avoid such crimes.

9.3 Others

(a) Holders of power of attorney

Management of a corporation is usually handled by the board of directors and by managers appointed by the board. In order to limit personal liability, responsibilities and authorities should be clearly set out in a set of internal organisational regulations. Those people authorised to sign on behalf of the corporation must be registered in the commercial register.

(b)   *Auditors*

The responsibility of the auditors is to ascertain whether the accounts and the annual financial statements and the consolidated financial statements, as well as the motion to the general meeting of shareholders with regard to the distribution of the profit in the balance sheet, comply with the law and the articles of association.

An ordinary audit is required if the corporation exceeds two of the following three conditions within two consecutive business years:

- a balance sheet total of CHF10 million;
- a turnover of CHF20 million; and
- an annual average of 50 full-time employment positions.

If the conditions for an ordinary audit are not met, a limited audit is required. The limited audit is less extensive and profound. With the consent of all shareholders, the limited audit may be waived if the company does not have an average annual number of full-time employment positions of more than 10.

The audit firm needs to be registered with the Federal Supervisory Authority of Audit Firms in Bern.[5]

10.   Business year, commencement of activities

The business year is defined in the articles of association. It does not need to coincide with the calendar year.

11.   Financial statements

The law prescribes a certain minimum structure for the balance sheet and the income statement. When preparing these documents, it is important to comply with the principles of orderly presentation of accounts (eg completeness, clarity, materiality, prudence, continuity). The company's position in terms of assets and profitability should be able to be assessed as reliably as possible from the documents. However, this does not mean that even a transparent set of accounts complies with the 'true and fair view' principle, since the valuation regulations enshrined in law permit the creation of hidden reserves.

Holding companies that meet the following criteria must prepare consolidated financial accounts each year. They must:

- exercise control, by means of majority voting rights or in some other way, over one or more companies; and
- have total assets of more than CHF10 million, turnover of more than CHF20 million or more than 200 employees.

No particular consolidation or valuation rules are foreseen by law, apart from the general principles of orderly presentation of accounts. However, in order to meet

---

5   See www.revisionsaufsichtsbehoerde.ch.

international requirements, it is permissible – and indeed common – for companies to use other standards, such as International Accounting Standards, US Generally Accepted Accounting Principles or comparable guidelines used within the European Union.

11.1 Company tax

The Swiss tax system is characterised by various levels of direct taxation: direct federal tax, cantonal taxes and municipal taxes.

The tax laws in the individual cantons are often very different from each other. The cantons were required to adapt their tax laws to the Federal Tax Harmonisation Law by January 1 2001. However, this harmonisation was not intended to make every canton adopt exactly the same tax legislation. Important decisions, such as the fixing of tax rates and tariffs, remain under the authority of the cantons.

Direct federal tax, cantonal and municipal taxes are levied on the income (profit) of a corporation. The capital is subject only to cantonal and municipal taxes.

Tax rates vary, depending on the activity of the company. In practice, a distinction can be made between operating companies, holding companies, management companies and principal companies, as set out next.

(a) *Operating companies*

Operating companies are enterprises that carry out trading, manufacturing or service activities. They are subject to ordinary taxation.

Tax is payable on the taxable net profit and the paid-in foundation capital, as well as on disclosed and taxed hidden reserves.

Type of tax	Capital and reserves	Tax rate
Direct federal tax	0%	8.5% of profit
Canton/municipality simple[a] tax (eg canton of Zug[b])	0.5‰	4% of profits up to CHF100,000 7% on profit in excess of CHF100,000

(a) Based on the simple tax, the canton, the municipalities and the church denominations levy multiples thereof (eg collectively, a company seated in the city of Zug had to pay 159.5% of the simple tax in 2005).
(b) On average, the canton of Zug has one of the lowest tax rate of all Swiss cantons.

(b) *Holding companies*

In contrast to direct federal tax, which provides only limited privileges for holding companies, the cantonal tax legislation provides privileged taxation for certain corporations, depending on their activities.

The term 'holding company' applies to those companies whose purpose is the ongoing management of investments in other companies and that conduct no business activity in Switzerland. In addition, the investments held or the revenues earned from them must represent at least two-thirds of the entire assets and/or income.

Holding companies are exempt from cantonal income tax and pay a reduced rate of capital tax. At federal level, and based on the income from significant investments in other companies, it is possible to claim a tax reduction (the so-called 'participation deduction'). In the same way, a tax reduction is granted at cantonal level for significant investments in other companies.

Type of tax	Capital and reserves	Tax rate
Direct federal tax[a]	0%	8.5% of profits
Canton/municipality (eg canton of Zug)	0.02‰	0%

(a) The confederation does not offer a holding privilege as such. It does, however, provide a participation deduction.

(c)   *Management companies*

A management company may be a domicile or mixed company. Domicile companies are characterised by the fact that while their business address is in Switzerland, they do not conduct any actual business activity in Switzerland. In particular, they have neither staff nor offices of their own. Mixed companies are companies whose business activity primarily relates to business abroad; any business activity in Switzerland itself is of a secondary nature.

For management companies, revenue from Swiss sources is taxed in full, whereas income from foreign sources is taxed proportionately, depending on the extent of the activity. Income from investments in other companies is tax exempt.

The business activity must be performed predominantly outside Switzerland – that is, at least 80% of both sales and purchases must take place outside that country (the 'bi-dimensional principle'). Exceptionally, purchases may be made in Switzerland as long as payment is on an arm's-length basis.

Mixed companies cannot be involved in their own production or distribution activities in Switzerland.

(d)   *Principal companies*

Principal companies process trading transactions with foreign subsidiaries and sister companies on a commission basis, and they allocate manufacturing orders to these foreign companies. For this kind of business activity, principal companies can claim a deduction at the level of direct federal tax for business conducted outside Switzerland.

The distribution of profits (eg in the form of dividends or other kinds of distribution) is subject to Swiss federal withholding tax, which is levied at source at a current (2009) rate of 35%. This tax may be refunded if a double-taxation treaty concluded with the recipient's country of residence provides for a refund.

Turnover from supplies of goods and services within the Swiss territory is subject to VAT at a current rate of 7.6% on gross sales. Liability for VAT arises when domestic gross sales reach CHF75,000 a year. For certain goods and services (eg newspapers, medicines, food and drink), the rate is 2.4%. Turnover derived from the supply of goods and services to customers abroad is exempt from VAT.

11.2 Annual accounts

(a) Documents

A business report must be prepared for each business year. It must contain the annual financial statement, the annual report and, where required, the consolidated financial statement.

The annual financial statement must be prepared in accordance with the principles of orderly presentation of accounts, in such a manner as offers the most reliable picture of the company's financial situation. It must also contain the previous year's figures. In particular, the proper rendering of accounts must observe the following principles:

- completeness of the annual financial statement;
- clarity and materiality of statements;
- prudence;
- continuation of the company's activity;
- consistency in presentation and valuation; and
- prohibition against the set-off of assets and liabilities, as well as of expenses and income.

The profit and loss statement must show operational and non-operational income, extraordinary income and expenses. The income statement must separately show revenue from deliveries and performances, financial income and profits from the sale of capital assets. The expense statement must separately show material and merchandise expenses, personnel expenses, financial expenses and depreciation expenses. The profit and loss statement must show the annual profit or loss.

The balance sheet must show current assets and capital assets, outside funds and equity.

If the company joins one or more companies under a common management (ie a group of companies) it must prepare consolidated financial statements.

(b) Audit report

The auditors must examine whether the bookkeeping and annual accounts, as well as the proposal to the general shareholders' meeting on the distribution of profits, comply with the law and the articles of association.

The auditors must provide a written report on the results of their audit to the general shareholders' meeting. They will recommend either that the annual accounts be approved with or without qualifications, or that they be rejected.

If, in the course of their examination, the auditors discover violations of law or the articles of association, they must report this in writing to the board of directors and, in important cases, to the general shareholders' meeting.

(c) **Approval and distribution of profits**

Each shareholder is entitled to a proportionate share of the profits shown in the balance sheet, to the extent that these are to be distributed to the shareholders in accordance with the law and the articles of association. Only the general shareholders' meeting is entitled to declare dividends. Dividends may be paid only out of balance sheet profits or out of reserves created for this purpose.

(d) **Deposit and publication**

In general, the business books and accounting records need not be made public. However, business books, accounting records and business correspondence must be preserved for a period of 10 years.

Once the annual financial statements and consolidated financial statements of listed companies have been approved by the general shareholders' meeting, they must be published in the Swiss *Official Gazette* or a copy must be sent to each person who requests it within one year of approval.

12. Company reorganisation

The Merger Law regulates mergers and de-mergers, the conversion of companies and the so-called 'transfer of assets and liabilities' (*Vermögensübertragung*).

The Merger Law provides for two methods of statutory merger. In a merger by absorption, one or more companies are dissolved and their businesses are transferred to an existing company. In a merger by amalgamation, all companies participating in the merger are dissolved and their businesses are transferred to a new company.

A company that is being taken over will be dissolved and deleted from the commercial register without being liquidated. Its businesses will be transferred to the surviving company by way of universal succession.

Various forms of de-merger may be distinguished. In a spin-off, two or more companies may be formed out of an existing company, which continues to exist. In a division, the businesses of a company are transferred to other companies and the existing company is dissolved.

In a conversion, the company continues to exist; it is merely the legal form that changes. Assets and liabilities, contracts and shareholders' ownership remain unaffected.

The transfer of assets and liabilities allows for the transfer and sale of part of a business or an entire business. It is a very broad concept, which may help achieve certain reorganisations or events that are not otherwise regulated by law.

13. Dissolution and liquidation

A company will be dissolved in the following situations:

- in accordance with the articles of association;
- by resolution of the general shareholders' meeting, executed in the form of a notarial deed;
- upon an adjudication of bankruptcy;
- by court order, where shareholders representing at least 10% of the share capital request dissolution for valid reasons (alternatively, the judge may

decide on another solution appropriate in the circumstances and acceptable to the interested parties); and

- in all other cases provided for by law.

The board of directors must apply for the dissolution to be recorded in the commercial register, except where the company is dissolved following an adjudication of bankruptcy or judicial decision.

The liquidation procedure begins with the preparation of a balance sheet. Creditors recorded in the books of the company or known in any other way must be informed of the dissolution by special notice and requested to file their claims. Unknown creditors and creditors whose domicile are not known are notified and requested to file their claims by way of publication in the *Official Gazette* and in any additional manner stipulated in the articles of association.

Distribution to the shareholders may not be effected until a year has elapsed since the date on which the call for the filing of claims was issued for the third time. As an exception, distribution may be made following a three-month period if a qualified auditor can confirm that all liabilities have been satisfied and that, under the circumstances, it may be assumed that no third-party interests are jeopardised.

After the liquidation has ended, the liquidators must notify the Mercantile Registry and request it to delete the company name from the commercial register.

14. Branches

Instead of incorporating a subsidiary in Switzerland, a foreign company may also establish one or several branch offices. Branch offices have a certain organisational and financial independence from the principal office: under Swiss law, a branch office can enter into contracts and execute and settle transactions in its own name, and can sue and be sued at its place of business. Legally, however, the branch office is part of the foreign parent company. If the foreign parent is liquidated or becomes insolvent, the effects of such liquidation or insolvency also extend to the Swiss branch office.

United Kingdom

David Kent
Taylor Wessing LLP
Nilesh Shah
Blick Rothenberg

1. Introduction

The United Kingdom boasts some of the most straightforward rules for company formation in the world, as recent rule changes have sought to make incorporation even simpler and the minimum share capital is £1.

The ease of company formation is one of the main reasons why the United Kingdom is the first port of call for an overseas company wishing to set up in Europe. Similarly, entrepreneurs choose the UK to start up their companies, hoping to raise venture capital or private equity funding or perhaps to become a vehicle that will eventually be listed or become part of a group listed on a UK public exchange. The straightforward rules encourage business growth.

English law (the law of England and Wales) is based on common law, which has grown and changed in accordance with its needs throughout the centuries. This makes the overall environment for business in the United Kingdom understandable and sensible.

This chapter is an introduction to company formation, regulatory and tax issues. However, to give it some balance the chapter also briefly reviews the steps following incorporation, namely stock options, the financial services regime, listing procedures, reorganisations, insolvency and the closure of a corporate entity. There are alternative suggestions for setting up and appointing consultants on a shoestring budget, together with a list of do's and don'ts.

2. Changes in company law

The law has been subject to many recent changes due to the implementation of the Companies Act 2006 (the 2006 Act), which will repeal much of the Companies Act 1985 (the 1985 Act). Some of the 2006 Act has been brought into force in stages, with many sections still due to be implemented in August and October 2009 (the changes in August 2009 are as a result of the implementation of the Shareholders' Rights Directive). As far as possible we have tried to flag the anticipated amendments; however, implementation dates are subject to change.

3. Types of company with limited liability

3.1 Which entity?

Overseas companies setting up in the UK have a choice of setting up a branch office or a private limited company (called a subsidiary if the owner is an overseas corporation). If the activities of the overseas company are non-taxable, a 'place of business' registration could be made. A branch is simply a registration of the overseas entity in the UK, whereas a private limited company will create a separate legal entity.

The most common choice of entity is the private limited company. The main benefit is that the company's shareholders (members) benefit from limited liability, so UK liabilities can be ring-fenced from those of the overseas parent company. There is also a commercial benefit to setting up a private limited company: UK and European companies are more familiar with this format and are likely to be more comfortable dealing with it as it has more of a permanent presence in the UK (branches can be closed down in one day). However, it costs more to maintain a private company due to the need to prepare annual accounts (see section 12 below) and it is more time consuming and costly to close a private company down.

3.2 Limited or unlimited company?

Section 3 of the 2006 Act divides companies in England and Wales into three categories:

- **Companies limited by shares.** The members' liability is limited to the value of their shareholding. Therefore, if their shares are fully paid up, the members do not have any further liability if the company is wound up and has outstanding liabilities. Companies limited by shares are the most common form of company in the United Kingdom and can be either a public or a private company.
- **Companies limited by guarantee.** The members' liability is limited to the amount the members have undertaken to contribute to the assets of the company, in the event of the company being wound up. Companies limited by guarantee are fairly rare in practice and are usually used by non-profit organisations. Private companies can be limited by guarantee and public companies can be limited by guarantee provided that they have a share capital. Companies limited by guarantee are not required to have the word 'limited' after their name.
- **Unlimited company.** An unlimited company means that there is no limit to the liability of the company's members and the members may be required to contribute all of their assets on a winding-up. Only private companies can be unlimited; for this reason, these companies are rare in practice.

3.3 Private or public limited company?

Companies limited by shares or by guarantee (with a share capital) can be either a public company or a private company. Private companies must have 'Limited' or 'Ltd' at the end of their name and public companies must use 'plc'.

The main difference between private and public companies is that a private company cannot offer any of its shares or debentures to the public and they cannot be listed on any stock exchange. A public company is subject to a minimum share capital requirement of £50,000 (or the euro equivalent), whereas a private company is not subject to a minimum and may have a share capital of as little as £1 (although private companies will usually have a share capital of £1,000).

Public companies are also subject to more onerous regulation. Public companies must:

- have at least two members;
- have a company secretary;
- hold annual general meetings,
- hold general meetings (as opposed to using a written-resolution procedure); and
- cannot file abbreviated accounts if they are a small or medium-sized company.

4. Limited liability partnerships

Limited liability partnerships (LLPs) were introduced into the United Kingdom by the Limited Liability Partnerships Act 2000. An LLP is a separate legal entity with limited liability similar to a private limited company; the LLP partners have a relationship that is analogous to that of a partnership so they are governed by a partnership agreement, there are no directors or shareholders and the LLP is taxed like a partnership. The general partner runs the business. The limited partners are not liable for more than they have put in, but they also have no power to run the business. These are complex entities to set up and operate. They are also beyond the scope of this chapter and detailed legal advice should be obtained as necessary.

5. Company law

5.1 The registered office

The registered office is the official address of the company and the address to which Companies House (the UK companies' registry) will send notices and reminders. The registered office must be:

- in England and Wales (if the company is to be registered there);
- in Scotland (if the company is to be registered there); or
- in Wales if the memorandum of association says that the registered office must be there.

The registered office must always be an effective address for delivering correspondence and documents to the company. Any change in address must be notified to Companies House on a Form 287. Until Companies House has entered this form onto its database, the change does not take effect.

A company with its registered office in England or Wales must send all documents to Companies House in London or Cardiff. A company with its registered office in Scotland must send all documents to Companies House in Edinburgh.

The officers of the company

The directors and the company secretary are officers of the company.

The 2006 Act requires that a private company must appoint at least one director, while a public company must appoint at least two directors. A sole director of a private company cannot also occupy the position of secretary of the company.

There are a few restrictions that prevent a person from becoming a director:

- the person must not have been disqualified from acting as a company director (unless they have been given permission by the court to act for a particular company);
- the person must not be an undischarged bankrupt (unless they have been given permission by the court to act for a particular company);
- the person must not be under the age of 16 (from October 1 2008); and
- at least one director must be a natural person, ie an individual (from October 1 2008). This avoids a corporate director from holding office as a sole director of a company.

Under the 2006 Act, a private company is no longer required to have a secretary but can appoint one if it wishes to do so. It should be noted, however, that where a company decides not to appoint a secretary, the duties previously carried out by the secretary will still need to be performed. The company secretary need not be a natural person.

A public company must appoint a secretary. The directors must ensure that the secretary is a person who appears to them to have the requisite experience and knowledge to fulfil the role.

Directors and secretaries do not have to be resident in the United Kingdom.

5.3 Authorised and issued share capital

Section 7 below provides further information on authorised and issued share capital.

5.4 Incorporation

Ready-made companies are available from company formation agents, whose names and addresses appear in business directories. The buyer and his professional advisers may choose between a ready-made company (ie one that has already been incorporated) or a custom-made company (ie the buyer will specify the company name, nominal share capital and objects of the company). The fastest option is generally to buy a ready-made company because trading may begin as soon as the transfer formalities are completed.

For those wanting to form a company themselves, the following documents, together with the appropriate registration fee (see section 5.12 below) must be submitted to Companies House:

- a memorandum of association;
- articles of association (except where Table A is adopted without modification – see section 5.6 below);
- a completed Form 10; and
- a completed Form 12.

5.5 The memorandum of association

The memorandum of association under the 1985 Act and the Companies Act 1989 is one of the documents of the company's constitution. It constitutes a company's charter with the outside world and in particular with the persons with whom it will transact, either directly or indirectly, in the course of its business. Provisions in the memorandum will override any contradicting or conflicting provisions in the articles of association (see section 5.6 below).

Under the 1985 Act, the subscribers to the memorandum are the first shareholders of the company. There must be at least one subscriber to the memorandum of a private company and at least two subscribers for a public company. By subscribing to the memorandum, the subscribers agree to take at least one share each in the company. Each subscriber must sign the company's memorandum in front of a witness, who must also sign this document, before sending it to Companies House.

The 1985 Act provides that the memorandum of association of a company must state:

- the name of the company;
- in the case of public companies only, a statement that the company is a public limited company;
- whether the domicile of the company is to be in England and Wales (ie it may be situated in either), in Wales (ie it may be situated only in Wales) or in Scotland;
- the objects of the company;
- where applicable, that the liability of the members is limited;
- in the case of a company limited by shares, the amount of authorised share capital with which the company is to be incorporated and how the shares are to be divided; or, for a company limited by guarantee, the amount each member undertakes to contribute to the assets of the company in the event of it being wound up;
- the names and addresses of the subscribers and, in the case of a company limited by shares, the number of shares to be taken by each (a minimum of one share must be taken by each subscriber).

The last three points above do not apply in the case of an unlimited company.

(a) Changes to the memorandum under the 2006 Act

Under the 2006 Act, any company incorporated from October 1 2009 onwards will have a memorandum that is a much simpler document and one that will look very different from that of a company registered under the 1985 Act. The 2006 Act retains the current requirement that individuals who wish to form a company must subscribe their names to the memorandum. However, this is all the memorandum will contain. The memorandum will simply state that the subscribers wish to form a company under the 2006 Act and have agreed to become members.

Matters that are currently contained in the memorandum, such as the company's name, will not need to be included in the memorandum after September 2009 but will either be dealt with in the articles or, in the case of the name, just recorded on the certificate of incorporation. The memorandum will essentially be a 'snapshot' of part of the company's constitution at the point of incorporation. It will therefore have no continuing relevance and it will not be possible to amend or update the memorandum.

For companies formed under the 2006 Act, from October 1 2009 onwards constitutional information of the type formerly set out in the memorandum will be set out in the articles. The 2006 Act provides that a company's objects will be unrestricted unless the articles specifically restrict them. This applies to both new and existing companies. Existing companies will not be required to amend their articles to reflect this change, but may do so if they wish.

The 2006 Act will also remove the requirement for a company to have an authorised share capital. For existing companies their current authorised share capital will be treated as a restriction in their articles of association, which can be removed by ordinary resolution. The 2006 Act will allow different currency denominations and different classes of shares denominated in different currencies. The only exception is that the initial minimum share capital requirement for a public company can only be met by shares denominated in either sterling or euros.

The 2006 Act will also remove the requirement for a public company to have at least two shareholders. With effect from October 1 2009 any type of company (and not just a private company) can be formed by a single person.

5.6   Articles of association

The articles of association set out the rules for the running and regulation of the company's internal affairs. The articles will commonly cover the rights of shareholders, the procedure upon an issue or transfer of shares, the rights attaching to shares, the appointment, removal and powers of the directors, and the conduct of board and general (shareholder) meetings.

A model set of articles for a company limited by shares is contained in 'Table A'. Table A applies to both public and private companies limited by shares and is contained in the Companies (Tables A to F) Regulations 1985 (SI 1985 No 805); it was amended by the Companies (Tables A to F) (Amendment) Regulations 2007 (SI 2007 No 2541) and The Companies (Tables A to F) (Amendment) (No 2) Regulations 2007 (SI 2007 No 2826). A company limited by shares can choose whether to:

- adopt Table A in whole or in part as its own articles of association;
- adopt Table A with modifications; or
- adopt its own articles.

If no articles are registered, then Table A will apply in its entirety and will automatically become the regulations of the company.

Table A comprises a set of regulations covering many – but by no means all – aspects of a company's internal affairs. It comprises 118 regulations covering the following range of topics:

- interpretation;
- share capital;
- share certificates;
- liens on shares;
- calls on shares and forfeiture;
- transfer of shares;
- transmission of shares upon the death or bankruptcy of a member;

- alteration of share capital;
- purchase by a company of its own shares;
- general meetings;
- notice of general meetings;
- proceedings at general meetings;
- votes of members;
- number of directors;
- alternate directors;
- powers of directors;
- delegation of directors' powers;
- appointment and retirement of directors;
- disqualification and removal of directors;
- remuneration of directors;
- directors' expenses;
- directors' appointments and interests;
- directors' gratuities and pensions;
- proceedings of directors;
- the company secretary;
- minutes;
- the company seal;
- dividends;
- accounts;
- capitalisation of profits;
- notices;
- winding-up; and
- indemnities to officers and auditors.

The regulations also contain other forms of articles: a private company limited by guarantee can adopt model articles as contained in Table C in the aforementioned range of tables, whilst an unlimited company can adopt model articles as contained in Table E.

Many private companies limited by shares find it convenient to adopt articles in a shortened format that incorporates Table A. Where a company chooses to adopt its own articles, it should be noted that no effect can be given to any regulations in the articles that conflict with any statutory requirements; and should any regulations in the articles conflict with any provisions in its memorandum of association, then the provisions of the memorandum prevail.

Under Section 9 of the 1985 Act, a company may at any time (but subject to its memorandum of association), by special resolution (75% majority) passed by the members, alter any or all of the conditions contained in its articles of association.

Each subscriber must sign the company's articles of association in front of a witness, who must also sign the document, before it is submitted to Companies House.

5.7 Changes to model articles under the 2006 Act

The 2006 Act has introduced the following with effect from October 1 2009:

- a simplified set of model articles for private companies limited by shares, which is more suited to the way smaller companies operate;
- a separate set of model articles for public companies limited by shares, with a clearer layout and drafting; and
- a set of model articles for private companies limited by guarantee.

The model articles for private companies limited by shares are divided into five principal areas:

- interpretation and limitation of liability (Articles 1 and 2);
- directors (Articles 3 to 20);
- shares and distributions (Articles 21 to 36);
- decision making by shareholders (Articles 37 to 47); and
- administrative arrangements (Articles 48 to 53).

Section 18 of the 2006 Act carries forward the requirement that all registered companies must have articles and they must be contained in a single document divided into consecutively numbered paragraphs. Companies are free to adopt, vary or exclude some or all of the model articles, subject to the provisions of the 2006 Act.

Under Section 19 of the 2006 Act, the Secretary of State may prescribe model articles for different types of companies and this will act as a default where a company has not registered articles or where its registered articles do not cover a particular matter.

Existing companies can continue without change to their articles or will be able to replace them with the new model articles if their members pass a special resolution to do so.

5.8 Form 10

Form 10 gives details of the first director(s), secretary and the intended registered office address. The company's directors must provide their full names and residential addresses, date of birth, nationality, occupation and details of other UK directorships they hold or have held within the last five years. Alternatively, if a confidentiality order has been granted, a service address must be given. Many prominent companies have achieved confidentiality orders.

As previously mentioned, a private company does not have to appoint a secretary, but should it decide to do so then the name and residential address of the secretary must be included in Form 10.

Each officer appointed and each subscriber (or their agent) must sign and date Form 10.

(a) Changes under the 2006 Act

With effect from October 1 2009, all directors and secretaries will be able to provide either a service address or a residential address for the public record. If a service address is provided, then the residential address will be kept on a restricted access register. In addition, from October 1 2009 directors will no longer be required to provide details of other UK directorships.

5.9 Form 12

Form 12 is a statutory declaration of compliance that confirms that all the legal requirements relating to the formation of a company have been complied with. It can be signed by the solicitor who is forming the company or by one of the people named as a director or secretary of the company.

Form 12 must be signed in the presence of a suitably qualified person (eg a commissioner for oaths, a notary public, a justice of the peace or a solicitor).

5.10 Registration

Once the memorandum and articles of association, together with Forms 10 and 12, have been signed and dated (they must all have the same date), they can be submitted to Companies House for registration, together with the appropriate filing fee (see section 5.12 below).

All company formation documents are subject to certain checks, including those necessary to ensure prospective officers are not on the Disqualified Directors' Register maintained by Companies House.

If the documents satisfy the examination and name acceptance tests, Companies House will incorporate the company and issue a certificate of incorporation, and the documents will appear on the public record for public inspection. The company is brought into existence when the registrar of companies issues the certificate of incorporation.

In addition, a public company requires a certificate (known as a Section 117 certificate) from the registrar before it may commence trading; this is done by way of a statutory declaration. The 2006 Act will replace the current statutory declaration with a statement of compliance, which does not need to be witnessed.

5.11 Summary of company formation under the 2006 Act

With effect from October 1 2009 there will be new registration requirements as set out in Sections 9 to 13 of the 2006 Act. The following will have to be submitted to Companies House:

- a new simplified memorandum of association in the prescribed form, authenticated by each subscriber. The memorandum will only contain the names of the subscribers (see section 5.5 above);
- an application for registration stating:
  - the proposed name of the company; and
  - the domicile of the registered office (ie England and Wales, Scotland or (as a new addition) Northern Ireland);
- whether the liability of the members is to be limited and, if so, whether by shares or by guarantee;
- whether the company is to be public or private;
- a statement of capital and initial shareholdings, containing the name and address of each subscriber to the memorandum together with the 'prescribed

particulars' of the rights attached to the shares. The prescribed particulars are rights to vote at general meetings, rights to participate in a distribution and rights regarding redemption;

- if the company is to be limited by guarantee, a statement of guarantee given by the founder members of the company to contribute to the assets of the company up to a specified amount in the event of it being wound up. The statement of guarantee should include the name and addresses of each subscriber to the memorandum;

- a statement of the company's proposed officers, being the first directors and the company secretary (unless, in the case of a private company, there is no company secretary). All officers will be able to provide service addresses and directors will no longer need to provide details of other UK directorships;

- a statement of the intended registered office address;

- a copy of the proposed articles of association (to the extent the company does not intend to use the model articles); and

- a statement of compliance that all requirements of the 2006 Act have been complied with. This replaces the witnessed statutory declaration (Form 12) and need not be witnessed.

If the registrar is satisfied that the requirements of the 2006 Act have been complied with, he will register the company and will issue a certificate of incorporation.

5.12 Costs of incorporation

The Companies House fees vary, depending on whether the incorporation is achieved by way of paper filing or software filing.

(a) *Paper filing*

The standard registration fee at the time of writing (2009) is £20 and Companies House aims to process documents within five days of receipt.

Companies House also provides a 'same day' service, which at the time of writing costs £50. The application must, however, be received before 3pm (Monday–Friday) and all the documents and any required supporting information must be acceptable. The completed statutory documents can be taken to Companies House offices at London or Cardiff (if the company is to have its registered office in England or Wales) or Edinburgh (if the company is to have its registered office in Scotland). The documents are inspected at the counter and, provided the necessary requirements are met, a certificate of incorporation is issued on the same day. When filing same-day applications by post, by courier or by hand, all envelopes must be clearly marked 'same day incorporation'.

Cheques must be made payable to Companies House.

In addition, when the statutory declaration comprised in Form 12 is made before a solicitor or commissioner for oaths or notary public, a fee is payable to him – which at the time of writing stands at £5.

(b)   Electronic filing

The standard Companies House fee for filing an application electronically is currently £15 and the same-day service is £30. To form a company using electronic filing, suitable software must be used. A number of formation agents for filing an application electronically provide this as a chargeable service. For more information about software and web filing, visit the Companies House website.[1]

5.13   Compulsory employer's liability insurance

Employers are responsible for the health and safety of their employees while they are at work. Employees may be injured at work or they, or former employees, may become ill as a result of their work whilst in employment.

Under the Employers' Liability (Compulsory Insurance) Act 1969, every employer carrying on business in the United Kingdom must insure against legal liability for death, bodily injury or illness sustained by employees while serving under a contract of service or apprenticeship where that injury or illness arises out of and in the course of their employment.

Employers must have employers' liability insurance where their employees are normally based in England, Scotland or Wales (including offshore installations or associated structures). If any employees are normally based abroad but spend more than 14 days continuously in the UK or more than seven days on an offshore installation, their employers will need employers' liability insurance. This is often overlooked by overseas companies sending employees to the United Kingdom on short-term assignments.

The purpose of employers' liability insurance is to protect an employer against claims for damages brought by employees for injuries or illness whether they are caused on or off site. The policy covers the employer's legal liability, including:

- negligence in failing to use reasonable care and skill in:
  - providing a suitable and safe plant;
  - providing a safe system of work;
  - providing a safe place of work; and
  - engaging suitable and competent employees;
- breach of statutory regulations (eg Health and Safety at Work Act 1974); and
- negligence of fellow employees (an employer will be vicariously liable if one employee negligently injures a fellow employee during the course of employment).

Employers must obtain the insurance from an authorised insurer: the Financial Services Authority (FSA) maintains a register of authorised insurers.[2]

An employer must be insured for at least £5 million (2009 threshold). However, depending on the risks and liabilities involved, insurance cover of more than £5 million may well be needed. In practice, most insurers offer cover of at least £10 million.

If the business is part of a group, a policy for employers' liability insurance can

[1]   www.companies-house.gov.uk
[2]   The FSA's website can be checked at www.fsa.gov.uk.

be taken out for the group as a whole. In this case, the group as a whole, including subsidiary companies, must have cover of at least £5 million.

A copy of the certificate of insurance must be displayed in a prominent place where the employees can easily read it. Since October 1 2008 employers may also display the certificate electronically. Employers choosing this method need to ensure, however, that their employees know how and where to find the certificate and that they have reasonable access to it.

An employer can be fined up to £2,500 for any day on which it does not have suitable insurance.

6. Corporate name

6.1 Choice of name

Many laws restrict a company's freedom to choosing its name, most notably the 1985 Act, the 2006 Act and the Business Names Act 1985.

As previously discussed, a public company's name must end with 'public limited company' or its abbreviation 'plc'; the name of a private limited company must, unless exempt, end with 'Limited', its abbreviation or the Welsh equivalent.

In addition, a name will be refused if its use would constitute a criminal offence or if the name itself is offensive. The approval of the Secretary of State is required if the proposed company name is likely to give the impression that the company is connected with the UK Government or any branch thereof. Approval is also required for sensitive words or expressions (enumerated in statutory regulations).

Words requiring the consent of the Secretary of State before they can be used in a company name fall into three categories:

- words implying national or international pre-eminence (eg British, England, English, European, Great Britain, International, Ireland, National, Scotland, United Kingdom, Wales);
- words implying business pre-eminence or representative or authoritative status (eg association, authority, board, council, federation, government, institute, institution, society); and
- words implying specific objects or functions (eg assurance, charity, chemist, co-operative, foundation, friendly society, fund, group, holdings(s), insurance, insurer, reassurance, stock exchange, trade union, trust).

There are also words or expressions where prior written approval to use them must first be obtained from the relevant body (eg charity, charitable, dental, dentistry, health centre, police, polytechnic, royal, university). A copy of the letter from the relevant body must be submitted to Companies House when incorporating the company.

The restricted names and relevant regulatory bodies or associations to whom permission to use a name must be applied, are set out in the Companies and Business Names Regulations 1981 (SI 1981 No 1685), as amended.

A name must not already exist on the registrar's index of company's names, as the Secretary of State may direct a new company to change its name if it is the same or too similar to a name already on the index.

The name can also be challenged in the tort of passing off (ie where a third party can prove that it has goodwill in its name and that the company is misrepresenting itself as that third party and thereby causing damage). A name may also be challenged if the name is identical or similar to an existing trademark. A person may object where the proposed name is the same as a name associated with the complainant in which he has goodwill or where it is sufficiently similar and suggests a connection between the company and the complainant.

In summary, it is prudent to check the proposed name against the registrar's index and against registered and unregistered trademarks.

If there is already a trademark registration that is identical or similar to the company name chosen and the company to be incorporated is in the same type of business as the existing company, the new company may face legal action for a trademark infringement. It is not possible to reserve a name in advance.

6.2   Amendment to company name

A company can change its name by special resolution in a general meeting or by use of the written resolution procedure if the company is a private company. Once agreed, the company must give notice to the registrar by forwarding to the registrar a signed copy of the resolution; and a copy of the amended memorandum and articles of association. These filings must be made at Companies House within 15 days of the special resolution being passed. The change of a company's name has effect from the date on which the new certificate of incorporation is issued.

6.3   Display/disclosure of company name

A company must display its registered name (as it appears in its memorandum of association) at its registered office and at any other place where it keeps its company records or carries on business (unless the location is used primarily for living accommodation). If the company has been dormant since its incorporation, it will be exempt from this requirement. The registered name must also be displayed continuously – except when the location where business is carried on is shared by six or more companies, in which case each company is then only required to display its registered name for at least 15 continuous seconds at least once in every three minutes.

The registered name must be disclosed in all business correspondence and documentation (hard copy, electronic, or any other form), including bills of exchange, letters, e-mails and websites. A company must also include its registered number, place of registration and registered office address in business letters and emails, order forms, and on its website.

A company may choose to adopt a business name (a trading name or 'dba' (doing business as)) by board resolution. The use of a business name is governed by the Business Names Act 1985 and is subject to similar requirements as are imposed on company names.

Parts of the 2006 Act come into force on October 1 2009 and make a number of changes to the existing law on using business names and changing company names. Most notably the 2006 Act grants companies the ability to change their name by any means provided for in their articles.

6.4 Rules to prevent opportunistic registration

From October 1 2008 the 2006 Act introduced new provisions allowing any person or company to object to a company name for 'opportunistic registration' if the company's name:

- is the same as a name associated with the complainant in which he has goodwill; or
- is so similar that its use in the United Kingdom would be likely to mislead by suggesting a connection between the company and the complainant.

7. Share capital

7.1 Introduction

Companies limited by shares must comply with the relevant provisions in the 1985 Act and the 2006 Act as to share capital, and set out below is an overview of the key provisions.

7.2 Authorised share capital

A company limited by shares is required by the 1985 Act to state in its memorandum of association the amount of the share capital with which the company is registered and the number and nominal value of the shares into which it is divided.

A company cannot issue more shares than comprised in its stated authorised share capital. However, Section 121 of the 1985 Act allows a company, with the consent of its shareholders, given by the passing of an ordinary resolution (over 50% of the members voting), to increase its authorised share capital.

The 2006 Act abolishes the requirement for a company to have an authorised share capital, which will allow the directors, subject to the restrictions on the issue of shares (see later in this section 7), to allot an unlimited number of shares. The relevant provisions come into force on October 1 2009 and will apply to companies incorporated after this date or existing companies that pass an ordinary resolution removing the existing restriction from their articles.

Although from October 1 2009 a company will no longer be required to have an authorised share capital, the company must still ensure that:

- shares have a fixed nominal value (eg £1). Section 542(1) of the 2006 Act states that any allotment of shares that does not have a fixed nominal value is void; and
- upon formation of a company with share capital, a statement of capital and initial shareholdings must be submitted to Companies House at the time of application for registration.

7.3 Issued share capital

The issued share capital of a company is the amount of share capital that the company actually has in issue (ie the number of shares that have been allotted to shareholders). The number of issued shares cannot exceed the authorised share capital of the company.

7.4   Allotment of shares

The directors may be authorised to allot relevant securities (being shares and any right to subscribe for, or to convert any security into, shares) by (a) the passing of an ordinary resolution or (b) the incorporation of such authority into the company's articles of association (Section 80(1) of the 1985 Act).

The authorisation must state the maximum amount of the relevant securities that the directors may allot and the date on which such authority will expire. The expiry date must be not more than five years from the date of the resolution or the date of incorporation of the company if the authorisation was incorporated in the articles of association upon incorporation (Section 80(4) of the 1985 Act).

A Section 80 authority authorising the directors to freely allot shares may be revoked or varied before the expiry date by the shareholders in a general meeting (Section 80(4) of the 1985 Act).

A private company may pass an elective resolution removing the time restriction, so that the necessary authority lasts indefinitely (Section 80A of the 1985 Act). Such authority must state the maximum number of shares to which it applies.

Part 17 of the 2006 Act sets out the new provisions relating to allotment of shares and will come into force on October 1 2009. Essentially, the current law is restated save with one major change, namely that from October 1 2009 directors will be able to allot shares (or to grant rights to subscribe for, or convert, any security into shares) where the company is a private company with only one class of share unless they are prohibited from doing do so by their articles of association (Section 550 of the 2006 Act). The directors do not have to be authorised by the shareholders, although the members have the right to restrict or prohibit the directors' authority to allot by incorporating the necessary provisions in the articles of association.

Section 629 of the 2006 Act states that shares are of one class if the rights attached to them are in all respects uniform.

When Section 550 of the 2006 Act comes into force, the elective resolution allowing shareholders to amend or remove the time limit on the directors' authority to allot securities will be repealed as it will no longer be necessary.

Directors of private companies with more than one class of shares and public companies may only allot shares (or grant rights to subscribe for shares or convert any securities into shares) if they have been authorised to do so by the passing of an ordinary resolution, or if such authorisation has been incorporated into the articles of association (Section 551of the 2006 Act).

The conditions of such authorisation are similar to those that apply under the 1985 Act, in that the authorisation must state the maximum number of shares to be allotted under it and the date on which it will expire. This date must not be more than five years from the date of authorisation or, where the authority is incorporated into the articles of association of the company, the incorporation of the company.

As from October 1 2009, Section 554 of the 2006 Act will also require that an allotment of shares is registered on the company books within two months.

Within one month of the allotment of new shares, the company must make a 'return of allotment' to the registrar of companies. Companies have, in accordance with Section 88(2) of the 1985 Act, been used to completing these returns, but upon implementation of Section 555 of the 2006 Act on October 1 2009, they must now be accompanied by a statement of capital. This will mean that the public register kept at Companies House will contain up-to-date information about a company's share capital.

Under Section 578 of the 2006 Act, which comes into force on October 1 2009, a public company must not allot shares following an offer of shares for subscription unless all the shares offered are taken up or the offer is made on the basis that it will go ahead even if all the shares offered are not taken up or if other conditions specified in the offer are met. It is not possible for the terms of the offer to override the requirements of this section. This protects those who apply for shares, by ensuring that if the increase in capital is not fully subscribed, the capital will be increased by the amount of the subscriptions received only if the conditions of the issue provide for it.

7.5 Pre-emption rights in relation to the offer of shares

Pursuant to Section 89(1) of the 1985 Act, a company proposing to allot equity securities must offer them first to existing shareholders on a pre-emptive basis (ie proportionately to their current shareholding). This right of first refusal allows the existing shareholders to preserve their percentage shareholding in the company when new shares are issued.

This statutory pre-emption can be disapplied for shares authorised to be allotted under Section 80 of the 1985 Act by the shareholders passing a special resolution or by incorporating the appropriate provision in the articles of association of the company (Section 95 of the 1985 Act).

A private company may exclude statutory pre-emption entirely and indefinitely by inclusion of the necessary provision in its articles of association or by passing a special resolution.

The relevant provisions of the 2006 Act (Chapter 3 of Part 17), which come into force on October 1 2009, restate the statutory pre-emptive process set out in the 1985 Act allowing a shareholder to protect his proportion of the total equity of a company.

7.6 Different classes of shares

A company may have more than one class of shares. The advantage is that different rights will usually attach to different classes of shares, making a certain class more attractive to shareholders and possibly allowing a premium to be paid for those shares.

Class rights can only be varied when the holders of three-quarters of the nominal value of the issued shares of the relevant class have given their written consent to the variations or have passed a special resolution approving the variation at a meeting of the relevant class (Section 125 of the1985 Act).

Section 127 of the 1985 Act provides that members amounting to not less than 15% of the members of the class affected and who did not consent to or vote in favour of the variation may apply to the court to have the variation cancelled.

Chapter 9 of Part 17 of the 2006 Act sets out the new law on class rights and largely restates the provisions of the 1985 Act. It allows the company to specify less demanding procedures for varying class rights in its articles of association.

7.7   Minimum capital requirements

(a)   Private companies

There is no prescribed minimum amount of capital for a private company. The vast majority of companies have an authorised and issued share capital of a £100 or £1,000 being the usual amounts with which a company is incorporated.

(b)   Public companies

A public company must have and maintain an allotted share capital of a nominal value of not less than the authorised minimum (Section 761 of the 2006 Act).

Section 763 of the 2006 Act defines the authorised minimum as £50,000 or the euro equivalent. The Companies (Authorised Minimum) Regulations 2008, which came into force on April 6 2008, prescribes the euro equivalent as €65,600. In accordance with Section 764(1) of the 2006 Act, the Secretary of State may alter the prescribed euro amount of the authorised minimum.

7.8   Nature of contributions

No company may allot shares at a discount to their nominal value. If shares are allotted at a discount to their nominal value, the allottee is liable to pay the company an amount equal to the amount of the discount together with interest (Section 100 of the 1985 Act). Section 580 of the 2006 Act, which comes into force on October 1 2009, restates the provisions of the 1985 Act.

Where shares are allotted at a sum greater than their nominal value, the excess above the nominal value is called the 'premium'. Subject to certain exemptions, the premium must be credited to a separate account called the 'share premium account'. This account forms part of the company's non-distributable reserves and can only be used for specified purposes or in accordance with the requirements relating to reduction of capital (Section 130 of the 1985 Act).

Part 1 of the 2006 Act comes into force on October 1 2009 and restates and amends the rules on the treatment of share premiums.

Shares allotted by a company, and any premium on them, must be paid up in money or money's worth (Section 99(1) of the 1985 Act). Money's worth includes goodwill and know-how. This position is restated by Section 585 of the 2006 Act and comes into force on October 1 2009.

A public company may only allot shares where they are paid up for at least one-quarter of the nominal value and the whole of any premium on it. Further, a public company may not allot shares as fully or partly paid up (as to nominal value or premium) otherwise than in cash if the consideration for the allotment is, or includes, an undertaking that is to be, or may be, performed more than five years after the date of the allotment (Section 102 of the 1985 Act). This provision is restated in Section 587 of the 2006 Act, which comes into force on October 1 2009.

Pursuant to Section 103 of the 1985 Act and subject to certain exemptions, a public company may not allot shares other than for cash unless:

- the non-cash consideration for the allotment has been independently valued;
- a report on its value has been made to the company during the six months

immediately before the allotment of shares; and

- a copy of the report has been sent to the proposed allottee.

The provisions of Section 103 of the 1985 Act are restated in Sections 593 and 594 of the 2006 Act, which come into force on October 1 2009.

7.9 Partial payments

(a) Private companies

Private companies may choose to allot shares that are nil paid or partly paid. Where shares are allotted and are not fully paid up, there remains an overriding liability on the shareholder to pay up the outstanding amount. A company may call for the shares to be paid at any time. Additionally, where a company is wound up the liquidator may, on behalf of the company, call for shares to be fully paid up.

(b) Public companies

Public companies are prevented from allotting any share unless at least one-quarter of its nominal value and the whole of any premium on it is paid up (Section 101 of the 1985 Act). Section 101 is restated by Section 586 of the 2006 Act and comes into force on October 1 2009.

7.10 Share transfers

Shares in a company are transferable in accordance with the company's articles of association and are subject to the provisions of the Stock Transfer Act 1963 and Section 544 and Part 21 of the 2006 Act.

(a) Formalities

A stock transfer form must be used to transfer shares unless the transfer is made in accordance with the regulations made under Section 207 of the Companies Act 1989 (currently the Uncertified Securities Regulations 2001 (SI 2001 No 3755)).

Under the Uncertified Securities Regulations 2001, title to securities may be evidenced and transferred without a written instrument in accordance with a computer-based system. The vast majority of shares in companies listed in the UK are held and transferred without the use of paper certificates in the CREST system.

When the shares are transferred, stamp duty at 0.5% of the value of the consideration is payable. A company cannot register a transfer of shares unless it has been, where appropriate, stamped by the Stamp Office.

Shares must be registered "as soon as practicable" and in any event, within two months of a transfer being lodged with the company (Section 771 of the 2006 Act). Where directors refuse to register a transfer, the transferee is entitled to be informed of the directors' reasons for refusal. Failure to comply with Section 771 is an offence, and the company and every officer in default will be liable to a fine.

Chapter 2 of Part 21 of the 2006 Act, which came into force on April 6 2008, includes sections giving the Secretary of State and the Treasury power to make regulations enabling title to securities to be evidenced without a written instrument.

No such action has yet been taken.

(b) *Restrictions*

The directors of a private company may, pursuant to Regulation 24 of Table A, refuse to register the transfer of a share:

- that is not fully paid up by a person of whom they do not approve;
- on which the company has a lien;
- if the transfer, the share certificate and such other evidence as the directors may reasonably require to show the right of the transferor to make the transfer is not lodged at the office or at such other place as the directors may appoint;
- if it is in respect of more than one class of shares; or
- if it is in favour of more than four transferees.

The articles of association of a private company may also extend the restrictions for registering a transfer of shares (eg to include restrictions on registering a transfer to a minor or a person of unsound mind).

(c) *Pre-emption on share transfer*

It is possible for private companies to incorporate pre-emption rights on the transfer of shares into their articles of association. Such pre-emption rights will offer dilution protections to the existing shareholders of the company and may include:

- the right for the existing shareholders or a class of shareholders to be offered the transferor's shares before they are offered to a third party;
- the right for the directors to refuse to register a transfer of shares to any third party whom they believe is a competitor or to any person who has not been offered the shares through the pre-emption process set out in the articles of association; or
- the right for the directors and/or the transferor to ask the company's auditors to certify the fair value of the shares.

Where the articles of association incorporate such provisions, they may also have provisions allowing existing shareholders to transfer their shares to permitted persons or companies, such as a spouse or child or another group company, without requiring the shareholder to comply with the pre-emption provisions in the articles of association.

8. Raising capital – public offers of securities

A company can seek to raise capital through an initial public offer (IPO) and admission of its securities to trading on an appropriate investment market. This is referred to as a 'listing', 'flotation' or 'quotation'.

The three principal London equity markets on which a company can list its shares are the Official List maintained by the UK Listing Authority (UKLA) (with admission to trading on the main market of the London Stock Exchange plc (LSE)), the AIM (operated by the LSE) and the Plus-quoted market (operated by Plus Markets plc).

In London, save for the largest new issues, the typical method of listing shares relating to an IPO is via a 'placing' of shares with institutions as opposed to a public offer. However, shares may also be listed via other routes. Importantly, shares in overseas listed companies and other companies with a wide spread of shareholders may be admitted to trading by way of an 'introduction' (ie where a company joins the market without raising capital in order to obtain the benefit of a trading facility for its securities, usually when there is already an established shareholder base).

These methods are not mutually exclusive and a listing application or admission may involve several methods. Where a company is already listed, further capital can be raised through a 'rights issue' or an 'open offer', for holders of existing securities to subscribe for new securities in the same proportion to their existing shareholdings. In a rights issue the offer is made by way of negotiable instrument whereas an open offer is not.

The choice of market may be influenced by a number of factors, including entry requirements, levels of regulation and liquidity.

8.1 The Official List

A company must apply to UKLA (UKLA is the Financial Services Authority (FSA), the competent authority for listing purposes under the Financial Services and Markets Act 2000) for its securities to be listed on the Official List and must apply to the LSE for its securities to be admitted to trading on the main market. An application for listing shares on the Official List must be accompanied by a prospectus.

Companies whose securities are admitted to trading on the main market will in particular be subject to the UKLA's Listing Rules, the Prospectus Rules and the Disclosure and Transparency Rules.[3]

8.2 AIM and PLUS quoted markets

In the context of AIM, an application for admission is made to the LSE. The AIM Rules for Companies (the AIM Rules) set out the rules and responsibilities for AIM-listed companies and regulate the process of admission to the AIM. The Prospectus Rules do not apply to the AIM unless an offer of securities to the public is being made.

Once a company's securities are admitted to trading on the AIM, it must continue to comply with the AIM Rules. The UKLA's Listing Rules do not apply and except in limited circumstances (including DTR 5) the Disclosure and Transparency rules do not apply to AIM companies.

In the context of the PLUS-quoted market, the procedure is the same save that the PLUS Rules are the applicable rules and the listing application is submitted to Plus Markets plc.[4]

9. Running a company

The board of directors is responsible for the day-to-day running of a company.

---

3   Together, these rules are set out at www.fsahandbook.info.
4   The full text of the AIM rules can be found at www.londonstockexchange.com and the PLUS Rules at www.plusmarketsgroup.com.

However, English law requires that certain decisions must be made by the members of a company by the passing of a resolution in a general meeting. Consent may be by way of ordinary resolution, special resolution, elective resolution or extraordinary resolution, and the type of resolution required will depend on the type of business to be transacted at the meeting.

9.1 Meetings of the members

A meeting of the members is called a 'general meeting' or an 'annual general meeting' under the 2006 Act (the terms 'extraordinary general meeting' or 'EGM' are no longer referred to). Private companies are no longer required by law to hold annual general meetings (although their articles of association may require such a meeting) but meetings may still be held if the members require them. Public companies are still required to hold an annual general meeting within six months, beginning with the day following its accounting reference date.

Section 281 of the 2006 Act requires that a resolution of the members of a private company must be passed either at a general meeting or by way of a written resolution (a public company cannot pass a written resolution).

Directors have the power to call a general meeting of a company under Section 302 of the 2006 Act. The articles of association of a company may contain provisions relating to the directors' ability to call general meetings (although the articles cannot prevent the directors from being able to call such meetings).

Members also have the power to require the directors to call a general meeting under Section 303 of the 2006 Act. Members who hold at least 10% of the paid-up share capital can request that the directors call a general meeting. If a company does not have a share capital, members who hold at least 10% of the voting rights can request that directors call a general meeting. If the company is a private company and 12 months have elapsed since the time of the last general meeting, the required percentage is only 5%. As at the date of writing (early 2009), it is noted that the Department for Business Enterprise & Regulatory Reform (BERR) proposes to amend Section 303 so that it applies to all companies, so members holding at least 5% of voting rights at a general meeting can require directors to call a general meeting (expected to come into force on August 3 2009 as a result of the Shareholders' Rights Directive).

Once directors become subject to the requirement to hold a meeting, they must call the meeting within 21 days and the meeting must be held within 28 days. If the directors fail to call the meeting within this time period, the members themselves (or any of them representing more than half of the total voting rights) may call a meeting at the company's expense, provided the meeting is called within three months of the date that the directors became subject to the requirement to call the meeting.

Resolutions at a general meeting will only be validly passed if notice of the meeting and the resolution has been given. The procedure outlined in a company's articles of association (if any) should also be followed.

9.2 Notice of meetings

Section 307 of the 2006 Act provides that if a company is a private company, it must give 14 clear days notice to its members of a general or annual general meeting. Public companies must give 21 clear days' notice of an annual general meeting and 14 clear days for any other general meeting. However there still may be circumstances where a company must still give 21 clear days' notice (eg when passing an elective resolution in accordance with Section 80A of the 1985 Act). A company's articles of association may require a longer period.

A private company may hold a general meeting at shorter notice if the members holding 90% in nominal value of the shares agree. The articles of association of a private company may increase this percentage to 95%. A public company may hold a general meeting on short notice if the members holding 95% agree.

Special notice of 28 clear days may be required in advance of a meeting. For example, special notice is required if a director is removed in accordance with Section 168 of the 2006 Act or an auditor is removed in accordance with Section 510 of the 2006 Act.

9.3 Types of resolution

The main types of resolutions that shareholders may need to pass are:

- **Ordinary resolution** – passed by a simple majority (ie more than 50% of those members who are entitled to vote and who vote in person or by proxy at a general meeting). A written resolution may also pass an ordinary resolution if it is signed by members representing a simple majority of the total voting rights of eligible members.
- **Special resolution** – passed by a majority of 75% of those members who are entitled to vote and who vote in person or by proxy at a general meeting where the required notice has been given and has included the text of the resolution and it is specified that it must be passed as a special resolution. A special resolution may be passed as a written resolution provided that the resolution specifies it is being passed as a special resolution and provided that it is passed by members representing not less than 75% of the total voting rights of eligible members.
- **Extraordinary resolution** – passed by 75% of those members entitled to vote and who vote in person or by proxy at a general meeting for which the required notice has been given. Extraordinary resolutions have generally ceased to exist and are only likely to be relevant if referred to in the company's articles.
- **Elective resolution** – passed by unanimous consent to amend the duration of the authority of directors to allot securities (Sections 80A and 379A(1)(a) of the 1985 Act). This is currently in force but is due to be repealed from October 1 2009. Furthermore, it now only applies to private companies.

9.4 Quorum

A quorum is required to conduct valid business at a general meeting. Unless the articles of association of a company state otherwise, Section 318 of the 2006 Act confirms that the quorum of a single-member company is one 'qualifying person'. If a company has more than one member, the quorum will be two qualifying persons.

Section 318 defines a 'qualifying person' to be a member of the company, a person appointed as a proxy of a member, or a person who is authorised to act as a representative of a corporation under Section 323 of the 2006 Act.

9.5 Written resolutions

A private company may pass resolutions by way of a written resolution. To pass such a resolution, signatures from a simple majority (more than 50%) of the total voting rights is required and if the resolution is a special resolution, signatures from not less than 75% of the total voting rights is required.

9.6 Derivative claims

Under Section 260 of the 2006 Act, a shareholder can bring an action on behalf of the company against a director (and/or a third party) in respect of the director's conduct that has given rise to a cause of action for the company. The cause of action must arise from an actual or proposed act or omission involving negligence, default, breach of duty or breach of trust by a director of the company.

However, the member must apply to the court for permission to continue a claim. The sections in Chapter 1 of Part 11 of the 2006 Act introduce a two-stage process. At the first stage the applicant will be required to make a case for permission to continue a derivative claim. The court will consider the issue on the basis of the applicant's evidence. The court must dismiss the application if the applicant cannot establish a case. At the second stage – but before the substantive action begins – the court may require evidence to be provided by the company.

Section 994 of the 2006 Act may be used if the court considers that the passing of a resolution may fall within the scope of unfair prejudice. A member may apply to the court by petition for an order under this section on the grounds that:

- the company's affairs are being, or have been, conducted in a manner that is unfairly prejudicial to the interests of members generally or of some part of its members (including at least himself), or
- an actual or proposed act or omission of the company (including an act or omission on its behalf) is or would be so prejudicial.

If the court is satisfied that a petition is well founded, it may order that the company regulates its affairs in the future.

More specifically, if a resolution has been passed that alters the company's objects clause of the memorandum of association, a member may challenge it under Section 5 of the 1985 Act, although this section will be repealed on October 1 2009.

9.7 Unfair prejudice

A member who considers that a company's affairs are being or have been conducted in a manner that is unfairly prejudicial to the interests of its members generally or of some part of its members (including at least that member) may apply to the court for an order under Section 994 of the 2006 Act. The court then has the power to make such order as it thinks fit that gives relief to the matters complained of, including an order requiring the company to:

- refrain from doing the act complained of;
- do an act the company omitted to do;
- authorise civil proceedings to be brought in the name or on behalf of the company;
- require the company not to make any alterations to its articles without leave of the court; or
- provide for the purchase of shares of any members of the company by other members or the company itself.

In practice, minority shareholders are most likely to use this last remedy.

10. Directors

When incorporating a company, the registrar of companies requires the company to submit a statement (in the prescribed form) naming the company's first directors. As and when the directors of a company change, the registrar of companies requires notification of the change (in the prescribed form), together with any new directors' particulars. The register of directors must also be changed.

The directors deal with the management of a company's business. Directors are the officers of the company and there is no separate division of roles as can be found in the United States and other jurisdictions. Decisions are taken collectively by a board of directors and a director should not act alone unless they are a sole director or they have been given this power expressly by the board. Decisions are made by a majority of the board of directors in a general meeting, or with unanimous consent by written resolution.

Both public and private companies must have at least one director who is a natural person (this is a new provision that came into force on October 1 2008 and there is a grace period until October 2010 for companies that had no natural persons as directors on November 8 2006). Private companies must have at least one director and public companies are required to have at least two. Directors must be at least 16 years of age (there is no maximum age requirement).

As mentioned before, public companies are required to have a company secretary. However, under Section 270 of the 2006 Act, there is no longer a requirement for a private company to have a company secretary, unless the articles of association state otherwise. Notwithstanding the removal of this requirement from law, many companies still choose to have a company secretary in place as the administrative burden remains the same.

10.1 Directors' liability to third parties

Generally, directors are seen as acting as an agent on behalf of the company and therefore in most cases it will be the company that has the liability rather than the director. However, a director may be held personally liable where::

- a director signs a contract personally as opposed to as agent of the company;
- a director has made a negligent or fraudulent misstatement about the company in order to deceive another party when negotiating a contract;
- a director is disqualified or acts in accordance with instructions from a person

he or she knows to be a disqualified director;

- a previous director of an insolvent company carries on another business under the same or similar name to the insolvent company in the 12 months before it went into liquidation; or
- a director is involved in wrongful trading or fraudulent trading.

If a member considers that a director is responsible for an actual or proposed act or omission involving negligence, default, breach of duty or breach of trust, a derivative claim may be brought under Section 260 of the 2006 Act by that member (see section 10.7 above).

10.2 Directors' powers

Any director can bind the company, whether or not they had actual authority to do so. A board of directors can delegate authority to a committee of board members or to an individual director, if the articles of association permit a company to do so.

Other powers that directors have are as follows:

- executive directors are usually employees of the company and are responsible for the day-to-day management. Executive directors may have been given their powers under their service agreement or a board resolution. An example is the managing director;
- non-executive directors provide an independent supervisory role to executive directors and are entitled to vote at board meetings. Non-executive directors do not have executive powers but are still subject to the same duties as executive directors; and
- a managing director is granted powers by the board and/or by the company's articles of association.

10.3 Directors' duties and conflicts of interests

Directors owe duties to the company and these duties now include statutory duties. The 2006 act sets out the duty:

- to act within powers (Section 171);
- to promote the success of the company (Section 172);
- to exercise independent judgement (Section 173);
- to exercise reasonable care, skill and diligence (Section 174);
- to avoid conflicts of interest (Section 175);
- not to accept benefits from third parties (Section 176); and
- to declare an interest, when it exists, in a proposed transaction or arrangement (Section 177) or in an existing transaction or arrangement with the company (Section 182).

At the first board meeting of the company, the directors must declare the nature and extent of their interest in the formation of the company and any ancillary matters, and also any other arrangements to be considered at the meeting. A director may also make a general declaration of interest in relation to specified persons or entities so that this will count for future meetings. It should also be noted that a director is also required to make a further declaration of interest if an initial declaration of interest proves to be, or becomes, inaccurate or incomplete.

For private companies incorporated on or after October 1 2008, a matter giving rise to a conflict of interest can be authorised by non-interested members of the board. This is provided that nothing in the company's constitution invalidates this. For public companies, the articles of association must include express provision enabling non-interested directors to authorise the matter giving rise to a conflict of interest.

Shareholders can also authorise conflicts of interest and, to a certain extent, a public or private company can include provisions in its articles of association permitting conflicts of interest.

10.4 Removal of directors

Under Section 168 of the 2006 Act, a director can be removed from office if the shareholders pass an ordinary resolution in a general meeting. However, special notice (a minimum of 28 clear days' notice) must be given to the shareholders before the meeting for the resolution to be effective. Section 169 of the 2006 Act provides that the company must send a copy of the notice to the director concerned. The director also has a right to be heard in relation to the resolution at the meeting and to send representations in writing to the company together with a request these are sent to the shareholders of the company (these rights are subject to there being enough time to circulate the representations and subject to the director concerned not abusing the rights conferred on him by Sections 168 and 169 of the 2006 Act).

The removal of a director is without prejudice to any right the director has to damages under his or her service contract.

The articles of association can outline a different procedure for the removal of directors than that stated in the 2006 Act. The procedure under the act is quite lengthy so many companies try to make the process simpler.

Before making a decision to remove a director from office, the company should bear in mind that if the director is also an employee of the company, the director can claim that he/she was constructively dismissed as a result of a breach of the employer's implied duty of trust and confidence.

10.5 Disqualification of directors

The articles of association of a company will normally outline the circumstances under which a director may be disqualified. For example, under Regulation 81 of Table A, the office of a director shall be vacated if:

- he ceases to be a director by virtue of any provision of the 1985 Act or 2006 Act (as amended) or he becomes prohibited by law from being a director;
- he becomes bankrupt or makes any arrangement or composition with his creditors generally;
- he is, or may be, suffering from mental disorder and his affairs have become subject to the jurisdiction of the court;
- he resigns his office by notice to the company; or
- he has been absent without permission from directors' meetings for more than six months, so the directors have resolved that his office be vacated.

The court also has the power to disqualify directors under the Company Directors' Disqualification Act 1985 (the CDDA) for a period of between two and 15 years. The CDDA only applies to directors of insolvent companies. If a director is disqualified, that person cannot be a director of a company, act as a receiver of a company's property, or directly or indirectly take part in the promotion, formation or management of a company unless he or she has the leave of the court. Nor can a disqualified director be an insolvency practitioner. Examples of conduct that can lead to disqualification are as follows:

- persistent breach of companies legislation (such as failure to file accounts, annual returns and other documents at Companies House);
- breach of competition law;
- conviction of fraudulent or wrongful trading (continuing to trade or failing to minimise the potential loss to the detriment of creditors at a time when the company was insolvent) or any other fraud in relation to the company; or
- being unfit to be concerned with the management of a company following insolvency.

11. Branches

11.1 General

In Great Britain, a branch or a place of business of a foreign company is considered to be a connected arm of the foreign company. The foreign company will be liable for all of the debts and liabilities of the branch or place of business unless it is incorporated as a separate limited company.

On or before September 30 2009, the overseas company must either make a branch registration or place of business registration as outlined at sections 11.2 and 11.3 below. From October 1 2009, Part 34 of the 2006 Act and the Overseas Companies Regulations 2009 (the 2009 Regulations) will implement a single regime for the registration of 'UK establishments', replacing the two-tiered approach for branches and places of businesses. From October 1 2009, whilst the documents required for registration of a UK establishment are likely to mirror those previously required for a UK branch or place of business, the form required to register the UK establishment will change. At the time of writing (early 2009), the 2009 Regulations remain in draft form and have not been finalised. Further details for practitioners are therefore awaited.

11.2 Branch registration (on or before 30 September 2009)

A branch is part of an overseas limited company organised to conduct business through local representatives in Great Britain rather than referring it abroad. Section 690A and Schedule 21A of the 1985 Act state that a company that is incorporated outside the United Kingdom and Gibraltar is required to register a branch in Great Britain within one month of its opening. Within this one-month period, the branch must deliver the following to the registrar of companies:

- Form BR1 detailing company specifics, including director (and secretary, if applicable) details and accounting period;

- a certified copy of the parent company's constitutional documents; and
- a copy of the latest set of audited accounts required to be published by parent law.

The requirement to file the accounts of the overseas company as part of the registration process and annually thereafter is key. A further holding company may need to be set up as many overseas companies do not wish to file their accounts on public record.

11.3 Requirement for registration in relation to foreign companies establishing a place of business in Great Britain (on or before September 30 2009)

The documents that are required to be registered by the registrar of companies at Companies House when establishing a place of business (which does not amount to a branch) are set out in Section 691 of the 1985 Act. The documents required include:

- a certified copy of the company's charter, statutes or memorandum and articles (with a certified translation if the original is not in English); and
- a completed Form 691, which must contain a list of the names, addresses and other information relating to the directors and secretary, and the name and address of at least one person resident in Great Britain authorised to accept service of process on behalf of the company and any notices required to be served on it.

A notary public or a commissioner for oaths must confirm the date at which the place of business was established and sign a declaration on the form.

The company must file any changes of the place of business with the registrar of companies under Section 692 of the 1985 Act.

11.4 Branch or place of business?

The main features that distinguish a branch from a place of business include:

- appearing to have a permanent presence;
- having managers present on the branch premises; and
- the ostensible capacity of the branch employees to conduct business with third parties that will bind the foreign company.

The question is whether the business activity in the United Kingdom is sufficient to constitute a permanent establishment for business purposes.

As indicated above, from October 1 2009, it will no longer be necessary to distinguish between the registration of a place of business and a branch, and it will be possible to make a single registration for a UK establishment.

12. Accounts

12.1 Accounting reference date

When incorporated, a company is automatically allocated an 'accounting reference date', which is the month end of the month in which it was incorporated. The accounting reference date is the date to which statutory accounts need to be drawn up and the date by reference to which the deadline for the submission of accounts to Companies House is determined.

A first accounting period runs from the date of incorporation through to the first accounting reference date. It is usually no less than six months and can be no more than 18 months long. Subsequent accounting periods then extend for the next 12 months, beginning the day after the end of the previous accounting period and running to the next accounting reference date.

UK legislation permits this allocated accounting reference date to be changed by the company's directors. For companies that form part of a group (whether domestic or international), it is often common for the accounting reference date be co-terminal with existing group companies for ease of any consolidation/group reporting requirements.

The accounting reference date may be changed by filing Form 225 with Companies House. Only changes to the current or immediately previous accounting period may be filed and Companies House must be informed of any new accounting reference date before the filing deadline of the related accounts.

As a general guide, it is possible to shorten an accounting period as often as the company wishes and by as many months as they wish; however, there are restrictions on the extension of a company's accounting reference period. The two significant restrictions are that the period must not be extended so as to be longer than 18 months from the start date of the accounting period and that it may only be extended, subject to specific conditions, once every five years.

12.2 Fiscal period

UK incorporated companies are required to prepare and file a UK corporate tax return with HM Revenue & Customs (HMRC). The statutory accounts and relevant accounting reference period are the starting point from which to prepare the associated corporate tax return(s). UK companies account for UK corporate taxes on a self-assessment basis.

For first accounting periods, a dormant corporate tax return will be prepared from the date of incorporation through to the date of the first expense incurred or revenue received, whichever is earlier. A second return would then be made up to the end of the accounting period or 12 months later, whichever the earlier. If necessary, for a first accounting period that is more than 12 months, a further corporate tax return may be prepared from the end of the previous return to the end of the accounting reference date. For subsequent active accounting periods that are 12 months in duration, just one corporate tax return will be prepared.

Corporate tax returns with a computation of the tax liability are required to be filed with HMRC within 12 months from the end of the accounting period.

12.3 Accounting records and statutory financial statements

The directors of a UK limited company are responsible for preparing an annual report and financial statements in accordance with applicable law and regulations. The accounting records are to be kept either at the company's registered office or at an alternative location that is considered suitable by the directors. They are to be made available for inspection at any time by the directors and the company secretary, if appointed.

Under UK company law, directors are required to prepare financial statements that comprise a balance sheet, a profit and loss account and supporting notes for each financial year, to the appropriate accounting reference date. These financial statements are prepared in accordance with United Kingdom Generally Accepted Accounting Principles (UK GAAP). They are required by law to give a true and fair view of the company's state of affairs and the associated loss or profit for that accounting period.

When preparing the financial statements, the directors are required to;

- select accounting policies and then apply them consistently;
- make judgements and estimates that are reasonable and prudent;
- prepare the financial statements on a going-concern basis unless it is inappropriate to presume that the company will continue in business;
- maintain proper accounting records for the company that at any time disclose with reasonable accuracy the financial position of the company and to ensure that they comply with the Companies Act 1985; and
- safeguard the assets of the company and take reasonable steps for the prevention and detection of fraud and other irregularities.

The profit and loss account must present a true and fair view of the company's affairs throughout the relevant accounting period and the balance sheet must do the same at the accounting reference date.

The financial statements, complete with directors' report, must be circulated to the shareholders for review and put to them at a general meeting for approval. It is possible for an elective resolution to be passed for a private company so that there is no longer that requirement. All companies must prepare a set of financial statements for their members and a set for filing with Companies House. For large companies, both these sets are the same; for small and medium-sized entities, there are certain disclosures that do not need to be reported on the set filed with Companies House. These are referred to as abbreviated accounts.

The deadline for filing financial statements at Companies House for accounting periods after April 6 2008 is nine months from the end of the accounting reference date for a private company and six months from the end of the accounting reference date for a public company. For long first accounting periods, the deadline is 21 months from the date of incorporation. When financial statements are filed at Companies House, they are available for public inspection.

12.4 Audit and group reporting

A UK company is required to have its statutory financial statements audited if it meets certain conditions. To qualify for an exemption, a company must first qualify as a 'small' company; and in order so to qualify it should not exceed two out of the three limits shown in the table overleaf.

Category	Small limits	
	Company	Group**
Turnover	£6.5m	£7.8m
Total assets	£3.26m	£3.9m
Employees	50	50

** Where the company is a parent of a group or a subsidiary, the size of the group is determined by adding the results of the parent and its subsidiaries together. The group limits can then be applied or, alternatively, the company limits if all intra-group trading has been eliminated.

12.5   Profits

(a)   *Distribution*

Dividends may only be paid to shareholders of a company out of distributable profits. In some instances, the company may have preferential share capital that gives a preferential right to those shareholders to a dividend ahead of other shareholders. The preferential dividend must be declared and paid out before a dividend is declared and paid on any remaining ordinary share capital. There is no withholding tax on dividends paid out by UK companies. If an overseas company holds shares in a UK company, then it may seek to receive relief from any potential double taxation arising on the underlying tax of distributed profits through the appropriate double-taxation treaty.

(b)   *Corporate taxes*

The level of taxable profits will, to an extent, depend upon the trading model adopted in the United Kingdom. The UK has transfer pricing legislation that dictates that transactions between connected parties need to be recorded at an arm's-length rate (ie the rate at which they would be recorded between independent entities). This is to prevent international groups from manipulating intra-group transactions so that profits may flow to the country with the most favourable tax rate.

The current rates of UK corporation tax are between 21% and 28%. For profits up to £300,000, the rate is 21%. For profits exceeding £1.5 million the rate is 28%. For profits between £300,000 and £1.5 million there is a sliding scale from 21% to 28%.

For companies that are deemed 'large', there is a requirement to pay corporate tax on account before the year end. A company is defined as 'large' for payment-on-account purposes if:

- its taxable profits exceed £10 million (or as appropriately divided by the number of associated companies in the worldwide group); and
- it was a 'large' company in the12 months preceding the period.

The profit limits as outlined above are reduced when there is more than one company under common control in the worldwide group. The profit limits for a UK company's corporate tax purposes are divided by the number of such companies held under common control.

(c)   *Business model*

If the UK business model were such that the UK company is providing solely marketing and technical support to a related company and is not receiving any third-party revenues, a fee would be charged to the related party for the services provided. The level of this fee would be based on certain conditions, such as the cost base in the UK, the nature of services provided to end customers of the related party and the level of responsibility/risk assigned to the UK company. This fee from the related party, less the associated costs incurred in the United Kingdom of providing these services and maintaining the UK company, would be subject to UK tax at the rates outlined above.

If the UK company is structured so that it can enter into contracts with third-party customers in its own name, then these revenues will be booked in the name of the UK company. Any intra-group licences/purchases/cost of sales/support services will be offset against these revenues, as well as all other UK-based costs associated with the UK company.

For UK companies that are part of a 'large group' under the UK domestic transfer pricing legislation, or who are entering into transactions with companies in certain 'high-risk' territories, a transfer pricing report will need to be prepared.

Written proof should be retained on file to demonstrate that the directors have satisfied themselves that all transactions with related parties have been recorded on an arm's-length basis. Signature of the annual tax return confirms that the correct procedures have been followed.

The proof usually comprises a functional and risk analysis of the businesses concerned, an analysis of the appropriate pricing model to be adopted and a benchmarking study for an arm's-length pricing policy. Since 2004, the UK domestic transfer-pricing legislation has been extended to apply to both domestic and international groups. Excessive amounts of interest paid to related parties by companies that are thinly capitalised (high debt–equity ratio) are also now caught by the transfer pricing legislation.

(d)   *Losses*

If a UK company incurs a trading loss in an accounting period, this may be carried forward indefinitely for offset against future taxable profits of the company, provided those profits are from the same trade. Trading losses may be carried back 12 months, again against profits of the company through the same trade.

Losses incurred by a UK company are generally not available for offset against overseas parent company profits.

12.6   **Value added tax**

VAT is a sales tax that is chargeable by businesses if they are making 'VATable' supplies (sales subject to VAT) above a certain threshold. The current threshold for registering for VAT in the United Kingdom is £68,000.

If the threshold has been exceeded in the previous 12 months or is expected to be exceeded in the near future, the business must notify the authorities and register for VAT. This will involve the business charging the appropriate level of VAT on its supplies of goods and services and being in a position to reclaim VAT incurred on purchases. VAT should not therefore be a direct cost to businesses; it does, though, have cash-flow implications and compliance costs.

From December 1 2008, the standard rate of VAT in the UK has been 15%, but this will revert to 17.5% after December 31 2009. There are two other reduced rates for certain items, which are currently 0% and 5%.

VAT returns are usually prepared and filed each quarter with the UK authorities. Detailed on such returns will be the VAT charged to customers and the VAT incurred on purchases relating to the UK company. The net amount, depending on whether more has been collected or paid, is either paid to the authorities or claimed back from them. VAT is ultimately a cost to individuals (end consumers) who are not registered for VAT or who are not in a position to reclaim the VAT incurred by them.

Where a UK company, after it has been registered as an entity but before it has been registered for UK VAT, incurs VAT in purchasing goods or services, it can recover this VAT for a period of up to six months prior to the date of obtaining the VAT registration. The goods must still be in its possession.

For a UK company transacting with overseas entities, the following issues are relevant:

- **Goods and services supplied to a company based outside the European Union.** If the UK entity sells goods to a non-EU entity, no VAT is chargeable as this is defined as an export. If the UK company provides services such as consultancy, technical support or marketing, these are not subject to UK VAT as they are regarded as 'Schedule 5' services, which fall outside its scope. These are regarded as being supplied in the country where the recipient is based. The provision of general management services would, however, be subject to VAT.

- **Supply of goods and services within the European Union.** A UK company registered for VAT does not have to charge VAT on the supply of goods or services to businesses in other EU countries, as long as they too are registered for VAT in their own country.

- **VAT on importation from outside the European Union.** VAT is due on the importation of goods into the United Kingdom from outside the European Union, which arises on the goods crossing the border. The entity that is the 'importer of record' is responsible for the payment of import VAT and any relevant customs duties. If that entity decides to register for UK VAT, then that VAT registration number will also act as the Trader Unique Reference Number (TURN) and is used on all import documentation to identify the importing entity.

12.7   Research and development tax incentives

The UK government currently provides some significant tax incentives for companies looking to undertake research and development (R&D) work in the United Kingdom. The aim is to encourage investment in R&D.

HMRC and BERR have issued guidance on the meaning of R&D for tax purposes. In broad terms, they are seeking advances in science and technology through the resolution of a scientific or technological uncertainty. The R&D should therefore not be something that is already available or could be made available by a competent professional working in the relevant field.

There are two R&D schemes, depending upon the size of the company. A company currently qualifies for the small and medium company scheme if it has:

- fewer than 250 employees; and
- either an annual turnover not exceeding £50 million or a balance sheet not exceeding £40 million.

If a company is a member of a group, the holding company and all companies in the group must together meet this definition. For R&D purposes any company that is not small or medium-sized under the above definition is a large company.

Small and medium-sized companies may currently claim a tax deduction for 150% of their R&D expenditure. For those companies with tax losses, an R&D tax credit can be claimed. This is a cash repayment from HMRC of up to £24 for every £100 spent on R&D, capped at the total amount of payroll taxes and social security paid for that particular accounting period. There are specific definitions of what expenditure qualifies for the R&D tax relief. The R&D work must not be subsidised by grants or subcontracted to the company by another entity. The company must also own the intellectual property rights arising from the R&D.

If all the conditions above are not met, then the company would qualify for the large company rate of deduction. Large companies may claim a current tax deduction of 125% of their R&D expenditure. Again, the definitions of what qualifies for this rate are quite specific. Large companies do not need to own the intellectual property rights arising from the R&D and where an overseas parent subcontracts to its UK subsidiary, the latter will only qualify for large companies' relief.

For both schemes, qualifying expenditure on R&D work must exceed £10,000 in a 12-month period; the expenditure should not be treated as capital and should relate to the trade of the company.

12.8 Payroll

A UK company with employees is required to operate a UK payroll scheme and register for Pay As You Earn (PAYE). Income tax for each employee is appropriately deducted at source through PAYE, along with employee National Insurance contributions (NICs) and paid across to HMRC. For the fiscal year to April 5 2010, employees' National Insurance is 0% for the first £5,720 of salary, 11% up to £43,888, and then for higher amounts a further 1% is charged.

Employers have to pay employers' NICs in addition to the gross salary paid through the payroll. For the year to April 5 2010, this is 12.8% of gross salary (above the initial £5,720, which has no Employers' National Insurance). The United Kingdom has entered into a number of reciprocal agreements with other countries under which, if an overseas national seconded to work in the United Kingdom continues to pay the equivalent of national insurance in his home territory, the employer and employee will be exempt from UK national insurance contributions. An exemption must be formally obtained and for an initial first period is unlikely to exceed a period of five years.

Payroll in the UK is typically run for salaried workers on a monthly basis, with hourly workers often paid weekly. The payroll year in the UK runs from April 6 to April 5 each year.

For the year to April 5 2010, employees receive a tax-free allowance of £6,475. Total earnings of up to £37,400 are then taxed at 20%, with earnings above £37,400 taxed at 40%.

13. Company reorganisation and insolvency

There are a number of ways that a company can reorganise its structure – and each method could warrant a chapter in its own right. Broadly speaking a company and its shareholders (or in certain circumstances its creditors) may reorganise by transferring all or some of the shares to other shareholders, or all or part of the business and assets to another company (usually another group company).

Fundamentally, the difference between the two routes is that when transferring shares there is no change to the company itself (although the identity of the shareholders will change) whilst on a transfer of assets the company will need to consider which assets (and indeed liabilities) will be transferred to (or assumed by) the transferee. Any assets or liabilities not transferred will remain with the transferor. This tends to make asset transfers more complex.

However, whether assets or shares are being transferred, there are a number of company laws and other issues that need to be considered – including, by way of example, the following:

- Will any customer, regulatory or other consents be required?
- Are directors complying with their statutory and common-law duties? (And particularly where a director is a director of both the transferor and transferee (not uncommon in group situations), he or she needs to be very careful about where duties lie.)
- Are there any solvency issues to consider? (See sections 16, 17 and 18 for a more detailed discussion on some of the issues.)
- Does the structure of the transaction (where intra-group) raise any concerns around returns of capital and unlawful dividends?

As well as the methods detailed above, the structures set out next are also commonly used to effect a reorganisation.

13.1 Capital reduction

Capital reductions are an effective way to, amongst other things, return surplus share capital to shareholders and to improve the distributable reserves of the company. Under the 1985 Act, a company wanting to reduce its issued share capital would usually do so via a court-approved capital reduction (which was a relatively costly and time-consuming process). Under the 2006 Act, a private company may now reduce its issued share capital using a much simplified solvency-statement procedure.

13.2 Scheme of arrangement

A scheme of arrangement is, put simply, an arrangement between a company and its members (or creditors) that often involves a transfer of shares to new shareholders and a reduction in capital through the cancellation of certain shares. Schemes of arrangement are required to be approved by the court, are costly and generally take a minimum of two months (and can take considerably longer, especially where the scheme involves a reduction in capital) – but can be a useful tool in group reorganisations (especially where there is a need to remove minority shareholders and/or solvency issues).

13.3 Section 110 of the Insolvency Act 1986

More unusually, a reorganisation may involve a scheme under Section 110 of the Insolvency Act 1986. Under a Section 110 scheme, a liquidator is appointed and the company is liquidated, pursuant to which its assets are transferred to two (or sometimes more) new companies. The new companies issue shares as consideration for the assets received and those shares are distributed to former shareholders. This route is generally used for tax reasons.

14. Administration

Administration is a short-term process. It lasts for no more than a year, unless extended by creditor agreement and/or court order. It is appropriate when a company has short-term cash-flow problems that indicate it is insolvent at a given time, but where there is residual value in the business. If in such circumstances there is a prospect that the company or business can be rescued as a going concern, protection from creditor action is required whilst rescue options are explored.

Administration can be commenced by a company's members, its directors, the holder of a qualifying floating charge (a charge that specifically refers to the relevant provisions of the insolvency legislation, that empowers the holder of the charge to appoint an administrator or administrative receiver and that relates to the whole, or substantially the whole, of the company's property) or by court order. Whichever of those routes is chosen, it must be proved that:

- the company is insolvent (ie it is unable to pay its debts as and when they fall due) and/or the value of its assets are less than the value of its liabilities (including contingent and prospective liabilities); and
- the statutory purpose can be fulfilled.

The statutory purpose of administration is: to rescue the company as a going concern; or, if that is not reasonably practicable, to achieve a better result for creditors as a whole than would be likely if the company were wound up; or, if that is not reasonably practicable, to realise property to make one or more distributions to secured or preferential creditors.

The effect of an administration is to impose a moratorium on creditor action. This means that, without the consent of the administrators or the court, and for the duration of the administration, no winding-up order can be made against the company, no goods can be repossessed, a landlord may not re-enter premises to forfeit a lease, no security may be enforced and no proceedings may be commenced or continued against the company.

Once a company is placed in administration, the administrator (who is an insolvency practitioner) is appointed. The administrator takes control of the company and manages the business and assets to achieve the statutory purpose. He is an officer of the court and has a duty to act in the best interest of all creditors. He does not, however, have the automatic power to distribute monies to unsecured claims, so administration is usually followed by another insolvency process where such a distribution is available.

15. Liquidation

There are two forms of liquidation available to an English company:
- compulsory winding-up by the court; and
- voluntary winding-up (members' or creditors').

15.1 Compulsory liquidation

A company can be wound up by a creditor on a petition to the court if that creditor can show that the company is insolvent, as set out above – normally by proving that the creditor is owed an undisputed amount of more than £750.

A company can also be wound up by the court on the petition of a creditor, director or contributory where it is just and equitable to do so. The Secretary of State also has the power to wind up companies if it is in the best interest of the public.

Commencement of winding-up is the date of presentation of the petition, rather than the date of the order itself. Any disposition of a company's property made after the commencement of winding-up is void, assuming that the company is in fact wound up, unless the court otherwise orders.

If the company is wound up, the matter is passed to the Official Receiver (part of the Insolvency Service). The Official Receiver will interview the directors and decide whether a meeting of creditors should be called to appoint an insolvency practitioner as liquidator.

15.2 Voluntary liquidation

(a) Members' voluntary liquidation (MVL)

MVL is where a company passes a resolution to wind up voluntarily on a solvent basis. An MVL can only take place when the directors make a statutory declaration that the company can pay all of its debts together with interest in full within a period not greater than 12 months of the date of the resolution. If such a statutory declaration is incorrect, this can be a criminal offence.

A company's shareholders can propose and pass a special resolution that the company be wound up voluntarily, appointing an insolvency practitioner as liquidator for the purpose of winding up the company's affairs and distributing its net assets, ultimately, to shareholders (as the company is solvent).

(b) Creditors' voluntary liquidation (CVL)

CVL is where a company is insolvent and its shareholders pass a special resolution to wind up voluntarily, without the involvement of the court. This resolution must be approved by the creditors in a meeting.

A company's board starts the process by convening a meeting for the shareholders to pass the special resolution that the company be wound up voluntarily and nominate an insolvency practitioner to act as liquidator.

The company's creditors must be given at least seven days' notice of the creditors' meeting, which itself must take place within 14 days of the shareholders' meeting. Notice of the meeting must also be published in *The London Gazette* and the local press.

The creditors then vote at the creditors' meeting for the appointment of the nominated liquidator or another liquidator of their choice. Voting is in accordance with the value of claims, to be agreed by the chairman of the meeting, who is normally the proposed liquidator. The creditors can also form a creditors' committee.

16. Receivership

Three are three forms of company receivership (excluding court-appointed receivers):

- Law of Property Act 1925 (LPA) receivership;
- fixed charge receivership; and
- administrative receivership.

16.1 LPA receivership

The LPA sets out rules relating to fixed charges over land granted by a company and gives a charge holder the power to appoint a receiver. The purpose of LPA receivership is to receive income from the land and to maintain the property. An LPA receiver is appointed by a charge holder under the provisions of a legal charge.

16.2 Fixed charge receivership

A fixed charge attaches to an identifiable asset (eg real property or fixed plant and machinery of a company). The charge holder can appoint a fixed charge receiver (who can be a surveyor rather than an insolvency practitioner if the only asset is land). The fixed charge receiver has all the powers (over the charged assets) of a receiver under the LPA, together with the powers that may be specified in the charge itself.

16.3 Administrative receivership

An administrative receiver is appointed pursuant to a floating charge over the whole (or substantially the whole) of the company's assets, that change having been created on or before September 15 2003. The Enterprise Act 2002, which came into force on this date, introduced changes to insolvency legislation, as a result of which an administrative receiver cannot be appointed if the floating charge was granted after September 15 2003, save for certain exceptions, including large-value (ie greater than £50 million) projects.

The administrative receiver is an insolvency practitioner who acts as an agent of the company over which he has been appointed. He is accountable to the charge holder who appointed him, not the general body of creditors. The administrative receiver, when appointed, takes control of the company, its business and its assets. His powers are set out in Schedule 1 of the Insolvency Act 1986 and the debenture pursuant to which he is appointed.

17.   Company Voluntary Arrang   (CVA)

A CVA is an agreement between a   any and its creditors for the company to pay a certain amount to its creditors, u   ally over a specific period of time, in settlement of its debts. It is usually used where a company has cash-flow difficulties but anticipates an improved future.

The directors of a company make a proposal for a CVA (usually drafted by an insolvency practitioner, the nominee supervisor of the proposal) to the company's creditors. The proposal describes the steps the company intends to take to meet the proposed settlement.

If the nominee believes the CVA may be approved, a creditors' meeting is called at which creditors vote on the proposal. More than 75% in value of those creditors voting (in person or by proxy) is required to approve the CVA proposal.

While the CVA proposal is being considered, 'small companies' (as defined in Section 247 of the 1985 Act) can obtain the protection of a moratorium, similar to that available to companies in administration.

If the CVA proposal is approved, it binds all creditors, whether or not they voted and whether or not they knew about it. If the proposal is approved, a creditor cannot take any steps to enforce his debt unless the CVA fails. He may exercise any rights he has against the company in relation to debts incurred that are not covered by the CVA.

If the CVA is approved, it is overseen by a 'supervisor' (an insolvency practitioner). The supervisor is not responsible for the trading of the company (if any), which remains the responsibility of the directors.

If the supervisor considers that the company is in breach of its obligations under the CVA, he can declare the failure of the CVA and usually has the power to apply to the court for the company to be wound up.

18.   Possible disqualification of directors on insolvency

Directors have a number of fiduciary duties set out in the 2006 Act. On an insolvency process, which does not include LPA or fixed charge receivership, the relevant insolvency practitioner is obliged to investigate and report on the company's directors' conduct to BERR.

BERR's Disqualification Unit will then consider the report and decide whether to pursue proceedings for disqualification of a director from acting in the promotion, formation and/or management of a company for a period of two to 15 years pursuant to the Company Directors' Disqualification Act 1986.

The various grounds for disqualification are set out in that act, but include wrongful trading, fraudulent trading, breach of fiduciary duties, and failure to keep proper accounts and records.

19.   Dissolution of companies

A company may be struck off the register of companies at Companies House and dissolved if:

- it has applied to the registrar of companies to be struck off; or
- the registrar himself concludes that the company is not carrying on business or is not in operation (eg a failure to file accounts and/or an annual return).

It is not normally appropriate for a company to apply for strike-off if it is insolvent, but such an application can be made if, amongst other things, the company has not traded or changed its name within the previous three months.

Notice of the application for strike-off must be given to the shareholders, all creditors (including contingent and prospective creditors) and employees, amongst others, who have the right to object. Failure to notify can be a criminal offence.

The company will be struck off if no objections are raised, following advertisement of the application in *The London Gazette*.

Even if a company is struck off the register and dissolved, creditors and others can apply to the court for the company to be restored to the register in certain circumstances. Thereafter, proceedings can be taken as if the company had not been dissolved.

20. Authorisation for regulated activities (financial services)

20.1 Definitions

A number of definitions need to be set out in relation to authorisation for regulated activities, as follows:

- 'Banking, investment and general insurance etc': the UK has a single regulator (the Financial Services Authority) under single legislation (the Financial Services and Markets Act 2000 (FSMA)) regulating nearly all financial services activities.
- 'General prohibition': a person is prohibited from carrying on a 'regulated activity' in the United Kingdom unless he is authorised or exempt (Section 19 of the FSMA). Breach is a criminal offence and resulting contracts are potentially unenforceable.
- 'Regulated activity' means a specified activity, relating to a specified investment or other financial product, that is carried on by way of business. Although there are certain exemptions, regulated activity generally includes:
  - deposit taking;
  - investment-related activities – for example: dealing in (buying/selling etc) investments as principal or agent; 'arranging' deals in investments; managing (on a discretionary basis) investments; advising on investments; providing or arranging custody of (safeguarding and administering) investments; agreeing to carry on any of the foregoing activities; establishing, operating or winding up 'collective investment schemes' (essentially, funds); or activities related to the Lloyd's insurance market. 'Investments' include shares, debt instruments (debentures), government securities, warrants, options, futures, contracts for difference and units in collective investment schemes;
  - general insurance-related activities – effecting and carrying out contracts of insurance, administering such contracts and insurance mediation;
  - regulated mortgage contract-related activities, including mortgage lending, administering and mediation;
  - issuing e-money; and

- other miscellaneous activities such as those relating to home reversion/purchase, stakeholder pensions and funeral plans.

20.2 How to obtain authorisation

Authorisation is obtained by applying to the FSA for 'Part IV Permission'. Applicants must satisfy the FSA that they meet certain 'threshold conditions', including being 'fit and proper' and having adequate (financial and other) resources. Regulated banks, investment firms and insurers established in an EU state with 'passporting' rights under certain EU single-market directives are automatically authorised (subject to notification and certain conditions).

Applications are paper-based (occasionally with FSA interviews) and typically take four to six months in total (FSA has six months under FSMA to determine a completed application).

Directors, senior management and other key personnel (including a compliance officer) must be approved and registered with the FSA as 'approved persons'.

20.3 Consumer finance

There is a separate regime for consumer finance business (other than FSMA-regulated mortgages), which is regulated under the Consumer Credit Act 1974 (CCA). Subject to some exceptions, the following activities require a licence from the Office of Fair Trading (OFT) and compliance with conduct rules under the CCA: consumer credit business (ie providing credit or otherwise being a creditor under a regulated credit agreement); consumer hire business; and certain ancillary credit business (including credit brokerage).

20.4 Controllers of FSA authorised firms

Anyone proposing to acquire 'control' of an FSA-authorised firm (such as a bank, investment firm or insurance company) must give prior notice to the FSA and wait for confirmation that it does not object before proceeding (or the expiry of three months from the notice without an objection). 'Control' has an extended definition here, but includes holding 10% or more shares in, controlling 10% or more voting power in, or holding a shareholding giving 'significant influence' over the management of, the firm or its parent undertaking(s).

20.5 Marketing – financial promotions

Marketing financial products and services is subject to restrictions under the 'financial promotions' regime. Persons who are not authorised by the FSA must not communicate a 'financial promotion' (essentially an 'invitation or inducement to engage in investment activity') in, into or from the United Kingdom, unless the communication falls within a statutory exemption or has been formally approved in advance by an FSA-authorised firm (Section 21 of the FSMA). The regime applies to all categories of products and services caught by the general prohibition, but it is even wider because the exemptions applicable to regulated activities are ignored.

Breach is a criminal offence and resulting agreements are potentially unenforceable.

There are more than 65 exemptions from the regime (eg financial promotions to FSA-authorised firms and other professionals to large corporates and certified high-net-worth/sophisticated individuals exceeding certain size thresholds).

20.6 Collective investment schemes

The special regulatory regime for funds and other pooled investment vehicles is defined in UK legislation as the 'Collective Investment Schemes' (CISs). These can be regulated or unregulated. Anyone setting up, managing or otherwise operating (or carrying on any other regulated activity in relation to) a CIS in/from the United Kingdom must usually be FSA authorised. Promotion of interests in a CIS is subject to the financial promotions restriction. FSA-authorised firms are also subject to special rules when promoting unregulated CISs.

21. Share incentives

When setting up a company in the United Kingdom, it may be desirable to provide share incentives for UK employees. If the company is to be a subsidiary of a non-UK company, the share options or share awards will generally be granted over the parent company shares.

There are two main areas of advice that must be sought for share awards or share options: UK securities laws and tax-related issues. Generally, a prospectus is not required for share options, but for share awards the necessary exemptions must be considered to ensure that a prospectus is not required. There are also rules on financial promotions, which usually necessitate changes to a non-UK parent plan before options can be granted to UK employees.

The tax-related issues are quite complex and require specific advice so the company, and the employees to some extent, do not end up paying substantial and unavoidable amounts of tax. The company will want to consider whether the share awards or share options can be offered in a tax-efficient manner. Certain types of plans can deliver returns to the employees of a capital nature (with a more favourable rate of tax) and other types of plans can deliver returns that are taxable as to employment income. Where employment income arises, there may also be the possibility of withholding taxes and employer and employee social security charges. There are ways in which the risk of the employer social security charges can be reduced for the employer.

The plans that can deliver capital returns include approved company share option plans, enterprise management incentive option plans, savings-related share option plans and share incentive plans. These all have different rules and qualifying requirements.

It is necessary to make reports of share awards and share options to HMRC; otherwise, there may be penalties or the tax status of the awards and options can be jeopardised.

22. Employment

22.1 Procedural requirements

Under Section 1 of the Employment Rights Act 1996 (the ERA), employees in the UK are entitled to be provided with a statement of the terms and conditions of employment. This statement must include certain prescribed information including the employee's salary, benefits, pension arrangements, holiday entitlement and grievance and disciplinary procedure. It is therefore advisable that all UK employees be issued with full UK employment documentation before commencing work.

For senior employees or those with access to confidential information or those who could potentially damage the company when or if they were to leave employment, it is important that companies consider implementing appropriate confidentiality and intellectual property protections, as well as robust post-termination restrictions.

It is also important that employers ensure that all UK employees have the right to work in the UK, because there are substantial liabilities for employers who are found to be employing illegal workers (up to £10,000 fine per illegal worker plus a potential jail sentence for directors of companies who 'knowingly' employ an illegal worker). Thorough checks should be made to ensure that all new-hires in the United Kingdom have the correct permission to work there.

22.2 Employees' rights in the UK

Employees in the United Kingdom (and in Europe generally) are afforded substantial protection during their employment. This includes protection from discrimination (on the grounds of age, gender, sexual orientation, gender reassignment, marital status, disability, race, national origin or colour) and harassment.

Those employees who have one year's continuous service also attain 'unfair dismissal' rights, meaning that employees have a right to be dismissed only if there is a fair reason for doing so and only after a fair procedure has been followed. If an employer fails on either of those tests, the employee can bring a claim in an employment tribunal (where the maximum compensation payable for unfair dismissal is currently £66,200).

Compensation for claims of discrimination is uncapped, but loss is only awarded on the basis of actual loss to the employee – there are no punitive damages for unfair dismissal or discrimination in the United Kingdom.

It is therefore very important that professional advice is taken before any steps are taken to dismiss a UK-based employee. It should also be noted that no settlement or compromise agreements with an employee will be binding unless countersigned by the employee's solicitors or ACAS (the Advisory Conciliation and Arbitration Service).

22.3 Employee v contractor

There is often a temptation for new companies setting up in the United Kingdom to avoid the formalities of having employees and labelling their workers as 'independent contractors'. However, if the reality of the working relationship is akin to that of employer and employee, the label the company places on the individual is irrelevant and the tax authorities can impose penalties on companies who have not properly accounted for PAYE and employer's and employees' NIC contributions.

Although no one factor can point to an individual being an employee as opposed to a contractor, the following are generally considered by UK courts/tribunals to suggest an employment relationship:

- mutuality of obligation (ie there is an obligation to provide work and an obligation to carry out that work);
- the individual's conduct being controlled by the company;
- the individual's equipment for carrying out their work being provided; and
- the individual not providing services to any other company.

In addition, an individual who is considered to be an independent contractor by the company but is considered to be an employee by HMRC or an employment tribunal will attain employee rights, such as unfair dismissal rights (see section 22.2) that the company may have assumed they do not need to worry about. This makes it more likely that the company will not have followed the correct procedures and can lead to costly additional liabilities.

23.   Venture capital

Venture capital is a term used to describe investments by funds, individuals and government schemes in companies in return for the issue of shares. Such investment is usually given to early-stage businesses that are unable to raise adequate funding. A usual investment in a venture capital transaction would be in the region of £1 million to £10 million.

Before any investment can be made, a company limited by shares must be established and those persons behind the business idea, usually referred to as the 'founders', would subscribe for shares in the share capital of the company. Care should be taken regarding the timing of the subscription by the founders if they are to be employees, to avoid any risk of income tax being payable on acquiring shares at less than market value. It is advised that specific tax advice is sought on this matter.

Sometimes an investment is made where all shareholders – both investors and those who have started the company – have the same rights. This is most likely when the investors are individuals (often referred to as 'business angels'). Here, changes may be made to the articles of association to ensure all shareholders are treated in the same way. There may also be an investment agreement under which some warranties are granted to the investors, and they are usually given some control rights.

When investments are made by funds (and sometimes by individuals) the terms may be more complicated with regard to both the return on investment and control rights. On completion of such an investment, new articles of association will be adopted by the company that incorporate a new class of preferred shares. The rights of these preferred shares may include:

- a preference above all other shareholders on a liquidation; or in a share or business sale, to receive an amount per share equal to the price paid for the share, plus any unpaid dividends;
- a preferential right to receive a dividend; and
- a first right to be offered newly issued shares or those that are subject to a transfer notice.

In addition to being allotted shares, on completion of an investment for preference shares the investors will usually require the company and existing shareholders to enter into an investment agreement. The investors will typically seek to protect their investment by requiring:

- that the company and the founders/senior management give warranties about the company and the information provided by the company to the investors. If these are breached, the warrantors will be liable to the investors;
- certain information rights about the company (eg to be sent monthly management accounts and receive an annual presentation of the business plan); and
- certain management controls that prevent the company from undertaking certain actions without the consent of the investors, for example the appointment of a new director or the incorporation of a new subsidiary.

Venture capital investments are returned to the investors in whole or in part through liquidation, IPO or trade sale.

24. Shoestring start-ups – do's and don'ts

Shoestring start ups can be a disaster because they are not well thought through. Each situation is different and legal advice should be sought to avoid difficulties at a later stage. Here are some possibilities and comments:

- Set up a limited company for £1, issue the share and produce the annual accounts without an audit as the UK turnover will most probably fall within the range for exemption (see section 12.4). It should be noted that the audited accounts exemption applies to the turnover of the group as a whole and not just the UK entity if the UK company is part of a large group of companies.

  Comment: ideal for small start-ups.

- Set up a branch of a dormant company overseas, which in turn is wholly owned by a trading company overseas. This structure will give limitation-of-liability protection up to the capital of the dormant overseas entity and protects the ultimate parent.

  Comment: very smart.

- Set up a branch of an overseas company.

  Comment: this is risky as there is no limitation of liability.

- Undertake business in the United Kingdom with an employee or consultant but with no registered entity: it is an unincorporated business.

  Comment: Do not do this without substantial advice. The consultant will probably be treated as an employee of an unregistered branch (see below).

- Appoint distributors/subcontractors without setting up an entity.

  Comment: the distributor/subcontractor must have a limited company or partnership (not husband and wife) in order to avoid employment of the individuals by the overseas company by an unregistered branch.

- Virtual entities are occasionally sold to overseas companies wishing to have a UK presence but supposedly without the cost of having an employee (to terminate in due course) or of a legal entity.

Comment: The reality is that none of this is actually true as the expenses are covered by an indemnity from the overseas company to the virtual office under which the overseas company pays for any and every liability as if the operation by the virtual company was wholly owned.

Do not appoint individuals as consultants because usually:

- they will be deemed employees;
- they should be paid after deduction of employment taxation (PAYE) and NICs payable by the employer and the employee; and
- you cannot terminate as you expect (see sections 22.2 and 22.3 above). and it can get very expensive. An entity is always going to be the safe route.

There is some doubt whether virtual offices shield an overseas company from taxation liabilities in any event. How will the employee of the virtual office company present himself to potential customers? If he uses a business card showing the name of the overseas company, then surely he is representing the overseas company in the United Kingdom as a branch in a taxable unregistered branch. A branch whether registered or not (in this case not) is a permanent establishment responsible for the payment of corporation tax on its profits. The overseas company therefore risks running a business in the United Kingdom for taxation purposes even though it thinks it is not doing so.

The virtual-office company faces serious tax issues on the exercise of stock options, ending up with the worst of all worlds. All exercises of options and grants of stock to employees will be subject to employment taxes and will be paid for by the overseas company under an indemnity in favour of the virtual office. It is only by setting up a UK subsidiary that the employer and employee could come within the benefits of the Enterprise Management Incentive (see section 23).

Most overseas companies would expect all intellectual property created by their UK employee to belong to them. Unless care is taken, the intellectual property rights created by an employee will belong to the virtual office company.

Lastly, as a practical matter, the overseas company is usually seeking to make an impression with customers and potential customers in the United Kingdom and Europe. What kind of message does it give to its customers by using a virtual office company rather than a purpose-built company or branch in its own name?

If a UK entity is owned by an overseas entity, there must always be an agreed method of trading for tax purposes whether a subsidiary or a branch is formed. Failure can result in months of anguish and the payment of additional professional fees to resolve the problems.

David Kent would like to thank the following individuals for their kind assistance in the preparation of this chapter: Karolina Plent, Sian Skelton, Lynn McCloghry, Charlotte Kershaw, Mark McCanney, Charlie Pring, Ann Casey, Neil Smyth, Clive Cunningham, Chris Jeffrey, Mark Barron, Jonathan Kent, Tim Stocks, Pascoe Simpson, and Lorraine Munday.

United States

John Reed
Edwards Angell Palmer & Dodge LLP
Bennet Hugh Silverman
Katz Wittenberg Levine & Silverman

1. Introduction

In the United States, with very limited exceptions, the formation and governance of corporations and other types of business entity is dictated by the legal regime of each of the 50 individual states, with each state providing several options, including some with limited liability on the part of the equity investors. As a general matter:

- the state governments regulate the governance or internal corporate affairs of business entities incorporated or formed in their respective states;
- the federal government regulates the securities markets and disclosures made to investors by publicly traded business entities (ie corporations whose securities trade on the New York Stock Exchange, NASDAQ or other exchanges); and
- within the structure of separation between the state and federal governments, there is some overlap:
  - pursuant to so-called 'blue-sky' laws, states to a much lesser degree also set standards for the offering and selling of securities;
  - pursuant to the Sarbanes-Oxley Act of 2002, the federal government mandates certain committees (eg audit committees and compensation committees) within the boards of directors of publicly traded companies; and
  - the stock exchanges themselves have rules that, for example, require a certain number of independent directors and also define such independence.

Although other types of wholly or partially limited liability entity are also available for consideration – such as general corporations, limited partnerships and Sub-Chapter S corporations – this chapter focuses primarily on Delaware limited liability companies due to:

- space limitations;
- the fact that a large proportion of alien non-residents (with respect to the United States) who choose to do business through the formation of a US business entity do so through limited liability companies; and
- the fact that for various reasons the state of Delaware is a jurisdiction of choice for forming such entities.

Nevertheless, single and even some multi-member limited liability companies conducting business in a state other than Delaware should always consider whether advantages might be achieved by forming a limited liability company in the state of its geographic focus.

Very few business activities preclude a US alien non-permanent resident from becoming an equity investor in a US business entity (eg an entity obtaining a licence for aircraft to fly in the United States), and this circumstance should be recognised and considered whenever a non-US person may seek to invest in a US business entity. However, one type of entity utilised more in the past – a corporation electing sub-chapter S status to avoid tax at the entity level and to pass tax consequences of entity profit and loss through for tax implication at the investor level – is not available to corporations having any non-resident alien shareholder (with respect to the United States). Further, in some jurisdictions limited liability companies are not permitted to engage in certain specific businesses, such as insurance and banking; and in most jurisdictions, prior approval of a designated official must be obtained before either a limited liability company or corporation may engage in certain types of endeavour, such as providing health or other professional services, insurance, banking and education.

Income generated by business entities incorporated in the United States can be subject to tax at the federal, state and local levels. Thus, a few state and local tax authorities do not recognise the limited liability company as being a flow-through tax entity and/or impose an unincorporated business tax upon federally recognised flow-through entities.

This chapter focuses on the commonly used limited liability company (LLC), commenting from time to time on general corporations. With regard to both limited liability companies and general corporations, the legal regime of the state in which the entity is formed mandates some of the content of the initial, typically bare-boned document (for general corporations, the initial document is called a 'certificate of incorporation'; for limited liability companies established under the Delaware Limited Liability Company Act (the Delaware act) the filing is called the 'certificate of formation'; for limited liability companies established under the New York Limited Liability Company Law the filing is referred to as the 'articles of organisation'). This allows other potentially very significant provisions to be added, some of which must be included at this point in order to be valid. The legal regime of the state of formation will also permit the incorporators or owners of a corporation (shareholders or stockholders) and the organisers or owners of a limited liability company (members) to vary some of the statutory laws and rules that would apply in the absence of a provision specifically dealing with an issue to fashion an entity whose procedures and governance closely follow the intent of the incorporators and organisers, and to meet the demands of other equity investors.

The statutes of a limited liability company generally provide greater flexibility in altering the statutory laws and rules because they emphasise principles of contract rather than broad fiduciary obligations that may be applied to corporate entities. Consequently, the limited liability company statutes found in each state provide:

- few mandatory terms;
- some 'default' terms (eg unless otherwise provided by appropriate organisational documents, the parties shall be deemed to have agreed to act

as that particular default rule provides. In Delaware, there are approximately 80 such default rules);

- many permissive rules (eg the parties may provide for X and if they do not so specifically provide then there is no agreement regarding point X); and
- some 'gaps' where the statute does not indicate whether or not the parties may make a valid provision.

Increasingly viewed as an attractive alternative to partnerships and general corporations, a limited liability company is a relatively new form of business entity. Stated simply, it is a business entity that provides its members with:

- the pass-through tax treatment of a partnership;
- limited liability principles of a corporation (commonly referred to as 'corporate veil' protection); and
- a large degree of ability to suit the organiser's desire to permit investors to participate in or to restrict management to a greater or lesser extent, or not at all.

All 50 states in the United States have limited liability company acts, which give members wide latitude to define the management structure and relationship between members of a limited liability company through a limited liability company agreement. Before they agree to invest in a limited liability company, potential non-organiser members should:

- understand the terms contained in the organisational documents, not only by the express provisions of those documents, but also those contained therein without mention and by virtue of statutory default rules;
- be happy to join an entity in which one or more permissible rules have not been included; and
- be satisfied with the tax consequences resulting from all such applicable rules.

Assuming that the limited liability company does not elect to be taxed as a corporation, there will be no entity-level tax for federal income-tax purposes. Similarly to partners in a partnership, the individual members are taxed on a personal level based on, among other things, the profits gained (or losses sustained) by that member in accordance with the company's allocation scheme contained in its limited liability company agreement (whether or not this is actually distributed). Given the significant flexibility provided by state limited liability company acts, limited liability companies enjoy a greater freedom in devising ownership and allocation regimes than corporations. Specifically, because most state acts do not contain limitations on capitalisation issues, members are free to agree contractually to a capitalisation structure in the limited liability company agreement. In those cases where a special allocation regime is not indicated in the LLC's documentation, a member of a company generally receives an ownership interest commensurate with the member's capital contribution to the company. The possibility of company members agreeing to be bound by a special allocation regime differs from stockholders of a corporation, who are required by statute to be treated the same within each class of shares.

Many state limited liability company acts allow members freely to assign their right to receive distributions from the company, although the assignees do not then become a member of the limited liability company without first obtaining the unanimous consent of the members. State statutes differ on this issue. Some allow members to override this prohibition by means of the operating agreement, while others provide that the restriction cannot be contracted around.

With respect to management, the default rule for most limited liability company acts is that a company is managed by each of its members, unless its agreement contains a provision that only one or more member-managers or non-member-managers will manage it.

This chapter provides an overview of limited liability companies in the United States by focusing on the popular Delaware Limited Liability Company Act (the Delaware act), initially enacted in 1992 and revised and updated several times since then. The act is often preferred, not only for its strong adherence to freedom-of-contract principles, but also due to its less stringent information requirements in organisational documents (thus preserving confidentiality, perhaps even from less informed potential members) and its default grant of jurisdiction to the Delaware Court of Chancery, widely renowned for its expertise with respect to complex business issues and the enforcement of contractual principles contained in organisational documents. In Delaware, by judicial decision, only the obligations of good faith and fair dealing cannot be avoided by the organisational documents. The following list identifies the number of new businesses formed in Delaware for each of the years listed:

- 2005 – 133,700;
- 2006 – 145,000;
- 2007 – 162,000; and
- 2008 – 122,000.

The formation of Delaware limited liability companies has increased steadily as a percentage of those new business formations. Nevertheless, due to the larger body of judicial precedent construing the authority of corporate management, companies with a large number of equity holders prefer to do business in the form of a general corporation rather than a limited liability company.

2. State limited liability company acts

In 1977 the state of Wyoming adopted the first limited liability company act in the United States. The state of Florida followed in 1982 with its own statute. Limited liability companies exploded in popularity in the United States following a ruling in 1988 by the Internal Revenue Service (IRS) that limited liability companies could be taxed as partnerships for federal tax purposes. (Rev Rul 88–76, 1988–2 Cum Bull 360). Today, limited liability company acts have been enacted in all 50 states and the District of Columbia. These acts tend to borrow liberally from their respective state's partnership and corporation laws. Consequently, courts will often refer to interpretations of similar provisions of corporation and partnership law to interpret the limited liability company or limited liability company operating agreement at issue.

Limited liability company acts provide the framework within which members can structure their business entity. As long as it does not conflict with the provisions of the applicable state limited liability company act, members can devise the organisation, management, allocation of profits, losses and distributions of the company by means of a company agreement, which binds members pursuant to contract law.

States are constantly amending their acts to keep pace with the evolution of these entities from a tax and organisational standpoint. Many states now permit single-member limited liability companies, continuity of life and free transferability of interests, unless otherwise provided for in a company agreement.

Delaware, widely known for its laws relating to corporations, enacted the Delaware act in 1992. The act was modelled on the Delaware Revised Uniform Limited Partnership Act. Each limited liability company may utilise a written agreement setting out the relationship between members as to the conduct of the company's business and affairs. The Delaware act provides members with a great deal of flexibility with respect to the provisions members may incorporate into their agreement. Under the act, a business can be formed as, or converted into, a limited liability company.

Under the act, members hold interests in a limited liability company and, unless otherwise stated, are not liable to third parties based solely on their status as a member. Further, the act explicitly provides that limited liability companies are taxed as partnerships for the purposes of state taxation, with the result that no income tax is imposed on the company entity (as distinct from its members).

Delaware has become the most popular forum for the creation of limited liability companies, given its relatively simple rules regarding formation, specific reference and abidance to the concepts of freedom of contract, and the well seasoned Delaware Court of Chancery as the default arbiter of disputes regarding the Delaware act and company agreements. This is consistent with its popularity within financial and corporate America with regard to general corporations. Indeed, Delaware has come to be known as the 'corporate capital of the world' for the following reasons:

- It is the state of incorporation for more than 62% of the Fortune 500 companies and more than half of all companies whose securities trade on the New York Stock Exchange, NASDAQ and other large exchanges.
- The Delaware Court of Chancery, which has statutory jurisdiction over directors and certain officers of Delaware corporations as well as the governance of business entities formed under its laws, has become the forum of choice in the United States for resolving corporate disputes. The Delaware Court of Chancery and the Delaware Supreme Court are nationally and internationally renowned, and both courts issue nationally significant corporate law decisions concerning challenges to the decisions of boards of directors, claims for breach of fiduciary duty, mergers and acquisitions litigation, issues of individual director and officer liability and other issues

arising under the corporate and business entity laws of the state.

- Its judicial system is consistently ranked number one among the 50 states in an annual assessment conducted by the US Chamber of Commerce, which notes the fairness, reasonableness, competency and impartiality of the judiciary, as well as its timeliness for resolving disputes.

3. Formation

A major attraction of limited liability companies, aside from the many beneficial characteristics borrowed from partnerships and corporations with respect to taxation and limited liability, respectively, is the ease of formation and wide latitude given to members in organising the company. Essentially, two material documents are required to form a limited liability company:

- the certificate of formation or articles of organisation (depending on the state statute); and
- the limited liability company agreement (the company agreement).

Typically, an agent may execute and file organisational documents and need not be a member of the company. The secretary of state of a jurisdiction in which such LLC organisational documents may be filed will often publish rules, guidelines or instructions relating to filing. The Delaware act allows for single-member limited liability companies, and further provides that a member may be a natural person, partnership, corporation, entity or association, or another limited liability company.

3.1 Certificate of formation or articles of organisation

Generally, a state's limited liability company act provides that a limited liability company is formed by filing a certificate of formation or articles of organisation with the secretary of state of the state in which the company is being formed. A certificate of formation typically sets out:

- the name of the company;
- the address of the registered office within the state; and
- the name and address of the company's domestic agent for service of process.

Although a company is required to provide a registered office in the state of formation, it generally need not have a physical presence in the state. The Delaware act does not require that a limited liability company be physically present in the state; nor does it require a domestic office or bank account, or that any of its members be residents of Delaware – or, indeed, the United States.

Most states, including Delaware, require the company name to include the words 'Limited Liability Company' or 'LLC'. Many states also allow the exclusive right to use a name to be reserved. If a company plans to use its name in multiple jurisdictions, it should consider determining at the outset whether that name is available in the jurisdictions in which it intends to conduct business (eg in New York both the corporate name register and limited liability company name register should be checked).

The certificate of formation must be signed by a person authorised to bind the limited liability company, although generally this may be a representative who need not be a member or manager. Unlike a general corporation's articles of incorporation, a limited liability company's certificate of formation is not itself required to indicate the management structure of the company or the relationship between its equity owners. Rather, the filing is a public notice of the company's existence. The Delaware act provides a higher level of confidentiality than most other state acts by its minimal disclosure requirements; specifically, it does not require the disclosure of members' names in the certificate of formation or other public organisational documents. Some other states require that the names of all members and the amounts of their capital contributions are stated on the certificate of formation. New York requires publication of the articles of organisation within 180 days of its filing in two newspapers for six weeks. The costs involved could exceed $2,000.

The general rule among limited liability company acts is that a company is formed when its certificate of formation is filed, thus increasing the speed with which a company can be formed. Given that a major purpose of a limited liability company is to provide its members with limited liability, a company (or any form of business entity) should avoid conducting business prior to the effective date of its existence. Further, a company agreement should be executed simultaneously with the filing of a certificate or articles to govern effectively the operation of the business and the relationship among members from its commencement, as well as provide proper authorisation for the individual executing the certificate of formation on behalf of the company. However, state limited liability company acts vary with respect to filing requirements and should be reviewed prior to filing.

As discussed more fully below, the management structure and relationship between members of a limited liability company, including voting rights, allocations, distributions, tax considerations and other items, are typically set out in the limited liability company agreement.

3.2 Limited liability company agreements

Limited liability companies are, first and foremost, creatures of statute and contract. An overriding principle of this form of business entity, and the statutes and rules that govern it, is freedom of contract. For example, Section 1101(b) of the Delaware act explicitly states that:

> [i]t is the policy of the [Delaware Limited Liability Company Act] to give the maximum effect to the principle of freedom of contract and to the enforceability of limited liability company agreements.

The limited liability company agreement is a contract by and among members wherein the relationship between members, management allocation scheme and tax issues, among other things, is defined. It is also a contract by and between the members and the limited liability company, thus making the company itself a party to the agreement. Although a written contract is preferable, some state limited liability company acts allow for non-written agreements. The Delaware act, recently amended in August 2005, provides that members, managers and assignees of a limited liability company are bound by a company's agreement, regardless of whether they executed the agreement. Consequently, where all parties have not properly executed a company agreement, the non-signing parties may still be bound by its terms. Delaware allows the modification of a manager's duty of care within the company agreement. Specifically, the act provides that the member's or manager's or other person's duties may be expanded, restricted or eliminated by provisions in the company agreement, provided that this does not eliminate the implied contractual covenant of good faith and fair dealing.

A written agreement will state the understanding between, and intent of, the members of the limited liability company and provide a foundation for interpreting future disputes relating to the company or its members. While Section 18–101(7) of the Delaware act states that a "written, oral or implied" agreement is enforceable, it is always preferable to sign a written company agreement stating the rights and privileges held by members, regardless of whether the applicable state act requires a formal written agreement.

(a)   *Nature of business permitted*

The business purpose of a limited liability company is stated in the company agreement. Under the Delaware act, there are virtually no restrictions on the types of business activity a limited liability company may pursue. Specifically, Section 18–106(a) of the act provides that "[a] limited liability company may carry on any lawful business, purpose or activity, whether or not for profit, with the exception of the business of banking, as defined in § 126 of Title 8". Unlike some other state limited liability company acts, the Delaware act expressly includes not-for-profit activities within the ambit of permitted business activities.

In some cases, members may wish to limit the parameters of the company's business purpose to avoid the future problem of the company expanding into types of business neither contemplated nor supported by its members. In that situation, a well-crafted statement of business purpose should refer to a specific activity or activities related or ancillary thereto to achieve its business purpose. However, a more general statement as to the nature of the company's business may be preferred by those entering into business transactions with a limited liability company to ensure that it has the power and authority to enter into the transaction.

(b)   *Members*

Members of a limited liability company are typically admitted as such upon the later to occur of:
- the formation of the limited liability company; or
- the time provided in and on compliance with the limited liability company agreement.

Typically, a member may join a limited liability company subsequent to its formation as long as the prerequisites set out in the company agreement have been met or, in the absence of any discussion within the agreement about additional members, the unanimous consent of the existing members has been obtained. Many state acts allow single-member companies and, consequently, contemplate a company agreement executed by only one party. However, the IRS does not recognise the existence of a single-member limited liability company for federal tax purposes. Consequently, all assets, liabilities, profits and losses are considered to be the personal assets, liabilities, profits and losses of its sole member.

In the absence of statutory corporate purpose-related or contractual restrictions, shares in a corporation are freely transferable and, generally, limited liability company acts provide that the benefits of a member's ownership interest are also freely transferable. However, this transferability entitles the assignee only to the benefits associated with membership, rather than to membership itself, which may be attached to other rights or obligations. Members may prefer to limit or control the transfer of benefits to third parties and may do so within the terms of the company agreement by requiring a certain level of consent from non-transferring members. This will often include language to the effect that consent will not be unreasonably withheld. This issue should be contemplated seriously by members in drafting the company agreement, as there are benefits and drawbacks to restricting the transferability of a member's economic benefits. While members may want to maintain economic benefits with those who have a voice in the company or potential obligations to it (unlike third parties, who simply enjoy the economic benefit of a member's interest), restricting the transferability of economic benefits arguably reduces the liquidity of a member's investment, thereby making it potentially less attractive to investors. Under the Delaware act, a company agreement may restrict the transfer of a company interest prior to the dissolution and winding-up of the company.

(i)   *Withdrawal*

Most limited liability company acts provide that a member may withdraw from a company in accordance with the conditions set out in the company agreement. Consequently, a company agreement should include a section relating to the withdrawal of members. Where a Delaware limited liability company does not provide a specific right of withdrawal, the Delaware act provides that a member may not resign prior to the dissolution and winding-up of the company.

(ii)   *Classes*

Generally, a company agreement may divide members into separate classes or groups with respect to rights (including those relating to voting), powers and duties. This allows great flexibility in devising the rights and benefits of ownership of the company, as well as the management structure. Given this flexibility, a company's ownership structure can resemble that of a corporation with preferred or non-voting stock.

(iii)   *Voting*

Members generally have the right to cumulative voting and pre-emptive rights, unless otherwise specified in a particular state act or company agreement. Section 18–302(b) of the Delaware act specifically provides that voting may be determined on a "per capita, number, financial interest, class, group or any other basis". Further, a company agreement may grant all, or certain members, of a specified group or class of members the right to vote separately or with all, or a specified group of, members and/or managers. In the alternative, the Delaware act states that a company agreement may provide that all or certain members of a specified class or group have no voting rights.

Although state limited liability company acts contain voting provisions, the company agreement should include a section dealing with the company's structure and the mechanics of voting by members. Given that the company agreement gives members the opportunity to design the voting requirements to their liking, this opportunity should be taken advantage of and included in the agreement rather than relying on any default rule of a state's act.

(c)   *Designation of tax matters member*

Limited liability companies that are taxed as partnerships for federal taxation purposes should consider designating a 'tax matters member' within the company agreement. Although all members of the company are entitled to review a company's tax return and audit report, the tax matters member will be responsible for preparing the company's tax return and audits. Pursuant to Section 6231(a)(7) of the Internal Revenue Code, which contains audit procedures for partnerships (and, consequently, limited liability companies taxed as partnerships), any tax matters member must be a member manager of the company. Section 6231(a)(7)–2 defines a 'member manager' as "a member of a limited liability company who, alone or together with others, is vested with the continuing exclusive authority to make the management decisions necessary to conduct the business for which the organization was formed".

(d)   *Management*

A limited liability company may be managed by all, some or one of its members or managers. Most company acts provide that, in the absence of a provision to the contrary, a limited liability company is managed by all of its members. The decision to be member-managed or manager-managed will typically be influenced by the type of business and how active members wish to be in the management of the company. Where members want to take a more hands-off approach, a manager-managed or managing-member-managed structure may be favoured. This may also occur when the company's business is complex and time consuming and members simply wish to be passive investors, or they are only offered such a position. Further, a member or manager is generally given statutory power and authority to delegate the member's or manager's rights and powers to manage and/or control the business affairs of the company. This authorises the creation of officer positions similar to those of a corporation (an option generally chosen by large limited liability companies with more complex business operations). This has the added benefit of indicating to outsiders the authority of the person acting on behalf of the company.

Where a company is member-managed, each member has statutory authority to bind the company. However, the company agreement may modify the default rule and explicitly indicate who is authorised to bind the company. Although state limited liability company acts contain voting provisions, the company agreement should include a section dealing with the company's structure and mechanics of voting by members. Members of a company should take advantage of the opportunity to implement the voting structure rather than relying on any default rule of a state's act.

Where a limited liability company is manager-managed, the company agreement should detail how the manager(s) will manage the company, rather than relying on default state rules. Generally, managers are given statutory authority to bind the company. As previously stated, however, the default rule in most states is that members also have the statutory authority to bind a company. Consequently, where a company is manager-managed, or managed by fewer than all of its members, a company agreement should explicitly state that some or all of the members do not have the authority to bind the company. In the event that managers will serve a function similar to that of directors of a corporation, bylaws governing their actions should be adopted and included in the company agreement.

The Delaware act provides that a non-resident of Delaware who accepts a position as manager of a Delaware company consents to jurisdiction in the Delaware courts for claims brought against the manager by members or member-managers for decisions made in the course and scope of running the company. This is so even if the limited liability company does not conduct business in Delaware but has merely been formed there, and even if the manager has never been there and has no connection with Delaware other than holding the manager's position.

Notwithstanding the consent to jurisdiction, unlike a Delaware general corporation which cannot by charter or bylaw preclude resolution in the Delaware Court of Chancery for disputes over the internal affairs of the corporation, a forum selection clause can be included in a limited liability company agreement to provide for resolution of any and all disputes in another jurisdiction or by arbitration.

3.3 Allocation plan, capital contributions and distributions

Members of a limited liability company have great flexibility in allocating profits and losses. A company agreement should specify the tax allocation and cash distribution rules relating to its members. Specifically, a limited liability company taxed as a partnership should set out:

- the initial amount in each member's capital account;
- the allocation plan relating to profits and losses; and
- the procedures for operational and liquidating distributions.

Typically, distributions by a limited liability company are made upon the occurrence of:

- benchmark events specified in a company agreement; and
- dissolution of the company.

Where a company does not specifically provide for distributions, members will not be entitled to any such distribution prior to resignation from, or dissolution of, the company.

Where a company agreement is silent as to an allocation plan, the default rule of a state's limited liability company act will dictate whether profits and losses are distributed based on the agreed value of a member's capital contribution or (eg as in Texas) based on a member's current percentage interest stated in the company's records. Members should fully consider tax issues relating to a company's particular allocation plan before implementing it (see section 4 below).

With limited exceptions, state acts allow members' capital contributions to take a variety of forms, including cash, property, services rendered or promissory notes. Most states require that a member's obligation to contribute capital to the company is in writing.

A company is generally authorised to make distributions of cash to its members as long as it is not thereby rendered insolvent (ie the company's ability to pay obligations as they fall due and to continue as a viable going concern is impaired). Although they vary from state to state, acts have default provisions relating to the distribution and allocation of profits and losses. Where a company agreement is silent on the issue, a company's allocations and distributions may be based on contributions, per capita sharing, *pro rata* profits or book value, depending on the default rule of the particular jurisdiction of formation. The Delaware act default provision relating to allocation of profits and losses provides for distributions based on the agreed value of a member's paid and unreturned contribution "as stated in the records of a limited liability company".

4. Taxation

4.1 Federal tax

As discussed, a major benefit of the limited liability company is its ability to be treated as a partnership for tax purposes. More than ten years ago, the IRS cast aside a test that analysed the corporate characteristics of a limited liability company to determine whether it should be taxed as a partnership or as a general corporation, and it adopted what is known as 'check-the-box' regulations. These were effective as of January 1 1997 and provide that, unless it elects to be treated as a corporation, a limited liability company with more than one member formed after the effective date will generally be treated as a partnership for federal tax purposes.

Single-member limited liability companies are regarded as similar to proprietorships in that the IRS does not recognise the single-member company as an entity separate from its sole member.

In the event that a company goes public, it will lose its pass-through tax treatment and be taxed as a general corporation. This is one of the reasons why limited liability companies generally convert to, or reincorporate as general corporations prior to a public stock offering. Also, the selling of assets or the conversion of a limited liability company to a general corporation to take it public may be taxable events. This chapter is not intended to address tax law in any detail and because the tax code is voluminous, often confusing and subject to change, tax experts should be consulted.

4.2 State tax

For state tax purposes, a limited liability company will generally receive the same tax classification as it does for federal tax purposes; however, this depends on the state. For example, Section 1107(a) of the Delaware act provides that, for state income tax purposes, a limited liability company "shall be classified as a partnership unless classified otherwise for federal income tax purposes, in which case the limited liability company shall be classified in the same manner as it is classified for federal income tax purposes".

A Delaware limited liability company pays no state income tax to the state of Delaware if it is merely formed there and does business elsewhere. Delaware currently (2009) imposes an 8.7% tax on income generated from business activity in the state.

4.3 Miscellaneous tax considerations

In general, a limited liability company is treated as a partnership for federal income tax purposes and its income passes through to its members. The members in turn are subject to federal income tax on their share. Members who are US persons are not subject to withholding on their share of company income, but are required to file quarterly estimated tax returns and pay any estimated tax. In addition, the operating income of a company will generally be subject to self-employment tax for its individual members. This is currently 15.3% for the first $106,800 and 2.9% on all income in excess of that threshold. If the company is engaged in a US trade or business, it is generally required to withhold and remit to the US Treasury 35% of the income allocated (whether or not actually distributed) to its non-US members. Each such non-US member will be required to file a federal income tax return (regardless of whether the member is allocated profits or losses, or has no income) and receive a federal income tax credit for any amount withheld. In addition, any member who is a non-US corporation may be subject to US branch tax at a current rate of 35%, subject to reduction under an applicable tax treaty with the United States.

In contrast to a limited liability company, a US corporation (other than an S corporation) is a taxpayer and pays federal income tax on its worldwide income. Such income is subject to federal income tax at various percentages depending on the amount of corporate income earned, and applicable state and local taxes also apply. The corporate federal income tax rates are outlined in the table below.

US corporate income tax

Income	Tax rates 2009
First $50,000	15%
$50,0001 to $75,000	25%
$75,001 to $100,000	34%
$100,001 to $335,000	39%
$335,001 to $10 million	34%
$10,000,001 to $15 million	35%
$15,000,001 to $18,333,333	38%
More than $18,333,333	35%

When a distribution is made to shareholders, they can also be subject to tax. Whether or not a shareholder is taxed on a distribution depends on:

- the amount of the distribution;
- the amount of the corporation's earnings and profits; and
- the shareholder's tax basis in the shares of the corporation (where 'tax basis' means the original cost paid by the investor for the investment (including expenses) that, when the investment is sold, is reported to the IRS for the purposes of calculating capital gains or losses).

Any distribution is taxed as a dividend first to the extent of the corporation's current earnings and profits (in general, the corporation's taxable income for the current year with various adjustments). To the extent the distribution exceeds the corporation's current earnings and profits, the distribution is taxable as a dividend to the extent of the corporation's cumulative earnings and profits (in general, all of the corporation's taxable income with various adjustments). The amount of the distribution that exceeds the corporation's current and cumulative earnings and profits is treated as a tax-free return of the shareholder's investment in the corporation (the shareholder's tax basis in the shares of the corporation). Any remaining amount of the distribution is taxed as a capital gain. Amounts that are taxed as a dividend are subject to a federal income tax of 15% for individuals and 35% for corporations. Dividends paid to non-US shareholders are generally subject to the 30% withholding tax; however, this rate may be reduced by an applicable tax treaty with the United States. A non-US shareholder will generally not be subject to federal income tax on capital gains, provided that shareholder is not present in the United States for 183 days or more in the year the gain is recognised, or is not engaged in a US trade or business.

For federal income tax purposes, if a member of a limited liability company is allocated losses in excess of the company's income, this may be able to be offset against other income of the member. In general, for a member to use such loss against other income, he or she must have an amount at risk in the company (tax basis in its interest) and must materially participate in the operation of the company. Even if the member does not, he or she may be eligible to use the loss to offset certain other qualifying passive income. In contrast, any loss generated by a corporation (other than an S corporation) will remain in the corporation and cannot be used by its shareholders.

5.   Company reorganisation

5.1   Merger or consolidation

A domestic limited liability company (ie a Delaware company) may merge or consolidate with or into one more other domestic companies or one or more other business entities. These include various entities organised under the laws of Delaware, other US states or foreign countries or jurisdictions. These entities are delineated by the Delaware act and include, but are not limited to, corporations, limited partnerships and foreign limited liability companies. The agreement of merger or consolidation may specify which entity shall be the surviving or resulting entity. Upon a merger or consolidation under the Delaware act, the surviving or resulting entity succeeds to the assets and liabilities of each of the constituent domestic companies or other business entities that merged or consolidated.

Unless modified by agreement, a merger or consolidation must be approved by members owning more than 50% of the then current interest in the profits owned by all the members of each domestic company that is to be merged or consolidated. If the company has separate classes or groups of members, then approval must be obtained by members owning more than 50% of the then current interest in the profits of each class or group.

For federal income tax purposes, a merger or consolidation of a company with another limited liability company or a partnership generally can be done on a tax-free basis. However, the merger or consolidation of a company with a corporation is generally a taxable transaction.

A company agreement may provide that, upon the occurrence of a properly protested merger, a sale of substantially all of the company's assets, conversion to a different form of business entity or domestication in another state, a company member may petition the Delaware Court of Chancery to have the member's interest bought out at fair market value as appraised by the court. This is similar to appraisal rights provided by the Delaware General Corporation Law to stockholders of general corporations.

5.2 Domestication

A limited liability company formed in a state other than Delaware may convert to a Delaware company. Similarly, a non-US business entity can, in accordance with the Delaware act, convert to and become a Delaware limited liability company. Prior to filing the necessary documents with the Delaware secretary of state, such domestication, as well as the company agreement that will govern the soon-to-be-domesticated entity, must be approved in accordance with the constitutive documents or other non-Delaware law then governing the entity.

Upon domestication, the limited liability company shall be subject to the Delaware act and will be deemed to have commenced on the date the non-US entity was originally formed. Like any other domestic limited liability companies, the domesticated entity shall succeed to the assets and liabilities of its predecessor non-US entity. However, unless otherwise agreed, the act of domestication does not dissolve the non-US entity, which can continue to exist in its jurisdiction of origin. Domestication does not affect the liabilities of the non-US entity incurred prior to its domestication, or the personal liability of any person. The interest-holding composition of the domesticated company is the same as the prior entity.

5.3 Transfer or continuance

A Delaware limited liability company may transfer to or domesticate in any other jurisdiction. The company may opt to discontinue or continue its existence as a Delaware company. If the company opts to continue its Delaware existence, the company is considered to exist under the laws of both Delaware and the jurisdiction to which the company transfers or domesticates. The procedure for effecting this, regardless of whether the company elects to maintain its Delaware existence, may be set out in the company agreement. Otherwise, the Delaware act provides that approval will be the same as that required for a merger or consolidation.

If a Delaware company transfers or domesticates out of Delaware and opts to discontinue its existence as a Delaware company, this does not affect the obligations, liabilities, or personal liabilities of any person that were incurred prior to the transfer or domestication. The interest-holding composition of the transferred or continued company is the same as that of the prior entity.

5.4 Conversion

The operative provisions of the Delaware act providing for the conversion of certain other business entities to a domestic limited liability company are substantially similar to the provisions of the act providing for the domestication of non-US business entities. The Delaware act identifies the following entities that can be converted:

- corporation;
- statutory trust;
- business trust or association;
- real estate investment trust; and
- common-law trust or any other unincorporated business, including a general or limited partnership or a foreign limited liability company (ie a US non-Delaware limited liability company).

The interest-holding composition of the converted company is the same as that of the prior entity. A conversion can generally be done on a tax-free basis for federal income tax purposes.

6. Resignation of members or managers

6.1 Members

A member of a limited liability company may resign as provided for in the company agreement, which may specify certain events that will trigger resignation of a member. Unless an agreement provides otherwise, a member may not resign prior to the dissolution and winding-up of a company. Under the Delaware act, however, membership ceases on events such as insolvency or bankruptcy, unless otherwise provided for in the company agreement. That said, the termination of a member does not mean that the company must be dissolved or its affairs wound up.

Subject to certain statutory exceptions, a member who resigns is entitled to such distributions as are provided for in the company agreement. If there is no such provision, the member is entitled to the fair value of his limited liability company interest, based on his right to a share in the company's distributions.

6.2 Managers

Like a member, a manager of a limited liability company may resign as provided for in the company agreement. However, this may provide that a manager does not have the right to resign. A manager may resign by giving notice to the members and other managers. The company may recover against the resigning manager for breach of the company agreement, in addition to any remedies available under the law, and offset distributions to which the manager is otherwise entitled by the amount of such liability.

7. Dissolution, winding-up and distribution of assets

7.1 Dissolution and judicial dissolution

A limited liability company can be dissolved as provided for in its company agreement, on events stated in the Delaware act, or if an order for judicial dissolution is entered. A limited liability company can be dissolved upon the expiration of a time period specified in the company agreement. If no such time period is specified, the company shall have perpetual existence unless dissolved by one of the other permitted means. These include:

- the occurrence of an event specified in a limited liability agreement;
- unless otherwise provided in the company agreement, by the vote of members owning more than two-thirds of the then current interest in the profits of the company owned by all the members (if the company has separate classes or groups of members, then approval must be obtained from members owning more than two-thirds of the then current interest in the profits of each class or group);
- at such time as there are no members of the company (subject to two exceptions provided in the Delaware act); and
- the entry of a decree of judicial dissolution under the Delaware act.

Only a member or manager of a limited liability company can petition the Delaware Court of Chancery for a decree of dissolution. This will be issued if the member or manager can establish that it is not practical to carry on the business of the company in conformity with the company agreement.

7.2 Winding-up

A manager or, if none, the members of company may wind up the company's affairs. A winding-up by the members must be approved by any members owning more than 50% of the then current interest in the profits. If the company has separate classes or groups of members, approval must be obtained by members owning more than 50% of the then current interest in the profits of each class or group.

Alternatively, a member or manager (or a creditor of the company) may petition the Delaware Court of Chancery for an order appointing a liquidating trustee or receiver to wind up the company's affairs, which may be issued upon a showing of good cause. The grounds for such a petition are that it is not reasonably practicable to carry on the business of the limited liability company because of:

- deadlocks;
- substantial disagreements over management decisions;

- litigation among the member/managers over management decisions or distributions; or
- similar events or circumstances that may impair the intended business and operation of the limited liability company and warrant dissolution.

Once a limited liability company is dissolved, the persons winding up the company's affairs may:

- prosecute and defend lawsuits;
- settle and close the company's business;
- dispose of the company's property;
- discharge or make reasonable provision for the company's liabilities; and
- distribute the remaining assets of the company to the members.

This may be done without affecting the previously agreed extent of liability of the company's members and managers, and without imposing liability on a liquidating trustee.

7.3   Distribution of assets

The Delaware act provides that upon the dissolution and winding-up of a company, its assets will be distributed and its liabilities satisfied in accordance with a mandatory statutory priority scheme. Upon winding-up, the company's assets are distributed:

- to creditors, including members and managers who are creditors. Distributions to creditors do not include distributions in satisfaction of liabilities for which the company has made reasonable provision. Neither do such distributions include payments to members and former members for amounts owed for interim distributions or distributions in respect of resignation from the company;
- unless otherwise provided in the company agreement, to members and former members for amounts owed for interim distributions or distributions in respect of resignation from the company;
- unless otherwise provided in the company agreement, to members for return of their contributions; and
- finally, to members *pro rata* in respect of their interests in the company.

With respect to a dissolved company, its liabilities, actual or contingent, are satisfied or provided for as follows:

- The company must pay or make provision to pay all known claims or obligations, which include contingent, conditional, or unmatured contractual obligations;
- The company must make provision that is reasonably likely to be sufficient to provide compensation in respect of pending litigation to which the company is a party; and
- The company must make provision that is reasonably likely to be sufficient to provide compensation in respect of unknown claims or claims that have

not arisen but that, based on known facts, are likely to arise or become known to the company within 10 years of dissolution.

Unlike the Delaware General Corporation Law, the Delaware act does not provide the option of a statutory 'safe harbour' for those distributing the dissolved company's assets. Prudence thus dictates that distributions should be made only after careful consideration, and likewise that provision for liabilities should not be approached in a cavalier manner. That said, members who unknowingly receive distributions in violation of the Delaware act are not automatically liable for the return thereof unless so provided by the limited liability company agreement or applicable law.

For federal income tax purposes, the dissolution of a limited liability company will generally be taxed to the extent that the sum of the cash and the fair market value of any marketable securities distributed to a member exceeds such member's tax basis in that member's ownership interest in the company. Any remaining tax basis of the member's interest will be allocated to the other property distributed to the member on dissolution.

8. Limitations on liability

A limited liability company is a non-corporate business entity that provides its owners with limited liability while at the same time allowing them to participate actively in the management of the company. In terms of the limitations on liability, a limited liability company can be considered roughly analogous to a partnership whose partners have limited liability. In similar fashion to the 'corporate veil' protection provided to shareholders of a general corporation, the Delaware act provides that no member or manager of a company is personally obligated in respect of any debt, obligation or liability of the company solely because that person is a member or acts as a manager of the company. This limitation on liability does not protect individuals from liability in tort or for acts of fraud or similar wrongdoing, even when the actions at issue are taken in the name of and on behalf of the company.

In an unusual statutory provision, pursuant to Section 630 of the New York Business Corporation Law, a New York corporation's 10 largest shareholders have personal liability for the payment of employee wages. Further, certain employment laws, such as a statute known as the 'wage payment and collection act' (versions of which have been passed by many states) may make certain managers personally liable for a wilful failure to pay employee wages.

A limited liability company can itself serve as a member or manager of another limited liability company, as a partner of a partnership or as a stockholder of a corporation. In those capacities, the separateness of the company will generally be respected. For example, the assets of a limited liability company that holds stock in a corporation are not at risk to satisfy claims against the corporation, solely because the company is a stockholder. Like any other stockholder, the company is at risk only to the amount of its equity investment. To the extent a limited liability company is liable for conduct as a participant in another business entity, the liability will be premised on the body of law governing the relationship, whether it be limited liability company law, corporate law, partnership law or other applicable law.

8.1 Specific protections for management

(a) Exculpatory provisions

The Delaware General Corporation Law allows a general corporation, in its certificate of incorporation, to provide for the elimination or limitation of directors' personal liability to the corporation or to its stockholders for breaches of directors' fiduciary duties. Such an exculpatory provision, when included in a corporation's certificate of incorporation or charter, shields directors from personal liability for certain breaches of fiduciary duty and business decisions. Specifically excluded from the scope of this protection, however, are breaches of fiduciary duty involving improper personal benefits for directors, bad-faith conduct or intentional misconduct, and certain unlawful issuances of dividends, stock purchases and stock redemptions. As a result, the claims for which directors are most often able to escape liability are:

- those involving alleged waste of corporate assets (conveying corporate property for inadequate consideration);
- those involving alleged inadequate disclosure of information to stockholders; and
- other claims relating to decisions about mergers and other corporate combinations.

By its terms, this provision of the Delaware General Corporation Law does not apply to officers of a general corporation and it remains open whether a corporation can provide such protection to officers in its charter notwithstanding the lack of an express statutory mandate.

Similar to the Delaware General Corporation Law, the Delaware act allows members of a limited liability company to limit the liability to the company's managers and members by agreement. For example, company agreements often limit the liability of members or managers for breaches of contract and other duties. The Delaware act specifically provides that a limited liability company's operating "agreement may provide for the limitation or elimination of any and all liabilities for breach of contract and breach of duties (including fiduciary duties) of a member", except that an agreement cannot purport to contract around liability for bad-faith breaches of the implied covenant of good faith and fair dealing that inheres in all Delaware contracts. However, decisions of the Delaware courts have set limits on the extent to which liability for breaches of fiduciary duty may be limited or eliminated, and it is now generally recognised that claims for fraud or bad faith cannot be precluded by language, no matter how specific, in a company agreement.

(b) Indemnification

In addition to exculpatory provisions, Delaware corporations can provide indemnification to directors and officers for expenses related to lawsuits and other proceedings to which directors or officers are parties, and that arise from a director's or officer's capacity. Where a director or officer is unsuccessful on the merits of a proceeding, indemnification is permitted. However, where a director or officer is successful on the merits of a proceeding, indemnification is usually mandatory. Indemnification is limited to cases where directors and officers acted in good faith and in a manner they believed to be in the best interests of the corporation.

When a corporation's charter or bylaws so provide, a director or officer may be entitled not only to indemnification but also to advancement of expenses, including attorneys' fees, upon providing the corporation with an undertaking to repay if it is later determined that indemnification is not legally available (ie a determination by a court that the director or officer engaged in fraud or a breach of loyalty or good faith to the corporation).

In lawsuits by or against third parties, directors and officers may be indemnified both for expenses incurred in connection with the lawsuit and for any amounts paid in judgment or settlement of the suit. However, in lawsuits by or on behalf of the company (ie derivative actions), directors and officers may be indemnified for expenses, but not for any amounts paid in judgment or settlement of the suit unless ordered by a court.

A person considering possible service on a board of directors or a position as an officer should obtain and, along with his counsel, carefully review the corporation's bylaws, any indemnification agreements and other corporation policies governing indemnification.

Similarities to the Delaware General Corporation Law are also contained in the Delaware act on the issue of indemnification. This contains broader language and states that a limited liability company "may, and shall have the power to, indemnify and hold harmless any member or manager or other person from and against any and all claims and demands whatsoever". A company agreement may also provide for the advancement of litigation expenses, including attorneys' fees.

(c) *Reliance on reports from advisers*

The Delaware General Corporation Law protects directors who, in the performance of their duties, rely in good faith on the records of the corporation or on information, opinions, reports or other statements provided to directors by officers, employees or committees of the corporation or by certain outside advisers, such as attorneys and auditors. Where particular business decisions fall outside a director's area of expertise, reliance on the reports or opinions of others may be required for a director to satisfy their duties adequately. This ability to rely on advisers can be particularly important to directors who serve on the company's compensation, audit or nominating committees. The foremost limitation on the principle of reliance is the requirement that reliance be in good faith. The good-faith qualification requires that directors not ignore 'red flags' raised in reports or opinions presented to them, and that they ask questions and demand additional information where necessary. In addition, reports or opinions received by directors must be pertinent to the decision at hand, and directors must be given adequate materials and time to consider those materials. Finally, if directors are to rely on officers and other advisers, they must be deliberate and careful when determining whom to appoint and upon whom to rely.

Again, like the Delaware General Corporation Law, the Delaware act provides that members and managers of limited liability companies:

shall be fully protected in relying in good faith upon the records of the limited liability company and upon information, opinions, reports or statements presented by another manager, member or liquidating trustee, an officer or employee of the limited liability company ... or by any other person as to matters the member, manager or liquidating trustee reasonably believes are within such person's professional or expert competence, including information, opinions, reports or statements as to the value and amount of the assets, liabilities, profits or losses of the limited liability company.

(d) Insurance

A corporation and a limited liability company may, but are not required to, provide insurance for directors and officers or managers against any liability that may arise as a result of their conduct. The corporation or company may provide this insurance regardless of whether it could indemnify the director or officer or manager, thus making insurance a potentially broader protection against personal liability than indemnification.

The primary limitations on insurance are found within the policies themselves. So-called 'director and officer liability' (D&O) insurance policies may differ widely from corporation to corporation and between insurance companies as to scope, coverage limits and deductibles; some companies do not even provide D&O insurance. A director or officer or manager should obtain and, along with his counsel, carefully review the insurance policy, if any, and the company agreement for inclusion of the management protection provisions, before agreeing to serve on a board or as an officer or as a manager.

8.2 Structural protections relating to creditors and other liabilities

Exculpatory provisions for limited liability companies and general corporations have been construed by the Delaware courts in the context of claims presented by creditors, with the courts holding that company managers and corporate directors are protected from claims of mismanagement and breach of fiduciary duty to the same extent as if the claims were being brought by members or stockholders. The courts have noted that creditors can pursue such claims on behalf of the company when the firm is insolvent because they are the beneficiaries of the remaining assets, but that the nature of the claim does not change. The courts have also noted that duties and obligations of a manager and director are at all times owed to the business entity and no special duties are owed to creditors who can protect themselves with provisions in the applicable debt instruments to create direct rights against the company, any member or manager by contract. Thus, under these judicial decisions, managers and directors will not face personal liability if their decisions are made in the good-faith exercise of business judgement.

Beyond exculpatory provisions for management, there are certain structural options provided by limited liability company acts that can protect assets from claims by creditors and other liabilities. The Delaware act permits a company agreement to establish a designated series of property or operations with separate business purposes or investment objectives, such that the debts, liabilities and obligations relating to a particular series would be enforceable only against the assets of such series and not against the assets of the limited liability company generally. Each series has separate members, managers, assets and liabilities, and business interests. The limited liability company and not the series will be treated as the legal entity under Delaware law. Theoretically, the limited liability company could avoid the debts altogether by allocating all the company assets to the various series within company.

Assets of a particular series may be protected if:

- the limited liability company agreement provides for the establishment of one or more series;
- separate and distinct records are maintained for each series and its assets are separate from the other assets of the limited liability company or any other series (and the limited liability company agreement so provides); and
- notice of such limitation of liability is set out in the company's certificate of formation.

However, a member or manager may agree to be personally liable for any or all of the debts, obligations and liabilities of one or more series. This structural protection applies to the legitimate operation of a business. The separation of assets and liabilities for the purpose of perpetrating a fraud, or the transfer of assets from one series to another to avoid a known or accrued liability (ie a fraudulent transfer), would not be deemed to fall within the protections provided by the Delaware limited liability company series structure.

Consistent with the general company goals of freedom of contract and flexibility, the company agreement can create numerous series within the limited liability company to accomplish diverse business objectives. The company agreement can provide for the future creation of additional classes or groups of members or managers not previously outstanding within a series, and it can also provide for the taking of any action, including amendment of the company agreement, without the vote or approval of any member or manager or class or group of members or managers.

Unless otherwise provided in the company agreement, any event that causes a member to cease to be associated with a series will not, in itself, mean that that member ceases to be associated with any other series, terminate the member's interest in the company, or cause the termination of the series even if the member was the last surviving member associated with the particular series.

Upon application of a manager or member of a series, the Delaware Court of Chancery may decree the termination of the series "whenever it is not reasonably practicable to carry on the business of the series in conformity with a limited liability agreement". The Delaware act also permits a foreign limited liability company (ie a non-Delaware company) that is properly registered to do business in the state of Delaware to provide for the establishment of a designated series of members, managers or company interests (provided that the application for registration as a foreign limited liability company so states) and for the limitation of liability for the debts, liabilities and obligations of a particular series to the assets of that series.

Each of the assets in a series company can operate independently of the limited liability company and avoid liabilities. The members of a limited liability company should be able to transfer freely assets and ownership interests from one series to another, provided that the purpose of the transfer is not to commit a fraud. The statutory language regarding series limited liability companies speaks not in terms of separate and distinct ownership, but rather in terms of separating assets and liabilities within the limited liability company. This provides for separate allocation of liabilities to one or more particular series if:

- the operating agreement and certificate of formation for the limited liability company so provide;
- separate records are kept; and
- separate accounts are maintained for each series.

Consequently, all of the assets of a limited liability company could be put into one series and all the liabilities into another.

As the creation of a series does not create a new legal entity, the limited liability company remains the legal entity under Delaware law and the certificate of formation should establish the authority of the manager of a particular series to bind the company and execute documents on its behalf. When dealing with the Delaware series limited liability company structure, careful attention must be paid to the certificate of formation and the operating agreement, and the ability to shift assets and liabilities among different series.

9.   **Overview of limitations on liability applicable to general corporations**
General corporations in the United States operate on a wide spectrum, from small privately held companies to publicly traded, billion-dollar, multinational corporations; but no matter what their size, they are subject to many formalities. For example, the relationship between management (board of directors) and the owners (stockholders) is fiduciary based, with the board of directors managing the company and the stockholders having little or no role in management other than the election of directors and the approval at stockholder meetings of amendments to the articles of incorporation and major transactions such as mergers. The fiduciary obligations owed to stockholders by management cannot be contracted away, and statutory requirements for things such as the holding of annual stockholder meetings, strictures with regard to the election of directors, amendments to the articles of incorporation and bylaws, notice periods, the sale of assets and the issue of stock must be strictly observed or written consents obtained in lieu thereof. If the corporation is a public corporation, it must comply with the Securities Exchange Act of 1934 and other federal securities laws in the United States, such as the Sarbanes-Oxley Act and the Securities and Exchange Commission. In addition, the exchange on which the corporation's securities are traded will have its own rules affecting the structure of management and the corporation's communications with stockholders. A review of these complexities could take up not just a chapter, but an entire book or volumes of books. Nonetheless, for someone seeking to do business or engage in a merger or acquisition in the United States, there are certain important legalities that warrant discussion and they are summarised next.

9.1 The business judgement rule

As previously noted, stockholders are entitled to 'corporate veil' protection, which means that unless the corporation was created or conducted with the intent of committing a fraud, the stockholders are not responsible for its liabilities or debts in the event of insolvency. With regard to Delaware corporations, mere ownership of stock in a Delaware corporation will not subject a stockholder to personal jurisdiction in the courts of the state of Delaware. However, a director or officer of a Delaware corporation is subject to personal jurisdiction in the Delaware Court of Chancery from actions alleging a breach of fiduciary duty or other wrongdoing committed in the course and scope of managing the corporation, even if the business is merely incorporated in Delaware and the director or officer has no other connection to the state other than holding the position of director or officer of a Delaware corporation.

In carrying out the business of the corporation, management is protected by the business judgement rule, which is the standard by which courts review most, but not all, director's decisions. The business judgement rule reflects the legal premise that decisions made by directors who are fully informed and free from conflicts of interest should not, and will not, be second-guessed by a court, even if the business decision under review turns out to have been 'poor'.

To receive a favourable presumption of the business judgement rule, a director must:

- be disinterested and independent (ie satisfy the fiduciary duty of loyalty);
- review and consider all pertinent information reasonably available (ie satisfy the fiduciary duty of care); and
- not act in a manner or with a motive prohibited by statute or otherwise improper, and at all times act in good faith when discharging fiduciary duties.

The fiduciary duty of loyalty concerns the qualities of disinterestedness and independence. As a general rule, courts consider a director to be 'interested' if he or she stands to receive a personal, financial or other benefit from a transaction that is not shared proportionately by the corporation's stockholders. Non-financial benefits can also create conflict, the most common of which is entrenchment (ie a director's desire for perpetuation of office). Directors are generally considered 'interested' when they have a unique or competing personal interest with respect to a given corporate decision or transaction.

Most typically, directors are considered not to be 'independent' where they are beholden to a person or entity that has a personal interest in the action under consideration. A director may be deemed 'beholden to' another where, as a result of personal, professional or financial relationships or dependence, the director cannot reasonably be thought capable of acting in the best interests of the corporation. In most cases, casual social ties or friendship, in the absence of other factors, will not create a lack of independence; however, close familial or financial ties or extensive professional and social ties may. Where present, or even potentially present, self-interest or a lack of independence may require that a director abstain from the decision-making process. Other steps aimed at ensuring that a director's potential conflict does not taint an otherwise valid exercise of directorial discretion include:

- the involvement of a disinterested and independent committee of directors; and
- stockholders' ratification.

The fiduciary duty of good faith is a subsidiary of the duty of loyalty; the Delaware courts have ruled that a director who acts in bad faith is disloyal to the corporation. Thus, the duty of good faith is something of a catch-all category, denying the protections of the business judgement rule to directors who, although not financially interested in a decision or transaction, act or fail to act out of a motive other than the best interests of the corporation. Conduct may also be deemed to be in bad faith where it is so far outside the realm of reason that it cannot be explained on any other grounds. Finally, sustained or systematic inattention to significant corporate issues or 'red flag' situations, potentially resulting in harm to the corporation, may also be deemed to be in bad faith. Steps that directors can take to avoid liability for claims based on allegations of bad faith include establishing internal reporting and control mechanisms to help maintain knowledge of events, or issues that may have a significant effect on the corporation.

The fiduciary duty of care concerns the quality of attention that a director is supposed to bring to management decisions, judged by a standard of reasonable prudence. To be deemed adequately informed regarding a given business decision, directors must have had access to all available information. Typically, as long as directors make a good-faith effort to undertake an investigation or gather pertinent information, courts will not second-guess their procedures. Such investigation and information gathering also contemplates a good-faith effort to review and understand that information. The question of what information is material to a given decision can only be answered based on the specific set of facts and circumstances of the decision. It may be prudent for directors to consult with management, attorneys or other advisers before making a decision. Section 141(e) of the Delaware General Corporation Law expressly allows directors to rely on corporate records and advice from professionals.

When directors fail to satisfy their duties, the transaction is not void but voidable; however, a heightened 'entire fairness' standard will be applied by a court if the transaction is challenged. Under such circumstances, the burden is on the directors to prove that the decision or transaction at issue is fair to both the company and its stockholders. Even if the transaction is approved by an independent special committee or a vote of a majority of the minority stockholders, business judgement rule protection is not available. Such procedural safeguards only shift the burden back to a stockholder-plaintiff to prove that the transaction was unfair, which means the substance of the transaction will be evaluated by a court. This is very different from transactions that are eligible for business judgement rule protection where the court merely evaluates whether a board was fully informed (duty of care) and whether a majority of the board was independent (duty of loyalty). Satisfying the 'entire fairness' standard is extremely difficult because the board must demonstrate fair process and fair price. Failure to establish the 'entire fairness' of the decision or transaction can render it void and lead to personal liability for directors.

Within this fiduciary structure, special rules and heightened scrutiny apply to certain structures and scenarios arising in mergers and acquisitions. For example, a business combination where a controlling stockholder sits on both sides of the transaction will also be subject to an 'entire fairness' review. When the company is subject to a hostile takeover and decides to take defensive action, such as the adoption of a 'poison pill' tactic, directors must satisfy what has come to be known as the 'Unocal' standard (derived from the 1985 Delaware Supreme Court case of *Unocal Corp v Mesa Petroleum Co*). This means that the board must demonstrate that the defensive action taken was reasonable in relation to the threat to the company and its business objectives. When a conscious decision has been made to sell the company or control of the company, or when market or other conditions make the sale of the company inevitable, the board operates in a so-called 'Revlon' mode (derived from the 1986 Delaware Supreme Court case of *Revlon Inc v McAndrews & Forbes Holdings Inc*). 'Revlon' mode obligates the directors to obtain the best price reasonably available for the stockholders. These special circumstances clearly become fact-intensive inquiries. The importance of complying with the above legal framework cannot be overstated, particularly if a merger or acquisition is later subject to legal challenge.

The functional protection of the business judgement rule is in addition to other protections, such as:

- exculpatory provisions in a corporation's charter for directors (see section 8.1(a));
- indemnification for both directors and officers (see section 8.1(b));
- the ability of directors and officers to rely upon corporate records and advice from professionals (see section 8.1(c)); and
- insurance (see section 8.1(d)).

9.2 Preventive measures

Preventive measures should be employed so as to avoid the need to invoke these protections. There is no blueprint for taking preventive measures to avoid being sued in the first instance or to avoid personal liability if a director is being sued for actions taken in the course and scope of his duties. Adherence to certain well-established 'best practices', however, can help to reduce the likelihood of liability. Such practices may include, but are not limited to, the following (some of which are already mandated for public companies by the Sarbanes-Oxley Act or stock exchange rules):

- establishing well-defined and conservative standards of director independence;
- setting a required number or percentage of independent directors, such as a majority;
- establishing term limits for directors;
- establishing a 'lead' independent director;
- considering the establishment of a chief governance officer position;
- maintaining separate chief executive officer and chairman positions;

- developing and initiating active compliance-monitoring systems, including the creation of a chief compliance officer who reports directly to the board;
- ensuring that the minimum expectations of director conduct standards, such as Sarbanes-Oxley or New York Stock Exchange or NASDAQ rules, are met;
- hiring and training directors with diverse sets of skills and backgrounds;
- evaluating the quality and effectiveness of board meetings, including the use of agendas, the preparation and distribution of materials, and the timing and length of meetings;
- keeping apprised of corporate governance trends and legislation;
- developing and implementing appropriately authorised committees and sub-committees to oversee and monitor areas of potential liability, such as executive compensation, director nomination, financial audits and regulatory compliance;
- prohibiting related-party transactions or requiring independent review of such transactions;
- creating and maintaining effective internal reporting systems for malfeasance or wrongdoing, including a 'whistleblower' policy;
- developing and adhering to a code of ethics;
- taking an active role in corporate disclosures; and
- maintaining open and active stockholder relations.

The authors would like to thank R Craig Martin, an associate in the Wilmington, Delaware office, and Robert E Baute Jr, an associate in the Providence, Rhode Island office of Edwards, Angell Palmer & Dodge LLP, for their valuable assistance in the preparation of this chapter.

Uruguay

Andrés Durán Hareau
Héctor Ferreira
Hughes & Hughes

1. Types of company with limited liability and applicable legislation

Several different corporate forms are available in Uruguay. However, investors usually opt for a corporation – whether locally organised or a branch of a foreign corporation – in the case of medium-sized and large companies, and a limited liability partnership in the case of smaller businesses.

Act 16,060, passed by the Executive on September 7 1989, sets out the system governing commercial companies, economic interest groups and consortia. This act regulates the different kinds of commercial company, with certain exceptions (eg financial investment corporations, financial intermediation corporations and tax-free zone users) that are governed by special laws and are subject to the provisions of Act 16,060 only in the absence of specific provisions in the relevant special laws.

The two main types of company with limited liability in Uruguay are:

- the corporation (*Sociedad Anónima*, SA); and
- the limited liability partnership (*Sociedad de Responsabilidad Limitada*, SRL).

The advantages and disadvantages of each depend on the nature of the business or activity to be carried out by the company.

As a general rule, partners' liability in a corporation or a limited liability partnership is limited to the capital they invest; however, in limited liability partnerships the partners may have subsidiary liability in certain cases (eg for labour and tax debts).

2. Incorporation procedure

2.1 Corporation

Corporations may be open or closed. An open corporation can raise public funds to pay its initial capital or increase its capital, is listed on a stock exchange and may incur debt by issuing securities to the general public. All other companies are considered to be closed corporations.

Corporations are incorporated though a single act or alternatively (but rarely) through public subscription. In the former instance, the memorandum of incorporation must be signed by the founding shareholders (at least two persons), who have full autonomy to draft the applicable bylaws (under Uruguayan law, the bylaws are synonymous with the memorandum of incorporation).

The Internal Auditorship of the Nation (*Auditoría Interna de la Nación* (AIN)) is the agency with responsibility for confirming the legality of the bylaws and compliance with the subscription and payment requirements. The bylaws must be submitted to the AIN for approval within 30 days of their execution.

The bylaws must also be filed with the National Trade Register within 30 days of their approval; an abstract of the provisions contained therein must be published within 60 days of such filing.

A corporation acquires legal personality upon execution of the bylaws. The company may then commence operating, provided that the words *'en formación'* ('in formation') are added to its name. The founding shareholders are jointly liable for any transactions entered into until completion of the applicable procedures.

'Off-the-shelf' companies (ie companies that have already been incorporated and registered before the competent authorities, without undertaking any previous commercial activity) may be purchased for the immediate commencement of operations.

2.2 Limited liability partnership

A limited liability partnership is incorporated through a single act, when the bylaws – which may be recorded in a public or private deed – are signed by the partners (at least two persons). As in the corporation, the bylaws must be filed with the National Trade Registry and an abstract of their provisions must be published. The limited liability partnership likewise acquires legal personality upon execution of the bylaws and can commence operations as long as the words *'en formación'* are added to the company name.

2.3 Proceedings prior to incorporation

(a) Corporate name

Any person – whether local or foreign, natural or legal – is entitled to reserve and register a company name that has not already been registered. To determine whether a proposed company name is similar to another name that is already in use, a search should be conducted of the national trade register in the case of a limited liability partnership, and of the national trade register and the AIN in the case of a corporation. The agency with responsibility for controlling and granting corporate names is the AIN in the case of an SA, and the National Trade Register in the case of an SRL. These agencies will reject any similar names unless the written consent of the existing company is obtained.

(b) Capital contributions

(i) Corporation

There is no minimum capital for a corporation. The capital may be contributed in cash or in kind. The founders must furnish the AIN with evidence of the injection of at least 25% of the authorised capital, and of their undertaking to subscribe the necessary amount to cover 50% of the capital (see section 7.3 below). There are no limits on equity contributions to the corporation as long as the authorised capital specified in the bylaws is not exceeded (in any case, the bylaws may be amended as many times as necessary, and there are no tax implications to having a large authorised capital).

(ii) *Limited liability partnership*
There is no minimum capital for a limited liability partnership. The capital may be contributed in cash or in kind. Each partner must pay at least 50% of his contribution in cash upon execution of the bylaws and must pay in the remaining 50% within two years. All in-kind contributions must be made available to the company upon execution of the bylaws.

(c) **Declaration of foreign investment**
There are no special requirements with regard to foreign investment. Foreign investors are treated identically to local investors.

(d) **Tax number for foreign partners/directors**
There are no special requirements with regard to tax identification. Foreign partners and foreign directors are treated identically to local partners and directors.

2.4   Incorporation

(a)   **Bylaws**

(i)   *Essential clauses*
Under Uruguayan law, the main issues that must be included in the bylaws are as follows:
- the names of the founding shareholders (corporation) or partners (limited liability partnership);
- the company name and domicile;
- the corporate purpose;
- the capital (in Uruguayan pesos);
- the nature and/or classes, amount, characteristics and conditions of issue of the shares (for a corporation);
- the total number of quotas and the number of quotas that correspond to each partner (for a limited liability partnership);
- the capital contributions;
- the term of the company;
- the regime for the distribution of dividends (corporation) or profits (limited liability partnership) and losses;
- the administrative regime, shareholders' meetings (corporations only) and internal controls, if applicable; and
- the value assigned to in-kind contributions and the manner in which the assets were valued (limited liability partnership).

(ii)   *Clauses not foreseen by law*
Additional provisions may be included in the bylaws as long as they are compatible

with Act 16,060. For instance, in the case of a corporation, special provisions on the transfer of shares may be included in the bylaws (see section 7.5 below). Other examples (for both limited liability partnerships and corporations) might include special provisions for the resolution of disputes (eg through arbitration), confidentiality and means of communication.

(iii)   *Optional clauses governed by law*
Numerous provisions may be altered or expanded, as long as this is not prohibited by Act 16,060. For instance, with certain exceptions a corporation may require larger quorums for the adoption of resolutions – of both the board of directors and the shareholders' meeting – than those provided by Act 16,060. In the case of a limited liability partnership, a 'continuity clause' may be included stating that if a partner dies, his quotas will be transferred to the surviving spouse or heirs instead of to the other partners or third parties. It is also possible to include rules on valuation of the quotas in order to ensure a fair price and to impose restrictions on their transfer.

(b)   **Execution of public deed**
The bylaws may be executed either in a private deed or in a public deed, before a notary public.

(c)   **Tax identification number**
Once the bylaws have been approved by the AIN (in the case of a corporation) and registered with the National Trade Registry, and an abstract has been published in the *Official Gazette*, the company must be registered with the Tax Office and the Social Security Office to evidence completion of the proceedings and to obtain a tax and social security number.

(d)   **Indirect taxes, incorporation fees and other levies**

(i)   *Corporation*
The taxes and other incorporation costs depend on the type of corporation and other variables, but generally average out at about US$1,000 (excluding fees for professional services). Off-the-shelf companies, which are immediately ready to operate with all initial taxes and costs paid, are available.

(ii)   *Limited liability partnership*
The taxes and other incorporation costs are approximately US$800 (excluding fees for professional services). Due to the characteristics of this type of company, the use of off-the-shelf companies is rare and is not recommended.

(e)   **Registration with the Mercantile Registry**
The bylaws, and amendments thereto, must be registered with the National Trade Registry.

(f)   *Legalisation of official books*

(i)   *Corporation*
All books required under Uruguayan law must be certified before the National Trade Registry. The official books required are outlined in the table below.

Corporate books	• Minutes of board of directors' meetings • Minutes of shareholders' meetings • Shareholders' meeting attendance book • Stock ledger
General commercial books	• Inventory book • Journal • Letter copybook

(ii)   *Limited liability partnership*
Limited liability partnerships with more than 20 partners are also required to keep the following books:
- partners' meeting attendance book;
- register of social participation; and
- minutes of partners' meetings (or board of directors' meetings, where appropriate).

In addition, all limited liability partnerships are required to keep the general commercial books listed above.

Again, the official books must be certified before the National Trade Registry.

(f)   *Declaration of start date and other tax declarations*
Such a declaration is done simultaneously with registration for tax purposes (see section 2.4(c) above).

3.   Number of shareholders

3.1   Corporation
There must be at least two founders of a corporation, whether natural or legal persons, and whether Uruguayan or foreign. However, following incorporation, a person can become the sole owner of 100% of the capital stock of the company.

3.2   Limited liability partnerships
There must be at least two founders of a limited liability partnership, whether natural or legal persons, and whether Uruguayan or foreign. The number of partners cannot exceed 50. A limited liability partnership cannot have a sole partner; this constitutes grounds for dissolution of the company. If, for any reason, a person becomes the sole partner in a limited liability partnership, he has one year to recruit at least one more partner before the company is dissolved.

4. **Corporate name – limitations**

There are no limitations on company names, with the exception of those that have already been registered (see section 2.3(a) above). Whatever the company name, the corporate form must be clearly indicated and included.

5. **Corporate domicile**

The bylaws must indicate the domicile of the company (ie the city or municipality in which the company's administration will be located). The company may have several particular locations within the domicile without any need to amend the bylaws. The bylaws may provide that the company may have branches within Uruguay and/or abroad.

6. **Corporate purpose**

Corporations and limited liability partnerships may have any legal purpose. Usually, the bylaws include very broad purposes to entitle the company to carry out any legal commercial, industrial or services activities. The purpose can also be strictly limited to a certain type of activity, and sometimes it is necessary, for certain types of activities, to have a specific and precisely defined purpose. In addition, a limited liability partnership cannot carry out certain commercial activities (eg financial intermediation and insurance).

7. **Capital stock**

7.1 **Minimum capital requirement**

(a) *Corporation*

There is no minimum capital requirement.

(b) *Limited liability partnership*

There is no minimum capital requirement

7.2 **Nature of contributions**

Capital may be contributed to corporations and limited liability companies either in cash or in kind. In-kind contributions include all assets of economic value, such as real estate, rights and credits. In all cases the contributed assets must be specific and enforceable in a judicial proceeding.

7.3 **Partial payments**

(a) *Corporation*

At the time of execution of the bylaws, the founding shareholders must subscribe at least 50% and pay at least 25% of the company's authorised capital. In the event of a capital increase, the shareholders are under no obligation to make a minimum subscription or payment.

(b) *Limited liability partnership*
Each partner must pay at least 50% of his contribution in cash at the time of execution of the bylaws and must pay in his contribution in full within two years.

7.4 Representation of shares

(a) *Corporation*
The capital stock must be represented by shares whose nominal value is expressed in local currency. These may take the form of bearer shares, registered shares evidenced by stock certificates (endorsable or non-endorsable) or book-entry registered shares, and may be owned by national or foreign individuals or legal entities. Shares may be also issued as common or preferred shares. Although at least two persons must incorporate the corporation, the whole corporate capital stock may be owned by a sole shareholder.

(b) *Limited liability partnership*
The partners of a limited liability partnership own participations (quotas) in the company, which are representative of its capital. These quotas have equal value and are indivisible; they cannot be represented by tradable certificates.

7.5 Transfer of shares

(a) *Restrictions*

(i) *Corporation*
In principle, the shares of a corporation may be freely transferred. However, the bylaws may impose restrictions on the transfer of nominative or book-entry shares, as long as such restrictions do not constitute an express or implicit prohibition on transfer. The transfer of shares, including bearer shares, may also be restricted through shareholder agreements that are registered with the National Trade Registry. The restrictions must be evidenced in the share titles and registered in the company ledger (for nominative and book-entry shares).

(ii) *Limited liability partnership*
Quotas may be freely transferred among the partners, without prejudice to any limitations stipulated in the bylaws. However, if a given transfer will affect certain majorities, the system for the transfer of quotas to third parties may apply.

Quotas may be transferred to third parties only where approved by partners representing 75% of the capital if the limited liability partnership has more than five partners, or by unanimous vote if the limited liability partnership has five partners or fewer. The quota to be transferred is not taken into account for such purposes.

If the partner seeking to transfer his quota fails to obtain the requisite majority, he can seek judicial authorisation of the transfer. This may be granted if the other partners' objections are considered unreasonable. However, the other partners, and the company itself, have a preferential right to purchase the quotas to be transferred, and they can eventually challenge the price of the relevant quotas.

(b)   Formalities

(i)   Corporation

There are no formalities for the transfer of bearer shares; transfer is effected by delivery of the shares, with no need to execute any agreement or sign any documents.

The transfer of nominative shares is effected by delivery and endorsement of the shares and registration of the transfer in the company ledger. To transfer nominative shares that are non-endorsable, it is necessary to execute a specific agreement of assignment, surrender the shares, issue new shares and register the change of ownership in the company ledger.

The transfer of book-entry shares is effected by registration in the register of book-entry shares.

(ii)   Limited liability partnership

The transfer of quotas requires amendment of the bylaws and registration with the National Trade Registry.

7.6   Tax on dividends

Dividends and gains paid or credited by corporate income tax (CIT) taxpayers to individual shareholders who are resident in Uruguay will be subject to personal income tax (PIT). This tax establishes that, as from July 1 2007, dividends and gains that are the product of incomes levied by CIT are subject to PIT at a rate of 7%. The Uruguayan company (a CIT taxpayer) will be the withholding agent for this tax. The same conditions and rate applies to non-resident income tax (NRIT) for dividends and gains paid by CIT taxpayers to foreign shareholders (individuals or entities).

However, when a company is a personal corporation (ie an SRL) the gains paid or credited will be exempt if the income of the company does not exceed UYUI4 million (approximately U$S385,000).

When dividends and gains are paid or credited by a CIT taxpayer to another taxpayer, the dividends and gains are considered to be exempt for the company that received the income. However, the PIT and the NRIT have established that if the first distribution is a product of incomes levied by CIT, those dividends and gains distributed by a CIT taxpayer who has been a beneficiary of dividends and gains distributed by other CIT taxpayers are subject to these taxes.

8.   Equity

8.1   Equity–capital ratio

Uruguayan law requires that a balance be maintained between a company's capital and its equity. Where losses reduce a company's equity to below 25% of the paid-up capital, this constitutes grounds for dissolution – unless the partners agree to reinvest or reduce the capital.

8.2 Convertible bonds

(a) Corporation

A corporation may issue bonds that entitle the holder to participate in the annual profits without being a shareholder (no more than 10% of the annual profits). These bonds may be converted into shares under certain circumstances and where a special reserve has been created by the corporation for this purpose.

(b) Limited liability partnership

Limited liability partnerships are not entitled to issue convertible bonds.

9. Administration

9.1 Limited liability partnership

The limited liability partnership does not have an independent administrative regime. Where a limited liability partnership has between two and 19 partners, it is basically managed in the same way as a partnership; where it has between 20 and 50 partners, it is basically managed in the same way as a corporation.

9.2 General shareholders' meeting

(a) Corporation

The highest corporate body is the shareholders' meeting. The ordinary shareholders' meeting examines and approves the company balance sheet, the allocation of profits and the appointment of members of the board of directors. A resolution of the extraordinary shareholders' meeting is required for the following:

- amendment of the bylaws;
- increase in capital;
- reimbursement of capital;
- merger, transformation or dissolution of the company;
- redemption, reimbursement or amortisation of shares; and
- other major issues.

(b) Limited liability partnership

In a limited liability partnership having between two and 19 partners, there is no formal general partners' meeting. Resolutions are taken through personal written consultation of each partner, unless otherwise stated in the bylaws.

Limited liability partnerships having between 20 and 50 partners must hold a general partners' general meeting, which is basically governed by the same rules as the shareholders' meetings of corporations.

(c) Quorum requirements

(i) Attendance

Corporation: An ordinary shareholders' meeting as originally scheduled will be validly constituted if attended by shareholders representing half of the voting rights plus one. An adjourned ordinary shareholders' meeting will be validly held regardless of the number of attendees.

An extraordinary shareholders' meeting as originally scheduled will be validly held if attended by shareholders representing 60% of the voting rights. An adjourned extraordinary shareholders' meeting will be validly held if attended by shareholders representing 40% of the voting rights. If this quorum is not met, a new meeting will be called to consider the same agenda, which will be validly held regardless of the number of attendees.

Limited liability partnership: In a limited liability partnership having between two and 19 partners, there is no formal general partners' meeting and so no quorum requirements apply.

The quorum requirements for limited liability partnerships having between 20 and 50 partners are identical to those that apply to corporations.

(ii)   *Voting*

Corporation: Resolutions of the shareholders' meeting are passed by majority vote; the exact majority depends on the issue under consideration and whether the resolution is to be taken by the ordinary or extraordinary shareholders' meeting. In some cases the law requires a certain majority, and a specific majority may also be required by the bylaws. The general principle is that resolutions must be passed by an absolute majority of the attendees. However, resolutions on major issues, which basically fall within the competence of the extraordinary shareholders' meeting, must be passed by absolute majority of all shareholders (ie, at least 51% of the paid-up capital). Blank votes and abstentions shall be treated as negative votes.

Limited liability partnership: In a limited liability partnership having between two and 19 partners, resolutions on major issues (eg change in corporate purpose, transfer of domicile abroad, transformation, merger, split-off, dissolution or the imposition of greater obligations or responsibilities on the partners) must be approved unanimously.

Other modifications to the bylaws require unanimous approval if the company has five or fewer partners, and approval by the majority of capital if the company has between six and 20 partners.

Other decisions are adopted by majority of the capital. The stipulations of the law have subsidiary application, unless otherwise stated in the bylaws.

The quorum requirements for limited liability partnerships with between 20 and 50 partners are identical to those for corporations.

(d)   Challenging resolutions

(i)   *Corporation*

Any resolution of the shareholders' meeting that is adopted in contravention of the law or the bylaws, or that might damage the company's interests or shareholders' rights, may be challenged. Directors, managers, members of the internal control body, the AIN and dissenting shareholders all have the power to initiate the relevant proceedings.

(ii)   *Limited liability partnership*

In the case of a limited liability partnership having between two and 19 partners, resolutions may be the subject of judicial challenge if they are adopted in contravention of the law or the bylaws.

The rules applicable to limited liability partnerships having between 20 and 50 partners are identical to those for corporations.

9.3   Administrative body

(a)   *Corporation*

Corporations are managed and administered by a board of directors; alternatively, a closed corporation may be managed by a manager (although this is rare), and a single-member board of directors is also possible. There are no legal requirements as regards the number of members of the board of directors. Directors (and managers):

- may be natural or legal persons;
- need not be shareholders of the company; and
- may be either Uruguayan nationals or foreigners, and have their domicile either in Uruguay or abroad.

In principle, directors must perform their duties personally, although they may empower another person to vote on their behalf (and this proxy is subject to no formalities).

The corporation is legally represented by the chairman, except as otherwise provided in the bylaws. The bylaws usually provide that the corporation is to be represented by the chairman or the vice chairman, or jointly by any two directors. If there is a single manager, the manager will represent the company.

In general, the board of directors has unlimited powers to manage the company and dispose of its assets. However, these powers may be limited under the bylaws or by resolution of the board of directors itself.

(b)   *Limited liability partnership*

Limited liability partnerships are usually managed by one or more managers, but they can also be managed by a board of directors. The managers need not be partners, and have the power to represent the company. If the partners do not appoint a manager, they can represent the company themselves. Where a board of directors is established, it is subject to the same rules as the board of directors of a corporation.

(c)   *Different systems of administration*

(i)   *Corporation*

The management of a corporation is entrusted to one or more managers or a board of directors. The shareholders' meeting will decide which management model to adopt and will specify the number of members of the board of directors, where applicable. Alternatively, the administrative system may be specified in the bylaws.

Meetings of the board of directors require a quorum of half of the members (rounded up where there is an odd number of members) plus one. Resolutions are adopted by majority vote of the attendees, unless a larger majority is required under the bylaws or the law.

(ii) *Limited liability partnership*

The management of a limited liability partnership is entrusted to one or more managers or a board of directors. The managers or directors may be Uruguayan or foreign, resident or non-resident and partners or not, and may be appointed directly in the bylaws or after incorporation.

The applicable system where the limited liability partnership is managed by one or more managers is that established in the "Partnerships" chapter of Act 16,060; where the company is managed by a board of directors, it is that governing corporations.

(d) *Term of office, resignation and removal of directors*

(i) *Corporation*

Directors or managers are elected for a specified term and may be re-elected indefinitely. The directors or managers are appointed annually by the shareholders' meeting, and they retain this position until new members are appointed or their resignation is accepted. They may resign at any time, with the approval of the shareholders' meeting. The shareholders' meeting can also remove directors from office at any time.

(ii) *Limited liability partnership*

There is no specified term of office for managers, who may be removed at any time. Nevertheless, the partners can establish a term of office in the bylaws or in the document through which the managers are subsequently appointed. Even where they are partners, the managers and company representatives may resign at any time, unless the other partners do not agree. Managers will also be liable for any damage caused if their resignation is deceitful or untimely. It is not possible to restrict the power to remove a manager unless the resignation is a condition of incorporation – and even then it will remain possible to remove a manager or representative for just cause.

If the limited liability partnership is administered by a board of directors, the same rules as govern corporations apply.

(e) *Directors' liability to third parties*

(i) *Corporation*

As a general rule, directors are jointly liable to the corporation, shareholders and third parties for all damage that results, directly or indirectly, from:
- violation of the law or the bylaws;
- poor performance of their duties (ie breach of the duty of loyalty or breach of the duty to act with the diligence of a "good businessman" – similar to the US 'business judgement' rule); or

- abuse of their authority, fraud or negligence (similar to a breach of the duty of care in the United States).

(ii) *Limited liability partnership*
The same conditions apply as in subsection (i) above, except that if the limited liability partnership has a manager, he will not be directly liable to third parties. Instead, the company will be liable and will then have the right to take action against the manager.

(f) **Non-competition**
In a case of a direct or indirect conflict of interest, a director or manager must disclose the situation – to the other board members, the internal controller, the shareholders' meeting (corporation) or the partners' meeting (limited liability partnership), as the case may be – and abstain from voting on related issues. A director who fails to do so will be liable for any damage caused to the company as a result. However, no liability arises where the director or manager obtains prior authorisation of the shareholders' meeting or partners' meeting to act.

(g) **Special duties of secrecy and loyalty**
Directors and managers must perform their duties with loyalty and with the diligence of a 'good businessman'. Anyone who breaches these fiduciary obligations shall be jointly liable to the company and the shareholders or partners for damage caused by their acts or omissions.

(h) **Civil and criminal liability**

(i) *Corporation*
The criminal liability of directors and managers is mainly governed by Article 76 of Act 2,230 and Article 12 of Act 14,095.

Directors and managers who are guilty of fraud or deception, or who violate the bylaws or Uruguayan law, may be subject to imprisonment for up to eight years and disqualification for up to 10 years, depending on the crime. The sentences of any accomplices will be reduced by half.

A director or manager is guilty of the crime of fraudulent corporate insolvency if he obtains an unjust benefit for his own benefit or that of a third party by hiding or dissipating company assets; this crime is punishable by between 12 months' and 10 years' imprisonment. Such persons will also be disqualified from holding a similar position for a period of between six months and five years.

Directors or managers who vote against incriminating acts and whose dissent is recorded in the minute book, and those who clearly evidence their opposition to such acts or are unaware of or do not participate in such acts, will escape criminal liability.

The provisions on civil liability are explored in sections 9.3(d) and (e) above.

(ii) *Limited liability partnership*
The managers and directors of a limited liability partnership will incur criminal liability under basically the same terms as the managers and directors of a corporation.

The managers and directors of a limited liability partnership will also have civil liability before the company and the partners for damage caused through breach of their duty of loyalty or breach of the duty to act with the diligence of a "good businessman".

9.4   Others

(a)   *Attorneys*

A corporation or limited liability partnership may grant all powers of attorney it deems necessary for the company's administration. However, the responsibilities of the board of directors are not diminished as a result of the delegation of authority. General managers and other key managers are usually granted powers of attorney to entitle them to represent the company.

(b)   *Controllers and internal auditors*

(i)   *Corporation*

A closed corporation may elect whether to have an internal audit committee or auditor, while an open corporation is required to appoint these officers. In the former case, the bylaws or the shareholders' meeting may appoint one or more auditors or an audit committee comprised of three or more members. In the latter case, the bylaws must make provision for the existence of an audit committee or auditor.

All corporations are subject to governmental control as regards:
- incorporation and amendment of the bylaws;
- any accelerated dissolution;
- transformation, merger or split-off; and
- any increase or reduction in share capital.

An open corporation is subject to governmental control as regards its operation and liquidation.

(ii)   *Limited liability partnership*

A limited liability partnership with fewer than 20 partners can choose whether to exercise internal control through an auditor or audit committee; where the company has 20 partners or more, the appointment of an auditor or audit committee is mandatory. In any event, limited liability partnerships do not fall under the control of the AIN.

10.   Fiscal year, commencement of operations

The fiscal year for all companies is one calendar year, but the closing date of the fiscal year may be decided by the board of directors or manager. Amendment of the fiscal year requires the approval of 51% of the shareholders. The fiscal year usually ends on December 31.

The company may begin activities immediately following registration with the

Tax Office and Social Security Office (even if the company is in formation). The activities of a corporation may continue indefinitely, while those of a limited liability partnership must not exceed 30 years in duration. The bylaws usually state that the duration of the company will be 30 years (in the case of a limited liability partnership) or 100 years (in the case of a corporation) from the date of incorporation.

11. Financial statements

11.1 Company tax

(a) *Corporation*
Corporations must pay:
- corporate income tax at a current (2009) rate of 25% on their net income earned in the national territory; and
- capital tax at a current rate of 1.5% on their net worth located or economically used in the national territory.

Foreign-sourced income and foreign capital are not subject to tax in Uruguay.

(b) *Limited liability partnership*
As for corporations.

11.2 Annual accounts
The annual accounts must be prepared in accordance with generally accepted accounting rules, and they must clearly reflect the company's economic situation and the profits earned or losses suffered.

(a) *Documents*
Within four months of the end of each fiscal year, the board of directors or manager must present the following information at a minimum, together with a summary of the year's activities:
- an inventory of the company's assets and liabilities as at the close of the fiscal year;
- the general balance sheet (economic situation and financial results); and
- the proposals for the distribution of dividends (corporation) or profits (limited liability partnership), if any.

(b) *Audit report*
Where an internal auditor has been appointed, the board of directors or manager must provide the auditor with the above documents at least 30 days before they are presented to the shareholders or partners. The auditor must then prepare a report setting out all observations or recommendations it deems relevant.

(c) *Approval and distribution of profits*
Dividends may be distributed if the balance sheet, as approved by the shareholders'

meeting or partners' meeting, as appropriate, shows a net profit. Dividends cannot be distributed before the losses of previous fiscal years have been covered. A corporation is obliged to distribute at least 20% of the net profits in each fiscal year. In certain circumstances, the dividends may be distributed in advance (eg, where there are sufficient reserves for this purpose or where the projected balance shows profits that exceed the dividend to be distributed).

(d) Deposit and publication

The documents must be deposited at the corporate headquarters and be made available to the shareholders or partners at least 10 days prior to the shareholders' meeting or partners' meeting. The shareholders' meeting or general partners' meeting must approve the documents within 180 days of the end of the fiscal year. The documents of an open corporation must also be sent to the AIN, and the balance sheet and the proposal for the distribution of dividends must be published.

12. Company reorganisation

Under Uruguayan law, a company may be:

- transformed into another type of company;
- merged into new or existing companies; or
- subject to different types of split-off.

Articles 104 to 142 of Act 16,060 provide specific rules on these different types of reorganisation.

Corporation: In all three sets of circumstances listed above, the participants must comply with several legal requirements and formalities (eg approval of the resolution on reorganisation by at least 51% of the paid-up capital, approval of special balance sheets, execution of agreements and/or amendments to bylaws, publication requirements). Ultimately, the approval of the AIN must also be obtained. The timeframe for the conclusion of proceedings will depend on the type and complexity of the deal, but it could range from three to 12 months.

Limited liability partnership: Where a limited liability partnership comes to have more than 50 partners, it has two years in which to transform itself into a corporation. If it fails to do so, the company must be dissolved, unless during this period the number of partners falls to 50 or fewer.

Where a limited liability partnership has fewer than 20 partners, a resolution on transformation, merger or split-off requires unanimous approval. Where the limited liability partnership has between 20 and 50 partners, the required quorums are identical to those required for a corporation.

13. Eventual partner separation

13.1 Corporation

In major cases involving a change to the company's structure or business, or its capital structure, dissenting shareholders have the option to withdraw from the company, in which case they will have appraisal rights.

Resolutions on the following must be approved by shareholders holding a majority of the voting rights, unless the bylaws require a higher majority:
- merger, split-off, transformation, extension or anticipated dissolution;
- transfer of the domicile abroad;
- fundamental amendment of the corporate purpose;
- increase in the social capital; or
- total or partial reintegration of the paid-up capital.

Dissenting shareholders will be allowed to withdraw from the company in all such instances, except in the case of anticipated dissolution or capital increase through liberated shares. The bylaws may stipulate that there is no right to withdraw from the company in a case of capital increase through new contributions. The right to withdraw from the company also arises in relation to the transformation of bearer shares into nominative shares, or the imposition of restrictions on the transfer of nominative shares.

In open corporations whose shares are traded on formal markets, the prospect of an increase in social capital, reintegration of paid-up capital, merger or split-off does not entitle dissenting shareholders to withdraw from the company (as long as the characteristics of an open corporation are unaffected).

In all other cases, dissenting shareholders and shareholders who abstain from voting or are absent during the vote, and who can provide evidence of their status as shareholders at the time of the meeting, may withdraw from the company, giving notice of their decision to the company within 30 days of the last publication of the resolution.

13.2 Limited liability partnership

Partners may separate from a limited liability partnership in the following cases:
- death, incapacity or disqualification of the partner (unless there is a continuity clause in the bylaws (see section 2.4(a));
- exclusion of the partner (in certain extremely serious cases, such as major breach of the bylaws); and
- exercise of the right of withdrawal (basically, the same as for a corporation).

14. Dissolution and liquidation

A company will be dissolved in the event of:
- an agreement of the shareholders or partners to this effect;
- expiry of the term;
- fulfilment of a condition for dissolution;
- fulfilment of the corporate purpose or impossibility to fulfil it;
- bankruptcy or judicial liquidation;
- losses that reduce the equity to less than 25% of the paid-up capital;
- merger or split-off, in certain cases;
- impossibility to operate or inactivity of the manager or corporate bodies, or impossibility to reach valid corporate agreements;
- continued illegal activity or commission of illegal acts of such significance as to distort the corporate purpose;

- a person becoming the sole partner in a limited liability partnership and failing to recruit at least one more partner within a term of one year; and
- all other cases provided by law.

Following dissolution, the board of directors or manager may act only in urgent matters and must adopt all necessary measures to initiate liquidation. The wording *'en liquidación'* ('in liquidation') must be added to the company name. The directors or managers will act as the liquidators of the company, unless otherwise provided by the shareholders or partners.

The liquidators will prepare an inventory and a balance sheet, which must be made available to the shareholders or partners at the company's headquarters. The liquidators will represent the company and will conclude all corporate issues that are pending as at the date of dissolution. The liquidators cannot initiate new business except where this is necessary for the purposes of the liquidation. They are entitled to execute all necessary acts for the sale of assets and the satisfaction of liabilities.

Once the liabilities have been satisfied, the liquidators will prepare a final balance sheet and a proposal for the distribution of assets, which must be approved by the shareholders' meeting or partners' meeting, as appropriate. The liquidators will then proceed to transfer the relevant assets to each shareholder or partner, and will notify the National Trade Register of the completion of proceedings.

15. Branches

A branch shares the same liability as its parent company. The legal representatives of foreign companies who open a branch in Uruguay also have the same responsibilities as the legal representatives of that type of company in Uruguay.

About the authors

John Aguilar Jr
Partner, Aguilar Castillo Love
jaq@aguilarcastillolove.com

John Aguilar Jr is a partner in the corporate/M&A department at Aguilar Castillo Love, a leading Central American law firm with six offices in the region. Mr Aguilar Jr has practised for more than 20 years in the Aguilar Castillo Love office in Costa Rica and is currently its managing partner. His focus is on corporate law, foreign investments, mergers and acquisitions, and taxation both locally and internationally throughout the network of offices in Central America.

Maria Luisa de Alarcón Elorrieta
Partner, JAUSAS
malarcon@jausaslegal.com

Maria Luisa de Alarcón Elorrieta has been a partner of JAUSAS since 1996. She specialises in corporate and tax law and provides national and international tax-planning advice, as well as personal income and corporate tax assistance, to clients on an ongoing basis. She also advises on value added tax and customs duties issues, tax investigations and appeals before administrative and judicial authorities.

Maria Luisa is a member of the Spanish Association of Tax Advisers and an arbitrator at the Barcelona Arbitration Court. She has spoken at several seminars on general tax legislation and is the author of a number of articles on tax and corporate law.

Hirokazu Amemiya
Associate, Kojima Law Offices
amemiya@kojimalaw.jp

Hirokazu Amemiya is a Japanese lawyer. He is a member of the Daini-Tokyo Bar Association. He has been with Kojima Law Offices since 2005.

L Fubara Anga
Partner, ÆLEX
lfanga@aelex.com

L Fubara Anga is a Partner in ÆLEX. He heads the banking, financial services and transportation practice groups. He advises on financial, corporate, commercial and fiscal matters that affect projects and companies in the oil, gas, power, aviation, telecommunications, maritime, banking and financial services sectors. He appears as counsel before all superior courts in Nigeria and has acted as counsel or party-appointed arbitrator in several arbitration proceedings.

Fubara Anga is admitted to practise law in in Nigeria, England and Wales, and Ghana. He was educated at Yale and Cambridge University. He is currently the Chairman of the Capital Markets Solicitors Association and Chairman of the Committee on Aviation of the Section on Business Law of the Nigerian Bar Association.

Michał Barłowski
Partner, Wardyński & Partners
michał.barłowski@wardynski.com.pl

Michał Barłowski is a legal counsel and senior

partner at Wardyński & Partners and he heads the firm's insolvency and restructuring group. He specialises in mergers and acquisitions, insolvency and restructuring matters and corporate law.

Michał often acts as a speaker on the above issues during international and local conferences. He has authored numerous articles on insolvency, corporate law and mergers and acquisitions, and he is the country correspondent editor of the journal *International Corporate Rescue* published by Chase Cambria.

Berth Brouwer

Senior Counsel, Boekel De Nerée NV
berth.brouwer@boekeldeneree.com

Berth Brouwer started his work as a lawyer at Boekel De Nerée in 1996. Until 2001 he specialised in company and real-estate law. After two years working in an international fund practice, he rejoined Boekel De Nerée as member of the real-estate practice group, further specialising in corporate real estate. Berth has broad experience in real-estate investment funds, development, public and private joint ventures, corporate law, contract law and litigation. His clients include both national and international real-estate companies. Berth has been senior counsel since 2008.

In 2005 Berth worked as a lecturer in corporate law at the Free University (Vrije Universiteit) in Amsterdam. He also regularly publishes on corporate and real-estate matters and is a member of the Dutch Litigation Association.

Esteban Burt

Partner, Peroni Sosa Tellechea Burt & Narvaja
esteban.burt@pstbn.com.py

Esteban Burt specialises in corporate and commercial law with an emphasis on mergers and acquisitions, joint ventures, foreign investments, and mining and petroleum concessions.

Álvaro Ivan Cala

Partner, Brigard & Urrutia Abogados S.A.
acala@bu.com.co

Álvaro Ivan Cala specialises in commercial contracts and corporations, including the securities markets, bankruptcy and dispute-resolution proceedings. Álvaro has extensive experience in litigation before civil and administrative courts and tribunals, and he offers general legal advice for local and foreign clients in drafting civil and commercial contracts and documents and in the incorporation of local companies, foreign company branches and subsidiaries.

He is a member of the International Bar Association.

Laura Carreño

Senior Associate, Brigard & Urrutia Abogados SA
lcarreno@bu.com.co

Laura Carreño has been an associate in Brigard & Urrutia since 2000 and is a member of its corporate law and due diligence team. She advises local and foreign clients in drafting civil and commercial agreements, in oil and gas regimes and in the incorporation of local companies, branches of foreign companies and subsidiaries.

Louise M Chau

Associate, Allens Arthur Robinson
Louise.Chau@aar.com.au

Louise Chau obtained her LLB from the University of Sydney in 2007 and was admitted to practise law in New South Wales, Australia, in 2008. She is now a lawyer in the corporate department of Allens Arthur Robinson.

Frederick John Chilton

Partner, Allens Arthur Robinson
Fred.Chilton@aar.com.au

Fred Chilton is a senior corporate and commercial partner with Allens Arthur Robinson, based in the firm's Sydney office. He is a graduate of the University of Sydney and Harvard University. He has held various positions in the International Bar Association and is a frequent speaker at national and international conferences.

Aakash Choubey
Senior Associate, Khaitan & Co
aakash.choubey@khaitanco.com

Aakash Choubey is part of Khaitan & Co's corporate and commercial practice, and he focuses on mergers and acquisitions, PE investments, franchising and foreign investment law.

Aakash has published articles in various Indian legal journals. He has authored and co-authored the chapters on India in several books.

Nuria Clemente Farré
Associate, JAUSAS
nclemente@jausaslegal.com

Nuria Clemente Farré has been a lawyer for JAUSAS since 1993. Her practice focuses on corporate law and mergers and acquisitions. She is responsible for the corporate law department, providing legal advice to foreign investors on company incorporation.

She has been appointed secretary of the board of directors of various companies and is a member of the Barcelona Bar Association.

Marco Consonni
Partner, Dewey & LeBoeuf
mconsonni@dl.com

Marco Consonni is a partner at Dewey & LeBoeuf, Milan, and the head of the communication and technology practice in Italy. He focuses mainly on corporate and commercial activity for international and domestic clients in the technology, communication, media, entertainment and advertising sectors. The work is frequently related to the incorporation of start-up companies and corporate vehicles for national and foreign clients, to corporate deals and business reorganisations. Marco also covers commercial contracts in the technology, media and communication fields.

Fernando Cuesta
Partner, Cuesta Campos y Asociados SC
fcuesta@cuestacampos.com

Fernando Cuesta has been advising clients in the area of corporate and business law for more than 10 years. He specialises in structuring, restructuring, acquiring and selling national and foreign-owned companies (private and public), and joint ventures (including special purpose entities). He also has experience in structuring, negotiating and documenting a broad range of international business transactions.

Alina Deiac
Attorney-at-Law, Pachiu & Associates
alina.deiac@pachiu.com

Alina Deiac is a member of the Bucharest Bar Association and a member of the National Union of Lawyers in Romania. Her area of expertise includes labour and corporate law as well as mergers & acquisitions.

Alina is also a contributor to several reviews and legal publications, covering a broad area of legal issues, mainly related to corporate, environmental and competition law. She is fluent in English and conversant in Spanish.

María Andrea Duque
Junior Associate, Brigard & Urrutia Abogados SA
mduque@bu.com.co

María Andrea Duque has been an associate in Brigard & Urrutia since 2007 and is a member of its corporate law team.

She advises local and foreign clients on the incorporation of local companies, branches of foreign companies and subsidiaries.

Andrés Durán Hareau
Partner, Hughes and Hughes
aduran@hughes.com.uy

Andrés Durán Hareau is a partner at Hughes & Hughes, Uruguay; he has also been a visiting lawyer at Slaughter and May, London, and worked at the legal division of the Inter-American Investment Corporation, Washington DC. He has vast experience in corporate M&A, financing transactions, and investment projects in Uruguay.

Mr Durán Hareau has been recommended as one of the leading practitioners in Uruguay by Chambers and Partners. He is a member of the International Bar Association, the New York State Bar Association and the Uruguayan Bar Association. He has authored or co-authored several publications.

Martin Eckert
Attorney at Law/Founding Partner, MME Partners
martin.eckert@mmepartners.ch

Martin Eckert is a founding partner of MME Partners with offices in Zürich and Zug. MME Partners advises foreign companies that aim to enter the Swiss market or to profit from Switzerland as a hub for their European or EMEA activities. Martin Eckert obtained his doctor of laws degree from the University of Zurich in 1992 and was admitted to the Bar in 1994. He is a member of the Swiss and Zurich Bar Associations.

Dr Eckert specialises in commercial law, international transactions and IT/IP law. He was formerly a judge at the Swiss Federal Appeal Commission of Intellectual Property, a clerk at the Register of Commerce and the Zurich Commercial Court. Dr Eckert is a board member of several Swiss corporations (banking, medical technology, IT, holding).

Héctor Ferreira
Senior Associate, Hughes & Hughes
hferreira@hughes.com.uy

Héctor Ferreira is a senior associate at Hughes & Hughes. His practice focuses on commercial law, corporate law, contracts, dispute counselling and commercial arbitration.

Mr Ferreira is an associate professor of commercial law at the Facultad de Derecho de la Universidad Católica del Uruguay, and an assistant professor of commercial law at the Facultad de Derecho de la Universidad de la República Oriental del Uruguay

He is a member of the American Bar Association and the Uruguay Bar Association. He is also an honorary member of International Bar Association. He is the author or co-author of several publications.

Ramón Macías Garcia
Partner, Cuesta Campos y Asociados SC
rmacias@cuestacampos.com

Ramón Macías Garcia has been practising corporate law in Mexico for more than 12 years. His areas of expertise include M&A, corporate, banking and finance, commercial contracts, tax and foreign trade.

Ramón has advised a variety of local and foreign companies (in the electronics, construction, banking and finance, automotive, retail and food sectors) during the formation of Mexican subsidiaries, joint ventures, M&A, financing contracts and real-estate transactions.

He has represented various banks and institutional lenders, documenting commercial finance transactions and preparing and negotiating security agreements.

Patrick Geeraert
Associate, NautaDutilh
patrick.geeraert@nautadutilh.com

Patrick Geeraert specialises in mergers and

acquisitions, advising several listed and non-listed companies.

He received his law degree from the Catholic University of Leuven in 1999 and obtained a masters degree in general management from the Vlerick Leuven Gent Management School the following year. After working on an assignment for the Brussels Stock Exchange (Euronext), he became a legal project manager and adviser with the business development department of the Brussels Airport Company. In 2003 he received an LLM from Northwestern University School of Law and he joined NautaDutilh the same year. He was also admitted to the Brussels Bar in 2003. He is currently a teaching fellow at the Catholic University of Louvain.

Marco Solano Gómez

Senior Associate, Aguilar Castillo Love

msg@aguilarcastillolove.com

Marco Solano Gómez is a senior associate in the corporate finance department at Aguilar Castillo Love. He has practised for more than 12 years in Costa Rica as well as in the offices of Sidley Austin and Greenberg Traurig in Washington DC and New York respectively, thus gaining exposure to cross-border transactions throughout the Americas. His practice focuses on corporate and financial matters, including structured finance, mergers and acquisitions, private equity and project finance.

Christian Bredtoft Guldmann

Attorney at Law, Kromann Reumert

cgu@kromannreumert.com

Christian Bredtoft Guldmann obtained his law degree from the University of Aarhus in 2000 and an MBA from INSEAD in 2006. He is a member of the Danish Bar and has held a right of audience before the Danish High Court since 2004. From 2003 to 2005, Christian was an external senior lecturer in property law at the University of Aarhus.

Christian's primary areas of work at Danish law firm Kromann Reumert are corporate law, mergers and acquisitions, and private equity. With his colleague Simon Krogh, Christian is responsible for, and coordinating, knowledge sharing at Kromann Reumert.

Peder Hammarskiöld

Senior Partner, Hammarskiöld & Co

Peder.Hammarskiold@hammarskiold.se

Peder Hammarskiöld specialises in M&A and capital markets, where he regularly works for both financial institutions and issuers. He acts for both Swedish and foreign clients. Over the years he has taken an active part in the Swedish corporate governance debate and regularly advises Swedish and international companies in this area of company law.

Peder has been a member of the Swedish Bar Association since 1985. He is the author of numerous articles in legal journals and magazines.

Guy Harles

Partner, Arendt & Medernach

Guy.Harles@arendt-medernach.com

Guy Harles is a founding partner of Arendt & Medernach and currently serves as its head of private equity. He specialises in corporate work, advising on the structuring of international transactions, private equity investments, corporate reorganisations, mergers and acquisitions, and corporate finance.

Guy presently serves as the president of the Luxembourg Association for Arbitration and Euroarbitrage.

Sandra Hein

Senior Associate, Hammarskiöld & Co

Sandra.Hein@hammarskiold.se

Sandra Hein is a senior associate of Hammarskiöld & Co. Her practice focuses on company law and dispute resolution. She has served as secretary in an investigation conducted within the Swedish Trade Ministry regarding the governance of state-owned companies. She is also the author of various articles on company law in Swedish and international publications.

Agustí Jausàs

Founder, JAUSAS
dsola@jausaslegal.com

Agustí Jausàs is the founder of the law firm JAUSAS, with offices in Barcelona and Madrid. He has authored several books on company law and is the editor of two international publications on agency and distribution agreements; he is also a regular contributor to specialist journals.

Mr Jausàs served for eight years as chairman of the International Bar Association's Sub-committee on Agency and Distribution, Section of Business Law, and for four years as co-chairman of the Committee on International Sales and Related Commercial Transactions. He has participated in many national and international conferences and seminars on international commercial law and on the regulation of agency and distribution agreements. He has also been very active in advising on the formation of subsidiaries in different jurisdictions.

Rabindra Jhunjhunwala

Partner, Khaitan & Co
rabindra.jhunjhunwala@khaitanco.com

Rabindra Jhunjhunwala is a corporate lawyer focusing on domestic and cross-border M&A, PE investments, venture capital fund work and foreign investments. He has published articles in various Indian and international legal publications.

Rabindra has been recommended by *Asian Legal Business, Which Lawyer?* and the *IFLR1000*.

Julian Juhasz

Partner, Squire, Sanders & Dempsey LLP
JJuhasz@ssd.com

Julian Juhasz is admitted to practice law in Canada, the Czech Republic and the Slovak Republic. He is the managing partner of the Squire Sanders Bratislava office. His qualifications make him particularly adept at leading cross-border transactions. He has worked on numerous financial transactions involving foreign and local lenders and local borrowers, and on many of the major merger and acquisition and project finance deals that have occurred in the Slovak Republic.

Alon Kaplan

Senior Partner, Alon Kaplan Law Firm
alon@kaplex.com

Alon Kaplan is the founder of the Alon Kaplan Law Firm, focusing on trusts and estates; international taxation; private banking; corporate law; agency and distributorships.

He is the academic coordinator of the STEP Diploma in International Trust Management at Tel Aviv University and has published numerous books and articles.

David Kent

Partner, Taylor Wessing LLP
d.kent@taylorwessing.com

David Kent leads a team specialising in advising emerging growth, listed companies and banks on corporate, IP and regulatory matters, mergers and acquisitions, joint ventures, strategic alliances, and the establishment and operation of businesses in the United Kingdom and Europe. He has contributed to numerous books and articles on inward investment. He is listed in *Legal Experts, Legal 500, Chambers* and *Who's Who*.

Péter Komáromi

Partner, Sándor Szegedi Szent-Ivány

Komáromi Eversheds

komaromi@sandor-advocat.hu

Péter Komáromi is one of the senior partners of Sándor Szegedi Szent-Ivány Komáromi Eversheds, Attorneys at Law, Budapest, which is a member of Eversheds International, a chain of law firms with offices across Europe, the Middle-East and Asia and more than 4,000 staff in 30+ locations. He has been in the legal business for almost 40 years and he has extensive experience in corporate law, media law, energy law, telecomms, project finance and international arbitration.

Saskia Konsbruck

Associate, Arendt & Medernach

saskia.konsbruck@arendt-medernach.com

Saskia Konsbruck is the head of the London representative office and an associate in the corporate and tax practice at Arendt & Medernach. She specialises in corporate work, advising major international companies, banks, private equity firms, hedge funds and other investors in structuring and financing cross-border public takeovers, private acquisitions and disposals, leveraged and management buyouts and reorganisation and refinancing.

Alexander Krilyszyn

Lawyer, Pistotnik Rechtsanwaltsgesellschaft mbH

a.krilyszyn@pistotnik.at

Alexander Krilyszyn will be admitted to the Bar in 2009. His main practice areas include corporate law, business law, contract law and litigation.

Simon Krogh

Attorney at Law, Kromann Reumert

sik@kromannreumert.com

Simon Krogh's primary areas of work with Danish law firm Kromann Reumert in Copenhagen are corporate law, mergers and acquisitions, private equity and energy law. With his colleague Christian Bredtoft Guldmann, Simon is responsible for, and coordinating, knowledge sharing at Kromann Reumert.

Simon obtained his law degree from the University of Copenhagen in 2004; he also holds an LLM from London University. Since 2007 he has taught company law as an external lecturer at the University of Copenhagen. Simon is a member of the Danish Bar.

Violetta Kunze

Partner, Djingov, Gouginski, Kyutchukov & Velichkov

violetta.kunze@dgkv.com

Violetta Kunze advises foreign clients on corporate and commercial law issues with a focus on corporate transactions, mergers and acquisitions, reorganisations and commercial agreements. She is also head of the telecommunications practice area group at her firm.

She graduated from the Law Faculty of the University of Sofia and holds a diploma from the Academy of American and International Law, Dallas, Texas. She is admitted to the Sofia Bar and is a member of Frankfurt am Main (Germany) Bar. Ms Kunze is fluent in Bulgarian, English and German.

Andreas Lachmann

Partner, Rotthege Wassermann & Partner GbR

a.lachmann@rwp.de

Andreas Lachmann is a graduate of the University of Marburg and Exeter University (UK) and is admitted as barrister for all regional and higher regional German courts. He became a partner of Rotthege Wassermann & Partner GbR in 2000, and is chief executive officer of the firm's RWP Consult GmbH. In addition to practising in the areas of corporate law, insolvency law and corporate restructuring, he is also chairman of the annual M&A International Lawyers' Conference.

Sophie Lim
Partner, Allen & Gledhill LLP
sophie.lim@allenandgledhill.com

Sophie Lim is a corporate and commercial partner in Singapore. Her areas of practice include advisory and compliance work for private and public listed companies. She is also involved in mergers and acquisitions, joint ventures, restructuring and employment law.

Dmitry Lyakhov
Attorney-at-Law, Russin & Vecchi LLP
russin@vladivostok.ru

Dmitry Lyakhov provides advice to clients on a wide variety of legal matters, specialising in civil law, commercial and corporate law, M&A, labour law and migration. He is a graduate of the Department of Jurisprudence of the Far-Eastern National University (Vladivostok, Russia). He is also an alumnus of the Institute for US Law (Washington, DC, USA).

Pasquale Gerardo Marasco
Associate, Dewey & LeBoeuf
pmarasco@dl.com

Pasquale Gerardo Marasco is an associate at Dewey & LeBoeuf, Milan. His practice focuses on contracts, opinions and litigation in the corporate and financial fields and frequently involves issues related to company law. He is the author of several articles and commentaries on civil and commercial law. He is also visiting professor at the University of Urbino.

Nicola Mariani
Corporate Partner, Dewey & LeBoeuf
nmariani@dl.com

Nicola Mariani is a corporate partner in Dewey & LeBoeuf's Paris office. His practice centres on French and cross-border merger and acquisition transactions, including public merger and acquisition transactions and transactions involving stock exchange matters.

Nicola has experience in negotiating complex commercial agreements and strategic alliances, including international joint venture agreements. He has successfully managed cross-border legal assignments requiring the selection and management of lawyers and professionals in several jurisdictions.

Evy Cynthia Marques
Associate, Felsberg, Pedretti, Mannrich e Aidar Advogados e Consultores Legais
evymarques@felsberg.com.br

Evy Cynthia Marques is a corporate finance lawyer at Felsberg, Pedretti, Mannrich e Aidar Advogados e Consultores Legais, a leading Brazilian law firm. She has an LLB and is currently studying for a masters degree in commercial law at the University of São Paulo, Brazil. She also has a postgraduate degree in Business Economics from the School of Economics, Fundação Getúlio Vargas (focused on capital markets) in São Paulo.

Rodrigo Rosenberg Marzano
Partner, Rosenberg Marzano, Marroquin Pemueller & Asociados
rmarzano@rrmmp.com

Rodrigo Rosenberg Marzano is currently a partner with Rosenberg, Marzano, Marroquin Pemueller & Asociados. He graduated from the Universidad Rafael Landivar as an attorney and notary public in 1983, and he went on to study at Cambridge University, obtaining his degree in international and comparative law in 1985. In 1986, he obtained a Masters degree in corporate, commercial and international tax law from Harvard University.

Mr Marzano served from 1998 to 2000 as vice-dean of the Law Faculty at the Universidad Rafael Landivar, and from 1996 to 2005 as president of the board of directors of the Guatemalan Centre for Arbitration and Conciliation.

Aurélie Maspétiol
Associate, Dewey & LeBoeuf
amaspeti@dl.com

Aurélie Maspétiol is an associate in Dewey & LeBoeuf's Paris office. Her practice focuses on M&A for financial and industrial investors and commercial contracts.

James McConvill
Associate, Appleby
JMcConvill@applebyglobal.com

James McConvill is an associate in the corporate and commercial department of Appleby. He specialises in banking and asset finance, and funds and investment services, advising banks, onshore law firms, investment companies, government bodies and other entities on a range of matters involving BVI commercial law.

Prior to joining Appleby, James was principal of The Corporate Research Group International, which provided consultancy services for corporate governance and corporate law. He was awarded a PhD in comparative corporate law and governance in 2006.

Neil Montgomery
Partner, Felsberg, Pedretti, Mannrich e Aidar
Advogados e Consultores Legais
neilmontgomery@felsberg.com.br

Neil Montgomery is one of the corporate finance partners at Felsberg, Pedretti, Mannrich e Aidar Advogados e Consultores Legais, a leading Brazilian law firm. He is a former Councillor of the British Chamber of Commerce and Industry in Brazil and Chairman of its Legal and Tax Committee. He is also a former associate of the City law firm Richards Butler, having worked in shipping and international trade & commodities and corporate finance departments in the City of London.

Mr Montgomery has authored many articles on corporate finance, international law, insurance,

reinsurance and arbitration and has spoken at corporate finance and international law events in Brazil and elsewhere. He is also a public sworn translator.

Yadira Moreno
Partner, Aguilar Castillo Love
ymc@aguilarcastillolove.com

Yadira Moreno is a partner in the corporate/M&A department of her firm. Her practice focuses on corporate law, taxation, mergers and acquisitions, and foreign investments. She also acts as general in-house counsel for a multinational company in the food industry. Yadira is currently the managing partner of Aguilar Castillo Love in Panama.

Amr ZA Motaal
Partner, Abdel Motaal, Moharram
& Heiza Law Firm
abdelmotaal@ammh-lawfirm.com

Amr Motaal is the senior partner in Abdel Motaal, Moharram and Heiza Law Firm, established in 1926. He is an Attorney-at-Law. His practice focuses on legal consultation, contracts, settlement of disputes and litigation. He is a legal advisor to Egyptian and foreign private and public entities and is the author of several legal treaties. He is listed as an arbitrator.

Mr Motaal is a member of official core committees drafting new laws in Egypt. He is member of the board of several entities and associations, including the Canada Egypt Business Council. He is currently the regional advisor of Pace Law Firm – Canada for Egypt and the Middle East.

Sizwe Msimang
Senior Associate, Bowman Gilfillan
s.msimang@bowman.co.za

Sizwe Msimang is a senior associate in Bowman Gilfillan's corporate department and advises on a wide range of corporate transactions, including mergers and acquisitions, joint ventures, financing arrangements and contract law, as well as exchange control.

Louis Néret
Associate, Dewey & LeBoeuf
lneret@dl.com

Louis Néret is an associate in Dewey & LeBoeuf's Paris office. His practice focuses on mergers and acquisitions (M&A), private equity transactions for financial and industrial investors, and commercial contracts.

Ng Shen Li
Senior Associate
Corporate & Commercial, Allen & Gledhill LLP
ng.shenli@allenandgledhill.com

Ng Shen Li is a Senior Associate in the corporate and commercial section at Allen & Gledhill LLP in Singapore. She has experience in corporate advisory work for private companies as well as corporate compliance for private and public companies. Shen Li has also advised on various corporate restructurings as well as employment and immigration law. In particular, she has been involved in the rationalisation of employment policies and documents of Singapore companies, the streamlining of the operations of multinational corporations, and schemes of reconstruction and restructuring of multinational corporations.

Marius Nita
Attorney at Law, Pachiu & Associates
marius.nita@pachiu.com

Marius Nita holds a BA in law from the University of Bucharest. He is a member of the Bucharest Bar Association and a member of the National Union of Lawyers in Romania. His area of expertise includes corporate law as well as mergers & acquisitions.

Marius is fluent in English and conversant in French.

Hiromasa Ogawa
Partner, Kojima Law Offices
ogawa@kojimalaw.jp

Hiromasa Ogawa is a Japanese lawyer. He is a member of the Daichi-Tokyo Bar Association.

He has been with Kojima Law Offices since 1993 and became a partner in 2000.

Yusuke Oyama
Associate, Hirakawa Sogo Law Office
oyama@hirakawa-law.jp

Yusuke Oyama is a Japanese lawyer. He is a member of the Daiichi-Tokyo Bar Association.

He has been with Hirakawa Sogo Office since 2009.

Eduardo Rosenberg Paiz
Paralegal, Rosenberg Marzano, Marroquin Pemueller & Asociados
erosenberg@rrmmp.com

Eduardo Rosenberg Paiz graduated from the Inter-American School of Guatemala. He is currently an undergraduate law student at Universidad Francisco Marroquin and works at Rosenberg Marzano, Marroquin Pemueller & Asociados as a paralegal.

Lynn F Pickard
Lawyer, Kojima Law Offices
pickard@kojimalaw.jp

Lynn Pickard is a New York lawyer who has practised in New York City, Seoul and Tokyo, for the past 30 years. He is admitted to the New York Bar (not admitted in Japan). He has been with Kojima Law Offices since 1987.

Marcelo Gustavo Pozzetti
Senior Associate, M & M Bomchil
marcelo.pozzetti@bomchil.com

Marcelo Pozetti works with local and international companies advising on mergers and acquisitions, the entertainment business and contractual matters (eg stock purchase, shareholders, technical assistance, transfer of technology, production, distribution and merger agreements). He also works with off-shore companies, investment funds, and the telecommunications and media sectors.

He was a professor of Commercial Law at the Universidad de Buenos Aires. He has participated in several seminars and has published a number of articles.

Dato' Johari Razak

Partner, Shearn Delamore & Co

jorazak@shearndelamore.com

Dato' Johari Razak has been involved in advising on mergers and acquisitions, joint ventures, restructurings and listing of public companies. He is currently the chairman of Ancom Berhad, Courts Mammoth Sdn Bhd and Daiman Development Berhad and a director of Hong Leong Industries Berhad, Nylex Berhad, Daiman Golf Berhad and Deutsche Bank (Malaysia) Berhad.

John Reed

Partner, Edwards Angell Palmer & Dodge LLP

JReed@eapdlaw.com

John Reed is a partner in the Wilmington, Delaware office of Edwards Angell Palmer & Dodge LLP, a full-service law firm with more than 600 attorneys and offices in major US markets, London and Hong Kong. He maintains an international business litigation and significant 'Delaware counsel' business law practice. His practice involves corporate counselling, pre-litigation counselling and high stakes corporate litigation.

He is listed in Delaware *Super Lawyers* and *Chambers USA: America's Leading Lawyers for Business*. John is a former Deputy Attorney General, and a frequent author and lecturer.

Orna Ronkin-Noor

Advocate, Alon Kaplan Law Firm

orna@kaplex.com

Orna Ronkin-Noor is an associate at Alon Kaplan Law Firm in Tel-Aviv. Her main practice areas are commercial law, corporate law, contract law, land and real estate, and estates.

She is a member of the Society of Trust and Estate Practitioners.

Jonathan Russin

Managing Partner, Russin & Vecchi LLP

jonathan.russin@russinvecchi.ru

Jonathan Russin has been advising clients on Russian legal issues since 1988. He is managing partner of Russin & Vecchi's Russian practice group, resident in Moscow, from where he directs the firm's offices in Moscow, Yuzhno-Sakhalinsk and Vladivostok. Mr Russin has advised US, European and Asian clients on the establishment of industrial and commercial activities in Russia. He has facilitated the creation of Western–Russian joint venture companies, and advised firms on Russian rules of corporate governance, on the resolution of disputes in a multicultural setting, and on compliance in Russia with the US Foreign Corrupt Practices Act and with the growing body of international and national laws against corruption.

Mr Russin specialises in international commercial and investment matters. He practised law in Latin America for two decades before establishing the firm's Russian operations. He is a graduate of Yale College and Yale Law School and a member of the bar of the District of Columbia. He has the highest rating in The Martindale-Hubbell Law Directory for legal ability and professional standards and is listed in *Who's Who in America* and *Who's Who in American Law*.

Georges Santoni-Recio
Managing Partner
Russin, Vecchi & Heredia Bonetti
gsantoni@rvhb.com

Georges Santoni-Recio is managing partner of Russin, Vecchi & Heredia Bonetti, one of the leading law firms in the Dominican Republic. His practice focuses on investment law, international trade, agency and distributorship law. He is a practising litigator, specialising in civil and commercial litigation, and also a practising arbitrator. Fluent in Spanish, English and French, he is well qualified to assist foreign clients in their business and litigation matters.

Mr Santoni-Recio is a graduate from the Universidad Nacional Pedro Henríquez Ureña (1982); he also holds a Masters degree in commercial law from the Université de Droit, d'Économie et de Sciences Sociales de Paris (1985). He is member of Meritas, the International Association of Lawyers, the American Bar Association, and the Dominican-French Chamber of Commerce.

Nilesh Shah
Senior Tax Partner, Blick Rothenberg
Nilesh.shah@blickrothenberg.com

Nilesh Shah is the head of tax at Blick Rothenberg, Chartered Accountants. He specialises in international corporate tax. Nilesh represents Blick Rothenberg on his regular trips to the United States, Canada and India, and he has spoken at professional conferences on a wide range of topics. He has helped many overseas companies successfully establish operations in the United Kingdom, advising on the correct tax structure as well as commercial considerations. Nilesh also has extensive transfer pricing experience, being involved in overseeing the preparation of reports as well as leading negotiations with the tax authorities on behalf of clients.

Tammy Shulman
Partner, Borden Ladner Gervais LLP
TShulman@blgcanada.com

Tammy Shulman has been practising corporate/commercial law for more than 20 years, with an emphasis on mergers and acquisitions, corporate reorganisations, public–private projects and commercial agreements. She holds degrees in both Civil and Common Law and is a member of the Bar of the Province of Quebec and the Province of Ontario, as well as the Canadian Bar Association and the International Bar Association. She has been peer-rated by Martindale-Hubbell.

In the Montreal office of Borden Ladner Gervais LLP, Canada's largest and one of its most respected national law firms, she is a member of the Legal Opinions Committee and the former chair of the Continuing Legal Education Committee.

Bennet Hugh Silverman
Partner, Katz Wittenberg Levine & Silverman
KWLandS@aol.com

Bennet Hugh Silverman has been a partner in the New York law firm of Katz Wittenberg Levine & Silverman since 1973. His practice centres on the representation of firms, governments and individuals concerned with international trade and investment, including shipping and the trading of agricultural commodities and manufactured products. Active in professional, fraternal, religious and community organisations, Bennet currently serves as co-chair of the International Sales Committee of the International Bar Association.

Marte Solberg
Associate, Brækhus Dege Advokatfirma ANS
Solberg@bd.no

Marte Solberg advises on a wide range of private law, especially contracts, employment law and company law. She has experience within environmental law, concessions and international trade.

Prior to joining Brækhus Dege Advokatfirma ANS she worked as an advisor in the Norwegian Ministry of Fisheries and Coastal affairs.

Francesco Spreafico
Associate, Dewey & LeBoeuf
fspreafico@dl.com

Francesco Spreafico is an associate at Dewey & LeBoeuf, Milan. His work covers corporate and commercial activity for international and domestic clients in the technology, communication, media, entertainment and advertising industry. He has advised foreign investors on the start-up of companies in Italy, mergers and acquisitions, and business reorganisations. He has also worked extensively with companies in transactional intellectual property-related matters, including technology licensing, trademark and copyright protection and enforcement, data protection and security.

Øystein A Sverre
Partner, Brækhus Dege Advokatfirma ANS
sverre@bd.no

Øystein Sverre has been a partner in Brækhus Dege since 1992. He has broad experience in all aspects of international business law

He has written two books on international tax and is the author of the Norwegian chapter of several international legal guides on tax law, corporate law and immigration law. He is on the board of directors of several Norwegian subsidiaries of foreign companies.

Paul Thaler
Managing Partner, Wenfei Attorneys-at-Law Ltd
Paul.Thaler@wenfei.com

Paul Thaler was one of the first foreign lawyers to practise in a leading law firm in China. He has more than 13 years of professional experience

there. In 2006, he established his own law firm to focus on China-related corporate work, international transactions and dispute resolutions. As a result of his long experience in China, Paul is a board member of various Chinese companies.

Vojtech Triska
Attorney at Law and Partner, Triska & Zak
office@aktz.cz

Vojtech Triska specialises in general commercial law, corporate law and IT/IP law. He has been a member of the Czech Bar Association since 2002.

Vojtech is a frequent author and lecturer on business law.

Claire van Zuylen
Partner, Bowman Gilfillan
c.vanzuylen@bowman.co.za

Claire van Zuylen is a partner of Bowman Gilfillan. She practises in the corporate department and specialises in insolvency and restructuring.

In 2007, Claire was one of *Practical Law Company*'s 'recommended' attorneys. She has been appointed to the editorial board of the quarterly journal published by INSOL (International Association of Restructuring, Insolvency and Bankruptcy Professionals). She is the author of numerous books and articles.

Mónica Villafaña Aquino
Associate, Russin, Vecchi & Heredia Bonetti
mvillafana@rvhb.com

Mónica Villafaña Aquino is an associate at Russin, Vecchi & Heredia Bonetti, handling the corporate division of the transactional department of this firm. Her practice focuses on corporate law, business, commercial law, and international negotiations. She has been involved in international transactions, including project financing, corporate restructures and major local mergers.

Mónica is an LLB graduate of Pontificia

Universidad Catolica Madre y Maestra (PUCMM) and in 2008 she was awarded a masters degree from the same university in corporate and business law. She is a member of the Dominican Bar and the Council of International and Comparative Laws Studious (COLADIC-RD). She is fluent in English.

Niels Walther-Rasmussen

Partner, Kromann Reumert
NWR@kromannreumert.com

Niels Walther-Rasmussen is responsible for the corporate department in Danish law firm Kromann Reumert in Copenhagen. His main fields of expertise are corporate law, financing, mergers and acquisitions, stock exchange regulations, securities law and private equity.

Mr Walther-Rasmussen holds law degrees from the University of Copenhagen (1978) and New York University. He is a member of the Danish Bar and the New York Bar, and he obtained the right of audience before the Danish Supreme Court in 1987. He is the author of a number of legal handbooks and other publications.

Jan-Willem Wiertsema

Partner, Boekel De Nerée NV
janwillem.wiertsema@boekeldeneree.com

Jan-Willem Wiertsema started his career as a candidate civil-law notary with Boekel De Nerée NV, becoming a partner in 2008. His practice covers many areas of commercial law and he specialises in mergers and acquisitions, banking and finance, and real estate. In the past few years he has been involved in a number of high-profile real-estate acquisitions and reorganisations.

Grace CG Yeoh

Partner, Shearn Delamore & Co.
gcgyeoh@shearndelamore.com

Grace Yeoh has wide experience in all areas of corporate and commercial advisory and drafting

work, including mergers and acquisitions, venture capital, takeovers, corporate restructuring, joint ventures, de-mergers, listings, regulatory issues and corporate governance, and corporate advisory and planning work.

Grace has featured as a 'leading individual' in recent editions of the *Asia Pacific Legal 500* and in a recent poll conducted by *Asia Law and Practice* (in June 2008). She is also named as a leading individual in the Corporate/M&A section of *Chambers Asia* and is a member of the Corporate and Commercial Law Committee and the GATS Committee of the Malaysian Bar Council.